The Cambridge Economic History of Modern Europe

Unlike most existing textbooks on the economic history of modern Europe, which offer a country-by-country approach, *The Cambridge Economic History of Modern Europe* rethinks Europe's economic history since 1700 as unified and pan-European, with the material organized by topic rather than by country. This second volume tracks Europe's economic history through three major phases since 1870. The first phase was an age of globalization and of European economic and political dominance that lasted until the First World War. The second, from 1914 to 1945, was one of war, deglobalization, and depression and the third was one of growing integration not only within Europe but also between Europe and the global economy. Leading authors offer comprehensive and accessible introductions to these patterns of globalization and deglobalization as well as to key themes in modern economic history such as economic growth, business cycles, sectoral developments, and population and living standards.

Stephen Broadberry is Professor of Economic History at the University of Warwick and a Co-ordinator of the Economic History Initiative at the Centre for Economic Policy Research. His recent publications include *The Economics of World War I* (2005, as co-editor) and *Market Services and the Productivity Race, 1850–2000: Britain in International Perspective* (2006).

Kevin H. O'Rourke is Professor of Economics at Trinity College Dublin and a Co-ordinator of the Economic History Initiative at the Centre for Economic History Research. His recent publications include *The New Comparative Economic History: Essays in Honor of Jeffrey G. Williamson* (2007, as co-editor), and *Power and Plenty: Trade, War, and the World Economy in the Second Millennium* (2007, with Ronald Findlay).

The Cambridge Economic History of Modern Europe Volume 2

1870 to the Present

EDITED BY

Stephen Broadberry

and

Kevin H. O'Rourke

CAMBRIDGE
UNIVERSITY PRESS

CAMBRIDGE UNIVERSITY PRESS
Cambridge, New York, Melbourne, Madrid, Cape Town, Singapore, São Paulo, Delhi

Cambridge University Press
The Edinburgh Building, Cambridge CB2 8RU, UK

Published in the United States of America by Cambridge University Press, New York

www.cambridge.org
Information on this title: www.cambridge.org/9780521708395

© Cambridge University Press 2010

First published 2010

Printed in the United Kingdom at the University Press, Cambridge

A catalog record for this publication is available from the British Library

Library of Congress Cataloguing in Publication data
Broadberry, S. N.
The Cambridge economic history of modern Europe / Stephen Broadberry, Kevin H. O'Rourke.
   p.   cm.
ISBN 978-0-521-88203-3
1. Europe – Economic history.   I. O'Rourke, Kevin H.   II. Title.
HC240.B6865   2010
330.94–dc22

2009050509

ISBN 978-0-521-88203-3 Hardback
ISBN 978-0-521-70839-5 Paperback

Contents

Figures

Tables

Contributors

Dudley Baines Department of Economic History, London School of Economics

Jörg Baten Department of Economics, University of Tübingen

Stefano Battilossi Department of Economic History and Institutions, Universidad Carlos III de Madrid

Andrea Boltho Magdalen College, Oxford

Stephen Broadberry Department of Economics, University of Warwick

Erik Buyst Centre for Economic Studies, Katholieke Universiteit Leuven

Albert Carreras Department of Economics, Universitat Pompeu Fabra, Barcelona

Nicholas Crafts Department of Economics, University of Warwick

Neil Cummins Department of Economic History, London School of Economics

Guillaume Daudin Université Lille-I and OFCE, Sciences Po

Barry Eichengreen Department of Economics, University of California, Berkeley

Jari Eloranta Department of History, Appalachian State University

Giovanni Federico Department of History and Civilization, European University Institute, Florence

Marc Flandreau Graduate Institute of International and Development Studies, Geneva

Juan Flores Zendejas Department of Economic History and Institutions, Universidad Carlos III de Madrid

James Foreman-Peck Cardiff Business School, Cardiff University

Piotr Franaszek Jagiellonian University, Cracow

Mark Harrison Department of Economics, University of Warwick and the Hoover Institution, Stanford University

Stefan Houpt Department of Economic History and Institutions and Instituto Figuerola, Universidad Carlos III de Madrid

Clemens Jobst Austrian National Bank

Camilla Josephson Department of Economic History, Lund University

David Khoudour-Casteras CEP II, Paris

Alexander Klein Department of Economics, University of Warwick

Gerhard Kling Bristol Business School, University of the West of England

Pedro Lains Institute of Social Sciences, University of Lisbon

Carol Leonard St Antony's College, Oxford

Jonas Ljungberg Department of Economic History, Lund University

Robert Millward Department of History, University of Manchester

Matthias Morys Department of Economics and Related Studies, University of York

Kevin H. O'Rourke Department of Economics, Trinity College Dublin

Albrecht Ritschl Department of Economic History, London School of Economics

Joan Roses Department of Economic History and Institutions, Universidad Carlos III de Madrid

Lennart Schön Department of Economic History, Lund University

Max-Stephan Schulze Department of Economic History, London School of Economics

Tobias Straumann Institute of Empirical Research in Economics, University of Zurich

Gianni Toniolo Duke University and Libera Università delle Scienze Sociali, Roma

Nicholaus Wolf Department of Economics, University of Warwick

Foreword

It would be unthinkable for American undergraduates to be offered courses in the economic history of their own state, rather than the United States as a whole. In sharp contrast, most existing textbooks on European economic history are country-specific, implying the risk that students will misinterpret continent-wide phenomena as having been purely national in scope, and as having had purely national causes. The time has come for a textbook on European economic history that takes an explicitly pan-European approach, with the material organized by topic rather than by country.

This project thus aims to provide a unified economic history of modern Europe, explicitly modeled on R. Floud and D. McCloskey's (1981) path-breaking *Cambridge Economic History of Britain*. Each chapter has been written by two or three leading experts in the field, who between them have been able to cover all of the three major European regions (northern Europe, southern Europe, and central and eastern Europe). Following the pattern established by Floud and McCloskey, we have broken down the project into two volumes covering the periods 1700–1870 and 1870–2000. Each volume contains chapters based on the dominant themes of modern economic history: aggregate growth and cycles; sectoral analysis; and living standards. The approach is quantitative and makes explicit use of economic analysis, but in a manner that is accessible to undergraduates.

This is a project that would have been simply unthinkable two decades ago. That there has always been a tradition of pan-European economic history is evident from a glance at the earlier volumes of the *Cambridge Economic History of Europe*, and many of the giants in the discipline represented there have provided us with sweeping accounts of the economic development of the continent as a whole. It is striking, however, that the later volumes in that series, from the Industrial Revolution onwards, tend to comprise a series of national histories, with a highly selective coverage of both countries and topics. Meanwhile, the quantitative economic history that was beginning to be written in European economics departments from the 1970s onwards was more often than not purely national in scope – which was perhaps inevitable, as economic historians started using their countries' national statistics to quantify economic growth over the long run. Furthermore, the number of cliometricians working outside of the British Isles remained comparatively small. The result was a European economic history profession that was both small and fragmented, especially when compared with our colleagues in North America.

How things have changed! A crucially important turning point came with the founding in 1991 of the European Historical Economics Society, which aimed to bring together quantitative economic historians from across Europe working in both economics and history departments. In 1997, the society launched the *European Economic History Review*, which has provided a common forum for economic historians across the continent. Another major breakthrough was the launching in 2003 of an Economic History Initiative at the Centre for Economic Policy Research in London, Europe's largest economics research network. In combination with EU funding for pan-European research initiatives, the result has been the development of a vibrant economic history profession in Europe, which can genuinely describe itself as "European."

We put our contributors through two grueling conferences at which we discussed chapter drafts: in Lund in 2006, and at the CEPR in 2007. We are naturally extremely grateful to the local organizers of both events. We would also like to thank all the contributors for the enthusiasm and stamina which they displayed on both occasions, and also for delivering their chapters in a timely fashion.

This project is an outgrowth of the EU-funded Marie Curie Research Training Network "Unifying the European Experience: Historical Lessons of pan-European Development," Contract no. MRTN-CT-2004–512439. It goes without saying that we are extremely grateful to the European Commission for their very generous financial support, without which this project could never have gotten off the ground. We are also grateful to the CEPR staff who provided such expert assistance in applying for the grant and administering this project. Much of the work on this book took place while Kevin H. O'Rourke was a Government of Ireland Senior Research Fellow, and he thanks the Irish Research Council for the Humanities and Social Sciences for their generous support.

Our training network was struck by tragedy in 2007, when one of our most respected and well-liked members, Stephan (Larry) Epstein, died suddenly, at the age of just forty-six. Larry is an enormous loss to our profession, and we will miss him greatly. These volumes are dedicated to him.

Stephen N. Broadberry
Kevin H. O'Rourke

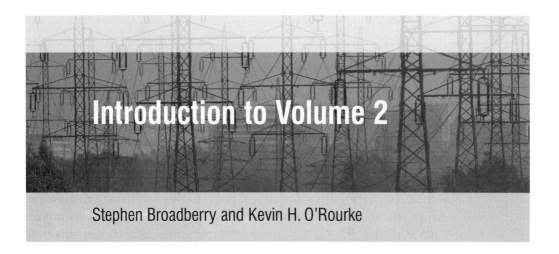

Introduction to Volume 2

Stephen Broadberry and Kevin H. O'Rourke

The economic history of Europe since 1870 can be divided into three phases. The first, which lasted until the First World War, was an age of globalization, and of European economic and political dominance worldwide. The Industrial Revolution, which was covered in Volume 1, led to the introduction of new steam-based technologies such as the steamship and railroad, which dramatically lowered transport costs, while the telegraph speeded the transmission of information. The Industrial Revolution also produced a dramatically asymmetric world, in which industrial output became increasingly concentrated in Europe and its overseas offshoots. Europe used the military power which flowed from this fact to dominate Asia and Africa politically, either through overt imperialism or in more indirect ways. The net result was a dramatic economic integration of Europe with itself and the rest of the world, despite trade policies which occasionally attempted to shield European farmers from overseas competition.

The promises which the Industrial Revolution had held out to ordinary workers were increasingly being realized across Europe during this period. According to the figures in Chapter 2, growth averaged a little over 2 percent per annum between 1870 and 1913. Real wages grew, and ordinary people lived longer, healthier and better-educated lives. While the period was certainly marked by business cycle fluctuations, governments on average found that the constraints imposed upon them by the gold standard were not excessively onerous.

The second era, which lasted from 1914 to 1945, was one of war, deglobalization, and depression: a "second thirty years war" during which Europe tore itself apart, and after which it would never regain its previous pre-eminence in world affairs. The period is a dismal confirmation of the cliché that "history matters": the roots of the interwar economic debacle, and therefore of the Second World War, can largely be traced back to the many national and international dislocations caused by the war of 1914–1918. The gold standard became unsustainable, although policy makers were slow to realize this, and the conflict created a host of protectionist pressures, as well as new borders along which these could be manifested. Meanwhile, the poisonous legacy of war debts and reparations would make international cooperation much more difficult, while the Russian Revolution of 1917 was an anti-globalization shock that continued to influence the world until the 1990s.

Economically, the period saw slow and extremely volatile growth, hyper-inflation, and mass unemployment, despite continuing technological progress and structural change. The economic misery of the period, and in particular the Great Depression, was a man-made event, and a testament to the power of economic policies to influence people's lives for better or for worse. The two-way interaction between politics and economics is a constant feature of the period: not only did bad policies create the Great Depression, but the unemployment of the period was directly responsible for the election of Adolf Hitler. Those who escaped the period's conflicts saw improvements in life expectancy and education, but war and genocide destroyed millions of lives.

The Europe which emerged from the ruins of the Second World War was overshadowed by the two main victors in that conflict, the United States and the Soviet Union, each with their own sphere of influence in the continent. The economic history of Europe from 1950 through the 1980s is one of a divided continent, characterized by two very different economic systems: communism in the east, and a mixed system combining markets and more or less activist states in the west. The post-war period saw a gradual rebuilding of international economic links between the non-communist industrial countries, and western Europe participated in this broader trend, while experiencing deeper regional integration of its own. This regional integration would come to include most of eastern Europe in the 1990s.

Both western and eastern Europe experienced rapid economic growth during the 1950s and 1960s: 1950–1973 was western Europe's golden age, and (as Chapter 12 puts it) eastern Europe's silver age. Both periods also experienced a subsequent slowdown, which in the case of eastern Europe was sufficiently destabilizing to lead to the collapse of the communist system at the end of the 1980s. The period after 1973 saw the oil shocks, stagflation, and the gradual emergence of a period of low volatility and steady growth which is now at an end (and which may, with the benefit of enough hindsight, eventually come to be regarded as one long, unsustainable boom).

The organization of Volume 2 reflects this globalization–deglobalization–reglobalization periodization, with one section devoted to each of these three epochs. So as to maintain comparability between periods, there are five chapters in each section. The first sets the scene, by discussing the globalization or deglobalization trends that characterized the era. There then follow chapters on economic growth, business cycles, sectoral developments, and population and living standards.

Before the First World War

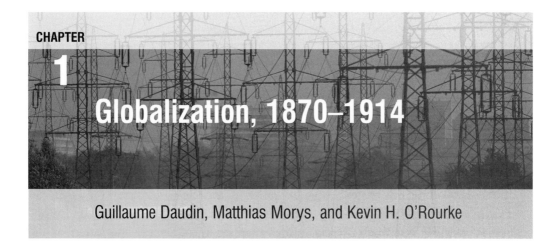

Globalization, 1870–1914

Guillaume Daudin, Matthias Morys, and Kevin H. O'Rourke

Contents

Documenting globalization

Introduction

The period from 1870 to 1914 represented the high-water mark of nineteenth-century globalization, which, as Chapter 4 in Volume 1 showed, had been developing since the end of the Napoleonic Wars. This chapter will explore several dimensions of this globalization, as well as its effects on the European economy. Since the topic is vast, our focus will be on the links between Europe and the rest of the world, rather than on the growing integration of the European economy itself, although that will be alluded to.

Nineteenth-century globalization involved increasing transfers of commodities, people, capital, and ideas between and within continents. The most straightforward measure of integration is simply the growing volume of these international flows, perhaps scaled by measures of economic activity more generally: for example, the ratio of commodity trade to GDP, or the number of migrants per head of population. Another measure is the cost of moving goods or factors of production across borders, and this cost will show up in international price gaps. Because it is less easy to measure integration in the international "markets" for ideas and technology, these flows are often not discussed in economists' accounts of globalization, but they are sufficiently important to be briefly considered here, problems of quantification notwithstanding.

Having documented the increasing integration of international markets in the late nineteenth century, we then discuss some of the effects of this unprecedented globalization. Finally, we turn to the question of how sustainable the relatively liberal nineteenth century world economy was: could globalization have continued unabated after 1914, had the First World War not intervened, or were there forces that would have undermined open markets even had that cataclysm not occurred?

Trade, 1870–1914

European international trade in current values grew at 4.1 percent a year between 1870 and 1913, as against 16.1 percent a year between 1830 and 1870.[1] In 1990 prices, European international trade grew at 6.8 percent a year (Maddison 2001, p. 362), with growth being particularly high in Belgium, Germany, Switzerland, and Finland (Table 1.1). The European trade to GDP

---

[1] Bairoch 1976, p. 77; Prados de la Escosura 2000 and personal communication with the author.

Table 1.1 European real trade 1870–1913

	1870 (million 1990 $)	Growth 1870–1913
Austria	467	+333%
Belgium	1237	+492%
Denmark	314	+376%
Finland	310	+415%
France	3512	+222%
Germany	6761	+465%
Italy	1788	+158%
Netherlands	1727	+151%
Norway	223	+283%
Spain	850	+335%
Sweden	713	+274%
Switzerland	1107	+418%
UK	12237	+222%
Weighted average		+294%
Weighted average, rest of the world		+379%

Source: Maddison 2001. Includes intra-European trade.

ratio, including intra-European trade, increased from 29.9 percent to 36.9 percent, while excluding intra-European trade it increased from 9.2 percent to 13.5 percent (Table 1.2), slightly more than the United States figure (12 percent in 1913).

Price evidence also shows impressive international integration during this period. Between 1870 and 1913, the wheat price gap between Liverpool and Chicago fell from 57.6 percent to 15.6 percent, and the London–Cincinnati bacon price gap fell from 92.5 percent to 17.9 percent. The period also saw US–British price gaps for industrial goods such as cotton textiles, iron bars, pig iron and copper falling from 13.7 percent to −3.6 percent, 75 percent to 20.6 percent, 85.2 percent to 19.3 percent, and 32.7 percent to −0.1 percent, respectively (O'Rourke and Williamson 1994). Prices also converged between Europe and Asia, with the London–Rangoon rice price gap falling from 93 percent to 26 percent, and the Liverpool–Bombay cotton price gap falling from 57 percent to 20 percent (Findlay and O'Rourke 2007, pp. 404–5). However, both Federico and Persson (2007) and Jacks (2005) point out that grain price convergence was if anything more impressive between 1830 or 1840 and 1870 than between 1870 and 1913.

International trade grew for many reasons. International freight rates declined steadily as a result of constant technical improvements and the growth in the use of faster and more regular steamships, especially after the opening in 1869 of the Suez Canal (which could only be used by steamships). However, as overland transport was much more expensive than water transport, the reduction

Table 1.2 Exports plus imports as share of GDP

	1870	1880	1890	1900	1913
Austria	29.0%	25.5%	25.2%	26.8%	24.1%
Belgium	35.6%	53.2%	55.6%	65.4%	101.4%
Denmark	35.7%	45.8%	48.0%	52.8%	61.5%
Finland	31.7%	50.8%	39.3%	47.6%	56.2%
France	23.6%	33.5%	28.2%	26.8%	30.8%
Germany	36.8%	32.1%	30.1%	30.5%	37.2%
Greece	45.6%	42.3%	39.4%	42.3%	29.4%
Hungary	19.4%	23.7%	22.1%	22.3%	20.8%
Italy	18.3%	18.3%	15.9%	19.0%	23.9%
Netherlands	115.4%	100.5%	112.3%	124.1%	179.6%
Norway	33.9%	36.1%	43.6%	43.4%	50.9%
Portugal	33.7%	43.8%	45.3%	48.9%	57.4%
Russia		14.4%	15.0%	11.4%	13.8%
Spain	12.1%	14.8%	18.8%	22.6%	22.3%
Sweden	29.4%	37.3%	44.9%	39.4%	34.7%
Switzerland		78.2%	81.9%	67.2%	64.5%
UK	43.6%	46.0%	46.6%	42.4%	51.2%
Best guess, European trade to GDP ratio	29.9%	33.4%	32.5%	31.9%	36.9%
Idem, net of intra-European trade	9.2%	10.7%	10.8%	11.1%	13.4%

Note: Ottoman Empire, Bulgaria, Romania, and Serbia not included.
Source: Bairoch 1976, and data kindly provided by Leandro Prados de la Escosura.

of internal transport costs through the development of railroads was crucial (Figure 1.1). As a percentage of the Chicago wheat price, the cost of shipping wheat to New York declined from 17.2 percent to 5.5 percent, while the cost of shipping it from New York to Liverpool fell from 11.6 percent to 4.7 percent (Findlay and O'Rourke 2007, p. 382). Railroads were particularly important in large countries such as Russia (Metzer 1974).

In addition, peace between the main powers between 1871 and 1914 promoted trade (Jacks 2006). The development of European formal and informal empires increased extra-European trade through the reduction of trade barriers, the inclusion of colonies in currency unions, and the better protection of (European) property rights (Mitchener and Weidenmier 2007). Meanwhile, the gradual spread of the gold standard dampened exchange rate fluctuations and reduced uncertainty in trade. Whether international currency arrangements such as the Latin Monetary Union (LMU) and Scandinavian Monetary Union (SMU) had an additional positive effect on trade is a matter of controversy (Estevadeordal, Frantz, and Persson 2003; López-Córdova and Meissner 2003; Flandreau and Maurel 2005).

Falling transport costs implied increasing potential market integration, but politicians always had the option of muting or even reversing this via protectionist

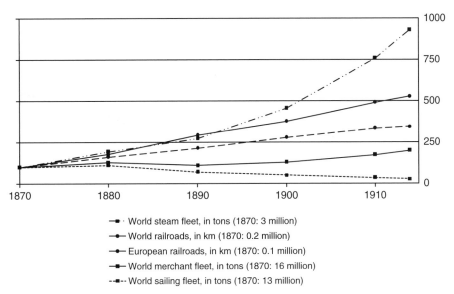

- — ▪ · World steam fleet, in tons (1870: 3 million)
- —◆— World railroads, in km (1870: 0.2 million)
- —◆— European railroads, in km (1870: 0.1 million)
- —■— World merchant fleet, in tons (1870: 16 million)
- --■-- World sailing fleet, in tons (1870: 13 million)

Figure 1.1 Transport infrastructure, 1870–1913 (index numbers, 1870 = 100).
Source: Bairoch 1976, pp. 32, 34

policies. Beginning in the 1870s Continental European countries raised barriers to trade in grain and other commodities (Bairoch 1989). Thus, Federico and Persson (2007) show that while grain prices converged among free trade countries during our period, this was more than counterbalanced by a substantial increase in price dispersion between free trade and protectionist countries.

As regards the pattern of trade, Europe as a whole was a net exporter of manufactures and a net importer of primary products, although this masks important differences among regions. At one extreme lay the United Kingdom, massively dependent on imported food and raw materials paid for with exports of manufactures and services. The rest of northwest Europe had a similar but less extreme specialization. Eastern and southern Europe, however, despite growing industrialization, still exported primary products and imported manufactures, net. The overall European deficit in commodity trade was partly balanced by net exports of services. To give an idea of their magnitude, the United Kingdom surplus in business services trade averaged over $800 million during 1911–13, as compared with a figure for total European exports of $11 billion in 1913 (Imlah 1952).

Capital flows, 1870–1914

International capital market integration was extremely impressive during this period. Europe was the world's banker (Feis 1930), and those regions with good access to European capital and abundant resources such as the USA, Canada,

Table 1.3 Foreign investment by England, France, and Germany, 1870–1913

	England			France	Germany
	Saving / GDP	Foreign investment / GDP	Foreign investment as % of saving	Foreign investment as % of saving	Foreign investment as % of saving
1870–79	12.3%	4.0%	32.5%	23.9%	10.2%
1880–89	12.2%	4.7%	38.5%	5.1%	18.8%
1890–99	11.0%	3.4%	30.9%	16.5%	12.1%
1900–4	12.6%	3.7%	29.4%	19.1%	8.3%
1905–14	13.1%	6.5%	49.6%	17.3%	7.5%
Net national wealth held overseas in 1914	32.1%				
Share of global foreign investment	41.8%			19.8%	12.8%

Sources: Feis 1930; Edelstein 1982, 2004; Maddison 1995, 2003; Lévy-Leboyer and Bourguignon 1990; Jones and Obstfeld 2001.

Argentina, and Australia prospered most between 1870 and 1913. There was also a smaller, but still important, transfer of capital from the western European core to the more peripheral economies of south, central, and eastern Europe.

For the UK, Edelstein (2004, p. 193) estimates that 32 percent of net national wealth was held overseas in 1913. This reflects four decades in which foreign investment as a percentage of (domestic) savings averaged roughly one third (Table 1.3). The UK committed, on average, some 4 percent of its GDP to capital formation abroad over a period of more than 40 years, an unprecedented phenomenon. Europe as a whole dominated foreign investment. In 1914, England (42 percent), France (20 percent) and Germany (13 percent), Belgium, the Netherlands, and Switzerland combined accounted for 87 percent of total foreign investment (Maddison 1995, p. 65).

Capital market integration has traced out a U-shape over the past 150 years (Obstfeld and Taylor 2004), with late nineteenth-century integration being followed by interwar disintegration and a slow move towards reintegration in the late twentieth century. According to Obstfeld and Taylor (2004, p. 55), foreign assets accounted for 7 percent of world GDP in 1870, but for nearly 20 percent from 1900 to 1914. The figure was only 8 percent in 1930, 5 percent in 1945, and still only 6 percent in 1960. However, it then shot up to 25 percent in 1980, 49 percent in 1990, and 92 percent in 2000. On this measure it was not until some time in the 1970s that the pre-1914 level of integration was recouped. Another measure of integration was suggested by Feldstein and Horioka (1980). International capital mobility breaks the link between domestic savings and domestic investment, as domestic savings can be invested abroad and domestic investment can be financed externally. Consequently, the weaker the relationship between domestic savings and domestic investment, the higher is international capital mobility. The U-shaped pattern emerges yet again from the data. A third measure looks at bond spreads. Bond spreads between peripheral economies, whether in Europe or elsewhere, and England, France, and Germany fell, on average, from some 5 percent in 1870 to only 1 percent in 1914 (Flandreau and Zumer 2004). Mauro, Sussman, and Yafeh (2002) have shown that emerging market bond spreads then were, on average, less than half of what they were in the 1990s, which demonstrates just how safe investors perceived foreign investment to be at the time.

Capital market integration was not a continuous process. As is true today, there were reversals which subjected capital-receiving countries to "sudden stops" (Calvo 1998). A first wave of financial integration came to an end with the Baring crisis of 1891. Capital receded dramatically for roughly a decade before massive foreign lending resumed again around the turn of the century.

What explains late nineteenth-century capital market integration? The absence of military conflict among the main lending countries between the Franco-Prussian War and the First World War certainly helped create and stabilize an atmosphere conducive to foreign lending. Another political explanation, by contrast, has been highly controversial. Marxists have long argued that late nineteenth-century capital exports and imperialism are only two sides of the same coin: excessive saving at home, generated by a highly unequal distribution of income, required outlets in underdeveloped countries, as domestic investment would have been subject to Marx's law of the falling rate of profit. This idea (associated with J. A. Hobson) prompted Lenin to declare imperialism to be the highest stage of capitalism. The contention of a connection between empire and capital exports was subsequently discredited, to be resuscitated recently by revisionist historians arguing for a more benign interpretation of imperialism. For example, Ferguson and Schularick (2006) argue that countries in the British Empire benefited from their colonial status through substantially reduced interest rates, presumably as a result of more secure property rights. But Table 1.4 raises doubts as to whether colonial affiliation mattered for the size and the direction of capital flows. All English colonies combined (excluding Canada, Australia, and New Zealand) received a paltry 16.9 percent of English capital exports, which is less than what the USA alone received (20.5 percent). The French and German experiences suggest the same, with colonies receiving only 8.9 percent and 2.6 percent, respectively, of the overall capital exports of their respective mother countries.

Table 1.4 Destination of English, French, and German foreign investment, 1870–1913

	England	France	Germany
Europe			
Russia	3.4%	25.1%	7.7%
Ottoman Empire	1.0%	7.3%	7.7%
Austria–Hungary	1.0%	4.9%	12.8%
Spain and Portugal	0.8%	8.7%	7.2%
Italy	1.0%	2.9%	17.9%
Other countries	2.5%	12.2%	
Total (Europe)	9.7%	61.1%	53.3%
Areas of recent settlement (outside Latin America)			
USA	20.5%	4.4%	15.7%
Canada	10.1%		
Australia	8.3%		
New Zealand	2.1%		
Total	41.0%	4.4%	15.7%
Latin America: Areas of recent settlement			
Argentina	8.6%		
Brazil	4.2%		
Total	12.8%		
Total (areas of recent settlement)	53.8%		
Other countries			
Mexico	2.0%		
Chile	1.5%		
Uruguay	0.8%		
Cuba	0.6%		
Total (Latin America)	17.7%	13.3%	16.2%
Africa	9.1%	7.3%	8.5%
Asia			
India	7.8%	4.9%	4.3%
Japan	1.9%		
China	1.8%		
Total (Asia)	11.5%	4.9%	4.3%
Rest	11.0%	9%	2%
Total	100.0%	100.0%	100.0%
Colonies	16.9%	8.9%	2.6%

Note: numbers for Russia and the Ottoman Empire include Asia. "Colonies" does not include Australia, Canada, or New Zealand.
Sources: Feis 1930; Stone 1999; Esteves 2007.

Turning to economic institutions and policies, a great deal of attention has been devoted to the gold standard (Bordo and Rockoff 1996) and, more recently, to sound fiscal policies (Flandreau and Zumer 2004). Adherence to gold is seen as having promoted global financial integration in two ways. First, it eliminated exchange rate risk. Second, it signaled that the government concerned would pursue conservative fiscal and monetary policies, which assured potential investors that returns were reasonably safe.

While economic institutions and policies can facilitate capital imports, they can never attract them if there is no genuine interest on the part of investors in what a specific country has to offer. This brings us to economic fundamentals as the main determinant in explaining the size and direction of flows. Over 50 percent of British capital exports went to areas of recent settlement (Table 1.4) where natural resources could be exploited, not to where labor was cheap (Africa and Asia). If New World land was to produce food for European consumers and raw materials for factories, railroads had to make it accessible, land had to be improved, and housing and infrastructure had to be provided for the new frontier communities. Clemens and Williamson (2004) provide econometric evidence in favor of this view, showing that British capital exports went to countries with abundant supplies of natural resources, immigrants, and young, educated, urban populations. While they also find that the gold standard and empire promoted foreign investment, supply and demand, rather than the presence or absence of frictions leading to price gaps between markets, were what was really crucial. The French and the German cases appear somewhat different and await further investigation. While foreign investment in Africa and Asia was rather unpopular in all three countries, France and Germany sent 61.1 percent and 53.3 percent, respectively, of their capital exports to other European countries. Investment in areas of recent settlement, by contrast, played a substantially reduced role for both countries.

Migration, 1870–1914

It is in the area of migration that the late nineteenth century was most impressively globalized, even compared with today. At the beginning of the century, intercontinental migration was still dominated by slavery: during the 1820s, free immigration into the Americas averaged only 15,380 per annum, about a quarter of the annual slave inflow. Twenty years later, the free inflow was more than four times as high as the slave flow, at 178,530 per annum (Chiswick and Hatton 2003, p. 68), and the numbers rose to more than a million per annum after 1900 (Figure 1.2), with Italians and eastern Europeans adding to the traditional outflow from northwest Europe. Some of the country-specific migration rates were enormous (Table 1.5): during the 1880s, the decadal emigration rate per thousand was 141.7 in Ireland, and 95.2 in Norway, while an emigration rate of 107.7 per thousand was recorded in Italy in the first decade of the nineteenth century. It should be noted that these figures are gross, not net, and that the extent of return migration varied over

Table 1.5 Migration rates by decade (per 1,000 mean population)

Country	1851–60	1861–70	1871–80	1881–90	1891–1900	1901–10
European emigration rates						
Austria–Hungary			2.9	10.6	16.1	47.6
Belgium				8.6	3.5	6.1
British Isles	58.0	51.8	50.4	70.2	43.8	65.3
Denmark			20.6	39.4	22.3	28.2
Finland				13.2	23.2	54.5
France	1.1	1.2	1.5	3.1	1.3	1.4
Germany			14.7	28.7	10.1	4.5
Ireland			66.1	141.7	88.5	69.8
Italy			10.5	33.6	50.2	107.7
Netherlands	5.0	5.9	4.6	12.3	5.0	5.1
Norway	24.2	57.6	47.3	95.2	44.9	83.3
Portugal		19.0	28.9	38.0	50.8	56.9
Spain				36.2	43.8	56.6
Sweden	4.6	30.5	23.5	70.1	41.2	42.0
Switzerland			13.0	32.0	14.1	13.9

Source: Hatton and Williamson 1998, Table 2.1.

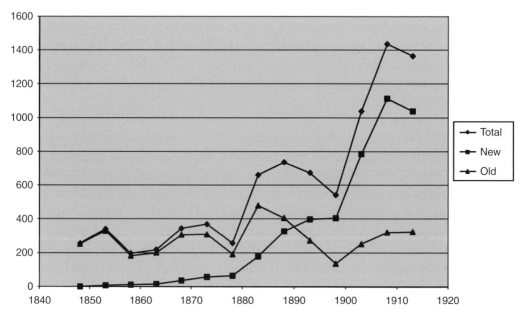

Figure 1.2 Average annual emigration from Europe, 1846–1915 (thousands). *Source:* Kirk 1946, p. 279. *Note:* "Old" means Britain and Ireland, Germany, Scandinavia, France, Switzerland, and the Low Countries. "New" means Italy, the Austro-Hungarian Empire, the Russian Empire, Iberia, and the Balkans.

time and across countries, rising from about 10 percent of the outflow initially to around 30 percent at the turn of the century (ibid, p. 70). While return migration was significant among Italians and Greeks, for example, it was very low among other groups, such as the Irish or eastern European Jews. In addition to these transoceanic migrations, there were significant migrations within Europe, for example from Italy to France, and from Ireland to mainland Britain. The average western European annual outmigration rate was 2.2 per thousand in the 1870s and 5.4 per thousand in the 1900s.

The causes of this mass migration are by now well understood (Hatton and Williamson 1998, 2005). On one level, the causes are obvious: the New World was endowed with a higher land–labor ratio than Europe, and hence American and Australian workers earned higher wages than their European counterparts. British real wages in 1870 were less than 60 percent of wages in the New World destinations relevant to British workers, whereas the equivalent figure for Irish workers was just 44 percent, and for Norwegian workers just 26 percent (Hatton and Williamson 2005, p. 55). The gains from migration were thus potentially enormous, and once the new steam technologies had lowered the cost of travel sufficiently, mass emigration became inevitable. This was particularly so because nineteenth-century immigration policy was relatively liberal, notwithstanding the policy developments which we will note later on.

On another level, there is the issue of what determined the timing of emigration streams from different European countries: why did emigration from relatively rich countries such as Britain take off before emigration from poorer countries such as Italy, where the gains to migrants were presumably higher? What explains the fact that so few French emigrated, while so many Irish and Italians did? What explains the initial rise, and subsequent decline, of emigration rates in several countries, documented in Table 1.5? Hatton and Williamson provide a simple explanation for all these questions, which can be represented in Figure 1.3. EM is a downward-sloping function relating emigration rates from a given European economy to home wage rates: as home wages rise, emigration rates should fall, *ceteris paribus*. The initial rise in emigration rates experienced in the typical economy (say from e_0 to e_1) must then have been due to rightward shifts in the emigration function, from EM to EM', since wages were rising (say from w_0 to w_1), not falling, in late nineteenth-century Europe. In turn, such rightward shifts were caused by a variety of factors. First, would-be emigrants were initially constrained by the cost of transoceanic transport, but as transport costs fell, more migrants were able to leave their homelands. Second, these poverty traps could also be overcome by previous emigrants sending home remittances or pre-paid tickets, thus directly financing the cost of travel. Emigration rates thus tended to increase as countries built up stocks of emigrants overseas, the so-called "friends and

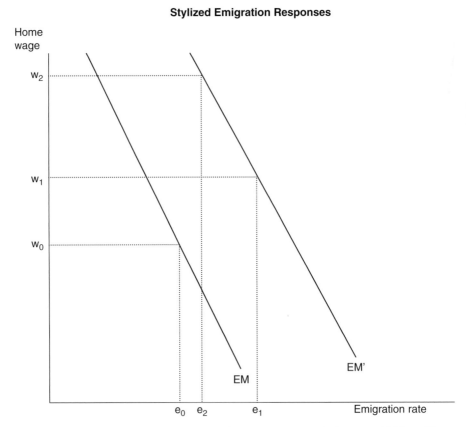

Figure 1.3 A stylized model of emigration. *Source:* Hatton and Williamson 1988, p. 36.

relatives" effect. Third, fertility rates were on the rise throughout Europe during this period, leading to an increase in the supply of young, mobile adults. And finally, it has often been argued that the industrialization documented in Chapter 3 of this volume led to workers being detached from the land, again increasing their mobility.

Rising fertility, structural transformation and falling transport costs thus increased emigration rates, initially in the richer economies whose workers could best afford the cost of transport, and then in poorer economies as living standards rose across the continent. This emigration was initially self-reinforcing, as a result of the friends and relatives effect: all these factors led to EM shifting rightwards. But eventually, the emigration function stabilized, and when this happened, emigration became self-limiting: by lowering labor supply at home, it pushed up real wages (say from w_1 to w_2), and economies thus moved up their EM schedules, experiencing lower emigration rates (e_2). Hatton and Williamson show that low French and high Irish emigration rates can be explained on economic grounds alone without appealing to cultural behavior in either country, since this one-size-fits-all European model explains most countries satisfactorily. Thus, high Irish emigration rates can be explained by the famine of the 1840s, which created a large Irish migrant stock in the New World, while low French rates can be explained by such factors as a precocious fertility transition. Economic rationality turns out to do a pretty good job of explaining European emigration during this period.

Trade in knowledge, 1870–1914

Economic globalization is not simply about the movement of goods or factors of production. It also includes technological transfers and the deepening of other intellectual exchanges.

Technology circulated relatively freely in the late nineteenth century. In Europe and in the Atlantic world, despite laws forbidding the emigration of skilled workers (repealed in the United Kingdom in 1825) and machinery exports (repealed there in 1842), technologies had been circulating for a long time. Textile mills around the world used similar machines, often imported from Britain (Clark 1987). Ship building, iron and steel, telegraph and telephone technologies transferred quickly, unless slowed by adaptation issues. Europe was internally exchanging new technologies, diffusing them – both to European off-shoots and to the rest of the world – and receiving new technologies, mainly from the United States. Japan was an especially keen learner (Jeremy 1991).

Several new factors increased the speed and the reach of technological transfers. Migration was easy. Imperialism allowed European entrepreneurs to invest overseas, taking advantage of low wages, with no fear of expropriation by hostile governments. The decline in transport and communication costs helped the diffusion of ideas, new goods, and machines. This last effect was especially important because more and more technology was embedded in machines rather than in individual know-how, even if training was still necessary. Firms could now export capital goods on a large scale. For example, Platt, a Lancashire firm, exported at least 50 percent of their cotton-spinning machines between 1845 and 1870 (Clark and Feenstra 2003). Explicit policies aiming at import substitution encouraged domestic technological emulation, with mixed success. Japan was able to replace its English suppliers of textile machinery, but France had difficulties in replacing its American telephone suppliers, and had to postpone the diffusion of this important technology.

To circumvent these restrictions and better protect their intellectual property, several firms set up production in foreign countries and transformed themselves into multinationals during this period. Sometimes the idea was to produce inside protected markets: for example, by 1911 International Harvester was producing harvesting machines in France, Germany, Russia, and Sweden as a result of those countries' protectionist policies (Wilkins 1970, pp. 102–3). Ericsson, a Swedish firm, and Western Electrics, an American firm, both had to establish overseas plants in order to win telephone contracts in various European countries (Foreman-Peck 1991). Sometimes direct foreign investment arose simply because, as the theory of the firm predicts, it proved difficult or impossible to transfer intangible assets such as new technologies abroad at "arm's length," via the market: thus Singer's attempts to profit from its invention of the sewing machine by licencing the technology to a French merchant proved a complete disaster, the latter refusing to pay what he owed, or even disclose how many sewing machines he was producing (Wilkins 1970, pp. 38–9).

The diffusion of technologies was also helped by the creation of international scientific and technical organizations. The Institution of Naval Architects was founded in 1860 in the United Kingdom, but organized meetings in different countries and through its membership created an international network of professional and learned bodies (Ville 1991). The number of international scientific conferences and organizations increased dramatically (Figure 1.4).

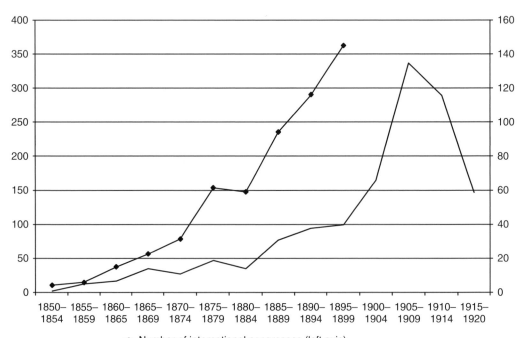

Figure 1.4 The rise of the international scientific community. *Sources:* Union des Associations Internationales 1957, 1960.

Paradoxically however, at the same time, science was seen as one of the weapons in the struggle between European nations. Besides straightforward military applications, academic activity was used as a diplomatic weapon. Inviting foreign scientists and participating in scientific congresses was part and parcel of the rivalry between France and Germany, as each hoped to tighten its links with allied and neutral countries, especially the United States (Charle 1994, ch. 8).

Governments increased formal technical cooperation. The International Telegraph Union was founded in 1865 and the Universal Postal Union in 1874. Humanitarian cooperation was expanded as well: the Red Cross was founded in 1863 and the first Geneva Convention signed in 1864. Most sovereign states, both European and non-European, joined these global institutions. Another form of rising globalization was the growing number of international exchanges and competitions. The World Fairs were official showcases for the technical prowess of each nation. The 1876 World Fair in Philadelphia was the first not to take place in Europe, and included official exhibitions from Japan and China. The first Venice Biennale took place in 1895. The modern Olympics began in 1896. The first five Nobel prizes were awarded in 1901.

Labor movements were increasingly globalized as well. Socialist ideals rejected nationalism and advocated the international defense of the interests of labor. The first International was founded in 1864 and the second in 1889, the latter having Japanese and Turkish members. The significance of these events is difficult to assess. International, especially pan-European, scientific and cultural cooperation among individuals had existed for a long time. De facto agreements about the rules of war and the management of public goods – e.g., the high seas – pre-dated the first globalization. To some extent, the heyday of elite cultural globalization was before 1870. Nationalist cultural identities gained in importance in the second half of the nineteenth century, leading to the fragmentation of cultural activities as they became more popular. The formalization of international cultural and scientific cooperation can be seen as an attempt to counteract the rise of nationalism, but in the end it was too weak for the task.

The effects of globalization

Globalization and factor price convergence

As we have seen, the late nineteenth century was characterized by booming commodity trade and mass migration from the Old World to the New. How did this influence income distribution within and between countries?

Let us begin with trade. According to Heckscher–Ohlin logic, the land-abundant and labor-scarce New World should have exchanged food and raw materials for European manufactured goods, and trade should have led to the wage–rental ratio, w/r, converging internationally. In New World economies, where w/r was high, w/r should have declined as farmers exported more, and manufacturing suffered from foreign competition. In land-scarce European economies, where w/r was low, it should have increased, as workers were hired by expanding manufacturing industries, and land rents were undermined by cheap food imports. Furthermore, trade should have led to absolute factor price convergence, with low European wages catching up on high New World wages, and expensive European land falling in price relative to cheap New World land.

By and large, these predictions hold good for the late nineteenth century (O'Rourke and Williamson 1999). Between 1870 and 1910, real land prices fell in countries such as Britain, France, and Sweden – in Britain by over 50 percent – while land prices soared in the New World. Furthermore, the forty years after 1870 saw substantial relative factor price convergence, with wage–rental ratios rising in Europe and falling in the New World (Williamson 2002a, Table 4, p. 74). Between 1870 and 1910, the ratio increased by a factor of 2.7 in Britain, 5.6 in Ireland, 2.6 in Sweden, and 3.1 in Denmark. The increase was less pronounced in protectionist economies: the ratio increased by a factor of 2.0 in France, 1.4 in Germany, and not at all in Spain. This suggests a link between trade and factor price trends, which is confirmed by both econometric evidence and CGE simulations. In turn, these wage–rental ratio trends implied that the European income distribution was becoming more equal, since landowners were typically better off than unskilled workers.

In addition to these Heckscher–Ohlin predictions, there was a more mundane reason why declining transport costs were good for European workers. In an era where a large proportion of laborers' incomes was still spent on food, cheaper transport meant cheaper food, and thus higher real wages. What was bad for farmers was directly beneficial to urban workers, then as now, which explains why, by and large, socialist parties tended to support free trade in Europe. British workers should have particularly benefited from free trade: not only did it lower the price of food, but any negative impact on agricultural labor demand would have had only a small effect on the overall labor market, given agriculture's small share in overall employment in Britain (just 22.6 percent in 1871). O'Rourke and Williamson (1994) estimate that British real wages rose by 43 percent between 1870 and 1913, and that no fewer than twenty percentage points of this increase can be directly attributed to declining transport costs. On the other hand, in more agricultural economies the net impact of cheap grain on wages could have been negative, if it sufficiently depressed agricultural employment and wages.

Migration was the dimension of globalization that had the greatest impact on European workers' living standards during this period. Figure 1.5 shows the

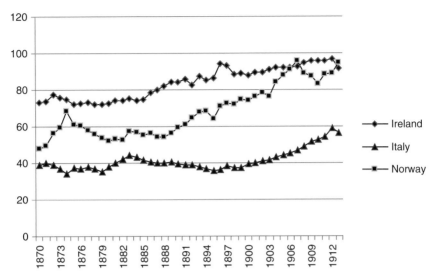

Figure 1.5 Wages relative to Britain, 1870–1913. *Source:* database underlying O'Rourke and Williamson 1999.

(PPP-adjusted) wages of unskilled male urban workers in three countries of mass emigration, Ireland, Italy, and Norway, relative to wages in the leading European economy of the day, Britain. Between 1870 and 1910, emigration lowered the labor force by 45 percent in Ireland, 39 percent in Italy, and 24 percent in Norway (O'Rourke and Williamson 1999, Table 8.1). The figure shows that living standards in these three economies rose more rapidly than in Britain. In Ireland, real wages rose from 73 percent to 92 percent of the British level during this period, while Norwegian wages rose from 48 percent to 95 percent. In Italy there was no convergence until the turn of the century, which is when Italian emigration rates exploded; thereafter, Italian real wages rose from 40 percent of British wages in 1900 to 56 percent in 1913. Similarly, Norwegian wages continually converged on US wages, while Italian wages converged after 1900; Irish wages converged over the period as a whole, although very rapid US growth in the final two decades of the period implied Irish divergence after about 1895.

Both econometric and simulation studies show that emigration was an important source of living standard convergence for countries such as Ireland. To what extent can these findings be generalized? Taylor and Williamson (1997) calculate the labor market impact of migration in seventeen Atlantic economy countries between 1870 and 1910. They find that emigration raised Irish wages by 32 percent, Italian by 28 percent and Norwegian by 10 percent. International real wage dispersion fell by 28 percent between 1870 and 1910, reflecting a convergence of poorer countries on the rich, but in the absence of the mass migrations international real wage dispersion would have increased by 7 percent. Wage gaps between New World and Old in fact declined from 108 to 85 percent during the period, but in the absence of the mass migrations they would have risen to 128 percent in 1910. The results suggest that more than all (125 percent) of the real wage convergence between 1870 and 1910 was attributable to migration. Even when allowance is made for the possibility that capital may have chased labor, lowering the impact of migration on capital–labor ratios, migration emerges as a major determinant of living standard convergence, explaining about 70 percent of it. Mass migration accounted for all of Ireland's and Italy's convergence on the United States, and for 65–87 percent of their convergence on Britain. The biggest lesson of nineteenth-century migration history is that emigration is of major benefit to poor economies (Williamson 2002b).

Capital flows, peripheral development, and core welfare

Assuming identical production functions with capital and labor as the only inputs, lower wages in the European periphery should have been due to lower capital-to-labor ratios, which in turn should have implied higher returns to capital. Did the European periphery attract capital imports as this logic suggests, and if so, did these capital imports have the desired effect of raising the capital-to-labor ratio and hence wages?

We shall start with Sweden, one of the few cases for which we have relatively reliable data. Capital imports after 1870 served to make the Swedish capital stock 50 percent bigger than it would have been in their absence, increasing Swedish real wages by 25 percent (O'Rourke and Williamson 1999). Sweden may have been the European country that benefited most from capital imports before the First World War. Denmark and Norway also benefited, albeit on a reduced scale as capital imports were substantially smaller.

These results cannot be easily replicated for other countries in the European periphery, owing to poor or contradictory data. This may be illustrated with reference to Austria–Hungary, by far the largest peripheral economy in pre-1914 Europe bar Russia. Looking from the "outside," i.e., considering the foreign investment of the European core countries, the dual monarchy seems to have enjoyed substantial capital imports (Table 1.4). A recent reconstruction of the Austro-Hungarian balance of payments, by contrast, concluded that, over the period 1880–1913, Austria–Hungary exported rather than imported capital (Morys 2006). Similar uncertainty surrounds the Italian, Spanish, and Portuguese cases, while there are indications that Ireland, another peripheral economy, also exported capital after 1870.

Even if some of the peripheral economies may turn out on closer examination to have imported capital, the general question remains: Why was the

European periphery not able to attract more capital from the European core? This is the nineteenth-century equivalent of the Lucas paradox: capital usually flows to rich rather than to poor countries today, despite the fact that wages are lower in poor countries (Lucas 1990). Three explanations have been offered for late nineteenth century Europe. First, lower labor productivity in the European periphery can potentially explain why capital did not flow there (Clark 1987). However, this only begs the question as to why labor productivity was lower in the European periphery. Second, non-adherence to gold may have dissuaded foreign investors. In support of the latter theory, the Scandinavian countries had the best record of adherence to gold among the peripheral economies. And finally, it may simply be that these countries were not as attractive to investors as the land-abundant New World.

We now turn to the capital-exporting core countries and ask what were the effects of capital flows on welfare levels there. Superficially, the answer seems straightforward. As investors preferred foreign investment opportunities to domestic ones based on their relative profitability, capital exports should have been beneficial to the core countries, lowering GDP (output) but raising GNP (income). However, some have argued that channeling funds abroad could have harmed the domestic economy. The 1931 Macmillan Report claimed that the City of London systematically discriminated against domestic borrowers, preferring instead to invest overseas. British industry, starved of capital, grew more slowly than it would otherwise have done. In other words, to the long-debated question why late Victorian Britain failed (as measured by its growth performance relative to the USA and Germany, its main economic rivals at the time) another debate was added: Did late Victorian capital markets fail?

In a monumental study, Edelstein (1982) showed that overseas portfolio investments yielded a higher realized return than domestic portfolio investments between 1870 and 1913. This result held true even when adjusting for risk. While this finding exculpated late Victorian and Edwardian investors (see also Goetzmann and Ukhov 2006), the question still lingered whether Britain could have done better by retaining more savings in the domestic economy, for example by imposing a tax on capital exports (Temin 1987). But here one must ask what were the real constraints facing the British economy at the time. Research has shown that entrepreneurs had strong internal sources of funding and easy access to local, provincial financing. Rather, what was missing was the highly skilled workforce required to take full advantage of the opportunities offered by the Second Industrial Revolution. Restrictions on overseas capital exports almost certainly would not have been the best way to encourage domestic, scientifically based industry; publicly supported general and technical education might have been.

The debate on the alleged trade-off between capital exports and domestic industry has also frequently neglected the positive externalities of European overseas investments benefiting European consumers. Since much of the investment went into the construction of railroads and other social overhead projects, it implied cheaper imports of foodstuffs and raw materials, which represented a major contribution to European core welfare.

Imperialism and European welfare

In 1880, European colonies (not including any part of Russia) ranged over 24.5 million square kilometers and had 312 million inhabitants. In 1913, they totalled 52.5 million square kilometers, more than a third of the earth's land surface, and had 525 million inhabitants. The United Kingdom, France, the Netherlands, Spain, and Portugal had been colonial powers for a long time. Belgium, Germany, and Italy now joined them. The United Kingdom controlled 93 percent of the surface and 87 percent of the population of these colonized territories (including dominions) in 1880, and 61 percent and 71 percent of the surface and population respectively in 1913 (Etemad 2006).

As noted earlier, Lenin, inspired by Hobson and others, suggested that the mature European economic system could only be sustained through imperialism. This argument has been discredited. Capital exports to colonies were important, but not dominant. Europe was self-sufficient in coal and nearly self-sufficient in iron ore and other minerals. Textile raw materials were more of an issue as cotton, for example, could not be produced in Europe in great quantities; but it was largely supplied by the United States. Colonial empires did not represent vital outlets for European goods either, absorbing less than 15 percent of all western European exports (Bairoch 1993).

Yet it is true that one of the driving forces behind imperialism was the influence of European traders, who saw in political control a way to facilitate their economic exchanges with African and Asian producers and consumers. Some industrialists also believed that the creation of a reserved market would be a suitable answer to international competition, and they managed to convince certain politicians, like Joseph Chamberlain (British Colonial Secretary from 1895 to 1903), Jules Ferry (French Prime Minister from 1880 to 1881 and from 1883 to 1885) and Francesco Crispi (Italian Prime Minister from 1887 to 1891 and from 1893 to 1896).

It is not certain that empires represented a net benefit for the European powers. The debate has centered on the British Empire, as it was by far the largest, and was the only empire controlling economically advanced settler colonies. According to Davis and Huttenback (1986, p. 107), private British investment in the empire after 1880 yielded higher returns than investment in the domestic economy, but smaller returns than investment in foreign countries. The direct cost of empires was limited, as the United Kingdom, like the other colonizers, tried to make its colonies pay for themselves and provided mainly disaster relief, funds for military campaigns, and shipping and cable subsidies. The indirect military cost was more important since, India excepted, the British Empire contributed very little to general military spending. While all these points have been extensively debated, the final word must go to Avner Offer (1993), who makes the obviously correct point that the military "debts" of the French and British empires were paid in full during the First World War.

To determine the effect of empire on European economic welfare, it is crucial to decide on the appropriate counterfactual (Edelstein 2004). Without formal imperialism, would Africa, Canada, South Asia, and Oceania have been as developed as they actually were, but with the ability to erect high tariff barriers against European exports, as did the United States? Or would they have been substantially less developed and less involved with the world economy? Was the alternative to a British Canada the United States, or Argentina? In the absence of empire, would the African states (as some imperialists feared) have remained independent backward territories, mostly closed to foreign trade, like Ethiopia? Depending on the answer to such questions, Edelstein has shown that the benefits of empire for the United Kingdom may have been somewhere between 0.4 percent and 6.8 percent of its GDP in 1913, up from −0.2 percent to 4.5 percent in 1870. These figures probably overestimate the benefits of imperial trade, as Edelstein assumes that there would have been no redirection of trade to compensate for lower imperial demand, but they do not take into account any impact of empire in facilitating emigration from the United Kingdom, especially to Oceania. No such calculation has been made for other European countries. Their empires were much smaller, but, as they were not committed to free trade, they could manipulate the terms of trade to maximize their commercial profits. For example, Portugal gained foreign currency from re-exporting African products through Lisbon. The net result was different for each country, but on the whole, whether positive or negative, it was probably small compared to the size of domestic economies (O'Brien and Prados de la Escosura 1998).

Even if the global economic effect of empires was small, they may have had an important redistributive role. Certainly the military and state apparatus benefited everywhere, while there was an obvious cost to taxpayers. In the United Kingdom, Cain and Hopkins (2002) have argued that the economic benefits of imperialism accrued mainly to "gentlemanly capitalists," the finan-cial and rentier interests of London and south-east England, to the detriment of more "modern" forces in the country such as industrial entrepreneurs. Elsewhere, some industrial exporting groups certainly benefited as well. On the whole, the European benefits from imperialism were small and uncertain.

More importantly, they were probably smaller than the costs of imperialism for colonized countries, although this remains an underexplored field of research.

Globalization backlash

Trade

While nineteenth-century European trade policy trends initially reinforced the impact of falling transport costs (Volume 1, Chapter 4), this changed after the 1870s as a result of the growing impact of intercontinental trade on factor prices. As we have seen, trade hurt European landed interests, and wherever these were powerful enough, the legislative reaction was predictable. In Germany, Bismarck protected both agriculture and industry in 1879; in France, tariffs were raised in the 1880s and again in 1892; in Sweden, agricultural protection was reimposed in 1888 and industrial protection was increased in 1892; in Italy, moderate tariffs were imposed in 1878, followed by more severe tariffs in 1887. As a grain exporter, Russia hardly feared free trade in agricultural products, but it was the first to backtrack from what had in any event been a rather half-hearted liberalization, increasing industrial tariffs substantially in 1877, 1885, and again in 1891. The purpose was to stimulate industrialization, and tariffs were combined with export subsidies for cotton textile producers. Austria–Hungary and Spain also sharply increased protectionism in the 1870s or 1880s. The Balkan countries had inherited liberal tariff policies from their Ottoman masters, but they too gradually moved towards higher protection, albeit at a slower pace than the Germans or Russians. The Ottomans themselves were allowed to slowly raise their tariffs, which reached 11 percent on the eve of the Great War (Bairoch 1989).

Some small countries remained relatively liberal: the Netherlands, Belgium, Switzerland, and Denmark, which transformed itself from a grain exporter to a grain-importing exporter of animal products. The United Kingdom also maintained free trade, despite the efforts of Joseph Chamberlain. What explains these exceptions? Economic considerations were surely important: countries such as Denmark and the United Kingdom, which retained agricultural free trade, were less vulnerable to the price and rent reductions which globalization implied. In the Danish case grain prices had been low to begin with, while the country was exceptionally well suited to meet the growing British demand for butter, eggs, and bacon, in part due to the success of its cooperative societies. In the British case, agriculture had already shrunk significantly, and further decline had little impact on the overall economy. Elsewhere, globalization undermined itself. Moreover, this switch towards agricultural protectionism would turn out to be permanent, the precursor of today's Common Agricultural Policy.

Immigration

While emigration benefited European workers, mass immigration hurt their counterparts overseas. Hatton and Williamson (1998) show that immigration lowered unskilled wages in the United States, although this is a *ceteris paribus* finding, since economic growth was raising living standards generally during this period. Nonetheless, the effects were large. Relative to what they would have been in its absence, immigration lowered unskilled real wages by 8 percent in the USA, 15 percent in Canada, and 21 percent in Argentina (Taylor and Williamson 1997). Counterfactual or not, such impacts did not go unnoticed, and the result was a political backlash, resulting in gradually tightening restrictions on immigration in the main destination countries (Timmer and Williamson 1998). For example, in 1888 the United States banned all Chinese immigration for twenty years, while in 1891 it banned the immigration of persons "likely to become public charges" as well as those "assisted" in passage (ibid., p. 765). The screw continued to be tightened on immigration until 1917, when a literacy test was imposed on would-be migrants, effectively blocking much of the low-skilled immigration of the day. Very similar trends can be discerned in Canada and Argentina. This shift away from a relatively laissez-faire immigration policy implied that interwar European economies no longer had the emigration safety valve that had helped sustain living standards during the population boom and slow transition to modern growth of the late nineteenth century.

Democracy, the gold standard, and capital flows

Global financial integration collapsed virtually overnight in the summer of 1914. Does it follow that pre-war levels of capital market integration would necessarily have been sustained in the absence of war?

Widespread – by 1913 almost universal – adherence to the gold standard was a central pillar of the pre-First-World War financial system. This implied a commitment to a policy of external balance, even when that coexisted with domestic economic imbalances, notably unemployment. According to Eichengreen (1992), one of the factors undermining attempts to reinstate the gold standard after 1918 was the fact that the war had given a boost to the extension of the franchise, and thus to workers' political power: it was no longer clear that gold standard discipline – i.e., raising the discount rate when needed – would be adhered to if this conflicted with domestic policy objectives. However, Eichengreen also notes that the franchise was already being extended before the war in many countries, and that unemployment was becoming a growing social issue. One can therefore speculate that, even in the absence of war, democratization would have ultimately succeeded in undermining the gold standard, and with it the foundations of the pre-war international financial system. Indeed, one could even interpret the extension of franchise as being in part a consequence of late nineteenth-century globalization, which gave rise to countervailing calls to regulate the market (Polanyi 1944). To this extent, one might yet again see globalization – the extension of the market – as having undermined itself.

Several objections could be raised against such reasoning, however. First, the single largest push for universal suffrage and democratization came, as Eichengreen says, in the wake of the First World War, not as a result of globalization. Second, even if the gold standard had proved unsustainable, this would not necessarily have implied the end of global financial integration. Today, most capital circulates among rich countries which are (with the notable exception of the Eurozone) no longer connected by fixed exchange rates. Indeed, as Obstfeld and Taylor (2004) point out, abandoning fixed exchange rates makes it possible for countries to pursue both independent monetary policies and a commitment to open capital markets. It was the attempt to combine fixed exchange rates with Keynesian macroeconomic policies which, in their view, condemned Bretton Woods capital markets.

Domestic policy responses

There were thus powerful political forces undermining late nineteenth-century globalization. However, European governments of this period did not just face a binary choice between open and closed international markets, between resisting or giving in to protectionist anti-globalization backlashes. Rather, there was a range of complementary domestic policies which governments could – and did – put in place during this period in order to shore up support for liberal international policies. Thus, Huberman and Lewchuk (2003) show that there was extensive government intervention in European labor markets in the late nineteenth century, a period that also saw a sustained rise in social transfers and the beginnings of what eventually evolved into the modern welfare state (Lindert 2004). A range of labor market regulations was introduced across the continent, for example prohibiting night work for women and children, prohibiting child labor below certain ages, and introducing factory inspections. The period also saw the widespread introduction of old-age, sickness, and unemployment insurance schemes. Moreover, this "labor compact" was more widespread in the more open European economies. Huberman and Lewchuk use this evidence to argue that unions were persuaded to back free trade, or openness more generally, in return for pro-labor domestic policies. In related work, Huberman (2004) finds that working hours in Europe and her offshoots declined between 1870 and 1913 as a result of labor legislation and union pressure, and that the decline was greatest in small open economies such as Belgium, where the Labor Party supported free trade after 1885 (Huberman 2008). Not only did governments not indulge in a race to the bottom during the late nineteenth-century globalization boom: in some cases governments cooperated so as to ensure a general raising of standards. Such was the case, for example, with the Franco-Italian labor accord of 1904, which raised labor standards in Italy as a *quid pro quo* for granting Italian workers in France benefits which their French colleagues already enjoyed.

To some extent, therefore, late nineteenth-century governments successfully managed the political challenges posed by globalization, sometimes defusing protectionist demands by means of domestic legislation, and sometimes giving in to them. World trade might have grown more slowly after 1914 than it did before, even had war not intervened, and the political challenges facing governments might have been exacerbated; but the 1920s and 1930s would have been utterly different had it not been for the Great War.

Aggregate growth, 1870–1914: growing at the production frontier*

Albert Carreras and Camilla Josephson

Contents

* We thank the participants in the RTN, especially those attending the meetings where first drafts of the book
were discussed. Very special thanks to Xavier Tafunell (UPF), who provided us with his database and who
should have been one of the coauthors, and to Steve Broadberry (University of Warwick), who assisted and
supported us at all the stages of the writing of the manuscript.

Introduction: from Marx to Marshall – and Lenin

Dominant views of the performance of the British and European economies during the first half of the nineteenth century were quite pessimistic. Growth was considered difficult to achieve. Conflict over distribution was perceived as fundamental, be it between landowners and the rest of the society, or between factory owners and workers. In his famous *Das Kapital*, as well as in many other writings, Karl Marx insisted on the inevitable decline of real wages. The discussions over what was to become known as the Industrial Revolution and the decline or fall of real wages were heated during those years, and have been so ever since. They constitute, in many ways, the permanent appeal of the phenomenon across disciplines and sensitivities: is economic growth worth the increase in inequality?

Sometime during the 1860s, there was a change in intellectual mood. Social conflict, polarization, and the fight over income distribution were no longer the only possible outcomes of economic life. There were cases of countries – nearly all the developed world – that were able to provide increased incomes to the entire population. There was economic growth without any single individual (or social group) paying a penalty for it. Growth was being diffused throughout the national economy. An increasing number of economies were enjoying this kind of growth. The world that Stanley Jevons, Karl Menger, Léon Walras and, a bit later on, Alfred Marshall were describing was the world whose economic performance we are now going to present. It was a growing world. For the first time in history, continuous and sustained economic growth was being diffused over most of Europe and also other parts of the world.

At the commanding heights of the European system of nation states welfare considerations were mixed with – and often secondary to – power goals.[1] The period from 1870 to 1914 starts with the Franco-Prussian war and finishes with the outbreak of the Great War – which later on came to be known as the First World War. Two major European wars define the period, and are not independent of what happens in between. The economic and social conflict view heralded by Marx was expanded into a view of conflict among imperial – i.e., European – nations by Lenin in his *Imperialism, The Highest Stage of Capitalism*. The switch from Marx to Lenin is still very present in the historiography on the period. But what must not be forgotten is the incredible amount of economic progress that happened during the period. The view of an expanding economy providing increasing welfare to everybody was very present among contemporaries, but it is only starting to be accepted among *our* contemporaries. We will focus on the amazing growth that was experienced,

---

[1] See Kennedy 1989.

its diffusion and its sources, in the context of the permanent competition among European nation states.

European growth performance: overall assessment

The period 1870–1914 is the classical era of European dominance. If we consider Europe in its wider definition (see below), European GDP was 46 percent of world GDP by 1870, and increased to 47 percent by 1913. European population jumped from 27 to 29 percent of world population. Average per capita GDP was 171 percent of the world average by 1870, and was still 165 percent by 1913. The only parts of the world that were challenging this hegemonic position were all settled by Europeans – the Americas, Australia, and New Zealand. They grew faster than Europe – increasing their share from 13 percent to 26 percent of world GDP, from 6.8 to 10.7 percent of world population, and from 184 to 240 percent of world per capita GDP. There was a more successful Europe outside Europe, epitomized by the United States of America. In what follows we will focus on European developments, but without losing sight of what happened in the United States.

The view of a continent made up of nation states fiercely competing among themselves for world supremacy has strong foundations. Countries compared their armed forces. Their strength depended both on the number of people that could be recruited into the army, and on the industrial capacity that allowed for better armaments. The combination of population and economic prosperity was starting to be assessed during those same years. What we now call Gross Domestic (or National) Product was a concept that started to be fully grasped at the turn of the century.[2] Its first label was "wealth," but we will refer to it as "product," "output," or "income."

Indeed, GDP was a very good proxy for national power – or military strength. From this perspective, Germany was catching up with the UK, and it did so in the early years of the new century. By 1908, German GDP was bigger than the UK's. Even Russia, thanks to rapid population growth, was catching up with Britain in terms of national power. Its growth from the early 1890s was spectacular. France was very worried because its welfare did not at all match with its power. Its destiny was increasingly closer to Austria–Hungary than to

---

[2] Domestic if we only account for incomes obtained within the country. National if we account for incomes obtained by nationals all over the world and spent within the country. The largest empires, such as the United Kingdom, had Gross National Products significantly higher than their Gross Domestic Products. Developing economies, like Spain or Sweden, with huge foreign direct investment and a lot of emigration, had GDPs significantly higher than their GNPs. In the following we will use only GDP; we do not have a database of homogeneous GNPs for all the European countries.

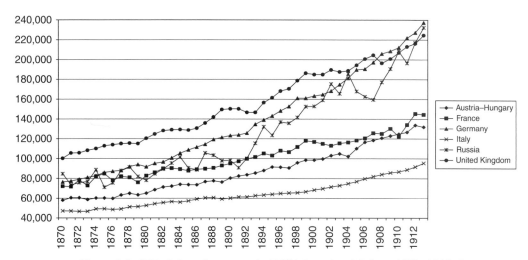

Figure 2.1 GDP of six major powers in 1990 international dollars, 1870–1914. *Sources:* see Appendix.

Germany. It comes as no surprise that Italy lay well below all the others. This was common knowledge at the time.

Figure 2.1 captures the core of the economic background of European political relations. But the Great War showed that there were two other big players: the Ottoman Empire and the United States. While we know a lot about the United States, our knowledge of the Ottoman Empire's real economic dimensions is much weaker.[3] Table 2.1 provides a comparison of the GDP of all these major powers. The USA overtook the major European power – the UK – shortly after 1870. By 1913 it was more than twice the size of the UK and almost double the size of Germany and Russia. By contrast, the Ottoman Empire, despite its huge territorial extension, was sparsely populated and quite backward.

Table 2.1 is informative with regard to another major element: the imperial factor. The major European powers had colonies. Most of the world was colonized by Europeans. Almost all of Africa and most of Asia consisted of European colonies. When the Great War came, the size of empires mattered. The UK with its Commonwealth succeeded in getting support from the colonies that were directly managed by the Colonial Office, such as India, and from the more autonomous, quasi independent, white-settled dominions, such as Canada and Australia.[4]

---

[3] Pamuk 2006.

[4] This mattered not only for food imports, as has been very well argued by Offer (1989). The human factor – soldiers – and financial support were also fundamental. For a summary see Ferguson 1991, and for a detailed economic analysis Broadberry and Harrison 2005a.

Table 2.1 Size of major European powers and world empires in 1913 (in billions of 1990 international (G–K) dollars and in million inhabitants

Country	GDP metropolis	Population metropolis	Population colonies	GDP colonies (in % of metropolis)	Estimated imperial GDP
United States	517.4	97.6	10.0	2	528
Germany	280.0	67.0	12.5	3	288
Russia	265.1	170.9	–	–	265
United Kingdom	229.6	45.7	394.4	146	565
France	129.0	39.8	47.6	23	159
Austria–Hungary	122.4	47.5	–	–	122
Italy	96.4	35.4	1.9	1	97
Spain	41.6	20.2	0.9	1	42
Belgium	32.4	7.6	11.0	20	39
Netherlands	22.0	6.2	49.9	181	62
Turkey/Ottoman Empire	18.3	13.0	12.3	40	26
Portugal	7.5	6.0	5.6	43	11

Sources: Broadberry and Klein 2008, cols. 1, 2; Etémad 2000, col. 3; Carreras 2006 (based on Maddison 2001, col. 4), but United States and Turkey/Ottoman Empire based on Maddison 2007.

With the incomplete information that we have, the power of the United Kingdom appears very impressive: there were 440 million inhabitants under the British Crown. The GDP of the British Empire was probably much larger than the German or Russian, and bigger even than that of the USA. The French Empire was also very large, but not enough to make France as powerful as Germany, while the Dutch Empire almost trebled the economic size of the Netherlands.

The main topic of this chapter is not the change in the overall size of the European economies – although this is a very interesting and related issue – but their growth performance, i.e., their increase in per capita GDP. From this point of view, the period was one of sustained growth for all of Europe. Growth was more widespread and more intense than in any previous recorded period. According to Maddison's (2007) data, the per capita growth rate for the continent was 0.12 percent between 1700 and 1820; it accelerated to 0.86 percent between 1820 and 1870, and accelerated still further to 1.22 percent between 1870 and 1913. By contrast, in the following period, across the two world wars, Europe performed worse, at 0.96 percent. Indeed, it was between the end of the Napoleonic Wars and the start of our period that Europe built up its economic leadership over the rest of the world; but the period from 1870 to 1913 displayed a sustained economic predominance that quickly expanded into political dominance – what was called imperialism.

Broadberry and Klein (2008) propose a wide definition of Europe that includes the Russian Empire (i.e., going beyond the Urals) and present-day Turkey. They find that European GDP (in constant 1990 dollars) grew at an annual rate of 2.15 percent, while population grew at 1.06 percent and per capita GDP at 1.08 percent. If we exclude Turkey, since most of its territory was in Asia (thinking in terms of the actual borders of the Ottoman Empire), almost nothing changes in terms of growth rates (0.01 percent in GDP and population, and nothing at all in GDP per capita). Exactly the same happens if we exclude the Balkan countries with poor yearly data (Bulgaria, Romania and Serbia). But if we exclude both Russia and Turkey, in order to focus on the countries that have only European territory, the changes are significant. The GDP growth rate is reduced by 0.05 percent and the population growth rate by 0.25 percent, but the GDP per capita growth rate increases by 0.21 percent.

The conventions are only conventions, and one could argue in favor of including the colonies of all the European empires. In that case, Russia beyond the Urals, the whole Ottoman Empire, and the British, French, German, Dutch, Belgian, Italian, Portuguese, Spanish, and Danish colonies would qualify – as in our exercise in Table 2.1.

In what follows we will normally restrict the definition of Europe to the countries that provide us with yearly historical national accounts, unless otherwise specified. This obliges us to leave out most of the Balkan countries: Turkey, Bulgaria, Romania, and Serbia, as well as Bosnia–Herzegovina. This means that we have quite reliable figures for Austria–Hungary, Russia, and Greece, but not for the countries south or east of these three.

In order to get a feel for the growth rates in all the countries that could qualify as European and the impact of excluding some countries, let us consider Table 2.2. There is quite a narrow range of experience for the growth rate of GDP, with the coefficient of variation being 0.24. The slowest growing economy was Portugal, at 1.20 percent per year, and the fastest was Serbia at 3.34 percent. The second slowest growing economy was Turkey at 1.48 percent and the second fastest was Germany at 2.90 percent. Among the larger economies, it is worth noting the 1.63 percent growth rate of France, the 1.86 percent of the UK, the 1.93 percent of Austria–Hungary and the 2.40 percent of Russia. The changes, even if they seemed spectacular to contemporaries, are not particularly impressive by modern standards. As is to be expected, the major contrast is between France and Germany.

In population growth, the range of experience was also quite small, although larger than for GDP growth, with a coefficient of variation of 0.42. The French case was exceptional, with an annual growth rate of 0.18 percent. At the other extreme, Serbian population grew at a rate of 1.99 percent. Far more important, the Russian population was growing at 1.60 percent, i.e., nine times faster than that of France. The second slowest growing population was in Spain, at 0.51 percent. The other

Table 2.2 Growth rates of GDP, population, and per capita GDP in Europe, 1870–1913 (%)

Country	GDP growth	Population growth	Per capita GDP growth
Austria–Hungary	1.93	0.79	1.14
Belgium	2.01	0.95	1.05
Bulgaria	2.84	1.45	1.37
Denmark	2.66	1.07	1.57
Finland	2.66	1.30	1.34
France	1.63	0.18	1.45
Germany	2.90	1.16	1.72
Greece	2.32	1.40	0.91
Italy	1.66	0.73	0.92
Netherlands	2.16	1.26	0.89
Norway	2.19	0.81	1.36
Portugal	1.20	0.71	0.48
Romania	2.20	1.25	0.93
Russia	2.40	1.65	0.81
Serbia	3.34	1.99	1.34
Spain	1.81	0.51	1.28
Sweden	2.62	0.70	1.90
Switzerland	2.50	0.87	1.67
Turkey	1.48	0.56	0.91
United Kingdom	1.86	0.88	0.97
EUROPE	2.15	1.06	1.08
Standard deviation	0.54	0.43	0.36
Coefficient of variation	0.24	0.42	0.30

Source: own calculations based on Broadberry and Klein (2008). Countries without yearly estimates between 1870 and 1913 are in italics.

major powers shared quite similar population growth rates: Austria–Hungary, 0.79 percent; the UK, 0.88 percent; and Germany, 1.16 percent.

Per capita GDP growth was even more similar across Europe. The slowest growing country was Portugal at 0.48 percent, a little less than half the European average. The fastest growing economy was Sweden, at 1.90 percent, less than double the European average but four times the Portuguese growth rate. The large economies were much closer together: Russia at 0.81 percent; the UK 0.97 percent; Austria–Hungary at 1.14 percent; France at 1.45 percent; and Germany at 1.72 percent. It is worth noting the good French performance and the poor Russian performance.

Was there any convergence among European countries during this period? Plotting initial (1870) GDP per capita against 1870–1914 GDP per capita growth rates suggests that there was no convergence at all. The correlation coefficient between both sets of data is as low as 4 percent. The data on yearly evolution do not change this view.

GDP growth rates were not at all stable. The 2.15 percent European average for the whole of the period conceals many differences across countries and over time. When we aggregate all these experiences into a European average we realize that there were some years of negative growth: 1871, 1875, 1879, 1885, and 1891. The year 1879 was the worst, with a decline in GDP of 2.5 percent. It was a very bad year in Russia and France, with GDP falling by more than 6.0 percent in both countries. It is worth mentioning that these extreme cases were not repeated after 1891 until 1913. GDP fluctuations became increasingly smaller. During the ten years before the outbreak of the Great War, growth rates became more stable, and positive. The contrast with the first decade of the period under consideration is striking. Economic progress brought about a more stable growth pattern.

Population growth is not the focus of this chapter. Nevertheless, it is necessary to emphasize that the 1.06 percent annual population growth for the whole period does not do justice to its changing chronological development. In the early 1870s, the average population growth rate was around 0.7 percent, while at the end of the period it was around 1.3 percent. During the 1870s population growth accelerated rapidly from 0.5 percent to 1.4 percent. But the 1880s and specially the 1890s were years of deceleration. Emigration is likely to be the main cause of this changing trend. The decline from 1.6 percent to 1.1 percent between 1909 and 1913 has the same cause. European population was growing as it was experiencing high fertility rates (except in France) and mortality rates were declining in most of western and central Europe.

The combination of GDP and population experiences provides a more nuanced assessment of GDP per capita. Figure 2.2 displays a highly fluctuating GDP. There were thirteen negative rates between 1871 and 1905. Only the eight years immediately before 1914 provided a stable growth period. It is rare to find many positive growth years in a row. The second longest experience happened between 1880 and 1884. It is fair to say that the overall trend was improving. The 1870s were much tougher than the 1900s. The 1880s (1.00 percent annual growth rate) were better than the 1870s (0.43 percent). The 1890s were even better (1.54 percent). The last thirteen years before the war were not as good (1.14 percent).

Growth was not smooth, and neither were prices. Just as with output, the range of variation was declining, but the variability was not insignificant, as can be seen in Figure 2.3. Yearly price variations were modest and they tended to decline. During the 1870s and early 1880s the variation was more important and the declining trend dominant. The following decade was less volatile, and after 1896 there was a switch to a regime with smaller variations, usually more within the positive range.

As with per capita GDP, convergence was very limited, but growth disparities were also quite small. The economy was highly integrated, as has been shown on many occasions, but further integration, and hence convergence, was

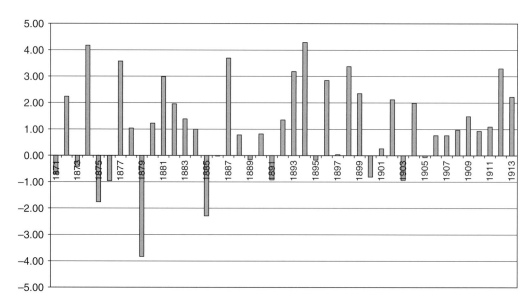

Figure 2.2 European per capita GDP growth rate, 1871–1914 (% per year). *Sources:* see Appendix.

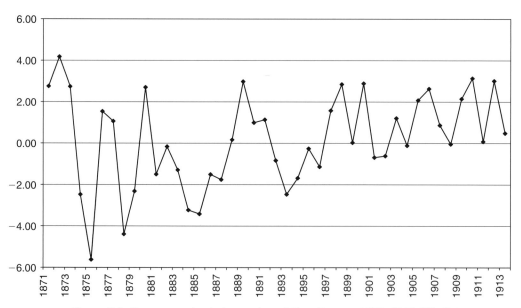

Figure 2.3 Consumer price index yearly variation, Europe, 1871–1913 (%). *Sources:* see Appendix.

very difficult to obtain. The political and ideological barriers were enormous, leading to the First World War.

As was suggested at the start of the chapter, the comparison with the United States seems the most natural. We compare European per capita GDP to the US

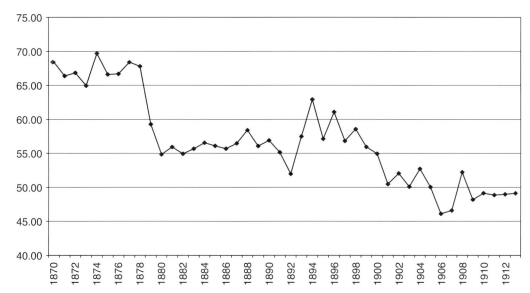

Figure 2.4 GDP per capita, Europe as a percentage of the United States, 1870–1913. *Sources:* Europe, see Appendix. For the USA, Maddison 2007.

series in Figure 2.4. Irrespective of the level, which deserves further exploration, the trend is very clear cut. The relative positions were stable until 1878, but in 1879 and 1880 there was a major decline. A new equilibrium was then found for the next decade. The 1890s were quite irregular, but towards the end of the century the series displays a new declining trend that led to a new and lower equilibrium.

The most important fact is the 1878–80 divergence, when there was an economic crisis in Europe and the US economy was booming. These were the early years of the agrarian depression, when poor harvests in Europe coincided with record highs in the USA. What economic historians call the agrarian crisis appears in the transcontinental comparison as a major source of divergence.

Europe, the dominant region of the world, was increasingly challenged by the overseas Europeans. Because the European-populated countries of the "Southern Cone," Oceania, and Canada never grew big enough to become real challengers, only the United States became a serious economic competitor. Its huge economic size only really became fully visible during the First World War, but it had been highly influential since 1880.

The changing composition of expenditure

When there is growth, there are also changes in the composition of output, and these changes are explored in detail in Chapter 3 of this volume.

There are also increases in real wages and in the standard of living, explored in detail in Chapter 5 of this volume. Because output produces incomes that are spent on all kinds of goods and services, expenditure patterns are also very sensitive to economic growth. We will present here some evidence on the changing expenditure patterns of the European economies. The usual classification of expenditure starts with a distinction between consumption –private *or* public – and investment – private *and* public. Besides consumption and investment, there is the final current-account balance with the rest of the world. All these figures are more difficult to obtain historically than figures for the output or income sides of GDP. Indeed, we only have them for ten countries (see Table 2.3). Accordingly, we will only provide a few hints about the direction and intensity of the changes.

The available data suggest that countries with balanced foreign sectors mostly experienced modest reductions in private consumption, stability, or moderate growth in public consumption, and substantial increases in

Table 2.3 Gross Domestic Expenditure patterns in Europe, 1870 and 1913 (% of values at market prices and at current prices)

Country	Private consumption		Public consumption		Investment (GCF)		X-M	
	1870	1913	1870	1913	1870	1913	1870	1913
Denmark (a)	83.6	82.1	6.2	6.3	8.0	12.5	2.1	−1.6
Finland (b)	77.8	84.3	6.4	8.3	12.4	12.0	3.5	−4.6
France (c)	80.9	82.8	9.0	7.1	10.3	12.2	−0.1	−2.1
Germany (d)	72.2	66.3	6.1	8.9	20.8	23.2	0.9	1.6
Italy	83.2	72.9	9.1	9.4	8.8	17.7	−1.0	0.0
Netherlands (e)	75.0	96.2	5.1	7.0	12.4	21.2	7.5	−24.4
Norway	80.4	73.0	3.9	5.8	12.2	20.7	3.5	0.5
Spain (f)	86.0	77.1	9.1	9.7	5.2	12.2	−0.3	1.1
Sweden	83.8	79.9	6.4	6.8	7.7	12.0	2.2	1.3
UK	82.6	76.2	4.8	7.5	7.7	7.5	4.9	8.8

Sources: Finland: Hjerppe 1996; France: Toutain 1997; the Netherlands: Smits *et al.* 2000; Spain: Prados de la Escosura 2003; Sweden: Krantz and Schön 2007; webpage. For all the others: Flora 1987. *Notes:* X and M normally correspond to goods and services. Investment is Gross Capital Formation; inventories are included. There is a +/− 0.1 rounding error.
(a) The amounts do not add to 100. The missing 0.8 represents consumption, but it is not assigned to private or public.
(b) GFCF. Stocks are mixed, as a statistical discrepancy, within exports of goods and services. Investment includes inventories.
(c) 1865–74 and 1905–1913. GFCF.
(d) 1872.
(e) They distinguish indirect taxes but do not assign them to consumption, investment, and imports. We decided to reduce them from GDE – meaning not GDE at market prices but GDE at factor costs (i.e., GDP).
(f) Constant 1913 prices.

investment. The stability or moderate growth in public consumption mirrored something very typical of nineteenth-century Europe: the stable size of public sectors. The rise in investment ratios was also a common feature, as was the declining trend in private consumption. What is interesting is the coexistence of countries with balanced foreign sectors and countries with highly unbalanced foreign sectors. This is the case of the Netherlands in 1913: the huge deficit (i.e., imports – of goods and services – were much larger than exports) allowed for a much larger proportion of both private consumption and investment. A key to understanding this imbalance is the huge inflow of earnings from abroad. They represented as much as 11.0 percent of GNE, and compensated for almost half the net import deficit.

National growth patterns: unity and diversity

In order to go deeper into the understanding of the growth experience of European countries, it is worth looking at their yearly development. Figure 2.5 displays the development of per capita GDP for Europe as a whole, and for three major regions: northwestern, southern, and central and eastern.

There is little doubt that the period was one of positive economic growth all over Europe. The average European performance was very close to southern Europe's. This region was dominated by the evolution of French GDP, with

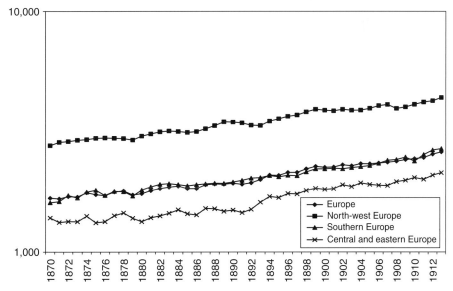

Figure 2.5 GDP per capita, Europe and its major regions, 1870–1913 in 1990 international dollars. *Source:* see Appendix. The regional definitions come from Broadberry and Klein 2008.

Italy's being clearly less important. North-west Europe was totally dominated by the United Kingdom's performance, and was well above the European average. Central and eastern Europe was a mix of Austria–Hungary, Germany, and Russia, with the latter being the most significant in terms of population. At first sight it is difficult to find much evidence of convergence. If we switch to another display of the same information using Europe = 100, and including the countries with poorer-quality data, the outcome is again quite clear, but there are hints of some convergence. All the countries keep their relative positions, and their positions relative to the European average are amazingly stable. There are very few dramatic changes. But for Switzerland, those that did occur happened after 1900.

The evolution of the coefficient of variation provides the statistical measure of the intensity of convergence (see Figure 2.6). The starting levels were around 45 percent, and the final levels declined to 40 percent. The trend was fairly flat until the end of the century. Only in the one or two decades preceding the First World War was a convergence trend clearly visible.

Another look at the same phenomenon can be provided by a systematic analysis of the convergence of eighteen European countries using the Barro and Sala-i-Martin (2003) formulation of beta and sigma convergence. Beta convergence refers to a negative relationship between per capita income growth and the initial level of per capita income, the beta coefficient indicating the

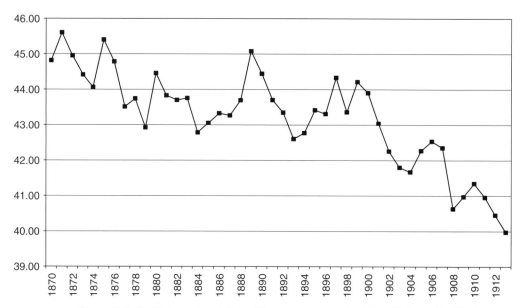

Figure 2.6 Coefficient of variation of European per capita, GDP, 1870–1913 (%). *Source:* see Appendix.

speed of convergence. If the beta coefficient is significantly negative in a sample of countries, this suggests that countries which start off relatively poor have a tendency to catch up with the richer ones. In the sample of countries considered here, the growth rate of per capita income is regressed on the level of per capita income in 1870. The results show that there was rather weak convergence in Europe during this period: the beta coefficient is 0.05 percent. However, when the estimates of convergence are separated for two time periods, one for 1870–90 and one for 1890–1913, it appears that convergence was stronger during the later period.

Sigma convergence refers to a narrowing of the dispersion of per capita income levels over time, as measured by the standard deviation or coefficient of variation. Examining sigma convergence for the same group of countries measured annually between 1870 and 1913, the conclusion is not quite the same as for beta convergence. Diminishing variance characterizes convergence, whereas increasing variance is a sign of divergence. In fact the variance of income per capita was larger during the later period, whereas it fell in the initial years after 1870.

The major issue at stake is that the usual vision of what happened to the national growth patterns during the nineteenth century is rooted in the experience of the early and mid-century, and not so much in the last decades. A cursory look at the decades preceding 1870 may thus be very interesting (see Figure 2.7).

Figure 2.7 includes the best available data series on per capita GDP from the end of the Napoleonic Wars to the outbreak of the First World War: the "pax

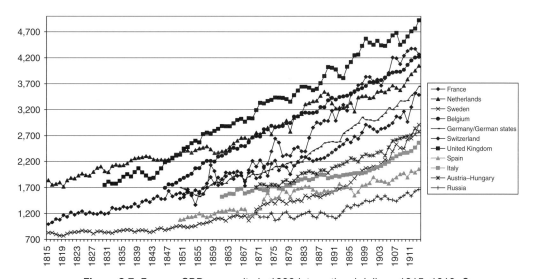

Figure 2.7 Europe: GDP per capita in 1990 international dollars, 1815–1913. *Source:* see Appendix.

Britannica" era. The most dramatic developments happened before 1870. In 1815, we start in a situation where the wealthiest economy in Europe (at per capita level) was still the Netherlands. By the mid-1840s the Netherlands had been overtaken by the United Kingdom, which grew much faster than the Netherlands for decades. After 1850 British dominance was undisputed. The second economy that managed to jump to Britain's economic speed was Belgium. Belgium was poorer than the Netherlands, but much more progressive. By 1860, the former had caught up with the latter, and by 1890 it had clearly outperformed it. The third country to take off was Switzerland. In the early 1850s Switzerland was poorer than Belgium, France, Germany, and Denmark. By the end of the same decade, apart from Belgium, it was leading this small group of countries. By the mid-1870s it was well ahead of all of them. By the end of our period it had even managed to outperform Belgium, becoming the second wealthiest European economy. We have mentioned the immediate followers: Denmark, France, and Germany. They shared a very similar growth pattern, but it was little Denmark that arrived in 1913 with higher GDP per capita, forging ahead of Germany and France during the "belle époque" years. It seems that France started to grow earlier than Germany, but there is still some uncertainty about this. The German states varied a good deal: some were very rich, others much poorer. By 1850, the average German GDP per capita was very close to the French level, and it remained so for the next quarter of a century. By the mid-1880s, the German advantage had become noticeable and remained so until 1913. Imperial Austria enjoyed similar income levels to France and Germany, but its growth rate was even lower than that of France. By 1913 Austria–Hungary was clearly behind France. The quadrangle that includes France, Germany, imperial Austria, and the smaller states of Belgium, the Netherlands, Switzerland, and Denmark constituted the developing Europe of the early nineteenth century. All of them joined the United Kingdom as developed nations at some stage during the nineteenth century. They were early industrializers. Italy, by contrast, quite possibly started the century among this same group, but lost ground throughout the nineteenth century.[5] After political unification in 1861, some growth was achieved, but not enough to catch up with the quickly developing economies of western and central Europe. Only from 1900 was there an acceleration in the growth rate – a big spurt – that allowed Italy to start to catch up with the leader, the UK. The real European periphery of the early nineteenth century provided a classic case of a peripheral country that took full advantage of its initial backwardness to

---

[5] Malanima (2003, 2006a, 2006b) argues forcefully for such a view. His data on income per capita suggest that Italy was as rich as the Netherlands in 1815. There is no consensus on this point, but his case for overall stagnation in Italy during most of the nineteenth century is convincing.

enjoy very quick growth: Sweden. Its first-rate performance during the thirty years prior to the First World War turned it into the most developed of the latecomers. But in 1913 Sweden was not yet among the club of the successful economies. As late as 1880 the odds also seemed favorable to Spain. But after 1880 Spain performed much worse than Sweden.[6] Much more important than Spain's failure to keep pace with the most dynamic European peripheral countries – the Nordic group – was the Russian failure. In 1870 Russia was a highly promising economy, fully embarked upon major political, social, and economic reforms. Its starting point was quite similar to that of Spain or Sweden. Thereafter Sweden did very well, Spain much less so, and Russia very poorly – the worst-performing European economy of the nineteenth century among those with medium or large populations. Because of Russia's sheer size and promise, the brakes on her late nineteenth-century growth have been studied by generations of historians. They are, in a nutshell, the problems of today's developing economies.

As any reader with historical knowledge will have noticed, we have been using a number of concepts that were defined precisely in order to describe what happened in Europe during the long nineteenth century. Walt Rostow (1961) coined the concept of "take off." Alexander Gerschenkron (1962) suggested a somewhat different concept, but christened it the "big spurt" – not so far away from the Rostovian take off! The diversity of national growth experiences in Europe is particularly striking between 1815 and 1870. Growth was being diffused according to patterns that need some explanation. Was the driving force the availability of natural resources? Was it, more precisely, the availability of coal and iron, as many authors, including Pounds (1957), Pollard (1981), and Cameron (1985), have taught us? Or was the critical feature the availability of a wider set of institutions – the Gerschenkronian growth prerequisites? Is there room for a human capital based explanation? Many think that this is the case – as O'Rourke and Williamson (1997) have argued. What role is left for economic policy? It is present in all the explanations – starting with Bairoch's (1976) case for the importance of protectionist trade policies – but no agreement has been reached on what would have been the best economic policy.

Because growth was intrinsically linked to national power, it is very difficult to disentangle growth-promoting policies from power-promoting policies, as Landes (1969) and Trebilcock (1981) have asserted. The dynamism of the small European economies is very telling for economics in general, and for development economics in particular, but contemporaries were much more worried about the race between the major economies. For all of them, size mattered a lot, as we stressed earlier. The largest economies have usually been seen as

---

[6] Carreras 2005.

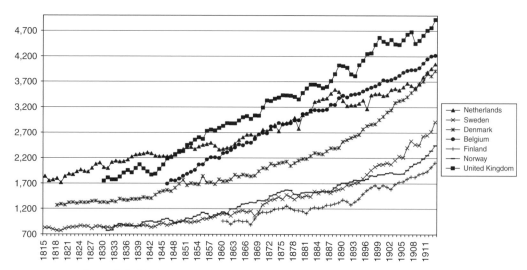

Figure 2.8 North-west Europe: GDP per capita in 1990 international dollars, 1815–1913. *Source:* see Appendix.

competing among themselves. They were major "powers," and their bench-marking was permanent – as was shown most explicitly in 1914.

Besides the major powers, Europe was made up of a number of neighbor-hoods. Location mattered from many points of view: natural endowments, trade, language, institutions, and technology, all depended heavily on geographical closeness. A very good vicinity was north-west Europe, consisting principally of the countries around the North Sea (see Figure 2.8). Nobody challenged the economic superiority and welfare of the UK, even if Belgium and the Netherlands were always close behind. Only little Denmark displayed the ability to grow at a much faster rate and to converge. Convergence allowed Denmark to reach the GDP per capita level of the Netherlands and to come close to that of Belgium. Of the other Nordic countries, all of them much poorer than the rest of the northwestern league, only Sweden was successful in its catching-up efforts during the quarter century prior to 1914.

Central Europe was a prosperous region (see Figure 2.9). Switzerland built up its economic leadership from the mid 1870s. It became closer in performance to Belgium and the Netherlands than to its other neighbors. By 1870, its per capita income distance to Austria and Germany was negligible, just as it was between Austria and Germany. It was only in the 1880s that Germany forged ahead of Austria. Hungary was never on a par with the rest of central Europe. Its position was substantially lower, even if its progress between 1876 and 1882 was impressive.

The well-managed Hungarian economy was the most advanced in eastern Europe. During the early 1870s, Hungary was very close to Finland or Russia (remember that Finland was then part of Russia). But Hungary went through

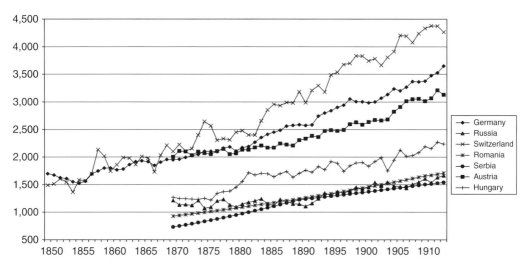

Figure 2.9 Central and eastern Europe: GDP per capita in 1990 international dollars, 1850–1913. *Source:* see Appendix.

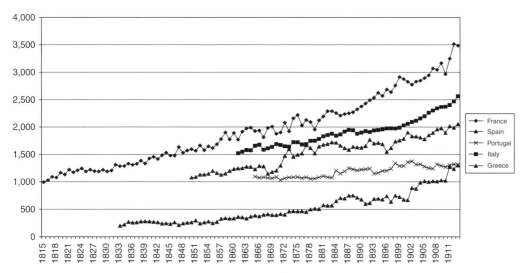

Figure 2.10 Europe: GDP per capita in 1990 international dollars, 1815–1913. *Source:* see Appendix.

the agrarian crisis of the late 1870s just as the United States did. As a major grain producer and exporter, Hungary became richer just when most of its neighbors were suffering from food shortages. Only the small Grand Duchy of Finland managed to perform better than Hungary after 1890. Russia was unable to catch up; so were the Balkan countries, at least according to the scarce quantitative evidence that we have.

The Mediterranean region – or southern Europe – was even more diverse than eastern Europe (see Figure 2.10). France was the leading country, well above all the others. Greece – just as it would be in eastern Europe – was the poorest. Apart from France, all were quite stagnant. Only Italy enjoyed rapid growth prior to the First World War. Greece made an effort to catch up, although starting from a very low level. Portugal and Spain did not catch up at all. Portugal seems to have been the least dynamic economy among the European peripheries.

Our knowledge of the poorest is, as might be expected, the most limited. The extreme peripheries were all poor, and it is probable that they were more or less around the same level. In our *numéraire* – 1990 international Geary–Khamis dollars – this means around 700 dollars. We must be skeptical of the Greek figures because they are so far below this level. In a Europe that was growing at a fairly even pace, it is rare to find poor countries growing well below the average. This seems to have been the case with Portugal, and also with Greece for many decades. Both deserve the kind of attention that has been given to Russia.[7]

Sources of growth: proximate and ultimate causes

Following Maddison's framework, we can distinguish between the proximate causes of growth that are easily accounted for (land, capital, labor, education, structural change, etc.) from the ultimate causes, which are more difficult to quantify (culture, institutions, values, etc.). We shall start by considering some of the most widely quoted proximate causes. We shall leave aside the contribution of structural change, which is considered in Chapter 3 of this volume.

Proximate sources of growth

The most traditional input for growth – land – did not increase much during the late nineteenth century. Our best estimates suggest a really small contribution. We know that the Netherlands increased its acreage thorough land reclamation. But the countries with the best data do not register significant contributions to growth from land.[8]

The second most obvious growth input is manpower. We will not go into detail on population issues in this chapter. But we do need to recall some basic facts. Population growth was rapid – 1.06 percent per year – in the whole of Europe. We lack proper data for a wide range of countries on activity rates, as well as on unemployment rates. But for some we have reasonable estimates of activity rates, which allows us to estimate employment. Generally speaking,

---

[7] See Reis 1993 and Lains 2003 for interesting interpretations of the origins of Portuguese underperformance.
[8] See the detailed account of this issue in Goldsmith 1985.

activity rates grew slightly.[9] We have a good dataset on average working hours for ten western European countries.[10] What the data show is a steady decline in working hours that appears to be more substantial than the growth in activity rates.

There has been a lot of research on the role of education in economic growth during the nineteenth century.[11] There are doubts about the contribution of formal education to growth prior to 1870. If there is any connection, it takes quite a long time to show up – perhaps as much as a generation. There is no doubt about the positive role of human capital, but there is much debate over what it is about human capital that really matters for growth (see Chapter 1 in Volume 1). Towards the end of the nineteenth century, formal education was becoming increasingly important.

The other major likely contributor to growth is physical capital. We have stock estimates for ten countries. This evidence underlines how similar the patterns of capital accumulation in Europe were during the period under consideration. Only Spain (1.8 percent) and France (1.4 percent) displayed trends well below the average (2.4 percent). Sweden (3.4 percent) and Denmark (3.3 percent) were in the opposite situation.[12] With this data we will make a first attempt to measure the contribution of various major inputs to growth.

Was there total factor productivity growth?

Estimating total factor productivity (TFP) growth for the whole of Europe between 1870 and 1913 is not an easy task. In the current state of knowledge, we can obtain estimates for eight countries that provide us with reliable data on GDP, employment, working hours, and capital stocks. These are the largest western economies – the United Kingdom, France, Germany, and Italy – and some of the middle and small-sized economies – Spain, the Netherlands, Sweden, and Denmark. Table 2.4 summarizes the results for each of them and for all of them together, as if they were a unified entity. We also report the European values for each concept, in order to get a rough assessment of what could change with a broader European database.

The results in bold provide the best available synthetic view of the likely TFP growth in western Europe.[13] The following row providing data for western Europe includes Belgium, Finland, Norway, and Switzerland, and is almost

---

[9] Maddison 1991.   [10] Huberman and Minns 2007, p. 548.   [11] Lindert 2004.   [12] Our own calculations.

[13] The TFP growth rate is pretty robust to the weighting assumptions. Although the most widely accepted weights are 70 percent and 30 percent for labor and capital, respectively, there are some cases where other assumptions have been made. In the case of a 65/35 weighting, the resulting TFP growth rate would be 0.85 percent. In the case of a 75/25 weighting, it would be 1.03 percent.

Table 2.4 TFP, 1870–1913 (growth rates or percentages, all %)

Country	GDP	Employment	Hours worked	Capital stock	TFP	GDP p.c.	TFP/ GDP	TFP/ GDP p.c.
Denmark	2.66	1.04	−0.53	3.29	1.32	1.57	84	49
France	1.63	0.20	−0.18	1.41	1.19	1.45	82	73
Germany	2.90	1.47	−0.43	3.12	1.24	1.72	72	43
Italy	1.66	0.58	−0.04	2.67	0.48	0.92	52	29
Netherlands	2.16	1.22	−0.25	3.14	0.54	0.89	61	25
Spain	1.81	0.52	−0.31	1.82	1.12	1.28	87	62
Sweden	2.62	0.71	−0.52	3.43	1.46	1.90	77	56
United Kingdom	1.86	1.15	−0.09	2.13	0.48	0.97	49	26
EUROPE-8	**2.04**	**0.85**	**−0.29**	**2.36**	**0.94**	**1.29**	**73**	46
W.Europe *	2.05	0.86	−0.32	2.36		1.29		
Europe Total	2.15					1.08		

Notes: TFP is calculated assuming a production function whereby labor's contribution is 70 percent and capital's contribution is 30 percent.
* "Western Europe" here means the western European countries with data on capital stocks or on employment and working hours. In addition to the eight considered in the table, they are Belgium, Finland, Norway, and Switzerland for employment; Belgium and Switzerland for working hours; Finland and Norway for capital stocks. GDP and GDP per capita data corresponds to the grouping of twelve.
Source: see text.

identical even if we do not have all the necessary information for each of these countries. We can assume that the overall picture would not change if we included them. We cannot say the same for the whole of Europe. The last row reminds us that overall GDP growth was 0.1 percent higher for the whole of Europe, and overall per capita GDP growth 0.2 percent lower. European TFP growth may have been different from the one that we have assessed – but not by very much.

The results are very interesting. At 0.94 percent per year, TFP growth for the whole period was impressive. It is even more impressive to see that TFP growth accounted for almost three quarters of GDP per capita growth. The diversity of experience was limited. There were five countries with higher than average TFP growth rates, but all of them were within a close range (1.12 to 1.46 percent). For these five countries – Denmark, France, Germany, Spain, and Sweden – TFP accounted for 72 to 87 percent of GDP per capita growth. Three other countries – Italy, the Netherlands, and the UK – shared very similar TFP growth rates (0.48 to 0.54 percent) and had a smaller share of per capita GDP growth (49 to 61 percent). Even these last ratios are fairly high by current standards. The comparison with GDP growth rates can be checked in the last column. France appears as the country getting the most TFP out of its GDP growth, followed by Spain and Sweden, all three well above the average.

Table 2.5 TFP growth, 1870–1913, Europe-8 (in %)

Period	GDP growth	Employment growth	Hours worked	Capital stock	TFP growth	GDP p.c. growth	TFP on p.c. GDP
1870–80	1.77	0.77	−0.32	2.15	0.81	1.08	75
1880–90	2.00	0.75	−0.40	1.99	1.16	1.33	87
1890–1900	2.17	0.88	−0.27	2.47	1.00	1.38	72
1900–13	2.17	0.98	−0.31	2.71	0.89	1.32	67

Sources: as for Table 2.4.

If we want to look for a parallel for TFP growth explaining such a high share of GDP growth or GDP per capita growth, we have to look to the Golden Age of the post-war era (see Chapter 12 in this volume). A significant portion of Europe was growing as fast as could reasonably be expected. We can say that these countries were growing at their full potential – at the production frontier. This happened both with countries that enjoyed relatively high GDP and per capita GDP growth rates like Germany, Sweden, or Denmark, and with countries with much more modest GDP outcomes like France and Spain. This strongly suggests that the economies were highly flexible, and allowed for a full exploitation of the economic opportunities to hand. We will quickly review these opportunities below. Meanwhile we advance the hypothesis that a wide range of the European economies of the time managed to grow at their full potential – very close to the production frontier.

Before this, let us briefly consider the temporal pattern of TFP evolution, displayed in Table 2.5. The smooth acceleration of GDP growth rates was eroded by a similar trend in employment rates and in capital stock. The overall effect was growing TFP from the first to the second decade, and a declining trend afterwards. TFP was most important in GDP and in per capita GDP growth between 1880 and 1890 and least important between 1900 and 1913.

Ultimate sources of growth

Scientific and technological progress

Science and technology are the *deus ex machina* of modern economic growth. The core of the explanation of the Industrial Revolution and of its diffusion lies in technological change (Landes 1969; Voth 2006). Behind it what we have is scientific change (Mokyr 2002). The determinants of scientific change are difficult to ascertain; Mokyr has made a big effort in this direction. What we do know is that patenting had something to do with it. Patents provide a financial incentive to inventors, especially those at the more applied end of the spectrum. Patents combine a property rights and a technological change view of both the rise of modern economic growth and its sustainability over time. There is much information on patenting from the middle of the nineteenth century, and in most countries much of the scientific and technological progress that occurred from this time onwards was patented.[14] A few small countries, most notably the Netherlands, opted out of the system and went for an open, non-proprietary approach. To all other countries, patents did matter – and perhaps they mattered even more to the Netherlands, but negatively. By 1913, two small European countries had a clear lead in patents granted per million inhabitants: Belgium and Switzerland (almost exactly the same: around 1,455/1,458). Denmark followed some way behind with 528. Not surprisingly, these three were the most successful countries after the UK. The Netherlands, with a dismal eighteen patents per million inhabitants in 1913, did not live up to its GDP per capita, but its patenting failure fits perfectly well with its inability to keep its past economic leadership and to enhance it. The Dutch failure in patenting mirrors its overall disappointing economic performance during the nineteenth century. The extreme Dutch position was exaggerated by the country's late return to a patent-based system for protecting intellectual property rights. The Dutch abandoned it in 1869 and only returned to normal practice by 1912. The patenting ranking of the other European countries by 1913 was (in declining order): Norway (488), France (401), Great Britain (364), Sweden (341), Italy (298), Austria–Hungary (214), Germany (202), Finland (143), Spain (88), Portugal (70), and Russia (15).[15]Germany's position was relatively low, but it has to be borne in mind that patenting laws were not identical throughout Europe. The German patenting system was very demanding, financially speaking, and fewer patents were granted per capita.

The development of patenting over time is at least as interesting as its cross-section (see Figure 2.11). With the available data to hand, the leaders in patenting by the end of the eighteenth century were Great Britain (no surprise), the United States, and France. The Netherlands was fourth, well below the other three. For three decades this was the situation. Some German states started to introduce patent laws during the Napoleonic Wars, Spain in 1820, Austria in 1821, and Belgium since its independence in 1830. Many others followed: Finland in 1833, Portugal in 1838, Norway, Russia, and Sweden in 1842. At the apex of the patenting era, the Netherlands repealed patenting (1869).

[14] See Moser 2005 for a discussion of the exceptions.
[15] All patenting data from Federico 1964. Population data from Mitchell 2003.

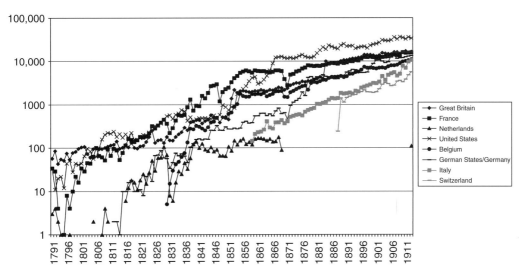

Figure 2.11 Total patents granted in Europe (selected countries) and the United States, 1791–1913. *Sources:* P.J. Federico 1964, but for Spain, Sáiz 2005.

Switzerland, which was uncertain, was very late and only started in the mid-1880s. It quickly became a major player in the field.[16]

The per capita figures in Table 2.6 provide a fascinating picture. The United States was the leader by the end of the eighteenth century and around 1830, but was overtaken by Belgium, which became the leader *c.* 1870 and remained so *c.* 1910. Switzerland, a latecomer in patenting law, was quite close to Belgium by 1910. The Netherlands was one of the initial players, and became European leader by 1830, but disappeared from the picture later on. France had a much more stable path as a top – but not in first position – European patenter, similar to the United Kingdom but for its very strong start. Among the small countries, Denmark and Norway also performed very well, while among the large countries Russia had a dismal perform-ance. All of this suggests that the Dutch failure to keep pace with the UK and Belgium could be related to institutional issues such as patenting.[17] The USA's successful catch-up could also be related to its precocious lead in patenting.[18]

Embedded technological change: investment performance

Technological change usually materialized through investment. Figure 2.12 displays the absolute effort realized at the European level (combining data

---

[16] All the information comes from Federico 1964, apart from Spain (Sáiz 2005).

[17] Van Zanden and van Riel 2004 elaborate on the slowness of Duch economic growth during most of the nineteenth century.

[18] Khan 2005.

Table 2.6 Patents per capita (decennial average per million inhabitants)

Country	1791–1800	1826–35	1866–75	1904–13
Austria–Hungary [a]		4.0	43.8	171.7
Belgium		4.8	386.5	1,194.3
Denmark		0.0	59.8	397.7
Finland		0.1	3.9	116.3
France	0.5	12.0	141.3	363.8
German states/Germany		2.2	20.9	186.5
Italy			17.5	185.8
Netherlands	0.5	15.7	15.2	1.9
Norway		0.0	24.5	486.2
Portugal				76.6
Russia		0.0	0.9	9.2
Spain		1.0	5.8	112.2
Sweden		0.0	35.0	348.5
Switzerland			0.0	971.7
United Kingdom	4.4	7.0	82.8	351.9
United States	5.6	39.0	300.0	344.1

Notes and sources: Population figures are mid-year estimates for 1801, 1830, 1870, and 1910. All come from Mitchell 2003, apart from the USA which is from Carter *et al.* 2006, the Netherlands 1800 and 1830, from Maddison 2007, and Spain 1830, from Nicolau 2005.
[a] Only Austria for 1865–75 and for 1904–13.

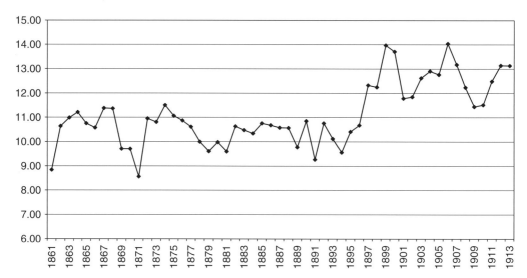

Figure 2.12 Europe, investment ratio, 1861–1913 (% of GDP). *Source:* see Table 2.3 and Appendix.

from the same ten countries as in Table 2.3). It provides a summary of the European experience with investment. Levels over the first three decades were relatively stable, but two major cycles are clearly visible, one in the 1860s and the other in the 1870s. Both were related to waves of railroad building all over Europe.

The late 1890s display a jump from 10 to 14 percent that was not completely reversed in the later period. This jump of the late nineteenth century was quite general, as were the two subsequent cycles leading to the 1906 and 1913 peaks. They were the substance of the second industrial revolution: electrification, new public services in the growing urban centers, chemicals, steel and engineering in manufacturing, and related developments.

The leading countries in absolute volumes of capital formation were Germany, the UK, and France. Interestingly enough, Germany was the leader most of the time. As a share of GDP (i.e., the investment effort or ratio), the Scandinavian countries, especially Norway and Denmark, were well ahead. Germany at the start of the period and Italy towards the end also made large efforts. Spain was clearly at the bottom of the investment ranking. These are features that square well with the rest of what we know.

Market expansion

Any account of the sources of TFP growth has to pay attention to market expansion – the most likely explanation at least since Adam Smith. Figure 2.13 provides part of the evidence. The measure of openness (exports + imports as a share of GDP) is a component of market expansion. According to evidence gathered from the whole of western Europe (Carreras and Tafunell 2008), openness jumped to 40.9 percent by 1913 from 27.6 in 1870, an increase of almost 50 percent. In 1870, openness had increased greatly compared to the

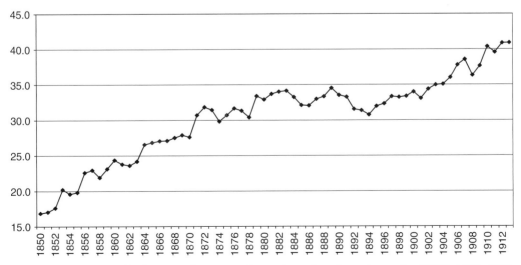

Figure 2.13 Openness in western Europe (exports + imports as a % of GDP), 1850–1913.
Source: Carreras and Tafunell 2008.

even lower 1850 starting point of 16.9 percent. The performance of the second half of the nineteenth century was not linear (see Chapter 1 in this volume). There were periods of modestly increasing openness in the 1870s and early 1880s, followed by periods of decline between 1883 and 1894 and a long period of expansion from 1894 to 1913. The combination of expanding output and expanding foreign trade allowed for the appearance and development of many markets that translated into efficiency gains of unknown magnitude.

Domestic trade also suggests the same phenomenon. The spread of railroads triggered very important expansions in trade volumes. The effect was fully at work in the most advanced countries by the middle of the nineteenth century, but it diffused towards peripheral countries later in the century. The available estimates of railroad freight traffic, in million tons, grew at 2.3 percent yearly in a group of eleven countries, excluding Germany and Russia. Measured in million ton-kilometers, railroads yield a 4.8 percent yearly growth for a group comprising Austria–Hungary, Finland, France, Germany, Norway, and Spain. Passenger traffic (millions of passengers) grew at 4.0 percent in a group of thirteen countries, including all the big ones apart from Germany. Postal mail grew at 5.1 percent in thirteen European countries (apart from Russia and a few peripherals). Telegrams grew at 5.6 percent in seventeen European countries, comprising all but a few Balkan states. All of these indices are proxies of market growth. All of them outperform GDP growth by various points and are suggestive of the importance of market expansion.[19]

Institutional developments

We switch now to one of the typical ultimate causes of growth. Institutions do matter, no doubt about it. But how much? Through what channels? These are much more difficult questions to answer. Late nineteenth-century Europe provides some evidence of the role of political institutions. The Polity IV database provides a quantitative assessment of political development along the autocracy–democracy continuum. The authors allocate from 0 to 10 points to democratic features, and from 0 to 10 points to autocratic features. The "Polity" index is the difference "Democracy less Autocracy." By definition the highest value is +10 (democracy without autocratic elements) and the minimum is −10 (autocracy without democratic elements). Of course, the Polity index is about distribution of power, representative institutions, extent of the franchise, but not about property rights and the rule of law. However, we may

---

[19] All the data in this paragraph come from Mitchell 2003.

infer that in a country with a proper democratic distribution of power, the rule of law should be present as well.

The countries that stand out as the most democratic by 1870 are Switzerland (Polity score: 10), Greece (9), Belgium (6), and the UK (3). All twenty-one others are in the negative range. The most autocratic are Russia and Turkey (−10). By 1913 there are twelve in the positive range and eight in the negative. The highest ranked are Switzerland, Greece and Norway (10), the UK, France, and Denmark (8), Belgium and Portugal (7), Spain (6), Sweden (5), Serbia (4), Germany (2). Bulgaria is the worst with a Polity index of −9.

While we may feel comfortable with Switzerland, Belgium, and the UK having high marks by 1870, what can we say about Greece? Our data suggest that Greece was not doing well at all. It was in the poor range, and not rising quickly. We can say the same of the two Iberian countries, Spain and Portugal, which reach high marks in 1913 and have greatly improved compared to 1870 (Portugal enjoys the second biggest improvement in Europe, just behind Norway). An alternative could be to obtain the average Polity index for the whole period. This is not an easy task, as the authors of the index have failed to deal with the turmoil years. The available data suggest that democratic regimes are usually prone to growth, but they can be even more prone to stability. Growth and stability may be complementary in advanced economies, but contradictory in backward ones.

Concluding remarks: growing at the production frontier

We know enough about the European economy between 1870 and 1913 to be quite confident about the aggregate growth rate, even if we are still searching for better data for a number of Balkan economies. The globalized European economy was in a "silver age." GDP growth was quite rapid (2.15 percent per annum) and widespread all over Europe. Even discounting the high rates of population growth (1.06 percent), per capita growth was left at a respectable 1.08 percent. Income per capita was rising in every country, and the rates of improvement were quite similar. This was a major achievement after two generations of highly localized growth, both geographically and socially. Indeed, the first two thirds of the century were characterized by highly localized growth spurts and the benefits were not diffused to most of the social fabric. By contrast, since 1870 or even earlier, the whole of Europe, with very few exceptions, was enjoying the advantages of the industrial age, with new products, cheaper food, improved transport and communication facilities, and better access to markets. Growth was based on the increased use of labor and capital, but a good part of it was due to improving total factor productivity – efficiency gains resulting from not-well-specified ultimate sources of growth. The proportion of increased income per capita coming from these sources suggests that the European economy was growing at full capacity – at its production frontier. It would have been very difficult to improve its performance. It is fair to say that the United States fared even better, but that was a truly exceptional achievement. Within Europe convergence was limited, and it occurred mostly after 1900. What happened was more the end of an era of big divergences rather than an era of big convergence. This did not seem sufficient to many – governments, elites and political and social movements – who were very anxious to fully reap the abundant profits of the new capitalist world. The road to August 1914 was paved with the ambitions of many. The expanding European economy of 1870–1913 was growing quickly enough to suggest to all the economic agents that all they had dreamt of was within their immediate reach, if only they had the will to take it. Crowned heads, populist leaders, arms manufacturers, as well as trade unions and minority political parties, played the sorcerer's apprentice. It is worth remembering that only Lenin fully seized the opportunity – and we know the outcome. All the others failed.

Appendix on sources

GDP, population, and per capita GDP data for the whole of western European and for each western European country come from Carreras and Tafunell 2004a, updated and expanded in Carreras and Tafunell (2008). More detailed information on sources and aggregation methods is available there. Data for Austria–Hungary are from Schulze 2000. Russian data after 1885 are from Gregory 1982, and earlier data from Goldsmith 1961. The limited data on the Balkans and the Ottoman Empire presented by Maddison (2007) are reviewed by Avramov and Pamuk (2006). Pamuk (2006) provides new data for some benchmarks. We have adjusted our estimates to the frontiers of the time set of benchmarks defined by Broadberry and Klein (2008). GDP data are always presented in international US $ at 1990 prices. This accounting procedure has been widely accepted for comparative purposes although most scholars are aware of its limitations (see Prados de la Escosura 2000 for an alternative measure). Western European consumer price index, openness, and investment ratios are from Carreras and Tafunell 2008.

Sectoral developments, 1870–1914

Stephen Broadberry, Giovanni Federico, and Alexander Klein

Contents

Introduction

Gross domestic product consists of a wide array of activities, and the structure of those activities has changed over time as the European economy has developed. Economists have long classified activities on the basis of a distinction between agriculture, industry, and services, although there has been less than complete agreement on which occupations to include in each sector (Clark 1951). In this chapter we will follow the modern European convention of including forestry and fishing together with farming as "agriculture," and include mineral extraction together with manufacturing, construction, and gas, electricity and water, in "industry." Services then covers all other activities, including transport and communications, distribution, finance, personal and professional services, and government. We will examine the development of the three main sectors and also consider the effects of the major structural shifts, as the share of the labor force declined in agriculture and increased in industry and services between 1870 and 1914.

For an economy to have high living standards, it is necessary to have high productivity in all sectors. However, it is also clear that the structure of the economy matters, because value added per worker is higher in some sectors than in others. Since agriculture has historically tended to be the lowest value-added sector, the share of the labor force in agriculture turns out to be a very good predictor of per capita income. In general, European countries that remained heavily committed to agriculture remained poor, while those that reallocated labor to industry and services became better off (Broadberry 2008).

Structure of the economy

Table 3.1 provides data on the sectoral distribution of the labor force between agriculture, industry, and services. For the sample of fourteen countries available in both years, the share of employment in agriculture declined from 51.7 percent in 1870 to 41.4 percent in 1913. The lowest share of the labor force in agriculture in 1913 was in north-west Europe and the largest share in central and eastern Europe. However, there was considerable variation within each region, ranging from just 11.8 percent in the United Kingdom to 82.2 percent in Serbia.

As the share of the labor force in agriculture declined, the shares in industry and services increased, and this trend can also be seen in Table 3.1. For the fourteen-country sample, the share of industry in employment rose from 26.9 to 32.3 percent, while the share of services increased from 21.4 to 26.3 percent. Looking at the cross-sectional variation in 1913, the share of industry was

Table 3.1 Distribution of the working population by major sector, 1870–1913

	Agriculture		Industry		Services	
	c. 1870	*c. 1913*	*c. 1870*	*c. 1913*	*c. 1870*	*c. 1913*
North-west Europe	31.7	20.9	35.0	39.5	33.3	39.6
Belgium	44.4	23.2	37.8	45.5	17.8	31.3
Denmark	47.8	41.7	21.9	24.1	30.3	34.2
Finland	75.5	69.3	10.1	10.6	14.4	20.1
Netherlands	39.4	28.3	22.4	32.8	38.2	38.9
Norway	49.6	39.6	22.9	25.9	27.5	34.5
Sweden	67.4	45.0	17.4	31.8	15.2	23.2
United Kingdom	22.2	11.8	42.4	44.1	35.4	44.1
Southern Europe	58.6	49.3	23.2	26.8	18.2	23.9
France	49.8	41.0	28.0	33.1	22.2	25.9
Greece		49.6		16.2		34.2
Italy	61.0	55.4	23.3	26.6	15.7	18.0
Portugal	65.0	57.4	24.9	21.9	10.1	20.7
Spain	66.3	56.3	18.2	13.8	15.5	29.9
Central and eastern Europe	56.6	54.9	25.8	24.4	17.6	20.7
Austria–Hungary	67.0	59.5	15.5	21.8	17.5	18.7
Bulgaria		81.9		8.1		10.0
Germany	49.5	34.5	29.1	37.9	21.4	27.6
Romania		79.6		8.0		12.4
Russia		58.6		16.1		25.3
Serbia		82.2		11.1		6.7
Switzerland	42.3	26.8	41.8	45.7	15.9	27.5
Total Europe	51.7	47.1	26.9	27.8	21.4	25.1
Total Europe (14 countries)	51.7	41.4	26.9	32.3	21.4	26.3

Notes: regional figures are weighted country averages within each region. Total Europe figures are calculated for the fourteen countries available in both years, as well as for the differing sample sizes. *Source:* Derived from Mitchell 2003 except as follows: Sweden: Krantz and Schön 2007; UK: Feinstein 1972; Germany: Hoffmann 1965.

highest in north-west Europe and lowest in central and eastern Europe. The share of the labor force in services in 1913 was also highest in north-west Europe and lowest in central and eastern Europe, but again with substantial variation across countries within each region.

Figure 3.1 shows a strong negative relationship between the level of per capita income and the share of the labor force in agriculture in 1913. It was already clear by this time that escaping from poverty required the reallocation of labor away from agriculture, so that modernizing governments across Europe adopted industrialization as a policy goal. However, the relationship between GDP per capita and the share of the labor force in industry was actually much less clear, as can be seen in Table 3.2. This table formalizes the

Table 3.2 Regression analysis of the relationship between GDP per capita and the sectoral allocation of labor, 1870–1992

	Agriculture	Industry	Services
Constant	9.47 (166.62)	7.10 (48.10)	6.72 (88.32)
Sectoral share of labor	−0.032 (−23.69)	0.041 (8.82)	0.047 (22.80)
R^2	0.795	0.349	0.782

Notes: The dependent variable is the log of GDP per capita in 1990 Geary–Khamis dollars. Figures in parentheses are t-statistics. Data are for up to twenty-two countries in 1870, 1913, 1929, 1938, 1950, 1973, and 1992, yielding 147 observations.
Source: Broadberry 2008.

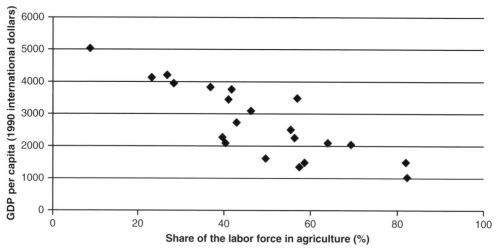

Figure 3.1 The relationship between GDP per capita and the sectoral allocation of labor in 1913. *Source:* Broadberry 2008.

relationship between GDP per capita and the sectoral allocation of labor, using regression analysis and pooling cross-sectional observations for a number of years between 1870 and 1992. The first column confirms the statistically significant negative relationship between living standards and the share of the labor force in agriculture, and also finds a significant positive relationship between GDP per capita and the share of the labor force in industry. However, notice that the fit of the equation, as measured by R^2, is much weaker for industry than for agriculture. Note also that the fit becomes stronger once again in the regression of GDP per capita on the share of the labor force in services.

These structural changes were occurring as a result of two main forces. First, within each country, as incomes rose, demand shifted proportionally away from agricultural goods, with relatively low income elasticities of demand, towards industrial goods and services, with higher income elasticities of demand. Second, falling transport costs permitted growing specialization along lines of comparative advantage.

Agriculture

Opportunities and challenges

Growth of population and income increased the demand for agricultural products. Total consumption of calories per capita increased, particularly in poor countries, and demand shifted away from cereals towards more income-elastic goods, such as livestock products in southern Europe and fruit and vegetables in northern Europe (Federico 2003a; Coppola and Vecchi 2006). The reduction in transport costs fostered trade in agricultural products, with a significant impact on relative prices. Although the real price of agricultural products remained broadly constant, the intersectoral terms of trade (the price of agricultural products relative to manufactures) improved in most countries (Williamson 2002a). Prices of crops (mainly cereals) declined relative to livestock in all European countries. Figures 3.2 and 3.3 show these trends in the intersectoral terms of trade and the relative price of crops to livestock for France, the United Kingdom, and the United States.

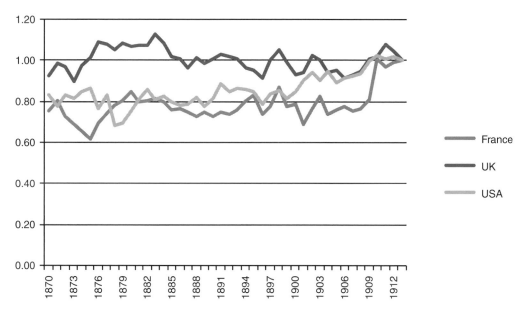

Figure 3.2 Intersectoral terms of trade, agriculture, industry, 1870–1913 (1913 = 1.00).
Source: Williamson 2002a.

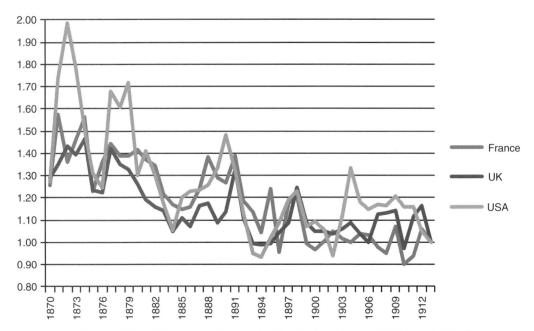

Figure 3.3 Relative prices of crops and livestock, 1870–1913 (1913 = 1.00). *Sources:* US Department of Commerce 1975; Levy-Leboyer 1979, Mitchell 1988.

The performance

The widely held view that European agriculture performed poorly during the period 1870–1913 is in need of revision. In Table 3.3, we see that the growth rate of gross output was quite high for the continent as a whole and also for the main regions. Although medium-term output trends were remarkably stable, production did nevertheless fluctuate quite a lot from one year to another, following the vagaries of the weather (Solomou and Wu 1999). In particular, there is some statistical evidence of a slowdown in growth between 1873 and 1896. However, the slowdown was not as serious as to warrant the label "Great Depression" (Saul 1969).

The country rankings of agricultural growth performance in Table 3.3 are also at odds with the conventional view. In fact, the best growth performance by far was recorded by Russia, where production increased by a factor of 2.5 over forty-three years, and the third highest increase was in Austria–Hungary. Clearly, these figures have to be considered with caution, but there is no doubt that Russia was a success story, as confirmed by the great increase in its agricultural exports (Stern 1960). Most countries increased agricultural production at a rate of around 1.0 to 1.5 percent per annum, exceeding or keeping up with the increase in their population. In only three cases (Portugal, the Netherlands, and the United Kingdom) did agricultural production per capita decline. Between 1870 and

Table 3.3 Agricultural production in 1913, by country

	Value added (£m)	Gross output (£m)	Share VA/gross output	Share livestock	Growth rate of gross output, 1870–1913 (% p. a.)
Austria–Hungary	383	414	0.925	0.262	1.88
Belgium	34	54	0.630	0.665	0.76
Denmark	36	67	0.540	0.940	1.62
Finland	15	18	0.833	0.746	1.56
France	516	587	0.879	0.426	0.62
Germany	526	575	0.915	0.698	1.56
Greece	18	20	0.900	0.363	2.12
Italy	326	352	0.926	0.307	1.14
Netherlands	30	56	0.536	0.591	0.65
Portugal	26	28	0.929	0.236	0.54
Russia	729	767	0.950	0.344	2.24
Spain	137	145	0.945	0.344	0.46
Sweden	37	44	0.841	0.661	0.96
Switzerland	31	35	0.886	0.795	0.70
UK	135	201	0.672	0.747	0.00
North-west Europe	287	440	0.653	0.748	0.88
Central and eastern Europe	1,132	1,132	0.904	0.429	1.91
Southern Europe	1,791	1,791	0.932	0.372	0.78
Europe	2,979	3,363	0.886	0.452	1.36
"World"	5,640	6,387	0.883	0.437	1.56

Notes: countries at their 1913 boundaries.
Source: Federico 2004.

1913, trade in primary products, which went almost entirely to western Europe, increased by a factor of 3.5. This increase fed Britons and allowed other western Europeans to improve their nutritional standards.

The proximate causes of growth: factor inputs and TFP

Table 3.4 shows that the growth of factor inputs contributed very little to the growth of agricultural output. There are some difficulties in measuring the total stock of land in use, because it is hard to be sure about the extent of pasture in use, but land under crop remained constant or fell in the west, and increased by only a few percentage points in the east. Again, there are difficulties in measuring the agricultural labor input because non-agricultural workers often helped

Table 3.4 Factor inputs and labor productivity in agriculture

	Land (millions of hectares)			Labor (millions of workers)			Labor productivity (UK in 1913 = 100)		
	c. 1850	c. 1880	c. 1910	c. 1850	c. 1880	c. 1910	c. 1880	c. 1910	Total growth
Austria–Hungary	20.2	25.6	26.7	13.8	14.9	15.5	16.8	28.9	1.725
Belgium		1.6	1.5	1.0	1.1	0.8	27.6	46.1	1.667
Bulgaria		1.8	2.5			0.9			
Denmark	2.0	2.4	2.9		0.95	0.5	23.7	79.0	3.341
Finland				0.4	0.45	0.6	20.7	26.6	1.288
France	34.3	32.7	29.6	9.1	8.6	7.7	48.6	74.0	1.523
Germany	24.4	26.2	26.2	8.3	9.6	10.5	34.8	52.4	1.506
Greece	0.85	0.9	0.9						
Italy	13.5	15.4	14.8		9.4	10.5	25.4	32.5	1.281
Netherlands	1.9	2.0	2.1	0.49	0.62	0.68	40.9	50.3	1.228
Norway					0.22	0.37			
Portugal	1.9		3.2		1.1	1.1	22.7	29.1	1.283
Romania	2.5		5.0			1.6			
Russia	82.5	103.8	113.4	17.6°	25.7°	37.0°			1.571°
European Russia			85.9						
Spain	16.0	15.8	19.1	4.5	4.9	4.4	25.6	33.7	1.314
Sweden		3.4	3.4	0.7	1.1	1.0	26.0	39.4	1.518
UK	8.0	8.0	6.7	2.0	1.6	1.5	87.9	100.0	1.137
India							9.3	10.5	1.136
USA							82.8	108.5	1.310

° males only.
Sources: land (acreage and tree-crops only), Federico 2005, Table 4.1. For European Russia, data from Anfimov and Korelin 1995: 61; Labor (males and females), Federico 2005, Table 4.16; labor productivity computed as ratio of GDP (averages 1878–81 and 1911–13) to workforce.

permanent agricultural workers at seasonal peaks; because the quality of work differed according to the age, sex, and skill of the worker, and because the number of hours worked or the intensity of work differed by country. Nevertheless, the labor force data show a pattern that is consistent with the pattern for land, with the number of agricultural workers staying constant or falling in the west and increasing only in the east. Note that this broad stability in the number of agricultural workers was consistent with a substantial fall in the share of the labor force in agriculture because of the increase in the population and the labor force.

Capital is the most difficult factor of production to measure accurately, but the available data on buildings, land improvements, and machinery rule out rapid growth, with the exception of Russia (Federico 2005, Table 4.7). Capital stock declined in the United Kingdom and rose at about 1 percent per annum in other west European countries. The effect of the diffusion of modern techniques can be detected in the growth of purchases outside agriculture. A simple measure of these purchases is the ratio between value added (which excludes them) and gross output (which includes them). As Table 3.3 demonstrates, the ratio in 1913 shows quite substantial differences among countries, which tally well with conventional views about the level of technical development in each country.

The combination of substantial production growth and relatively slow increase in inputs implies a healthy growth of total factor productivity (TFP). Federico (2005, Table 5.5) finds an average rate of TFP growth for ten European countries of 0.7 percent per annum, which corresponds to a cumulated 30 to 40 percent increase over the 1870–1913 period. This is broadly consistent with the findings of Van Zanden (1991) and suggests that European performance compared quite favorably with that of the countries of western settlement over the same years, with TFP in agriculture growing at a rate of 0.2 to 0.5 percent per annum in the United States.

The underlying causes of growth: technical progress or market integration?

Most authors attribute growth in TFP to technical progress, and there were some important technological innovations in nineteenth-century European agriculture. Fallow practically disappeared from western Europe, with the conspicuous exception of Spain, although it remained important in the east (Antsiferov 1930, p. 16; Bringas Gutiérrez 2000, Table I.3). Tools improved, with iron ploughs replacing wooden ones in backward countries and with better design improving performance and reducing the need for draft power in more advanced areas. Mechanization proceeded more slowly, with the steam thresher the only "modern" machine widely used in the early twentieth century (Federico 2003b). However, there was a major breakthrough from the 1860s, as the chemical industry made new products such as ammonium sulphate and calcium-cyanamide available at lower and lower prices, and fertilizer consumption per hectare increased dramatically (van Zanden 1994, Table 4.7; Federico 2005, Table 6.3).

Before simply assuming that all TFP growth was due to technical progress, it is important to consider the possible role of the more efficient allocation of resources, as a result of the growing development of markets, including commercialization and market integration (price convergence). There is a substantial literature on market integration, at least for wheat (Jacks 2005; Federico and Persson 2007) and some work on commercialization (Federico 1986). However, the effects of these developments on agriculture have hardly been explored. The only exception (Grantham 1989) focuses largely on the pre-railroad age in France. To what extent did integration cause relative prices to change and to what extent did production adjust via local specialization? To be sure, there is evidence of the growth of specialized production around the cities or in some well-endowed areas, such as the south Italian and Spanish vineyards. Also, there was a modest increase in the share of livestock in total gross output, from 41 to 46 percent, consistent with the increase in its relative price (Federico 2004). However, much more detailed data would be needed to provide a comprehensive assessment of the real impact of commercialization and globalization and its importance relative to technical progress.

The role of institutions

By and large, farmers were left to themselves. Support for technical progress was very limited and although land reform was much debated, very little action followed, except in Ireland. Even intervention in product markets was relatively modest. This statement may seem surprising in the light of the conventional view of a protectionist backlash to the grain invasion from the United States (O'Rourke 1997). However, it is important to remember that (1) Russia rather than the United States was the main invader in most European markets, at least for wheat; (2) tariff barriers on wheat were erected in only a few continental countries and were not particularly high; (3) wheat accounted for only 15 to 20 percent of total output, while the rest of agriculture was affected much less by global competition.

Many historians blame institutions for what they perceive as the disappointing performance of European agriculture, arguing that common ownership of land and traditional contracts, such as sharecropping, hindered innovation. However, the empirical evidence for such a proposition is at best mixed, as can be seen from the following two examples. First, sharecropping is often blamed for the poor performance of Mediterranean agriculture (Sereni 1968). Landlords are said to have been more interested in accumulating land than in making productivity-increasing investments, while tenants were too poor to risk anything. However, econometric tests on Italian data have failed to find any effects of contracts on productivity (Galassi 1986; Galassi and Cohen 1994). Second, in Russia, serfdom was abolished only in 1861 and land ownership was vested in the peasant commune, the *obschina* or *mir*, where periodic redistribution of land is usually seen as having hindered investment or innovation (Gerschenkron 1966). But the *obschina* was actually rather flexible (Gregory 1994), and agricultural output grew rapidly in Russia while it stagnated in Britain, where the institutional framework was most developed. This example reminds us that the catching-up perspective suggests that we should expect a negative relationship between the growth rate and the starting level of

productivity. Since Britain had the highest level of agricultural labor productivity in Europe in 1870, slow productivity growth was only to be expected.
Similarly, the low initial level of productivity in Russia opened up the opportunity of rapid catching-up growth. Also, institutions are only one possible
reason for the failure of a country to catch up, since other factors such as land
quality and economic policy also play their part.

Industry

Europe's industrial production, 1870–1913

Industrial production generally grew faster than GDP in Europe between 1870 and
1913, as Europe developed and agriculture declined in relative importance.
Table 3.5 presents data on the average annual growth rate of industrial production,
by countries grouped together in the main regions. The scope for rapid catching-up
growth was greater in the less developed parts of Europe, which in 1870 had still
not embarked upon the development of modern industry. In central and eastern
Europe, Germany, Austria–Hungary, and Russia all recorded rapid growth rates of
industrial output as they began the process of catching up on Britain, the most
highly developed country in Europe. In north-west Europe, the Netherlands and
Sweden also began a sustained period of industrial development from around 1870.

Table 3.5 Growth of industrial production, 1870–1913 (% per annum)

Country	Growth rate	Country	Growth rate	Country	Growth rate
North-west Europe		*Southern Europe*		*Central and eastern Europe*	
Belgium	2.5	France	2.1	Austria–Hungary	2.8
Denmark	3.4	Italy	2.7	Germany	4.1
Finland	4.1	Portugal	2.4	Russia	5.1
Netherlands	3.0	Spain	2.7	Switzerland	3.2
Norway	3.3				
Sweden	4.4				
United Kingdom	2.1				

Note: growth of industrial production in Switzerland is for the period 1891–1913.
Sources: Belgium: Gadisseur 1973; Denmark: Hansen 1974; Finland: Hjerppe 1996; Netherlands:
Smits, Horlings, and van Zanden 2000; Norway: unpublished data kindly made available by Ola
Grytten; Sweden: Krantz and Schön 2007; United Kingdom: Feinstein 1972; France: Crouzet 1970;
Italy: Fenoaltea 2003; Portugal: Lains 2006; Spain: Prados de la Escosura 2003; Switzerland:
unpublished data kindly made available by Thomas David; Austria–Hungary: Schulze 2000;
Germany: Hoffmann 1965; Russia: Goldsmith 1961.

Table 3.6 Per capita levels of industrialization, 1870–1913 (UK in 1900 = 100)

	1860	1880	1900	1913
North-west Europe				
Belgium	28	43	56	88
Denmark	10	12	20	33
Finland	11	15	18	21
Netherlands	11	14	22	28
Norway	11	16	21	31
Sweden	15	24	41	67
United Kingdom	64	87	100	115
Southern Europe				
France	20	28	39	59
Greece	6	7	9	10
Italy	10	12	17	26
Portugal	8	10	12	14
Spain	11	14	19	22
Central and eastern Europe				
Austria–Hungary	11	15	23	32
Bulgaria	5	6	8	10
Germany	15	25	52	85
Romania	6	7	9	13
Russia	8	10	15	20
Serbia	6	7	9	12
Switzerland	26	39	67	87
EUROPE	17	23	33	45

Source: Bairoch 1982, pp. 294, 330.

However, being backward is not sufficient for the achievement of rapid industrial growth, and many relatively poor countries, particularly in southern Europe, recorded unimpressive rates of growth in industrial output.

It is therefore important to consider both levels and growth rates when assessing economic performance. Russia, for example, shows rapid industrial growth after 1870, but starting from an extremely low level of industrialization. In Table 3.6, we thus see that despite this very rapid industrial growth after 1870, Russia had still reached only 17.4 percent of the UK level of industrialization on a per capita basis by 1913.

Table 3.6 provides a good summary of the industrial development gradient within Europe, with the UK the most heavily industrialized country and Belgium, France, and Switzerland also substantially more heavily industrialized than Europe as a whole throughout the whole period 1860–1913. Sweden and Germany started the period with below-average levels of per capita industrialization, but ended it with significantly above-average levels. Although per capita industrialization increased in all countries, the level remained relatively low in much of Europe.

European industrialization can thus be thought of as geographically concentrated in a series of Marshallian districts. Marshall (original edition 1920) explained the spatial concentration of industrial production through external economies of scale, which he attributed to learning (knowledge spillovers between firms), matching (thick markets making it easier to match employers and employees), and sharing (giving firms better access to customers and suppliers in the presence of significant transport costs) (Duranton and Puga 2004).

One potential explanation for these patterns is simply geographical, with an important role for natural resource endowments. In particular, it would be difficult to understand patterns of industrial location at this time without taking account of mineral deposits. Put simply, much industrial development in the age of iron and steam took place around coal and ore fields, although this is not always particularly well captured by the boundaries of nation states (Pollard 1981: xiv–xv).

However, the period after 1870 also saw the development of a new scientific approach to industry, which began a process of freeing industry from the constraints of location around natural resource deposits. This trend was reinforced by falling transport costs. The importance of science was most obvious in the development of wholly new industries such as synthetic dyestuffs, based on new chemical processes, or electrical goods, based around a new source of energy (Chandler 1990; Landes 1969). However, it also affected many old industries, such as brewing, where research could improve both processes and products, and iron, where research led to the utilization of new ores and to better products, such as varieties of steel. Also, the development of "mass production" in engineering industries on the basis of the assembly of interchangeable parts made it possible to replace skilled craft labor by machinery, threatening the position of established producers and creating opportunities for newly industrializing nations without a large stock of experienced workers.

The "Second Industrial Revolution" thus offered countries with little previous industrial experience the opportunity to replace established producers through the more rapid development and adoption of new technology. This revolution was also associated with a growth in the concentration of industry, as large firms came to dominate the production of many of the new science-based industries (Chandler 1990; Hannah 1983). However, the extent of these trends, which became stronger after the First World War, should not be exaggerated for the pre-1914 period (Broadberry 1997; Scranton 1997).

Performance of countries and regions

The United Kingdom was Europe's most industrialized country in 1860, in terms of the absolute level of production as well as on a per capita basis. However,

Britain's very dominant position in world export markets on the basis of early industrialization was vulnerable to competition from follower countries, and was challenged during the period 1870–1913 by Germany and the United States. However, as Broadberry (1997) notes, there has been a tendency to overstate failings in British industry at this time, and to ignore success stories. First, comparative labor productivity in manufacturing as a whole changed little between the three major industrialized countries of Britain, the United States, and Germany during the period 1870–1913. So the proximate cause of the faster industrial output growth in Germany compared with Britain was simply the faster growth of the labor input, with labor productivity in Britain and Germany remaining broadly equal. Labor productivity in manufacturing in both countries remained substantially lower than in the United States, where higher labor productivity has usually been attributed to labor scarcity and natural resource abundance, leading already by the mid-nineteenth century to the development of a machine-intensive technology that was not well suited to European conditions (Habakkuk 1962; Broadberry 1997). Second, although Germany did very well in a number of heavy industries, such as chemicals and iron and steel, where labor productivity was higher than in Britain and where Germany took an impressive share of world export markets by 1913, there were also lighter industries such as textiles and food, drink and tobacco, where Britain retained a substantial productivity advantage and remained strong in world export markets (Broadberry and Burhop 2007).

The traditional view of French industry during the late nineteenth century was that it was relatively backward and, in contrast with Germany, failed to catch up with Britain (Kindleberger 1964; Landes 1969; Milward and Saul 1977). Nevertheless, this generally negative assessment of French industrial performance was tempered by the fact that the pace of industrial output growth picked up after 1895, particularly in sectors based on the new technologies of the Second Industrial Revolution, such as electrical engineering, electrometallurgy, electro-chemicals, and motor vehicles (Caron 1979, pp. 135–60; Lévy-Leboyer and Bourgignon 1989, p. 105). However, the revisionist views of O'Brien and Keyder (1978, p. 91), who claimed that levels of industrial labor productivity were higher in France than in Great Britain for most of the nineteenth century, surely went too far in rehabilitating French industrial performance. Taking both output and employment from census sources, Dormois (2004) finds that in 1906, output per worker in French industry was just 74.1 percent of the British level. The French may have found an alternative path to the twentieth century, based on small family firms catering to niche markets, but it was not without its costs in terms of living standards (O'Brien and Keyder 1978, p. 196; Caron 1979, pp. 163–70).

Austria–Hungary had a relatively low level of industrialization per capita, as can be seen in Table 3.6, but the empire nevertheless produced a significant share of Europe's industrial output on account of its size. In fact, levels of economic development within the imperial territories varied widely, with Austria (Cisleithania) generally more industrialized than Hungary (Transleithania), and with considerable variation even within Austria (Milward and Saul 1977; Pollard 1981; Komlos 1983; Good 1984). Although early quantitative research indicated a very rapid growth rate of industrial output in the Austrian part of the empire, subsequent research has modified this picture. Whereas Rudolph (1976) suggested an industrial growth rate of 3.8 percent per annum for the period 1870–1913, the addition of a wider range of industries and the use of improved value added weights has reduced this to 2.5 percent (Komlos 1983; Schulze 2000). Allowing for a faster rate of growth in Hungary, however, produces a rate of industrial growth for the empire as a whole of 2.8 percent per annum, reported here in Table 3.5 (Schulze 2000). Downward revision of the industrial growth rate by later researchers was concentrated particularly in the period before 1896, leading to an unfortunate resurrection of the term "Great Depression" for a period when output did not fall but continued to grow (Komlos 1978; Good 1978). The catching-up perspective creates an expectation that Austria–Hungary ought to have experienced rapid industrial growth to catch up with the leading European industrial nations at this time. From this perspective, Austria–Hungary clearly underperformed between 1870 and 1913.

We have already noted in our discussion of Table 3.6 that Russia was a very backward economy in the middle of the nineteenth century, so her rapid rate of industrial growth between 1870 and 1913 (see Table 3.5) conforms to the predictions of the catching-up framework. The experience of Tsarist Russia led Gerschenkron (1962) to formulate a number of propositions concerning the link between backwardness and economic development. These included (1) a greater role for the state, substituting for the lack of private entrepreneurship, (2) a greater focus on capital goods industries to compensate for a lack of consumer demand, (3) a greater role for banks in directing scarce capital into industrial projects, and (4) a greater role for imported technology. Gerschenkron attached little importance to agriculture, which he saw as almost immune to change in backward societies. Although some of Gerschenkron's generalizations do seem to fit the Russian case well, others have not stood up so well to quantitative scrutiny (Falkus 1972, pp. 57, 61–74; Gregory 1982, pp. 133–4; Gatrell 1986, p. 144).

The catching-up perspective suggests that we should expect a similar performance from the countries of the northern and southern peripheries of Europe. In Table 3.6 we see that in 1860 per capita levels of industrialization in Italy and Iberia were similar to levels in Scandinavia. Industrial growth rates in Table 3.5, however, were much higher in the Scandinavian than in the Mediterranean countries. In particular, Sweden stands out as having experienced a very rapid phase of industrial growth, achieving by 1913 a level of industrialization on a par with the European core. This is a notable case of leap-frogging thanks to the technologies of the Second Industrial Revolution, drawing particularly on Sweden's abundant supply of hydroelectric power (Pollard 1981, pp. 233–6). The relatively slow overall rate of industrial growth in Italy and Iberia masks some regional sparks of industrial development, most notably in a triangle between Genoa, Milan, and Turin, and based again on hydro-electric power (Pollard 1981, pp. 229–32).

Developments in particular branches

Industry covers a wide range of activities, and we shall now survey briefly a number of important sectors, highlighting the contributions of the major European producers. We begin with coal, the major source of energy in the age of steam. As noted earlier, industry was heavily concentrated around coalfields during the nineteenth century, so it is not surprising to see in Table 3.7 that Britain was Europe's major coal producer throughout the period, followed by Germany. Belgium, a very small country but an early industrializer, was over-taken by Germany, France, and Russia as these much larger countries industrial-ized. Although Britain remained Europe's largest coal producer, and increased her output significantly, labor productivity stagnated, with technological and organizational changes merely offsetting diminishing returns, as pits were sunk ever deeper and coal was mined further from the pithead (Greasley 1990). Although European production was still increasing, coal from the New World was already being mined in more favorable geological conditions and taking an increasing share of world production (Svennilson 1954, p. 107).

In iron and steel, major technological developments drew on science, with wrought iron increasingly being replaced by varieties of mass-produced steel, following the introduction of the Bessemer process in 1856, the Siemens-Martin (open hearth) process in 1869, and the Thomas (basic) process in 1879 (Svennilson 1954, p. 121). The general picture of Germany leap-frogging Britain is illustrated in Table 3.7B, which shows output of pig iron among Europe's main producers. Allegations of entrepreneurial failure in Britain have been exaggerated, since account must be taken of iron ore reserves and demand-side factors such as protective barriers raised in the rapidly growing markets of Germany and the United States, combined with Britain's continued free trade policy (McCloskey 1971; Tolliday 1991). The Russian growth spurt of the 1890s is also evident, with Russia overtaking France before the French forged ahead again after 1900 (Gatrell 1986, p. 153; Caron 1979, pp. 158–9). Austria–Hungary was also a major iron and steel producer despite a low per

Table 3.7 Europe's major producers of some important industrial products

A Coal (millions of metric tonnes)

	1870	1880	1890	1900	1913
United Kingdom	112	149	185	229	292
Germany	26	47	70	109	190
France	13	19	26	33	41
Russia	1	3	6	16	36
Belgium	14	17	20	23	24
Austria–Hungary	4	7	10	12	18

B Pig iron (thousands of metric tonnes)

	1870	1880	1890	1900	1913
Germany	1,261	2,468	4,100	7,550	16,761
United Kingdom	6,059	7,873	8,031	9,104	10,425
France	1,178	1,725	1,962	2,714	5,207
Russia	359	449	928	2,937	4,641
Belgium	565	608	788	1,019	2,485
Austria–Hungary	403	464	965	1,456	2,381

C Sulphuric acid (thousands of metric tonnes)

	1870	1880	1890	1900	1913
Germany	43	130	420	703	1,727
United Kingdom	590	900	870	1,010	1,082
France	125	200	–	625	900
Italy	–	–	59	230	645
Belgium	–	30		165	420
Netherlands	–	–	–	–	320

D Raw cotton consumption (thousands of metric tonnes)

	1870	1880	1890	1900	1913
United Kingdom	489	617	755	788	988
Germany	81	137	227	279	478
Russia	46	94	136	262	424
France	59	89	125	159	271
Austria–Hungary	45	64	105	127	210
Italy	15	47	102	123	202

E Beer (thousands of hectoliters)

	1870	1880	1890	1900	1913
Germany	23,700	38,572	52,830	70,857	69,200
United Kingdom	–	44,955	52,100	60,010	58,836
Austria–Hungary	9,993	10,957	14,117	21,471	24,070
Belgium	7,794	9,239	10,771	14,617	16,727
France	6,499	8,227	8,491	10,712	12,844
Russia	–	–	–	5,872	11,612

Source: Mitchell 2003.

capita level of industrialization. Like Russia, Austria–Hungary was dependent on the large home market, with a railroad construction boom providing a substantial boost to demand (Milward and Saul 1977, pp. 304–6).

Between 1870 and 1914 the chemical industry was transformed on the basis of scientific research. The production of inorganics that had been manufactured on an industrial scale since the early nineteenth century was revolutionized by innovations such as the replacement of the Leblanc process by the Solvay process for soda ash, and the introduction of electricity as an important agent in chemical processes (Svennilson 1954, p. 162). However, of more significance for the long-run development of the industry was the synthesis of organic (carbon-based) products, such as dyestuffs, pharmaceuticals, perfumes, and photographic chemicals (Svennilson 1954, p. 163). Since the synthesis of organic products required large quantities of inorganic chemicals, the production of sulphuric acid (Table 3.7C) can be taken as an indicator of the general state of Europe's national chemical industries (Svennilson 1954, pp. 163–4). As in other heavy industries, Germany overtook Britain, although the scale of the German advantage towards the end of the period is understated, since Germany was much more dominant in organic products, where Switzerland was the only serious competitor. In synthetic dyestuffs, for example, Germany produced 85.1 percent of world output in 1913 (Svennilson 1954, p. 290). The chemical industry remained relatively underdeveloped in eastern Europe, with neither Russia nor Austria–Hungary featuring among the major producers. Small, relatively rich countries such as Belgium and the Netherlands were also significant producers, alongside France, while Italy showed strong growth from the 1890s.

The Industrial Revolution began in cotton textiles, which continued to be an important branch of European industry until 1914. Britain remained the largest producer in the world despite some inevitable loss of market share as other countries industrialized (Sandberg 1974). The switch from mules to rings in spinning and from the power loom to the automatic loom in weaving removed some of the skill from the production process, and enabled countries with a less skilled but cheaper labor force to compete with Britain, in line with Vernon's (1966) product cycle model. Broadberry and Marrison (2002) emphasize the importance of external economies of scale in the British industry, which was highly localized in Lancashire, but consisted of around 2,000 spinning and weaving firms. The product cycle perspective also helps to understand the high output figures achieved towards the end of the period in low-wage countries such as Russia and Austria–Hungary, with Russia almost catching up with Germany, and with Austria–Hungary ahead of Italy and not too far behind France (Gatrell 1986: 160; Milward and Saul 1977, p. 238).

The home market was more important for the food, drink, and tobacco sector, although even here tradability was increasing with urbanization and the emergence of a substantial urban working class demanding more processed foodstuffs. Data on beer production are available on a consistent basis (Table 3.7E), and suggest a strong link to home market size and per capita income, with the highest levels of production and consumption in Germany and Britain, and with substantial production also in Austria–Hungary, France, and Russia. Although the possibility of transporting such a heavy and perishable product was limited, a small country such as Belgium was able to export to neighboring countries. Of course, it must be borne in mind that France produced large quantities of wine for export as well as for home consumption, so that more general data on production of alcoholic drinks would show a much bigger contribution from the Mediterranean countries, including Italy, Spain, and Portugal (Pinilla and Ayuda 2002).

Services

Europe's service sector output, 1870–1914

Most economic histories of the period 1870–1914 pay little attention to services, apart from railroads and banks, which are seen as supporting industry. The national accounting approach allows us to place the contributions of the railroads and banks in the wider context of the service sector as a whole, and to bring out the contributions to consumers as well as to industrial producers. Railroads moved people and agricultural produce as well as industrial goods, and it was not the sole purpose of banks to provide cheap loans to heavy industry. Furthermore, in addition to transport and communications and

finance, services also comprised the important sectors of distribution, professional and personal services, and government.

Regional developments

The most highly developed service sectors were in north-west Europe, particularly Britain and the Netherlands, where high productivity was achieved in
the specialized and standardized supply of services in a highly urbanized
environment. In sectors where international trade was possible, this played
an important role in increasing the size of the market and allowing economies
to benefit from the division of labor. High productivity required the "industrialization" of services, involving a transition from customized, low-volume,
high-margin business, organized on the basis of networks, to standardized,
high-volume, low-margin business with hierarchical management (Broadberry
2006). In some sectors, such as shipping and insurance, this involved the
emergence of large firms in classic Chandlerian fashion, but in others, such as
investment banking, it involved Marshallian external economies of scale for the
financial districts of London and Amsterdam, on the basis of large numbers of
small firms (Broadberry and Ghosal 2002; van Zanden and van Riel 2004,
pp. 305–19). Large firms also grew in importance in a number of sectors where
international trade was impractical, such as retail distribution, retail banking,
and the railroads.

Germany was a land of contrasts. Although it contained some modernized
service sectors such as the railroads and the universal banks, which have been
highlighted in the literature, the continued importance of agriculture and the
associated low levels of urban agglomeration limited the extent of the market
for specialized services. Distribution remained dominated by small wholesalers and retailers, and although Gerschenkron (1962) focused on the role
of the universal banks in directing funds into heavy industry, a balanced
overview of the banking sector as a whole has to take account of the many
small institutions that made up the bulk of the German banking sector, and
which pulled down the average productivity performance (Guinnane 2002;
Broadberry 2004).

The service sector in Italy during the late nineteenth century bears a certain
resemblance to its German counterpart, with the railroads playing an important role in the unification of a new state that was keen to foster modernization,
and with universal banks channeling resources into heavy industry (Milward
and Saul 1977, pp. 243–7, 260–4). However, recent research has tended to play
down the contribution of these two sectors to economic growth, with Cohen
and Federico (2000, p. 72) pointing out that Italy's per capita railroad mileage

was still only one-half that of France in 1913, while Fohlin (1998) claims that Italy's universal banks tended to support large, established companies rather than provide venture capital to small, promising firms.

The existing literature on services in the Habsburg Empire is also heavily oriented towards the railways and the banks. The Austro-Hungarian railway system was one of the largest in Europe, although this owed more to geography than to high levels of economic development (Milward and Saul 1977, p. 304). In Gerschenkron's (1962) work, the banks are seen as playing an important role in mobilizing capital for industry and the railroads. However, they became less involved in financing investment in industry and the railroads after the crash of 1873 (Rudolph 1976).

Developments in particular sectors

This section will focus on the major private services of transport and communications, finance, and distribution. Within a national accounting framework, the other parts of the service sector are housing, which is simply an imputed rent; government, which remained relatively small throughout this period; and domestic service, which still accounted for around 10 percent of service sector output in the more advanced parts of Europe before the First World War (Deane and Cole 1962; Hoffmann 1965).

Table 3.8 provides some indicators of activity in Europe's transport and communications sector on the eve of the First World War. Railroads are often seen as playing an important role in integrating national economies in the nineteenth century, and were in many cases actively promoted by governments seeking to speed up the process of industrialization (Gerschenkron 1962). The largest railroad systems were inevitably in the countries covering the largest geographical area, with Central and eastern Europe claiming the three largest systems within the empires of Russia, Germany, and Austria–Hungary. Western Europe was more fragmented politically, with the next largest systems being in France, the United Kingdom, and Italy.

For freight traffic, the social savings of the railroad are calculated as the extra cost of transporting the quantity of freight shipped on the railroads by the next best alternative (Fogel 1964). Social savings estimates on freight are shown for a number of European and non-European countries in Table 3.9, based on surveys by O'Brien (1983) and Herranz-Loncán (2006). Note first that the estimates for Belgium, England and Wales, France, Germany, and Russia are consistent with Fogel's expectation of relatively small social savings where a good alternative system of transport such as inland waterways existed. Social savings were large only where there was no good system of inland waterways, as

Table 3.8 Indicators of European transport and communications activity, *c.* 1913

	Railroad track open in 1913 (km)	Merchant ships registered in 1910 (1000s of net tons)	Telegrams sent in 1913 (millions)	Telephone calls in 1913 (millions)
North-west Europe				
Belgium	4,678	191	9.5	138
Denmark	3,868	547	3.9	227
Finland	3,560	411		
Netherlands	3,305	534	7.1	170
Norway	3,085	1,526	4.0	170
Sweden	14,377	771	5.0	434
United Kingdom	32,623	11,556	88.5	1,098
Southern Europe				
France	40,770	1,452	67.1	396
Greece	1,584	447	2.0	3
Italy	18,873	1,107	25.3	230
Portugal	2,958	114	5.0	7
Spain	15,088	789	6.6	35
Central and eastern Europe				
Austria– Hungary	43,280	510	37.8	568
Bulgaria	2,109		2.3	8
Germany	63,378	2,903	64.3	2,325
Romania	3,549		4.3	20
Russia	70,156	723	45.0	900
Serbia	1,958		2.4	6
Switzerland	4,832		6.5	69

Sources and notes: Railroads from Mitchell 2003, except railroad track open in Austria–Hungary, from Bachinger 1973, pp. 301, 482; shipping from Kirkaldy 1914, Appendix XVII and Mitchell 2003; telegrams and telephone calls from Foreman-Peck and Millward 1994, p. 109.

in Spain. Note secondly that the social savings of the railways increased over time, due to technological progress, which led to freight rates on the railways falling relative to freight rates on inland waterways.

There was no scope for international competition in railroads, so that relatively underdeveloped countries in eastern Europe had the largest systems on account of their geographical size. In shipping, however, international competition was possible, allowing the most efficient providers to gain market share. Data on the net tonnage of the main European merchant fleets are shown in Table 3.8. By far the most successful nation in shipping was the United Kingdom, which operated

Table 3.9 Social savings on freight transport by railroad

	Date	Social savings as a percentage of GNP
Belgium	1846	1.0
England and Wales	1865	4.1
England and Wales	1890	11.0
France	1872	5.8
Spain	1878	3.9–6.4
Spain	1912	18.9
Germany	1890s	5.0
Russia	1907	4.5
USA	1859	3.7
USA	1890	8.9
Mexico	1910	24.9–38.5

Sources: O'Brien 1983, p. 10; Herranz-Loncán 2006, p. 854.

around 35 percent of the world merchant net tonnage throughout the period 1870–1913 (Kirkaldy [1914]). The next largest shipping nation was Germany, with less than 10 percent of world net tonnage, while the third largest was Norway. Indeed, the Scandinavian countries, despite their relatively small populations, had a strong comparative advantage in shipping at this time.

Turning to telecommunications, international competition was not possible at this time, so that population and income per capita were the main determinants of the level of activity, as with the railroads. The highest levels of activity, shown in Table 3.8, were in the large, rich countries of Britain, France, and Germany, but the poorer large countries such as Russia, Austria–Hungary, and Italy also show large volumes of business. By 1913, telephones were becoming more common, and there is some evidence to suggest that public sector telecommunications monopolies delayed the development of the telephone system to protect their investments in the older telegraph technology (Foreman-Peck and Millward 1994, pp. 97–111; Millward 2005, pp. 103–4).

Table 3.10 provides some indicators of activity in finance and distribution in 1913. Financial activity is represented by banknotes in circulation and commercial bank deposits. Since estimates for individual countries are in national currencies, it is necessary to convert them to a common currency (US dollars) in order to make international comparisons. Again population size and per capita income were important determinants of activity. However, per capita income had a negative effect on the circulation of banknotes but a positive effect on the scale of bank deposits, since the degree of financial intermediation increases with the level of economic development (Bordo and Jonung 1987). Hence large, backward economies such as Russia and Austria–Hungary had high levels of banknote circulation, whereas even small but highly developed

Table 3.10 Indicators of European financial and commercial activity in 1913

	Banknotes in circulation ($m)	Commercial bank deposits ($m)	Merchandise exports ($m)
North-west Europe			
Belgium	206	451	717
Denmark	44		171
Finland	0.2	120	78
Netherlands	125	117	413
Norway	29	159	105
Sweden	63	429	219
United Kingdom	177	5,231	2,555
Southern Europe			
France	1,093	2,200	1,328
Greece	47	40	23
Italy	537	330	485
Portugal	95		38
Spain	373		183
Central and eastern Europe			
Austria–Hungary	505	164	561
Bulgaria		33	94
Germany	691	2,526	2,454
Romania	82		130
Russia	770	1,308	783
Serbia			18
Switzerland	61	355	226
EUROPE			

Sources and notes: Banknotes and deposits: nominal values in national currencies from Mitchell 2003, converted to US dollars using exchange rates from Svennilson 1954, pp. 318–19; merchandise exports: nominal values in national currencies from Mitchell 2003, converted to US dollars using exchange rates from Svennilson 1954, pp. 318–19. Adjustment for re-exports from Maddison 1995, Table I-1.

economies such as Belgium had quite high commercial bank deposits. Note that the United Kingdom, with the most highly developed financial sector, had very high levels of commercial bank deposits but very low levels of banknote circulation. The City of London established a dominant position at the center of world finance in the second half of the nineteenth century, which it retained until after the First World War, despite challenges from Berlin and Paris as well as New York (Lindert 1969; Kynaston 1995).

To capture levels of activity in distribution, it is necessary to turn to indirect indicators such as the level of exports and domestic consumption of agricultural and manufactured products. Table 3.10 provides comparative data on merchandise exports. The most successful European exporters were the United

Kingdom, Germany, and France, whose exports dwarfed those of the large eastern economies, Russia and Austria–Hungary. Even the small nation of Belgium had exports that were larger than Austria–Hungary's and close to the Russian level. Furthermore, if re-exports were to be added in, the Netherlands would also feature as a major international wholesale distributor, on account of its links with Indonesia. While wholesale distribution tended to remain in the hands of entrepreneurial merchant houses, the process of industrializing services went further in retailing, which saw the emergence of large-scale organizations, including cooperative societies as well as department stores and multiple (or chain) stores (Broadberry 2006). This shift towards large-scale distribution was dependent on the process of urbanization, and therefore proceeded more rapidly in industrialized areas than in more rural societies.

Conclusion

This chapter reminds us that GDP consists of a wide variety of activities, and that prosperity depends both on achieving high productivity in each sector and on allocating resources efficiently across sectors. In general, we find that within Europe between 1870 and 1914, achieving high productivity overall required shifting labor out of agriculture and into industry and services. Although the literature has tended to focus on industrialization as the main way out of economic backwardness, the growth and modernization of the service sector was of at least equal importance. Indeed, much of the process of achieving high productivity in services required a kind of "service sector industrialization," with provision on a high-volume basis, in a standardized form, using modern technology, overseen by hierarchical management.

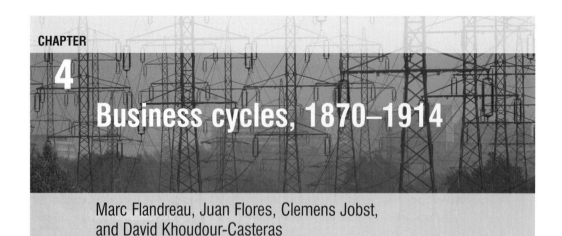

Business cycles, 1870–1914

Marc Flandreau, Juan Flores, Clemens Jobst,
and David Khoudour-Casteras

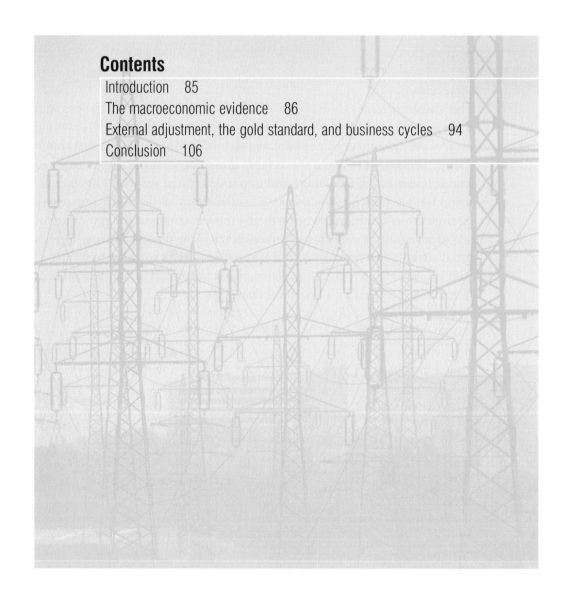

Contents

Introduction

The following survey concerns itself with the interaction between business cycles and the international economy in the "heyday" of capital flows, trade integration, and global migration before the First World War. Some years ago Alec Ford provided a defining survey of issues pertaining to business cycles in the classical age of the gold standard (Ford 1989). As a result of Ford's work, any discussion of business cycles during the last quarter of the nineteenth century has inevitably focused on the operation of the gold standard, and on the conduct of monetary policy in a gold standard system, or just next to one.

But this perspective is not without confusions and ambiguities. As Ford emphasized, and as subsequent writers have repeatedly rediscovered, the diversity of experiences within the gold standard *period* (a period which included many individual cases of *floating* exchange rates) is so large that it is extremely difficult to generalize. The exchange rate regime, trade flows, capital flows, and monetary policies are indeed relevant to the subject matter of "business cycles" before the First World War. But beyond that, generalizations are difficult.

Providing a comprehensive yet balanced survey of issues is a daunting challenge. As an alternative, this chapter provides a simplified guide to critical problems. Readers therefore should not expect to find in the following pages anything like an update of Alec Ford's article. Rather, they will be provided with perspectives, gleaned from the research frontier, on where we think knowledge is heading.

There are two ways to interpret Alec Ford's article. The conventional reading sees it as an essay in Keynesian economics that countered the Panglossian view of contemporary neo-classical or monetarist writers such as McCloskey and Zecher (1976, 1984) according to which everything was for the best in the best possible world of the gold standard. Against this backdrop, Ford showed that there were some problems with accounts of a smooth operation. A connoisseur of the Argentine experience, he knew that in some important parts of the world the gold standard had been a flirt, not a marriage. This pushed him to provide a geographic perspective on the operation of the gold standard, whereby adjustments in "core" or "peripheral" countries complemented or at times contradicted one another.

Another, not inconsistent, emphasis is to think of Ford's essay as an attempt to persuade scholars to take a more careful look at the microeconomics of monetary regimes, by which we mean not only monetary institutions, discount rates and the like, but more generally the microstructure of markets, in which these policies are implemented. In particular, his emphasis on the relevance of the institutional underpinnings of the conduct of monetary policy suggests taking a serious look at how exchange rate systems under the gold standard "really worked."

The rest of this chapter is organized in two parts: the division may be artificial, but it helps us keep repetitions at a reasonably low level. The first section surveys the macroeconomic record. It documents what we know, what we ought to know, and what we will probably never know about the fluctuations of the international economy before the First World War, with special emphasis on Europe. The second section guides the reader through a number of relevant issues pertaining to the mechanisms and institutions through which disturbances were transmitted, spread, or amplified throughout the world. We then offer our conclusions.

The macroeconomic evidence

Reconstructing historic business cycles

The years between 1870 and 1914 were characterized by sustained increases in GDP per capita in most parts of Europe. However, the growth process did not proceed smoothly. It exhibited considerable volatility over the short run. This was true for all key macroeconomic variables: production, employment, investment, price and wage levels, etc. The apparent regularity in economic ups and downs sparked the interest of contemporary observers and economists.

Today, students of business cycles can rely on a large number of macroeconomic time series provided by national statistical offices according to international standards that allow cross-country comparisons (or at least we are told so). However, national accounting data, like the concept of a national economy, are a relatively recent invention. While political economists have been interested in the calculation and comparison of national income since the seventeenth century (Maddison 2003), annual or quarterly GDP dates only from the first half of the twentieth century (Studenski 1958; Fourquet 1980).

Research on early periods therefore depends on series reconstructed *ex post*. There has been a considerable effort in recent decades to trace output and income series further back in time, to refine the existing series, and to increase the number of countries covered. The reconstructed series, however, can only be as good as the underlying contemporary statistical material. The main inputs for historic national income and production series are the censuses on population, industry, workforce etc., which became increasingly widespread over the second half of the nineteenth century (Tooze 2001). These were undertaken from time to time, allowing reasonable inferences about long-term growth trends.[1]

---

[1] Although there has been considerable debate about and revisions of nineteenth-century trend growth rates: see Chapter 2 in this volume.

The situation becomes trickier when short-term fluctuations in output and other macro variables are considered. While for some industrial sectors, such as coal and iron, output figures are available on an annual basis, a significant part of estimated GDP typically derives from more or less (in)accurate interpolations between benchmark years (see, e.g., Kuznets 1961). Some interpolations use related (or 'proxy') series, e.g. cotton imports for yarn output, which may reflect long-term trends accurately but suggest incorrect cyclical behavior. Production in sectors not (well) covered in the available censuses, e.g. handicrafts or some services, have to be extrapolated from other sectors with possibly different cycles, introducing further sources of error.[2]

Some students of historic business cycles (BCs) have therefore concentrated on industrial production (IP) as the most reliable subcomponent of GDP (A'Hearn and Woitek 2001; Craig and Fisher 2000). An alternative strategy is to collect many different indicators that are thought to be related to fluctuations in output but that are more readily available, with higher frequency or further back in time. This approach has a long tradition. Juglar (1862) dated cycles using central bank credit, interest rates, and money in circulation, but also wheat prices, tax receipts, and the number of marriages and births. Business cycle research in the interwar years continued along these lines and strove to assemble a large number of disaggregate indicators of economic activity (Burns and Mitchell 1946).

When using a large number of indicators, the key issue is how to detect a common trend among the possibly contradictory tendencies in the individual series. There are different techniques for constructing such a diffusion index. The National Bureau of Economic Research (NBER) uses its own judgement when dating the American business cycle, relying not only on real GDP but also on real income, employment, and retail sales. A simple, automatic, procedure would be simply to look at whether the majority of the indexes are increasing or declining. More complex statistical tools allow the estimation of one or more underlying (and non-observable) factors that are driving changes in the observed variables (see Sargent and Sims 1977 for an early contribution). The underlying factor "growth," for instance, may affect output and imports positively while affecting unemployment negatively. In contrast to the simple dichotomy between expansion and recession, factor models allow more precise tracking. They also recognize the existence of several underlying trends, e.g., an international and a regional business cycle. While using available information efficiently, such synthetic indexes are not a

---

[2] A classic case, but in the American context, is Romer, who demonstrated (1989) that the long-run decline of US GDP volatility was an artefact of changes in the procedures used to reconstruct historic GDP data. This is the stuff annual GDP series are made of and it is easy to see that it rules out a high degree of trust in conclusions from covariation across countries.

panacea. In particular, they cannot be readily interpreted in economic terms or compared across countries, if the primary data on which they are based differ. Comparison across time is also difficult, as is de-trending, since the extraction of a "trend" affects measurement of the "cycle" (see, e.g., A'Hearn and Woitek 2001).

Evidence of national and international business cycles

The ups and downs of the economy provoked the interest of observers and economists at an early stage. In 1862, Clément Juglar (1819–1905) described trade cycles with an average period from peak to peak of seven to nine years. Nikolai Kondratiev (1892–1938) identified longer "Kondratiev" waves that are about fifty to sixty years long. They were popularized in the work of Joseph Schumpeter (1883–1950). Simon Kuznets (1901–85) added a cycle with an intermediate length of around twenty years.

A powerful piece of evidence which came quite early to their attention was the covariation of real prices. As can be seen in Figure 4.1, prices experienced similar long-run trends throughout Europe, declining between the mid-1870s and mid-1890s and then increasing until the First World War. While the first era has been occasionally referred to, perhaps improperly, as the "Long Depression," the post-1895 inflation, which was accompanied by rapid growth, is known to some as the "Belle Epoque."

More recently, economists have become skeptical about reference to "business cycles" and have preferred "fluctuations." Observed movements are much more erratic than a sine or cosine wave, and in fact, such perfect predictability would offer profit opportunities and lead to the disappearance of the cycle.[3] The more agnostic approach is evident in the characterization of Burns and Mitchell (1946), who define business cycles as recurrent, but not periodic, fluctuations in aggregate economic activity with a length of more than one and fewer than twelve years.

The real business cycle (RBC) literature tries to demolish the concepts of trend and cycle altogether and argues that long-term growth and short-term variability of output must be explained within a unified model based on micro-economic foundations (Kydland and Prescott 1982). Empirical regularities that look like cycles result from behavioral responses to random exogenous impulses. The empirical work has concentrated on the properties of macro time series, such as volatility (standard deviation), persistence (auto-correlation),

---

[3] An example of this is Barsky and DeLong's (1991) discussion of the "Gibson Paradox," i.e., the positive association between prices and nominal interest rates. They explain it as the result of imperfect forecasts by agents.

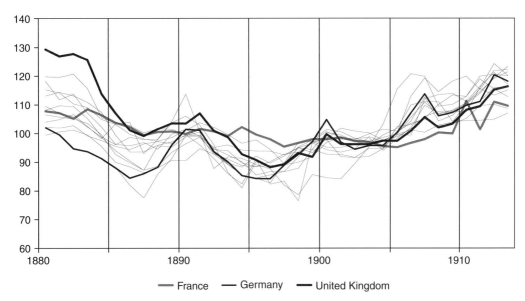

Figure 4.1 Price levels (1890–1913 = 100). Fifteen countries, exchange rate adjusted. *Note:* price levels in national currencies converted at FF exchange rate. Countries included are Austria–Hungary, Belgium, Denmark, Italy, Netherlands, Norway, Portugal, Russia, Spain, Sweden and Switzerland. France, Germany and the United Kingdom are tagged in the graph. *Source:* authors' calculation based on Flandreau and Zumer (2004).

and comovement with other time series (correlation). While conceding the irregular nature of economic fluctuations, many authors continue to view business cycles as a useful empirical approximation.

Many studies of business cycles between 1870 and 1914 proceed by comparing the record of that period with those of other subsequent periods. A major question is whether or not changes in the macro policy regime (like the introduction of countercyclical monetary and fiscal policies) have reduced the volatility of business cycles after the Second World War (compare Chapter 14 in this volume). The question can also be put the other way round: Why did macro policy regimes change repeatedly over time? From this point of view, it is policy that is endogenous to structural volatility or the process generating the shocks that economies are subjected to. Bayoumi and Eichengreen (1994) try to disentangle three explanations of changing policy regimes: political preferences and institutional mechanisms (e.g., are politicians willing to accept high interest rates to defend an exchange rate peg?), stability of the underlying economic environment (e.g., are there exogenous asymmetric shocks to economies, such as the 1970s oil shocks?), and the capacity of the economy to adjust to such shocks (e.g., will prices and wages adjust swiftly?).

It is conventional to map the chronology of monetary and fiscal policies into broad historical "regimes," which are labeled with reference to monetary arrangements. Thus the "gold standard" period before 1914 is compared with the "Bretton Woods" era (1945–71) and the period of "floating exchange rates" (1971–"now"). For lack of a well-identified dominant monetary regime (it saw the reconstruction and subsequent collapse of the gold standard), the period between 1918 and 1939 is cautiously, if appropriately, dubbed the "interwar" period.

Notwithstanding Romer's (1989) caveat, which recent studies tend to overlook, existing works on business cycles over time concur that they were less volatile before the First World War than during the interwar years, but more volatile than after the Second World War (Backus and Kehoe 1992; Bergman, Bordo, and Jonung 1998).[4] Basu and Taylor (1999) argue that volatility during the Bretton Woods period was comparable to the levels seen before the First World War. These studies also come to similar conclusions with regard to the behavior of the various components of GDP. Investment was (as it is today) two to five times more volatile than GDP, depending on the country and period, while consumption in most countries was slightly less volatile than GDP (Basu and Taylor 1999). The current account appears to have been most volatile before 1914. Backus and Kehoe (1992) report similar results for the trade balance. Persistence (autocorrelation) is generally low for income, consumption, and investment, but high for the current account. A high persistence in the current account implies that capital can flow one way for a prolonged period of time. Persistence was much lower during the interwar and Bretton Woods years, which may reflect limits on capital movements.

How did country cycles interact? Individual country chronologies often contain references to international events such as changes in foreign interest rates or financial panics. Increasing integration of goods and financial markets should have made national business cycles more and more interdependent according to the degree to which specialization and risk sharing coupled or decoupled individual country cycles, as we shall discuss later. The empirical analysis of international business cycle synchronization poses at least as many technical challenges as the extraction of national cycles from growth data. Again, the choice of statistical and econometric method can affect results (Bordo and Helbling 2003). A first approach starts from the traditional concept of the NBER reference cycle and derives a coefficient of concordance correlation, basically a measure of whether the cycles in two countries are in the same

---

[4] Romer found that traditional estimates overstated pre-Depression volatility, and hence the decline in volatility after the Second World War. All these comparisons of volatility in different periods may of course now have to be revisited, in the light of the worldwide economic crisis which began in 2008.

phase – expansion or recession – at about the same time. Based on such an approach, Morgenstern (1959) found that the UK, French, and German cycles regularly aligned before 1914. The use of reference cycles has the advantage of being relatively straightforward and avoiding the pitfalls of different detrending procedures. At the same time, the discrete expansion/recession classification precludes the use of many standard statistical tools and detracts from a number of interesting aspects such as the magnitude (in addition to the direction) of the comovement.

A logical alternative is thus to explore the correlation of output across countries. Based on contemporaneous correlation between output fluctuations, Backus and Kehoe (1992) were much more skeptical about short-run comovements, finding positive correlation among the Scandinavian economies but mostly zero or negative values for Germany, Italy, and the UK. Basu and Taylor (1999) similarly look at correlations of GDP and various components with the US economy and find a low level of comovements before 1914. It might however be asked whether the USA is a good reference point for the global growth pattern in the pre-1914 years. On the contrary, Craig and Fisher (1992, 1997, 2000) find increasing levels of correlation in GDP, industrial production, and imports for their sample of countries.

Study of common factors does provide an alternative measure of business cycle synchronization. The underlying mechanism can be either the existence of common shocks that affect all countries (like the oil-price shocks in the 1970s) or country-specific disturbances that spill over to the other economies, or both. An example is provided by the study by Bergman *et al.* (1992) of the determinants of business cycles in the Scandinavian countries, Denmark, Finland, Norway, and Sweden. For the late nineteenth century, they find evidence consistent with the existence of both a regional business cycle, specific to the four Nordic economies and reflecting their high level of integration, and a world business cycle (which they proxy by the USA, UK, Germany, and Japan). Bordo and Helbling (2003) compare the results from discrete and continuous correlation measures and a factor model and in none of the three cases do they find business cycles to be correlated on average before 1914. All measures, however, show an increasing degree of synchronization over the course of the twentieth century.

A'Hearn and Woitek (2001) criticize these approaches because they cannot distinguish between correlations at different lengths of the cycle. Countries may not be correlated over a short 3–5 year cycle, but well correlated over a 7–10 or 15–20 year cycle such as the one Kuznets (1958) had posited for the UK and the USA, a result more recently extended to a large number of countries (Solomou 1998). Using spectral analysis, A'Hearn and Woitek decompose various series of industrial production into cycles and find that most countries experienced 7–10 year cycles, while evidence in favor of 3–5 year cycles is much weaker. They also find strong comovements over 7–10 years, while shorter 3–5 year cycles appear little correlated between countries. This result may help reconcile the perception of contemporaries with the weak statistical evidence referred to earlier.

One of the reasons why results differ across studies is that they use different samples. Country choice is often constrained by data availability. Few studies differentiate between countries on the basis of structural features or exchange rate regimes, even though the exchange rate regime is often used as the primary criterion in the chronology. Bordo and Helbling (2003) use an *ad hoc* classi-fication of countries into "core" and "periphery" as well as various geographic criteria. The result of low output correlation, however, seems to be robust to different specifications for the pre-1914 period. A'Hearn and Woitek (2001) use more explicit structural criteria to classify countries on the strength of trade links and the monetary regime. They show that business cycle correlation rises along with trade. They also find higher correlation among countries that had a convertible currency throughout the period.[5] From this perspective, Morgenstern (1959) and Huffman and Lothian (1984) show that there was a significant correlation among the levels of economic activity of the countries that belonged to the gold standard before the First World War. Flandreau and Maurel (2005) argue that participation in monetary unions and in fixed exchange rate regimes before the First World War I induced comovement in business cycles.

Before we proceed, it may be useful to provide some summary elements. Tables 4.1, 4.2, and 4.3 show the correlation coefficients between short-term interest rates, yields on government bonds, and contemporaneous GDP growth rates, respectively, for fifteen European countries between 1880 and 1913.

We observe a strong correlation among the short-term interest rates of countries that belonged to the gold standard over a long period, which is consistent with the hypothesis of efficient and integrated markets. Countries with flexible exchange rates were naturally more disconnected from those of the three leading powers (France, Germany, and the UK).

We also see a strong correlation among long-term interest rates within that group. To the extent that these long-term rates reflect default risks, the evidence is consistent with the fact that the three countries experienced no sovereign debt crises and were thus less vulnerable to speculation than the other group. As can be seen, other low-sovereign-default-risk countries also exhibited strongly correlated nominal interest rate correlations.

---

[5] It is noteworthy, however, that bilateral correlation measures show that Spain and Austria had well-correlated cycles despite their inconvertible currencies.

Table 4.1 Correlation coefficients among short-term interest rates, 1880–1913

Bel	Den	Fra	Ger	Gre	Ita	Net	Nor	Port	Rus	Spa	Swe	Swi	UK	
0.69	0.43	0.39	0.69	-0.16	0.37	0.53	0.40	0.16	0.27	0.03	0.48	0.50	0.52	A–H
	0.69	0.75	0.85	-0.13	-0.01	0.83	0.47	-0.05	0.52	-0.18	0.52	0.62	0.76	Bel
		0.50	0.79	-0.60	-0.45	0.76	0.66	0.12	0.49	-0.14	0.91	0.63	0.49	Den
			0.56	0.17	0.12	0.53	0.62	-0.21	0.52	-0.45	0.30	0.35	0.72	Fra
				-0.24	-0.16	0.80	0.58	0.06	0.61	-0.13	0.75	0.76	0.78	Ger
					0.19	-0.25	0.02	-0.35	0.25	-0.21	-0.43	-0.43	-0.08	Gre
						-0.12	0.00	0.17	-0.19	0.03	-0.29	-0.25	0.08	Ita
							0.42	0.17	0.47	0.07	0.61	0.61	0.71	Net
								-0.27	0.43	-0.37	0.77	0.55	0.57	Nor
									-0.21	0.49	0.21	-0.19	-0.24	Por
										-0.22	0.40	0.33	0.52	Rus
											-0.05	-0.14	-0.40	Spa
												0.64	0.51	Swe
													0.66	Swi

Note: list of countries: Austria–Hungary (A–H), Belgium (Bel), Denmark (Den), France (Fra), Germany (Ger), Greece (Gre), Italy (Ita), Netherlands (Net), Norway (Nor), Portugal (Por), Russia (Rus), Spain (Spa), Sweden (Swe), Switzerland (Swi).
Source: authors' calculations based on Flandreau and Zumer 2004.

Table 4.2 Correlation coefficients among yields on government bonds, 1880–1913

Bel	Den	Fra	Ger	Gre	Ita	Net	Nor	Port	Rus	Spa	Swe	Swi	UK	
0.76	0.86	0.84	0.78	-0.21	0.51	0.78	0.71	-0.42	0.78	0.74	0.76	0.68	0.39	A–H
	0.92	0.72	0.88	-0.34	0.12	0.86	0.84	-0.52	0.57	0.34	0.52	0.92	0.68	Bel
		0.86	0.95	-0.53	-0.37	0.92	0.96	-0.59	0.27	-0.51	0.53	0.93	0.86	Den
			0.66	-0.21	0.38	0.73	0.58	-0.54	0.71	0.37	0.70	0.80	0.36	Fra
				-0.54	0.08	0.89	0.96	-0.59	0.67	0.34	0.51	0.84	0.81	Ger
					0.53	-0.57	-0.57	0.61	-0.38	0.26	0.16	-0.43	-0.61	Gre
						0.03	-0.25	0.38	0.07	0.62	0.78	-0.32	-0.42	Ita
							0.83	-0.61	0.72	0.39	0.38	0.78	0.69	Net
								-0.57	0.44	-0.50	0.35	0.83	0.82	Nor
									-0.66	0.11	-0.10	-0.56	-0.75	Por
										0.41	0.33	0.23	0.49	Rus
											0.50	-0.46	-0.06	Spa
												0.33	0.07	Swe
													0.82	Swi

Note: list of countries as for Table 4.1.
Source: as for Table 4.1.

These results are in sharp contrast with the result of computing direct GDP growth correlation coefficients across European countries. While some correlations can be rationalized with reference to proximity or commonality of main export markets (such as the correlations shown across the Scandinavian

Table 4.3 Contemporaneous correlation in real GDP growth, 1880–1913

Bel	Den	Fra	Ger	Gre	Ita	Net	Nor	Port	Rus	Spa	Swe	Swi	UK	
0.34	0.19	0.01	-0.50	-0.18	-0.30	-0.29	0.37	0.63	-0.22	-0.36	0.35	-0.06	-0.56	A–H
	0.30	0.17	-0.47	-0.27	-0.17	-0.13	-0.04	0.12	-0.26	-0.34	-0.12	0.14	-0.56	Bel
		0.57	-0.14	0.42	0.22	-0.02	0.34	-0.22	-0.44	0.28	-0.01	-0.45	-0.24	Den
			-0.03	0.57	0.39	0.00	-0.02	-0.55	-0.53	0.66	-0.27	-0.27	-0.07	Fra
				0.20	0.28	0.22	-0.26	-0.52	0.15	0.18	0.02	-0.08	0.67	Ger
					0.11	0.36	0.26	-0.49	-0.04	0.51	-0.34	-0.48	0.33	Gre
						-0.38	-0.18	-0.37	-0.36	0.71	0.07	0.14	0.26	Ita
							0.24	-0.55	0.15	0.06	-0.43	-0.39	0.56	Net
								0.09	0.13	-0.03	0.44	-0.76	-0.08	Nor
									0.24	-0.67	0.34	0.24	-0.63	Por
										-0.52	-0.03	-0.14	-0.08	Rus
											-0.17	-0.06	0.46	Spa
												-0.14	-0.18	Swe
													-0.08	Swi

Note: Russia 1885–1913 and Switzerland 1899–1913 only.
Source: as for Table 4.1.

economies), it is hard to make anything of the results in Table 4.3. As stated earlier, the quality of the data may explain this result. But the lesson may nonetheless be the apparent disconnection between nominal integration and financial integration, on the one hand, and the real economy on the other hand.

External adjustment, the gold standard, and business cycles

When an international regime appears to be working well, two alternative explanations are conventionally encountered. According to one of these, virtuous policies are to be praised. The other points to favorable circumstances. Discussion of the pre-1914 era conforms to this pattern. Some have argued that monetary policies were at the heart of the success of the international gold standard, and claim that the gold standard "worked well" because monetary policies adhered to the "rules of the game." Others emphasize globalization, experienced in terms of factor and commodity price integration that facilitated international adjustment and prevented monetary authorities from having to confront difficult situations (McCloskey and Zecher 1976, 1984; Bayoumi and Eichengreen 1994).

One complication is that students of the international monetary system of the pre-1914 period have often fallen prey to a dangerous illusion – that this regime was characterized by particularly orderly adjustments and was in general a smooth operation. But a more careful scrutiny suggests that the operation of this regime was anything but smooth, with the period displaying exchange rate crises, speculation, and financial turmoil.[6] There was only a fairly brief period, say between 1895 and 1913, during which everything worked relatively easily, with fixed exchange rates holding well both in normal times and in periods of crisis, while an increasing number of countries joined the gold standard.

To adhere to the idealized version of the pre-First World War period would be misleading. But it nonetheless remains true that, when we make pair-wise comparisons with later periods, the era stands alone in that a large number of developed countries managed to stay durably committed to a monetary policy whose long-run target was exchange rate stability and whose short-run objective was either convertibility of banknotes into gold bullion or (equivalently) fixity of their price in gold-convertible currencies. This was maintained without the kind of dislocations that were to occur during the interwar period, or the recurrent speculative crises of the 1990s. It is in that sense – in that narrow sense only – that we can write about the "mystery" of the smooth operation of the international gold standard. What follows provides a number of hints on how the gold standard really worked.

The gold standard and monetary policies

A commonplace of academic discussions of monetary policy under the gold standard is the conventional reference to the "rules of the game." We hasten to say that they did not exist before 1914, but were invented by observers of the monetary and financial cataclysms during the war and the interwar period. Starting with the Cunliffe Committee of 1918, economists developed a variety of fantasies regarding how and how well the gold standard had worked. Greater morality was one. It was speculated that the efforts of central banks to pass on rather than sterilize variations in the gold reserve were a critical ingredient in the success of the adjustment mechanism. This was in contrast with the interwar period, they said, and Nurkse (1944) reported evidence of rampant sterilization in interwar policy making. But then Bloomfield (1959) demonstrated that sterilization was just as pervasive during the pre-war period.

Bloomfield's findings laid the foundations of a new literature. In its latest development, this literature attempts to reconstruct from first principles the actual set of rules by which monetary policies were conducted before the First World War.[7] There is still some way to go until this literature can be said to have delivered systematic insights. But at this stage, it already provides more

---

[6] See Flandreau, Le Cacheux, and Zumer 1998, Flandreau 2003b, and the following paragraphs.

[7] See, e.g., Flandreau 2004, Chapter 4, and Reis 2007.

explicit microeconomic, institutional and political underpinnings to discussions of the adjustment mechanism.

The early contributions by Ford (1960, 1981) and Lindert (1969) are critical landmarks in this research effort. They emphasized the existence of asymmetrical adjustment under the gold standard, ascribed to different degrees of financial centrality. The key term here (coined by Lindert) is "relative pulling power." Some central banks were more equal than others when it came to attracting foreign money – they had more "pulling power." Ford noted that the adjustment mechanism worked differently depending on the type of country one was looking at: Adjustment was easier in the "center" (Britain), more difficult in the "periphery" (Argentina).

Ford (1960) had a quite specific mechanism in mind, ascribing most of the difficulties to the volatility of the terms of trade stemming from highly concentrated exports. But the logic of asymmetrical adjustment is perhaps more general than he suggested. To see why, let us examine the simple adjustment mechanism in a two-country world. We start with the traditional emphasis on relative price movements creating an initial external imbalance.[8] Country A has accelerating inflation, which leads to a shift in trade patterns and a trade deficit. In principle, with passive monetary policies, equilibrium could be restored over the long run as deficits lead to gold outflows from country A and subsequent relative price deflation. But monetary authorities may help by raising the interest rate. This policy brings domestic prices into line with international prices. Perhaps more importantly, it has the short-run effect of helping to finance the external deficit by attracting foreign capital.

Suppose now that we change the setting in one critical dimension. We assume that the currency of country A is a local currency, while that of country B is an international currency. That is, foreign investors do not hold any balances (time deposits, short-term credits, long-term debt, and the like) that are denominated in currency A. As a result, a raising of the interest rate by the central bank of country A will have no effect on foreigners and can only work through repatriation of foreign balances by residents of country A and deflation of the domestic economy. This would be completely different from what would happen in country B, since currency B is an international currency. In such a setting, external adjustment is bound to be asymmetrical.

The previous example matches a key empirical feature of the international financial system of the pre-1914 period. "A" may stand for Argentina, and "B" for Britain. There was no market, in London, for peso bills, but there was a substantial market in Buenos Aires for sterling bills. The insight is that missing markets matter. The reason for the asymmetry in the international adjustment

---

[8] Eichengreen and Flandreau 1997.

mechanism points to underlying microeconomics.[9] Going down that route, we would expect adherence to the gold standard to be more continuous and sustained in countries whose currencies enjoyed a certain amount of international circulation. Countries with an international currency could avoid the pains of adjustment through domestic deflation and as a result were more inclined to become faithful adherents of the international gold standard.

Flandreau and Jobst (2005) have provided evidence that bears upon this issue. Focusing on the international reach of the bills of exchange originating in a given market, they provide a systematic ranking of countries between "core" and "periphery." Three large European economies (Britain, France, and Germany) together formed the core of the international monetary system of the time. The authors also identify a group of intermediary countries whose currencies had a regional circulation. Other European nations feature prominently in this group. It is tempting to relate this finding to the relative consistency with which the policies of the gold standard were adhered to throughout Europe.

Emphasis on the microeconomic structures in which monetary policy is conducted is also central in the "modern synthesis" on monetary policy in the period before the First World War.[10] This synthesis has emphasized certain features that make central bank operations under the gold standard part of a broader family of theoretical insights that belong under the "target zone" heading initially developed to deal with Europe's Exchange Rate Mechanism (Krugman 1991a). Target zones or currency bands are arrangements whereby central banks undertake to keep the exchange rate fluctuations within a certain range. The "gold points," which reflected the cost of shipping bullion between two markets, provided a currency band of that kind, between countries that were on gold. The exchange rate could not rise or fall above the price at which it would become more advantageous to purchase gold against notes in one market, ship it to the other market, and resell it against notes.[11]

Target zone theory is useful because it suggests that currency bands provide a trade-off between exchange rate stability and policy autonomy. This is best understood by studying what happens in the ideal case of a perfectly fixed and perfectly flexible exchange rate regime. In a perfectly fixed exchange rate regime, there cannot be any degree of policy autonomy. Domestic money

---

[9] Related research includes recent work on the so-called original sin problem. For details on the extent of this problem in Europe, see Flandreau and Sussman 2005.

[10] See Eichengreen and Flandreau 1997 for an early statement.

[11] Because the ERM was not a credible arrangement, and because it exhibited some special features such as a pre-defined fluctuation band, adaptation of the target zone framework to the gold standard period requires some qualifications, which are occasionally overlooked, creating confusion. One is that, unlike in modern target zones, central banks during the gold standard period never committed to support the currency at a pre-set price, but only to guarantee the convertibility of notes into specie.

supply, interest rates, etc. are endogenous. It is often emphasized that countries that choose to peg their currency to gold lose the flexibility of exchange rate adjustments. The Mundell "trilemma" states that it is impossible to reach at the same time more than two of the three following objectives: monetary policy autonomy, exchange rate stability, and free capital mobility. By contrast, countries that maintain exchange rate flexibility are able to cope with external disequilibria by letting the exchange rate bear the brunt of the adjustment.[12]

So a currency band may provide the best of all worlds. Suppose, for instance, that the foreign interest rate rises above the domestic interest rate. In a fixed exchange rate system domestic authorities must follow suit. But in a currency band, monetary policies can avoid adjusting domestic conditions. Instead, they let the exchange rate go. This can happen because, provided that speculators trust the monetary authorities' commitment to go on paying their notes in gold, they will bet on an eventual appreciation of the currency. The smaller return from lower domestic interest rates is compensated by expected capital gains after the currency recovers. One important implication of this is that, owing to the leeway that it afforded to central banks, individual countries could enjoy a measure of insulation from international shocks, despite the existence of quasi-fixed exchange rates.

The following example, dealing with the experience of Austria–Hungary, illustrates this logic (see Flandreau and Komlos 2006 for details). In 1907, a violent financial crisis shook the New York financial market and reverberated in a number of European centers. This led to a global liquidity squeeze and to gold outflows, which central banks in the most exposed countries had to meet through interest rate hikes. In Berlin, the central bank (Reichsbank) raised its rate from 5.5 percent to 6.5 percent on November 1 and again to 7.5 percent on November 11.

The Austro-Hungarian Bank had a fixed exchange rate against the mark and ought to have followed suit. But, as contemporaries soon noted, the currency band protected it. As they observed, the spot rate in florins per mark was below parity at the onset of the crisis and therefore the exchange rate was "strong." At the same time, however, the forward rate was above the spot rate, implying that the market expected the florin to depreciate. When the crisis hit, the authorities let the exchange go. As a result, the exchange rate became "weak" (it went above parity). But forward rates now traded *below* spot rates. This reflected market anticipation that the spot exchange rate would recover. Thus, by letting the exchange rate go, the monetary authorities induced speculators to play the florin up in forward markets.

---

[12] Catão and Solomou 2005 report a significant contribution of effective exchange rate fluctuations to the adjustment mechanism during the gold standard period for those countries that were not on gold. See also Catão (2006).

The benefit from this was that the Austro-Hungarian monetary authorities were able to tolerate a large spread of their base rate against the German official interest rate, despite the two countries being on the gold standard. That spread reached 250 basis points in the middle of November and stabilized at 150 basis points. The expected capital gains for money market investors had enabled the central bank to avoid raising the interest rate and thus secure a non-negligible measure of monetary autonomy. Contemporary and subsequent commentaries have suggested that this policy was deliberate, reflecting a high degree of sophistication and understanding of the possibilities of cyclical management (Federn 1910; Einzig 1937; Flandreau and Komlos 2006). Figure 4.2 summarizes this by showing the relation between the exchange rate and market expectations regarding future changes of the currency. It exhibits a negative slope, implying that the market expected appreciation when the currency was weak and depreciation when it was strong.

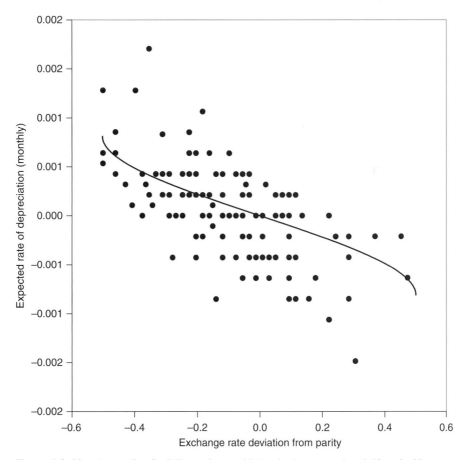

Figure 4.2 Monetary policy flexibility under a gold standard currency band. (Austria–Hungary 1901–14, monthly data). *Source:* authors' calculation based on Flandreau and Konlos 2006.

This Austro-Hungarian episode brings to the fore an important element of current discussions of the adjustment mechanism: for stabilizing speculation to take place and investors to support the policies of Austro-Hungarian monetary authorities, there had to be a deep and liquid market for Austro-Hungarian bills as well as a well-functioning market for forward exchange. Perhaps unsurprisingly, Austria-Hungary does indeed feature in the "intermediary" category, closer to the core of the international financial system than to its periphery, and the success of its experience, while it admits credibility as a precondition, was perhaps more profoundly influenced by its degree of monetary development and international financial integration.[13]

Globalization, business cycles, and the adjustment mechanism

An era of exceptional integration

Figure 4.3 depicts the evolution of three indicators measuring integration in commodity, labor, and capital markets over the long run. Commodity market integration is measured by computing the ratio of exports to GDP. Labor market integration is measured by dividing the migratory turnover by population.

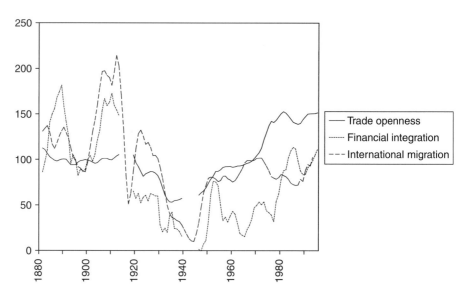

Figure 4.3 Trade openness (continuous line), financial integration (dotted line), and migration indicator (1880–1996, 1900 = 100). *Source:* authors' computations, from a variety of sources.

[13] For more details on the development of foreign exchange markets in Austria–Hungary on the eve of the First World War, see Jobst 2009.

Financial integration is measured using Feldstein–Horioka estimators of current account disconnectedness.[14] The benchmark year for the indices is 1880.

One striking result is the degree of integration achieved during the years before the First World War, and it can be related to the decline in transaction costs. Market integration and limited trade barriers played a significant role in increasing international competition (Broadberry and Crafts 1992). The decrease in transportation costs and technical progress in refrigeration brought to Europe products from all around the world (meat from Argentina, cereals from the United States, wool from Australia).[15] The contribution of capital market openness to financial integration is another obvious element (Nurkse 1954; Edelstein 1982). Previous authors have noted the process of international convergence in real wages and interest rates.[16]

Integration and business cycles: Caveats

Some remarks are in order. First, even if one takes the view that transaction costs were reduced and external adjustment easy, the question of the relative integration of alternative markets remains open. The presumption is that the more fluid markets ought to have borne the brunt of the adjustment. The interest in understanding the operation of global markets during this period is not obliterated by reference to "automatic adjustment" in "perfect markets."

Secondly, it is noteworthy that economic development remained unbalanced. There was a contrast between rich countries in north-west Europe (in particular France, Germany, and the United Kingdom), which exported capital, and southern and East European countries, consisting of rural economies with a substantial scope for catch-up. Consequently, it is not possible to consider European economies as a homogeneous whole, affected by symmetric shocks, and with a perfect timing in the transmission of cycles. Therefore, as already mentioned, the geography of international transmission of business cycles remains an intriguing matter.

Thirdly, a distinction ought to be made between comovements and external adjustment. Integration may ease the process of external adjustment without necessarily operating through greater business cycle synchronization. In some cases, market integration promotes specialization (Krugman 1991b), with the

---

[14] Bayoumi 1990; Flandreau and Rivière 1999; Bordo and Flandreau 2003; Obstfeld and Taylor 2003.

[15] An open issue is whether the gold standard did feed back to integration. Some scholars have argued that the gold standard system reduced transaction costs and generated a safer environment, spurring trade and capital flows (Lopez-Cordoba and Meissner 2003; Jacks 2006). On the other hand, Yeager (1976) emphasizes pre-commitment problems in floating exchange rate regimes and the incidence of gold standard adherence on the credibility of liberalization in the absence of other coordinating mechanisms. Flandreau and Maurel (2005) report evidence of colinearity between the gold standard and openness, supporting Yeager's interpretation.

[16] Flandreau, Le Cacheux, and Zumer 1998; O'Rourke and Williamson 1999; Dowrick and DeLong 2003; Obstfeld and Taylor 2003.

consequence that country-specific shocks become more frequent, contributing to de-synchronization between individual business cycles. Eichengreen (1992d) follows Ford in noting that less developed countries, mainly specialized in the production of a narrow range of commodities, had to face market disturbances that resulted in dramatic fluctuations in their terms of trade. Flandreau and Maurel (2005) find evidence that trade integration had a negative effect on business cycle comovements in late nineteenth-century Europe.

Fourth, the question of whether these flows were stabilizing or destabilizing remains open. Bloomfield (1968) argued that short-term capital flows increased towards the later part of the period, generating increasing stress. Ford (1981) suggests that capital flows could be helpful or destabilizing depending on the period. He suggests the existence of a cycle, driven by exports from the center economy (Britain), which in turn led to offsetting capital and labor exports to the New World. Kindleberger (1985), following Schumpeter (1939) and Morgenstern (1959), notes that the annual volume of international investment before 1914 was closely linked to business cycles, in both sending and receiving countries.

Factor movements and adjustments

To what determinants did factor flows respond? Consider capital first. While the capacity that investors had in a system of free capital mobility to shift portfolio around explains the current and irretrievable lack of systematic data on bilateral capital flows, data on origination provide some hints. They suggest some biases. At the turn of the century, British capital exports were mainly concentrated in the New World and settler countries. French and German capital was concentrated in Europe. Fishlow (1985) argues that British capital looked for development-oriented investments, directed mainly to railroads and other infrastructure, whereas continental investment was focused on revenue finance, benefiting governments and current expenditures in Europe and the Middle East. Esteves (2007) argues that German investment responded to the same factors as the British. Flandreau (2006) argues that European investment was "home biased" in the sense that colonial status gave preference to particular countries by providing them with an institutional framework favoring their "willingness to pay," thus making colonial borrowing safer for metropolitan investors than for others.[17] Regalsky (2002) links the boom of French exports with investment in South America. Easterlin (1968) also demonstrated that capital exports and migration went hand in hand. Clemens and Williamson (2004) find that these factors with regard to British capital exports were mainly schooling, natural resources, and demography.

---

[17] Accominotti *et al.* (2008) provide additional evidence that bears upon this issue.

Another way to look at this is to study the determinants of sovereign bond prices. Bordo and Rockoff (1996) argue that adherence to the gold standard reduced a country's external borrowing costs and suggest that the gold standard acted as a "good housekeeping seal of approval." Flandreau and Zumer (2004) find that, once they control for policy performance (indebtedness and fiscal track record), the effect of being on the gold standard disappears. They show that the two main factors that reduced financing costs in borrowing countries and caused interest rates to converge were growth and inflation rather than fiscal discipline. This combination, after 1895, became a powerful force that improved fiscal sustainability.[18] There was thus an element of self-sustained expansion, as accelerating growth fueled inflation that wiped out earlier debts.

On the labor front, the capacity of markets to operate smooth adjustments through price movements ought not to be exaggerated. Downward nominal wage reductions were resisted by trade unions at a time when a significant number of labor market reforms and social insurance schemes were adopted (Huberman and Lewchuk 2003). Phelps Brown and Browne (1968) argued earlier that while business booms were generally followed by an increase in labor earnings, wage cuts in depression periods were marginal and asymmetrical. Hatton (1988) finds that wages in the United Kingdom were less flexible between 1880 and 1913 than at the end of the twentieth century.

In this context, international labor flows provided an alternative. Jerome (1926) found that they were strongly related to business cycles.[19] When economic conditions at home worsened, people headed towards more prosperous areas either within Europe itself or more importantly in the New World, in particular, the United States. By contrast, an improvement in economic activity and employment came with a decrease in emigration. Likewise, return migration responded to business fluctuations. Recent immigrants were the most exposed to economic reversals, and were therefore prone to come back to their home country during recessions (Gould 1979).

Panic (1992) argues that for countries on gold, capital mobility and international migration were substitutes: while more advanced countries could rely on capital flows to cope with their disequilibria, more backward nations had to lean on labor movements. Khoudour-Castéras (2002, 2005) argues that there was a trade-off between nominal exchange rate fluctuations and international migration. The example of Austria–Hungary is particularly striking. After the adoption of the gold standard by monetary authorities, there was a significant change in migration patterns (Figure 4.4).While exchange rates tended to

---

[18] A similar intuition is examined in Flandreau, Le Cacheux, and Zumer 1998. They find that real interest service on sovereign debts decreased drastically after 1895.

[19] See also Thomas 1954; Gould 1979; Hatton and Williamson 1998.

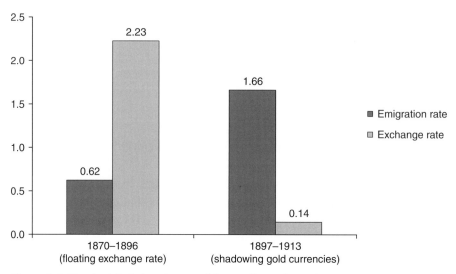

Figure 4.4 Standard deviations in annual Austro-Hungarian emigration and exchange rates before and after fixed exchange rate. *Source:* authors' computations, based on Khoudour-Casteras 2005.

stabilize after 1896, emigration flows increased and became more volatile. Labor mobility addresses labor market imbalances across regions, and helps to sustain a fixed exchange rate regime.[20] Khoudour-Castéras (2005) shows that emigration in deficit countries helped to finance current account deficits. Moreover, remittances that migrants sent back home contributed to restoring equilibrium (Fenoaltea 1988; Esteves and Khoudour-Castéras, 2009).[21]

Financial crises and contagion

Figure 4.5 compares an indicator of default risk in "emerging markets" on the left-hand axis with the Feldstein–Horioka measure of financial openness on the right-hand axis in inverted scale.[22] When this indicator moves up, it reveals a tendency for current accounts to close down, as would happen in a regime of financial autarky (limited financial integration). The co-movement of the two measures reveals that the greater the default risk in emerging markets, the less open was the global financial system. The visual impression is also of a succession of waves of increased financial integration and declining risk premia. Earlier writers (Abramovitz 1961; Ford 1962) have conventionally identified three

---

[20] This is consistent with the theory of optimum currency areas developed by Mundell (1961).
[21] In some cases, remittances could turn out to be carriers of instability, as illustrated by the impact that the collapse of the Brazilian currency in the early 1890s had on Portugal's balance of payments (Lains 1995).
[22] This is the Feldstein–Horioka test (which correlates saving and investment). See Bayoumi (1990) for an early use.

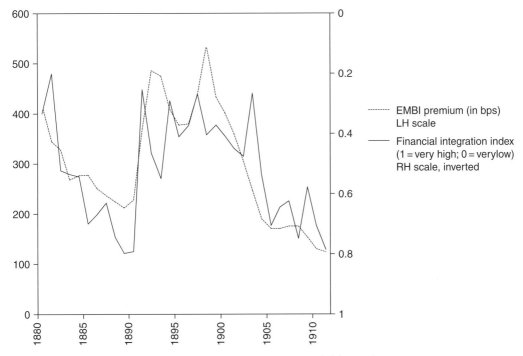

Figure 4.5 Financial integration and governments' risk premiums.

capital booms: the 1860s, with a peak in 1872 followed by a fall until 1878; the 1880s, with a peak in 1888 and then an abrupt shutdown of global capital markets after 1890 and their gradual reopening afterwards, leading to the globalization of the Belle Epoque which ended with the First World War. The circumstances in which the last cycle collapsed are somewhat peculiar, but the first two shared several features. In both cases, the financial crisis disrupted international capital flows and led to sovereign default on outstanding debt payments and other painful adjustments that included banking or currency crises.

The Barings crisis occupies a special position. As Figure 4.5 shows, during the years that followed the Barings crisis, capital exports from Great Britain and other financial centers fell abruptly. The Barings crisis was surrounded by a number of other events, but there is a strong suggestion that it was responsible for what happened in the early 1890s (Wirth 1893; Kindleberger 1989).

Sharp falls in capital exports have attracted much scholarly interest recently and are designated as "sudden stops."[23] Sudden stops are global credit

---

[23] Calvo, Izquierdo, and Mejía (2004) define sudden stops as "sharp contractions of international capital flows." According to Catão (2006), sudden stops before 1914 were the concern of many countries, irrespective of their income level or financial development. Esteves and Khoudour-Castéras (2009) argue that European migrants' remittances helped to reduce the impact of sudden stops in periphery countries by offsetting the negative effects of unexpected capital outflows.

crunches. When a shock occurs in global capital markets, highly leveraged investors may be reluctant to sell certain categories of assets and as a result curtail their lending to others (Calvo 1999). In the early 1890s, some observers argued that German banks that were long on Latin American securities after the Barings crisis threw away their more liquid Austro-Hungarian securities, causing problems to the Habsburg monarchy, just as described in models of sudden stops.[24] Earlier research has also pointed to the critical contribution of supply-side factors to the contraction that followed the Barings crisis (Joslin 1963; Kindleberger 1985). The fall in capital exports from London strongly affected third countries, both within and outside Europe. Bordo (2006) finds that the negative impact of sudden stops before the First World War could reach 4 percent of GDP, when coupled with financial crises.

The process through which financial crises spread from country to country is known as *contagion*. Contemporaries wrote about what they called the "reverberation" of the Barings crisis.[25] Recent literature has discussed the existence of contagion and contagion channels for the spread of financial crises in the nineteenth century. Triner and Wandschneider (2005) argue that there was some contagion from Argentina to Brazil. Bordo and Murshid (2000) compare correlation coefficients in yields for a group of countries in the six months prior to and after the Barings crisis and find no significant increase in correlation coefficients. Similarly, Mauro, Sussman, and Yafeh (2002; 2006) explore comovement in emerging market bond spreads during the period 1870–1913 and report a striking lack of contagion following the Barings crisis.[26] Flandreau (2003a, 2003b) and Flandreau and Zumer (2004) find that, following the Barings crisis, debt burdens were monitored more carefully than before. The crisis also created opportunities for new banks to enter the market using new signaling techniques in the shape of heavy spending on information acquisition. Global risk perceptions, which were shared by investors in leading markets, appear to have been a powerful driver of the global economic cycle.

Conclusion

This chapter has surveyed a number of issues pertaining to the outlook of business cycles in the late nineteenth and early twentieth centuries. First, we emphasized the chasm between financial and nominal integration and comovement on the one hand, and the apparent disconnect of real variables. Secondly

---

[24] Flandreau (2003a).   [25] See Flandreau (2003a); Kindleberger (1987).

[26] They suggest that the nineteenth century was contagion free. Flandreau and Flores (2009) use the same methodology to find that comovements were stronger during the 1820s than in the late nineteenth century.

we found that the much-emphasized role of the exchange rate regime in bringing about comovement has been vastly exaggerated. Serious qualifications to the notion that the gold standard "unified the world" include evidence of specialization that pushed towards desynchronization of business cycles, central banks' ability to play on tiny differences of exchange rates to secure a substantial amount of policy autonomy, and so on.

We also came across a wealth of further issues that need to be examined more carefully in the future. In particular, we think that microeconomic aspects of the global financial system may have weighed much more heavily on the record of business cycles than macroeconomic arrangements such as the exchange rate regime.

On this account we noted that our survey repeatedly came across the relevance of supply factors in the global money market. We encountered it when we emphasized the importance of the geography of international liquidity in shaping individual countries' responses to global disturbances. We encountered it again when we discussed the global cycles in the supply of capital, which we said displayed "sudden stops," as was the case in the follow-up to the Barings crisis. We encountered it finally when we argued that reputational variables and government policies interacted in a decisive fashion to generate the long cycle of the Belle Epoque. It is our feeling that these features played a critical role in shaping policy outlooks and should be the topic of future work.

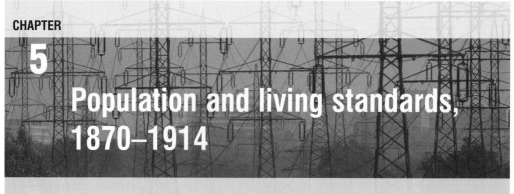

CHAPTER

5

Population and living standards, 1870–1914

Carol Leonard and Jonas Ljungberg*

Contents

* The authors gratefully acknowledge useful advice and comments from George Alter, Leonid Borodkin, Steve Broadberry, Bob Millward, and Kevin O'Rourke. Remaining flaws are ours.

Introduction

Those who lived through the half century before 1914 experienced tremendous changes in living conditions. This can be said not only for the early-industrializing regions of Europe, but also for many peripheral areas, particularly in the north. Whereas early industrialization had ambiguous effects on living standards, by the late nineteenth century the time had come for the mass of the population to share in the increasing supply of goods and opportunities. Changes were profound indeed and influenced almost all areas of daily life: railroads opened up for commuting; networked systems for piped water and sewerage systems made household work easier in cities and larger towns; in most of Europe elementary education came to encompass all children and, in combination with modern newspapers as well as scientific breakthroughs such as germ theory, rational knowledge influenced society in a new way; moreover, new consumer goods such as canned food, ready-made clothes, the bicycle, etc. appeared on the market; around the turn of the century telephones and electrification emerged and contributed to a revolution in everyday life, even though still only a few people had direct access to these innovations. However, this chapter will deal only indirectly with these novelties of the late nineteenth century and instead focus on more basic aspects of living standards, embracing population developments including health, household patterns, and income distribution.

Total population

Estimates indicate that the total population of Europe (excluding Turkey) amounted to some 314 million in 1870 (Chapter 10 in Volume 1). By 1913 population numbers had increased by around 50 percent to 471 million (calculated from Maddison 1995). That corresponds to an average annual population growth rate of just below 1 percent (0.95 percent), which probably meant a slight acceleration over the preceding half century (0.78 percent). Russian population increased even more rapidly, by 1.5 percent per annum between 1867 and 1913, due to a sharp decrease in mortality rates. Russia's case highlights the larger observation that one should be careful to avoid connecting rapid population growth closely with industrialization and rising living standards. For example, rapid population growth in Finland began before industrialization in the eighteenth century, and was nearly as fast as in Britain during the Industrial Revolution. To take another example in the period that we are dealing with here, the high population growth in Tsarist Russia took place in a mostly agrarian context. In Britain, on the other hand, population growth began to decelerate in our period. That was in part due to a decline in the fertility rate, and to some extent also to emigration (see Chapter 1 in this volume). Besides emigration, the decline in fertility was a factor that held back population growth. The European fertility decline is discussed at some length in Volume 1, Chapter 2. However, in 1870, in most western European countries, ranging from Italy to Sweden, the number of children per woman was still around five. In 1910 this number had fallen to between three and four, and to fewer than three in England. In parts of the south (Iberia, Greece) and the east (Poland, Hungary) the number of children was slightly higher but there too a decline occurred. Also slightly lagging behind, but catching up with the general decline by the late 1890s, was Tsarist Russia. Thus this period saw a decisive and largely pan-European fertility decline.

Mortality decline and longer lives

Notwithstanding massive emigration and fertility decline, the population of Europe grew rapidly up to 1914. The most important reason for rapid population growth was that people survived to higher ages, or in other words, mortality declined. Probably the most telling description of the mortality decline is the lifetime a newly born child might expect. We know that today the expected lifetime, or *life expectancy*, is around eighty years in the advanced countries and below fifty only in poor countries where warfare has constrained progress (Afghanistan) or AIDS has shortened life expectancy, as in many countries in Sub-Saharan Africa. To be sure, an exact calculation of life expectancy requires detailed demographic data, and figures are not available for all countries for our period. However, Table 5.1 highlights the change over the half century before 1914.

By 1870, only Scandinavia had achieved a life expectancy above or close to fifty years. Even in richer western European countries, such as Germany, France, and the Netherlands, a baby could not expect to live more than thirty-five years. Further to the east and south of Europe, this was still the case towards the end of the century. In Russia, life expectancy is estimated to have been even lower and did not improve after 1890. However, in large parts of Europe, life expectancy increased by more than ten years up to the threshold of the First World War, in the Netherlands by as much as nineteen years over a period of four decades. At that point in time life expectancy had risen to well above fifty years in north-west Europe, and over forty everywhere else except for Russia. Even though life expectancy seems to convey very concrete information, one must consider that it is an abstraction built upon the assumption that newborn

Table 5.1 Life expectancy in European countries, 1870–1914

	Years	Late nineteenth century		Years	Early twentieth century	
		Males	Females		Males	Females
Austria	1868/71	32.7	36.2	1909/12	43.5	46.8
Belgium (HMD)	1870	40.1	41.7	1913	50.6	54.3
Bulgaria				1900/05	42.1	42.2
England and Wales	1871/80	41.4	44.6	1910/12	51.5	55.4
Estonia				1897	41.9	45.5
Denmark (HMD)	1870	45.0	47.0	1913	57.6	60.1
Finland	1881/90	41.3	44.1	1901/10	45.3	48.2
France	1870	33.7	37.7	1913	49.4	53.5
Germany	1871/81	35.6	38.5	1910/11	47.4	50.7
Iceland (HMD)	1870	34.5	42.5	1913	56.6	61.2
Italy (HMD)	1872	28.5	29.5	1913	47.9	48.8
Luxembourg				1913	48.0	52.6
Netherlands	1871/75	36.5	38.2	1911/15	55.3	57.4
Norway	1871/75	47.4	50.4	1911/15	56.3	59.6
Poland (B&M)	1890	37		1910	42	
Russia (M)	1838/50	25	27	1904/13	32.4	34.5
Spain	1900	33.9	35.7	1910	40.9	42.6
Sweden	1870	43.2	46.8	1913	57.2	60.0
Switzerland (HMD)	1876	38.4	41.8	1913	52.5	55.9

Source: Max-Planck-Gesellschaft 2007 The Human Life-Table Database (www.lifetable.de), where detailed sources are given; countries marked HMD, *Human Mortality Database*. University of California, Berkeley (2008), www.mortality.org; Poland: data sources for Bourguignon and Morrisson 2002 at www.delta.ens.fr/XIX/; Russia: Mironov 1999b, pp. 209–10 and note 212.

children over their lifetimes will experience the same mortality as that prevailing in the actual year or period. Another aspect of this measure is that it is highly sensitive to mortality in younger years, which means that a child in Austria who, in the early 1870s, attained the age of ten could expect to live beyond the age of fifty-five instead of below thirty-five. Similarly, at the same time in Norway, those who had survived to ten could expect to live to be older than sixty instead of barely fifty. Thus ten years of childhood added another twelve years in Norway but more than twenty years in Austria. This discrepancy is mostly due to the difference in infant mortality, that is, mortality during the first year of life. Infant mortality is an important factor in the big differences in life expectancy across Europe from 1870 to 1914, but its decline is only part of the explanation for the fact that human lives became longer. Before we discuss in more detail changes in living conditions that determined the mortality decline, we will present a picture of European living standards with the help of the Human Development Index.

An assessment of living standards: the Human Development Index

So far we have discussed living standards from the perspective of population changes, ranging from life expectancy and health to migration. A widely used indicator of living standards in a country is, of course, GDP per capita. It describes the level of economic development. As a measure of living standards, it has clear limitations. These are highlighted by the Human Development Index (HDI), developed by the United Nations Development Program (UNDP) and applied to the more recent state of welfare globally. Besides GDP per capita, the HDI takes account of life expectancy and the distribution of knowledge in the population, each variable contributing a third to the index. Knowledge, in turn, is measured in two ways: literacy in the adult population and enrollment of teenagers in secondary education. Table 5.2 highlights GDP per capita as well as the HDI and the change between 1870 and 1913. For the

Table 5.2 GDP per capita and Human Development Index in European countries, 1870 and 1913

	GDP per cap. 1870	GDP per cap. 1913	Rate of change, % p.a.	HDI 1870 (UK 1913 = 100)	HDI 1913 (UK = 100)
Denmark	2003	3912	1.63	79.5	102.5
Netherlands	2757	4049	0.80	75.5	100.8
UK	3190	4921	0.97	77.6	100
Switzerland	2102	4266	1.80	80.0	99.8
Sweden	1662	3096	1.79	75.0	99.5
Norway	1360	2447	1.04	70.5	98.0
Germany	1839	3648	1.56	71.9	95.3
France	1876	3485	1.28	71.9	94.3
Ireland	1775	2736	1.01	–	93.0
Belgium	2692	4220	1.00	72.8	91.6
Czech lands*	1164	2096	1.38	–	84.0
Hungary	1092	2098	1.53	–	78.7
Austria	1863	3465	1.48	51.4	77.8
Italy	1499	2564	1.11	41.6	75.3
Finland	1140	2111	1.43	37.1	69.9
Spain	1207	2056	0.73	46.7	65.4
Bulgaria	840	1534	1.41	–	62.6
Russia	943	1488	1.07	–	53.6

* "Czech lands" include Slovakia as regards GDP per capita. Rate of change is calculated as the fitted trend to the time series and may not exactly agree with the trend between start year and end year, except where data for the intermediate years are missing, as in the cases of Ireland, Czechoslovakia, Hungary, Bulgaria and Russia.
Notes: ranked according to HDI position in 1913. GDP per capita in 1990 purchasing power parity-adjusted, international dollars.
Sources: Maddison 2007, Historical Statistics, www.ggdc.net/Maddison/; Crafts 2002 and calculations.

sake of comparison, we have recalculated the HDI figures so that they are all relative to the level in the richest country, the United Kingdom, in 1913.

It is striking that there is no perfect match between the HDI and GDP per capita rankings. In 1913 the UK was by far the richest country, but countries in north-west Europe, plus Switzerland, challenged the British in terms of the HDI. The continental pioneer of industrialization, Belgium, was in the top group of income levels but lagged behind in living standards as measured by the HDI. Moreover, the Scandinavian countries Norway and Sweden roughly matched the Belgian level of the HDI at the beginning of the period and were far above it by the end, though still lagging distinctly behind in income levels. Further to the south and east in continental Europe, Italy and Austria were richer than Norway and Sweden, respectively, yet far below in HDI levels. The huge differences in life expectancy across Europe have already been highlighted and these explain a large part of the discrepancies in HDI levels.

It can also be seen in Table 5.2 that the countries at the bottom of the welfare league in 1913, Spain, Bulgaria, and Russia, had by that time attained levels of income comparable to those of the medium-income countries forty years earlier. As regards HDI levels, they had overtaken the earlier levels of Austria and Italy but still suffered from a living standard below that prevailing in northwestern Europe around 1870.

All in all, rapid improvements took place all over Europe between 1870 and 1913, unprecedented in both time frame and geographical scope. Economic growth was not the only factor, as is clear from the far from perfect correlation between GDP per capita and HDI level. Differences in literacy and schooling are one part of the mismatch. Of no less significance are differences in life expectancy. The classical explanation proposed that improvement in nutrition and living conditions reduced mortality (McKeown 1976). Growing national income and its fair distribution should drive progress. However, a closer analysis of data, particularly for age-specific mortality, found that view too simple, although there is still no consensus (Schofield and Reher 1991; Riley 2001). We shall now examine factors affecting health and mortality.

Modernization, urbanization, and living conditions

Urbanization completely changed traditional ways of life, and thus we start the broader discussion about modernization and the changes in living conditions with urbanization. Migration is the result of people searching for new opportunities. Besides the great emigration, there also occurred internal European migration, moving peasants from rural to urban areas.

The urban population, defined as those living in communities of at least 10,000 inhabitants, comprised 15 percent of the European population in 1870 (Chapter 10 in Volume 1). Differences were substantial between the highly developed north-west, where England and Wales led with 43 percent urban dwellers, and the sparsely populated northern and eastern areas of Europe. In 1869, 9.5 percent of Russians were resident in urban areas with at least 10,000 inhabitants (Mironov 1999, pp. 313–15). In Scandinavia, only 5.5 percent of the population qualified as urban, although definitions of urbanization differ. If one takes a lower level of 5,000 inhabitants as the threshold, urbanization in Scandinavia varied between 10 and 25 percent, and was about 60 percent in England and Wales, with 23 percent as the European average. At the end of our period, in 1914, the urbanization rate in Europe as a whole had increased to 25 percent (or 38 percent with the weaker definition). Given the rapid overall population increase, this meant a significant acceleration of urban growth and in absolute numbers the inhabitants in large towns and cities increased from 47 to 118 million (72 to 179 million with the weaker definition). It is well known that Germany exhibited an extremely rapid urbanization, particularly in the Ruhr area. Regional migration, from east to west, was important in Germany and the number of inhabitants in the Ruhr grew fourfold in our period. The largest towns of the Ruhrgebiet, which at the turn of the century (1800) had been scarcely more than villages with a combined population of less than 40,000, a century later approached one and a half million. However, even in more peripheral parts of Europe, urbanization accelerated, the outstanding case being Tsarist Russia where quite a few previously ordinary towns grew to impressive urban centers, and the urban population increased to 15.3 percent by 1914 (Mironov 1999a, p. 315). With a weaker definition of urbanization, including settlements of 2,000 or more, the urban percentage in Russia reached 32.3 (Mironov 1999a, p. 318). Table 5.3 gives an overview of the European urbanization based on data for 99 important cities or towns. It is striking that the wave of urbanization extended also to regions where industrialization had only just begun. However, in the center of Europe – Britain, France, Italy, and the Czech lands – urban growth was moderate as well as in the Iberian peninsula and Ireland.

City life brought new habits. Traditionally the household was both a consumption and a production unit. Modernization and urban life made it more of a consumption unit. However, children continued to contribute to household income. Although primary schooling was universal, except in Portugal, the Balkans, and Russia, it was not yet a full-time occupation and few stayed in school beyond the age of fourteen. Thus there was a family life-cycle pattern of income, where the children took over the income-earning role of the mother before they finally left home and formed their own families. In 1900, in the

Table 5.3 Major cities or towns in Europe: their numbers and growth

	Total number	Number > 200,000 in 1910/11	Annual rate of change in percent	
			1800/1 – 1870/1	1870/1 – 1910/1
Austria	1	1	1.75	2.25
Belgium	2	2	1.78	2.12
Bulgaria	1	0	–	4.30
Czech	1	1	1.06	0.89
Denmark	1	1	0.84	2.86
Finland	1	0	1.53	4.43
France	8	5	1.43	1.69
Germany	16	16	1.85	3.11
Greece	2	0	–	5.09
Hungary	1	1	1.90	3.75
Italy	9	7	0.54	1.47
Ireland	2	2	1.05	1.82
Netherlands	3	2	0.61	2.54
Norway	1	1	2.75	3.27
Poland	7	7	1.41	2.95
Portugal	1	1	0.37	1.57
Romania	1	1	2.15	2.21
Tsarist Russia	21	10	1.31	3.12
Serbia, Croatia	2	0	0.27	3.32
Spain	4	3	0.87	1.63
Sweden	2	1	1.10	2.47
Switzerland	2	0	1.57	2.28
United Kingdom	10	10	1.99	1.59
Europe, this sample	99	69	1.25	2.27

Source: Mitchell 2003 – those towns or cities which had a quarter of a million inhabitants in 1900/1, or half a million in 1960/1, or "otherwise important." 1870/1 figures for Barcelona, Seville, and Valencia have been interpolated. Ireland includes Northern Ireland; Poland includes Wroclaw, which at the time was German Breslau; Tsarist Russia includes currently independent republics.

textile district of Ghent in Belgium, wives typically earned 20–30 percent of household income initially. As time passed, children came to contribute a full half, and the father contributed the rest. Working teenagers, living with their parents, were the rule long after the end of our period. By 1900, in most of industrialized Europe including Russia, legislation barred labor under the age of twelve. Almost everywhere, however, protective laws did not extend to small artisan workshops. Generally there was not much legislation on working conditions before 1900 except for child and female labor. Remarkably, legislation in Russia did not lag behind and in 1897, the working day was limited to 11.5 hours and night work to 10 hours, although overtime was allowed

(Janssens 2003, pp. 73–4; Tugan-Baranovsky 1970, pp. 313, 329, 341–2). Elsewhere, working hours were not limited, except for the British Act restricting them to nine hours a day in 1873. This Act seems not to have had much of an impact, although British male workers even in 1870 worked about 500 hours less per year than their counterparts in other western European countries. Compared with today, working hours in western Europe were unbelievably long: 3,200 hours against 1,600. By 1913 working hours in western Europe had converged towards the British standard, and in France a ten-hour working day was enforced by law in 1904. Significant differences remained, however, with the Netherlands having the longest and Spain the shortest hours (Huberman 2004).

Legislation also focused on female labor. In 1878 Germany forbade female work in mines and prescribed three weeks' maternal leave after childbirth, supplemented from 1887 by an allowance. In Russia, night work by women and children in the textile industries was prohibited in 1885. Following the Berlin Conference on legal harmonization in 1890, more countries regulated female work in the following year. Germany forbade female night work, doubled maternity leave to six weeks, and limited the working day for women to eleven hours. Britain prescribed four weeks of maternity leave, and France in 1892 legislated the eleven-hour day for women and forbade female night work in factories. Maternity leave had to wait in France, but before the end of the period female factory workers were laid off six weeks before and six weeks after childbirth (Kintner 1985; Rose 1996; Canning 1996; Stone 1996) With urbanization and industrialization, the age-old bourgeois ideal of the male breadwinner family gained a cultural hegemony in places even before 1914 (Janssens 1997, 2003). In Britain it obviously did, since only 10 percent of married women are reported to have been in the labor force in 1901, as against 40 percent of French wives (Frader 1996). Although the first figure may be too low and the latter an exaggeration, the higher propensity of French married women to work for pay was probably more the outcome of a lower wage level in France than of deliberate female emancipation. In Germany women, and increasingly married women, streamed to the factories during the rapid late nineteenth-century industrialization (Canning 1996). The wage level interacted with the propensity of married women to join the labor market. In Russia, after the Emancipation of the serfs in 1861, the rise in relative wages gradually swelled the female labor force. In the province of Moscow by 1898, a full quarter of adult women worked outside the village in non-agricultural labor (Pallot 1991, p. 167). In Britain and the Netherlands, where wages were comparatively high, fewer wives worked outside the household. In Belgium and France, female labor-force participation varied between industrial districts. Where mines and metal-working industries dominated, female workers were few. In textile districts they could dominate the workforce, and wages also were much lower. In France, there was a vociferous debate within the labor movement over the "family wage" which would bring about the male-breadwinner household (Frader 1996). It was not introduced, but after the turn of the century the employment of French women outside agriculture stagnated. One might presume that the decline was brought about by the behavior of married women. Statistics on employment by gender and sector are provided by Mitchell (2003). The accuracy and consistency of the data can be questioned for some countries, but the overall picture is probably about right. Since reported employment in agriculture is highly dependent on its structure, whether based on hired labor or self-employment, only employment outside agriculture has been considered here. It should be noted that the share of employment is not equal to the labor-force participation rate (which is the usual indicator), and there is no fixed relation between them. Say that the female share of employment is 30 percent and there are as many women as men of productive age; then if 90 percent of the males are active, the female labor force participation rate will be 39 percent, but if only 80 percent of the males are active, the female rate is 34 percent.

As shown in Table 5.4, few countries exhibit big changes in the gender distribution of employment, and the trend differed among countries and over time. Among the more populous countries, Italy experienced a sharp decline in the female share of non-agricultural employment during the late nineteenth century – so sharp that it had an impact on the European level. If Italy is excluded, the female share in non-agricultural employment was stable at 30 percent in Europe, as represented by these fifteen countries. This is equal to a female labor force participation rate of at most 40 percent, and since a majority of unmarried women certainly worked, the share of non-agricultural, married women working outside the household should not be too far from the figures in Table 5.4. Thus it was fairly stable over the period 1880–1910. However, the employment statistics certainly under-report female domestic labor, which actually persisted and grew during the late nineteenth century, due to out-sourcing of work in the expanding clothing industry. Consequently the male-breadwinner household was slow to appear and was not yet the pattern in 1914 (Honeyman and Goodman 1991). There was no historical turning point when married women returned from the factories; the lower female than male labor-force participation rate was rather an outcome of individual life cycles. Married women withdrew from the labor force as the family grew and the children began to earn money.

City life not only changed habits and household patterns, but also had a severe impact on health. The "urban penalty" meant that mortality was significantly higher in large towns and cities than in the countryside, and continued to be so throughout the period in large parts of Europe. Moreover, at the

Table 5.4 The share of females in non-agricultural employment

	1880	1900	1910	Deviating year
Ireland	47.9	–	40.8	
Britain	33.8	31.5	31.6	1881, 1901, 1911
Belgium	33.0	29.3	32.1	
Netherlands	25.1	26.4	26.3	1889, 1899, 1909
France	34.4	37.4	36.2	1886, 1901, 1911
Germany	18.3	20.1	21.5	1882, 1895, 1907
Switzerland	26.4	34.4	38.6	1890
Austria	35.4	29.4	31.4	
Hungary	34.6	29.0	27.1	
Italy	42.5	31.7	29.4	
Spain	24.5	23.6	20.0	1877
Portugal	40.1	20.9	33.3	1890, 1911
Denmark	50.4	35.0	38.3	
Norway	40.0	40.2	40.5	1875
Russia		18	27	1914
Sweden	17.9	29.4	30.3	
Finland	31.3	31.7	35.9	
Europe, this sample	**32.1**	**29.7**	**29.7**	As above
- excl. Italy	**30.3**	**29.5**	**29.8**	

Source: Calculated from Mitchell 2003. Decrease by at least one percentage point in italics. For Russia, Barber and Davies 1994, p. 92.

beginning of the period deaths exceeded births in Italian, French, and Russian cities. Thus urban growth was entirely dependent on the inflow of migrants. However, as indicated by the previous discussion about the increase in life expectancy, circumstances improved over the period 1870–1914. A comparison of mortality in England and Germany, and of the specific causes of death at different ages, highlights important factors in the mortality decline. We have separated the two most common causes of death: respiratory diseases, including tuberculosis, and digestive diseases. Other, communicable diseases such as smallpox, scarlet fever, typhoid fever, diphtheria, and whooping cough, which previously had claimed many lives, were now of secondary importance. That also meant that there were fewer of the epidemics that had been an ineradicable scourge in human history. Table 5.5 shows the dismal statistics for the ten largest towns as well as for the whole of both countries.

What is striking in Table 5.5 is not only that there was an "urban penalty," at least early in the period, but also that there was a "German penalty." Even by 1900 mortality in Germany had not come down to the English level of the 1870s. The age distribution was, however, very different in the two countries and for all ages above one year, the German mortality in 1900 was lower or about the same as in England at the beginning of the period, and was

Table 5.5 Mortality (per 10,000) in Germany and England and Wales, due to certain causes and at certain ages in large towns and country-wide

	Germany			England and Wales		
	Ten largest towns 1877			*Ten largest towns 1871–80*		
	Infant	Child	All	Infant	Child	All
Digestive	1,717.1	75.9	61.3	320.8	30.9	22.4
Respiratory	3,34.2	90.5	67.3	386.4	95.1	48.2
All causes	3,417.9	408.0	267.7	2,031.8	421.4	240.2
	Whole country (Prussia) 1877			*Whole country 1871–80*		
	Infant	Child	All	Infant	Child	All
Digestive	1,131.6	78.0	49.5	241.7	22.1	20.0
Respiratory	96.1	35.1	46.3	317.9	67.3	37.6
All causes	2,327.7	417.3	256.8	1774.1	311.9	212.7
	Ten largest towns 1900			*Ten largest towns 1901–10*		
	Infant	Child	All	Infant	Child	All
Digestive	1,367.8	34.6	38.5	248.5	15.5	7.9
Respiratory	385.3	93	56.9	361.6	129.3	50.5
All causes	2899.0	239.1	199.6	1699.7	347.8	168.2
	Whole country (Prussia) 1900			*Whole country 1901–10*		
Digestive	1,369.0	58.4	49.0	180.0	19.7	5.7
Respiratory	221.5	58.4	52.1	312.4	99.3	40.8
All causes	2,582.2	246.2	223.1	1,501.7	263.1	153.6

Source: Vögele 1998, Tables 12–13, 16–17, 20–3. Infant is age 0–1, child 1–5. Some of the included German towns, for example Munich, Nuremberg, and Hamburg, were not situated in Prussia. Vögele also reports German mortality in 1907, but by then the classification of death causes had changed in some cities so that the figures are not comparable.

approaching the contemporary English level above the age of five. Among children aged between one and five, mortality actually had become lower than in Britain, as seen from the figures in the "Child" columns. Thus, the "German penalty" shifted more and more towards a persistently higher mortality among the youngest children.

A similar development, continuing the German–English comparison, can be seen in an urban–national comparison within Germany. The "urban penalty" shifted more and more towards an "infant penalty," and in 1900 urban mortality was so much lower, among those who had survived the first year of life, that overall mortality in the large cities was below the average for the country. Nevertheless, urbanization contributed to an increase in the country-wide infant mortality rate, and the toll from digestive diseases in 1900 was the same in the country as in the largest cities. Considering the causes, it is clear that digestive disease, mainly diarrhea, was the worst killer behind the "German penalty" and, broadly speaking, stood behind the whole gap in German–English infant mortality, town and country alike. Respiratory diseases took more lives in England as well as in the German cities than on average in Germany. However, despite a minor retreat of tuberculosis, mortality due to other respiratory diseases increased in Germany and the difference between the largest cities and the rest of the country narrowed. This is probably connected with rapid urbanization on a broader scale in Germany, whereas England always had a more urban character outside the ten largest cities.

In England the "urban penalty" changed very little, in relative terms, and by the end of the period the overall mortality was still 10 percent higher in the largest cities. Thus we might summarize the picture as an "urban penalty" and a "German penalty," both due to a large and increasing "infant penalty."

Infant mortality was higher in Germany than in most other European countries. In Figure 5.1 Germany has been grouped together with Austria

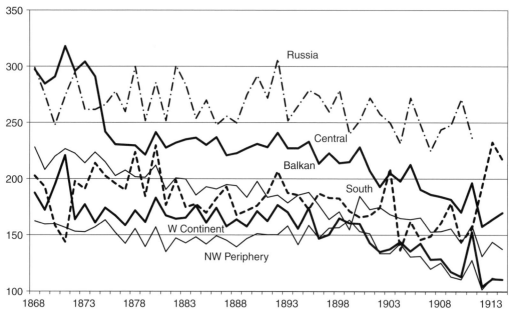

Figure 5.1 Infant mortality in parts of Europe, 1868–1914. Per 1,000 born. *Source:* calculated from Mitchell 2003. Central: Austria, Germany, Hungary (1891–); Balkan: Bulgaria (1892–1912), Romania (1868–1903; 1912–), Serbia (1888–1910); South: Italy, Spain (1868–70, 1878–88, 1900–); W Continent: Belgium, France, Netherlands, Switzerland (1871–); NW Periphery: Denmark, Ireland, England and Wales, Norway, Scotland, Sweden. IMR for each country has been weighed with its population in 1870 and 1913, which may deviate from the actual number born.

and Hungary in "central Europe," and this region had significantly higher infant mortality not only than other advanced parts of Europe but also than poorer regions. Russia was the worst case, but other eastern countries such as Bulgaria and Serbia had significantly lower infant mortality than Germany–Austria–Hungary. In most regions a decline occured first in the 1890s. One exception was the south, with both Italy and Spain showing a slow but steady decline throughout the period. Another exception among individual countries was the Netherlands, which, even more than Italy, showed a steady decline over the whole period. The remarkable sharp drop in the central European region in the mid-1870s highlights the huge differences within Germany; the drop is due to a decline in the German series which in turn comes with the inclusion of Prussia, whereby more weight is given to northern and western Germany. Despite that drop, central Europe stayed at a higher level throughout the period – although the Balkans showed a steep rise in the very last years – due surely to Romania being the sole representative of this region in 1913–14. Until the turn of the century Romania had a lower infant mortality than Germany, but it then lagged behind in the decline and had huge variations between the years. A key factor for explaining the huge differences in infant mortality is the extent to which the babies were artificially fed, which in combination with deficient hygiene and handling of food made them much more exposed to disease.

However, as already noted, there is no consensus on the causes of the mortality decline (Corsini and Viazzo 1997). Insights can be gained by considering the European pattern of infant mortality and feeding practices from the perspective of social improvements in the period 1870–1914.

Sanitary conditions, childcare, and the progress of knowledge

Clearly, the increase in the urban population of Europe from close to 50 million to almost 120 million over the period 1870–1914 must have put a strain on housing. New migrants to the cities found their residence in attics or in cellars, and living spaces and beds were shared by many people. In Russia, urban living conditions were overcrowded and insanitary. In St Petersburg, workers tended to live in barracks, and the number of people living in each room or cellar was twice that in Berlin, Vienna or Paris (Barber and Davies 1994, p. 93). Nevertheless, the "urban penalty" disappeared during the late nineteenth century in Russia and overall mortality became even lower in urban than in rural areas (Mironov 1999, p. 190). In other words, in Russia, as elsewhere, conditions probably improved, even though the improvement was very uneven. Similarly, in England before the start of our period, in the 1840s, 40,000 people, or 20 percent of the population, in Liverpool lived in cellars. Liverpool and

Manchester were probably the worst places. About this time, the public health movement for improvement of sanitary standards began, and Manchester seems to have led the way with local regulations on housing, for example, forbidding housing people in cellars in 1853. At the national level, the Public Health Act came in in 1875 and Belgium and France, at about the same time, also made legislative efforts to improve housing standards (Burnett 1991). The migration to towns and cities propagated an intense housing construction effort, but in many areas it nevertheless fell short of demand. In Berlin in 1880, more than 100,000 people, or about a tenth of the population, lived in cellars. Social statistics evolved with the public health movement, and in Berlin mortality was registered with specification by floor. In the mid-1870s the risk of dying on the fourth floor, under the roof, or in the cellar, was about 25 percent higher than on the first floor. Ten years later, in the mid-1880s, general mortality had declined but still the risk of dying in the attic or the basement was about 15 percent higher (Vögele 1998, p. 148). Similarly, in Glasgow as late as 1911, the mortality in one-room dwellings was twice as high as in apartments with four or more rooms (Burnett 1991). Probably more than housing as such, these figures indicate the importance of social class for mortality.

Housing standards slowly improved, yet this cannot be credited with more than a minor part of the mortality decline. Probably of greater importance than the housing itself were central water networks and sewerage systems. Traditionally, the water supply in cities had been provided by wells and fountains where citizens themselves or water porters fetched the water. Where central piped water networks existed in 1870 only a minority of the houses were served. If Britain and France started earlier, Germany caught up in the construction of entire supply systems. In 1870, only 15 percent of German towns and cities with more than 25,000 inhabitants had a central water supply system. In 1900, all towns of that size had one and so did nearly half of the smaller towns. The coverage was, however, another matter since the completion of the systems took time. For example, Berlin began construction in 1853, and twenty years later about half the buildings were connected, whereas London did not attain the same coverage until the 1890s (Spree 1988, pp. 133ff.; Brown 1988; Goubert, 1988; Vögele 1998, pp. 151ff.). Not only Germany caught up with Britain and France. Big cities over large parts of Europe began construction of central water systems at about the same time, between 1860 and 1890. In a sample of twenty-one cities in continental Europe from Finland to Italy and Romania to Netherlands, fourteen began water networks in this period, three earlier, and four after 1910. One of the early starters, Madrid, did not retire its last water porter until in 1912 (Juuti and Katko 2005). Water closets and sewerage systems came, broadly speaking, at about the same time as central water supply although with variations. In

England and Germany, water closets and sewerage systems typically came ten to twenty years after central water supply (Brown 2000; Vögele 1998), but in other parts of Europe the development seems more often to have been contemporaneous (Juuti and Katko 2005). In Russia, even though by 1910 in Moscow a central water supply had been installed, for those who lived outside the "Garden Ring," the central area of the city, water porters were still a critical feature of life (Bradley 1985, p. 67). Central water supply and sewerage meant large improvements in urban sanitary standards, although these were not always very sustainable since problems were exported from town to country. Sometimes the sewerage polluted freshwater sources: for example, the Thames, which supplied parts of London and the Seine, which supplied Paris. Since purification of the water did not become satisfactory until the twentieth century, sanitary progress was not clear cut.

No doubt the central water supply had a tremendous impact on living standards, probably saving more household labor than later innovations such as the washing machine (Svensson 1995). However, the less significant impact on health and mortality may be due to the deficient quality of the water. The ten largest towns and cities in England and Germany were about equally endowed with central water supplies in the early twentieth century, but digestive diseases continued to be a "German penalty" not only among infants but in the entire population, although other death causes had been significantly reduced in Germany compared to England, as discussed above (see Table 5.5).

Of course it was a combination of factors that caused mortality decline. As shown above, life expectancy was not closely correlated with GDP per capita. McKeown (1976) emphasized improved nutritional standards as a key factor. An estimate for the German population shows that the caloric intake of the total population improved by about 30 percent between 1870 and 1914 (Twarog 1997). Although gross intake is of great importance for living standards and health, it is what is actually digested that matters. Exposure to disease, in particular at an early age, greatly influences human ability to use nutrition, and therefore influences health throughout life (e.g., Bengtsson and Dribe 2005, p. 348). Thus there is no linear relationship between the availability of foodstuffs and demographic indicators.

Emphasis here falls on the impact of infant mortality on life expectancy. Maybe variations in child nursing across Europe provide a clue to understanding the factors that drove the increase in life expectancy. Infant mortality in Russia was strongly affected by child-rearing practices. The children of Great Russian women were breastfed only briefly and graduated somewhat early to solid foods, which led to extraordinarily high rates of infant deaths from diarrheal diseases (Hoch 1994, p. 69). Similarly, the low level of breastfeeding distinguished German child rearing. Avoidance of breastfeeding was more common further to the east and south in Germany as well as in the neighboring central European countries, all with high infant mortality (Newman 1906, p. 235; Kintner 1985; Morel 1991; Vögele 1998, p. 82). The reader may recall Figure 5.1, where the inclusion of north-west Germany in central Europe showed up as a sharp drop in infant mortality. Instead of mother's milk, babies were nourished with cow-milk or pap, often prepared by chewing bread and feeding it to the baby through a tube. Given the deficient storage of the food and the breeding of germs in the utensils, contagion in the infants was inevitable. In Berlin in 1885, mortality was seven times as high among artificially nursed babies as among the breastfed. Knowledge about nursing and caring improved but still in 1910 the difference was 4.4 times (Vögele 1998, p. 82). Often women's work in factories, not only in Germany, meant a reduction in breast-feeding, which had a disastrous impact on infant mortality (Morel 1991; Vallin 1991). Artificial feeding was not the only alternative to breastfeeding. Infants were also left to wet-nurses. This was a common practice in France, and in particular in Paris where, in 1869, 41 percent of all babies were handed over to wet-nurses in the countryside who, moreover, often handfed the step-babies (Guttormsson 2002, p. 265; Newman 1906, p. 234). By contrast, where infant mortality was the lowest, in Ireland, Scotland, and Scandinavia, breastfeeding was overwhelmingly the dominant practice (Newman 1906, pp. 221ff.).

Was it, then, just piecemeal improvements in several factors, from nutrition to housing and sanitary conditions that brought about the decline in mortality? A comparative perspective suggests that this is not a satisfactory explanation. If it were, the correlation across Europe between GDP per capita and life expectancy would have been close to perfect. Instead, human behavior determined a society's responsiveness to improvements for the benefit of health and the decline of mortality.

Some attention must be given to what was going on within the household. There, infants were breastfed or fed on cow-milk and pap, or outsourced to wet-nurses. The household was also the locus of personal hygiene and the handling of food. At least since the beginning of the public health movement in the early nineteenth century, filth had been fought, and cleanliness was the ideal. However, diseases were believed to spread through *miasmas* (bad smells), and this belief constrained efficient prevention, for example in the handling of water. A much-cited example is the discovery, by the London physician John Snow, that cholera was being transmitted from a public well contaminated by the leakage from the privies in a nearby yard. That was in the 1850s, and it would be another decade before Louis Pasteur provided scientific proof of the germ theory, as opposed to miasmas and the ancient belief that new life could emerge spontaneously in organic material. Pasteur, himself a chemist, opened the way for modern medicine with antisepsis and the identification of specific germs as the causes of certain diseases (Biraben 1991). Germ theory was not immediately accepted: it was engineers and not physicians who drove the construction of central water supplies and sewerage (Vögele 1998, p. 163). Neither did improved medical treatment significantly contribute to the mortality decline before 1914. Nonetheless the impact of the new knowledge on human behavior was immense, not least in households, and this propelled much of the improvement in health (Mokyr 2000). The age-old belief that disease was sent by God was replaced by knowledge about the causes and by pre-emptive behavior. Rejecting fatalism and pious approval of what "the Lord gave and the Lord hath taken away," parents began actively to promote the survival of their children (Guttormsson 2003). Improved care of infants was also pushed by infant welfare centers, set up in Germany after 1900, by British Medical Health Officers, and by doctors such as George Newman, who in 1906 published the remarkable book *Infant Mortality. A Social Problem* (Kintner 1985; on Newman, see Galley 2006 and Woods 2006).

New knowledge propelled the ideology that propped up the so-called male-breadwinner household. Historically that concept is a misnomer that draws attention away from the contribution of women to the development of the modern household. Certainly much of the agitation, for example, for a family wage or for legislation on female work had a patriarchal motive and tone that denounced women's individualism (Honeyman and Goodman 1991; Frader 1996). But it is to fall into a discriminatory trap to ignore the modern household's role in promoting health – and reducing mortality. The label "modern household" is not intended to denounce its gender division of labor, which still today is predominantly traditional, but to emphasize that it took advantage of a new technology. The new knowledge about hygiene, germs, and, after the turn of the century, vitamins and minerals was diffused to the public. Books and journals spread the message of "domestic science." And it had an impact. Diffusion was also enhanced through schooling, which encompassed almost the entire new generation in most of Europe. "While the absorption of the full behavioral implications of germ theory took decades, what is surprising is how relatively quick and complete its triumph was by 1914, delivering sharp declines in infectious disease decades before the introduction of antibiotics" (Mokyr 2000, p. 17). The middle classes were the first to adopt the new practices and to gain from improvements in health. Poorer *arrondissements* in Paris in 1891 had 71 percent higher infant mortality than the wealthier. Two decades later the difference had grown to 135 percent. In Prussia, also in 1891, the differential in infant mortality between working-class families and civil servants was 31 percent – and two decades later it had increased to over 90 percent (Morel 1991). Knowledge and habits worked their way down the social ladder, however, and health improved generally with the passing of time.

A comparison of inequality

The discussion of household patterns, social class and health leads to another aspect of living standards: income distribution. During the initial period of modern economic growth in Europe, inequality seems to have widened and large sections of the population suffered from deteriorating incomes (Pamuk and van Zanden, Chapter 9 in Volume 1). After 1870, economic growth gained momentum and income levels increased. What about inequality? If income gaps are wide in a rich country, one can conclude that poverty is not rare. If gaps are moderate in a medium-income country poverty probably is rare. In a low-income country high equality nevertheless means ubiquitous poverty. Comprehensive statistics on income and earnings are rare before the First World War, which is why international comparisons for this period have to rely on less precise estimates. Available for most countries are real wage data for manual labor, and for a bundle of countries there are also purchasing power parity-adjusted real wages, making levels comparable across countries. We will use such data in combination with GDP per capita for a shorthand estimate of European income inequalities. "Wages" is a term applied in most countries to the remuneration of urban unskilled labor, but in the case of (less urbanized) Finland it applies to "manual outdoor workers"; for Sweden it is average male wages in manufacturing, and for Russia it is wages of workers in agriculture. Let us first give the picture and then discuss its validity and limitations.

The basic idea is that the ratio *real wage/GDP per capita* (hereafter w/y), gives information about income distribution. Most important, it allows a comparison not of the absolute numbers but of relatives over time and space. Over time is simple, since if the ratio w/y increases it means that manual workers are getting a larger share of national income, and there is a decrease in inequality. Where w/y falls, inequality increases. Moreover, if we can compare wage and GDP per capita levels across countries, that will allow a comparison of income distribution in the countries involved. Thus a measure of comparative equality is derived:

$$Equality = \frac{W_j/W_{uk}}{Y_j/Y_{uk}}$$

If the real wage in country j is, say, 95 percent of the real wage in the United Kingdom, whereas GDP per capita is only 85 percent of the UK level, then manual workers in country j have a larger share than their British counterparts, and equality is higher in country j. Conditions in the UK, the most advanced country at the time, are taken as the standard for comparison. Since the pattern we find is quite different for the period before and after 1890, this year is taken as the reference year and Table 5.6 shows the results.

Table 5.6 Comparative income, real wage and equality levels in European countries (UK 1890 = 100)

	Relative GDP/ cap. 1890	Relative real wage 1890	Equality 1870	Equality 1890	Equality 1913
Serbia	20.6	44.0	277.4	217.5	167.8
Portugal	28.1	47.2	122.0	168.0	151.4
Russia	27.6	40.8	118.2	150.0	99.0
Finland	34.4	51.5	130.2	149.7	157.5
Germany	60.6	85.4	139.0	140.9	115.0
Spain	40.5	55.1	192.9	136.0	136.4
Sweden	52.0	66.3	97.7	127.5	101.0
Norway	42.6	52.8	96.5	123.9	140.3
France	59.3	71.9	109.5	121.2	99.6
Belgium	85.5	96.6	105.4	113.0	94.6
Netherlands	82.9	85.4	83.9	103.1	74.7
Denmark	62.9	64.0	76.0	101.7	115.7
United Kingdom	100	100	82.6	100	80.7
Italy	41.6	38.3	63.8	92.1	83.6
Europe, this sample	44.1	53.8	89.3	121.9	119.0

Notes: ranked according to inequality in 1890.
Sources: GDP per capita, as for Table 6.1; Yugoslavia stands in for Serbia here. Real wages, Williamson 1995 but Finland Heikkinen 1997; Russia, Leonard (forthcoming); Serbia, Palairet 1995; Spain, Simpson 1995; Sweden Bagge, Lundberg, and Svennilson 1935). Simpson's series behaves very similarly to that in Williamson 1995 but deviates starting in 1900, where the level is inferred from Williamson. For Russia and Serbia the PPP has been inferred from this model: *real wage* $= \alpha + \beta_1$ *GDPc* $+ \beta_2$ *wgrowth* $_{1870\text{–}90}$.

A few things stand out. First, inequality was particularly noticeable in the United Kingdom and in 1913 only the Netherlands was more unequal. Second, the poorest country, Serbia, was also the most equal, although inequality steadily increased. These two observations are in line with the so called *Kuznets curve*, which presumes increasing inequality during early industrialization and then, in the maturing industrial society, a resurgence of a more equal income distribution. However, a third observation points counter to the Kuznets curve. In the period 1870–90 all countries except Serbia, Spain and, maybe, Germany experienced increasing equality. Moreover, thereafter, in 1890–1913, all countries except Denmark, Norway, Finland and, maybe, Spain, experienced a clear decrease in equality. For Europe as a whole, as represented by the countries in table 5.6 weighted by population shares, equality also increased in the first period and was roughly stable in the second.

A limitation of the Kuznets curve is that it is a generalization confined to a closed economy, whereas the observed pattern should be seen in the perspective of globalization and the Second Industrial Revolution. From about 1870, railroads and falling transport costs made Russian and American grain competitive in European markets. Previously prices had been low in the producing peripheries, but due to the foreign demand prices now increased and led to expanded cultivation. In the consuming centers, however, cheap imports led to falling prices. The twofold effect was to allow higher wages for Russian agricultural day labor as well as higher real wages for European workers (O'Rourke and Williamson 1999; Borodkin, Granville, and Leonard 2008). After 1890 smoothly falling price levels changed into a mild inflation that acted as a brake on real wages, at the same time as the Second Industrial Revolution shifted demand to more skilled labor (Goldin and Katz 1998; Svensson 2004). Whether the change from deflation to mild inflation in the 1890s was caused by increased production of gold, which was minted to a larger quantity of money, or by increased pressure on available resources is not settled. To some extent, globalization continued to contribute to equality, primarily through emigration, which made labor a more scarce resource in Europe. That is highlighted by increasing equality in three of the Nordic countries after 1890. However, even in the fourth Nordic country, Sweden, emigration pushed up wages and living standards, but since the growth of GDP per capita reached a very high rate the result was nevertheless decreasing equality (O'Rourke and Williamson 1995; Ljungberg 1997). Largely unaffected by the pattern displayed over most of Europe, from Britain to Russia, was Serbia. Unaffected by market integration and the Second Industrial Revolution, Serbia's income distribution followed the path of the early Kuznets curve with rising inequality.

To what extent is the above picture of European income distribution valid? First it must be said that the quality of the data, for both GDP per capita and real wages, leaves room for improvement. Without going into detail, quality issues probably affect cross-country levels and may influence country rankings. However, the general pattern – whereby equality increased before 1890 and decreased thereafter – is probably robust by our measure. The w/y measure may require caution in that it reduces income distribution to the wage share of unskilled workers. If the size and level of earnings of the skilled and professional income earners vary between countries, this will affect income distribution and w/y. Since skilled and professional labor contribute more to GDP, their expansion causes a rise in GDP per capita and depresses equality, explaining why the richest countries were the least equal. Thus, w/y indicates the gap in regard to the lowest income earners but says little about the structure of the income distribution. However, during this period unskilled workers made up a sizeable share of all income earners and in want of more precise measures w/y makes sense. Economic growth in Europe from 1870 to 1913 elevated income levels and reduced inequality up to the 1890s. The acceleration of growth in the 1890s, however, exacted a price in stable or slightly increasing inequality; in Russia this price was dramatic.

Conclusion

The half-century before 1914 saw tremendous changes in living conditions across Europe. No doubt one could list a series of innovations as well as manifestations of human mobility that changed everyday life to no less an extent than in the current era of globalization and the IT revolution. However, the most striking, and often overlooked, evidence of the change is, we would suggest, increased life expectancy. Whereas a European born in the 1870s could expect an average lifetime of only about thirty-five years, barely more than a generation later, on the eve of the First World War, life expectancy was around fifty years. These figures are simply the averages of country observations in Table 5.1, without consideration of the numerous Russian population, making up roughly a quarter of the European population in 1870 and a third in 1913, which even at this latter date had not attained a life expectancy of thirty-five. Since infant mortality was the most important cause of the low life expectancy, one should note, first, that there were large variations across Europe and, secondly, that a decrease in infant mortality moved largely in parallel – though, again, this was less marked in Russia. Differences in income levels cannot explain the variations in infant mortality, however; a major cause was the extent of breastfeeding. The decrease in infant mortality, particularly from the turn of the century in 1900, however, cannot be explained by breastfeeding practices but largely by improved sanitary standards in urban areas as well as improved hygiene within the household. The role of women in the latter, as mothers and housekeepers, is often overlooked or even ridiculed, despite its monumental importance. Moreover, not least for women, quality of life improved when they could bear three instead of five or more children and have a much higher probability of seeing them grow up.

New knowledge and its diffusion to broad layers of the population was key to the improvement in living standards. The scientific proof of germ theory, which overturned old conceptions about disease and contagion, was fundamental for the change of habits as well as for medicine – although the impact of the latter was still marginal.

Of course modern economic growth opened up possibilities for improvement, for example, through investments in piped water and sanitary systems. Moreover, economic growth was more evenly distributed than during preceding periods. Globalization, with emigration and imports of cheap food, became a lever for increased real wages and greater equality in western Europe. However, technological change, such as electrification, increased the demand for skills and human capital and thus stemmed the further development towards equality. In Russia particular conditions even made income gaps widen dramatically. The shadow of this development is still seen a century later – and beyond.

II The world wars and the interwar period

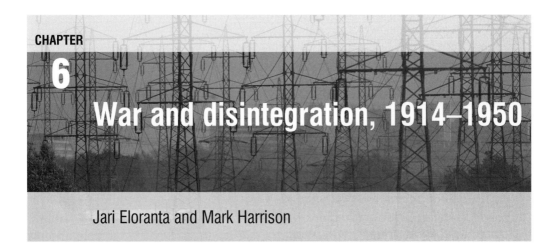

War and disintegration, 1914–1950

Jari Eloranta and Mark Harrison

Contents

Introduction

Between 1914 and 1945 Europe's economic development and integration were interrupted and set back by two world wars, and its regional patterns were brutally distorted by combat, exterminations, migrations, and the redrawing of borders.[1] The First World War (the "Great War" of 1914–18) set more than thirty countries into conflict with each other and led to ten million premature deaths. It was dwarfed only by the Second World War (1939–45), in which more than sixty countries waged war and the war prematurely ended the lives of more than fifty-five million people (Broadberry and Harrison 2005b). As for who fought whom, there were limited continuities: in both wars, Germany, Austria, and Hungary fought Britain, France, and Russia for much of the time. Other allegiances changed. For ease of reference, Table 6.1 lists the European countries that were in or out of each war and, if in, on what side.

Although punctuated by an "interwar period," the two wars can be understood as a single historical process. The process was global but the European dimension was fundamental to it. Thus, Europe was the main theatre of a vast thirty-year conflict of empires and nationalisms. The first War was fought primarily by European powers in Europe; some non-European participants and colonial polities played a minor role while others intervened late in the process. It produced a fragmented continent that had spent vast amounts of physical and human capital; the countries at its center were ensnared in reparations and debts, and incapable of returning to political and economic stability. The second began in Asia but quickly spread across the world to Europe, and most participants understood that the conflict in Europe would be decisive for the outcome. The German historian Ernst Nolte (1965) was the first to define these three decades as a European "civil war." He saw it as a war launched from Russia in 1917 by communist terror and aggression, to which German National Socialism and racial genocide were a defensive response. This is not our view; if any country launched the war it was Germany, first in 1914 and again in 1939, for a variety of reasons. Undoubtedly, however, it makes sense to view the two wars and the interwar period as a continuous process – and we also find the destruction of moral limits that Thucydides first associated with civil strife.

Our period was one of economic and political instability. The average growth rates of most European states were modest compared with their performance

---

[1] The authors gratefully acknowledge the advice and comments of the collaborators in this volume, in particular Joerg Baten, Robert Millward, Leandro Prados de la Escosura, and Kevin O'Rourke, and thank them for their willingness to share their knowledge and understanding.

Table 6.1 Taking sides: belligerents and neutrals in two world wars

	First World War	Second World War
Albania	Neutral	Anti-Comintern Axis
Austria	Central Powers	Annexed to Germany
Belgium	Occupied by Germany	Occupied by Germany
Bulgaria	Province of Austro-Hungarian Empire	Anti-Comintern Axis
Czechoslovakia	Province of Austro-Hungarian Empire	Occupied by Germany
Denmark	Neutral	Occupied by Germany
Estonia	Province of Russian Empire	Occupied by USSR
Finland	Province of Russian Empire	Anti-Comintern Axis
France	Entente	Occupied by Germany
Germany	Central Powers	Anti-Comintern Axis
Greece	Entente	Occupied by Italy
Hungary	Central Powers	Anti-Comintern Axis
Ireland	Province of United Kingdom	Neutral
Italy	Entente	Anti-Comintern Axis
Latvia	Province of Russian Empire	Occupied by USSR
Lithuania	Province of Russian Empire	Occupied by USSR
Netherlands	Neutral	United Nations
Norway	Neutral	Occupied by Germany
Poland	Province of Russian Empire	Occupied by Germany and USSR
Portugal	Neutral	Neutral
Romania	Province of Austro-Hungarian Empire	Anti-Comintern Axis
Russia/USSR	Entente	United Nations
Serbia/Yugoslavia	Province of Austro-Hungarian Empire	Occupied by Germany
Spain	Neutral	Neutral
Sweden	Neutral	Neutral
Switzerland	Neutral	Neutral
Ottoman Empire/Turkey	Central Powers	Neutral
United Kingdom (UK)	Entente	United Nations

before 1914 or after 1950 (Maddison 1995); Angus Maddison (2001) describes these years as "a complex and dismal period, marked deeply by the shock of the two world wars and an intervening depression." Eric Hobsbawm (1996) viewed the extreme political and military outcomes of this period as characteristic of the decadence and economic failures of the twentieth century. But that is not the whole story. Bradford DeLong (2000) and Alex Field (2003, 2006) have stressed that the massive rises in living standards in the second half of the twentieth century were enabled by technological advances that continued in an unbroken stream through the most dismal episodes of the first half. In Europe as elsewhere, the rate of technological improvement remained high throughout our period and exceeded nineteenth century benchmarks in spite of military, economic, and demographic disaster (Ferguson 2006). In short, whatever it was that came to an end in 1914, it was not the forces underlying economic growth.

Globalization, empire, and war

In the nineteenth century globalization and empires were inextricably linked. None other than the Russian revolutionary leader Lenin, writing in 1916 (Lenin 1916; reprint 1963), noted the association between the rise of global markets, global enterprises, and global colonial empires.

In the early twentieth century the great powers all regarded colonial empire as an entirely legitimate national pursuit. For illustration, Table 6.2 shows the world's colonial dependencies. In 1913, Europeans were the greatest imperialists in the history of the world, with 30 percent of the world's population living in European colonies outside Europe that spread across more than two fifths of the world's land surface. In the same year Britain alone, which accounted by itself for one fortieth of the world's population and one five-hundredth of its land surface, claimed sovereignty over 400 million people and thirty-three million square kilometers of Africa, Asia, America, and Australasia. Its empire, including both self-governing dominions such as Canada and Australia and colonial dependencies such as India and Nigeria, embraced almost one quarter of the world's population and a quarter of its land surface. Other European powers, chiefly France and the Netherlands, and after them Belgium, Germany, Italy, Portugal, and Turkey, lagged far behind. Outside Europe, the United States administered some neighboring islands, as did Japan, in addition to its Korean colony (see also Huntington 1996).

In 1938, a quarter century later, almost nothing had changed. Germany and Turkey had lost their little empires as a result of the peace treaties that followed

Table 6.2 Colonial dependencies in 1913 and 1938: populations and land surfaces

	1913		1938	
	Population (millions)	Land surface (million km^2)	Population (millions)	Land surface (million km^2)
British dominions	19.9	19.5	30.0	19.2
British colonies	380.1	13.5	453.8	15.0
French colonies	48.4	10.7	70.9	12.1
Dutch colonies	44.1	2.1	68.1	1.9
Other European colonies	54.1	11.5	33.0	8.3
European powers' colonies and dominions, total	546.5	57.2	655.9	56.5
Non-European powers' colonies	28.8	0.6	75.7	1.9
The World	1,810.3	134.4	2,168.0	134.4

Sources: Harrison 1998a; Broadberry and Harrison 2005a.

the First World War. Italy and Japan were in the first stages of their expansion across the Mediterranean and the Pacific respectively. But these are barely apparent in the figures. Indeed, looking at the world from Berlin, Rome, or Tokyo, the lack of change in the balance of the world's colonial possessions was the problem: the old colonial powers had failed to give way to the aspirations of the new imperialists.

In fact, the pursuit of colonies by the rising powers, combined with the defense of their colonies by the established ones, contributed to repeated crises in the global equilibrium among the powers and was perceived to be to a large extent responsible for the two world wars. In the process the very idea of empire lost its legitimacy. The legitimacy of empire had never been strong among the colonial populations, and its decline became marked within the United States, the foreign policy of which became decidedly anti-colonialist. By 1950 whole-sale decolonization, by consent or by force, was already under way within the British, French, and Dutch empires, the only ones of any significance that remained. This is another sense in which the two world wars formed a single historical process that began in 1914 and ended in 1945 (Modelski and Thompson 1996).

Since Lenin it has been fashionable to link world trade and world empires with the causes of the two world wars. The truth is more complex, however. Neither globalization nor imperialism directly caused the war to break out in 1914. Norman Angell had argued in his 1909 bestseller *The Great Illusion* (reprint, 1972) that the increased economic interdependence of the great powers would make any major international conflict an impossibility, or at least bring it to a quick conclusion. Globalization had increased the interde-pendency of regional and global players, thereby increasing the costs of war. Specifically, increased openness had made the European states more vulnerable to the interuption of imported supplies of food and materials. By raising wages, economic growth had made the maintenance of standing armies more expen-sive. Businessmen across Europe were not pushing for war and its outbreak came as a shock (Ferguson 1999). But there were also countervailing factors. One was the industrialization of warfare, which increased the destructive efficiency of military equipment and gave industrialized states a bigger bang for their bucks (McNeill, 1982; Ferguson 2001). Finally, the very fact of increased vulnerability to economic disruption heightened the propensity of the likely participants to gamble on a rapid offensive, once war became probable (Rowe 2005).

John Hobson (1993) has shown that both the United Kingdom and Germany spent less on their armed forces than most great powers. John Keegan (1999) describes a Europe thrust into war by communication failures and irreversible war plans based on tit-for-tat responses that were designed for the "age-old

Table 6.3 Military spending of the Great Powers in peacetime, 1870–1913 and 1920–38

Country	Military spending, % of GDP		Military spending, % of central or federal government expenditures	
	1870–1913	1920–38	1870–1913	1920–38
Austria(–Hungary)	3.5	0.9	12.0	5.8
France	3.7	4.3	25.9	22.4
Germany	2.6	3.3	54.1	23.8
Italy	2.8	4.4	21.7	25.4
Russia (USSR)	3.9	7.1	27.9	11.9
UK	2.6	3.0	37.5	16.3
Six-country mean	3.2	3.8	29.9	17.6
Japan	5.0	5.7	32.2	20.1
USA	0.7	1.2	29.4	22.4
Sixteen/seventeen country mean	2.7	2.8	33.3	18.0

The sixteen-country mean for 1870–1913 includes Austria(–Hungary), Belgium, Denmark, France, Germany, Italy, Japan, Netherlands, Norway, Portugal, Russia, Spain, Sweden, Switzerland, the UK, and the USA; the seventeen-country mean for 1920–38 adds Finland.
Sources: see Eloranta 2002b, p. 110, for details.

quest for security in military superiority." The First World War was no accident, however. Historians have tended to hold Germany particularly accountable for the pre-1914 arms race and the subsequent diplomatic breakdown (e.g., Berghahn 1973). Niall Ferguson (1999, 2001) has noted that, having started the arms race, Germany was unable to compete against its rivals, and was led therefore to gamble on a pre-emptive strike in 1914. Thus, the pre-war arms race, stimulated by the competition for colonies, was a principal cause, whereas the industrialization of armaments production contributed mainly to the length and destructiveness of the war.

The arms race that led towards war in 1914 is not remarkable for its economic dimension. The Industrial Revolution, combined with the fiscal reforms of the nineteenth century, enabled western states to increase military spending without excessively burdening their economies. We provide two standardized measures of defense spending: the "military burden" on national resources (percent of GDP) and the "defense share" of budgetary means (percent of central government expenditure). In the period before 1914 most countries carried heavier military burdens than in the early nineteenth century. Within Europe, as Table 6.3 suggests, the great powers carried somewhat heavier burdens than others; the average military burden on the GDPs of the six great powers was 3.2 percent, compared with 2.7 percent for the whole sample. Notably the United States, the emerging economic leader, devoted less than one percent of GDP to its armed forces (Eloranta 2003).

The arms race was fueled by both rivalry and restraint. While some countries pushed up military spending to keep abreast of their rivals' efforts, others did the same to exploit the relative restraint of the British and American economic giants. The origins of the Great War are often seen in the consolidation of two confrontational alliances; however, when the statistical evidence is inspected for evidence of strategic interaction we find that the alliances themselves were ultimately inefficient and almost irrelevant to national spending decisions (Eloranta 2007).

A different picture emerges when we turn to the causes of the Second World War. In the interwar period, military burdens were on average higher than before 1914 but, as Table 6.3 suggests, military spending was overtaken everywhere (except Italy) by other spending categories. As a result budgetary defense shares were almost uniformly lower, often much lower. Not reflected in the table are national variations in the timing of rearmament; the Soviet Union and Japan began to rearm at the end of the 1920s and Germany at the beginning of the 1930s. Most others delayed intense rearmament until the mid-1930s. Hitler raised Germany's military burden from below 2 percent in 1933 to nearly 20 percent in 1938. The Japanese rearmament drive was still more impressive, with a 23 percent military burden and more than 50 percent defense share in 1938. Mussolini was less successful in rearmament as well as in his efforts to realize the new Roman Empire, with Italy's military burden reaching no more than 5 percent in 1938. Achieving high rates of military output before that time, as in the Soviet Union, was of doubtful military value, since the rapid pace of technological change made many of the armaments produced earlier obsolete within two or three years.

Some states oscillated between policies of disarmament and rearmament. Many smaller states did not begin active rearmament until after 1935, but some already had high military burdens in the 1920s (e.g., Portugal and Finland). Sweden started the period with a high defense share, which declined noticeably by the end of the 1930s. A member of the League of Nations from the beginning, Sweden exemplifies an active pursuit of disarmament. According to Ulf Olsson (1973), Sweden's rearmament was slow to react to the worsening international security climate, and its military burden remained below 2 percent until 1939. It thus resembles the slow reaction of the United States to the new arms race in the late 1930s (Eloranta 2002b).

Relatively high military spending was not a guarantee of military success or the security of borders. Military spending determined only the increment to one of four dimensions that, according to Samuel Huntington (1996), produce military power. This was the quantitative dimension (men, arms, and resources). The other three are the technological (effectiveness of the equipment); the organizational (deployment and morale of the troops); and the societal (ability and willingness to apply military force in various situations). Military activity itself takes place at four different levels – political, strategic, operational, and tactical – of which the political sphere contains the funding decision (Millett *et al.*, 1988). Germany, for example, put forth the quantitative resources, invested heavily in various civilian and military technologies, had the required organizational structures and training, and whipped the society into a condition ready for war in the 1930s. French policy makers, although convinced in the 1920s that French security required high military spending, were unable to maintain this spending at a competitive level in the 1930s, which may have contributed to the technological weaknesses of the French forces in the Second World War. In addition, their military strategies were ill-attuned to the war of maneuver that was about to be unleashed.

The ascendancy of the authoritarian nations and their military spending began in the mid-1920s, and accelerated after 1933, with Germany quickly tipping the balance. It appears that the international system was destabilized by the dispersion of military power in the 1920s. The United States failed to exercise credible military leadership commensurate with its economic power. In European democracies, domestic military spending decisions were driven more by producer lobbies than by external security concerns (Eloranta 2002b).

The outcome of the renewed rearmament competition was the Second World War. Where did the drive to war come from? There were both new and old elements in the mixture. Something in continuity with the period before 1914 was rivalry for colonies. The British, French, and Dutch defended their empires. The Soviet Union defended the frontiers of the former Russian Empire. The Japanese looked to create a new empire, first to the north in Manchuria and Siberia, then, when the Soviet Union proved too difficult an adversary, turning south to the British, French, and Dutch colonies. The Italians looked to build an empire around the Mediterranean, from North Africa to the Balkans and Greece. And Germany looked towards eastern Europe and Russia for complementary resources and markets and an ethnically restructured living space. To realize these plans the Japanese moved first (into China), then Italy moved (into North Africa), and finally Germany (into eastern Europe). If Lenin had been alive, he would have recognized the picture. The imperial powers were redividing the world by force. Driving the imperial rivalry, however, was something new.

War, development, and dictatorship

Before 1913 the richest countries in Europe were becoming more democratic, while aristocratic and monarchical institutions were weakening in poorer

Table 6.4 Political regime and economic development in Europe across two world wars: numbers of countries

	With GDP per head	
	Above median	Median or below
Polity 2 index, 1913		
Above zero	7	5
Zero or below	3	5
Polity 2 index, 1923:		
Above zero	9	5
Zero or below	0	5
Polity 2 index, 1938:		
Above zero	9	2
Zero or below	2	9
Polity 2 index, 1950:		
Above zero	11	3
Zero or below	1	10

Countries are Albania (1950 only), Austria (not 1938), Belgium, Bulgaria (not 1923), Czechoslovakia (not 1913 or 1938), Denmark, Finland (not 1913), France, Germany, Greece, Hungary (not 1923), Ireland (not 1913), Italy, Netherlands, Norway, Poland (not 1913), Portugal, Romania (not 1923), Russia/USSR (not 1923), Serbia/Yugoslavia, Spain, Sweden, Switzerland, Turkey, and UK. The Polity 2 index subtracts autocracy scores from democracy scores, and also fixes standardized scores, to create a composite index of the political regime suitable for time series analysis, with values ranging from +10 (strongly democratic) to −10 (strongly autocratic). *Sources:* Polity IV data-set from www.systemicpeace.org/polity/polity4.htm; GDP per head in 1990 international dollars from Maddison 2001.

countries such as Greece, Serbia, Spain, Portugal, and Turkey. In so far as democracies rarely fight each other, the prospects for peace in Europe should therefore have been improving. We measure the political regime using the Polity 2 index (based on the Polity IV data), which subtracts autocracy scores from democracy scores to create a composite index of the political regime with values ranging from +10 (strongly democratic) to −10 (strongly autocratic). Table 6.4 compares the degree of democracy with the level of economic development achieved. It shows that in 1913 seven of the ten countries with GDP per head above the European median had achieved a positive Polity index – and so had half of the ten poorer countries. The First World War was launched, however, by the mobilizations of the least democratic powers in Europe: the monarchies of Germany, Austria–Hungary, and Russia.

Losing the Great War destroyed the legitimacy of the regimes that launched it. In Germany, Austria, Hungary, and Russia, the monarchies fell; Germany and Austria became markedly democratic, Hungary mildly so, and Soviet Russia not at all. Where democracy developed, however, it was fragile. The circumstances of the 1920s and early 1930s could hardly have been less favorable, and by the late 1930s the new democratic constitutions had been overridden by a new kind of dictator in Germany, Austria, Italy, Spain, Portugal, and most of eastern Europe, while Russia had gone over from monarchical to communist absolutism with hardly a pause for breath. Table 6.4 shows the stark division of Europe that had developed by 1938: most rich countries continued to uphold democracy, but most poor countries had succumbed to authoritarianism. Finally, the post-Second World War settlement left the continent just as polarized between rich democracies and poor dictatorships as before, with communists taking the place of fascists across eastern and south-eastern Europe.

The new ingredient in interwar imperial rivalry was totalitarianism, a term that the political theorist Hannah Arendt applied to the most oppressive regimes of the twentieth century: National Socialist Germany and communist Russia. According to Juan Linz, a *totalitarian state* has: (1) centralized political power; (2) an exclusive ideology that the leader uses as an instrument both for purposes of political identification and as a guide to action; and (3) mobilization of the citizenry for collective purposes, channelled through a single party using brutal violence against real or perceived opponents (Boesche 1996; Linz 2000). It remains debatable whether the structures of National Socialism and communism were so similar that one concept could cover them both. The consequences were similar but not identical. In the Soviet Union, Stalin created a state-owned command economy under a ruthless political dictatorship. His victims were chiefly his own subjects, whether killed by neglect in the famine that followed the forced collectivization of the countryside or killed by design during the Great Terror. Using state controls, he built up heavy industry and invested in new military technologies; in the mid-1930s the Soviet Union was possibly the biggest defense producer in the world. At the same time the secret record of Stalin's foreign policy has been shown to be "passive-aggressive" rather than expansionist (Barber and Harrison 2005).

Hitler's regime also exemplified the notion of totalitarian control. He added the explosive elements of anti-Semitism and racial purification to the traditional ideals of German nationalism and imperialism. His ascent to power in 1933, beginning with an election victory and rapid assumption of the role of dictator, was preceded by the economic collapse of the Great Depression. German unemployment reached staggering proportions in 1932, with one third of the labor force out of work. Hitler's appeal was based on promises to restore Germany to prosperity and imperial domination, hatred of the Jews, and fear of the communists at home and in the Soviet Union. He consolidated his power by silencing his enemies and building an efficient police state. His policies reduced unemployment and aimed to make the economy self-sufficient for war. He did not aspire to total control over economic life, but was ready to squeeze living standards and real wages for the sake of rearmament (Tooze 2007). He withdrew Germany from the League of Nations, and his decisions to remilitarize the Rhineland in March 1936 and annex Austria were among the death blows to the League's credibility. His main target was colonial expansion (Kennedy 1989; Abelshauser 2000). Compared with Stalin's, his policies killed more people by intention and fewer by accident. More of his victims were in other countries. But he still killed millions of his own citizens.

Compared with the totalitarianism of Hitler and Stalin, the regimes of the Italian and Iberian fascists, although bloody and repressive, do not really measure up. In Italy Mussolini was appointed prime minister in October 1922, after the fascists' march on Rome. He took several years to overcome parliamentarism and the other political parties and he never achieved central-ized control of his polity as did Hitler and Stalin. Nor did he secure a rearma-ment advantage for Italy in the 1930s as he had hoped. Similarly, in Portugal, where authoritarianism was on the rise from 1926, António de Oliveira Salazar only gradually acquired dictatorial authority after becoming prime minister in 1932. In Spain Primo de Rivera's dictatorship of 1923–30 marked the first authoritarian experiment; after a short-lived republic and a brutal civil war, Francisco Franco returned Spain to dictatorship in 1939. In eastern Europe, the Baltic, and the Balkans, the 1930s brought the general rise of authoritarian governments, often led by prominent generals and populist leaders (Lee 1987; Saz 1999).

The evidence shows, however, that regime shifts were not associated with structural changes in these countries' military spending behavior. Although authoritarian, they did not accumulate the centralized powers necessary for massive rearmament. Compared to those of Germany and Japan, for example, Italy's military burden in the late 1930s remained meager (Eloranta 2002b). Other authoritarian states failed to resolve the tension between a revisionist ideology and the requirements of survival in the international arena. Their domestic popularity rested heavily on the promise of more security and pro-tectionist trade policies, but in the 1930s they adopted only weak foreign and commercial policy positions. In the Second World War, however, especially in eastern Europe, they tended to side with the Axis.

Waging war

The two world wars placed the economies of Europe under immense strain. What did this mean? The war demanded huge resources. In both wars, tens of millions of men and guns flung millions of tons of explosives at one another

Table 6.5 Wartime GDP (percent of pre-war)

	Percent of 1913		Percent of 1938	
	N	1917	*N*	1944
Europe, total	16	90	19	96
Of which, countries that:				
Stayed out	7	97	6	112
Won	*2	100	2	99
Lost	7	75	11	91
Former British colonies	4	105	4	207
Former Iberian colonies	8	100	14	124

European countries that stayed out are, in the First World War: Denmark, Netherlands, Norway, Portugal, Spain, Sweden, and Switzerland; in the Second, Ireland, Portugal, Spain, Sweden, Switzerland, and Turkey. Countries that won are in the First World War: France and UK (with regard to Italy, see the note to this table); in the Second: UK and USSR. Countries that lost, meaning that their governments surrendered or their territory was entirely occupied, are, in the First World War: Austria, Belgium, Germany, Hungary, and the Ottoman and Russian Empires (including Finland); in the Second: Austria, Belgium, Bulgaria, Denmark, Finland, France, Germany, Greece, Italy, Netherlands, and Norway. Former British colonies are, in both wars: Australia, New Zealand, Canada, and the United States. Former Iberian colonies are, in the First World War: Argentina, Brazil, Chile, Colombia, Mexico, Peru, Uruguay, and Venezuela; in the Second: Argentina, Brazil, Chile, Colombia, Costa Rica, Cuba, El Salvador, Guatemala, Honduras, Mexico, Nicaragua, Peru, Uruguay, Venezuela.
*Excludes Italy for reasons mentioned in footnote 1. If Italy is included, then 100 becomes 107.
Sources: Maddison 2001, except that for GDP in 1917 we add estimates for Hungary from Schulze 2005, p. 86, and for Russia from Gatrell 2005, p. 241; for the Ottoman Empire we use a figure of two thirds of 1913 based on Pamuk 2005, p. 120, but the aggregate figure in the table is not sensitive to this assumption.

using huge machines to do so – battleships, aircraft, and tanks. The demands that this occasioned could be met chiefly by producing more, by importing more, and by consuming and investing less.

The scope for producing more in wartime was limited, and in practice most countries produced less in wartime, not more, despite determined attempts to mobilize their economies. Table 6.5 compares the European belligerents with three "control" groups: the neutral countries of Europe, the former British colonies of North America and Australasia that joined the war actively from a distance, and the former Iberian colonies of South America that remained neutral or, if they joined in, did so in name only. In both wars European output fell absolutely, while the more distant regions held their ground or gained. Within Europe the countries that were occupied or defeated suffered most. In almost all regions the loss of output associated with the Second World War was less than that during the First, an exception being the disastrous condition of the Soviet economy in 1944. In these terms the success in the two wars of the

Table 6.6 The mobilization of national resources in two world wars (percent of GDP at current prices)

	Government spending		Military spending	
	1913	1917	1939	1943
France	10	50	...	...
Germany	10	59	23	70
Italy	...	...	8	21
Soviet Union	...	...	*17	61
United Kingdom	8	37	15	55

*1940; figures are in constant 1937 prices.
Sources: Broadberry and Harrison 2005b, p. 15; Harrison 1998b, p. 21.

United States and Canadian economies, which more than doubled their GDPs from 1938 to 1944, was exceptional.[2]

Since total output was inelastic to the needs of the war, military needs imposed a tremendous squeeze on capital spending and household consumption. Table 6.6 shows figures for a restricted sample of belligerent countries. Setting to one side the huge methodological problems of valuing the consumer cost of the war effort statistically, it is clear that by the twentieth century the main belligerent countries had found ways of diverting between one third and two thirds of total output to warfare. To remove the necessary purchasing power from civilian markets they used a wide variety of instruments: higher taxes were important, and so were war bonds that promised repayment after victory. Also of importance were direct controls on consumption and corporate activity that rationed civilian access to everything from food and textiles to machinery, fuels, and strategic materials.

The unit of mobilization was for the most part the national economy. Part of the story is also the way in which international trade was diverted to meet the national purposes of warfare. In wartime the great powers mobilized their young men for military service and their industries for war production. As a result they ceased to supply commercial exports to the world market; as far as they could, they sucked in food, fuel, and war goods from external sources, including their respective colonial empires and their neutral trading partners. These had to accumulate credits that, they hoped, would continue to be good in the post-war period. Only one great power was comparatively rich enough to wage war and keep up an external surplus at the same time: the United States, which supplied its allies in two world wars by doing so.

---

[2] The Italian data report a miraculous increase in GDP in the First World War; surely a statistical anomaly, as discussed by Broadberry (2005).

The existence of alliances created the scope for mobilization at a supranational level. Twice in this period a victorious coalition stretched around the northern hemisphere from the western seaboard of the United States through Great Britain to Russia, whose territory completed the circle across northern Europe and Asia to within a few miles of Alaska. Britain and the United States supplied financial and material aid to their allies on a large scale, particularly to France and Italy in the First World War and to the Soviet Union in the Second. By combining the abundant capital of the richer economies with the abundant military manpower of the poorer ones, they maximized total fighting power from the given resource endowments of their coalition. In fact, on both occasions the winners integrated and coordinated their economic and military resources with much greater effect than the losing countries, which mobilized and fought to a considerable extent in isolation from each other. But it is also true that the winners started with endowments that were superior in both quantity and quality.

In some poorer countries the relevant scale of mobilization became subnational. The strain of mobilization was such that efforts to integrate and coordinate a nationwide war effort failed. Instead, national economies pulled themselves apart. This tended to happen where agriculture was only partially commercialized and remained largely in the hands of small-scale subsistence farmers. Under the pressure of wartime mobilization this section of the economy displayed a tendency to "secede from the nation." The immediate symptom was usually the emergence of urban famine. When working families in wartime Hamburg or Petrograd could no longer buy food, the main reason was not the lack of food in the economy as a whole, but the growing reluctance of farmers to sell at any price, given the lack of industrial commodities to buy in exchange. As a result, the true scale on which mobilization could be carried out in practice was not the national economy but just the local urban economies that came under the direct control of the central government. Legally the government could claim jurisdiction over the countryside, but its economic sovereignty was de facto much more limited; it could no more command the resources of the farming households a few miles from the city limits than it could control the business decisions of manufacturers and traders in neutral countries the other side of the world (Harrison 1998b; Broadberry and Harrison 2005b).

The economic disintegration of the Austro-Hungarian Empire during the First World War illustrates this theme. The two kingdoms of Austria and Hungary were ruled by a single emperor in Vienna but had separate governments, legal systems, and currencies. More important than outward differences was an economic asymmetry: Austria was richer and more industrialized than Hungary. To mobilize its industries for war, Austria needed the surplus food products of Hungarian farmers, but was unable to supply Hungary with manufactured civilian goods on the same scale as in peacetime. As a result, trade between the two kingdoms tended to shrink; the food stayed in the Hungarian countryside while the Austrian cities were unable to scale up industrial production because of the lack of food and raw materials. At the same time two things happened. Coordination between the kingdoms of the empire deteriorated, and at the same time, within each kingdom, the farmers went their own way (Schulze 2005). If Austria–Hungary could not coordinate itself, what chance did it have of achieving coordination with the other Central Powers?

Germany's experience of conquest in the Second World War provides another case. Germany's intention was to seize a colonial empire in eastern Europe and convert the Ukraine and European Russia into a food surplus region, chiefly by killing or starving a large proportion of the inhabitants and forcing many of the survivors to flee beyond the Urals (Kay 2006). The failure to achieve a quick victory over the Soviet Union prevented this master plan from being fully implemented; even so, the German occupation authorities made the most determined efforts to exploit the agricultural resources that fell under their control. But these resources proved exceptionally difficult to mobilize, even at gunpoint (Liberman 1996). Almost by accident, at the same time most of western Europe fell into German hands. During the period of occupation, Germany's imports of food from rich, industrialized France ran at several times the level of its food seizures in Russia (Milward 1965). This illustrates again the difficulty of mobilizing resources when they remained in the hands of low-productivity subsistence farmers.

In the two world wars, the only low-income country to defend its economic integrity under serious attack was the Soviet Union in the second conflict. More than a decade earlier, Stalin and his associates had drawn the appropriate lesson from Russia's defeat in the First World War: small-scale peasant farming was Russia's Achilles heel in wartime (Simonov 1996). Stalin had launched a drive to secure state control over the peasant farmers and their food surpluses by collectivizing the farms. The campaign was carried through at huge cost in lives, and the farming system that resulted was hated and inefficient (Davies and Wheatcroft 2004). But it achieved its goal in the sense that, when war broke out again, the peasant farmers no longer had the freedom to withdraw from the market. When food was critically short, when there was absolutely not enough food in the country to keep everyone alive and millions starved, the soldiers and war workers had enough to eat (Barber and Harrison 1991; Harrison 1996). Stalin had converted the peasants into residual claimants on their own produce. As a result, when the fate of the country was on a knife edge in 1942, the economic system did not break down and the Soviet war effort sustained itself at the most critical moment of the war.

The mobilization advantage of the richer economies is equally evident in food consumption. During both world wars, for example, despite submarine blockade the British fed themselves quite healthily and sufficiently, if monotonously, partly from their own capital-intensive commercialized agriculture, which responded speedily and flexibly to mobilization requirements, and partly from the other side of the world (Olson 1963). In the United States in the Second World War, as Hugh Rockoff (1998) has observed, consumers did not have more butter, but they did have more ice cream.

The world wars took economic warfare, traditionally limited to siege and blockade, to a new level. Blockade continued to be practiced, but economists from Olson (1963) to Davis and Engerman (2006) have argued that its force was easily vitiated by direct countermeasures as well as economic mobilization and substitution. Germany overcame the British blockade of its ports in the First World War in part by exploiting overland trade with neutral neighbors, including Britain's trading partners. The Allies successfully used naval convoys in both wars to protect merchant vessels against Germany's submarine warfare, and so maintained the integration of the Allied war effort. Conversely, for Germany the submarine construction program in both wars was enormously expensive, and a direct cost of the gamble to resort to unrestricted submarine warfare in 1917 was that the United States entered the war on the side of the Allies.

In the Second World War heavy long-range aircraft provided the capacity to bombard the enemy's rear. Between 1940 and 1945, the Allied air forces dropped two million tons of bombs on Germany; 40 percent of these were aimed at German industrial and transport facilities and another 30 percent at urban areas (Zilbert 1981). The strategic bombing of Germany was meant to dislocate the war economy and destroy the will to fight. Firebombing cities ran into diminishing returns as the war progressed; it did not break the will of the people and sometimes even had the opposite effect (Brauer and Tuyll 2008). It also had little effect on war production, since it primarily destroyed civilian resources and increased the workers' readiness to make sacrifices. The daylight bombing of industry and transport became possible late in the war and proved more effective. Even so, German industrial facilities continued to expand because new investment more than kept pace with the war damage (Abelshauser 2000). Strategic bombing did increase German production costs, and it forced a huge diversion of German resources from ground attack in the east to air defense in the west. The air campaign was also extremely expensive for the Allies to maintain, however, resulting in frequent disputes about its priority compared with direct support for the Normandy landings. In general, economic warfare did not determine the outcome of any conflict, but may have shortened the duration (Førland 1993).

Aftermath

The consequences of war arrived in two instalments, postmarked 1918 and 1945 respectively. There were some common features, primarily their heavy costs. Both wars resulted in large losses of life and of human and physical capital. The effects of the two wars on economic institutions and post-war performance were quite different, however. The First World War cast a long shadow over interwar economic development that international institutions failed to disperse. Unresolved tensions eroded the possibilities of returning to a normal world, and Europe became fatally polarized between wealthy and poor, democracies and dictatorships. Domestic and international reforms that accompanied the ending of the Second World War, in contrast, helped to alleviate the economic and political problems that plagued Europe after 1918. The aftermath of the second war was quite different. The international economy recovered quickly. The Cold War began, but in spite of it Europe entered a post-war golden age; consumers prospered, at least for a while, on both sides of the Iron Curtain.

The human losses of the First World War were terrible enough: nearly ten million soldiers died in battle and from other causes. Of 5.4 million Allied military deaths more than half were Russian and French. Of the four million on the side of the Central Powers, Germany and Austria–Hungary contributed three quarters (Broadberry and Harrison 2005b). These losses cannot be valued in all their human dimensions. To the extent that they represent human capital that had a replacement cost, however, they can be valued financially and compared with other material losses. This is shown in Table 6.7. Germany,

Table 6.7 Physical destruction in Europe in the First World War: selected countries (percent of pre-war assets)

| | Human capital | Physical capital | | | |
		Domestic assets	Overseas assets	Reparations bill	National wealth
Austria–Hungary	4.5	6.5	…	…	…
France	7.2	24.6	49.0	…	31.0
Germany	6.3	3.1	…	51.6	54.7
Italy	3.8	15.9	…	…	…
Russia	2.3	14.3	…	…	…
Turkey and Bulgaria	6.8	…	…	…	…
United Kingdom	3.6	9.9	23.9	…	14.9

Source: Broadberry and Harrison (2005b).

Table 6.8 Physical destruction in Europe in the Second World War, selected countries (percent of assets)

	Human assets	Physical assets	
		National wealth	Industry fixed assets
UK	1	5	...
USSR	18–19	25	...
Germany	9	...	*17
Italy	1	...	10
Japan	6	25	34

*West Germany only.
Source: Harrison 1998b.

and Turkey and Bulgaria together, each lost more than 6 percent of their pre-war human capital. The table also shows that there was a tendency for human losses to be exceeded, proportionately, by losses of physical capital. The exception was Germany, the territory of which was spared fighting. The heaviest destruction of physical capital took place in France which, being already rich and industrialized, had most to lose.

Turning to the losses associated with the Second World War we can give a more complete account that includes civilian as well as military deaths. Even taking this into account, the losses of this war dwarfed those of the First. This is most certainly the case for civilian mortality, since relatively few civilians suffered premature death during the First World War. In contrast, in the second at least fifty-five million people died prematurely, more than half of them civilians. More than forty million were citizens of Europe. Germany and Yugoslavia lost one in ten, the Soviet Union one in seven, and Poland one in five of its pre-war population. As a proportion of the European total, three fifths were citizens of a single country, the Soviet Union, which lost twenty-five million (for figures see Urlanis 1971, pp. 294–5, except for the Soviet Union itself on which see Harrison 2003). This was not accidental; part of Germany's plan was to bring about a large reduction in the population of the Soviet Union, in order to free up food supplies for Germany.

The financial dimension of human loss may be compared with what we know about other material and financial losses using Table 6.8. These figures show that the rate of human losses was highly variable, and in the Soviet case astonishingly heavy. Despite this, it was exceeded everywhere by the rate of physical destruction, made possible by new destructive technologies such as strategic bombardment from the air, used alongside traditional means.

Ethnic displacement and racial killing were features of both world wars. The main episode of note in the First World War was the deportation of Armenians eastward from Anatolia in 1915/16. The stated policy of the Young Turk government was to seize their property and walk them to the Syrian desert in the south. There is uncertainty over the number of deaths that resulted (from 300,000 to 1.5 million), and the precise combination of deaths arising from hunger, lack of shelter, and disease with killings in the massacres that accompanied the deportations (Simpson 1939; Zurcher 2000). In the Second World War there is no doubt about the German intention to kill Europe's Jews, some in Germany and western Europe but most in Poland and the USSR, from 1942 onwards (but the timing, as well as the internal and external triggers of the decision, are still debated). Adolf Eichmann, its chief organizer, put the number of deaths resulting at six million. In addition, the Nazis murdered hundreds of thousands of other "undesirables," including homosexuals, Gypsies, socialists, and mentally or physically disabled persons.

Still more complex and variable was the impact of the two wars on institutions and policies. The First World War ended the liberal order of the nineteenth century and began a phase of deglobalization. Production and consumption for total war relied on securing vital strategic materials, raw materials, and food, and this led countries to restrict exports and expand imports when possible. The belligerents also used the denial of trade as a weapon of war, seeking to bring the enemy to its knees through blockade and starvation. International commodity markets disintegrated and the volume of world trade declined (Maddison 1995).

More generally, in the first half of the century, mercantilist motivations and instruments became more prominent in Europe than at any time for a hundred years. The scramble for resources provoked by the First World War was replaced in peacetime by a scramble for liquidity. The longer-term impact of the First World War on international trade was disastrous. Globally, the share of trade in GDP fell from 22 percent in 1913 to 15 percent in 1929 and only 9 percent in 1938 (Estevadeordal, Frantz, and Taylor 2003, p. 595). As for Europe, exports declined relatively and stagnated absolutely after the war; despite the initial recovery of world trade, European exports in 1929 remained below the level of 1913 (Maddison 1989). Protectionism of both agriculture and industry gained popular support. By the mid-1920s tariffs were substantially higher than they had been in 1913 in Bulgaria, Czechoslovakia, Germany, Hungary, Italy, Romania, Spain, Switzerland, and Yugoslavia. Once the Great Depression took hold, beggar-my-neighbor policies in the hands of increasingly nationalistic governments, and the consolidation of autarkic regional trading blocs, completed the process of trade disintegration. The new restrictions on trade in the 1930s usually came in the form of quotas rather than tariffs. Trade treaties and relations became subjugated to the economic and military interests of the rearming European nations (Kindleberger 1973; Kennedy 1989; Findlay and O'Rourke 2007). Europe's share of world manufacturing continued to decline, and European trade recovered only modestly by the end of the 1930s. By 1950, in contrast, all regions of the world economy, Europe included, began to share the benefits of restored trade and renewed commitments to liberalization (Maddison 1995).

A notable exception to interwar protectionism is found in the arms trade. Military exports collapsed as the First World War drew to a close, but rebounded in the early 1920s and grew substantially until the Great Depression. After the Depression military exports recovered faster than world trade as a whole despite falling prices, which resulted partly from the worldwide deflation and partly from increased competition as smaller nations entered the market. Czechoslovakia and Sweden, followed by Belgium and Norway, were the rising military exporters of the 1930s; by 1935 Czechoslovakia led the way with a quarter of the market for small and medium armaments, smaller shares going to Sweden and Belgium (Eloranta 2002a). The UK maintained its traditional domination of the trade in heavier equipment such as warships. Attempts to regulate the arms trade usually fell far short of professed goals, partly because of opposition from domestic producer lobbies (Krause 1992; Krause and MacDonald 1993).

Interwar economic and political instability and the rise of authoritarian regimes can be seen as extensions of the First World War and the Great Depression (Feinstein et al. 1997). Many institutional failures were rooted in the Versailles Peace Treaty of 1919, which created many new democracies and the appearance of a "new Europe." The core of the treaty, however, inflicted collective punishment on the former Central Powers and set up a cause for German nationalist resistance in the 1930s, while failing to meet the demands of many participants.

The interwar European economy was additionally stressed by war debts. The United States had provided war loans worth millions of dollars to Britain and France. In turn, the British and French had extended their own credits to Italy and Russia. As a result, the poorer countries in the coalition were able to continue fighting long after they would have run out of their own resources. Interwar economic and political relationships were bedevilled by this network of debts, most of them eliminated sooner or later by default. During the Second World War a similar pattern emerged in that the United States eventually made billions of dollars of economic assistance available to Britain and the Soviet Union, and Britain had its own much smaller Soviet aid program. The difference is that, after an early pause for consideration, all the wartime assistance among the Allies was rendered free of charge, so that no substantial post-war indebtedness arose.

The institutional failures of the interwar period can perhaps best be observed in the performance of the League of Nations, established in 1920. The eighteen founder members held sway over 74 percent of the world's population and 63 percent of its land area, but did not include the United States, which had turned to isolationism. The record of the League was one of failure to respond to various acts of aggression, Japanese, Italian, and German, over the next two decades. There were several factors to this failure, including the differing disarmament and security goals of the key members, the absence of some key great powers (for example, the United States), and the failure to provide credible security guarantees for the member nations.

The fear of repeating this failure hung over the United Nations, established in 1945 by the victorious Allied coalition. The rapid emergence of the Cold War made a repetition seem more than likely. For example, the first proposals for disarmament were not initiated until the 1950s, with little chance of actual success (Jolly *et al.* 2005). There were two major differences, however. One difference is that whereas the United States had stood aloof from the interwar League, in the post-war UN the United States was the new and economically powerful hegemonic leader. Another was the additional dimensions of new institutions for multilateral coordination after 1945. The UN was complemented by other bodies that emerged in the immediate post-war period: the Bretton Woods system of exchange rate coordination under the International Monetary Fund, the International Bank for Reconstruction and Development (later the World Bank), and the Marshall Plan, which provided economic aid for rebuilding post-war Europe. Bretton Woods became the anchor of post-war stability and economic expansion until the early 1970s (Maddison 1995, 2001).

Between 1948 and 1951 the United States poured $13 billion (about $100 billion at 2003 prices) into the economies of western Europe. This massive aid package was named after its designer, US Secretary of State George C. Marshall. Its purpose was to help Europe recover from the devastation of the war period and at the same time promote the alternative to socialism. Most eastern European nations had been converted into Soviet satellites, or did not want to irritate the Soviet Union by accepting this aid. In western Europe, in contrast, the Marshall plan boosted economic cooperation in the region and helped to embed the recovering economies into policies of trade liberalization and market integration (Ritschl 2004).

In this context it is not surprising to find that post-war economic recovery after 1918 was strained and slow, whereas after 1945 it was generally rapid. Table 6.9 shows that Europe's neutrals and victors generally took more than

Table 6.9 Years to recovery of pre-war GDP per head from the final year of war

	N	First World War	N	Second World War
European Countries that:				
Stayed out	7	3.4	6	1.3
Won	4	3.4	2	1.5
Lost	10	9.7	16	4.4

Countries that stayed out are, in the First World War: Denmark, Netherlands Norway, Portugal, Spain, Sweden, and Switzerland; in the Second: Ireland, Portugal, Spain, Sweden, Switzerland, and Turkey. Countries that won are, in the First World War: France, Greece, Italy, and UK (including Ireland); in the Second: UK and USSR. Countries that lost, meaning that their governments surrendered or their territory was entirely occupied, are, in the First World War: Austria, Belgium, Bulgaria, Czechoslovakia, Germany, Hungary, Romania, Russia, Serbia, and Turkey; in the Second: Albania, Belgium, Bulgaria, Czechoslovakia, Denmark, Finland, France, Germany, Greece, Hungary, Italy, Netherlands, Norway, Poland, Romania, and Yugoslavia.
Source: Maddison 2003.

three years after 1918 to return to the 1913 benchmark of GDP per head, while the losers took nearly a decade to do so. In comparison, economic recovery after 1945 took place at almost lightning speed. This was one early sign that the world after 1945 would be truly different.

Conclusion

In the first half of the twentieth century European globalization came to an abrupt halt. It was replaced by protectionism, nationalism, war, and killing and destruction on an immense scale. In the middle of the century, globalization was resumed, and the European economies began to converge on much higher and more uniform income levels.

After two world wars, three things had changed. First, European economic growth, integration, and prosperity had lost their association with empire. It would no doubt have surprised Europe's nineteenth-century leaders, had they lived to see it, to find that it proved possible to acquire wealth and wield influence without claiming imperial sway over vast numbers of faraway peoples and their lands and oceans.

Secondly, Europe's leaders had a new sense of the importance of cooperation. They now cooperated with the United States in economic recovery, exchange rate coordination, and tariff reduction, with each other in laying new foundations for European integration, and with developing countries in decolonization and development assistance.

Third, Europe's leaders had learned to use the power of the state to regulate economic life. In wartime, governments had wielded immense authority over their people, production, and consumption. There is at least some reason to see the effectiveness of this power as directly linked with the level of development of the economy: as the economy became richer, the potential scope of government authority became wider and more effective. It did not follow that government ought to use this authority in peacetime as in wartime just because it could, although some thought so. One particular reason that they thought so was the unexpected success of the Soviet command economy in mobilizing to defeat Nazi Germany. Learning the appropriate limits of government control over the market economy in turn became a major challenge of the post-war period.

Business cycles and economic policy, 1914–1945

Albrecht Ritschl and Tobias Straumann

Contents

Introduction

The Great War of 1914–18 constituted a major rupture for the economies of Europe in several respects. It marked the end of almost a century of uninterrupted economic growth. It ended a long period of near-universal currency stability, and set in motion a painful process of deglobalization. It brought about an age of highly politicized labor relations. And it ushered in an era in which sharp fluctuations in economic activity and persistent mass unemployment became the dominant experience of everyday life.

While the beginning of this dramatic period can clearly be identified with the First World War, its effects lasted beyond the end of the Second. Throughout the interwar period, the economies of Europe remained far below their historical growth paths. Full recovery from this long-lasting depression occurred only during the golden age of the 1960s. But not all of the displacement from historical trends that took place after the First World War was ultimately corrected, and some of the changes became permanent. In the more developed economies of Europe, a marked upward shift in labor's income shares occurred after 1918. To this must be added compression of wages and of the personal income distribution in general. Both favored low incomes and reduced the shares taken by top earners. Most of these distributional shocks of the early interwar period have proved permanent and are still visible in the economies of Europe today. Monetary conditions were also fundamentally altered after the First World War. Some of the changes were temporary. Most prominent among these were the dramatic hyperinflations which hit the former Central Powers and their successor states in the early 1920s. Equally temporary were the deflationary waves elsewhere in Europe in the early 1920s, and more universally in the early 1930s. Other regime changes in monetary conditions were more permanent, most importantly the aborted attempt to reconstruct the gold standard in the 1920s. The traumatic consequences of this experience had far-reaching consequences for the reconstruction of the monetary system after the Second World War. More persistent also was the notable reduction in the freedom of international capital flows, and later of foreign trade.

The period between the world wars also marked a sea change in macroeconomic policy. In contrast to the nineteenth century, where modest policy intervention had been the accepted norm, activism in economic policy now became the order of the day. State intervention in the markets for goods, factors of production, and money quickly became widespread. In this context, institutions were created that often acquired constitutional status, in some cases with effects that have lasted up to the present. Not all of the policy experiments after the First World War were equally long-lived, however. Attempts to achieve monetary stabilization with paper currencies were quickly abandoned, and an – albeit half-hearted – return to gold took place in the mid-1920s. A second transition to paper currencies in the early 1930s was only marginally more successful, this time not because of inflation but rather because of increasingly tight capital controls and import quotas which in most parts of Europe suffocated international trade and capital movements. While these trade restrictions were dismantled with relative ease after the Second World War, only in the 1970s was a solution found that combined regional fixed exchange rate blocs with liberalized capital movements.

Economic planning began as an improvised response to shortages during the First World War, but soon acquired systemic character in a number of European countries. Industries were nationalized or supervisory state agencies created, attempting to exert political control both at the macro and the micro levels, and to reduce the exposure of the national economy to business fluctuations. Again, the effects of these changes were long-lived, with lasting macroeconomic impacts. Deregulation of state-controlled sectors, as well as divestment from state-owned industries, lasted almost to the end of the twentieth century. The end of the Soviet system in eastern Europe, where economic planning and the abolition of private property rights had been driven to the extreme, is but the most evident case in point.

Economic policy was itself a dimension of international conflict during the period from 1914 to 1945. Economic warfare was never quite off the agenda of national policy makers during the interwar years. Conflicts over German reparations seriously affected monetary policy and trade relations, as well as international capital flows during the 1920s (Temin 1989). To an even stronger degree, the economies of Europe were overshadowed by Germany's aggressive stance and war preparations in the 1930s.

With political intervention came the attempt to deepen the theoretical understanding of its effects. The interwar period saw the invention of macroeconomics as a separate sub-field of economics. It soon extended from the new Keynesian theory of unemployment to public sector economics, balance of payments theory, and monetary economics. At the same time, rapid progress was made in welfare economics. Shaped by the traumatic experience of the interwar years, the economic analysis generated in this period was skeptical about market forces, dismissive of the power of monetary and exchange rate policy, and highly optimistic about the power of the state to intervene in economic activity, be it through fiscal policy, financial repression, or a combination of the two. Again, the consequences were far-reaching, as this mindset shaped an interventionist approach to macroeconomic policy that prevailed far into the 1970s.

Given the highly pathological nature of our period of interest, there has never been a shortage of attempted economic interpretations. Explaining the Great

Depression after 1929 has even come to be regarded as the "holy grail" of macroeconomic theory (Bernanke 2000). Given the complexity of the phenomenon and the multiplicity of rival explanations, any attempt to describe the business cycle of the period from 1914 to 1945 will necessarily have to be eclectic, walking a fine line between the single-mindedness needed to achieve analytical depth and the imprecision required for providing a *tour d'horizon*.

This chapter sets out to review Europe's macroeconomic performance between 1914 and 1945. It highlights key stylized facts and surveys some of the most prominent attempted explanations. The second section looks at a salient feature of this period: the highly persistent deviation of aggregate output per capita from its long-term growth path after 1914. Inspection of these data suggests a business cycle chronology that holds for most of the countries for which we have data. The third section reviews monetary factors and highlights the instability of the nominal side of the economy in this period. The fourth turns to social conflict as one driving force of the interwar business cycle, and looks at its consequences. These include the displacement of factor shares after the First World War in key European countries, the shortening of the industrial working week, as well as concomitant declines in income inequality. The fifth section documents the interplay between macroeconomic fluctuations and international trade and capital flows. The sixth turns to foreign policy and international conflict as a possible driving force behind much of the interwar business cycle, and argues that its influence was pervasive. The seventh concludes with remarks on the two dimensions of conflict that shaped the macroeconomic performance of the interwar period. Far from constituting a normal business cycle, economic fluctuations during the period between 1914 and 1945 were primarily driven by two forces that shaped events and profoundly altered the economic constitution of the European polity. One was social conflict and the institutions and labor market responses it created. The other was international conflict and the deglobalization of the European economy that it caused. Influenced by these two forces, the interwar period exhibited highly pathological macroeconomic performance, but was formative for the European economy during the second half of the twentieth century.

Identifying the European business cycle

The interwar period saw a succession of short-term business cycles, and at the same time was a long-term recession from historical productivity trends. This downward deviation began during the First World War and continued until the end of the Second. In the three decades after 1914, Europe's economy was in

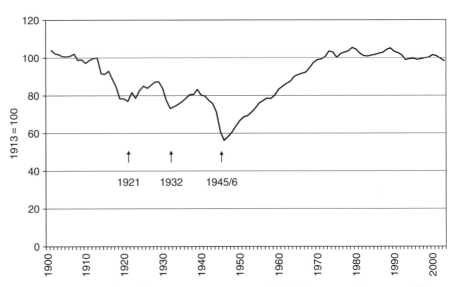

Figure 7.1 Europe's Great Depression and recovery, 1913–73: western European GDP per capita relative to 1.95 percent growth trend. *Source:* calculated from data in Maddison 2003.

recession relative to trend during fourteen years, and cumulatively lost forty percent of its potential output (see Figure 7.1).[1]

Mirroring this development, the recovery from this depression, commonly referred to as the post-war Golden Age, lasted to the 1970s. Why Europe's economic reconstruction after the First World War remained incomplete, precipitating a Great Depression lasting thirty years, is one set of issues to be addressed in this chapter.

Embedded in Europe's long-term depression were three short-term recessions. The first lasted from 1914 to 1921, the second from 1929 to 1932, and the third from 1940 to 1946.[2] With two of these recessions linked to the world wars themselves, this would leave one true interwar recession.

Yet the aggregate European picture conceals major regional differences. Germany and most countries in Continental Europe were seriously affected by the First World War recession, suffering output declines of up to 25 percent relative to pre-war levels. By contrast, Britain and Italy experienced a wartime boom. A major international recession in 1920/21 decreased national output in these two countries quite severely (by 20 and 25 percent, respectively), but was

---

[1] Figure 7.1 assumes 1.95 percent annual trend growth in GDP per capita, close to the 2 percent that is commonly regarded as trend growth in neo-classical growth theory. The slight downward deviation from the accepted stylized facts is caused by slightly lower trend growth in Britain. See on this Crafts and Mills 1996 and Crafts and Toniolo 1996, arguing for a break in British growth in the interwar period. Data in Figure 7.1 are calculated for the fourteen European countries for which annual data are provided in Maddison 2003.

[2] The evidence in Figure 7.1 seems robust to alternative assumptions about trends. Using, e.g., an HP filter with the parameters suggested by Ravn and Uhlig 2002 leads to broadly the same chronology.

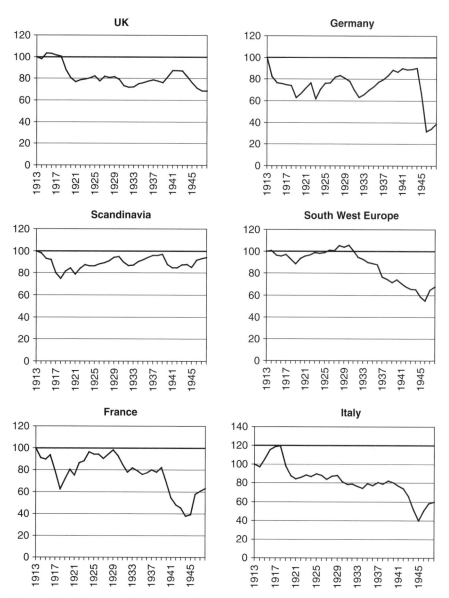

Figure 7.2 GDP per capita relative to 2 percent growth trend (1913 = 100). *Source:* calculated from data in Maddison 2003.

hardly noticeable in most of Europe. During the rest of the 1920s, the econo-mies of Continental Europe recovered well, coming close to or even super-seding the historical productivity trend (Figure 7.2). The two big exceptions are Germany and Britain, where recovery remained grossly incomplete: relative to a 2 percent productivity trend, neither country had recovered to much more than 80 percent of its potential by 1929.

The international recession of 1929 affected the whole of Europe, albeit in rather unequal measure. By the mid-1930s, the depression had reduced much of Europe to the low utilization of potential that had characterized Germany and Britain already in the 1920s. For most of these economies, the late 1930s were a time of relative stagnation or further deterioration, which accelerated in south-west Europe with the Spanish Civil War (1936–9) and elsewhere with the Second World War (1939–45). Three major exceptions to this regularity stand out: Germany, Britain, and Scandinavia. In all three cases, recovery back towards the trend began in 1933.[3] This recovery was most complete in Scandinavia, which grew back almost fully to trend by 1939. Germany experienced vigorous recovery to 1939, but was unable to continue on this path during the Second World War. Britain was hit less hard than Germany by the recession of 1929–32 and accordingly had a more muted recovery. During the Second World War, however, Britain's position relative to trend improved and quickly reached parity with Germany's.

With a view to these distinct regional patterns, four groups of analytical issues suggest themselves. First, there is the question of what drove the recession of the First World War, and why its regional effects on the economies of Europe differed so widely. A second set of questions relates to the speed and degree of economic recovery from that War. A third group relates to the depression of the early 1930s, and to the question of why recovery remained confined to a few places, while the rest of Europe experienced continued depression throughout the 1930s. The fourth set of questions relates to the deepening recession during the Second World War. For all of these phenomena, a variety of explanations have been offered in the respective national and comparative literatures. While it is not possible here to review the many national cases in detail, certain common patterns do emerge. The following sections will consider the most prominent of these in turn.

Monetary factors in the interwar European business cycle

While monetary calm reigned in most of Europe during the classical gold standard era of the late nineteenth century, Europe's monetary and financial systems emerged battered from the First World War. All countries had suspended gold convertibility in 1914, and wartime inflation had pushed price levels up by 50 percent or more. After the war ended, inflation was still rampant in the weak democracies that had been newly established in Central Europe. In

---

[3] In the undetrended series, Britain's recovery begins a year earlier. Relative to trend, however, this year was still one of recession.

other countries where the political environment was more favorable, post-war monetary stabilization met with the new phenomenon of downwardly rigid wages, itself partly a consequence of newly introduced collective wage bargaining schemes. Deflation in these countries combined with rising unemployment and low rates of output growth, or even outright recession as in Italy or Britain. Monetary stabilization in Europe took almost a full decade after the war, and was just completed when the recession of 1929 struck.

Hyperinflation was rife in Germany as well as in Austria, Hungary, and Poland. The first two were the former Central Powers, while the latter two had regained their independence after the dissolution of the Habsburg monarchy and the reversal of the eighteenth-century partition of Poland between Russia, Prussia, and the Habsburgs. Inflationary war finance, deficient tax systems, new customs borders, and the concomitant decline of trade, as well as political turmoil towards the end of the First World War, all contributed to monetary instability in these countries. By 1919 or 1920, price levels had already increased tenfold or more compared to 1914 (Figure 7.3a). As a consequence, the middle classes' savings in nominal assets had essentially lost their value, and most of the war debt had been annihilated. Yet in all of these countries, the transition to hyperinflation only came after inflation had performed its fundamental economic function of wiping out the war debt. One major factor contributing to this delayed outburst of post-war hyperinflation was the inability of the newly formed states to enforce effective taxation. Political and fiscal stabilization in the hyperinflation countries of the 1920s indeed went hand in hand, and monetary stabilization followed once order had been restored to public finances (Sargent 1982; Dornbusch 1987). Austria and Hungary were the two economies that had been particularly hard hit by the disintegration of the Habsburg Empire. With international help and rigorous public spending cuts, they stabilized in 1922 and 1924, respectively. Germany stabilized in late 1923, after internal revolts had been crushed, an understanding with France on accepting mediation in the conflict over reparations had been reached, and emergency legislation had been passed to restore order to the government budget. Poland's stabilization was delayed by war with Russia, and later by trade conflict with Germany. Poland's first, abortive attempt to join the gold standard in 1924 was followed by successful stabilization in 1926. In all cases, currency stabilization proved successful, as Figure 7.3a bears out: price levels did not spiral out of control again until the Second World War or after.[4]

Britain, like most of the neutral countries of the First World War, returned to gold at the pre-war parity, reversing wartime inflation. As in the USA, deflation

---

[4] In the German case, the inflationary trauma was a major factor in avoiding currency devaluation in the 1930s, motivating policy makers to impose capital controls instead: see Borchardt 1984.

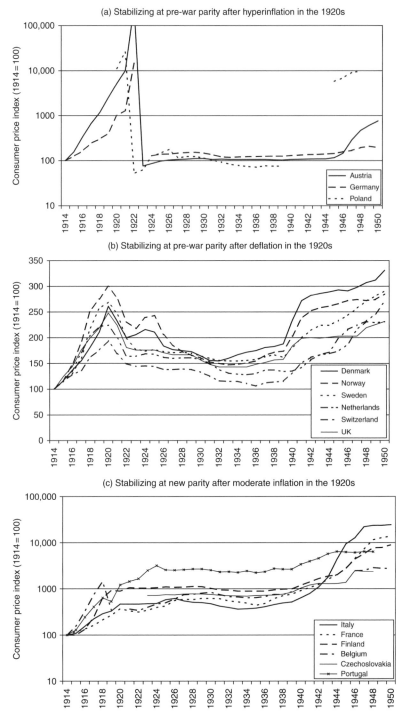

Figure 7.3 Post-war inflation, stabilization, and inflation recurrence in Europe. *Source:* calculated from data in League of Nations 1931, 1940; Mitchell 2003; Lains 2003.

from wartime price levels was substantial but failed to restore pre-war prices. By the end of the 1920s, consumer prices in these countries were on average still 50 percent higher than in 1914, well in line with the USA. Again, stabilization was successful: in most of these countries, the price levels of 1925 were not surpassed again before the Second World War (see Figure 7.3b). Wartime inflation after 1940 broadly repeated the pattern of moderate inflation from the First World War, with the important exception that no post-war deflation occurred in these countries after 1945.

A number of countries, led by France, took the middle way and allowed prices to increase seven- to tenfold during the First World War, without experiencing post-war hyperinflation, and also without attempting to return to pre-war gold parities. During the interwar period, price levels in these countries fluctuated around the levels attained in the early 1920s. As a consequence, war-related debts issued in domestic currency, as well as nominal savings, lost much of their value. This group of economies proved markedly less resistant than the others to the recurrence of wartime inflation during the Second World War, as Figure 7.3c shows.

The monetary policy choices of the various European countries after the First World War have attracted much scholarly attention. Britain's decision to accept post-war deflation to prepare for the return (ultimately in 1925) to the pre-war parity has been criticized ever since Keynes warned against the consequences of deflating. Downward wage rigidities, he argued, would increase real wages and thus translate deflation into depression.[5] This link between the recession of 1920/1 and deflation after World War I is nowadays widely accepted.[6] Indeed, countries that experienced inflation at the time were spared from this recession.[7] On the other hand, the same countries had seen the trough of their respective deep recessions around 1918/19 (see Figure 7.2 above). In addition, post-war deflation gained momentum in Britain only after the depression had set in,[8] just as post-war inflation in Continental Europe picked up speed only after the recovery had begun. Whether post-war deflation was indeed the cause of recession thus continues to be an open issue.

At the same time, Keynes' argument went, a British return to gold parity after an insufficient degree of price deflation would increase the real exchange rate relative to those countries that did not deflate, or that stabilized after going through hyperinflation. Relative price levels in Europe did vary considerably after the return to gold in the late 1920s, and the evidence does indeed bear out some of this claim. Figure 7.4 shows real exchange rates vis-à-vis the British

---

[5] On the discussions among experts before Britain's return to gold, see Moggridge 1969.

[6] See, prominently, Eichengreen 1992b and Feinstein, Temin, and Toniolo 1997.

[7] For Germany, this point has been made by Holtfrerich 1986 and Webb 1989.

[8] This point was made by Cole and Ohanian 2002 and earlier by Broadberry 1986.

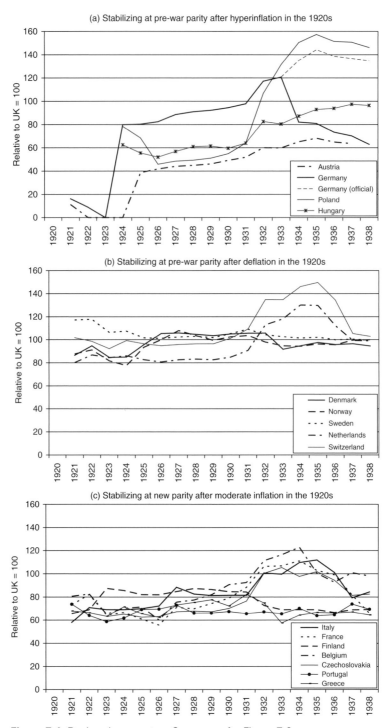

Figure 7.4 Real exchange rates. *Source:* as for Figure 7.3.

pound, taking the level in 1913–14 to be equal to 100. The choice of a pre-war benchmark reflects an assumption that purchasing power parity more or less held at that date; thus, real exchange rates below or above 100 reflect under- or overvalued currencies. The real exchange rates are derived from the price level data in Figure 7.3, and nominal exchange rates, in the usual manner. Figure 7.4a suggests strong currency undervaluation relative to the pound for the hyper-inflation countries (albeit far less so for Germany). Currencies that stabilized at the pre-war parity were on the whole quite close to purchasing power parity with the pound, with the Netherlands as the only exception of some importance (Figure 7.4b). Currency stabilization at less than the pre-war parity coincided with substantial undervaluation, as evidenced in Figure 7.4c.

The undervaluation of the French franc has attracted much scholarly attention, not least because of the implicit accusation that France manipulated the gold standard for its own political ends. More recent scholarship has pointed to French domestic instability and inflation as a source of currency instability in the 1920s: see Mouré 1991, Prati 1991, and Sicsic 1993. Whatever the political motives, it is apparent that France was not an isolated phenomenon. Under the gold standard of the late 1920s, violations of purchasing power parity were prevalent in countries that had stabilized at lower parities, and were not quickly corrected by market forces.

On the whole, it appears that those countries that stabilized at new parities fared substantially better in terms of unemployment in the 1920s than the others. Figure 7.5 shows indexes of unemployment (1932 = 100) for the same country groups as before (unfortunately the data are not comparable across countries, which is why we focus on trends rather than levels). The unemployment experience of the countries stabilizing after hyperinflations was mixed (Figure 7.5a). Countries that had gone through deflations to stabilize at pre-war parities often suffered protracted unemployment already in the 1920s (Figure 7.5b). In contrast, those stabilizing at lower rates enjoyed near-full employment in the 1920s (Figure 7.5c).

All European countries were badly affected by the adverse shock that came with the international depression after 1929. However, the crisis affected them in unequal measure and at different times. As Figures 7.3 and 7.4 bear out, the crisis was not primarily a deflationary or real exchange rate shock: deflationary tendencies in the gold parity countries were already well under way in the 1920s and just accelerated again after 1929, while real exchange rate movements did not really matter until 1931/32. Figures 7.1 and 7.2 bear out a strong output shock after 1929, although the timing of this shock seems far from uniform. The unemployment data in Figure 7.5c broadly confirm this: on the whole, the countries that stabilized below par in the 1920s were latecomers to the depression of the 1930s. Compared to their good performance in the 1920s, they were also harder hit by the depression, and for the most part took longer to recover in the 1930s.

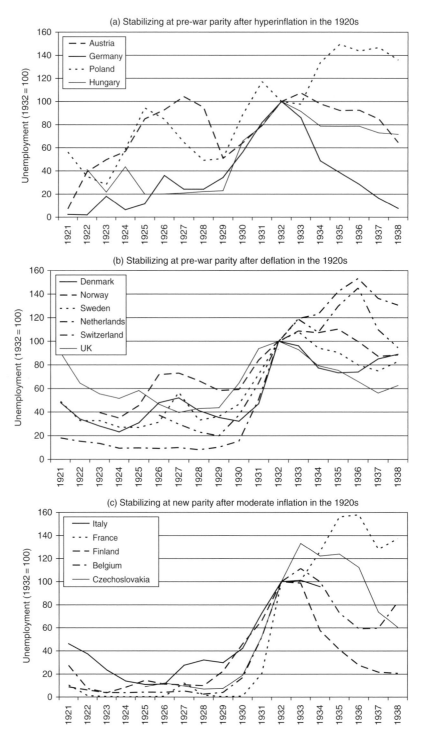

Figure 7.5 Unemployment. *Source:* calculated from data in League of Nations 1931, 1940.

To what extent the economic collapse after 1929 was driven by monetary policy is still debated. Monetarist orthodoxy has blamed the decline, as well as most of the depression as such, on contractionary monetary policy in the USA in the late 1920s (Friedman and Schwartz 1963). Critics have pointed out that Europe, notably Germany, created its very own deflationary pressures (Temin 1989). The credit-oriented view that prevails in most of the discussion today sees reduced American capital exports as the proximate cause of monetary contraction in Europe (Kindleberger 1973; Feinstein, Temin, and Toniolo 1997). Clearly, fixed exchange rates and generally high capital mobility under the restored gold standard of the 1920s acted as a mechanism that quickly transmitted the shock through Europe (Choudri and Kochin 1980; Bernanke 1995). Central banks across Europe reacted to reserve losses by tightening monetary policy according to the rules of the game of the gold standard. Fiscal policy played its part by tightening public budgets and compensating for lost tax revenue with spending cuts. In a matter of two or three years, price levels across Europe decreased by up to a quarter.

Yet the seemingly obvious connection between deflation and unemployment is less than easy to find in the data. Research on the dynamic Phillips curve would suggest short-term trade-offs between inflation and unemployment that allowed monetary policy to have effects until the natural rate of unemployment is restored (Clarida, Gertler, and Gali 1999). Yet while there was ample variation in both unemployment and inflation during the interwar period, no systematic pattern seems to emerge in the data, even if the 1920s and the 1930s are looked at separately. The picture emerging from Figure 7.6 is rather that the natural rate of unemployment moved quite independently of inflation, irrespective of whether or not a country was on gold.[9]

Downward-spiralling prices increased the pressure on the banking system, as well as on central banks' currency reserves, a pressure which became politically unbearable in 1931. In May 1931 Austria faced a banking crisis, and a run on the central bank was only narrowly averted.[10] In July, Germany partly suspended convertibility after a bank run, forcing her international short-term creditors to roll over existing loans.[11] Partly as a consequence of seeing her loans to Europe frozen, Britain was forced to abandon gold in September. This truly revolutionary step – Britain had always been on gold in peacetime since the 1720s – marked the effective end of the gold standard.[12] Governments all across Europe soon scrambled to either let their currencies float or protect them behind a firewall of capital controls, often doing both and embarking on

---

[9] Much more rigorous analysis would be needed to substantiate this point further. However, standard econometric procedures confirm the conclusion. This is left as an exercise to the reader.

[10] See Schubert 1991.   [11] See Schnabel 2004; James 1985, 1986.

[12] The literature on this is huge. For a discussion see Eichengreen 1992b.

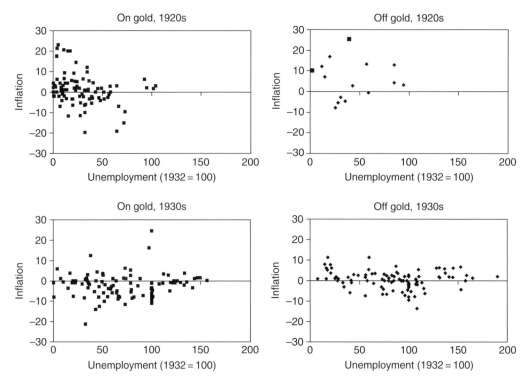

Figure 7.6 The inflation/unemployment trade-off. *Source:* see previous figures. Large boxes in 1920s: inflation is $y \times 10^3$.

competitive devaluation. The countries of Scandinavia had pegged their currencies to sterling. Many countries in Continental Europe followed Germany in abandoning convertibility, so that whatever parity they adhered to became a mere *numéraire* without much economic meaning. Only a small group of countries held out in a French-dominated gold bloc, which collapsed in 1936.

There is general agreement that, just as the gold standard transmitted the recessionary impulses internationally, breaking the "golden fetters" (Eichengreen 1992) contributed to recovery. Eichengreen and Sachs (1985) as well as Bernanke and James (1991) argue for a connection between the speed of recovery from the depression and the departure from gold. According to this consensus, those countries that maintained their commitment to the gold standard incurred overvaluation of their currencies, were forced to keep interest rates high, and paid for this with sluggish and delayed recoveries. Figure 7.7a shows inflation and GDP growth in the 1930s separately for countries on and off gold. While there is a weak positive within-group correlation in both cases, the countries off gold exhibit higher overall GDP growth, as expected. Figure 7.7b examines the correlation between a currency's overvaluation relative to sterling and its GDP growth in the 1930s. Contrary to expectation, no

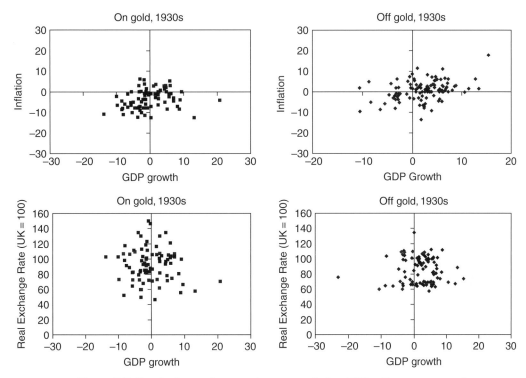

Figure 7.7 Devaluation and economic recovery in the 1930s. *Source:* see previous figures.

(a)   Inflation and growth

(b)   Real exchange rates and growth

within-group correlation seems to emerge (although, to repeat, countries off gold experienced higher GDP growth). Instead, real exchange rates among the devaluing countries appear to cluster around two levels, parity with sterling and undervaluation of around 70 percent, without any clear-cut growth advantage for either group. This is a puzzle: while countries that devalued had higher growth in the 1930s, neither induced inflation nor changes to external competitiveness, exploiting incomplete exchange rate pass-through, suggest themselves as a reason. Wolf (2008) has argued that the decision to devalue was largely driven by other considerations, and may have been endogenous to both inflation and currency undervaluation. The evidence in Figure 7.7 would be consistent with that view.

By the late 1930s, the process of abandoning the gold standard had come to a close. The main characteristic of the new currency system was the prevalence of bilateral exchange agreements that often subjected long lists of goods to quotas and an elaborate system of split exchange rates. While not the first country to move to such agreements, Germany became the center of this system after 1933, and tried to exploit it for its economic war preparation.[13]

Thus monetary factors, being the most prominent interpretation of the interwar depression today, contribute to its explanation in varying measure. Deflationary monetary policy is still popular as an explanation of the recession of 1920/21 in the UK and USA. Yet, as we have seen, deflation without depression was widespread in Europe after the First World War, casting some doubt on this explanation. In contrast, the role of fixed exchange rates in spreading the depression after 1929 is undisputed. Countries that broke with the gold standard in the 1930s fared better than those which did not. Yet the mechanisms behind this appear to be less than obvious.

Social conflict and the interwar European business cycle

Before 1914, most economies of Europe resembled the model of the nineteenth-century market economy, with little or no welfare policy and no institutional role for trade unions. Also, most European societies still had large employment shares in agriculture, so that the task of providing insurance against old age or sickness was largely still borne by the family.

After the First World War, many countries saw their social institutions and labor markets being reshaped very swiftly, and with far-reaching consequences. In the more advanced economies, the eight-hour day became the norm in industry almost universally. Unionization and the right to strike were now institutionalized, or at least became common practice.[14] This had the effect of altering the wage-setting mechanism away from bilateral towards collective bargaining. In the wake of this institutional change, wage shares in national incomes went up markedly compared to the pre-war period.[15]

At the same time, the beginning of active welfare policy and the gradual introduction of unemployment insurance increased the replacement ratio, i.e., the level of welfare benefits relative to the going wage. Some countries in Europe instead experimented with generous minimum wages, arguably with similarly adverse results.

All these factors – the increased bargaining power of unions, the rise in replacement ratios, the introduction of minimum wages – have been held responsible for persistent unemployment and a slow pace of recovery in the

[13] See Ellis 1941. A review of the literature is Ritschl 2001.
[14] See the comparative evidence on trade unions collected by Bain and Price 1980.
[15] See Broadberry and Ritschl 1995 for evidence on Britain and Germany.

early 1920s.[16] Similar explanations have also been offered for the persistence of the depression into the 1930s.[17] A case in point is the pro-labor policy of the Blum government in France beginning in 1934.[18] There is also the claim, now widely accepted, that welfare policies and labor-friendly wage mediation by the state contributed to the economic demise of Germany's Weimar Republic.[19]

The expansion of the welfare state and the adoption of labor-friendly wage-setting mechanisms in the early 1920s went hand in hand with major political convulsions in much of Europe. Everywhere, labor movements gained political influence and used it to promote the rights of organized labor, as well as universal suffrage and women's rights. In spite of attempts to find a compromise with organized labor during the First World War, monarchies everywhere on the continent were toppled in revolutionary processes, with the exception of the Netherlands and Scandinavia, which had been neutral in the war and where the transition to democracy was managed peacefully. Under threat from the extreme left, which had taken power in Russia (and briefly in Hungary and parts of Germany), right-wing movements formed in many parts of Europe. These movements would share the revolutionary impetus of the left and appeal to similar strata of the population. Yet they typically combined populist welfare policies with aggressive economic nationalism. Over time, the weak democracies that formed in continental Europe after the First World War increasingly came to feel the pressure from revolutionaries on both the left and the right. Before the Second World War, most of these countries had succumbed to authoritarian rule from the right. These regimes used the revolutionary impetus from the early 1920s, copying the model of Italian fascism, but rescinded the rights of organized labor. Trade unions were dissolved and labor was put under state-controlled umbrella organizations. The participation of women in the labor force was again discouraged, and agriculture received special promotion at the expense of further industrialization. Still, industrial wage shares did not drop back to the levels of 1913; all the dictatorships of Continental Europe built their legitimacy on pro-labor pretensions, and mostly refrained from cracking down on the material gains that labor had received in the 1920s as strongly as on their political organizations.

Soviet labor policies departed radically from the western European model in the 1920s. But not unlike the right-wing dictatorships that later emerged in Europe, the Soviet regime suffocated independent labor movements and their

---

[16] The seminal contribution on the effects of unemployment insurance in Britain is Benjamin and Kochin 1979. Broadberry (1986) emphasized the effects of unionization and the eight-hour day on labor supply and wage rates.

[17] In the context of a stochastic growth model with labor market frictions, Cole and Ohanian (2002) again stress the rise in the replacement ratio, combined with workers' decreased sectoral and regional mobility, as a main factor steering the UK away from its long-run trend in the 1920s and 1930s.

[18] Beaudry and Portier (2002) employ a framework related to that of Cole and Ohanian.

[19] Borchardt (1991 [1982]). Fisher and Hornstein (2002) obtain similar conclusions in a stochastic growth framework.

political representations, and instituted state-controlled umbrella organizations in their place. The effects of these policies on the material well being of the industrial working class seem doubtful. Collectivization of agriculture according to the same principles entailed human costs that arguably amounted to several million lives (Davies and Wheatcroft 2004).

While the labor market paradigm is useful in explaining post-war turmoil as well as the weak recoveries of the 1920s and the 1930s, it appears somewhat less successful in explaining the universal recession of 1929–32. High-wage policies that may have adversely affected unemployment were in force quite evenly across Europe, yet the depth and the persistence off the 1929–32 recession varied a good deal. In addition, recovery back towards historical trends was strongest in Scandinavia, where stringent pro-labor-market regulation was in effect in the 1930s, and in Germany, where quite the opposite was true.

International trade

In most European countries, the pre-1914 period was generally a time of moderate tariffs, which were often levied more for fiscal reasons than in order to protect home markets. Economic warfare during 1914–18 reduced trade to minimal levels, notably through the Allied blockade and – to a lesser extent – through German submarine warfare and other counter-blockade measures. As a consequence, international trade was severely depressed in Central Europe at the end of the war, but far less so in western Europe with its access to the Atlantic Ocean. This wartime difference in trade appears to explain to a large extent the different timing of the wartime recession in Central and western Europe, discussed above.[20]

Restoration of commercial trade after the First World War was generally sluggish, partly owing to the German reparations conflict and the developing hyperinflations in central Europe. Tariff conflicts between Germany on the one hand and Poland and France on the other hand further delayed the recovery of trade in the mid-1920s. In eastern central Europe, trade was further inhibited by the erection of tariff barriers between the former parts of the Habsburg monarchy. In addition, post-revolutionary turmoil in Russia and the establishment of a state monopoly in foreign trade seriously damaged central Europe's trade with Russia.

---

[20] Ritschl (2005) documents a tight relationship between declining imports and decreasing output in Germany during the First World War. Disruption of imports to the British war economy, although at times substantial, was far less in magnitude (Broadberry and Howlett 2005).

As a consequence, trade had not fully recovered to its 1913 levels by 1929. The general decline in overall trade volumes was accompanied by changes in the country and commodity structure of trade. Deprived of many of her overseas assets, Britain struggled to maintain balance of payments equilibrium in the 1920s, and lost major export markets for her declining staple industries of the nineteenth century. Germany developed massive import surpluses during the hyperinflation, a tendency that continued throughout the 1920s almost without interruption.

The beginning of the international depression quickly depressed trade volumes once again. Short of foreign credit inflows that had supported its trade deficits in the 1920s, Germany adopted a policy of drastic deflation, and generated high trade surpluses after 1930, thus transmitting a strong recessionary impulse throughout Europe.[21] Worries about foreign exchange reserves spread in 1931 and led to the widespread adoption of bilateral trade and exchange agreements, thus effectively linking trade flows to capital controls. The protectionist Smoot-Hawley tariff of 1930 in the USA, as well as the British Commonwealth's Ottawa preferences of 1932, added to the protectionist impetus. Germany's transition to tight capital controls and trade quotas in 1933 cemented the new trade regime. As a consequence, international trade in the 1930s failed to recover fully from the recession, and the degree of openness of Europe's economies fell to its lowest levels since the middle of the nineteenth century (Table 7.1). At the same time, the imbalances on capital account that had characterized the 1920s almost disappeared. Achieving equilibrium in the balance of payments and the balance of trade simultaneously became a

Table 7.1 Regional distribution of world trade, 1913–1937 (exports, million 1990 US dollars)

	1913 (in %)		1928 (in %)		1937 (in %)	
Europe (including Russia)	58.9	139,198	48.0	160,516	47.0	152,284
North America (Canada and USA)	14.8	34,977	19.8	66,213	17.1	55,406
Latin America	8.3	19,615	9.8	32,772	10.2	33,049
Asia	11.8	27,887	15.5	51,833	16.9	54,758
Africa	3.7	8,744	4.0	13,376	5.3	17,172
Oceania	2.5	5,908	2.9	9,698	3.5	11,340
Total	100.0	236,330	100.0	334,408	100.0	324,009

Source: Our calculations using data from Kenwood and Lougheed 1992 and Maddison 1995.

---

[21] Ritschl 2002b, 2003.

paramount economic policy goal in the 1930s, and was implemented through policy fiat rather than through market forces.

The trade policies of the 1930s were not just motivated by financial concerns. Import substitution policies targeted sectors thought to be strategically important. Agricultural protectionism aimed to improve self-sufficiency in order to confront future wartime blockades. As a consequence, substantial resources were invested in building up industries in sectors ranging from steel to chemicals and textiles, thus diverting and substituting trade for the sake of war preparation. This also implied major redistribution of incomes to domestic agriculture and to the import substitution industries. This in turn had the effect of slowing down the relative decline of agricultural employment, and of channeling substantial parts of the pool of unemployed into the new, war-related import substitution industries. In this way, Europe in the 1930s fell back into a state of mercantilism, forgoing the gains from trade for the sake of increased national self-sufficiency, a policy goal that was incompatible with market processes.

Capital flows, international conflict, and the interwar European business cycle

Between the 1860s and 1914, international politics had remarkably little influence on economic fluctuations in Europe. Europe's advanced countries did attempt to use capital exports and direct investment in the periphery of Europe to their strategic advantage.[22] Yet most of the economic rivalry between Europe's great powers found its outlet in colonial adventures. Closer to home, the prevailing doctrine was to refrain from using state intervention in markets as a lever to gain the upper hand in international rivalries. An exemplary case was the "commercialization" of France's reparations to Germany after the war of 1870/1.[23] France issued bonds on international markets, paid off the Germans, and thus transformed its political debt into a purely commercial one. Germany used part of the proceeds to back its new currency, the mark, which it linked to Britain's gold standard rather than to the French-dominated bimetallic system. Still, discriminatory practices in monetary policy were mostly absent. An atmosphere prevailed in which money and financial markets were seen as a matter for experts, to be sheltered from political interference. Under the classical gold standard that originated in the 1870s, cooperation among central banks continued even in times of

[22] Fishlow 1985; Davis and Huttenback 1986. For more recent debates, see Flandreau, Le Cacheux, and Zumer 1998; Ferguson and Schularick 2006.
[23] White 2001.

heightened political tension between their governments, notably in the crises of 1907 and 1911.[24]

All this changed dramatically with the First World War. Schemes for punitive reparations were drawn up on both sides during the war. Germany's ruthless financial exploitation of occupied Belgium served as a model for future financial warfare. Large-scale territorial changes were envisaged, and policy proposals discussed in German government circles even suggested the ethnic cleansing of large swathes of eastern Europe.[25] Given such scenarios, the armistice of 1918 and the economic conditions attached to it look less radical than they might seem at first sight.

Historians have long argued that the feud over German reparations and its twin, the inter-allied credits owed to the USA by France and Britain, over-shadowed financial relations between 1919 and 1932. The interference of political matters at times seriously impaired the normal functioning of international capital markets, and undermined domestic stability in some of the core countries. The reparations bill of 1921 is held to have contributed to tax revolt, civil unrest, and the transition to hyperinflation in Germany (Feldman 1993). Germany's refusal to pay reparations at the stipulated rates played a part in destabilizing the French budget in the early 1920s, with consequences for the franc that lasted throughout the decade.[26] American-brokered stabilization of Germany under the Dawes Plan of 1924 set capital flows between Germany and international markets in motion again.[27] Yet it provided no final settlement and left the future of the controversial inter-allied debts open. French refusal to service these debts to the USA unless these were fully securitized by future German reparations led to an American credit ban on France. This had the effect of cutting the French off from the American market and motivated France's much-criticized policy of hoarding gold, which in turn contributed to destabilizing the interwar gold standard.[28]

Capital flows between the USA and Europe during the second half of the 1920s were nevertheless substantial. Many of these credit flows were directed to Germany, which on balance absorbed the entire net capital exports from the USA during the second half of the 1920s.[29] For half a decade, Germany turned

---

[24] Representative of a large literature is Eichengreen 1992a.

[25] The seminal work on Germany's long-term war aims is Fischer 1967.

[26] Schuker 1976b; Prati 1991; Hautcoeur and Sicsic 1999.

[27] Among other things, the Dawes Plan internationalized Germany's central bank, protected its new currency from reparation transfers, provided a major international loan, and designed a new reparation schedule that was quite favorable to the Germans. However, it provided no final settlement.

[28] See Schuker 1976a on the political fallout of the Dawes Plan. A contemporary treatment of the interconnection between the two types of debt is Boyden 1928. On the political constraints of French currency policy at the time see Mouré 1991.

[29] See Ritschl 2002b.

into the world's largest net capital importer, enabling the Germans to pay all reparations under the Dawes Plan on credit.[30]

Historians have argued that the Germans abused the Dawes Plan to over-borrow in international markets;[31] sovereign debt theory would suggest that they had every incentive to do so.[32] As a result, Germany's foreign debt, including the current value of reparations, stood somewhere near 80 percent of GNP in 1929 when the international recession broke out.

Monetary and financial crisis management under the informal rules of central bank cooperation established in the nineteenth century would have dictated swift and discreet support for the German currency once difficulties arose. Such cooperation as existed during the interwar period clearly failed to provide these services.[33] The attempted ersatz commercialization of German reparations in the Dawes Plan had seemingly succeeded in decoupling international politics and financial relations for a while. With the much stricter Young Plan of 1929/30, the former link between the two was firmly re-established. Being essentially a payback scheme for inter-allied war credits, the Young Plan aligned French and British interests in shedding their war debt with America's interest in avoiding default on these credits. At the same time, it implicitly – and, one could argue, belatedly – placed Germany under Allied financial control, and thus inextricably intertwined any future monetary rescue operations under the gold standard with the German debt and reparation problem.[34]

To depoliticize central bank cooperation under these circumstances, the Bank of International Settlements was created. However, classical-style, discreet central bank cooperation proved impossible when, after two years of forced deflation and austerity, the German payments crisis broke out in 1931.[35] Plans for financial assistance were quickly loaded with political issues, and it soon became apparent that no debt relief was possible without addressing the deeper issues underlying the Young Plan. A temporary way out of the deadlock was only achieved after the USA proposed a one-year moratorium on all political debt, thus finally accepting the link between reparations and inter-allied debt. The price for this political arrangement in lieu of central bank cooperation was the imposition of capital controls in July of 1931, and thus Germany's exit from the gold standard.

---

[30] See Kindleberger 1973 for a discussion of this debt recycling mechanism.

[31] Link 1970; Schuker (1988).   [32] Ritschl 2002a.

[33] This is a central theme in Eichengreen's (1992) account of the interwar depression. On the wider theme of interwar central bank cooperation, see Clarke 1976. A rather more critical perspective is Mouré 2002.

[34] Ritschl 2002a.

[35] On this and the following, see the detailed account of the German crisis in James 1985 and 1986. Toniolo (2005) documents the attempts to implement cooperation at the nascent Bank of International Settlements in spite of political intervention from all sides.

German debt problems and international conflict continued to plague financial markets throughout the mid-1930s. Negotiations over reparations were delayed to mid-1932, provoking further deflationary measures in both France and Germany. In the wake of the end to German reparations in August 1932, France and Britain declared default on their inter-allied war debt to the USA (December 1932). Germany defaulted on increasing portions of her commercial debt and obtained rescheduling deals on others. By 1935, the average default rate was between 80 and 90 percent.[36] As a consequence, international financial relations in Europe were channeled into a network of increasingly tight capital and exchange control agreements.[37] Before the Second World War, trade and payments in large parts of Europe had become a matter of politics and bureaucratic interference, creating a new, extreme version of mercantilism whose principal aim was to utilize trade as a weapon in international conflict.

Conclusion

The interwar period witnessed a long-term downward deviation from Europe's output and income growth trends, a truly Great Depression that lasted from 1914 to 1945 and that had no comparison in the nineteenth century. In it were embedded three severe recessions, each of which would probably have qualified as the deepest European recession since the Industrial Revolution, had it not been for the next, even deeper one. This chapter surveyed some of the most prominent interpretations of these recessions. It argued that this highly pathological period of European economic history cannot be analyzed separately from two dimensions of conflict that ravaged Europe at the time. One is international conflict, represented by Germany's two wars against its neighboring countries. The other is social conflict, connected mainly to the increasing role of labor movements and the concomitant changes in the distribution of income, but also to the first spread of civil rights and the changing role of women. Both dimensions of conflict strongly impacted on business cycle outcomes in the interwar period.

Social conflict is one key variable that may have steered the economies of Europe away from their previous long-term growth path: unionization, the eight-hour day, and the expansion of welfare benefits all changed the balance of bargaining power in labor markets, increased wage shares, and lowered profit margins. Social conflict was also a key factor in the rise of authoritarian regimes all across Continental Europe, which tried to reverse the results of the 1920s by

---

[36] Klug 1993.   [37] Einzig 1934; Child (1958).

forcing economic growth at the expense of living standards – usually achieving the latter policy goal, but not necessarily the former.

International conflict was paramount in the war-related recessions of 1914–18 and again in 1940–5. But it also played a decisive part in the failed attempts to stabilize the European economies during the interwar years. This chapter has argued that continuing conflict over Germany's reparations seriously impaired the functioning of international financial markets in the interwar period, and also prevented central bank cooperation from defusing the crisis of the gold standard in 1931. The German debt default that began to unfold in the spring of 1931 turned a serious, but potentially manageable, crisis of the European interwar monetary system into a catastrophe with long-term consequences. Under the pathological political conditions prevailing in Europe during the interwar period, it is hard to see how a more robust international financial architecture could have been designed that would have produced significantly better outcomes.

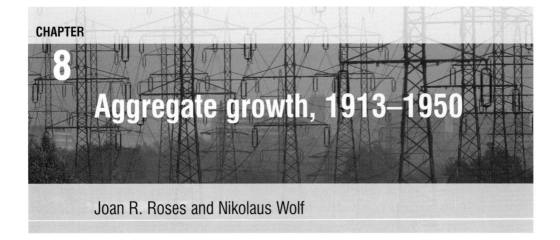

Aggregate growth, 1913–1950

Joan R. Roses and Nikolaus Wolf

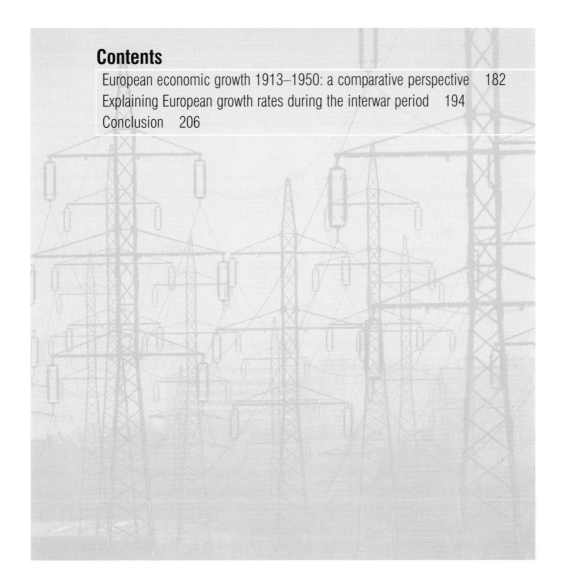

Contents

European economic growth 1913–1950: a comparative perspective

From 1913 to 1950 the European growth record was rather poor. The "Second Thirty Years War" (Churchill 1948, p. xiii), or the period from the beginning of the First World War in 1914 to the end of the Second World War in 1945, stands in sharp contrast to the following Golden Age of Growth between about 1950 and 1973 (see Chapter 12 in this volume). And indeed, the rates of economic growth across European countries were "unusually" low: they seem to distinguish Europe from other parts of the world during that time span, but also stand out compared to Europe's growth experience from about 1870 to 1913. A substantial literature has pointed to several key factors that may account for this slowdown of growth rates in Europe. Not surprisingly, a central role is attributed to the occurrence of two devastating wars that raged in the center of Europe over a third of the entire period 1913–1950 (Svennilson 1954). The remaining twenty years have often been characterized as a time of political turmoil and, in many cases, misguided macroeconomic policies; and, related to this, a general failure to coordinate policies between countries, which prevented Europe from fully realizing its economic potential (Feinstein, Temin, and Toniolo 1997).

To see how policies and coordination failures affected economic growth, we need to understand how large Europe's potential for growth actually was after the First World War. In a nutshell, the economic potential of Europe rose considerably between 1913 and 1950, driven by technological, organizational, and sectoral change, by the accumulation of physical capital, and by the formation and accumulation of human capital. There is plenty of evidence for significant technological progress during the 1920s and 1930s. The period saw the beginnings of mass motorization, advances in chemical and electrical engineering, the construction of an extensive road network, the emergence of commercial aviation, and crucially the electrification of large parts of the European economy, including some of the most remote rural areas. European industry underwent a broad process of modernization, including many firms that attempted to introduce and adapt new methods of American-style standardized mass production (Chandler 1990). Moreover, the share of agriculture declined in all European economies between 1913 and 1950, with labor moving into the more productive industrial and service sectors, especially in northern and western Europe (see Chapter 9 in this volume). The governments of newly created states all aimed at a rapid economic development of their largely backward countries, and the records show rising school enrollment and numbers of students, high and in some cases rising participation rates in labor markets, and a steady growth of the European population.

So why did Europe not enter into a Golden Age of Growth earlier, in the 1920s? Europe's cultural history, especially the "golden twenties" or "les années folles," intriguingly reflects the tensions between the vast unexplored possibilities of modern life and looming disaster. The First World War brought the liberal economic order of the late nineteenth century to an end, foreshadowed by increasing protectionism in large parts of the Atlantic economy (Kindleberger 1989; Findlay and O'Rourke 2003) and the first signs of dissolution of the central European empires from the 1880s onwards (Schulze and Wolf 2009). Protectionism continued after the war. Many tariffs, quotas, and other restrictions on trade installed during the war remained in place in the 1920s. This, together with limits on migration and declining capital mobility, inevitably led to a misallocation of resources across states. The failure to resolve the international issue of war debt and reparations (Ritschl 1998) and tensions due to the emergence of new states and the redrawing of political boundaries (Rothschild 1974; Broadberry and Harrison 2005) are most often discussed in this context (see Chapter 7 in this volume). Any existing attempts to improve international policy coordination, such as the re-establishment of the gold standard as a monetary system in the late 1920s, surrendered to economic nationalism or club formation during the Great Depression (Eichengreen 1992). In a similar vein, mass migration, which had favored wage convergence between Europe and the New World during the first globalization (Hatton and Williamson 1998), fell sharply as war and depression halted the previous trend and immigration policies entered a new age of restriction. Not only did restrictive immigration policies proliferate in the receiving countries, like the United States and Australia, but also some sending countries like the Soviet Union introduced severe emigrant restrictions (Chiswick and Hatton 2005). To some extent these coordination failures can be related to increased costs of political coordination within states due to the extension of the political franchise and the associated rebalancing of political power during and after the First World War (Nurkse 1944; Eichengreen and Temin 2000).

In what follows we shall survey the European growth experience during the interwar years, with a special focus on the period 1920–38. That is, we shall largely exclude the direct effects of the two wars and their immediate aftermath. Nevertheless it will become clear that both the legacy of the First World War and the foreshadowing of the Second World War had strong indirect effects on economic growth in the 1920s and 1930s. Given that the time span under consideration is relatively short, we shall remain largely descriptive and exploit as far as possible the large cross-sectional variation in growth rates across European countries. First we shall sketch the general picture of European economic growth from 1913 to 1950. Then we shall briefly present some theoretical background to sharpen our focus on possible explanations for different growth experiences, and discuss several explanations for aggregate

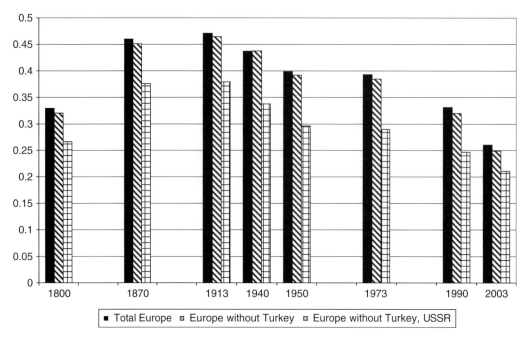

Figure 8.1 The share of "Europe" in the world economy. *Source:* based on Maddison, 2007.

growth in interwar Europe. Finally we shall summarize the evidence and reach some general conclusions.

European growth performance: intertemporal comparisons

Let us start by putting the European experience between the wars in a wider perspective. Figure 8.1 shows Europe's share in the world economy (GDP measured in 1990 International Geary–Khamis dollars). Here we distinguish three concepts of "Europe": first, all European countries including Turkey and the USSR, secondly, Europe without Turkey, and thirdly, Europe without either the USSR or Turkey.

The interwar years mark the beginning of a decline of Europe's share in the world economy after a longer period of expansion since the Industrial Revolution. At its zenith around 1913, Europe (including Turkey and the USSR) accounted for 47 percent of world GDP. By 1950, after two world wars and the interwar period, this share had decreased to about 40 percent. It is notable that the relative decline of Europe in the world economy could not be reversed despite spectacular growth rates during the "golden age" of economic growth from 1950 to 1973. After this, Europe's share in the world economy declined even faster, to about a quarter around 2000. Obviously, a

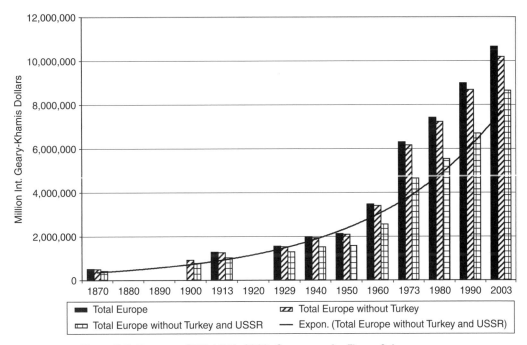

Figure 8.2 European GDP, 1870–2003. *Source:* as for Figure 8.1.

main driver for this relative "decline" is found in the economic development of hitherto stagnant economies in Asia and other parts of the world, with a largely positive impact on the European economy. A more optimistic picture emerges from Figure 8.2, which contrasts GDP shares with the levels of European GDP (measured in million 1990 International Geary–Khamis dollars) from 1870 onwards.

No matter what aggregate is considered, the European economy grew by a factor of about 20 between 1870 and 2003. If compared against a long-run trend (based on "Europe" *without* Turkey and the USSR) extrapolated backwards from 2003, the interwar years stand out as a period of rather poor economic performance. This underperformance against a long-run trend is even more visible when we consider the development of GDP per capita, which will be our focus on the following pages: While the standard of living continued to increase across Europe during the interwar years, the rate of increase was low if put in a long-run perspective (see Figure 8.3).

The aggregate data mask another feature of the interwar years, namely a significant increase in the variance of growth rates in the period 1913–50 compared to 1870–1913, both in the cross-section of European countries and in a short-run business-cycle perspective (see Chapter 7 in this volume).

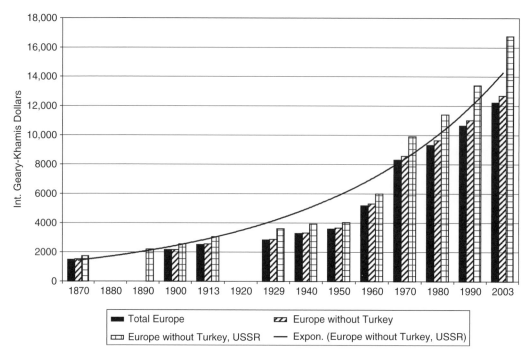

Figure 8.3 European GDP per capita, 1870–2003. *Source:* as for Figure 8.2.

European growth performance: spatial comparisons

The long-run perspective on the interwar growth experience raises several related issues. First and foremost, what accounts for the marked slowdown in GDP per capita growth in Europe after 1913? The long-run decline of Europe's share in the world economy suggests that European growth may have been adversely affected by the rise of strong competitors in world markets overseas (especially the USA and Japan). While there is certainly an element of reverse causation, overseas competition can only in part explain the slowdown in growth rates, because the share of Europe continued to decline even during the golden age of exceptionally high growth rates. Also, the large variation in intra-European experiences indicates that some country- or country-group-specific factors affected growth rates. As stated in our introduction, among these factors was the degree to which a country was involved in the two wars. Table 8.1 shows the year in which European countries regained their 1913 levels of GDP per capita and their involvement in the First World War.

The defeated Central Powers recovered significantly more slowly from the war than members of the winning coalition, which in turn were outperformed by war neutrals such as the Netherlands, Norway, and Spain during the 1920s. The data also show that among the winners, the UK and Romania did not

Table 8.1 Recovery of GDP per capita to levels of 1913 in twenty-seven European countries

Country	GDP per capita 1922 relative to 1913 (%)	Year when 1913 level regained	Participation in WWI
Austria	83	1927	loser
Belgium	105	1922	winner
Denmark	106	1922	neutral
Finland	98	1923	neutral
France	103	1922	winner
Germany	91	1926	loser
Italy	102	1922	winner
Netherlands	114	1919	neutral
Norway	109	1919	neutral
Sweden	94	1924	neutral
Switzerland	108	1920	neutral
United Kingdom	94	1924	winner
Ireland	95	1928	independence (from winner)
Greece	123	1919	winner (but enters into war with Turkey 1919)
Portugal	114	1921	winner
Spain	111	1920	neutral
Albania	n/a	n/a	independence (from loser)
Lithuania	n/a	n/a	independence (from loser)
Latvia	n/a	n/a	independence (from loser)
Estonia	n/a	n/a	independence (from loser)
Bulgaria	59 (1924/1913)	1937	loser
Czechoslovakia	96	1923	independence (from loser)
Hungary	91 (1924/1913)	1925	loser
Poland	79	1926	independence (from loser)
Romania	72 (1926/1913)	1959	winner
Yugoslavia	99	1922	independence (from loser)
Russia/USSR	n/a	1933	loser

Source: Maddison 2007 and own calculations.

perform particularly well; the UK experienced a severe post-war recession and recovered only slowly, while Romania's per capita GDP did not grow at all during the interwar period. Countries that gained independence during or immediately after the war such as Czechoslovakia, Poland, and Ireland had quite diverging experiences. Some did exceptionally well, including the two (of three) new Baltic states for which sufficient data are available (Latvia and Estonia), while the economies of Ireland and Yugoslavia developed very slowly. In what follows, we will focus on the growth performance of twenty-seven European countries between 1920 and 1938. Table 8.2 shows their average annual growth rates over that time span, including the corresponding standard deviations for various periods.

Table 8.2 Average annual rates of growth (GDP per capita) in twenty-seven European countries and the USA

Country	1913–50 (StdDev)	1920–29 (StdDev)	Year of recovery – 1929 (StdDev)	1929–38 (StdDev)
Austria	0.18 (0.17)	4.93 (0.04)	2.68 (0.02)	−0.43 (0.07)
Belgium	0.70 (0.07)	3.99 (0.05)	2.75 (0.03)	−0.50 (0.03)
Denmark	1.55 (0.06)	2.74 (0.05)	3.53 (0.04)	1.41 (0.02)
Finland	1.89 (0.07)	4.94 (0.03)	3.97 (0.02)	3.09 (0.04)
France	1.12 (0.12)	5.16 (0.07)	5.33 (0.02)	−0.59 (0.05)
Germany	0.17 (0.16)	4.49 (0.09)	3.43 (0.04)	2.32 (0.07)
Italy	0.84 (0.09)	0.83 (0.05)	2.52 (0.03)	0.77 (0.04)
Netherlands	1.06 (0.13)	3.22 (0.02)	4.81 (0.06)	−0.89 (0.04)
Norway	2.15 (0.06)	2.71 (0.06)	3.75 (0.07)	2.55 (0.05)
Sweden	2.10 (0.04)	3.71 (0.03)	3.98 (0.03)	2.22 (0.04)
Switzerland	2.04 (0.06)	4.44 (0.03)	4.44 (0.03)	0.10 (0.03)
United Kingdom	0.93 (0.04)	1.22 (0.04)	2.42 (0.04)	1.44 (0.03)
Ireland	0.63 (0.02)	1.36 (0.02)	3.12 (0.01)	0.86 (0.03)
Greece	0.50 (0.12)	2.49 (0.01)	2.50 (0.01)	1.48 (0.05)
Portugal	1.33 (0.06)	3.17 (0.08)	2.99 (0.08)	0.91 (0.07)
Spain	0.25 (0.06)	2.92 (0.03)	2.92 (0.03)	−4.72 (0.09)
Albania	0.57 (–)	n/a	n/a	n/a
Lithuania	n/a	n/a	n/a	
Latvia	n/a	5.31 (0.11)	n/a	4.10 (0.12)
Estonia	n/a	2.75 (0.10)	n/a	3.30 (0.06)
Bulgaria	0.19 (–)	5.23 (0.11)	n/a	3.35 (0.09)
Czechoslovakia	1.40 (–)	5.04 (0.05)	5.95 (0.04)	−0.68 (0.06)
Hungary	0.45 (–)	5.17 (0.08)	5.17 (0.08)	0.78 (0.05)
Poland	0.93 (–)	5.24 (0.07)	8.38 (0.04)	0.34 (0.09)
Romania	−1.04 (–)	−2.91 (0.03)	n/a	0.83 (0.05)
Yugoslavia	1.04 (–)	3.11 (0.03)	3.37 (0.03)	−0.06 (0.06)
Unweighted average	**0.91 (–)**	**3.43 (–)**	**3.90 (–)**	**0.88 (–)**
Weighted average	**0.72 (–)**	**3.21 (–)**	**3.69 (–)**	**0.53 (–)**
Russia/USSR	1.76 (–)	n/a	n/a	4.87 (0.05)
USA	1.61 (0.09)	1.94 (0.04)	1.94 (0.04)	−1.32 (0.09)

Source: Maddison 2007 and own calculations.

The impression we get from Table 8.2 is that of a very heterogeneous development: the average annual rate of growth over the entire period 1913–50 was 0.72 percent (weighted by population), but varied from a maximum of 2.15 percent (Norway) to a minimum of −1.04 percent (Romania). Over the entire period, only three Nordic countries (Norway, Sweden, and Finland) and the neutral Switzerland grew faster than the United States and the USSR, with growth rates of, respectively, 1.61 and 1.76 percent annually. Only four other European countries (Denmark, France, Czechoslovakia, and Yugoslavia) grew at rates over 1 percent per year, while the remaining countries failed to reach even these low levels of growth.

But there were some regularities. Broadly speaking, all European countries (except Romania) shared the experience of relatively high growth rates during the 1920s. Also, Europe was rapidly converging with the United States during that decade, with a weighted average of 3.21 percent per annum compared to 1.94 percent per annum observable on the other side of the Atlantic. Up to ten countries grew at rates above four percent per year and only four countries (Britain, Ireland, Italy, and Romania) grew at rates below that of the United States. This strong growth can only partially be explained by reconstruction growth after the First World War, because growth rates stayed quite high even when the 1913 levels were regained (compare Table 8.2, columns 2 and 3). It is also noteworthy that several neutral states that had not experienced any major destruction during the war grew faster than the European average, notably Sweden and Finland in Scandinavia and Switzerland. In these three cases, growth was accompanied with visible changes in the structure of the economy: in Sweden and Switzerland a major shift towards higher value-added industries (Krantz 1987; Siegenthaler 1987 respectively), in Finland a significant industrialization following political independence (Hjerppe and Jalava 2006). We will return to these factors later.

Table 8.2 also shows clearly that the Great Depression was a watershed for Europe's economic development. During the second decade of the interwar period growth slowed down in all European countries, but somewhat less so in Scandinavia, the UK, Latvia, and Estonia. While most governments attempted to protect their economies from further exogenous shocks by raising tariff barriers, introducing capital controls, and the like, the Scandinavian countries, and interestingly also Estonia and Latvia, managed to coordinate an early exit from the gold standard with the UK in late 1931, and outperformed the rest of Europe. This illustrates how macroeconomic policy and its cross-border coordination mattered during the interwar years: "the timing and extent of depreciation can explain much of the variation in the timing and extent of economic recovery" (Eichengreen 1992, p. 232). Germany's growth performance in turn overstates the improvements in the standard of living during that period, because it was already from 1934 onwards largely driven by massive rearmament policies at the expense of rising government debt and low nominal and real wages in a strictly regulated labor market (see Ritschl 2002a).

Finally, our panel of European countries shows some interesting distribution dynamics that are not visible from the above figures and tables (for more on this see Epstein, Howlett, and Schulze 2000). Table 8.3 shows the ranking of sample countries according to their GDP per capita for 1922, 1929, and 1938.

While the UK lost her leading position to Switzerland and the Netherlands during the 1920s, she nearly caught up again by the late 1930s due to the

Table 8.3 Distribution dynamics: Country ranking according to GDP per capita, 1922, 1929, 1938

1922		1929		1938	
Country	GDP per capita	Country	GDP per capita	Country	GDP per capita
UK	4637	Switzerland	6332	Switzerland	6390
Switzerland	4618	Netherlands	5689	UK	6266
Netherlands	4599	UK	5503	Denmark	5762
Belgium	4413	Denmark	5075	Netherlands	5250
Denmark	4166	Belgium	5054	Germany	4994
France	3610	France	4710	Belgium	4832
Germany	3331	Germany	4051	Sweden	4725
Sweden	2906	Sweden	3869	France	4466
Austria	2877	Austria	3699	Norway	4337
Norway	2784	Norway	3472	Latvia	4048
Italy	2631	Italy	3093	Estonia	3771
Ireland	2598	Czech.	3042	Finland	3589
Estonia	2311	Ireland	2824	Austria	3559
Spain	2284	Estonia	2802	Italy	3316
Finland	2058	Latvia	2798	Ireland	3052
Czech.	2006	Spain	2739	Greece	2677
Greece	1963	Finland	2717	Hungary	2655
Latvia	1929	Hungary	2476	Poland	2396
Portugal	1430	Greece	2342	Spain	1790
Poland	1382	Poland	1994	Portugal	1747
Yugoslavia	1057	Portugal	1610	Bulgaria	1595
		Yugoslavia	1364	Yugoslavia	1356
		Bulgaria	1180	Romania	1242
		Romania	1152		
		Albania	926		
No data on Albania, Bulgaria, Hungary, Romania				No data on Albania, Czechoslovakia	
Poorest as % of richest: 22.8		Poorest as % of richest: 14.6		Poorest as % of richest: 19.4	

Source: Maddison 2007 and own calculations.

prolonged stagnation of the Swiss and the Dutch economies after the depression. Apart from this, the most remarkable changes include the steady improvement in the relative positions of the Scandinavian countries, especially during the 1930s; the positive development of Latvia and Estonia (while the estimates here might be on the high side); and the relative and even absolute decline of Austria and Spain. The Balkan countries, along with Romania and also Portugal and Spain (after the devastating Civil War; see Prados de la Escosura 2005) remained at the European economic periphery, while Greece and Poland started to improve their positions in the 1930s. Taken together, this suggests that there was little overall convergence during the interwar years. Nevertheless, there may have been "conditional" convergence – conditional on country- or country-group specific factors that affected the pace of productivity growth via structural change, schooling, the propensity to save and invest, and the like. To explore more systematically how such factors can explain Europe's growth during the interwar years, we shall introduce briefly some background on the economic theory of growth.

Some theoretical background

Why do some countries prosper, while others suffer from stagnation? To answer this question, it is useful to consider the benchmark neo-classical growth model, first developed by Solow (1956) and Swan (1956; for a good exposition see, e.g., Barro and Sala-i-Martin 2003, ch. 1). In the benchmark model with labor-augmenting technological progress, growth of per capita GDP is driven by the rate of technological change and capital accumulation, which is subject to diminishing returns. The production function is typically specified as a Cobb–Douglas function of the form:

$$Y = K^\alpha (AL)^{1-\alpha}, \tag{1}$$

where Y is GDP, K is capital, L is labor, and A is the level of technology.[1] A central prediction of this model is convergence: everything else (including technology) being equal, poorer economies grow at higher rates than richer economies owing to diminishing returns to capital accumulation. Therefore, all economies should in the long run converge in terms of income per capita and productivity. Note that the model crucially assumes that the markets for labor, capital, and technology transfer are efficient. Imperfections in domestic or international markets would affect the speed of convergence, for example because good access to international capital markets can foster capital accumulation in poor countries, while richer countries can earn higher returns on their savings by lending to the poor (Barro, Mankiw, and Sala-i-Martin 1995). Moreover, the model predicts that changes in the savings rate (the proportion of output used to create more capital rather than being consumed) and the rate of capital depreciation affect the levels of output and transitional dynamics, but not the long-run rate of growth. If savings and depreciation rates or the rate of technological change differ across countries, the model predicts convergence conditional on these differences, a prediction that receives much more

---

[1] This formulation of technology is described as "labor-augmenting" because it raises output in the same way as an increase in the stock of labor, which is essential for the existence of a steady-state.

empirical support than that of un-conditional convergence (see the debate between Baumol 1986 and DeLong 1988).

While it provides a convenient starting point, the benchmark model needs to be further modified to be useful for empirical analysis. Mankiw, Romer, and Weil (1992) propose an augmented model that includes human capital formation interacting with labor as an input factor, for example through schooling, and show that this provides a better description of cross-country income differences over time. Recent research has mainly focused on the microeconomic foundations of growth, including the idea of endogenous growth due to endogenous innovation (Romer 1990) or benefits from proximity (Krugman and Venables 1995); others have stressed the effects of sectoral change (Broadberry 1998) due to technological differences between sectors, and the impact of market inefficiencies. The current consensus is that differences in efficiency are at least as important as factor accumulation in explaining income differences across countries. This is robust to attempts to improve the measurement of human capital, to account for the age composition of the capital stock, to sectoral disaggregations of output, and to several other robustness checks (Caselli 2005). Directly related to this is the large literature in the wake of Abramovitz (1986), who observed that cross-country growth patterns are characterized by catch-up to technological leaders. The scope for catch-up in turn depends on the "social capability" of a country and "technological congruence" between countries. From this perspective national policies and institutions, but also the market size of a country, are not neutral but are closely associated with long-run economic growth rates (North 1990; Mauro 1995; Engerman and Sokoloff 1997; Hall and Jones 1999; Acemoglu, Johnson, and Robinson 2002; Easterly and Levine 2003).

Generally speaking, there are two approaches to evaluating the explanatory power of these theoretical concepts, both starting from the benchmark neoclassical growth model. One approach attempts to test the key prediction of convergence, controlling for conditioning factors such as differences in savings or investment rates, the stock or formation of human capital, and differences in institutions or market size (see Sala-i-Martin, Doppelhofer, and Miller 2004). This typically takes the form of estimating:

$$\ln\left(\frac{y_T}{y_0}\right) = a + b(\ln(y_0)) + \sum_{i=1}^{J} c_i \ln(X_i) + \varepsilon, \qquad (2)$$

where y is GDP per capita (that is per population), T denotes the time of the last observation, and 0 the starting point, X represents conditioning factors, and ε is an error term. The dependent variable is the growth rate of per capita income, which is negatively related to the initial level of income (y_0) if there is convergence, indicated by b < 0. This means that countries which start off richer grow more slowly, while countries that start off poorer grow more quickly. The inclusion of conditioning variables allows for other factors to offset this process of catching-up or convergence.

The other approach is that of growth accounting, following Tinbergen (1942) and Solow (1957). The rate of growth of levels of GDP or GDP per unit of labor input is decomposed into the growth contributions of production factors and changes in productivity. Typically, the underlying model is specified as a Cobb–Douglas production function:

$$Y = AK^{\alpha} L^{1-\alpha}. \tag{3}$$

Note that two identifying assumptions are usually made in this framework. First, the technology parameter A is interpreted as Total Factor Productivity (TFP) and assumed to be "Hicks-neutral" instead of labor-augmenting (or "Harrod-neutral"), such that technological change would be unbiased with respect to capital and labor. Secondly, the production function is assumed to feature constant returns. Define labor productivity as y = Y/L, and capital intensity as k = K/L. Given this, the growth rate can be approximately decomposed as follows:

$$\ln\left(\frac{Y_{t+1}}{Y_t}\right) = \ln\left(\frac{A_{t+1}}{A_t}\right) + \alpha\ln\left(\frac{K_{t+1}}{K_t}\right) + (1-\alpha)\ln\left(\frac{L_{t+1}}{L_t}\right) \tag{4}$$

or equally as:

$$\ln\left(\frac{y_{t+1}}{y_t}\right) = \ln\left(\frac{A_{t+1}}{A_t}\right) + \alpha\ln\left(\frac{k_{t+1}}{k_t}\right), \tag{5}$$

where the growth rate of A (TFP) is always calculated as the residual, given that we have data only on Y, K, and L. The formulation in (5) shows that the growth of labor productivity can be decomposed into changes in TFP and changes in capital intensity (or "capital deepening"). This can also be expressed in terms of GDP per capita, which differs from labor productivity according to the participation rate defined as employment per head of population. The resulting estimates of TFP have often been interpreted as approximations of technological progress, but some caveats are important. First, any mis-measurement of factor inputs or outputs will affect the estimated TFP. Second, any mis-specification of the functional relationship, for example when in fact there are increasing returns to scale, or if the aggregate production function changes over time due to sectoral change, or when technological progress is biased, will equally affect the results. Finally, changes in "TFP growth" can also reflect changes in policies and the institutional environment, given that TFP is calculated as the residual. Nevertheless, accounting of this sort is useful to develop a general idea about the factors that drive economic growth.

Explaining European growth rates during the interwar period

Was there conditional convergence?

We start with a test of the strongest possible hypothesis from neo-classical growth theory: unconditional convergence. As a first step we simply plot the average annual rate of growth between 1913 and 1950 against GDP per capita in 1913, as in (2), without controlling for any conditioning factors. As shown in Figures 8.4–8.7, we can reject the idea that there was unconditional convergence across European countries, both for the full period 1913–1950 and for any of the sub-periods.

The relationship between initial income and growth was very weak. Given the evidence from Table 8.3, this is hardly surprising. The absence of unconditional convergence over the years 1913–50 can easily be explained by the fact that both rich and poor countries were involved in the wars and experienced destruction and reconstruction growth that were largely unrelated to their 1913 levels of development. Note, however that there is a weakly negative relationship between growth and initial income during the period of peace. In this light we can explore whether there was convergence in

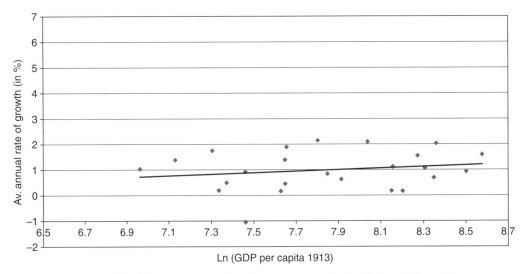

Figure 8.4 Was there unconditional convergence, 1913–50? Twenty-three European countries and the USA.

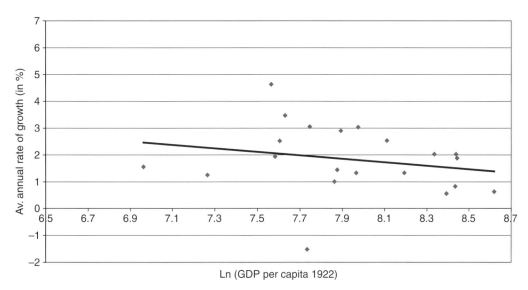

Figure 8.5 Was there unconditional convergence, 1922–38? Twenty-three European countries and the USA.

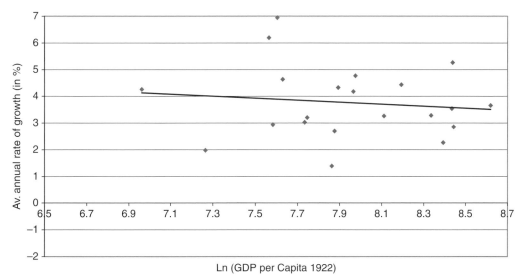

Figure 8.6 Was there unconditional convergence, 1922–9? Twenty-three European countries and the USA.

1920–38 conditional on country-specific factors. But what factors conditioned growth rates? As outlined earlier, there are many possible candidates.

The empirical literature on economic growth faces a serious "small-sample" problem: because sample sizes for regressions on the determinants of long-run

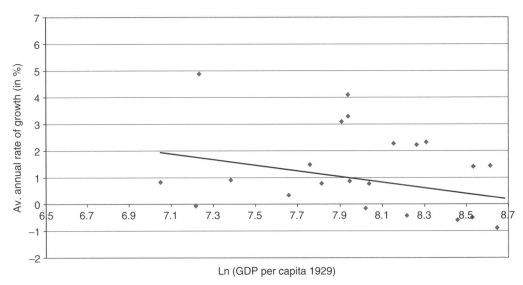

Figure 8.7 Was there unconditional convergence, 1929–38? Twenty-three European countries and the USA.

growth rates are typically small compared to the number of variables proposed by the theoretical literature, parameter estimates can often be far from the "true" parameters of the data-generating process. This problem is especially severe in the case of interwar Europe, as the number of countries for which sufficient (reliable) data are available is extremely limited, while on the other hand the number of possible causes for (slow) growth in interwar Europe is exceedingly large. Given this, one could either refrain entirely from the idea of putting economic theories to econometric tests, or try to narrow the focus of the analysis using some "out-of-sample" information. Such information is provided by a "meta-analysis" by Sala-i-Martin, Doppelhofer, and Miller (2004), who employ a Bayesian Averaging of Classical Estimates (BACE) approach to weight the relevance of sixty-seven explanatory variables as proposed by various economic models. Their results are based on the growth experience of eighty-eight countries for the years 1960–96 and several million randomly drawn regressions. They show that three variables have a particularly high explanatory power for growth of GDP per capita, namely the rate of primary school enrollment, which captures human capital formation; the relative price of investment goods, which captures physical capital accumulation; and the initial level of income. Some geographical and institutional variables also help to explain growth rates, but to a lesser extent.

On these grounds, we can augment the neo-classical benchmark model by measures of primary school enrollment and the investment environment. Enrollment rates are estimated as the share of children of school age (5–14) who attended primary schools in a given country over the years 1920–39, where we use a data-set from Benavot and Riddle (1989). Moreover we will use lagged enrollment rates (ten years earlier) instead of contemporaneous rates, to take account of the fact that primary school enrollment should affect the economy only with a time lag, of about ten years on average, before children enter the workforce. We lack reliable data on the price of investment goods relative to the general price level, but capture investment dynamics by an index based on per capita consumption of steel and cement, which we derived from Svennilson (1954). The per capita consumption data allow us to specify this index relative to the UK with UK 1925–9 = 100. Hence, it contains relevant variations both over time and in the cross-section. Moreover, for some European countries we have estimates of capital stocks from Madsen 2007. Table 8.4 shows how school enrollment rates, investment indices, and capital stocks developed over time. There were apparently vast differences in the formation of human capital and in the conditions for investment across European countries, which should have affected their growth performance.

We can explore conditional convergence in two steps. We first estimate, again for a sample of twenty-three European countries, the relationship between annual growth, income in the preceding year, changes in schooling (with a ten-year lag), and investment using simple OLS. Next, we calculate the counterfactual growth rate, controlling for the varying effects of schooling and investment, and plot this against initial income. The results indicate that European countries did – *ceteris paribus* – converge somewhat over the interwar period, conditional on the differences in human capital accumulation and in investment conditions (see Figure 8.8).

The estimated effect of initial income on growth implies, for example, that on average the difference between a rich and a poor country in 1922, say Belgium and Finland, would be halved after twenty-three years (we estimate a beta of about 0.029; see Barro and Sala-i-Martin 2003, ch. 1). Good conditions for capital investment and rising rates of primary school enrollment could speed up this convergence. In fact, Finnish GDP per capita in 1922 was 47 percent of the Belgian level, but sixteen years later had already reached 74 percent. By contrast, GDP per capita in Greece in 1922 was 55 percent of the Belgian level, which was virtually unchanged in 1937/38. To some degree this can be explained by the fact that both school enrollment rates and investment grew relatively faster in Finland than in Greece. However, our results also suggest that the effect of human and physical factor accumulation on growth was quite limited.

Table 8.4 Primary school enrollment and investment dynamics, 1922–38

	Primary school enrollment rates		Per capita consumption of cement and steel (UK 1925–9 = 100)		Change in capital stock
	1922	1938	1922	1938	1938 as % of 1922
Austria	0.70	0.71	44	117	91
Belgium	0.62	0.73	127	191	125
Denmark	0.41	0.67	75	114	157
Finland	0.26	0.51	37	119	180
France	0.86	0.79	72	93	148
Germany	0.73	0.73	101	229	119
Italy	0.45	0.59	48	79	209
Netherlands	0.70	0.74	79	127	135
Norway	0.69	0.72	81	129	161
Sweden	0.67	0.64	56	168	188
Switzerland	0.71	0.70	63	122	130
United Kingdom	0.78	0.82	54	162	172
Ireland	0.78	0.87	34	86	–
Greece	0.40	0.53	7	37	–
Portugal	0.19	0.27	12	29	–
Spain	0.35	0.36	30	45 (1935)	184
Albania	Na	Na	Na	Na	–
Lithuania	Na	Na	Na	Na	–
Latvia	0.22	0.37	Na	Na	–
Estonia	0.14	0.27	Na	Na	–
Bulgaria	0.41	0.73	9	28	–
Czechoslovakia	0.71	0.66	32	92	–
Hungary	0.53	0.64	30	40	–
Poland	0.24	0.57	23	47	–
Romania	0.34	0.59	17	34	–
Yugoslavia	0.20	0.42	19	29	–

Sources: see text.

Growth accounting and productivity performance

We now turn to a growth accounting framework where we decompose growth rates into the contributions of factor accumulation and changes in productivity, which is useful for exploring the relationship between economic potential and realized growth. To do this for a country, we need estimates of its total stock of capital and good measures of its total labor input, and these data do not exist for all European countries in the interwar period. Madsen (2007) provides estimates of capital stocks and total hours worked for several European countries, which we will use in the following analysis, together with GDP estimates from Maddison 2007. No data on eastern European countries are available, so the following results do not represent the entire European continent.

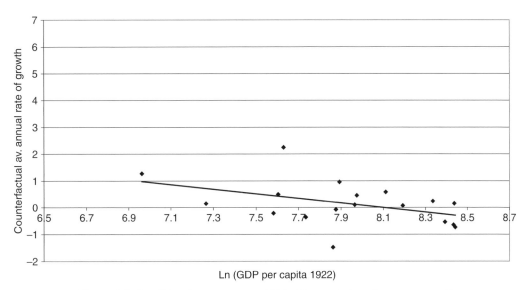

Figure 8.8 Conditional convergence, 1922–38, twenty-two European countries.

As usual, we decompose the growth of GDP into the contribution of changes in capital stock, changes in total labor input, and the growth of TFP according to equation (4). Note that the changes in labor input are measured in terms of total hours worked, defined as total employment (full-time equivalents) times the average number of hours worked in a given country and a given year. All estimates are based on country-specific capital shares, given at the end of Table 8.5, with an assumption of constant returns to scale.

Three results from this exercise stand out clearly. First, the contribution of growth in total labor input to GDP growth was generally small – in some cases even negative – reflecting an upward trend in labor productivity together with changes in labor market policies such as the introduction of the eight-hour working day in Germany in 1918. Secondly, when we consider growth in the 1920s (starting in 1922, when most countries had regained their pre-war income levels), we find that growth rates were typically higher in the 1920s than in the decade before the Great War, and this difference can mainly be attributed to increases in TFP growth. Thirdly, the significant slowdown in growth during the 1930s was driven by a combination of slow capital accumulation, slow or negative growth in total labor input, and low TFP growth.

A different way to estimate TFP is to decompose the growth in labor productivity into its components. Table 8.6 shows the decomposition of labor productivity into TFP and capital deepening according to equation (5).

However we look at it, our measure of TFP is certainly incomplete, for example because we did not distinguish between TFP and changes in human

Table 8.5 Growth accounting for western Europe, 1900–38 (% growth per year), according to equation (4)

1900–14				
	Capital accumulation	Total hours worked	TFP	GDP growth
Belgium	1.08	0.50	−0.22	1.35
Denmark	1.35	0.27	1.76	3.38
Finland	1.10	0.37	0.85	2.32
France	0.55	−0.15	0.60	1.00
Germany	1.30	0.35	−0.08	1.57
Italy	1.80	−0.37	1.86	3.30
Netherlands	0.92	0.65	0.73	2.30
Norway	1.41	0.46	0.84	2.70
Spain	1.22	−0.48	0.80	1.53
Sweden	1.12	0.92	−0.08	1.96
Switzerland	1.01	0.52	0.37	1.90
UK	0.65	0.60	0.21	1.46

1922–29				
	Capital accumulation	Total hours worked	TFP	GDP growth
Belgium	0.86	0.13	2.61	3.60
Denmark	1.17	1.01	2.20	4.39
Finland	1.42	0.70	3.42	5.54
France	1.36	0.40	4.19	5.95
Germany	0.56	−1.72	5.22	4.06
Italy	2.40	0.01	1.00	3.41
Netherlands	0.95	1.14	2.50	4.59
Norway	0.98	−0.04	3.72	4.67
Spain	1.95	0.27	1.45	3.68
Sweden	1.22	2.00	1.78	5.00
Switzerland	0.83	0.18	4.56	5.57
UK	1.53	0.88	0.72	3.13

1929–38				
	Capital accumulation	Total hours worked	TFP	GDP growth
Belgium	0.30	−1.06	0.72	−0.04
Denmark	0.91	1.18	0.12	2.20
Finland	0.97	1.05	1.80	3.83
France	0.53	−2.23	1.30	−0.40
Germany	0.40	0.55	2.01	2.96
Italy	1.12	−0.44	0.88	1.55
Netherlands	0.37	0.12	−0.17	0.33
Norway	1.62	0.24	1.24	3.10
Spain	0.83	−0.29	−4.31	−3.78

Table 8.5 (cont.)

1929–38				
	Capital accumulation	Total hours worked	TFP	GDP growth
Sweden	1.34	−0.14	1.35	2.55
Switzerland	0.31	−0.49	0.74	0.56
UK	1.35	0.73	−0.20	1.88

1922–38				
	Capital accumulation	Total hours worked	TFP	GDP growth
Belgium	0.56	−0.50	1.61	1.68
Denmark	1.03	1.10	1.10	3.23
Finland	1.18	0.89	2.56	4.63
France	0.92	−0.99	2.66	2.59
Germany	0.48	−0.52	3.52	3.48
Italy	1.72	−0.23	0.94	2.43
Netherlands	0.65	0.60	1.09	2.33
Norway	1.32	0.11	2.41	3.84
Spain	1.36	−0.03	−1.60	−0.27
Sweden	1.28	0.87	1.55	3.70
Switzerland	0.55	−0.17	2.54	2.92
UK	1.44	0.80	0.23	2.47

Country-specific capital shares in order of table (from Madsen 2007): 0.37, 0.37, 0.33, 0.38, 0.40, 0.38, 0.32, 0.47, 0.35, 0.33, 0.33, 0.44.

capital via education, and because the measurement rests on some debatable assumptions. Nevertheless, the indicated patterns in TFP and factor accumulation are highly suggestive. The rapid increase in TFP during the 1920s reflects the existence of many unused opportunities to increase the efficiency of Europe's economies at the end of the war, especially along two dimensions: technological change and sectoral change. Many new technical possibilities had emerged during the war, in most cases already prior to the war, and their diffusion across Europe, from one region to another and from one industry to another, started in the early 1920s. Two innovations easily stand out as the most important here: the internal combustion engine and new applications of electricity, which in combination revolutionized mechanical motive power in industry, transport, and agriculture. Table 8.7 gives the production and number of private and commercial cars in use in four leading European car-producing countries and the United States, 1923 to 1950. Table 8.8 shows the changes in total energy production between 1922 and 1950 in Europe and the United States.

Table 8.6 Decomposing labor productivity growth for western Europe, 1900–38 (% growth per year), according to equation (5)

1900–14			
	Capital deepening	TFP	Labor productivity (GDP per total hours worked)
Belgium	0.78	−0.22	0.56
Denmark	1.19	1.76	2.95
Finland	0.92	0.85	1.77
France	0.64	0.60	1.23
Germany	1.07	−0.08	0.98
Italy	2.02	1.86	3.89
Netherlands	0.61	0.73	1.35
Norway	1.00	0.84	1.84
Spain	1.48	0.80	2.28
Sweden	0.66	−0.08	0.58
Switzerland	0.75	0.37	1.12
UK	0.18	0.21	0.39

1922–29			
	Capital deepening	TFP	Labor productivity (GDP per total hours worked)
Belgium	0.78	2.61	3.39
Denmark	0.59	2.20	2.79
Finland	1.08	3.42	4.49
France	1.11	4.19	5.30
Germany	1.69	5.22	6.91
Italy	2.40	1.00	3.40
Netherlands	0.41	2.50	2.91
Norway	1.02	3.72	4.74
Spain	1.80	1.45	3.25
Sweden	0.22	1.78	2.00
Switzerland	0.74	4.56	5.30
UK	0.85	0.72	1.57

1929–38			
	Capital deepening	TFP	Labor productivity (GDP per total hours worked)
Belgium	0.93	0.72	1.65
Denmark	0.23	0.12	0.34
Finland	0.45	1.80	2.25
France	1.90	1.30	3.20
Germany	0.04	2.01	2.05
Italy	1.38	0.88	2.26

Table 8.6 (cont.)

	1929–38		
	Capital deepening	TFP	Labor productivity (GDP per total hours worked)
Netherlands	0.32	−0.17	0.15
Norway	1.41	1.24	2.65
Spain	0.99	−4.31	−3.32
Sweden	1.41	1.35	2.76
Switzerland	0.55	0.74	1.29
UK	0.78	−0.20	0.58

	1922–38		
	Capital deepening	TFP	Labor productivity (GDP per total hours worked)
Belgium	0.86	1.61	2.47
Denmark	0.40	1.10	1.50
Finland	0.75	2.56	3.31
France	1.53	2.66	4.19
Germany	0.82	3.52	4.34
Italy	1.86	0.94	2.80
Netherlands	0.36	1.09	1.45
Norway	1.23	2.41	3.63
Spain	1.37	−1.60	−0.23
Sweden	0.85	1.55	2.40
Switzerland	0.64	2.54	3.17
UK	0.82	0.23	1.05

Country-specific capital shares in order of table (from Madsen 2007): 0.37, 0.37, 0.33, 0.38, 0.40, 0.38, 0.32, 0.47, 0.35, 0.33, 0.33, 0.44.

By implication, these technological changes deeply affected the sectoral structure of Europe's economy. New techniques in the field of electricity raised the efficiency of electricity production from coal and water, while the development of high-voltage transmission made this electrical energy available even in remote parts of the European countryside. Simultaneously, the motor vehicle (as truck, bus, or private car), together with improvements in road networks, allowed the transportation of goods and people between remote areas and the urban agglomerations more cheaply and rapidly than ever before (Svennilson 1954, ch. 2).

Technological change contributed to the increase in labor productivity via several channels. For one thing, lower unit costs of energy and cheaper transport raised labor productivity in all sectors of the economy and thereby raised incomes. Moreover, given the low income elasticity of demand for food, the

Table 8.7 Cars produced and used in four major European economies, 1923–49

		Passenger cars (1000)		Commercial vehicles (1000)	
		Production	Use	Production	Use
UK	1923	71	384	24	259
	1929	182	981	57	428
	1938	341	1944	104	583
	1949	412	1961	218	896
Germany	1923	31	98.6	9	53.5
	1929	117	422	39	155
	1938	277	1272	65	384
	1949	104 (FRG)	352	58 (FRG)	329
France	1923	–	294	–	155
	1929	211	930	42	366
	1938	200	1818	27	451
	1949	188	1200*	98	750*
Italy	1923	–	53.8	–	24.5
	1929	–	170	–	52.7
	1938	59	289	8	83.6
	1949	65	267	21	214

*own estimate.
Sources: Svennilson 1954; Mitchell 2003:

Table 8.8 Energy production in Europe and the United States, 1922–50 (billion kilowatt-hours)

	Europe			United States		
	Hydro	Thermal	Total	Hydro	Thermal	Total
1922	24.5	36.0	60.5	21.3	39.9	61.2
1929	43.7	70.3	114.0	–	–	116.7
1937	65.3	106.2	171.5	48.3	98.2	146.5
1950	112.1	189.1	301.2	101.0	287.7	388.7

Source: Svennilson 1954.

demand for labor in agriculture declined relative to the labor demand of other sectors. The share of agriculture in total employment declined significantly during the 1920s, and continued to decline during the 1930s, though at a slower rate. This sectoral change of employment, out of agriculture into industry and services, had an additional effect on aggregate labor productivity, due to the fact that sector-specific labor productivity was higher in industry and services than in agriculture (see Broadberry 1997 and Chapter 3 in this volume). This also implied changes in the geographic distribution of economic activities across

Europe, for example because improved access to energy and new transport facilities opened up new opportunities to reap the benefits of low labor costs in rural areas for industrial expansion. An interesting example of this is the rise of Bavaria from a backward rural economy to a leading industrial region of Europe, which started in the 1920s (Salin 1928). With hindsight, we know that the economic possibilities opened up by electrification and motorization were huge and would transform every part and region of Europe over the next decades.

The role of coordination failure

Some of the changes that occurred during the 1920s were supported by economic policies. Most European governments saw the need to transform their economies after the Great War to adapt to the circumstances of peace and help their industries to catch up with the technological leaders. Some early "corporatist" organizations emerged in the early 1920s, such as the Zentral-Arbeitsgemeinschaft (ZAG) in Germany that sought to help economic recovery via new rules for collective bargaining, or the Reichskuratorium für Wirtschaftlichkeit (RKW) that aimed at fostering technological and organizational change across the German economy (Shearer 1997). They had some similarities to the "corporatist arrangements" established after the Second World War, which are mentioned among the factors that helped to unleash Europe's economic potential during the "golden age" (see Eichengreen 1996a and Chapter 12 in this volume). In eastern Europe, where agriculture was typically still the dominant economic sector, most governments attempted to implement policies that would simultaneously increase agricultural productivity and help to develop the industrial sector – with limited success (see Aldcroft 2006). On an international scale, the 1920s saw many efforts to coordinate economic policies across borders, especially with respect to the position of Germany after the war. While the level of tariff protection remained high after the war, international capital markets experienced a remarkable recovery with a stabilization of most currencies by about 1926, the de facto establishment of the gold-exchange standard as an international monetary system in 1928, and new arrangements on reparation payments and war-debt settlements with the Young Plan in 1929. However, the fragility of these international arrangements quickly became apparent.

As a counterpart to Europe, the United States had experienced an economic boom during the late 1920s, fueled to a large extent by the vast prospects of economic growth following electrification and mass motorization at home and overseas. When this boom ended in October 1929, the European economy split along the fault lines of protectionism and economic nationalism that were already visible much earlier. Some European countries were quick to swap the gold-exchange standard for a currency arrangement with their main trading partners, while others feared a relapse into hyperinflation similar to the early 1920s (see Wolf 2008). The London monetary and economic conference convened to coordinate a policy response to the economic crisis failed to prevent the further fragmentation of Europe's economy, exemplified by Germany's move to autarky (see Chapter 7 in this volume). This inward movement of economic policies blocked further sectoral change, limited the mobility of capital and labor, and significantly slowed the diffusion of technology (Madsen 2007).

Conclusion

Let us try to summarize the evidence on aggregate growth in interwar Europe. Notwithstanding the devastation of two world wars, the twenty years of relative peace in Europe after 1918 were characterized by missed opportunities. The European economy continued to grow, and growth was fueled by several sources. To start with, many countries experienced a push for modernization that was implied by the process of reconstruction after the First World War but went far beyond that. The new states in eastern Europe made great efforts to modernize their economies and encourage a transition to industrialization, but with mixed success. Many new technical possibilities had emerged during the war, in most cases already prior to the war, and their diffusion across Europe from one region to another and from one industry to another started in the early 1920s. Among the many innovations of that period, the internal combustion engine and new applications of electricity easily stand out as the most important. In combination they revolutionized mechanical motive power in industry, transport, and agriculture, driving the levels of investment and energy consumption. Moreover, many European countries accumulated a large stock of human capital over the last decades of the nineteenth century and continued to do so during the interwar years, as seen in a secular rise of primary school enrollment rates. We showed that neo-classical growth theories need to be modified for the impact of institutions and policies if they are to be useful. We found some evidence for (conditional) convergence as well as evidence that primary school enrollment and the conditions for investment were important factors, similar to broad international evidence on economic growth after 1950. From a growth accounting perspective we found that the relatively strong performance during the 1920s was mainly driven by increases in TFP, which in turn can be related to technological and structural change. However, the vast potential from these manifold sources for growth was poorly exploited due to a failure to coordinate economic policies, especially during the 1930s. Conflict over the redistribution of economic and political power in the wake of the First World War slowed down investment or channeled resources into unproductive employment in preparation for another armed conflict. A much-needed coordination of cross-border economic policies failed in many instances, resulting in an increase in protectionism and fragmentation of labor and capital markets that prevented an efficient allocation of resources across the continent. Instead, the economic policies of the 1930s turned increasingly inwards, blocking further sectoral change and significantly slowing down the diffusion of technology both within Europe and between Europe and the United States as the technological leader. Once these political obstacles to growth were removed, Europe would be ready to enter a golden age of economic growth.

9

Sectoral developments, 1914–1945

Erik Buyst and Piotr Franaszek

Contents

Introduction

In contrast to the relative macroeconomic stability of the pre-1913 period, the era between 1914 and 1945 was hit by a series of severe shocks. The First World War not only caused major devastation and disruption, but also redefined the role of government in economic life. Although the command economies imposed in many European countries during the hostilities were largely dismantled after the armistice, the tone was set for more nationalistic economic policies in the decades to come. The carving up of eastern Europe into a dozen or so independent states out of the ruins of the Habsburg and Russian empires only made matters worse. In parallel, the number of separate currencies and tariff units increased substantially, while the newly created Soviet Union isolated itself from the rest of the world. The fragmentation of Europe contrasted sharply with the large homogeneous home market of the United States. It gave American corporations an unseen advantage in the adoption of high-volume methods in both industry and services.

In the first half of the 1920s many countries in Europe struggled with huge debt problems, monetary chaos, and waves of inflation and deflation. The economic turmoil, in combination with social and political unrest, stimulated the emergence of inward-looking economic policies. After a short period of relative stability in the late 1920s the Great Depression arrived. Massive unemployment, currency disorder, and devastating financial crises aggravated the general trend towards economic nationalism and even autarky. European economic disintegration ultimately paved the way for a new world war.

The main structural changes

Table 9.1 provides an overview of the distribution of the labor force in most European countries over the three traditional sectors of agriculture, industry and services between c. 1913 and c. 1950. These figures must be used with caution due to border changes, differences in the classification of subsectors over time and across countries, and inconsistencies in the treatment of female labor. The case of Russia/USSR is not taken into account because the few figures available are not sufficiently comparable over time.

Despite the succession of severe macroeconomic shocks during the period under consideration, the process of structural change observed in Chapter 3 of this volume continued almost unabated. The share of employment in agriculture in Europe as a whole decreased further, from about 47 percent in 1913 to 36 percent in 1950. The relative positions of most countries did not change much through time. The United Kingdom, Belgium, and Switzerland remained

Table 9.1 Distribution of working population by major sector, 1913–50 (%)

	Agriculture			Industry			Services		
	c. 1913	c. 1930	c. 1950	c. 1913	c. 1930	c. 1950	c. 1913	c. 1930	c. 1950
North-west Europe	**22.5**	**17.7**	**13.4**	**39.3**	**40.6**	**44.2**	**38.2**	**41.7**	**42.4**
Belgium	23.2	17.7	12.5	45.6	46.4	48.7	31.3	35.9	38.8
Denmark	43.1	35.8	25.4	25.0	27.5	33.7	31.9	36.7	40.9
Finland	78.5	69.8	46.6	12.0	15.9	28.1	9.5	14.4	25.3
Ireland	47.5	45.0	33.1	25.5	22.8	30.7	27.1	32.2	36.2
Netherlands	28.6	20.8	19.6	33.1	36.8	37.4	38.3	42.3	43.0
Norway	40.0	35.6	26.1	26.2	26.6	36.6	33.8	37.8	37.3
Sweden	48.3	36.3	20.5	26.9	32.3	41.1	24.8	31.5	38.4
UK	10.2	6.0	5.1	45.1	46.5	49.1	44.7	47.5	45.8
Southern Europe	**50.8**	**43.1**	**40.7**	**27.6**	**29.8**	**30.2**	**21.5**	**27.2**	**29.1**
France	41.0	35.6	31.8	33.1	33.3	32.8	25.9	31.1	35.3
Greece	57.1	61.1	51.3	18.7	18.0	20.7	24.2	20.9	28.0
Italy	55.7	46.8	42.2	26.8	30.8	32.1	17.5	22.4	25.7
Portugal	57.4	52.1	48.5	21.9	19.2	25.1	20.7	28.7	26.5
Spain	66.6	45.5	49.6	16.3	26.5	25.5	17.0	28.0	24.9
Central and eastern Europe	**54.6**	**50.1**	**43.4**	**27.5**	**27.8**	**32.3**	**17.9**	**22.0**	**24.3**
Austria (*)	36.0	33.5	32.9	37.5	32.8	37.1	26.6	33.7	30.0
Bulgaria	82.4	81.9	77.4	8.1	8.2	10.5	9.4	9.9	12.1
Czechoslovakia (*)	40.9	37.5	37.8	37.4	37.7	37.5	21.7	24.8	24.7
Germany	37.1	29.0	21.0	41.2	40.4	45.8	21.8	30.6	33.1
Hungary (*)	59.7	54.8	47.8	20.2	24.9	29.8	20.1	20.3	22.4
Poland (*)	77.5	67.3	57.6	9.6	17.5	23.1	13.0	15.2	19.3
Romania	80.0	80.7	70.1	8.1	9.3	16.8	12.0	10.0	13.1
Switzerland	26.9	21.3	16.6	45.9	45.0	47.0	27.2	33.7	36.4
Yugoslavia (*)	82.2	79.7	66.9	11.0	11.2	18.2	6.7	9.0	14.9
EUROPE	**46.6**	**41.0**	**35.7**	**30.0**	**31.2**	**34.3**	**23.4**	**27.8**	**30.0**

(*) 1920

Source: Mitchell 2003; Prados de la Escosura 2003.

far less agricultural than the rest of Europe. At the other extreme we find the Balkan countries, where even in 1950 more than two thirds of the labor force was engaged in farming. Moreover, in the Balkans the absolute number of people working in agriculture continued to increase until the 1930s.

The share of industry continued to grow, so that by 1950 employment in the secondary sector was roughly equal to that in agriculture. The speed of industrialization differed considerably from country to country, however. In the Nordic countries the share of the secondary sector in employment rose rapidly so that the gap with the "industrial core" – the United Kingdom, Belgium, Switzerland, and Germany – diminished substantially. In eastern Europe some countries experienced a catch-up movement, but the distance from the "core" remained very large. On the other hand, the share of industry stagnated in France, Austria, Czechoslovakia, and Greece.

The largest beneficiary of the relative decline of agriculture in Europe as a whole was the service sector. Several countries clearly did not follow the pattern pointed out in the famous writings of Colin Clark (1951). This author claimed that modern economic growth implied the following stages: first an agricultural society was transformed into an industrial economy, and then a shift occurred towards a service economy. The "industrial core" of Europe indeed went through these phases, but the Netherlands was an early exception to the rule. During the 1913–50 period Denmark, France, and Greece also shifted a substantial share of their labor forces directly from agriculture to the tertiary sector.

Agriculture

General tendencies

An analysis of European agricultural production between 1914 and 1945 reveals three distinct periods with different levels of crop and animal production, reflecting political events and the world economic situation. The first period spans the First World War. The second period is the interwar years, comprising the 1920s, the Great Depression, and recovery until the late 1930s. The third stage was the Second World War. The acreage of arable and tree crops in Europe stagnated between 1910 and 1938 at around 149.5 million hectares. In the meantime the acreage of pasture decreased by 0.6 million hectares – from 82.1 to 81.5 million. The number of cattle and oxen grew from 93.3 to 104.3 million; the number of pigs from 65.9 to 79.9 million; and the number of sheep and goats from 112.5 to 138.7 million between 1913 and 1937 (Federico 2005).

The rate of change in gross output between 1913 and 1938 shows that agricultural production grew faster in north-west Europe than in the south and east (Table 9.2). At the same time agricultural prices declined on average by 32 percent. In 1930 the agricultural workforce in Europe was about 63 million. But the number of workers as well as the percentage of the working population in agriculture varied significantly between countries (Table 9.1). There were substantial differences in the average amount of land per worker (Table 9.3): in several European countries it remained roughly constant or even declined during the interwar period, but it increased in the UK

Table 9.2 Agricultural production, by country (1913 = 100)

	Europe	North-west Europe	Southern Europe	Eastern Europe
1920	75.5	80.4	97.9	59.3
1921	75.3	82.3	96.1	57.1
1922	81.4	86.4	101.8	66.0
1923	84.9	86.4	105.9	73.4
1924	87.0	90.1	102.2	76.4
1925	95.7	93.0	111.5	91.8
1926	94.6	88.8	108.0	95.7
1927	100.6	98.2	108.5	99.8
1928	103.3	101.6	107.0	103.5
1929	108.4	104.9	117.2	108.8
1930	104.1	102.8	104.2	105.7
1931	104.8	107.5	109.5	99.3
1932	102.6	105.6	120.2	90.9
1933	106.5	114.3	109.5	95.5
1934	106.5	114.4	111.0	94.8
1935	107.3	110.4	115.1	100.0
1936	102.7	112.5	94.2	94.5
1937	111.6	108.1	107.2	117.9
1938	112.6	116.0	106.4	111.2

Source: Federico 2005.

Table 9.3 Land per worker, by country (hectares)

Country	1910	1938
Belgium	1.88	1.69
Denmark	5.80	4.82
France	3.84	3.80
Germany	2.50	2.22
Italy	1.41	1.44
Netherlands	3.09	1.67
Portugal	2.91	2.46
Spain	4.34	4.10
Sweden	3.40	3.80
United Kingdom and Ireland	4.47	5.21

Source: Federico 2005.

Table 9.4 Rates of growth in Total Factor Productivity, by country

Country	1910 – 1938
Belgium	0.96
Germany	0.64
Ireland	1.55
Italy	0.42
Spain	1.11
United Kingdom and Ireland	1.17

Source: Federico 2005.

(by 0.74 hectares) and in Sweden (by 0.40). The average annual rate of TFP growth for the period 1910–40 was 1.16 percent (Federico 2005 and Table 9.4).

The First World War

As the First World War progressed, its nature and scope effected far-reaching changes in European agriculture. Military mobilization and requisitioning of farm horses was not compensated for by mechanization, as industrial capacity was diverted to the production of armaments. For the same reasons, chemical industries limited the output of artificial fertilizers, which, given reduced animal stocks, could not be sufficiently offset by natural fertilizers. Theatre-of-war operations caused widespread destruction of farmland, losses of livestock, and damage to farm buildings. All these factors resulted in reduced farm acreage and a drop in crop production (Figures 9.1 and 9.2). As a corollary, farm produce quickly rose in price, which, however, failed to restore a balanced market. Direct warfare brought about an agricultural decline in affected countries (Broadberry and Harrison 2005b).

Faced with the impossibility, during wartime, of making up for the food deficits with imports, most governments resorted to active interventionist practices. Instruments of agricultural policy, while effective in peacetime, proved a complete failure during war. Consequently governments tried to use administrative orders to regulate food prices by rationing sales and imposing a state monopoly. In Germany towards the end of 1914, fixed wholesale prices were introduced for grain; to maintain them, the government resorted to requisitioning. The following year saw the introduction of a state monopoly over grain, potatoes, and cattle fodder. Faced with continuing shortages on the food market and rising profiteering, governments introduced rationing of commodities, some of which were replaced by substitutes. To some extent, Germany's tight nutritional spot was alleviated by the plundering of foodstuffs from conquered territories in the east.

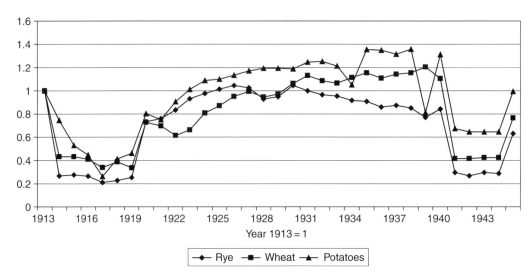

Figure 9.1 Rye, wheat, and potato areas in Europe, 1913–45. *Source:* Mitchell 2003.

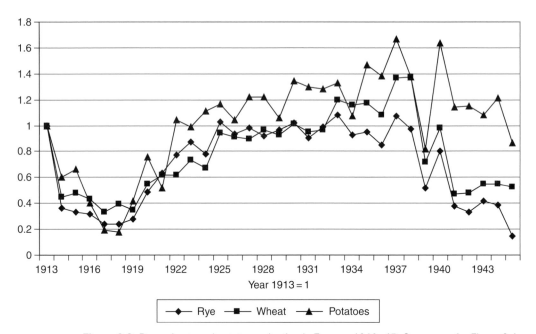

Figure 9.2 Rye, wheat, and potato production in Europe, 1913–45. *Source:* as for Figure 9.1.

Similarly, in France in 1915 and 1916, the government secured a right to control the pricing of agricultural produce, complete with the authority to confiscate grain and flour. In 1917, rationing was introduced for cereal products and sugar, and three "meatless" days per week were instituted. The British government stimulated domestic agricultural output by increasing the arable land area (for example, by converting gardens and orchards to grain-producing fields) and by taking measures to increase land yields. This policy was implemented by a state-ordained increase in official prices for produce. In April 1917 a bill was passed guaranteeing minimum prices for agricultural produce and minimum wages in agriculture. Farmers were supported with supplies of artificial fertilizers, machinery, and livestock. With these measures in place, the government succeeded in curbing excessive price hikes and profiteering.

Things were much tougher for agriculture in eastern Europe. The mobilization of 7.5 million men in Russia badly hit the productive capacities of farmsteads, given their low level of mechanization. The country's cropland shrank from 93.5 million hectares in 1913 to 78 million in 1917, when German troops captured a large area of Russia. Stocks of cattle and sheep declined, although the number of pigs grew from 15.8 million in 1913 to 19.3 million in 1917 (Antisferov 1930).

The interwar period

After the First World War ended, almost all of Europe was engulfed by hunger. All countries suffered from food shortages, as needs were huge. Rural areas directly affected by warfare were devastated. Buildings lay in ruins, machinery was in disrepair, fields had been burned; cattle, pigs, and horses were all in short supply. In large areas average crop yields had fallen due to poor cultivation in wartime. A serious hindrance was the structure of land holding, which was particularly adverse in eastern and southern Europe. That was why agricultural reforms were introduced to alleviate the prevailing disproportionate systems of ownership. The impact of such agricultural reforms on production capacities varied greatly across countries. Within a few years from the end of hostilities, European agriculture was rebuilt.

As a result of the shortage of agricultural produce in Europe, the significant decline in food prices which occurred in many parts of the world in 1920–1 was less acute there. Moreover, positive developments in world agriculture from 1922 helped to rebuild profitability in European food production. Nonetheless the following year still did not see European production recovering its pre-First World War volume. For rye it was 25 percent lower; 15 percent lower for wheat, 22 percent for barley, and 11 percent for oats (Figure 9.2). Pre-war production levels were not attained until 1923–4 (Federico 2004). In subsequent years they rose further, accompanied until the second half of the 1920s by a similar trend in industry. With that, there was a much more rapid growth in crop production for industry than for consumption. This did not apply only to wheat production, which rose greatly. One reason for this was the disappearance from the market of the largest grain exporter – pre-war Russia. The Americans tried to take advantage of the situation by exporting large amounts of grain to Europe. Some European countries also significantly increased their wheat output, among them Hungary, Romania, Yugoslavia, and Bulgaria. At first this was consistent with rising prices for agricultural produce. However, in time the increased supply of crops exceeded the expected demand. In some countries, especially the wealthier ones, the demand for grain was falling as a result of a shift in consumption patterns away from cereal products, especially bread. To offset the drop in revenue, producers responded by increasing production. This naturally led to mounting overproduction, resulting in falling prices by the mid-1920s. Between 1927 and 1929 the drop was 17 percent in Warsaw, 14 percent in Berlin, 8 percent in Paris, and 15 percent in Liverpool.

Meanwhile agriculture's share of GDP declined. In the UK the proportion was 6.3 percent in the first half of the 1920s, but later in the decade it fell to 3.6 percent. In Sweden, in the ten years after the war, agriculture's share shrank from 13 percent to 11 percent. Yet in poorly industrialized nations, agriculture continued to account for a major share of national product. For example, in the late 1920s the Baltic states derived as much as 80 percent of their GDP from agriculture, and the figure was even higher for the Balkans and Romania.

The interwar period was marked by the appearance of an entirely new economic system, including a new type of agriculture, in the form of the USSR's communist economy. When the Bolsheviks seized power they proceeded with the redistribution of private and church land holdings to smallholders or landless peasantry. Approximately 11 percent of land was seized by the state and about 3 percent was assigned to collective farming. Faced with an economic slump of huge proportions, the government introduced a so-called New Economic Policy (NEP) in 1921. Its elements as applicable to agriculture included ceasing to seize the fruits of peasants' labors and introducing a tax system, first in kind, and from 1924 in cash. Farming communities also received farm machinery and credit support. Almost overnight, this about-turn in policy resulted in attempts to rebuild Russian agriculture and restore severed links between rural and urban markets. When it seemed that the NEP had paved the way for successful further development, the government launched collectivization, which was bound to curtail agricultural production (Davies and Wheatcroft 2004).

As the great economic crisis struck, agricultural production suffered a major setback. The slump was more severe and lasted longer than in industry. It was particularly acute in the agricultural countries of southern and eastern Europe (Poland, Hungary, Romania, Italy), where the depression continued until 1935. The situation on world food markets did not noticeably improve until the latter half of the 1930s (Svennilson 1954).

Agriculture at the time of the Great Depression was characterized by steady or even rising output. In western Europe there was a systematic increase in the

cultivated areas devoted to wheat, sugar beets, and fodder crops needed for
animal breeding. Agricultural development was much slower in central and
eastern Europe. If the average level of agricultural production in Europe (other
than the USSR) in 1925–9 is represented as 100, by 1929 it had climbed to 108
and by 1933 to 112. Of course figures for different countries and crops varied.
The growth in production came about as a result of farmers' response to a rapid
decline in agricultural prices. As prices fell, farmers tried to maintain their
incomes and standards of living by producing more. Yet the rising supply
inevitably caused further price drops. As a result, for the same amount of
produce sold, a farmer would receive less money compared to the previous
year. One of the most palpable effects of this was to freeze or even set back
farming techniques, with reduced use of artificial fertilizers and the replacement of machinery by increasingly cheap human labor. The plight of European
villages was compounded by the fact that farm produce was falling in price
more rapidly than industrial goods, a process sometimes described as the
opening of the price scissors. To purchase the same amount of industrial
goods, pay his taxes, pay back any loans, and pay insurance premiums, a farmer
had to sell increasing amounts of produce, up to twice or three times the pre-
crisis volume. Within agriculture, the drop came sooner and was steeper for
arable produce than for livestock. For that reason some farmers switched to
animal breeding (Feinstein, Temin, and Toniolo 1997).

As a consequence of the Great Depression, large capitalist farms became
unprofitable as costs exceeded expected revenues. Crops were left in the fields
or destroyed. Smallholdings, which consumed much of what they produced,
pursued a course of action called hunger supply, whereby peasants had to sell
their crops to get enough money to pay tax or buy industrial goods although
they themselves were suffering from hunger. The situation occurred very often
in central and eastern Europe during the Great Depression, when the gap
between prices of agricultural and industrial goods increased very fast. Many
farms went bankrupt or passed to creditors. In European agricultural countries
this considerably weakened domestic markets. The Great Depression caused a
surge in rural unemployment, leading to further impoverishment of farmers. It
became obvious that nothing short of structural change in the economy could
alleviate rural poverty; the solutions offered included forced industrialization
(in Poland, such an attempt was the creation of the Central Industrial Region).

The situation on world food markets improved noticeably in the later 1930s.
Rural populations enjoyed a rise in purchasing power, but food prices grew
more slowly than those of manufactured goods. In 1934–8, average annual
arable production in Europe (without the USSR) was about $4.6 billion, while
pastoral production amounted to more than $5.6 billion. Total average
European agricultural output made up approximately 30 percent of the world's

agricultural production. In the same period, the Soviet Union's arable output was worth $2.85 billion and its pastoral output about $1.2 billion.

In Europe foodstuffs constituted about 98 percent of total agricultural production. High levels of production were achieved in western European countries – Denmark, Holland, Belgium, Great Britain, and Germany – where yields reached from twenty to thirty quintals of wheat per hectare. The same countries also used the most artificial fertilizers, with all of Europe responsible for about 63 percent of their entire world consumption.

The Second World War

During the Second World War, with a need to feed the army and general population of the Reich, the German authorities at first tried to foster an increase in agricultural production. They aimed to develop the cultivation of industrial and root crops, even at the expense of grain. They also supported animal breeding. But as the demand for food rose sharply, and supplies of farm machinery and artificial fertilizers could not keep up, in 1942 Germany began large-scale predatory exploitation in the conquered territories. A ruthless system was instituted, including confiscation, requisition, and levies. While this policy was especially acute in eastern Europe, its adverse effects were felt in agriculture all over Europe. The result was a fall in crop production. While the average French yield in the second half of the 1930s was 15.6 quintals of wheat per hectare, in 1944 it was two quintals less. Similarly in Czechoslovakia wheat yields fell from 17 to 13.3 quintals per hectare. In Austria at the same time the decline was 3 quintals. Nonetheless, every year more and more produce was shipped from conquered territories to the Reich. This was achieved largely by restricting consumption in the conquered territories by introducing food rationing, banning free market exchange, and keeping incomes low. While in January 1943 the caloric value of German food rations was 1,980, it was 1,765 in the Netherlands, 1,320 in Belgium, 1,080 in France, and in the General Government (part of German-occupied Poland) it was only 855, less than a half the German level (Harrison 1998a).

Great Britain was forced to boost its own farming due to the difficulties of securing food from abroad: potato crops rose by about 80 percent and grain crops by as much as 90 percent during the war. Increases were also obtained in fruit and vegetables grown in small gardens. Pastoral farming fared worse, for while the number of cattle grew, a shortage of fodder adversely affected the number of pigs. All in all, such policies ensured that potatoes and bread continued to be freely available, and average consumption did not differ greatly from the pre-war level. In 1943 in the Soviet Union, grain crops in *sovkhoz* and *kolkhoz* farms were below four quintals per hectare. Although by 1945 the yield had grown to 5.1 in *kolkhozes* and 6.7 in *sovkhozes*, that was still only about 60 percent of pre-war levels.

Industry

The general picture

During the period under consideration, industrial production in Europe as a whole grew considerably slower than in the decades prior to the First World War, but there were large regional differences (see Table 9.5). The Nordic countries and the Netherlands continued to record rapid growth rates as they pursued their catch-up on the "industrial core," a process that in many cases had started in the late nineteenth century. At the other extreme, Belgium and

Table 9.5 Per capita levels of industrialization, 1913–38 (UK in 1900 = 100)

	1913	1928	1938
North-west Europe			
Belgium	88	116	89
Denmark	33	58	76
Finland	21	43	59
Ireland	-	23	40
Netherlands	28	61	61
Norway	31	48	76
Sweden	67	84	135
United Kingdom	115	122	157
Southern Europe			
France	59	82	73
Greece	10	19	24
Italy	26	39	44
Portugal	14	18	19
Spain	22	28	23
Central and eastern Europe			
Austria		56	64
Bulgaria	10	11	19
Czechoslovakia		66	60
Germany	85	101	128
Hungary	-	30	34
Poland	-	22	23
Romania	13	11	11
Switzerland	87	90	88
Yugoslavia	12	15	18
EUROPE		76	94

Source: Bairoch 1982.

Switzerland – two small but highly industrialized countries in 1913 – had fallen prey to relative stagnation. In addition, the manufacturing sectors of the Iberian Peninsula and in some countries of central and eastern Europe displayed little dynamism, despite their low initial levels of per capita industrialization. Thus the process of industrial convergence did not make much progress between 1913 and 1938. It only materialized within north-west Europe.

The First World War seriously disrupted Europe's industrial development from several, often interrelated, points of view. First, military requirements boosted production in sectors such as steel, engineering, shipbuilding, and chemicals. Once hostilities came to an end not all of this increased productive capacity could find a market. Shortly after the armistice the problem of excess capacity became even worse as France and Belgium decided to rebuild their destroyed or dismantled steel and engineering industries on an even bigger scale.

Secondly, during the war the insatiable demand for military expenditure and transport problems prevented European belligerents from supplying their traditional export markets in the normal way. These difficulties encouraged European neutrals and some more advanced overseas countries, such as Australia, Canada, and South Africa, to pursue import substitution policies. Moreover the United States and Japan seized the opportunity to increase their sales to Asia and Latin America. Consequently the European belligerents faced reduced export opportunities after the war, which often gave rise to structural trade imbalances (Wrigley 2000; Broadberry and Harrison 2005a). In these circumstances it is not surprising that the call for protectionism became louder.

On top of these adverse structural elements, the outcome of the war and differences in exchange rate policies profoundly affected relative industrial performance during most of the 1920s. Exhaustion and widespread socio-political upheaval plunged the defeated nations – Germany, Austria, and Hungary – into a deep post-war crisis. Inflation produced a fast but short-lived recovery, since prices soon spiraled out of control. As money lost its vital functions the manufacturing sector once again slid into a sharp recession. In the second half of the 1920s a new recovery emerged. During that period Germany managed to push through an impressive rationalization process in the steel, machinery, and chemical industries. Unfortunately this effort was to a large extent financed via an unsustainable accumulation of foreign debt (Ritschl 2002a).

Austria and Hungary continued to cope with the adverse effects of the collapse of the Habsburg Empire in an increasingly protectionist environment. The case of Czechoslovakia illustrates, however, that the argument should not be stretched too far. After some initial difficulties Czechoslovakia registered one of the most impressive growth rates in manufacturing production in Europe. Admittedly, the newly created state had inherited the most industrialized parts of the former Habsburg Empire, but nevertheless it was a landlocked country surrounded by usually not so friendly neighbors. Innovative production techniques played an important role in the country's success story, as is illustrated by the spectacular rise of the Bat'a Shoe Company. It became a world leader in 1928 by applying American methods of mass production, vertical integration, and modern welfare policies (Teichova 1988).

Industrialization in the Balkans benefited from a general drive towards import substitution. The flip side of the coin was duplication of productive capacity and diseconomies of scale, so that many companies could only survive behind high tariff walls. In some countries artisan output grew faster than factory production. An interesting exception was the export-oriented oil production and oil refining in Romania, but this sector remained an enclave of modern industry. Elsewhere, food processing and textiles dominated the picture. For strategic reasons chemicals, engineering, and metallurgy could often count on state support. Yugoslavia substantially expanded its mining of copper, lead, zinc, and chromium (Berend 2006).

France and Belgium, although on the winning side, registered a low level of output in 1920 as their main industrial areas had been destroyed or dismantled during the war. Reconstruction, however, proceeded swiftly, and by 1924 manufacturing output had already surpassed its pre-war level. Economic growth benefited from the fact that both countries, and also Italy, hesitated to impose harsh deflationary measures in order to restore their pre-war parities. Continuous inflationary pressures undermined confidence in their currencies, so that on various occasions their exchange rates fell even faster than the rate at which domestic prices increased. French, Belgian, and Italian exporters took advantage of the resulting currency undervaluation in two ways. First, they gained market share by selling somewhat below the international price level (usually expressed in American dollars or pounds sterling). Secondly, they increased profit margins, as domestic input prices took time to adjust.

Currency stabilization in 1926 marked the beginning of the end of export-led growth. Although both the French and Belgian franc were pegged to the gold standard below their purchasing power parities, entrepreneurs realized that the time of "easy profits" was fading away. In response they used the large profits of the early 1920s to launch large-scale investment programs to modernize their plant and equipment. The capital goods industries expanded particularly quickly (Buyst 2004; Dormois 2004). Italy's performance in the late 1920s was far less impressive, as Mussolini stabilized the lira at a highly overvalued rate (Cohen and Federico 2000).

The neutrals and the belligerents that were spared large-scale devastation during the war – the United Kingdom and Italy – generally entered the 1920s with a level of industrial output that was at least as high as in 1913. Despite these favorable starting conditions the United Kingdom, Denmark, and Norway suffered from slow growth during most of the 1920s. They imposed severe deflationary measures intended to restore "normalcy" – a return to the gold standard at the pre-war parity – as soon as possible. High taxes and tight credit conditions, however, put downward pressure on domestic demand, while an overvaluation of the currency undermined international competitiveness. Finally, price deflation increased the real debt burden on both governments and corporations.

Nevertheless exchange rate policies cannot be blamed for all evils. The Netherlands and Sweden also imposed deflation, but achieved impressive growth rates in manufacturing output in the late 1920s. Much depended on the structural characteristics and flexibility of the economy. Both countries proved very successful in developing new industries, such as electrical engineering and artificial fibers (the Netherlands) or machinery and consumer durables (Sweden). Britain, on the other hand, faced adverse structural developments. Because of its early lead in industrialization, British manufacturing was still highly specialized, in cotton textiles, coal mining, iron and steel, and shipbuilding. Moreover a very large share of the output of these industries was exported, which made Britain particularly vulnerable to changes in the international environment. In this context stagnating demand, import substitution in traditional markets (India, Continental Europe), and growing competition from the United States and Japan dealt a heavy blow to the British staple industries. As a result, unemployment remained stubbornly high, which in its turn provoked social unrest and impeded structural change (Maizels 1965; Broadberry 1997).

For obvious reasons the newly established Soviet Union was a special case. In 1920, industrial production came to a virtual standstill as a result of an extremely brutal civil war. War communism introduced not only tight government control over the economy, but also nationalization of key manufacturing sectors. Once the anti-communist forces were defeated, Lenin allowed entrepreneurs more autonomy again, especially in the lighter industries. Although this New Economic Policy proved successful, in 1928 Stalin dramatically changed course. He launched five-year programs based on central planning, full nationalization, self-reliance, and forced industrialization. The extraction of agricultural surpluses and forced savings were aimed at speeding up production in the machinery and heavy industries (Allen 2003).

During the Great Depression all European countries – except the Soviet Union – suffered from a substantial decline in industrial output. Germany was undoubtedly one of those hit hardest because of a sudden drop in foreign lending, harsh deflationary policies, and a savage financial crisis. Exploding unemployment undermined the credibility of the already weak Weimar Republic, which ultimately gave way to Nazi dictatorship. Four-year plans more or less structured the rearmament effort, which boosted heavy industry.

Production of consumer goods recovered only slowly as tight regulation kept down real wages. For the same reason the famous *Autobahn* construction programs primarily served propaganda purposes because the Reich had relatively few cars to use them. Exchange controls and autarkic policies completed the picture of an emerging war economy (Ritschl 2002a).

In many other countries, the speed of recovery depended to a substantial degree on the exchange rate regime adopted (Eichengreen and Sachs 1985). Countries that devalued their currencies against gold at an early stage recovered much earlier than those that clung to the gold standard. A typical example of the first category was Britain. It abandoned the gold standard in September 1931, which enabled the Bank of England to introduce a policy of cheap money. Low interest rates stimulated the building industry and related sectors, such as the production of bricks and cement. The consumer goods industries also benefited from cheap money and the continuous extension of the electricity supply throughout the country. Finally, the steep fall of sterling vis-à-vis many continental European currencies gave British exporters a competitive edge, although the effects of this should not be overstated. The Imperial Preference system imposed in 1932 allowed British manufacturers to avoid direct competition with continental Europe (Broadberry 1986).

The Nordic countries, which traditionally maintained strong commercial links with Britain, followed the Bank of England's example and also experienced a strong recovery from about 1933. Sweden complemented low interest rates with a substantial increase in public spending, but the major stimulus came from exports: iron ore – mainly to Nazi Germany – consumer durables, paper, and pulp – mainly to Britain.

The gold bloc – France, Belgium, the Netherlands, Italy, Switzerland, and Poland – on the other hand decided to maintain their gold parities. Loss of competitiveness, deflation policies, and capital flight wreaked havoc and by the end of 1936 the bloc had collapsed. Many of these countries devalued too late to benefit from the general recovery of the world economy in the mid-1930s. Already in the course of 1937 a new recession struck. French industrial output, for instance, never regained its 1929 level. But there were exceptions to this bleak picture. Oil refining recorded spectacular growth rates in the 1930s and became one of the major sectors of the French economy (Smith 2006).

In the early 1930s most central and eastern European countries suffered from mounting agricultural protectionism, rapidly worsening terms of trade, and a foreign debt crisis. Lack of foreign reserves limited their imports of manufactured products, which dealt a heavy blow to the industrial exporters of the area, Austria and Czechoslovakia. Poland experimented with state ownership of a number of industrial enterprises, especially in chemicals, armaments, and steel production. The effort was part of a broader plan to set up a central industrial region between Crakov and Lvov. Yugoslavia also tried to create an industrial heartland around its iron ore fields. In both cases the impact on overall industrial structure and performance was rather limited (Turnock 2006).

While most European economies sank into the mire of the Great Depression, the Soviet Union experienced a rapid growth in industrial output. But the picture varied enormously from sector to sector. Between 1927 and 1940 pig iron production quadrupled and the new blast furnaces emulated best American practice. But the consumer goods sector lagged far behind. In the early 1930s, food processing, woolen textiles, and the leather industry suffered from the collapse of agriculture. At the end of the decade an arms build-up squeezed the civilian economy (Allen 2003).

During the Second World War, all territories occupied by the Nazis were exploited to serve the German war effort. Poland and the occupied parts of the Soviet Union suffered heavily from plunder and scorched earth tactics. Many prisoners of war, and also ordinary citizens, ended up as slaves in German factories. In western Europe, exploitation was less brutal but more effective through forced labor, high occupation taxes, and deliveries of raw materials – such as French iron ore – steel, and chemicals. Due to lack of investment and maintenance, many productive assets were run down. In Germany, on the other hand, the industrial capital stock in May 1945 was one third larger than in 1939, despite intensive Allied strategic bombing (Harrison 1998a).

Developments in certain sectors

In relative terms, coal remained by far the largest provider of primary energy in Europe during the interwar period. In absolute terms, however, coal output stagnated. A first reason was that in the manufacturing sector steam engines were rapidly being replaced by cheaper, more compact and flexible, electric motors. Of course, power plants also used coal, but not in a symmetric way, as hydro-electricity remained important and the energy efficiency of thermal power plants increased by leaps and bounds. Secondly, the bunkering trade suffered from the slow but continuous substitution of oil-burning for coal-burning ships and from the stagnation of international trade. Similarly, in railway transport, electric and diesel traction threatened the hegemony of the traditional steam locomotive. Moreover, railway companies faced increased competition from cars, trucks, and buses. Finally, the iron and steel industry grew considerably more slowly than before 1913 and also substantially increased its energy efficiency (Svennilson 1954).

Britain's coal mining was disproportionally hit by these long-term developments because it was very export-dependent (Table 9.6a). It traditionally supplied most of the bunkering coal; it now faced import substitution policies

Table 9.6 Europe's major producers of coal, steel, electricity, and chemicals, 1913–38

A Coal (millions of metric tons)

	1913	1920	1929	1938
United Kingdom	292.0	233.1	262	230.6
Germany (*)	154.0	140.8	177	186.2
Russia/USSR (*)	28.0	6.7	36.6	115.0
France (*)	43.8	24.3	53.8	46.5
Poland	n/a	31.7	46.2	38.1
Belgium	22.8	22.4	26.9	29.6

B Steel (millions of metric tons)

	1913	1920	1929	1938
Germany (*)	14.3	9.3	18.4	22.7
Russia/USSR	4.9	0.2	4.9	18.1
United Kingdom	7.8	9.2	9.8	10.6
France (*)	7.0	3.1	9.7	6.2
Italy	0.9	0.8	2.1	2.3
Belgium	2.5	1.3	4.1	2.3

C Electricity (gigawatt hours)

	1913	1920	1929	1938
Germany	8.0	15	30.7	55.3
USSR	1.95	0.5	6.2	39.4
United Kingdom	2.5	8.5	17.0	33.8
France	1.8	5.8	15.6	20.8
Italy	2.0	4.0	9.6	15.5
Norway	n/a	5.3	7.8	9.8

D Chemicals (in percentages of the value of world production)

	1913	1920	1929	1938
Germany	24.0	16.0	17.6	21.9
United Kingdom	11.0	10.2	9.3	8.6
USSR	3.0	3.6	5.7	8.2
France	8.5	6.7	7.6	5.6
Italy	3.0	3.1	4.3	4.1
Belgium	2.5	2.0	1.9	1.7

(*) 1913: interwar boundaries
Source: Svennilson 1954; Mitchell 2003.

in Continental Europe and the rise of new exporters such as Poland. But domestic factors also played a role. The sector was highly fragmented, which impeded scale economies and retarded mechanization compared, for instance, with the German coal industry.

From a long-term perspective, steel consumption in Europe continued to grow, but at a slower pace than before 1913 (Table 9.6b). Nevertheless the sector struggled with structural overcapacity. Wartime expansion, reconstruction of even bigger plants in the devastated areas of France and Belgium, and import substitution policies – often financed by governments – contributed to the problem. Downward pressure on prices was the obvious effect. Companies responded to the difficult market conditions not only by mergers, especially in Germany, and increases in productivity, but also by making arrangements that reduced competition.

National cartels were soon followed by the so-called first and second International Steel Cartels. Initially these international syndicates only united the leading producers of Continental Europe, but in the course of the 1930s their British and American colleagues joined in. Their main aim was to restrict output according to a quota system. The system was complemented by a set of bilateral agreements heralding the principle that domestic markets should be reserved for domestic producers. The success of these acts of collusion is reflected in the fact that domestic prices could often be raised substantially above the international level. Governments not only approved this search for monopoly power, but sometimes became heavily involved in the steel sector, for example in Nazi Germany and Italy (Munting and Holderness 1991).

The motor industry was certainly a promising new sector. Nevertheless the introduction of mass production methods pioneered by Henry Ford proceeded slowly in Europe. Consequently, the productivity gap between the United States and the Old Continent remained huge. On the supply side, workers clung to craft-based flexible production techniques to safeguard their autonomy and skills. On the demand side, the European market was fragmented by high tariffs, so there was simply no mass market for cars (Broadberry 1997). As a result, production costs in Europe remained relatively high, which together with lower incomes compared to the USA, explains why car ownership remained rather limited. Despite these weaknesses some positive developments took place. A strong concentration movement considerably reduced the number of European car producers. In addition high taxation of vehicles and motor fuels favored the development of the typical European compact car.

Electrical engineering was another success story. Many inventions of the late nineteenth century were only fully exploited in the interwar period. Major improvements in the transmission of electricity over long distances favored the construction of large-scale energy-efficient power plants. Thus Paris was mainly served from power stations located at the coalfields along the Belgian border, and the industrial centers of the Po Valley used hydro-power generated in the Alps. As increasing quantities were distributed through the same network, unit costs fell even further, which stimulated the demand for electricity from both industrial and household users (Svennilson 1954 and Table 9.6c).

In industry, steam engines were rapidly replaced by electric motors. In parallel the production of generators, transformers, switchboards, and other electrical equipment expanded swiftly. Philips became a very successful international producer of electric lamps. The production of radios and household appliances – washing machines, electric heaters, vacuum cleaners, etc. – also proceeded quickly, but struggled with the same problems as the European motor car sector. Fragmented markets reduced the possibilities of mass production. As a result, many domestic appliances remained unattainable even for the lower middle classes.

The First World War tremendously shook up the chemical industry. Until 1913 Germany held a virtual monopoly on the production of certain organic chemicals, such as synthetic dyestuffs and drugs (Table 9.6d). During the war the Allied countries, especially Britain, launched a large-scale effort, supported by the government, to build up a domestic chemical industry. Britain, for instance, faced embarrassing shortages of dyes for uniforms and pharmaceuticals to treat the wounded. The Allies also seized German patents and factories abroad. After the armistice the import substitution process continued in other European countries, so that excess capacity loomed. Pressure on prices and cooperation agreements during the war facilitated the formation of national cartels. In 1925 the major German chemical firms merged into IG Farben. This move, and the rapid recovery of German chemical production based on new technological breakthroughs, led to a similar merger in Britain whereby Imperial Chemical Industries or ICI was formed. These two giants soon pushed through various international agreements that would largely regulate world trade in chemicals. As with the steel industry, governments often supported these attempts to escape competition and declining prices (Travis 1998).

Services

The general picture

As shown in Table 9.1, employment in Europe's tertiary sector grew rapidly in the 1913–45 period. Although the share of services in employment rose faster in southern, central, and eastern Europe, the gap with north-west Europe remained large. Britain and the Netherlands remained at the top of the ranking, while the share of Balkan countries and Poland did not exceed 20 percent. In this section we will focus on shipping, rail and road transport, financial services, and distribution. Less can be said about personal services. In high-income countries domestic work and religious services continued to decline in importance, in favor of education, medical, and social services (Krantz 1988; Thomas 2004). Education is considered more extensively in Chapter 10 of this volume.

Developments in certain sectors

During the First World War many countries could no longer rely on the international shipping services provided earlier by Britain and some other belligerents. The United States and several European neutrals therefore decided to build up or expand their own merchant fleets. In addition, the Versailles Treaty required Germany to surrender most of its shipping capacity to the Allies. Germany responded to this challenge by quickly reconstructing its merchant fleet. So in the early 1920s world tonnage was much larger than in 1913, while world trade had barely recovered to its pre-war level. Market forces could not solve the structural problem of overcapacity, since many governments intervened through subsidies, preferences, and even the establishment of state fleets. In Britain the shipping lines consolidated into the "Big Five." As was often the case in the interwar period, strategies to limit competition soon reached an international level. The large shipping lines successfully regulated freight rates through the shipping conference system.

Britain was disproportionally hit by these developments and could never regain its dominant role in shipping: its share of the world fleet fell from 40 percent in 1913 to 26 percent in 1939 (Table 9.7). The shift away from coal-fired to oil-fired ships added to Britain's problems. Before the First World War, British vessels bringing grain and other raw materials to Europe could ship British bunker coal outward. As the bunkering trade declined, British ships lost an important cost advantage vis-à-vis Greek and other competitors. In the

Table 9.7 World merchant fleet, 1913–39 (millions of gross tons)

	1913	1920	1929	1939
United Kingdom	18.3	18.1	20.0	17.9
United States	4.3	14.5	13.5	11.4
Germany	4.7	0.4	4.1	4.5
France	1.8	3.0	3.3	2.9
Seven European countries *	7.6	9.0	14.3	16.7
World total	43.1	53.9	66.4	68.5

* Italy, Netherlands, Sweden, Denmark, Norway, Greece, and Spain.
Source: Svennilson 1954.

expanding oil tanker business Norwegian shipowners took the lead. In these circumstances the British merchant fleet became more and more dependent on seaborne trade within the empire (Broadberry 2006).

In most of north-west Europe, the golden age of railroads was clearly over. The length of the railroad network stagnated, and passenger and freight traffic, expressed in passenger-kilometers or ton-kilometers, grew at a much slower rate than before the First World War. In Britain, freight transport even declined because of the problems indicated earlier in the old staple industries. In all high-income countries, the railways suffered from the breakthrough of road transport, especially in passenger traffic and over short distances. Cars, trucks, buses, and coaches provided more flexible transport at ever cheaper prices (Table 9.8).

In most countries the railroad companies were either state-owned or maintained close links with the government. They used their political influence to push through various kinds of restrictive measures against road traffic. Tightening of licensing systems restricted new entry, and high taxes on motor vehicles and fuel raised operating costs. Nevertheless it would be unfair to blame only the railroad companies. Early movers into the road transport business also gained from restricting entry (Millward 2005).

Table 9.8 Europe's most motorized countries (number of motor vehicles per thousand inhabitants), 1922–38

A Passenger cars

	1922	1926	1930	1935	1938
France	5.1	14.3	26.0	37.7	41.9
United Kingdom	7.4	16.9	24.5	33.0	38.7
Denmark	5.4	18.0	22.0	24.9	29.4
Sweden	3.9	12.7	17.0	17.5	24.9
Germany (*)	1.3	3.4	7.8	12.7	20.7
Belgium/Luxembourg	3.8	6.5	12.9	12.9	18.6

B Commercial vehicles

	1922	1926	1930	1935	1938
France	2.4	7.5	9.1	12.0	12.2
United Kingdom	3.0	6.0	8.6	10.4	12.1
Denmark	1.5	5.2	9.0	10.6	11.4
Sweden	1.2	3.6	6.7	8.0	9.8
Belgium/Luxembourg	0.8	5.4	7.2	7.3	9.6
Netherlands	0.4	3.5	6	5.9	6.4

* 1938 including Austria and Sudetenland.
Source: Svennilson 1954.

In eastern Europe the picture looked substantially different. In the early 1920s many countries had to adjust their railroad networks to the new borders. Poland, for instance, inherited three different railroad systems. Once these problems were more or less solved, railroad networks, and usually also railroad traffic, continued to expand. Motor transport remained of limited importance. In many regions, horses and donkeys were still widely used as draft animals (Ambrosius and Hubbard 1989; Turnock 2006).

The First World War and its aftermath seriously shook up the financial sector. International financial leadership passed from London to New York, and within Europe the banking sector was seriously weakened in countries that had fallen victim to hyperinflation. In Germany, for instance, the universal banks had to loosen up their traditional grip on heavy industry. In many countries the banking world responded to these and other challenges by new merger waves. Oligopolistic behavior sneaked in, whereby big banks competed more on service than on price. In this context, increasing the number of branches was a successful strategy to lure new clients. The rise of large financial networks also put a premium on efficient organization, standardized procedures, and functional specialization (Thomas 2004).

Eastern Europe, the backyard of Viennese banks during the Habsburg Empire, became in the 1920s a battleground for British, French, Belgian, and German financiers. These foreign investors did not provide share capital, but granted short-term loans to local institutions (Turnock 2006). In the early 1930s this foreign capital was hastily withdrawn, which wreaked havoc on the eastern European banking system. While governments tried to save the bigger banks, many small ones went bankrupt (Cottrell 1997).

The banking crises of the early 1930s did not remain confined to eastern Europe, but ravaged most of the continent. In order to save the financial system, the Weimar Republic de facto nationalized almost all big German banks. In Italy and Belgium the universal banks were required to split up into deposit banks and holding companies. In the Italian case, many industrial shares held by these private holdings ended up in the hands of IRI, a public holding company (Toniolo 1995). In several countries confidence in private banks was so shaken that deposits never recovered before the Second World War. Governments established public credit institutions to fill the gap, but also to extend their influence over investment flows (Feinstein, Temin, and Toniolo 1997).

Where distribution is concerned, it is necessary to make a distinction between, on the one hand, wholesale merchants who organize a country's international trade, and on the other, domestic wholesalers and retailers. It is clear that the volume of goods passing through traditional merchant houses was hit by the rise of economic nationalism. The overall decline in the degree of openness of the European economies – although less pronounced for the

Table 9.9 Telecommunications

A Telephones per 1,000 inhabitants

	1913	1932
Denmark	42	98
Sweden	39	93
Norway	31	70
Germany	19	46
United Kingdom (*)	16	46
France	7	30

B Radio licenses per 1,000 inhabitants

	1938
France	195
United Kingdom	181
Denmark	176
Sweden	146
Belgium/Luxembourg	126
Netherlands	112

* 1913: Britain only.
Source: Millward 2005.

Scandinavian countries – was only one setback. The growing importance of state trading and of international marketing organizations under the direct control of big manufacturers also adversely affected the merchant houses. Nevertheless it was not all gloom and doom. The rapidly increasing complexity of exchange control systems and the myriad of trade arrangements allowed merchant houses to realize more value added per international transaction.

In high-income countries large-scale retailers – cooperative societies, department stores, and chain stores – continued to gain market share at the expense of small shops. Nevertheless the position of unit retailers remained relatively strong in time-sensitive goods, such as fruit and vegetables, tobacco, confectionery, and newspapers and magazines. During the Great Depression many laid-off workers tried to escape unemployment by setting up small shops or pubs that were often barely profitable (Peeters, Goossens, and Buyst 2005). The traditional *Mittelstand* did not welcome this additional competition in a shrinking market, and called more loudly than ever for protective measures. In Germany and elsewhere the government passed regulations which restricted entry, especially for large-scale retailers (Braun 1990). All these elements contributed to deteriorating productivity.

Population and living standards, 1914–1945[*]

Robert Millward and Joerg Baten

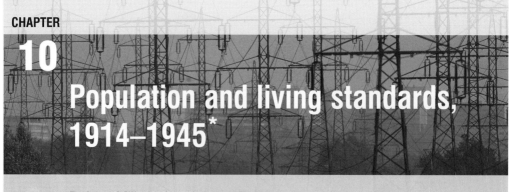

Contents

[*] A longer version of this chapter may be obtained by writing to the authors. Our thanks go to participants in the Lund workshop on population in July 2007 organized by Jonas Ljungberg, to the editors, to Nikolaus Wolf, and to other participants at the Third RTN Summer Symposium, London, October 2007.

Introduction

The 1914–45 period was littered with civil wars, famines, economic depression, population displacements, ethnic cleansings, and World Wars, and yet a clear long-term demographic trend can be discerned. The total population of Europe rose from nearly 500 million in 1913 to nearly 600 million by 1950, a result of mortality falling more than fertility. In 1913 there were still very large differences in birth and death rates across Europe's regions, with the highest in eastern and southern Europe. Despite massive short-term shocks, the next thirty years were marked by huge overall declines in mortality and fertility and by a considerable narrowing of the differences across countries. One task of this chapter is to explain these developments.

A second distinctive feature of the period was the great movements and displacements of population within Europe. The underlying economic force was a large shift from agriculture to industry, matched by the move from villages to towns which is analyzed in a later section. Equally important were political forces linked to the collapse of the three multicultural empires (Ottoman, Russian, Austrian–Hungarian) which, together with the military expansions and contractions of the German Reichs in the two world wars (see Chapter 6 in this volume), led to huge population displacements, ethnic cleansings, and deaths from war, famine, and deportation.

What effect did these massive changes have on living standards? Over the whole period, real incomes rose, as did life expectancy, literacy, and education levels. We will examine how these developments varied across countries and how they were reflected in new measures of living standards, such as the human development index, and in biological indicators such as the height of individuals.

Public health and the transformation of life expectancies

Historical demographers often characterize the period since the eighteenth century as one of a huge demographic transition in Europe. Population growth was initially modest, since high birth rates were offset by high death rates, the latter a product of numerous epidemics, harvest failures, and poor sanitation and medical care. A decline in both rates started in the nineteenth century, but the 1914–45 period witnessed a very steep decline to a regime of low birth and death rates. It was interrupted by the 1940s baby boom, but by the late twentieth century the new phase of very slow population growth was confirmed. These demographic changes were not Malthusian. Fertility fell even though income levels were rising. The fall in mortality was due, as we shall see, as much to environmental improvements as to rising nutritional levels, which, in the Malthusian world, followed subsistence crises.

The long-term decline in mortality started in the second half of the nineteenth century more or less everywhere in Europe (see Chapter 5 of this volume). After a slow start in the late nineteenth century, the decline was steep and pervasive between 1914 and 1945. More than a half of the rise in life expectancy over the 120 years from 1850 to 1970 occurred in the thirty years after 1914. Figures 10.1 and 10.2 plot the death rates from 1900 for five-year periods (in order to display the long-term trends) for a selection of countries with continuous time series.

A wide range of mortality experience existed at the start of our period, with the levels higher in eastern and southern Europe. Deaths in the period 1910–14 ranged from 13 per 1,000 population in Denmark and the Netherlands to 28 in imperial Russia and, on some estimates, over 36 in Turkey. What followed in Russia was quite remarkable. The Russian data have been the subject of much debate but, after careful scrutiny of the sources, Wheatcroft (1999) is convinced that there was a steep fall in the death rate. Despite the prevalence of famines, wars, and forced labor movements, the death rate had fallen to 11 by 1948. The combination of massive short-term welfare losses and a secular rise in life expectancy was, says Wheatcroft, highly unusual. Although the Russian case is dramatic, the mortality decline was also abrupt and late in Germany, while some of the features can be discerned in many other countries and the changes are consistent with the fact that the period is one of convergence. Our Figures are somewhat congested, but that very congestion tells its own story. By the late 1940s many countries had moved into a range of 9 to 14 deaths per 1,000 population. Of course crude death rates mask changes in the age composition of the population. Of note is that infant deaths saw a huge fall and a rate of decline which continued after 1950 (see Chapter 15 in this volume). As Figures 10.3 and 10.4 show, in 1910–14 infant deaths varied from 66 per 1,000 live births in Norway to about 150 in many large European industrial towns and even more in Hungary and the other parts of eastern Europe. Although there was not as much convergence as in the other age groups, infant mortality did exhibit the most precipitous fall of all and was the major element in raising life expectancy. In 1910 life expectancy at birth was about 55 years in Denmark, England, and Wales and as low as 37 years in Russia and probably less than 35 in Turkey. By 1950 a majority of people had a life expectancy of 65 years or more (Shorter 1985; Caselli, Meslé, and Vallin 1999).

In looking for causes, it is important first to note the key medical dimensions of ill health and mortality. At the turn of the century, the major health problems lay in infectious diseases, especially tuberculosis for the 15–64 age

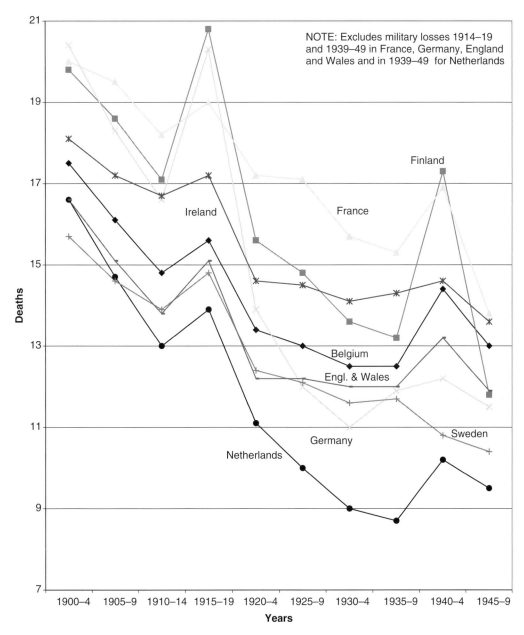

Figure 10.1 Mortality in northern and western Europe 1900–49 (contemporary boundaries; number of deaths per 1,000 population). *Source:* Mitchell (1976; 2003).

group; other diseases of a mainly airborne variety (influenza, bronchitis, pneumonia) for those less than five years old; and diarrheal and congenital defects for infants. The reliability of these disease categories and the associated statistics varies considerably. The data for Italy and England and Wales

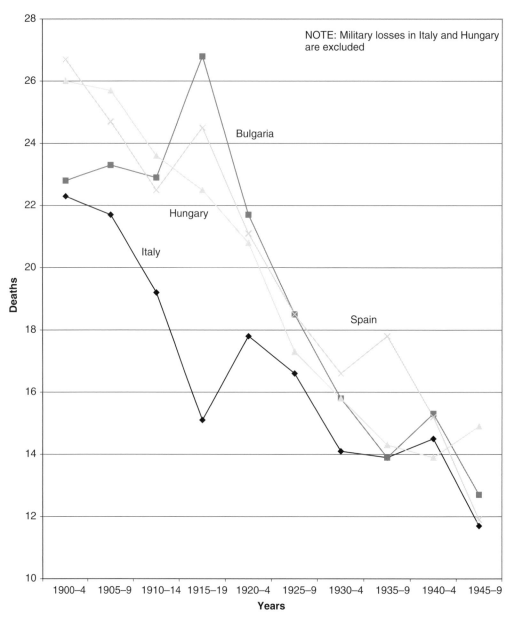

Figure 10.2 Mortality in southern and eastern Europe, 1900–49 (contemporary boundaries; number of deaths per 1,000 population). *Source:* Mitchell (1976; 2003).

are as good as any and they indicate that, of the gains in life expectancy between 1911 and 1951, about one half arose from reduced mortality from airborne diseases and a further quarter from reduced diarrhea, enteritis, and the diseases and congenital defects associated exclusively with infancy and

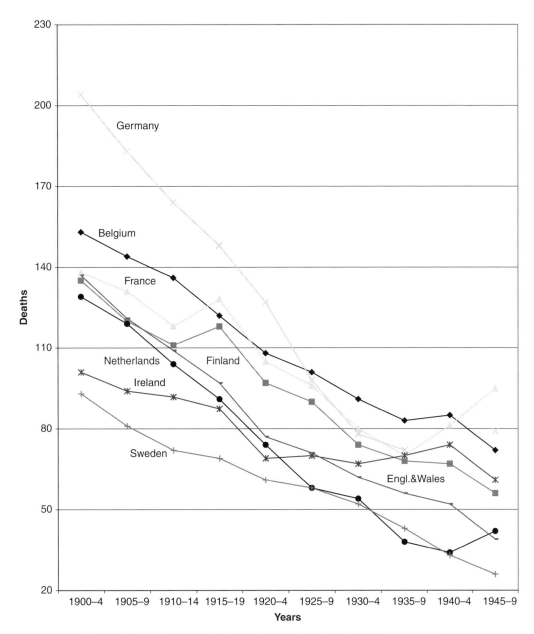

Figure 10.3 Infant mortality in northern and western Europe, 1900–49 (contemporary boundaries; number of deaths of infants under one year, per 1,000 live births). *Source:* as for Figure 10.1.

early childhood. Italy experienced a larger fall of diarrhea and enteritis than England and Wales (where the fall had occurred in the late nineteenth century) and a smaller fall for the other categories. Similar patterns have been documented for many other countries, including the Netherlands,

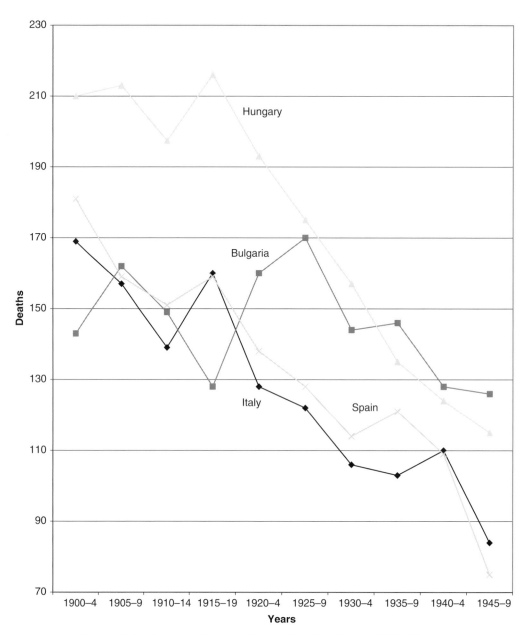

Figure 10.4 Infant mortality in southern and eastern Europe, 1900–49 (contemporary boundaries; number of deaths of infants under one year, per 1,000 live births). *Source:* as for Figure 10.1.

Denmark, Germany, Spain, and Portugal. An interesting contrast is between the Czechoslovakian provinces of Bohemia and Moravia and the economically less advanced Slovakia and sub-Carpathian Ruthenia. As a mirror image of western and eastern Europe, all these provinces saw a decline in infectious diseases and a rise in the "modern" cardio-vascular and cancerous ailments in the 1900–50 period, but the point in time at which the latter became more important than the former was much later in the eastern provinces (Caselli 1991; Mášová and Svobodný 2005).

Very few of these improvements arose from scientific advances in medical knowledge. Vaccines like Bacillus Calmetten Guérin (BCG) and drugs like Streptomycin, for TB, emerged in our period but had little impact before 1945. The same can be said for gynecological care. The major health improvements lay in (a) reduced exposure to disease via better housing, sewerage, and water supplies, and (b) increased ability to resist disease through higher nutritional status, a product of food intake and past exposure to disease. Infant mortality depended also on the condition of the fetus, itself linked to the health of the mother.

The beginning of the mortality decline in the late nineteenth century has generated a considerable literature about the role of nutrition versus public health (cf. Chapter 5 in this volume), but there has been hardly any debate about why the very steep decline and convergence occurred between 1914 and 1945; or why it did not occur earlier or indeed later. It is important, we think, to focus on the coalescence of favorable forces from the first decades of the twentieth century in the areas of sanitation, housing, health education, and counseling, as well as on the very strong, continuing rise in the health of mothers. Improvements in public health required funding and in particular investment in sewerage, drainage, and water supply systems. It seems that, notwithstanding all the rhetoric of the nineteenth-century public health movements, the major spending efforts did not occur until the 1890s and early 1900s, and even later in some countries. These were big capital works programs, the major impact of which would be spread over the next fifty years or so. In many German cities, for example, water quality was still poor at the turn of the century, privies were common, and the spread of water closets had a long way to go. The evidence about the delays is clear for England and Germany and is probably symptomatic of what was happening in other parts of north-west Europe, whilst for southern and eastern Europe these investments came even later (Bell and Millward 1998). An equally important factor for infant mortality was the large increase in support for mothers, which again dates from the early 1900s. Infant health movements swept the continent in the decade or so before the First World War. There were more midwives, childcare centers, promotion of breast-feeding, more brochures and counseling, and all supported by legislation passed in the 1900–14 period (Brown 2000).

The decline of fertility and family size in the late nineteenth century (see below), reduced the numbers susceptible in the home, and this trend was well into its stride by 1913. Then there was the interwar housing boom, which created more space for living and working. In most countries the nineteenth century saw little relief from overcrowded conditions, often exacerbated by poor personal hygiene. Government involvement was largely a matter of regulating standards, though this did mean that most new houses had better access to sewers and water supplies and lower occupancy rates. There was a major housing boom in many countries in the 1920s. An important part was played by municipalities supported by state grants and subsidies and targeting lower-income families, slum clearance, and new houses. In German towns with populations of 5,000 or more, local authority capital expenditure on housing rose from 900 million marks in 1913/14 to 149,000 million reichmarks in 1925/26 and 205,000 million in 1928/29. As a proportion of all municipal expenditure on new construction and property, housing rose from 0.02 percent in 1913/14 to 25 percent in 1925/26 and 23 percent in 1932/33. Even in a very rural country like Ireland, capital expenditure on housing by local government rose tenfold, from £ 34 per 1,000 population at the start of the interwar period to £ 346 by 1936–8. In England and Wales, much richer countries, it rose from £ 67 to £ 1,109. Capital investment in housing was not limited to the public sector; indeed, in some countries the rise in privately financed home ownership exceeded the rise in municipal housing. In the period 1911–51, the housing stock in Britain rose by 60 percent and population by 21 percent. In Ireland the stock rose by only 6 percent but the population was falling, so here again occupancy rates were improving. A final piece of evidence about the enhanced role of public health, water supplies, and housing may be found in the pattern of all UK capital formation over the long period 1890–1945. Aggregate investment in these three key sectors rose to equal that for the whole of UK industrial investment in the 1890s and early 1900s. In the 1920s and 1930s, mainly because of the rise in housing, they became the dominant element of UK investment (Mitchell 1988; Balderston 1993).

The fact that the data for these sectors are readily available for the British Isles and Germany is not an accident, since they were often seen as pioneers in public health. The substantial investment in public health and hygiene during the Weimar Republic has been characterized as part of the creation of an embryonic welfare state, a *Sozialstaat*. The messages about clean, more spacious houses, factories, and hospitals and investment in sanitation, housing, and water supplies were taken on board in the economically less developed parts of Europe. The *zemstvos* (local governments) of imperial Russia, with their emphasis on public health and hygiene, were influenced by the sanitary movement in the west and continued under the Soviets. There was a substantial increase in medical personnel, hospitals, and centers for TB, VD, and childcare in the 1920s. In Spain the improvements in hygiene and health in the 1920s have been attributed to the institution of public health programs. "Social medicine" was seen as combining the social sciences with medical knowledge but, with malaria rampant in rural areas, the Spanish government's commitment to improving the lot of the peasantry had to be assured. New Ministries of Public Health were established in Yugoslavia and Czechoslovakia, where however the emphasis on collective efforts, so necessary to public health measures, had to confront resistance from the traditional private medicine practiced by the doctors. The damaging delays in conquering malaria in Macedonia (this was not achieved until the 1960s) has been attributed to the educational problems of implanting a culture of public health (Stachura 2003; Emmons and Vucinich 1982, Chapter 8; Dugec 2005; Zylberman 2005).

All these factors reducing exposure to disease (and indirectly raising nutritional status) took place whilst food intake and real incomes were on an upward path, albeit not a very steep one. These developments will be discussed in more detail later in this chapter, but in the meantime we may note that both GDP per head and real wages were generally higher in 1950 than in 1913. There were of course great differences across different income groups; the depression of the early 1930s saw wages stagnate and many were unemployed. On the other hand, because of falling fertility and thereby falling numbers in the 0–15 age bracket, the ratio of dependants to the working population was actually falling, so that the need to finance unemployment was, in aggregate at least, offset in part by the smaller needs of the 0–15 year group. A further result of income increases, as well as the emergence of large-scale refrigeration techniques, was that the ratio of meat consumption (and hence protein) to cereals generally rose in this period. Overall however it does not appear that rising real incomes could have been the major element in the huge fall in mortality. Russia is a poignant illustration of the fact that the local food situation (in time and place) cannot explain the downward trends in mortality. The First World War lasted from 1914 to 1917 in Russia. It was followed by civil war and famine 1917–22, another famine in 1931–3, and the period 1942–5 has also been classed as one of famine. Yet the long-term decline in mortality in Soviet Russia was steeper than in most other European countries.

The very large fall in infant mortality was a product of three factors. First was improved support and counseling for childcare already noted. Secondly, the improvement in the physical environment reduced infants' exposure to disease. Third and possibly most important was the health of mothers. The latter, and hence the condition of unborn babies, improved rapidly during the late nineteenth century. The smaller number of births which accompanied fertility decline (see below) probably also eased the health of mothers and hence the condition of babies. Mortality levels fell faster for females than for males in the nineteenth century; and by 1913 female mortality was generally lower than that of males, except for the 5–49 age group. Thereafter the decline in female mortality was so steep that by 1950 it lay below that for males for all age groups. Females were less exposed to direct losses in military combat and less susceptible to alcohol; their rank in family hierarchies was rising as agriculture and mining (with their male-dominated cultures) declined and women became paid employees in the war periods and in textiles more generally.

Improvements in public health, housing, and real incomes occurred everywhere, but in eastern and southern Europe there was more to overcome given their initial high levels of mortality. On the other hand, as we have seen, knowledge of the relevant childcare, sanitary, and public health measures was spreading. Notwithstanding deglobalization in capital and goods markets, the 1914–45 period was one where good health practices were known and spreading. The more benign health environment of north-west Europe was attainable, and most countries had come close to it by 1950. The main exceptions seem to prove the point. The persistent very high death rates in less economically developed regions, such as Albania and southern Italy, have been attributed to deficient sanitary conditions, hygiene norms, and medical support. In Turkey the long-term decline in mortality did not start until after the Second World War. The continuing high level of infant mortality in southern Italy meant that the aggregate figure for Italy as a whole did not fall below 100 infant deaths per 1,000 live births until after the Second World War. Albania was of course a region with all the signs of an underdeveloped country whilst in Italy (because of the favorable attention to the north in reconstruction after the First World War and in fascist policy thereafter), most of the socio-economic indicators showed the south–north gap widening in the first half of the twentieth century. But these regions were the exceptions. For most of Europe, convergence in life expectancy was nearly complete.

Family and work: economic factors in fertility decline

In the first half of the twentieth century, birth rates declined steeply – a collapse similar to that for mortality. The fall was so strong that, despite the decline in mortality, many countries became worried about population stagnation and "natality" programs flourished. In Table 10.1 the data for a sample

Table 10.1 Birth rates, 1890–1939 (births per 1,000 population)

	1890–9	1900–9	1920–9	1930–9
Norway	30.1	27.9	21.0	15.4
Scotland	30.3	28.7	22.3	18.1
Spain	34.8	34.4	26.7	23.1
Bulgaria	38.8	41.4	36.9	27.2
Russia (in Europe)	49.3	47.2	39.4	35.3

Source: Mitchell 2003.

of countries illustrate how the signs of decline were present in the late nineteenth century, and also that the decisive fall was in the 1920s and 1930s. In the early 1900s there was still a wide range of birth rates, from fewer than 30 per 1,000 population in northern and western Europe to 41 in Bulgaria and nearly 50 in European Russia. As we shall see, France and Ireland, for contrasting reasons, were distinct outliers at the bottom end, at 19 and 23. In general the propensity to marry was greater and the age of marriage lower in eastern Europe. In 1920, some three quarters of women aged 20–24 were still single in western Europe while in eastern Europe three quarters were married. In Romania, Serbia, Bulgaria, and Hungary less than 5 percent of the population in the age range 45–49 was celibate, about half the rate found in northern and western Europe (Hajnal 1965).

The leading lights of the well-known European Fertility Project at Princeton University placed the decisive downturn for a large cluster of countries in the 1890s (Coale 1986). France started much earlier. Several countries in eastern and southern Europe did not start their long-term decline until the 1920s: Russia, Spain, and Portugal. A few regions, southern Italy being the best example, had to wait until after the Second World War and, on one estimate, the fertility level in Turkey was actually rising, from about 5.4 births per mother in 1923 to just over 7 in 1930–5 (Shorter 1985).

Changes in birth rates can arise from changes in the age composition of the population, particularly in the number of females in the childbearing age range of 15–49. Young readers will also perhaps need to be reminded that most births in this period took place within marriage. Even if one relates the number of births to the number of women in the 15–49 age group, as we do in the following figures, there is still then the problem that such overall fertility measures may change simply because the numbers getting married change and/or if the rate of illegitimacy changes. During our period illegitimacies remained, with some exceptions, roughly constant at about 10 percent of births. Also the age at which people married had been fairly constant for a long time. It did not change until the marriage boom of the late 1930s and 1940s. For the most part, then, the main changes in overall fertility levels shown in Figures 10.5 and 10.6 reflect changes in levels of marital fertility. The data are for a selection of countries with continuous series and relate to five-year periods in order to draw attention to the long-term trends. They record for each period (e.g., 1910–14) the number of babies a woman would have borne during her childbearing years (15–49) if she bore them at the rate all women did in that period (1910–14).

For many countries in 1910–14, the range was 3 to 4.5 births per mother; it had fallen to about 2.5 in the late 1930s. This is a fall of about 40 percent, with distinct signs of convergence: the more rapid decline in marital fertility in eastern and southern Europe was reinforced, in terms of convergence, by a rise in marriage rates in northern and western Europe from the late 1930s. That marriage boom raised the central range of overall fertility levels to about 2.8 children by the 1940s. Conditions of war and reconstruction helped, but this baby boom was a temporary phenomenon and the fertility levels of the 1930s proved to be a better indication of twentieth-century trends. Fertility levels had fallen, in some countries, to only about two children per mother in the 1930s, as they were to do in the latter part of the twentieth century. Allowing for child deaths, that meant a reproduction rate less than 2, that is, below that necessary to maintain the population, in the absence of wars, immigration, etc.[1] A rough calculation suggests that in 1900 the death rates were such that the reproduction rate needed to sustain a population was about 3.4 children, a figure that, with death rates themselves declining, fell to 2.8 just before the First World War, 2.5 in the 1920s, 2.4 in the 1930s, and about 2.1 in the second half of the twentieth century. On that basis, the time period when each country first hit the decisive bottom line was (ignoring the war years) as follows:

Pre-1914: France
1920–9: Austria, Germany, Sweden, Switzerland, UK
1930–9: Belgium, Czechoslovakia, Denmark, Norway.

For the rest of Europe it was much later – from the 1960s onwards. Of course, in several western European countries there was a marriage and baby boom from the 1940s, linked in part to the Second World War, and this raised reproduction rates above the target level; but from the 1970s the previous patterns emerged. In our period, 1914–45, low rates led to worries in Denmark about the approach of "extinction." In fascist Germany the nation was deemed to be under threat as the fertility level fell below 2 in the early 1930s, but, allowing for

---

[1] Note that it is common for demographers to focus on the "gross reproduction rate" which is similar to the fertility measure in Figures 10.5 and 10.6 but counts only female births, so that the benchmark net reproduction rate (the gross rate less the expected deaths of females up to age 49) is 1 (unity). The rough calculations in the text for sustaining reproduction rates are based on Chesnais 1999 and on age-specific female death rates in the UK.

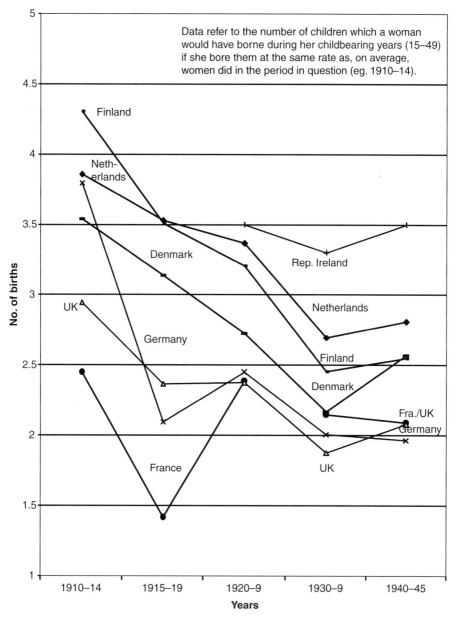

Figure 10.5 Fertility in northern and western Europe, 1910–45 (contemporary boundaries; average number of births per woman aged 15-49). *Source:* Chesnais (1999, p. 106). The entries for Republic of Ireland and the UK 1910–14 (which excludes S. Ireland) are estimates.

mortality, the reproduction rate had actually fallen below 2 in 1922. Natality programs flourished in many countries, though the exaltation of motherhood and family life took a racist tone in Germany. Aryans were encouraged to propagate but not Jews and Slavs.

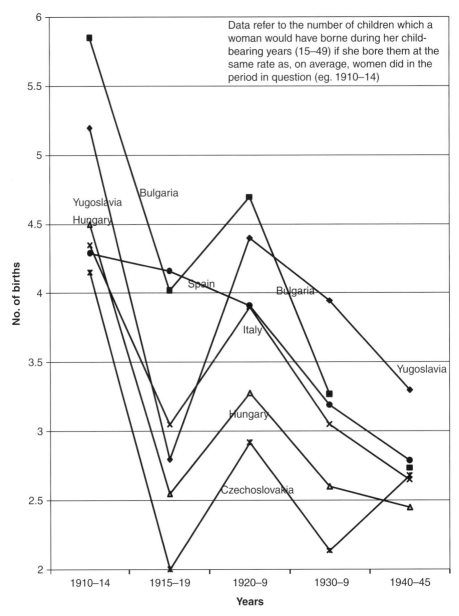

Figure 10.6 Fertility in southern and eastern Europe, 1910–45 (contemporary boundaries; average number of births per woman aged 15-49). *Source:* as for Figure 10.5. The entries for Czechoslovakia 1914–19, Italy 1910–39, and Yugoslavia 1910–19 and 1940–5 are estimates.

How can one account for the huge fall in fertility from 1914 to 1945 and the tendency to convergence? Before looking at the economic issues, it is important to recognize that the fertility decline was strongly conditioned by socio-cultural factors. This is not surprising, in that family size was affected by the age of marriage and by birth control practices within marriage. The decline in fertility in this period is often termed "parity specific" in that it involved controlling family size after some target number of children had been achieved (Coale 1986). Unlike the involuntary control that occurs during breast feeding and owing to wars etc., it required a willingness to use contraceptive techniques. Demographers have agreed that there was nothing new here, in that *coitus interruptus* and abstinence had been used for a long time, and high-quality inexpensive condoms were apparently widely available in, for example, Germany by the early twentieth century. It was the willingness of adults to use these methods that was important, and recent interview evidence from old people suggests that many of the negotiations between partners were tacit and with uncertain aims (Fisher 2000; Guinanne 2003).

In sum, we might expect fertility to decline more rapidly in middle-class and non-catholic areas, and to be enhanced by the spread of family planning programs and increases in educational enrollment and literacy rates. At the same time, the pace of decline, its spread and convergence, were strongly determined by economic forces. We suggest that a coalescence of four forces accounts for the great decline in average fertility (roughly 40 percent over the thirty years 1914–45) and the convergence of levels by the late 1940s. First is the fact that as mortality declined, a given target family size could be achieved by a smaller number of births. The crucial long-term decline in infant mortality started in the early 1900s, by which time child mortality had been falling in many countries for some thirty years, enough experience to trigger off commitments to a smaller target number of births. In England and Wales, for example, in 1871 there were 72 deaths per 1,000 boys less than five years old, a figure that had fallen to 47 by 1911 and continued thereafter to fall to 23 in 1926 and to 7 in 1950. Similar patterns of child mortality have been recorded in France, Sweden, Norway, Germany, and Castile in Spain. The experience of the two outliers reinforces the point. If French families had the same target family size as other European families, then, given that they already had relatively low fertility levels by the end of the nineteenth century, we would expect adjustments to the mortality decline to be the smallest of all. That is what happened – France experienced the lowest decline in fertility between 1914 and 1945, and by 1950 it was no longer an outlier. Ireland also showed only a small decline in fertility. This was no doubt due in part to strong catholic traditions, but it should also be noted that its relatively healthy rural expanses meant there were only 38 male child deaths per 1,000 in 1871 and it was not until 1926 that the recorded levels in Ireland, England, and Wales converged at 23. Since, finally, the decline in mortality was steepest of all in many eastern European countries, that would make some contribution to inducing faster falls in fertility in these countries and hence to convergence.

The second key factor in 1914–45 was the large structural change in the European economies which reduced the significance of sectors like agriculture, cottage industry, and outwork, where the labor value of children was high and the merging of work and home made good economic use of mothers' time. Shifts out of these sectors to service employment and factories reduced the labor value of children and raised the time cost of rearing them. A key indicator here is the percentage of the male labor force in agriculture. There were huge differences in 1911, matching some of the differences in fertility levels. Agriculture's share ranged from 11 percent in Britain and 24 percent in Belgium to over 65 percent in Poland, Finland, Romania, Bulgaria, Russia, Turkey, and Serbia. The large fall over the 1911–50 period was accompanied by some convergence, such that the major bunching by 1950 was of countries whose agricultural share lay between 20 percent and 40 percent. Of note are the large declines in Austria, Russia, Finland, and Poland, which also saw some of the largest declines in fertility. The modest declines in the agricultural sectors of southern Italy and southern Spain were matched by their modest declines in fertility. Turkey lost 20 percent of its population during the First World War, including large numbers of urban dwellers, and was thereby more rural after the war than before.

Thirdly, there is evidence of increasing participation of females in the labor market, raising the cost of children in terms of mothers' wages and use of time. Female employment was always high in textiles in the late nineteenth century; the decline in fertility was noticeably early in the Czech lands of Bohemia, a big textile area, and was rapid and substantial in the English textile towns (Millward and Bell 2001). In Turkey, over half the textile labor force in the 1930s was female; it was an urban-based industry and fertility was distinctly lower in urban areas. Employment in secretarial, teaching, and other service jobs rose throughout Europe in the interwar period. The late 1930s saw a clearly rising number of women in full-time employment in Germany. Data for married females in Britain indicate a labor market participation rate of 12 percent for those aged 15–24 in 1911, and this rose to 18.7 percent by 1931 and 36.6 percent by 1951. For those aged 25–64 it rose from 9.7 percent in 1911 to 10.0 percent in 1931 and 22.5 percent by 1951, much of which could have been the effects of war (Matthews, Feinstein, and Odling-Smee 1982, Table C.3). An interesting case is southern Italy, where in the first half of the twentieth century female paid employment actually fell (because of a decline in textiles and owing to fascist policy), providing an additional element in the very slow decline in fertility levels.

The fourth factor was the growing awareness of developments in family planning; an important element here was the rising literacy rates in eastern and southern Europe and rising school enrollments generally. Literacy rates were already 90 percent or more in northern and western Europe in 1913. In Spain the rate was only 52 percent, in Finland 59 percent, Italy 62 percent and Austria 66 percent. These were all countries with fertility levels of four births or more per mother. By 1950 the literacy rates were over 80 percent, in Finland 90 percent and in Austria 99 percent. The relatively low levels of literacy still found in Turkey (32 percent), Portugal (56 percent), Yugoslavia (45 percent), and Albania (46.2 percent) were reflected in their fertility levels, which were the highest in Europe in 1950 (Crafts 1997). Fertility levels also remained high in catholic regions such as Ireland and parts of the Netherlands, which witnessed very strong campaigns against family planning. Ireland and Portugal still had relatively low income levels and saw much emigration. Ireland saw a strong increase in educational enrollments in our period, but many young people emigrated, leaving behind a population containing many men and women who did not marry until their forties.

Ireland was in fact a single outlier within western Europe in still having a very low marriage rate by 1950. The marriage boom in western Europe from the 1930s was a major break with the past. For centuries the age of marriage in western Europe, which fluctuated in response to economic conditions, had not shown a decisive long-term trend, upwards or downwards. The early age of marriage in eastern Europe characterized by Hajnal (1965) as a region to the east of a line from Trieste to St. Petersburg – was associated with a culture of extended families, though its origins may have lain in the relative abundance of land. The nuclear family household was more characteristic of western Europe, and the economic independence with which it was associated required couples to have a good prospect of an independent income. A large family size threatened family income per head, and the traditional method of safeguarding that income was by delayed marriage. It seems likely that the decisive shift to earlier marriages in western Europe from the 1930s, although it followed the world depression, was a consequence of the new willingness and ability to control fertility within marriage. This is supported by evidence from as early as the 1860s of a fertility decline in some departments in France being followed by rises in nuptiality in those same departments (Watkins 1986). The number of people who got married in 1913 varied from 10 per 1,000 population in Ireland to 18 in Hungary and Romania. Such marriage rates rose decisively in Scandinavia, Austria, the British Isles, and the Netherlands, and by the 1940s many countries were in the range 16–21. The rates in eastern Europe were somewhat higher but, despite a slight rise, Ireland was still an outlier (together with Greece), with only 11 persons per 1,000 population getting married in 1950.

Economic migration

The most striking feature of population change in this period was not so much its growth over time as movements within Europe. The population increase was modest when compared to the rise in the late nineteeth century, especially since the large overseas emigration of that century petered out in the face of immigrant quota restrictions in the USA from the 1920s and of the economic depression of the 1930s. Russia, Yugoslavia, and the rest of eastern Europe suffered most from the two world wars, but did see their population rise by nearly 40 million. In north-west Europe it rose by slightly more. The remaining 20 million increase in southern Europe constituted the largest proportionate change. Italy, Spain, Portugal, and Greece all experienced some decline in fertility, but it remained higher than in the rest of Europe.

The most harrowing dimension of migration was the forced movements associated with population displacement and ethnic cleansing which were themselves closely linked to the political impact of the two world wars (see Chapter 6 in this volume). Here we shall focus on economic migration, which, we should emphasize from the start, was not primarily directed to permanent agricultural employment. Some people from northern Italy did settle in south-west France but they were the exception. There were many agricultural settlement and colonization schemes promoted by national governments – Germany, Poland, Yugoslavia, Russia – but they all failed. The key driving forces in economic migration were industrialization and the growing gap in income levels between the Americas and Europe. This gap had induced a peak overseas emigration rate of over one million persons per annum in the first decade of the twentieth century (Table 10.2). The highest rates were in Italy, where the underdeveloped south was the main source; similar push factors operated in Ireland, Portugal, and Spain. Britain was also a major source of emigration both to the Americas and to the Commonwealth (Canada, Australia, New Zealand, etc.) and this was given an extra boost by the support provided in the 1922 Empire Settlement Act. Latin America continued to welcome immigrants and 3 million arrived between 1921 and 1940. For many Europeans, however, the USA's 1921 and 1924 Quota Laws were a body blow. They limited immigration to 0.16 million persons per annum, and its allocation across countries to the national origins of the US population, thereby effectively discriminating against Italy, Russia, and Poland. Whilst 12.4 million Europeans entered the USA between 1901 and 1921, this fell to 2.8 million between 1921 and 1940 (Faron and George 1999). Moreover, the nationalistic policies of Germany and Italy made for active discouragement of emigration. The exceptions were Jews, who were allowed to move or, if they were not, escaped – the main non-economic overseas migration of the interwar period.

Table 10.2 Overseas emigration from Europe, 1901–50 (annual average, 1,000 individuals)

	1901–10	1911–20	1921–30	1931–40	1941–50
Italy	361.5	219.4	137.0	23.5	46.7
Britain & Ireland	315.0	258.7	215.1	26.2	75.5[a]
Austria	111.1[b]	41.8[b]	6.1	1.1	na
Spain	109.1	130.6	56.0	13.2	16.6
Russia	91.1	42.0	na	na	na
Portugal	32.4	40.2	99.5	10.8	6.9[c]
Sweden	32.4	8.6	10.7	0.8	2.3
Germany	27.4	9.1	56.4	12.1[d]	61.8[e]
Poland	na	na	63.4[f]	16.4[g]	na
Norway	19.1	6.2	8.7	0.6	1.0[a]
Finland	15.9	6.7	7.3	0.3	0.7
Denmark	7.3	5.2	6.4	10.0	3.8
France	5.3	3.2	0.4	0.5	na
Switzerland	3.7	3.1	5.0	4.7	1.8[h]
Belgium	3.0	2.1[i]	3.3	2.0	2.9
Netherlands	2.8	2.2	3.2	0.4[d]	7.5[a]

[a] 1946–50.
[b] Austria–Hungary.
[c] Includes emigration to European countries 1941–9.
[d] 1932–6.
[e] West Germany.
[f] Incomplete data.
[g] 1931–8.
[h] Includes emigration to European countries 1941–4.
[i] Excludes 1913–18.
Source: Mitchell 2003.

The major economic opportunities for emigration in the interwar period therefore lay in the industrializing regions of Europe, and into them large numbers flowed from rural areas in the same countries or from other European countries, with only a small trickle of non-European immigrants. The 1920s was an especially active decade, but the world depression of the 1930s reduced the opportunities in urban areas. Some idea of the size of the shift may be given by a crude calculation that the share of the male labor force in agriculture over all Europe fell from about 55 percent in 1910 to 40 percent in 1950. Given the total European population figures recorded earlier, rural areas would have had over 80 million more inhabitants in 1950 if the agricultural share had remained at 55 percent; over one half is accounted for by the shift to industrial employment in Russia.

De Santis and Livi Bacci (2005) have shown that in Italy the tendency to emigrate from any given region was greater, the larger was the share of agriculture in that region's economy and the lower was output per head.

There is little doubt that this applied to Europe generally. The general movement was from the south and east to the west, typified by what happened in Czechoslovakia. The net outflow in 1921–30 from the eastern provinces was 1.2 million from Slovakia and 0.15 million from Carpathian Ukraine, while the industrialized western province of Bohemia had a net inflow of 0.03 million, rising to 0.33 million in the 1930s (Kulischer 1948). For Italy, the industrial centers in the north, such as Milan and Turin, replaced the USA as the destination for emigrants from the south, in the same way as Britain became the main destination for the Irish, and Spain also saw a massive shift from the south and west to the Basque area, Catalonia, and the center. Even France, one of the least urbanized countries in north-west Europe, saw the share of its population living in villages fall from 56 percent in 1911 to 45 percent in 1951. In 1911 only 27 percent of those aged forty-five were born in a different department from the one where they lived; by 1932–6 it was 37 percent. The main destinations were the Ile de France and other industrial areas into which the net inflow was about 1 million persons during the years 1920–31. Within Poland, there was considerable movement in the 1920s from the center and south to western regions which promised access to the sea and industry. In 1918–21 some 0.9 million moved from former Russian and Austrian Poland to the (former German) western regions of Poznan and Pomerania, where "Polonization" was more successful than the attempt at Germanization had been in the years before the First World War. In the 1930s, with urban outlets and overseas emigration closed, many central and southern areas of Poland were seen to be overpopulated, with 79 persons per square kilometer, about double the density of France.

Nor were the migrations limited to transfers within countries. There had always been movements of seasonal agricultural labor across the French, German, and Russian borders, but industry now attracted those willing to stay. The main emigrants were from Poland, Italy, the Balkans, Russia, Spain, and Portugal, and the main destinations were northern France, the Ruhr, and ports like Rotterdam and Hamburg. In Germany in 1914 there were already half a million Poles, Ukrainians, and Byelorussians, accounting for 90 percent of the foreign labor force. They reinforced the internal rural exodus which in the 1930s saw the armament factories emerge as an important destination. From 1935 they were being built in the safer central zone and in the Berlin suburbs. By that time, with unemployment rising, new immigrant labor was being curtailed, though in 1939 there were still half a million foreign workers. However, the most striking feature of the interwar cross-border economic migration was the flow to France. Faced with significant war losses and a long prior history of stationary population levels, it opened its doors to foreign labor (though entry permits were required). The emigrants entered mining, building, chemicals, steel, and public works; over 60 percent of the labor in the Longwy steelworks in 1929 was foreign. Some 0.6 million Poles entered in the 1920s and up to 0.4 million Spaniards. Residents of foreign origin in France rose by 1.7 million from 1911 to 1931, by which time they totaled 3.3 million or 7.9 percent of the French population (Bardet 1999).

Changes in income and human development

In the last sections of our survey, we will consider how all these developments affected people's welfare. We use three different measures of welfare development: (1) GDP growth as a proxy for purchasing power increase, (2) the Human Development Index (HDI) as a more comprehensive measure to include life expectancy and education, (3) human stature as an indicator of the quality of nutrition and health. Mapping these indicators will offer an overview of a large number of European countries simultaneously.

The increase in purchasing power during this period contains a number of paradoxes. Given the terrible destruction of the two world wars, the Great Depression after 1929, and the economic disintegration during the whole interwar period, we would not expect much growth in purchasing power. But national incomes did grow substantially and Foreman-Peck (1983) has argued that the wide diffusion of new basic technologies such as electricity and the internal combustion engine, while already developed before the First World War, still led to income gains from their application in many fields. Moreover (as we saw above), Europe benefited during this period from the demographic gift of having a modest share of the population who were children or elderly persons who were not working.

The typical measure of purchasing power is GDP per capita. The UK was clearly the richest country in Europe in 1913, with almost $ 5,000 measured in 1990 dollars (Maddison 2001). In the next group, between $ 3,500 and $ 4,500, we find Switzerland, Belgium, the Netherlands, Denmark, Germany, France, and Austria. The poorest countries were those in the Balkans, Turkey, and the Russian Empire. The growth of GDP per capita between 1913 and 1938 is displayed in Figure 10.7. In the map, we have recalculated all contemporary statistics to match modern borders. This makes the maps more easily readable for the modern reader, and facilitates comparisons of pre- and post-First World War.[2]

---

[2] Before the war "Austria–Hungary" was a large empire consisting of southern Poland, the south-western Ukraine, north-western Romania, Slovakia, the Czech lands, Hungary, Austria, and the northern parts of later Yugoslavia (and a small part of Italy). The Russian Empire included Finland and parts of today's Poland. The German Empire stretched to today's territories of Poland, Russia (East Prussia, eastern part), part of Denmark, and France (and small parts of Belgium and of later Czechoslovakia). Ireland was still part of the UK before the First World War, and the Ottoman Empire still existed. In the interwar period, Czechoslovakia was one country, as was Yugoslavia, and Poland was situated further east compared to today's position. Germany still had some eastern territories such as Silesia, East Prussia, and Pomerania.

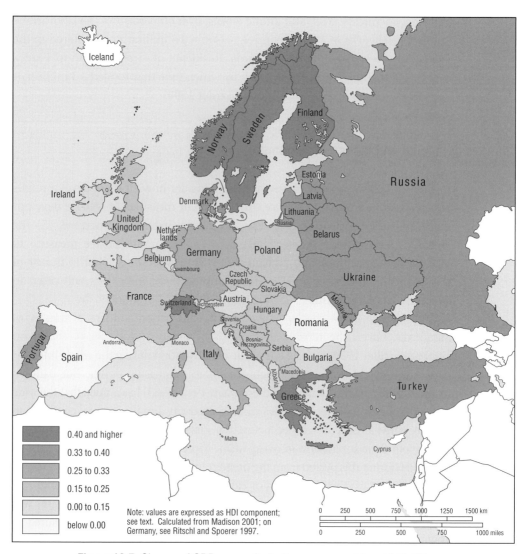

Figure 10.7 Change of GDP per capita in European countries, 1913–38.

In Figure 10.7, GDP in 1990 dollars is measured as an index, making it comparable with the HDI maps discussed later; it ranges between 0 and 1.[3] Note that both Germany (under the Nazi government in 1938) and parts of the Soviet Union may not have provided entirely reliable statistics. In most countries the change of purchasing power was positive between 1913 and 1938. Only Spain, which experienced a civil war in 1936–9, and Romania, which suffered heavily from rural overpopulation and unsuccessful reforms, showed a decline

---

[3] 0 is set equal to the log of $ 100 and 1 equals the log of $ 40,000.

in GDP per capita between 1913 and 1938 (Feinstein, Temin, and Toniolo 1997). Very modest were the increases in Bulgaria, Austria, Belgium, and Ireland. The strongest growth can be found in Scandinavia, Switzerland, and Greece; the countries of the Soviet Union, Turkey, and Portugal also performed relatively well, as far as we can tell from their GDP statistics. The latter three countries were converging from initially quite low levels of purchasing power.

Another way to measure living standards is by the Human Development Index (HDI). The idea behind this is to include life expectancy and education levels as well as purchasing power. As the aim of this chapter is to bring living standards and population development together, this index is particularly attractive. Its calculation takes into account minimum and maximum levels of three components:

(a) GDP per capita in 1990 dollars, ranging from $ 100 to $ 40,000
(b) Life expectancy, ranging from 25 years to 85 years
(c) Primary school enrollment and literacy, from 0 to 100 percent.

There is a debate about whether the HDI should include declining marginal utility effects of GDP per capita – that is, it is clear that 100 additional dollars for a person close to starvation provides more additional utility than 100 additional dollars for a millionaire. As a compromise, the most recent version of the HDI employs (as we do) the log of GDP per capita in order to account for those effects. Another issue is whether political freedom, human and gender-specific rights and capabilities, inequality, environmental quality, etc. should also be included, and a number of extended HDI versions have been suggested. However, given the scarcity of historical data and a preference for simplicity, we will present the standard form of the HDI in the following, and discuss the stature indicator separately below (the only difference being that our HDI is calculated on the basis of schooling only, not literacy plus schooling).

What were the major changes in educational spending during the interwar period? Germany continued to have a strong educational sector in the 1920s, but the Nazis changed the contents in the 1930s to serve their political aims, making previous progress obsolete. The Soviet Union pursued similar aims, but given the low level of public schooling before the First World War, its record of educational achievements still looks impressive. Some of the previous parts of the Habsburg Empire, such as Hungary and western Romania, were not able to keep the level of primary schooling when they experienced serious economic crisis in the 1920s (Lindert 2004). Finally, the southern European world was quite divided. Italy, for example, achieved remarkable progress in education (relative to low pre-First World War levels), but the Portuguese state did not invest much in education during the 1920s.

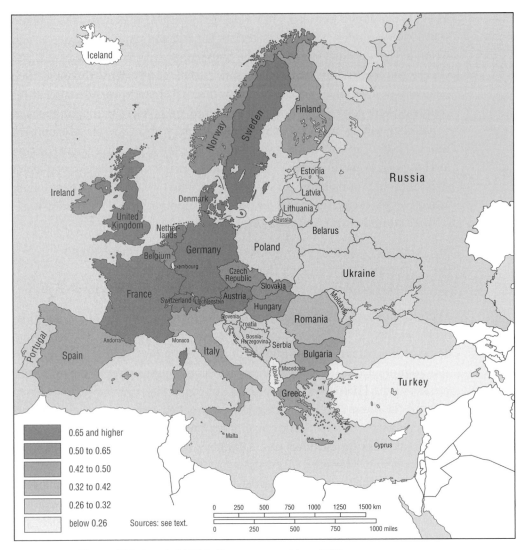

Figure 10.8 Level of HDI in European countries, 1913.

Looking at the year 1913, that is, before the wars and interwar distortions, we find a strong core–periphery structure in Europe (Figure 10.8). The group with the highest HDI values consists of the UK, France, Germany, Austria, Switzerland, the Netherlands, Denmark, and Sweden. The reasons for inclusion in this group vary. In the UK, for example, a high GDP is the key element, Germany and France feature particularly well in education, and in Scandinavia life expectancy was quite high, compared with national income. Also high are the values for Hungary, Belgium, Ireland, Norway, and the Czech and Slovak territories (they share one value, although Slovakia may in fact have been less

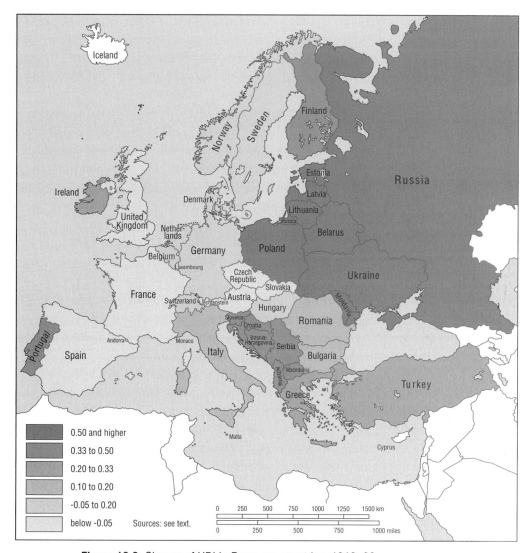

Figure 10.9 Change of HDI in European countries, 1913–38.

developed). At the other extreme, the regions of the Russian and Ottoman Empires, as well as Portugal, performed badly, and the Balkans were also quite modestly developed. The historical change between this early core–periphery structure in 1913 and 1938 was dramatic (Figure 10.9). Of particular note is the rise of the Soviet Union: according to the statistics available, its education system developed rapidly, as the communist government aimed at requiring all children to attend school, and mortality declined dramatically. The increase in life expectancy and GDP, as recorded in the official statistics, was remarkable. Apart from the Soviet Union, other initially less developed countries such as Poland, others on the Baltic, Portugal, and to a lesser extent the Balkan countries and Turkey, increased their HDI values, whereas the European core made the smallest gains and in some cases even declined; Lindert (2004) argues that France had particularly high pre-war schooling values, and the country may have lost some educational coverage up to 1938.

We can conclude that GDP per capita and HDI showed signs of convergence within Europe during the interwar period. eastern Europe in particular improved in welfare until 1938. But some rich countries such as Switzerland and Sweden also achieved substantial GDP growth. The change of the HDI in contrast shows some unequivocal convergence, which was to a large extent driven by educational efforts in the east.

Height as an indicator of living standards, 1914–1945

The study of human stature is another approach to measuring welfare development. This concept has also been termed the "Biological Standard of Living," as it tends to be correlated with most biological dimensions of welfare such as health, life expectancy, and nutritional quality (Komlos 1985; Steckel 1995). The height of any one individual tells us little about her/his well being, as there is much genetic height variation among individuals. However, the average of a large number of height measurements can reveal much about the quality of nutrition and health. There is a large literature on these "anthropometric" welfare measurements, which uses a wide range of sources (Fogel 1986; Steckel and Floud 1998; Komlos and Baten 2004).

The amount of research by economic historians on height in the early twentieth century is actually quite limited. We know more about the cycles of height during the eighteenth and nineteenth centuries than in the early twentieth century. This is understandable, given that for the eighteenth and nineteenth centuries other living standard indicators, such as GDP per capita and real wage estimates, are in particularly scarce supply. For the interwar period of the twentieth century those indicators are again problematic, as the Stalinist Soviet Union, Nazi Germany, and some of the war economies regulated prices and wages and so the purchasing-power-based indicators are less than reliable. Height research has many strengths and some weaknesses, but offers the largest added value when other welfare measures are unreliable or unavailable.

Previous research on the early twentieth century focused strongly on Britain, for which Harris (1988) studied the development of schoolchildren during the years of high unemployment. On the Soviet Union, a number of studies have been published in a special issue of the *Slavic Review*. The interpretations of the Soviet anthropometric record are quite controversial. Wheatcroft (1999) finds a positive trend in the Central Russian male heights, and attributes this to welfare improvement and success of communist policies. Taking the opposite view, Komlos (1985) compares the Soviet height record with those of a number of other countries and finds that while the trend was positive, it was not impressive in international comparisons. Other countries, Komlos argued, performed much better. Given the global spread of hygienic and medical knowledge, small upward trends of height in this period can be an indication of disappointing developments. Only a comparison with a worldwide trend, which is not yet available, will yield a correct interpretation. Mironov (1999c) aimed at explaining the positive height trend, especially during the 1950s, by the enormous reduction in fertility. He also suggests a number of adjustments to Wheatcroft's height record, given that a very large number of above-average height Soviet soldiers died during the Second World War, which was biasing the early height estimates downwards. Moreover, some older individuals were included among the early cohorts.

Turning to another undemocratic and inhuman regime of the time, Baten and Wagner (2003) studied the biological standard of living during the early Nazi period in Germany. They found that, in quite ironic contrast to the Nazi insistence on tall Germanic body properties, the heights of German schoolchildren actually stagnated or slightly declined during the Nazi period, in contrast to other European countries. In a similar vein, life expectancies developed much less favorably than in France, the USA, or other countries, and some diseases spread much more than in other countries (diphtheria, for example, and most nutrition-related diseases). The reason behind these developments was the disintegration of food markets in Germany due to autarky and market interventions. Moreover, investments in public health developed much more slowly than in other countries; even poorer countries such as Hungary started vaccination campaigns against diphtheria earlier and were more successful than Germany.

While those individual country studies are instructive, we need to discuss the broad picture for all of Europe. We first consider the time trends of height (in centimeters) in different European regions (Figure 10.10). It should be noted that these figures are interpolated to a considerable degree; therefore some short-term movements are not visible. But the broad trends and the degree of height growth yield substantive information.

Initially, in 1910–14, there was a "tall" group in Europe (Scandinavia, the UK, and Ireland), a middle group of central, south-eastern, eastern, and western Europe, and a "short" group of southern European countries. The "tall" groups had a very favorable nutrition, which consisted of substantial amounts of protein and calcium (contained in milk, for example), and a high educational standard. In general, heights trended upward in all of Europe during the early

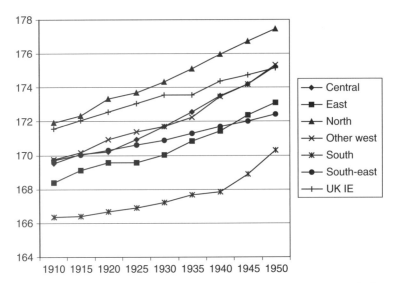

Figure 10.10 Heights in European countries, 1910–50 (in centimeters). *Source:* Baten 2006. Definitions: the years on the horizontal axis are the start years of a five-year birth period. north = DK Denmark, SE Sweden, NO Norway, FI Finland; UK IE UK and Ireland; south: CY Cyprus, GR Greece, IT Italy, ES Spain, PT Portugal; south-east: AL Albania, BG Bulgaria, RO Romania, YU Yugoslavia; central: DE Germany, AT Austria, CH Switzerland; east: CZ Czech Republic, HU Hungary, PL Poland, SK Slovakia, and previous Russian Empire countries RU; other west: NL Netherlands, BE Belgium, FR France.

twentieth century, but the rate of increase was somewhat different in different regions. The least growth can be found in the south-east and the British Isles. The UK and Ireland together fell clearly back into a middle group, and south-east Europe fell from the middle group to the shortest height group. Southern Europe converged upward, as nutrition, education, and health improved. What are the reasons for this development? Well, clearly the UK lost its prominent position as the "workshop of the world" during the early twentieth century. Moreover, the UK was the world's largest food importer in the pre-war period, and it may have suffered considerably from the great trade disruptions during periods of war and depression. The Balkans, on the other hand, had initially a fairly good nutrition (relative to their low income) from subsistence farming in the remote mountains of Bulgaria, Montenegro, and Albania, but strong population growth and slow productivity change ate up each initial advantage. The Scandinavian countries were among the leaders in developing the classical European welfare state, which had quite a positive impact on the health of the poorer strata of society. Whilst stature did not decline in eastern Europe, it did not show much convergence with Scandinavia or other countries with more favorable anthropometric values. The development of the Soviet Union dominates the estimate for eastern Europe. While increasing more strongly than the Balkans, eastern European stature development was not exceptionally strong. The positive effects of the communist schooling efforts, which showed up in the discussion of the HDI above, cannot be found in the pre-1950 height record. However, this cannot be simply attributed to communist economic development. The German armies which invaded the Soviet Union in 1941 also destroyed much of the capital stock and other growth components.

Other interesting developments which can be seen in this figure are the modest southern European height development before 1940 – probably influenced by the civil war in Spain, among other factors. In a similar vein, the socialist and communist experiments also contributed after 1945 to the poor development in south-east Europe. Together with the southern Europeans, the south-eastern Europeans became the shortest on the continent; but southern Europe started to improve its position. In central Europe, Germany faltered from its long-run growth trend during the First World War and its aftermath, whereas the nutritional problems of the 1930s and 1940s are not visible in the maps (perhaps owing to the catch-up growth during the early post-war period, or to imprecise estimates).

Even as late as the early twentieth century, proximity to protein (cattle, milk, etc.) explained a lot of the variation of height, because those who lived close to this kind of agricultural specialization could consume the bottleneck factors of protein and calcium at relatively low prices. In Scandinavia, for example, this proximity advantage was strong, even if income was not as high as in England.

During the interwar years, income also became important for height, and protein proximity lost its significance for longevity. Hence there is a gradual switch from protein proximity to income and other factors (such as public health) over time as determinants of biological welfare. Was there convergence in heights between 1910 and 1935? Interestingly, in this period of market disintegration, there was divergence rather than convergence in heights (Figure 10.11). As the economies no longer exported as much of their staples of comparative advantage, consumption temporarily increased in those countries of high protein supply, whereas it declined in the Mediterranean economies. The picture is much more mixed when we move from the late interwar period to the 1950s: Some countries of initially lower heights, such as Greece, Russia, and Spain, started to improve considerably, whereas Sweden and Norway had lower than average growth. But there were also counterexamples on both sides, such as Denmark and the Netherlands among the initially tall nations. Most notably, Turkish heights did not increase at all, in spite of the large scope for catch-up.

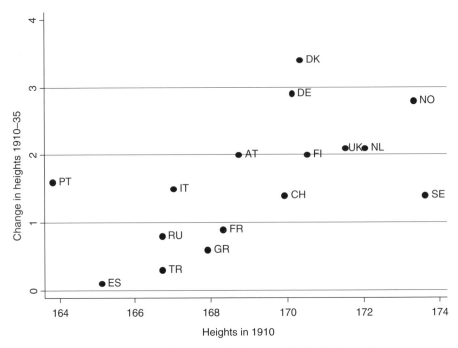

Figure 10.11 Height level *c*. 1913 and height change *c*. 1913–35 (in centimeters).
Note: Country abbreviations are explained below Figure 10.10.

Conclusion

The 1914–45 period will be remembered mostly for the devastation of two world wars, the collapse of major imperial systems, a major economic depression, and civil wars in Russia and Spain. Research studies show how these disasters had major short-run effects on incomes; and, where income data are unreliable as in Nazi Germany and Soviet Russia, new indicators of stature reveal the stagnation of living standards. In this light, the fact that over the whole forty years, population rose by nearly 100 million, income per head by over 25 percent and average individual height by more than four centimeters, was remarkable. European society seems to have had strong powers of recovery; after each conflict and population displacement there was an early resumption of long-term trends. Indeed the macro movements in population and incomes were perhaps less important than some of the more qualitative dimensions of living standards – life expectancy, family size, literacy, education – and changes in the structure of economies wherein industrialization promoted major economic migrations from agriculture to industry, from villages to towns, from the poorer agricultural economies of southern and eastern Europe to western European industrial regions.

The Human Development Index records major advances in this period, with a distinct convergence of eastern and southern Europe towards the levels in north-west Europe. Income growth was not the most important underlying factor. Much more important was how incomes were spent and how governments intervened. Infant mortality fell dramatically and was a major element in life expectancy, rising by about 40 percent – a product mainly of public health expenditure, better housing, and a mushrooming of counseling and support for mothers and of childcare. Knowledge of the key parameters was being spread throughout eastern and southern Europe, which were able to catch up. The fall in infant mortality induced mothers to have fewer children, a trend enhanced by the large fall in the share in the economy of those sectors, like agriculture, which traditionally used much child labor, and by the significant rise in the labor market participation of females which, in conjunction with the increased training needs of children, raised the opportunity cost of having children. The eastern and southern European countries which were able to catch up with northern and western Europe experienced a greater decline in the share of the traditional sectors, a major distinguishing feature of this period.

III From the Second World War to the present

The economic impact of European integration

Barry Eichengreen and Andrea Boltho*

Contents

* The authors are grateful to Albert Carreras, to the editors, and to participants in a CEPR-hosted 2007
Summer Symposium for numerous helpful comments; the usual disclaimers apply.

Introduction

An important part of western Europe's post-Second World War success story was its rapid integration into the world economy as well as its rapid integration with itself. The Great Depression, protectionism, and the war had reduced foreign trade to the levels recorded just before the First World War. In 1947–8, for instance, the volume of western European exports was barely above what it had been in 1913 (Svennilson 1954). As for capital movements, they had virtually come to a standstill, in a world riddled with inconvertible currencies and rigid controls on foreign exchange flows. Sixty years later, the volume of exports had been multiplied by fifty, free trade prevailed in both western and eastern Europe, and the degree of openness had reached unprecedented levels, as had the extent of intra-European trade, while capital movements were almost completely free. Indeed, a significant number of countries had gone as far as doing away with their domestic monies in favor of a new common currency – the euro.

The rising importance of foreign trade over the period is documented in Figure 11.1, which shows the share of exports in GDP for western Europe in constant prices. The series, after dipping in the interwar years, rises very sharply after 1950 to levels that by 1973 had already overtaken those achieved during the last phase of globalization at the beginning of the twentieth century. The rise in the trade share is even more spectacular in the last few decades. And while Europe's share of world output (measured at purchasing power parity, or ppp) declined quite rapidly through the period, the same was not true for Europe's share of world trade (Figure 11.2). This had fallen from almost 60 percent in 1870 to barely a third in 1950, but it rose again in the 1950s and 1960s, fluctuated in the 1970s and 1980s, and only began gently declining in the early 1990s, as a number of formerly relatively closed emerging economies entered into world markets. One important reason lying behind this resilience was the much greater share taken by intra-European exchanges (Table 11.1). Of the world's three major trading areas, Europe is today by far more integrated than either the Americas or the Asia-Pacific zone.

The same may well be true of capital movements; the dearth of data on country-by-country flows makes it more difficult to reach firm conclusions in this area. As mentioned above, the period began with severe restrictions on capital transactions which were relaxed only very slowly between the 1950s and the 1970s. The jettisoning of controls accelerated in the 1980s, and free capital movements were given further powerful boosts by the EU's 1992 Single Market Program and the creation of the euro. Probably the best indirect indicator of this gradual opening is provided by so-called Feldstein–Horioka tests (Feldstein and Horioka 1980). These look at the simple relationship between gross domestic saving and investment rates. A near-perfect correlation (as would

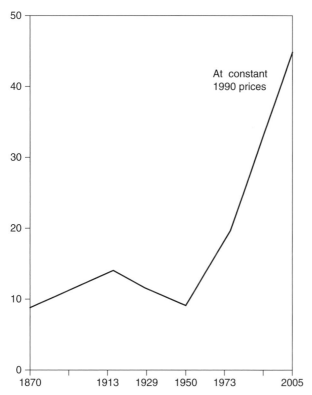

Figure 11.1 Western Europe: exports/GDP (in percent). *Sources:* Maddison 1995; IMF, International Financial Statistics; OECD, National Accounts; World Bank, World Development Indicators; WTO, International Trade Statistics; authors' estimates.

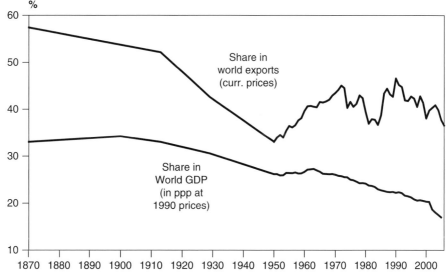

Figure 11.2 Share of western Europe in world GDP and exports. *Sources:* Maddison 1995, 2003; WTO, Statistics Database.

Table 11.1 The importance of intra-European trade

	(Share of intra-trade in total)			
	Intra-western Europe	Intra-total Europe[a]	Intra-Americas	Intra-Asia-Pacific
1938	52.2	61.4	33.3	...
1950	49.3	58.7	53.9	...
1970	67.3	73.9	46.9	35.1
1990	72.2	75.2	47.8	41.7
2008	...	76.6	57.2	50.1

[a] Including eastern Europe and Soviet Union (CIS in 2006).
Sources: GATT International Trade and WTO International Trade Statistics (various issues).

Table 11.2 Capital mobility in western Europe

Simple Feldstein–Horioka tests for capital mobility[a]	
	Fourteen western European countries
1950–9	0.78
1960–9	0.76
1970–9	0.63
1980–9	0.58
1990–2006	0.48

[a] The data show the value of the β coefficient in simple regressions of the form $I/Y = \alpha + \beta \, S/Y$, where I/Y and S/Y stand for the current price shares of gross investment and gross savings in GDP. For more detail see text.
Sources: Feldstein and Horioka 1980; OECD National Accounts and Economic Outlook Data Base (various issues).

be expected in a closed economy) is at least suggestive of the absence of free capital movements; lack of correlation, conversely, shows that countries can supplement their domestic savings by borrowing abroad, or, alternatively, are able to freely lend their excess savings to the rest of the world.

Table 11.2 presents some very simple tests of this relationship over half a century for fourteen western European countries. The lower the figure shown (i.e., the lower the coefficient linking gross investment to gross savings in a simple linear regression), the closer western Europe would be to perfect capital mobility. The evidence, as it stands, suggests that this is still far from being the case and/or that portfolio preferences have a strong bias in favor of domestic assets. It also points, however, to a gradual and fairly steady move towards greater mobility from the 1950s to the mid-2000s.

The reasons for these various trends are numerous. Falls in transport costs and improvements in communications are likely to have helped to raise trade and encourage capital mobility. More importantly, economic growth must have contributed strongly. In rapidly growing economies, demand spills over into imports, while productivity gains create new and cheaper products and hence potential exports; also, as growth proceeds, financial systems become more sophisticated and the distorting influence of controls more costly. Equally, of course, rapid involvement in international exchanges adds to growth by raising demand, stimulating competition, promoting technological spillovers, and attracting foreign direct investment.

Yet most observers of post-war Europe would add a further institutional explanation for the Continent's successful opening and integration: the process of economic and political unification. The abolition of tariffs on intra-European trade, the dismantling of non-tariff barriers, and the abolition of capital controls must surely have been one further important, indeed crucial, contributor to the process. From the timid beginnings of the European Coal and Steel Community (ECSC) to the eastward enlargements of 2004 and 2007, Europe has moved from a club of six countries to a union of twenty-seven (Table 11.3). Indeed, it might well grow to 30 or more over the next decade. According to conventional wisdom, had this process not occurred, the integration story that has just been briefly sketched out could never have happened. And in the absence of that integration story, surely, the growth that was recorded would also have been a good deal more modest. But is this conventional wisdom necessarily justified?

Table 11.3 Some major steps in Europe's unification

	Importance of the area		
	Number of countries	Population (millions)	Share of Europe's total GDP^a (%)
1957 Signing of Treaty of Rome	6	167	49
1973 First enlargement	9	257	68
1981 Entry of Greece	10	271	69
1986 Entry of Spain and Portugal	12	322	77
1990 German unification	12	346	82
1995 Further expansion	15	373	88
2004 First East European enlargement	25	456	95
2007 Entry of Bulgaria and Romania	27	489	96

^{a} At constant 1990 prices; the Europe GDP data include estimates for eastern Europe (excluding the former Soviet Union).
Source: Groningen Growth and Development Center (GDDC), Total Economy Database, January 2008; Maddison 2003.

Approach

The view that regional integration was one of the leading processes shaping the development of the European economy after the Second World War is very common. Contributors to the literature generally take one of two approaches to identifying its effects. Exponents of the narrative approach point to influential individuals (Monnet, Schuman, Delors), key events (the decisions to form the ECSC, sign the Treaty of Rome, establish the Single Market), and underlying forces (the preference of export and banking interests for trade and financial liberalization, the acquiescence and even support of the USA for European integration), implying that things would have turned out quite differently in their absence. Those taking a quantitative approach employ data for a cross-section of countries, regressing measures of economic performance – the growth of, say, output, exports, or employment – on their standard determinants, augmented by measures of a country's participation in the EU. Here the assumption is that the impact of integration on the economy can be captured by setting the EU membership variable to zero and in effect comparing the statistical performance of member states and other countries, controlling for their other observable characteristics.

Both approaches have limitations. In the narrative approach the conclusion that things would have turned out differently in the absence of key individuals or events typically remains implicit, and how exactly they would have differed is unspecified. Things might have indeed been different had, for example, Monnet not been a committed Europeanist, an able diplomat and first head of the ECSC. But these observations beg the question of how precisely the actual and hypothetical would have diverged. Without Monnet, would the ECSC never have been created, and would Europe have been unable to sustain its recovery from the Second World War? Or would other mechanisms have been devised for locking Germany into Europe, freeing her heavy industries from production ceilings, and reactivating Europe's principal source of capital goods? Might not alternative avenues have led as successfully to the Treaty of Rome? And, if not, how then would Europe have developed? Would European countries have ended up trading less with one another and more with the United States? Would the Common Agricultural Policy (CAP) have failed to develop, and if so would the price supports and import restrictions imposed at the national level instead have been more or less generous?

Similarly, in the quantitative approach the belief that the impact of European integration on, say, exports can be captured by setting the EU membership variable to zero rests on the assumption that the degree of integration is exogenous and everything else is equal. But, in reality, exports and integration were simultaneously determined as part of a larger historical system. Not only did the liberalizing influence of the EU encourage intra exports, but the growth of intra-regional trade lent further stimulus to the deepening and development of the EU. In this setting, estimating the effect of an endogenous variable like EU membership is not simple.

In this chapter we take another approach. Rather than imagining that one can analyze the impact of European integration by imagining that a particular integrationist initiative did not occur but that everything else of substance remained unchanged, we set up a counterfactual world. We ask, for example: if the ECSC had not been created, would European countries have found other ways of restarting production and trade in their iron and steel industries? If the Common Market had not been established, would western Europe have found other ways of increasing its intra trade? Rather than simply imagining the non-existence of a specific initiative and assuming that nothing else would have changed we explicitly consider how the entire system would have adapted in its absence. In this sense we follow economic historians like Fogel (1964) in attempting to fully specify the counterfactual.

We also seek to counter the triumphalist bias in previous accounts of the integration process (often written by individuals "present at the creation") by seeing how far we can push the hypothesis that little would have differed economically in the EU's absence. It is our hypothesis that the EU *did* matter for the development of the European economy. By seeing how far we can push the thesis that it didn't (adopting assumptions that work to minimize its effects), we are biasing our procedures against our preferred conclusions. Here again we are drawing on Fogel's approach to counterfactual analysis.[1]

The second section outlines in more detail our analytical framework. We then turn to the counterfactual exercises. In each case we imagine that a pivotal event did not occur, or that a particular factor that encouraged integration operated less powerfully or not at all. We then envisage how the integration process and the economy would have developed in its absence. The concluding section reviews what we have learned.

Analytic considerations

A first way of framing counterfactuals is in terms of the determinants of economic growth. In early neo-classical models like that of Solow (1956) – developed at the

---

[1] Recall that Fogel (1964) wished to argue that the impact of the railways on American living standards was small. He could thus adopt any assumption of convenience, no matter how unrealistic, so long as this worked to exaggerate the change in American living standards that would have taken place in the absence of the railways. In our case, we wish to argue that the impact of the European Union on European living standards was non-negligible. Thus, we want to see how far we can push the argument that, in the absence of the EU, the difference in European living standards would have been disappearingly small, either because the economic impact of the EU was negligible or because, in its absence, Europeans would have found other ways to reach the same ends.

same time as the European Economic Community (EEC) was being established – the level of income per capita depends on the aggregate savings rate (domestic savings determining domestic investment in this period of low capital mobility), and the rates of population growth and technical progress. In this restrictive framework, the key variable through which European integration affected steady state levels of income (and growth for a transitional period) would have been by encouraging savings. By fostering peaceful cooperation between France and Germany, it could have promoted a sense of security that resulted in higher savings and investment rates. By facilitating the speedier relaxation of wartime controls, it could have encouraged firms to reallocate resources to more profitable activities and stimulated additional corporate savings. These mechanisms, however, most plausibly operated in the 1950s; it is more difficult to see how they could have been of first-order importance in later years.

One possible exception to this last statement is the formulation in which savings, investment, and profitability depend on wage pressure (Bruno and Sachs 1985; Armstrong *et al.* 1991) and wage pressure is affected by integration. One might imagine that the more competitive environment created by freer cross-border trade would, for instance, have encouraged wage moderation. The problem for this linkage is that the period famous for wage moderation was one when European integration was in its infancy and import competition was still limited. The period when integration-linked competition intensified, with the completion of the customs union, was also the period when wage moderation was notoriously lacking. Similarly, in recent years, and despite monetary union, there have been very different nominal and real wage trends in different euro-area countries – contrast Italy and Portugal with Germany, for example – suggesting that wages are more heavily determined by national factors than Europe-wide processes.

In the Solow formulation, the rate of technical progress is exogenous and therefore unaffected by factors like European integration. In subsequent growth models, technological change was endogenized and linked to, *inter alia*, the rate of growth of exports. Models of export-led growth (e.g., Little, Scitovsky, and Scott 1970; Myrdal 1970) suggest that learning by doing is faster in export-linked activities; they thus suggest that Europe's creation of a customs union and then a Single Market, by speeding the removal of cross-border barriers to trade, could have stimulated learning, led to technological spillovers, and increased productivity growth. In so far as higher productivity meant higher profits, there also would have been a stimulus to additional capital formation, leading to faster growth and still higher incomes. And, to the extent that technological progress is embodied in capital equipment, the result could have been an even faster rate of growth. In this class of endogenous growth models, a shock like the creation of the Single Market can shift the economy to an entirely new growth trajectory, in which not just the level of income and output but the growth rate itself is permanently higher (Baldwin 1989).

The models considered so far tend to assume that markets are perfectly competitive. If this assumption is relaxed, economic integration can have further effects. One channel of transmission would be through economies of scale, fostered by larger markets. Another would build on the idea of X-efficiency (Leibenstein 1966), and suggest that EEC policies, by intensifying cross-border competition, could have stimulated the development and adoption of new techniques and modes of corporate organization by forcing firms to innovate or die. Further effects could come through improvements in institutions. "Good" institutions promote development. In an integrated Europe, demonstration effects from countries with "superior" institutions might have encouraged the adoption by other governments of better practices and policies. Similarly, Brussels might have been able to encourage reforms stimulating more pro-competitive behavior or more market-friendly policies than would otherwise have occurred.

Thus, alternative models of economic growth point to potential impacts on saving, investment, profitability, exports, the determinants of technical change, and corporate and institutional reform as channels through which European integration could have had an impact (possibly a substantial impact) on the rate of economic growth. The changing focus of these models suggests that the relative importance of different channels may have also changed over time, with the tendency for the EEC to enhance security and boost savings having been more important at the beginning of the period and its efforts to enhance competition and encourage measures boosting efficiency being more important more recently. These models also suggest that integration mattered most for outcomes (in other words, that the counterfactual would have been very different) in so far as it operated through channels emphasized by models of economic growth with endogenous technical change, or in models stressing the role of trade in increasing competition.

Following a large literature, the preceding discussion takes policies as exogenous and asks: How would economic outcomes have differed in the absence of the policies actually observed? In the same way as new growth models endogenize technical change, new political-economy models endogenize policies. One tradition – the so-called adding-machine model – takes policies as a function of the self-interest of sectors or factors of production (Moravcsik 1998; Frieden 2006). The EEC developed the CAP because agriculture was still an important source of employment and production in the 1950s and 1960s; it adopted a Social Charter enshrining the rights of workers because workers were well organized through Social Democratic parties and trade unions; it eventually mandated free capital mobility because financial capital became increasingly influential. The common element in these applications is that policies flow from the sectoral composition of activity which, in turn, flows from factor proportions. Thus, unless the policies of European integration have a first-order impact on, say, the capital/labor ratio, they cannot have a first-order impact on policies.

Again, these observations point to the question of what is the relevant growth model: in Solow-type models, there is a tendency for factor proportions to settle down not far from the initial equilibrium following a shock. Thus, if a particular set of policies had not been adopted then it is plausible to think that self-interested lobbying by the same factors that had, in reality, brought about those policies would have led governments to devise close substitutes in a counter-factual world. By contrast, in new growth models a counterfactual change in policy can lead to a very different capital/labor ratio and a very different sectoral composition of production. One can then imagine that the lobbying and the policies that would result might be very different.

The other tradition in the literature on European integration assumes that policy outcomes are shaped by particular individuals with agenda-setting powers. Policies are endogenous with respect to their actions. Thus, the literature empha-sizing the influence of, *inter alia*, Monnet, Schuman, De Gaulle, and Delors posits that policies would have been very different in their absence. If this is one's approach, then one needs merely to trace out the implications of counterfactual policies (presumably, the *status quo ante*) in one's preferred growth model. Alternatively, scholars writing in the tradition of Haas (1958) suggest that early policy choices and institutional developments importantly shaped subsequent policy options. Policy itself was path dependent, in other words. If Monnet and Schuman had not been there to create a European bureaucracy to regulate the coal and steel industries, there would not have been a Treaty of Rome. If Delors had not been there to help create the Single Market, there would not have been a single currency, since there were positive spillovers, both economic and political, from economic to monetary integration.

Whichever of these approaches is adopted, imagining the counterfactual is no easy task. Depending on the growth model one regards as relevant, counter-factual policies might have had either very large or very small effects. And depending on the model of policy one regards as pertinent, one can imagine the counterfactual policies might have been very different, or differed little if at all, from those actually observed.

Some counterfactuals

Here we apply the counterfactual method to different stages in the European integration process, starting with the European Payments Union (EPU) and the

ECSC, proceeding through the Common Market, the EMS, and the 1992 Single Market Project (SMP), and concluding with European Monetary Union (EMU).

The European Payments Union

The EPU of 1950 was the first significant post-war step in European integration. Exchange controls had been used for regulating the balance of payments during the war and in the second half of the 1940s. Now eliminating exchange controls and making currencies convertible on current account (that is, allowing them to be freely bought and sold for trade-related purposes) was a precondition for reconstructing intra-European trade and creating a common market.

But in seeking to restore current account convertibility, European countries faced a coordination problem. Imagine that one country had unilaterally freed up imports and exports by making its currency freely available for such transactions. Residents would have indulged their pent-up demands for imported goods, but exporters would still have been unable to sell their products abroad (since other countries had not similarly relaxed their exchange restrictions). The danger of a worsening trade balance would thus have discouraged governments from liberalizing unilaterally.

The EPU solved this problem by encouraging governments to coordinate this transition. The participating countries – essentially recipients of US Marshall Plan aid – agreed to adopt a Code of Liberalization committing them to jointly phase out exchange controls and other discriminatory trade measures over a period of years. The Organisation for European Economic Cooperation, or OEEC (which evolved into today's OECD), administered that code. The USA contributed $500 million through the Marshall Plan to provide adjustment assistance to countries that experienced temporary balance-of-payments problems in the course of liberalizing, as Germany did in 1951. A Managing Board, composed of independent financial experts, monitored the governments' compliance with their commitments and administered emergency assistance.

Full current account convertibility was gradually restored over the course of the 1950s. Meanwhile, intra-European trade expanded robustly from roughly $10 to $23 billion. The counterfactual is that, in the absence of the EPU, trade liberalization would have lagged and exports would have grown more slowly. Economic expansion and adjustment would have suffered and performance would have been less satisfactory.

It is hard to dispute the importance of trade in the golden age of European economic growth (1950–73). Without the ability to export, it would have been impossible for countries to restructure along comparative advantage lines. Learning-by-doing, which was heavily export-linked, would have been slower.[2] Productivity growth being slower, rates of capital formation would have been lower. And a more sluggishly growing economy would have meant less enthusiasm for other regional initiatives.

But it is possible to dispute the assumption that trade would have stagnated in the absence of the EPU. If the advantages of reconstructing Europe's trade were so strong, then other means might have been found to this end. The obvious alternative was the International Monetary Fund (IMF). The IMF's Articles of Agreement similarly obliged countries to restore current account convertibility within five years of the Fund's coming into operation. As events transpired, the IMF had limited influence in the late 1940s and early 1950s. The USA essentially prohibited the recipients of its Marshall aid from also borrowing from the IMF, which would have constituted double dipping and undermined American conditionality. Indeed, the EPU can be thought of as the Marshall Plan administrators' targeted response to this very ban (recall that $500 million of Marshall Plan funds were used to capitalize the EPU). With no EPU – which in the aforementioned sense implies no Marshall Plan – the ban on borrowing from the IMF need not have followed.[3] Without EPU adjustment assistance, there would have been more help from the IMF. Liberalization by different European countries would not have been coordinated as closely, since an IMF-led process would have been less Europe-centered.[4] If, as a result, they had not been able to expand their trade with one another, at least as quickly, they would have still been able to trade with the USA. This form of trade would presumably have grown more quickly.

Thus, the relevant counterfactual is not no EPU and all other institutional arrangements unchanged. Rather, it is no EPU and an expanded role for the IMF in pressing for current account convertibility and providing emergency financing to countries experiencing trade balance difficulties. It is somewhat faster expansion of Europe's trade with the USA, offsetting in part the somewhat slower expansion of intra-European trade. European countries would still have been able to raise their exports and to restructure along lines of comparative advantage. It is not clear that learning effects and rates of capital formation would have been all that different.

---

[2] These points are developed in detail in Eichengreen 1996b.

[3] This additional counterfactual is beyond the scope of this chapter, but it is addressed in DeLong and Eichengreen 1992.

[4] That said, it would still have been Europe-centered to a considerable extent. The IMF had a European managing director and European countries had fully a third of the seats on the Fund's executive board.

The European Coal and Steel Community

The heavy industry community centered on France and Germany (and including Italy and the Benelux) was the next significant step in European integration. As Gillingham (1995, p. 151) put it, the ECSC was based on a new idea: supranationality. Membership required transferring sovereign powers to a new European authority. A working paper produced under Monnet's direction provided the basis for a June 1950 conference which established the new High Authority. Monnet's blueprint sought to empower this body to promote competition, steer investment, create a single market, and eliminate all subsidies, quantitative restrictions, and cartel-like restraints on trade. Imagine, however, that Monnet had not come up with this idea and Schuman had not developed it further. How would the European economy have differed as a result?

In terms of the pricing, production, and profitability of coal and steel and the investment in capacity and technology that flowed from them, little would have been different. Following the 1950 conference, governments moved quickly to avoid having to cede their control of taxes, subsidies, and tariffs on coal and steel products to the High Authority. Contrary to Monnet's aspirations, the ECSC did not create a single market. In coal, subsidies and price controls at the national level remained pervasive, since governments regarded subsidized energy as essential for social stability (fuel costs figuring importantly in household budgets) and for their development plans; the High Authority could do nothing about it. In steel, tariffs were harmonized rather than eliminated; European markets continued to be segmented by residual restraints on intra-European trade. A concrete indication of the ECSC's failure to create a common market in steel among the Six was that German exports to the members of the so-called common market grew less quickly than its exports to other European countries. This change in trade patterns was precisely the opposite of what one would have expected if the community had had strong trade-creating effects. As a result, the ECSC did little if anything to stimulate technological and organizational change.[5]

Another community aim was to promote competition by breaking up large producers and pre-Second World War cartels. But it is hard to argue that Europe's coal and steel industries would have been less competitive in the absence of the ECSC. The deconcentration of German heavy industry never occurred, since US officials recognized that a radical reorganization of German ownership was incompatible with their desire for an immediate increase in production in response to the outbreak of the Korean War. As for collusion, a new organization to replace the old German cartel of coal producers was

[5] Gillingham 2003, p. 27.

established as soon as the so-called common market in coal was created. The International Steel Export Cartel was then formed in Brussels in 1963 to regulate prices both in Europe and third markets, and began by setting price minimums for some 15 percent of total community production. The evidence thus suggests that the ECSC had little ability to restrain the recreation of cartels along pre-war lines. It is hard to imagine that cartelization and concentration would have been significantly greater in its absence.

Might there be subtler reasons why prices, production, and profits – and therefore the development of the European economy – would have differed under the counterfactual? Authors like Gillingham (1995), Berger and Ritschl (1995), and Eichengreen (1996b) have argued that, without the ECSC, France and the other victorious powers would not have acquiesced in the removal of ceilings on German industrial production. As Gillingham (1995, p. 152) puts it: "The great achievement of the ECSC ... was to have made the revival of Germany acceptable to its former victims ..." It created at least the myth, if not the reality, that the industries on which the country's military prowess hinged had been placed under supranational control. In its absence, the conclusion follows, ceilings on German steel production would have been maintained in order to make France and other western European countries feel secure.[6] But with such ceilings, a key precondition for European economic growth would have been missing, since the German machine-building industry was critical to the recovery of not just Germany but also other western European economies that relied on German capital goods.[7] And slower economic growth could have resulted in serious economic and social consequences, for example increasing labor militancy, as labor struggled for a larger share of a more slowly growing pie, and more support for left-wing governments, both of which could have depressed the high investment rates that were one of the key economic motors of the so-called golden age.[8]

But this pessimistic counterfactual assumes that, in the absence of the ECSC, no other mechanism could have been found to reconcile the economic and political advantages of freeing German heavy industry from production ceilings with France's desire for security. In so far as the USA saw the elimination of

---

[6] An alternative formulation is that in the absence of the ECSC a revived German steel industry would have led to quick remilitarization and the rapid renewal of military conflict. We regard this counterfactual as implausible: not just France and Germany but also the USA were prepared to go to great lengths to prevent the outbreak of another war.

[7] This scenario is most plausible for the first half of the 1950s, when the steel-producing capacity of the Ruhr provided essential inputs into German machinery production. By the second half of the decade, additional capacity had been added in Europe's coastal regions and elsewhere, making Ruhr capacity less essential. From this point the argument would have to be that without high employment and growth in the Ruhr, the rate of growth of the German economy as a whole would have been less, dragging down aggregate demand and growth rates Europe-wide.

[8] These assumptions might seem extreme. But this is an example of how we adopt assumptions with the effect of accentuating the difference between the actual and counterfactual in order to reinforce our point.

restraints on German heavy industry as critical to geopolitical stability, it is likely that America and its European allies would have found another solution to this problem. For example, there might have been more support in both the USA and France for putting German troops under some sort of European command. Monnet himself drafted a plan for a joint European army following the outbreak of the Korean War. One can imagine that the French would have dropped their opposition to a European Defense Community in the absence of the ECSC and that this would have produced much the same result.

Alternatively, one can imagine that the USA would have guaranteed French security in the absence of the ECSC by maintaining more troops in Germany. NATO had already been established, not just to provide security against the Red Army but to tie the hands of "would-be mischief-makers" within western Europe itself.[9] A related possibility is that the French would have demanded and the USA would have agreed to delay adoption of the German state treaty, which terminated the operations of the Allied High Commission, beyond the actual date of May 1955.

The other important effect ascribed to the ECSC is that it paved the way for the Treaty of Rome. Without the High Authority, the Council of Ministers, the Common Assembly, and the High Court of the ECSC, it is said, it is hard to imagine that as part of the Treaty of Rome the same six countries would have envisaged the creation of a Commission, a Council, a Parliament, and a Court of Justice. In the counterfactual world with no ECSC there might well have been no Treaty of Rome. But answering the question how much difference this would have made for the development of the European economy requires considering another counterfactual.

The Common Market

Europe's great achievement following the Treaty of Rome was to complete its Common Market, which entailed eliminating tariff barriers to intra-Community trade. However, quantitative restrictions were still used to limit trade in sensitive sectors (e.g., agricultural products produced by powerful farm lobbies, or selected industrial goods whose domestic production was seen as essential to national security). Barriers behind the border (product standards and regulations) were also maintained initially.

Despite such lingering restrictions, intra-European trade saw an impressive expansion. The share of intra-exports of the Six rose from 35 to 49 percent between 1960 and 1970. The problem with ascribing this to the Common

---

[9] Gillingham 2003, p. 23.

Market is that Europe's economies were expanding robustly throughout the 1960s – growth was even faster than in the 1950s – and not merely because members of the EEC enjoyed increased freedom of trade. Given income elasticities of demand for imports and exports greater than unity and the tendency of countries to trade disproportionately with their neighbors, it is not implausible to think that the main effect ran from higher incomes to greater trade, and greater intra-European trade in particular, rather than from the creation of the Common Market to greater trade and from there to higher incomes.

The conclusion of the great majority of the studies which have tried to separate the various influences is, however, that the customs union did make a difference and that this difference was welfare-enhancing, since trade creation was significantly larger than trade diversion, particularly in the early years of integration. For example, the estimates of Bayoumi and Eichengreen (1997) imply that trade among the Six in 1953–73 grew 3 percent per annum faster than can be explained by their other economic characteristics and the behavior of other countries. As a result, growth in the Six may have been boosted by one third of a percentage point per annum, resulting in a 1969 GDP level some 4 percentage points higher than otherwise (Eichengreen 2007). Indeed, applying the results of Frankel and Romer (1999) roughly doubles the size of this figure (ibid.). Alternative estimates have attempted to quantify the increased scope for economies of scale. Owen (1983), extrapolating from his detailed microeconomic work on three sectors (cars, trucks, and white goods), puts the total GDP gain of the customs union (including trade creation effects) at 3 to 6 percentage points in 1980.

These and other not dissimilar estimates are clearly very tentative. They nonetheless suggest significant gains, to which could be added further, if small, favorable effects coming from increased foreign direct investment attracted by the large size of the market, and improved terms of trade; this last gain, of course, would have come at the expense of other countries (Petith 1977). As a very rough guess, it could thus be argued that the customs union may have boosted the GDP of the original six members by, say, 5 percent by the mid-1970s. Against this should be set the welfare losses arising from the CAP. These were almost certainly substantial for the UK, once it entered the EEC, but are unlikely to have been very significant for the original Six (as indirectly suggested by the very small amount of trade diversion that seems to have occurred, according to most estimates, between 1958 and 1973).

Not all of these gains and losses can, however, be attributed to the Common Market since, in its absence, the participating countries might have found other ways of satisfying their appetite for more product variety and hence greater trade, and would probably have gone on protecting their farmers. But while it is relatively easy to argue that what the ECSC accomplished would in all like-lihood have occurred even in its absence, and that, similarly (given the impor-tance of agriculture at the time) a fair amount of protection in this area would have materialized irrespective of the CAP, the same is probably less true for the customs union. Though pressures for liberalizing trade had been a constant since the war and would have continued in the 1960s under American pressure, there was strong opposition in several countries as scarce factors and/or weak sectors feared for their incomes and jobs.[10] In Germany and Italy the politicians overcame this opposition by appealing to the need for European integration.[11] France, which had deep misgivings about fully freeing trade in industrial goods (Bonin 1987), did so only because the Treaty of Rome allowed it to achieve several other more political aims (Milward 1992). And while it is true that the Kennedy Round of trade negotiations lowered tariffs substantially, it can be argued that having a single large negotiator facing the USA instead of several smaller countries eased the process (Davenport 1982).

Sapir's (1992, p. 1500) judgment that "the process of EC integration was a catalyst in the reduction of Europe's external protection" seems appropriate. Similarly, while some scale economies in the durable goods sector would surely have been reaped even in the absence of the customs union, rapid trade integration must have helped. All these are reasons for thinking that the level of output in a counterfactual world where the Common Market did not exist would almost certainly have been somewhat lower than the one that was actually recorded. A very rough guess could put the figure at perhaps 3 to 4 percent of GDP – a welcome, if perhaps only limited, addition to living stand-ards that were already growing very rapidly.

A final argument about the effects of the Common Market is that without it there would have been less pressure to stabilize intra-European exchange rates following the breakdown of the Bretton Woods System. Had intra-European trade been lower, policy makers would have worried less about the tendency for exchange rate variability to depress intra-European imports and exports. Hence there would have been less pressure to create the EMS. The limitation of this argument is that empirical studies have failed to find a first-order negative impact of exchange rate variability on the volume of intra-European or world trade. Alternatively, and more plausibly, had European countries not removed barriers to cross-border transactions in agricultural goods, it would not have been necessary to harmonize agricultural support prices and hence to stabilize

---

[10] In the event, of course, the unforeseen rapid growth of intra-industry trade greatly mitigated any such potential costs.

[11] Interestingly, the main opposition to the customs union in Germany came not from protectionist but liberal interests. Erhard was against any form of trade discrimination and German industry was in favor of free access to the world market (Milward 1992). In Italy, on the other hand, industry feared that, deprived of protection, it would be decimated by German competition (Corbino 1964; Sylos-Labini 1970).

exchange rates in order to avoid creating incentives for cross-border arbitrage. The problem here is whether to ascribe Europe's appetite for exchange rate stability to EEC policies like the CAP or to memories of the economically and politically disruptive effects of haphazard exchange rate movements in the 1930s – memories that would have persisted and presumably influenced policy even in the absence of the EEC. And even if one accepts the argument that no Common Market would have meant no EMS, answering the question how much difference this would have made for the development of the European economy requires considering yet another counterfactual.

The European Monetary System

The next important step in the road to European integration was the late-1979 attempt to stabilize exchange rates via the EMS. The system had a perceptible impact only until August 1993, when the permitted fluctuation bands for each currency were moved from 2½ to 15 percent. Up until then, and with the exception of the September 1992 episode when the Italian lira and the British pound left the Exchange Rate Mechanism, the EMS was broadly successful in achieving its main aim: exchange rate stabilization. It is true that currency realignments were numerous in the years to 1987, but academic studies have shown that, overall, member countries' exchange rates fluctuated significantly less than the currencies of other developed economies which did not at the time benefit from similar arrangements (Artis and Taylor 1994; Hu, Jiang, and Tsoukalas 2004).

The impact on longer-run growth is likely, however, to have been negligible. For one thing, as already mentioned, the available evidence suggests that exchange rate variability reduces trade only very modestly, if at all. Hence any gain from the greater stability that was achieved would have been small. In addition, it could be argued that such gains could have been more than offset by the (presumably) higher interest rate volatility that pegging the exchange rate should have caused. Interestingly, however, one of the studies quoted above, which established that exchange rate fluctuations were dampened, also found that, contrary to expectations, interest rate variability was no higher than it was at the same time in the control group of other non-EMS industrialized countries (Artis and Taylor 1994). One plausible explanation for this apparent paradox lies in the likelihood that financial markets saw the system as reasonably credible and therefore did not engage in speculative portfolio shifts that would have elicited from the authorities interest rate responses designed to preserve existing parities.

The EMS's second main contribution was to reduce inflation in countries such as France and Italy. It is doubtful, however, that this would have had an important effect on longer-run growth. Both countries would almost certainly have reduced their rates of price increase, albeit over a longer time horizon, even in the absence of the EMS.[12] Any EMS-specific gain could only have come if the "sacrifice ratio" (the amount of extra unemployment needed to squeeze out any reduction in inflation) had been lowered thanks to credibility effects. Devolving de facto monetary policy control from national central banks to the Bundesbank might, it was argued at the time, lower the inflationary expectations of French and Italian workers and thus speed up disinflation. But the available research shows that, contrary to what seems to have happened on financial markets, no such credibility bonuses emerged: inflation declined because unemployment rose, not because wage and price setters were convinced that a "regime change" had occurred (Egebo and Englander 1992). Financial markets may have seen the EMS as a credible system; labor and product markets seem to have been much more skeptical.[13]

A final EMS contribution was, of course, the one of paving the way for eventual monetary union. While earlier attempts, such as the Werner Plan of 1970, were shelved in the aftermath of the Bretton Woods collapse, the EMS was seen by most observers as a step towards that ultimate goal, and not just because it aimed at stable exchange rates. An important feature of the period was the gradual acceptance by countries such as France and Italy (but also Spain and others) of macroeconomic policies that put a premium on monetary stability and, in particular, on low inflation and orderly public finances. Both of these were seen by Germany as *sine qua non* conditions for its acceptance of eventual monetary integration. Whether this stepping-stone role would justify a more upbeat assessment of the EMS's contribution to Europe's growth depends on how one assesses EMU's impact on the area's welfare.

The 1992 Single Market Program

The origins of the SMP go back to the early 1980s, a period in which growth had faltered and the EEC had become bogged down in CAP and budgetary rows. A 1985 White Paper called for a removal of non-tariff barriers (tariffs having already been abolished), such as restrictive regulations and product standards inhibiting cross-border competition, as well as the free movement of factors of production. Approved in 1986, it presided over a gradual liberalization and deregulation process through the next twenty years.

---

[12] Indeed, in the case of France, it has been argued that the relentless pursuit of a "franc fort" policy within the EMS may well have kept unemployment well above desirable levels (Blanchard and Muet 1993).

[13] This finding also matches similar UK and US results, suggesting different responses by financial and labor markets to what might be characterized as "regime changes" (Buiter and Miller 1981; Blanchard 1984).

The rationale was to enhance efficiency and stimulate growth by intensifying product- and factor-market competition. In goods markets the principle of mutual recognition was used to ensure that products in compliance with consumer-safety standards in one member state were automatically deemed to be in compliance elsewhere in the Community. National preferences were similarly reduced, or challenged by the European Commission in the Court of Justice. In factor markets, controls on cross-border capital flows were removed to create a level playing field for investors and establish a more competitive environment for financial institutions.

The "Cecchini Report" (Emerson *et al.* 1988) calculated that full implementation of the SMP's provisions could boost EC output by 2½ to 6½ percent of GDP over the next decade or so, via resource reallocation, scale economies, and, most importantly, a higher degree of competition. In addition to this one-off gain, even more optimistic estimates suggested that a permanent GDP growth bonus of between one quarter and nearly one percentage point was also attainable thanks to the higher income, savings, and investment that the SMP would have brought about (Baldwin 1989).

The empirical evidence for such so-called endogenous growth models is not very strong, however (Crafts 1992a) and few now believe in permanent growth effects arising from institutional changes such as those outlined above.[14] Even the initial "Cecchini Report" assessment of likely SMP effects has been scaled down significantly by more recent research. Thus, an early estimate for the period to 1994 found that, as for the Common Market, trade creation had dominated trade diversion, but put the gains at somewhere between ½ to 1½ percent of GDP (Allen, Gasiorek, and Smith 1998). A later Commission estimate thought that, by 2002, the overall positive impact had been of the order of 1½ to 2 percent of GDP (European Commission 2002), very much in line with what more skeptical observers had already anticipated at the time the SMP was launched (e.g., Peck 1989). Some further gains can probably be expected, since not all the SMP's provisions have yet been implemented; but any remaining effect is likely to be quite small.

While the probable benefits of the SMP thus look significantly smaller than those apparently achieved by the Common Market, they are not insignificant. Yet, as with so many other aspects of European unification, they might well have been reaped even in the absence of Commission initiatives. The 1980s was a period that saw a good deal of domestic liberalization and deregulation in Europe. To take just one example, the interventionist French government had relaxed some of its tight hold over the financial sector well before the SMP was launched. More broadly, the Fraser Institute's Economic Freedom Index, which "measures

---

[14]   For an exception, see Henrekson, Torstensson, and Torstensson 1997, a study that finds a permanent growth effect for the EC (and EFTA), but does so using dummy variables to quantify the impact of integration.

the degree to which the policies and institutions of countries are supportive of economic freedom" (Gwartney and Lawson 2006, p. 3), shows that the EC countries deregulated their economies faster between 1980 and 1990 than they did between 1990 and 2000. It is thus quite plausible to argue that efforts to liberalize and open economies further might have been made in any case.

That said, it is hard to imagine that European countries would have moved as far or fast in deregulating product markets in the absence of the SMP. National governments were prepared to remove subsidies only if they were assured that their neighbors would do likewise, so that domestic firms would not be placed at an unfair competitive disadvantage. The EC's institutions helped to coordinate these decisions and secure governments' commitment to them. Often "Europe" was used as a shield against domestic opposition to deregulation. Thus, the German telecommunications reform commission shifted the onus for difficult measures onto EC officials, helping to overcome opposition to deregulation from the Bundespost and the unions (Moravcsik 1998). French governments similarly saw pursuing domestic reforms in the context of Community liberalization as a way of shifting responsibility for painful actions.

In addition, two aspects of the SMP might not have occurred (or might have occurred only very partially) in its absence. One was the push to open public procurement to foreign firms, a push imposed by Brussels on mostly very reluctant member states. It is true that the efforts many countries were making at the time to reduce their budget deficits might have led them to seek economies by resorting to cheaper imports, but any such effect would almost certainly have been much more drawn out. The other was the (earlier and unrelated) legal decision that standards and regulations adopted by partner countries should be mutually recognized, a decision taken by the European Court of Justice in 1979. This greatly facilitated the SMP's task of doing away with non-tariff barriers. Here too, one might have expected that efforts at harmonization would have proceeded even in the absence of the SMP (as they are, for instance, proceeding, albeit very slowly, between the USA and the EU), but mutual recognition is a far faster and infinitely less bureaucratic procedure than harmonization. Both of these practices thus seem to have been genuine achievements of the European integration process. As an upper esti-mate it could thus be argued that perhaps half of the SMP's gains, as estimated by the Commission in 2002, might not have been obtained in its absence.

European Monetary Union

The EMU has clearly been (and still is) Europe's most ambitious project since the Treaty of Rome. Originally entered into by eleven countries on January 1,

1999 (sixteen by 2010), it has involved devolving monetary policy to a supra-national (and fiercely independent) European Central Bank (ECB), while also constraining, at least in theory, the use of fiscal policy by limiting the size of budget deficits and public debt/GDP ratios.[15]

After a decade of operation, the verdict on EMU's achievements is still open. Both growth and inflation in the Eurozone have been somewhat lower than in, for instance, the USA and the UK, though higher than in Japan. Financial integration has been very rapid and trade integration has risen further. Yet, at the same time, significant divergences in economic performance have emerged, in particular among some of the countries of the European periphery. Thus, Finland, Ireland, and Spain have grown rapidly at least until the 2009 recession, spurred in part by low real interest rates; Italy and Portugal, on the other hand, have hardly grown at all, held back, in particular, by high real intra-euro exchange rates.[16]

EMU's contribution to the growth of the European economy may come through three channels: higher investment rates because of greater confidence and a lower cost of capital; increased X-efficiency encouraged by rapid intra-Eurozone trade growth; and further efficiency gains brought about by institu-tional reforms spurred by the increased competitive pressures that countries are now facing within a single currency area. The evidence, so far at least, does not suggest major effects in any of these areas.[17]

Nominal interest rates have clearly been very low by historical standards, largely reflecting low inflation. Real interest rates have, similarly, been well below the levels recorded in the 1980s and 1990s and this may have stimulated investment. It is difficult, however, to attribute such developments to EMU. World inflation and nominal and real interest rates have all been low during the EMU's first decade, reflecting global forces (e.g., the widespread switch to central bank independence, increased international trade competition, world financial deregulation, the large East Asian and OPEC current account sur-pluses) that have little to do with the creation of EMU. The latter could still have had favorable effects had it created a climate of greater confidence in future growth and stability. This too, however, seems to have been lacking. For several years, in the early 2000s, the Eurozone went through a phase of very modest growth, while more recently, the difficulties of Italy and Greece, in

---

[15] These constraints were initially enshrined in the Maastricht Treaty and therefore apply to all EU member countries. They are, however, somewhat more binding for EMU members because of the perceived potential negative externalities that an overexpansionary fiscal policy could generate in a monetary union.

[16] A common nominal interest rate and exchange rate, in the presence of still diverging inflation rates, has clearly led to diverging performance across the area. In theory, the growth of high-inflation countries, while benefiting from low real interest rates, should be held back by the appreciation of their exchange rates, and *vice versa* for low-inflation countries. In practice, in open economies in which financial markets are still highly regulated (such as those of Italy, but also of Germany), the impact of interest rate changes on activity is muted, while exchange rate changes can have powerful effects.

[17] For a survey of the growth effects of EMU, see Barrell *et al.* 2008.

particular, have sown the first doubts about the perennity of the present monetary arrangements. Neither development was, or is, conducive to increased confidence.

One area in which EMU's contribution to investment is highly likely to have been positive is the creation of a vast and liquid financial market that may well have lowered the cost of capital (Freixas, Hartmann, and Mayer 2004). This has been particularly the case in the bond market. For the public sectors of the Eurozone countries, bond yield differentials have been greatly reduced, allowing much lower budget deficits (and hence higher savings) than would otherwise have been the case, at least in those (many) countries with high public debt/GDP ratios. The private sector saw a boom in corporate bond issues in the years immediately following the introduction of the single currency, a boom that was more pronounced in the euro area than elsewhere in Europe (Rajan and Zingales 2003). This must have had a favorable impact on investment and hence on growth. The size of the effect is, however, likely to have been very small. For one thing, investment is not particularly interest-rate elastic. For another, any favorable effects have probably been limited to a sub-sample of the corporate sector, namely large companies.

A second channel of transmission could come through increased trade integration fostered by the single currency and promoting resource reallocation and greater X-efficiency, along the lines already looked at in the sub-section on the Common Market. Initially, it was expected that such effects would be small: since the move to floating exchange rates following the Bretton Woods break-down seemed to have hardly dented the growth of world trade, it followed that the move to fixing parities should have had only a minor trade-stimulating effect. This consensus view was then shaken by research that showed that currency unions boosted intra-union exchanges by a factor of three relative to the trade of countries not participating in such monetary unions (Rose 2000). Adapted to the experience of the Eurozone, research in the same vein suggested that future trade gains, while not as large, could still raise trade by 50 percent or more (Rose and van Wincoop 2001). Indeed, even the ultra-skeptical UK Treasury, in an evaluation of the costs and benefits of British participation in EMU, concluded from such estimates that membership could boost the country's per capita income growth rate by as much as 0.2/0.3 percent per annum for some twenty to thirty years (HM Treasury 2003).

The Eurozone has seen a significant expansion of its intra-zone trade, but the orders of magnitude so far are a good deal less than those suggested by such studies. In a review of the evidence, Baldwin (2006a, 2006b) has pointed to some problems with the earlier optimistic estimates and concluded that trade may have risen by some 5 to 15 percent between 1999 and 2003 over what might otherwise have been expected. More importantly, he also argued that this rise derived mainly from the increased trading activities of small and medium-sized firms which now faced lower fixed costs in intra-Eurozone trade. This effect is in the nature of a one-off adjustment, suggesting, therefore, that further large gains on this score are highly unlikely. That benefits have accrued would thus seem undoubted. Their impact on the level, let alone the growth rate, of output seems, however, on the basis of the available evidence, to have been very small so far and is likely to remain so.

Finally come growth effects that stem from institutional changes designed to make member countries more market friendly and spurred by the increased competition inevitable in a monetary union. Firm evidence in this area is difficult to come by. The OECD and the World Bank have both tried to quantify the importance of regulation and other restrictions in hampering competition in labor and product markets. A selected sample of their results is presented in Table 11.4. This shows (unweighted) averages for the Eurozone and for a group of five other western European countries not participating in the single currency. The overall impression is that there has been some reform in EMU countries, but this has not been noticeably faster than in the non-EMU ones, especially given the much more liberal nature of the latters' economies.[18] For the one indicator for which evidence is available for the 1990s (strictness of employment protection), it would appear that reform had been significantly more rapid in the decade preceding monetary union than it has been since. And, according to the World Bank, deregulation seems to have been very limited over the years 2003–7.[19] A similar impression is conveyed by the already mentioned Economic Freedom Index produced by the Fraser Institute – for the years 2000–7, this shows, if anything, a slight regression for the Eurozone.[20]

The overall verdict is thus only mildly positive. The single currency has undoubtedly provided greater financial stability to those member countries that were in the past prone to high inflation and rapidly depreciating exchange rates. It has also helped create a large capital market which has almost certainly reduced the cost of raising money for both governments and companies. It has,

---

[18] Taking the percentage "improvement" (i.e., shift towards less regulation) for all the fourteen indicators for which the World Bank provides data in both 2003 and 2008–9, results in an average change for the Eurozone countries of some 12 percent, as against a small change in the opposite direction for the other European economies. But then the latter were, in 2003, some 40 percent less regulated than the former.

[19] The World Bank has also produced a "regulatory quality" indicator for a longer time span (1996–2008). This attempts to measure "the ability of the government to formulate and implement sound policies and regulations that permit and promote private sector development" (Kaufmann, Kraay, and Mastruzzi 2007, p. 5). Here too, the years 1996–2000 saw a sharp increase in the pace of deregulation in the Eurozone, but in the years 2000–08, only little progress in contrast to the experience of other west European industrialized countries.

[20] An alternative, and somewhat more erratic, Freedom Index (Heritage Foundation 2009) paints a different picture, however. For the years 1999–2008 it shows faster deregulatory activity in the Eurozone than elsewhere in western Europe.

Table 11.4 Regulatory reform in western Europe

OECD indicators[a]

		Employment protection	Regulation[b]
Eurozone[c]	late 1980s	3.19	...
	late 1990s	2.66	2.26
	2003	2.52	1.57
Other W. Europe[d]	late 1980s	2.51	...
	late 1990s	1.94	1.72
	2003	1.94	1.31

World Bank indicators[a]

		Labor market rigidities[e]	Starting a business[f]	Closing a business[g]	Enforcing contracts[h]
Eurozone[c]	2003	45.5	26.5	67.6	494
	2009	37.1	11.4	68.6	557
Other W. Europe[d]	2003	28.4	10.6	73.3	224
	2009	20.4	8.5	76.3	397

[a] Unweighted averages.
[b] Average of four indicators: barriers to entrepreneurship, product market regulation, barriers to trade and investment, extent of state control.
[c] Excluding Cyprus, Luxembourg, Malta, Slovakia, and Slovenia.
[d] Denmark, Norway, Sweden, Switzerland, and UK.
[e] Average of difficulties in hiring, in firing, and of the rigidity of hours worked.
[f] Average of number of procedures and duration (in days).
[g] Financial recovery rate (%).
[h] Duration (days).
Sources: Conway, Jarod, and Nicoletti 2005; OECD, Employment Outlook 2004; World Bank, "Doing Business", http://www.doingbusiness.org.

in addition, led to somewhat faster trade integration than would otherwise have occurred, and it may also have spurred some regulatory reforms that might not have been adopted without it, though the evidence in this area is more mixed. None of these changes, however, is likely to have had much more than a very small effect on the area's growth rate or even level of output.

Would things have looked very different had EMU not occurred? While the de facto monetary union linking the greater Deutschmark area (Germany, the Benelux, and Austria) might, conceivably, have adopted a single currency, it is highly unlikely that France, let alone Italy or Spain, would have joined such an arrangement. Hence, the (small) gains from trade and from the expanded capital market that EMU generated would not have been forthcoming. Similarly, given trends in the dollar and in oil prices, and frequent political uncertainty, there

would almost certainly have been much less financial stability in several countries, noticeably so Italy and possibly also Spain, an economy that by 2007–8 had
recorded a current account deficit of some 10 percent of GDP.

Yet, paradoxically perhaps, Italy in particular might in such circumstances
have followed more deliberate reform policies at home than it actually did.
When the lira depreciated sharply in 1992, or when joining EMU was seen as a
national goal, the Italian authorities took fairly drastic monetary and fiscal
measures designed to reduce inflation and rein in the budget deficit. When all
pressures on the exchange rate and on the interest rate were removed thanks to
the single currency, Italy's deficit began growing again, pension reform was
diluted, and public expenditure was not trimmed (while Spain allowed its
national savings rate to plummet).[21] Necessary reforms, in other words, were
almost certainly postponed, and any future adjustment might turn out to be
more costly than it otherwise would have been. While it may be far-fetched to
suggest that EMU's contribution to Italy's welfare, in particular, may have been
negative (after all, net interest payments on the country's public debt fell from
more than 10 to less than 5 percent of GDP between the mid-1990s and the
mid-2000s thanks to the drop in long-term interest rates that EMU membership brought about), a final verdict will have to wait.

Conclusion

European integration, starting with the ECSC, proceeding through the establishment of the Common Market and the EMS, and culminating (if that is the
right word) with the completion of the Single Market and the creation of the
euro, is one of the most visible, controversial, and commented-on aspects of
Europe's development since the end of the Second World War. It is hard to
imagine that Europe's economy would have developed the same way without it.
Or is it?

This brief survey of the economic impact of European unification began by
taking a skeptical standpoint. We have tried to see how far we can push the
argument that European living standards, growth rates, and economic structures would have been little different in the absence of the institutions and
processes that have culminated in today's EU. This entailed two steps. We
argued, first, that in standard growth models trade and other forms of integration that were central to the European process have only a relatively minor (and
temporary) impact on economic growth; in endogenous growth models the
effects can be larger, but the empirical evidence for such models is not

---

[21] And thanks also to the complacent attitude of financial markets to the country's massive public debt.

particularly robust, suggesting that not too much weight should be given to their predictions. And even if research could point to relatively large effects, we then argued that many of these might well have occurred even without the integration process, since economic forces would almost certainly have pushed for freer trade, stable exchange rates, and less regulation in Europe in any case. The *ex-ante* hypothesis was thus that the economic (as opposed to the political) impact of European unification has been limited.

In a sense this argument is an application of the Coase Theorem, and as such it is subject to all the limitations of that famous proposition. The Coase Theorem proposes that the allocation of property rights has no implications for the efficiency of economic outcomes, because interested parties can always make side payments sufficient to reallocate resources and rights in a more efficient direction. In the present instance it implies that where a particular allocation was needed for efficiency, governments, banks, firms, and households would have found other ways of achieving it in the absence of the EU. And where an allocation was inefficient, governments, banks, firms, and households would have been quick to find ways around it. But Coase's result obtains only when there are no liquidity constraints, no transactions costs, and no uncertainty. Yet in Europe uncertainty was and is pervasive, transactions costs were and are far from negligible, and agents were and are liquidity constrained. All these are reasons for thinking that the actions of the EU and the outcomes of the integration process have mattered for the development of the European economy.

Thus, while it would still seem to be true that the growth effects of economic unification can never match those arising from changes in the rate of technological progress, it would appear that not everything that happened on the economic integration front in western Europe over the last half century would have happened anyway. Trade would no doubt have grown, but the decision to create a Common Market – a decision that went against the interests of powerful lobbies in most of the original six member countries – might well not have been taken without the political drive to unification. While Europe's revealed preference for relatively stable exchange rates would almost certainly have led to attempts similar to those of the "Snake" arrangements of the second half of the 1970s or of the EMS, the move to monetary union goes well beyond schemes to manage exchange rates. By giving up their monetary policies, the EMU countries have ceded sovereignty in what many see as one of the principal prerogatives of a state.[22] It is inconceivable that such a step would have been taken had there not been a strong political will to pursue integration.

---

[22] For some EMU members, of course, that sovereignty was somewhat limited, given their financial integration with Germany: "As European Vice President Christofferson noted in late 1989 after the Bundesbank raised its discount rate, the other central banks of Europe had about 45 minutes of sovereignty" (quoted in Cooper 1990, p. 277).

It is more difficult to quantify the effects of the process. The approach followed was in the nature of a two-step assessment. First, potential channels of transmission between a particular episode and economic growth were selected and evaluated (often using estimates available in the literature). Then, we made an attempt to see what part of those evaluations reflected genuine unification effects, additional to what, using educated guesses, might have occurred anyway. By design, these attempts went in the direction of minimizing the positives in an attempt to bias the conclusions away from our priors.

The bottom line is that the growth effects stemming from exchange rate efforts (the EMS and EMU) were limited, although for EMU the jury is still out. The same was not true of trade, however. Both the Common Market and the SMP probably boosted output in the EU by more than might have been expected on the strength of the trade liberalization that was occurring in the world at the time. A rough guess suggests that EU GDP is some 5 percent higher today than it would otherwise have been (an impact of the EU on European incomes similar to that Fogel found for the impact of the railroad on US incomes). Whether this is a large or small number is ultimately for the reader to judge.[23]

A final positive contribution of European unification comes from its attractiveness to non-member countries. The economic successes since the 1980s of Spain and, to a lesser extent, Greece and Portugal may well have owed something to the strengthening of democracy and openness which membership of the EU imposed. Even more importantly, the promise of eventual membership that Brussels provided to eastern Europe after the fall of the Berlin Wall must have contributed strongly to the anchoring of both democracy and economic reform in the Accession countries. In many ways, that promise acted as an extremely successful "structural adjustment program," as also confirmed indirectly by the much less satisfactory performances of those east European countries that have (so far?) been left out, be this in the former Soviet Union or in the former Yugoslavia.

The overall economic verdict is thus cautiously favorable. Integration has clearly not been a panacea for the Continent's economic ills, as claimed by some of its proponents. But it has bestowed some benefits. It is difficult to see how it could have been otherwise. After all, few would doubt that the USA's prosperity today owes at least something to it having been a single market and a monetary union for many decades.

---

[23] It is a good deal more modest than a recent estimate which suggests that the "GDP per capita of the EU would be approximately one-fifth lower today if no integration had taken place since 1950" (Badinger 2005, p. 50), but such estimates assume that virtual autarky would otherwise have prevailed.

A final argument is more political in nature. According to many, the major achievement of European unification was not a somewhat higher level of GDP, or even monetary union, but lasting peace in western Europe. For instance, without Franco-German reconciliation (a major by-product of economic integration), conflict would have returned to the Continent as it had always done in the past. The most appropriate counterfactual in such a scenario would be the Europe of the interwar years, against which what happened looks like a spectacular improvement. Yet, however plausible this view may have seemed to a generation that had lived through two world wars, it ignores another political factor that, on its own, would almost certainly have made for west European cooperation even in the absence of economic integration efforts, namely the Cold War. The threat of a communist take-over (particularly felt in the 1950s in countries such as France and Italy) would surely have made otherwise querulous nations close ranks, all the more so given the USA's pre-eminent role in aiding and cajoling its much poorer and weaker European partners. Peace in post-war Europe almost certainly owes much more to Stalin and Truman than it does to Monnet or Schuman.

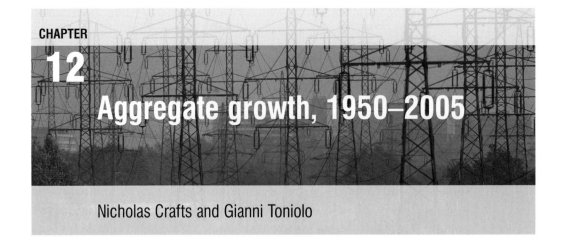

Aggregate growth, 1950–2005

Nicholas Crafts and Gianni Toniolo

Contents

Introduction

Since the Second World War, western Europe has experienced an unprecedented period of growth, but its performance relative to Asia and the United
States has seemed less impressive in recent decades than in the early post-war
period. eastern Europe did much less well, as communism was unable to
sustain similar improvements over the long run and the initial years of transition to market economies proved difficult; but the region has seen rapid
growth in recent years. Against this background, variations in the performance
of individual countries also catch the eye: for example, the "Celtic Tiger" phase
of growth in Ireland and the long period of relative economic decline in the UK.
The objective of this chapter is to describe Europe's post-war growth performance, understand its main causes and, in the process, also explore what economists, historians, and policy makers can learn about modern economic
growth from European successes and failures.

Our analysis is informed by two conceptual approaches. The first of these
focuses on the microfoundations of growth in terms of incentives to invest and
innovate, and draws on endogenous growth theory. The key ideas are captured
in Figure 12.1 which is adapted from Carlin and Soskice 2006. Here the
downward-sloping (Solow) line represents the well-known inverse steady-
state relationship between technological progress (x) and the capital intensity
of the economy (k) for a given savings rate in the neo-classical growth model.
The upward-sloping (Schumpeter) line reflects the endogeneity of technological progress, based on the assumption that with a higher capital-(and output)
to-labor ratio a larger market makes innovation potentially more profitable.
The equilibrium rate of technological progress is established by the intersection
of these two lines and, in turn, this determines the rate of economic growth.

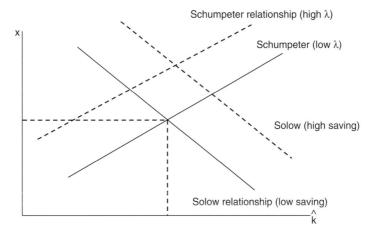

Figure 12.1 Endogenous growth

Figure 12.1 implies that the rate of innovation increases when the Solow and/ or the Schumpeter line shifts upward. In the former case, this will be the result of an increased rate of investment, which has growth rate effects, unlike the neo-classical model in which technological progress is exogenous. In turn, investment will respond to changes in the economic environment which affect its expected profitability. In the latter case, the increased innovation rate will be the result of an increase in innovative effort for any given market size, which will reflect such changes as greater technological opportunity, lower R&D costs, increased appropriability of returns, and intensified competitive pressure on managers. An improvement in any one of these with no change in the rest would give higher λ. The implication of Figure 12.1 is that the growth rate will be affected by institutions and policies.

The second set of ideas on which we draw is that of catch-up growth in the tradition of Abramovitz (1986). This literature highlights the fact that growth may be very rapid in phases where countries start from a low initial level but are able to catch up with the leaders by reducing gaps in capital intensity and technology. This implies that scope for catch-up must be taken into account in evaluating growth performance. Abramovitz stressed that catch-up is by no means automatic but depends on "social capability" and "technological con-gruence." The former relates to the incentive structures which influence the effective assimilation of new technology, and the latter to the cost effectiveness of technologies that might be transferred from more advanced countries. In terms of Figure 12.1, Abramovitz can be thought of as seeing catch-up oppor-tunities as potentially shifting the Schumpeter line upwards, but by how much depends on social capability and technological congruence. A phase of success-ful catch-up growth will tend to be one in which investment is highly profitable and will also see outward shifts of the Solow line.

The post-war history of economic growth in both western and eastern Europe has seen different episodes with largely coincident time patterns. In western Europe, the period 1950–73 is conventionally known as the "golden age of economic growth"; it was followed by a period of slowdown and then, from the mid-1990s, by the era of the "New Economy." This gives rise to classic questions which can usefully be addressed in the light of the theoretical approaches outlined above. These include the following: "why did Europe experience the golden age and why did it come to an end?"; "what accounts for relative success and failure across countries in different periods?"; "why has Europe failed to complete its catch-up to the United States?"; "what is different about growth in the era of information and communications technology (ICT)?"

In eastern Europe, we can distinguish a communist "silver age" of growth ending in the early 1970s, followed by slowdown culminating in collapse at the end of the 1980s, and the subsequent transition to catch-up growth in a market economy. Here too classic questions are apparent: "why did the communist era lead in (Abramovitzian terminology) to falling behind rather than forging ahead?"; the linked, but distinct, question "why did the communist era end so abruptly?"; "how does catch-up in the transition economies compare with earlier experience elsewhere?"

European growth in long-run perspective

This section seeks to establish the basic facts of European economic growth taking a long-run perspective and using the standard periodization employed by Maddison (2003). We both review aggregate European performance and offer a preliminary view of catch-up and convergence across countries.

Table 12.1 reports the combined growth performance of sixteen western European countries, and provides comparison with the United States. Long-run growth has been formidable: in 2005 real GDP per capita in western Europe was about ten times the level in 1870. The growth rate has been quite variable – the golden age of 1950–73 stands out as an era of extraordinarily rapid growth, which in part represents recovery from a period when growth had been undermined by the world wars and the Great Depression. The post-golden age slowdown period has seen growth which by pre-1950 standards looks quite good.

Table 12.1 also shows that from 1820 to 1950 real GDP per capita in the United States pulled a long way ahead of that in western Europe, which was at 96 percent of the American level in 1820 but had fallen to 48 percent by 1950. The golden age saw a catch-up such that by 1973 western Europe had reduced the gap markedly and was at 68 percent of the United States level. Since 1973, however, growth rates have been virtually the same on both sides of the Atlantic, and the western European catch-up in real GDP per capita has stalled while still far from complete. Most countries share in the overall European ups and downs between periods, but there are some notable exceptions. For

Table 12.1 Levels and growth rates of real GDP per capita: western Europe and United States ($ 1990 GK and % per year)

	Western Europe	United States		Western Europe	United States
1820	1205	1257	1820–70	0.98	1.34
1870	1962	2445	1870–1913	1.33	1.82
1913	3461	5301	1913–50	0.78	1.61
1950	4582	9561	1950–73	4.06	2.45
1973	11431	16689	1973–2005	1.86	1.91
2005	20589	30519			

Sources: GGDC 2007; Maddison 2003, updated from website.

example, the first industrial nation, the UK, saw growth slow down in the late nineteenth century; Norway, Sweden, and Switzerland escaped the worst effects of war and had relatively strong growth in the 1913–50 period; while Ireland spectacularly bucked the trend to slow down in the late twentieth century. The long run has seen some notable changes in the rank order of countries, most obviously the relative decline of the UK.

Table 12.2 shows that the ratio of real GDP per capita in the top compared with the bottom country has fallen since 1950, so that in 2005 it was about 2, while eleven countries were clustered within 9 percent of the median. There has been a clear tendency towards β-convergence since 1950 such that, on average, countries with low initial income levels have grown more quickly. Generally speaking, however, over the long run countries in southern Europe have persistently had relatively low levels of real GDP per capita. On the other hand, peripherality now appears to be less of a handicap – in some cases at least, as the rise of Ireland and Norway confirms.[1]

Table 12.3 presents data comparable to Table 12.1 for the aggregate of eastern European countries for which Maddison 2003 and GGDC 2007 present long-run estimates, and also for Russia/USSR. In eastern Europe over the long period since 1870 real GDP per capita has risen by less than in the west, about seven times (five times in Russia) compared with ten times. Levels of real GDP per capita have always been well below those in western Europe and over time the gap has widened, especially since 1973. Obviously, this was partly attributable to the collapse in output at the end of the communist period and the delay before catch-up growth started in the transition economies, but slow growth was also very much the case in the 1970s and 1980s. In the golden age, however, communism delivered growth rates only a little below those in western Europe, although this is not so impressive once the much greater scope for catch-up is taken into account.

The USSR was clearly always a long way below the United States in terms of real GDP per capita – about 30 percent in 1950 and 36 percent in 1973 – and, despite a promising start, in the golden age only reduced the gap very slowly. The growth rate of 3.35 percent per year for this period reported in Table 12.3 compares quite unfavorably with the achievements of western European countries like Italy or Spain, which started out with relatively low income levels. A similar point emerges in Table 12.4, where Czechoslovakia is seen to have grown at 3.08 percent per year – almost 2 percentage points per year lower than Austria. At the end of the "silver Age" in 1973, all countries except

---

[1] Measured in terms of real GDP per capita, the figure for Ireland in 2005 was $ 27,295, i.e., just ahead of Norway. However, Irish GDP is distorted by transfer pricing encouraged by the corporate tax rules, and GNP is a more appropriate measure for recent performance (Cassidy 2004).

Table 12.2 Levels and rates of growth of real GDP per capita in western European countries ($ 1990 GK and % per year)

	1950	1973	1950–73
Switzerland	9064	18204	3.08
Denmark	6943	13945	3.08
UK	6939	12025	2.42
Sweden	6739	12494	3.06
Netherlands	5971	13081	3.45
Belgium	5462	12170	3.54
Norway	5430	11324	3.24
France	5271	13114	4.04
West Germany	4281	13153	5.02
Finland	4253	11085	4.25
Austria	3706	11235	4.94
Italy	3502	10634	4.95
Ireland	3453	6867	3.03
Spain	2189	7661	5.60
Portugal	2086	7063	5.45
Greece	1915	7655	6.21

	1973	2005	1973–2005
Switzerland	18204	22972	0.74
Denmark	13945	24116	1.73
Sweden	13494	22912	1.68
West Germany	13153	20576	1.41
France	13114	22240	1.67
Netherlands	13081	22531	1.72
Belgium	12170	21953	1.87
UK	12025	22417	1.96
Norway	11324	27219	2.78
Austria	11235	22036	2.13
Finland	11085	22121	2.18
Italy	10634	19252	1.88
Spain	7661	18166	2.74
Greece	7655	14868	2.10
Portugal	7063	13954	2.15
Ireland[a]	6867	23019	3.84

[a] The Irish figure is for GNP in 2005
Sources: GGDC 2007; and West Germany from Statistisches Bundesamt Deutschland 2007.

Czechoslovakia were below Ireland, which at that time had the lowest level of real GDP per capita in the west. In 2005, East Germany was just below Portugal, then the lowest western European country.

Table 12.5 provides estimates of cross-section equations of the form:

$$GYP = \alpha + \beta(Y/P)_0$$

Table 12.3 Levels and rates of growth of real GDP per capita in eastern Europe and Russia/USSR ($ 1990 GK and % per year)

	Eastern Europe	Russia/USSR		Eastern Europe	Russia/USSR
1820	683	688	1820–70	0.63	0.63
1870	937	943	1870–1913	1.39	1.06
1913	1695	1488	1913–50	0.60	1.76
1950	2111	2841	1950–73	3.81	3.35
1973	4988	6059	1973–2005	1.14	0.14
2005	7174	6336			

Source: GGDC 2007; Maddison 2003.

Table 12.4 Levels and rates of growth of real GDP per capita in eastern European countries ($ 1990 GK and % per year)

	1950	1973	1950–73
Czechoslovakia	3501	7041	3.08
Hungary	2480	5596	3.60
Poland	2447	5340	3.45
East Germany	2102	5753	4.47
Bulgaria	1651	5284	5.19
Yugoslavia	1551	4361	4.59
Romania	1182	3477	4.79
Albania	1001	2273	3.62

	1973	2005	1973–2005
Czechoslovakia	7041	10704	1.32
East Germany	5753	13800	1.56
Hungary	5596	8857	1.45
Poland	5340	8476	1.46
Bulgaria	5284	7147	0.96
Yugoslavia	4361	5582	0.79
Romania	3477	3992	0.44
Albania	2273	3476	1.34

Sources: GGDC 2007; and Statistisches Bundesamt Deutschland 2007.

where GYP is the rate of growth of real GDP per capita and $(Y/P)_0$ is the level of real GDP per capita at the start of the period measured as a percentage of that in the leading country. Since no other variables are included, this is an unconditional convergence regression in which the null hypothesis of no β-convergence is rejected by a significant negative coefficient on $(Y/P)_0$. Unlike earlier periods, β-convergence is evident in the 1950–73 period and less evident after 1973; the estimates imply a rate of convergence of a little over 2 percent per year in the golden age, but 1.5 percent per year thereafter.

Table 12.5 Unconditional convergence regressions: eastern and western Europe

	1950–73	1973–2005
Western Europe		
Constant	6.340	4.091
	(14.519))	(9.450)
Initial GDP/capita as % USA	−0.045	−0.030
	(−5.572)	(−4.898)
R²	0.667	0.605
Western and eastern Europe		
Constant	6.468	3.858
	(15.309)	(8.397)
Initial GDP/capita as % USA	−0.047	−0.027
	(−6.442)	(−4.096)
Eastern Dummy	−1.334	−2.084
	(−3.932)	(−6.374)
R²	0.643	0.637

Source: own calculations based on data in Tables 12.2 and 12.4; t-statistics in parentheses.

When eastern European observations are added to the cross-section the estimated coefficient on initial income is virtually the same, but for the post-1950 periods an eastern European dummy variable is significantly negative. The regression confirms the point made earlier: communist countries underperformed in the golden age and, allowing for initial income levels, their growth was about 1.3 percentage points lower than that of their western European counterparts.

In Table 12.6, the regression analysis of unconditional convergence is repeated using data on regional GDP per capita in western Europe. Not surprisingly, the basic results are very similar to those obtained in Table 12.5. Again, unconditional β-convergence is observed in both periods, but at a slower rate after 1973. When country dummy variables are added to the regression, it is interesting to note that estimated coefficients suggest quite large differences among growth outcomes in the golden age, though not post-1973. Normalizing for scope for catch-up, West Germany, Spain, and Italy seem to have overperformed and the United Kingdom to have underperformed.

Growth accounting estimates

Growth accounting can be used to benchmark the sources of growth by imposing a standard production-function formula. This allows comparisons both among countries and over time and is a useful diagnostic for the

Table 12.6 Unconditional convergence regressions: western European regions

	1950–73	1950–73	1950–73	1973–2005	1973–2005	1973–2005
Constant	6.660	5.292	5.633	3.218	2.340	2.419
	(39.755)	(17.567)	(13.926)	(19.608)	(9.731)	
Initial GDP/capita	−0.051	−0.029	−0.035	−0.019	−0.008	−0.011
% leader	(−14.487)	(−7.521)	(−6.294)	(−7.870)	(−3.396)	(−3.396)
Spain		0.920	0.826		0.793	0.660
		(3.537)	(2.975)		(4.243)	(3.350)
West Germany		1.046	0.917		−0.229	−0.265
		(4.346)	(3.683)		(−1.247)	(−1.514)
UK		−0.833	−0.798		0.195	0.082
		(−3.539)	(−3.198)		(1.088)	(0.469)
France		0.169	0.167		−0.044	−0.028
		(0.766)	(0.765)		(−0.263)	(−0.176)
Italy		0.716	0.645		0.085	0.023
		(3.017)	(2.661)		(0.492)	(0.131)
Density			0.0002			0.0002
			(1.895)			(2.930)
Distance to			−0.0001			0.0001
Luxembourg			(−0.462)			(0.807)
R²	0.713	0.870	0.873	0.420	0.662	0.696

Sources: own calculations based on GDP per capita relative to national average for France, Italy, Netherlands, Spain, the UK, and West Germany for set of same eighty-five regions obtained from Molle 1980, Martínez-Galarraga 2007, and Eurostat, *Regional Statistics*, various issues. These relativities were then applied to national estimates for real GDP per capita reported in Table 12.2. Density (= population/land area) was calculated from the same sources. Distances to Luxembourg are from www.mapcrow.info plus intercept of 100 km. t-statistics in parentheses.

evaluation of growth performance. The traditional methodology is based on a Cobb–Douglas production function:

$$Y = AK^\alpha L^\beta$$

and the Solow residual measure of total factor productivity (TFP) growth is computed as:

$$\Delta A/A = \Delta Y/Y - s_K \Delta K/K - s_L \Delta L/L$$

where s_K and s_L are the factor income shares of capital and labor, respectively, which are taken to be 0.35 and 0.65 in the benchmarked studies reported below. The contribution of labor force growth can be refined by taking labor quality into account rather than simply measuring the crude quantity of labor. So it is quite standard to take account of the education of the labor force by converting years of schooling per worker into an augmented labor input.

The basic growth accounting equation can be converted into an expression that accounts for the rate of growth of labor productivity as follows:

$$\Delta(Y/L)/(Y/L) = s_K\Delta(K/L)/(K/L) + \Delta A/A$$

i.e., in terms of contributions from capital deepening and TFP growth.

It should be noted that TFP does not equate to technological progress even though the latter is a major component of the former. Two important reasons for this are improvements in the efficiency with which inputs are used and economies of scale, which both show up in the Solow residual. Slightly less obvious is that the underlying rate of technological progress may not feed through into productivity improvements, because the economy does not always operate at optimal capacity owing to adjustment costs and fixed factors of production.

In episodes of catch-up growth, strong labor productivity growth is based on a combination of substantial capital deepening and rapid TFP growth from a starting point where capital per worker and, especially, the level of TFP are both relatively low. The former reflects a history of a shortfall of savings and investment; the latter is partly a consequence of technology gaps, but also partly of inefficient use of factors of production.

Table 12.7 reports growth accounting estimates for the sources of economic growth in western European countries in three periods: the latter part of the golden age, the subsequent period of slowdown, and the recent past when ICT became important. The golden age era of rapid catch-up was indeed a period when both capital deepening and TFP growth contributed greatly to labor productivity growth. In fact, in the majority of countries TFP growth made the larger contribution. This was not based to any significant extent on domestic R&D but rather on a combination of technology transfer, structural change, economies of scale, and fuller utilization of factors of production as post-war reconstruction was completed (Temin 2002).

Similar estimates are not generally available for eastern European countries, but it is possible to construct crude estimates for the USSR. As Table 12.7 shows, the striking feature of catch-up growth in the communist world is that, if standard growth accounting assumptions are adopted, it relied much more on "extensive growth." While the capital deepening contribution to growth in the golden age was similar or a bit lower, TFP growth was decidedly inferior, such that its contribution was very weak compared with countries like Ireland or Italy with similar catch-up potential.[2] A comparison between Tables 12.7 and 12.8 shows that catch-up growth in golden age western Europe owed a

---

[2] It has been suggested that this may be an artefact of the methodology, and that the USSR is better described in terms of a production function with a very low elasticity of substitution between capital and labor and thus severely diminishing returns to capital (Weitzman 1970). Allen (2003) provides a convincing rebuttal of this claim, noting that the technological possibilities were similar in west and east and that there is clear evidence of massive waste of capital in the Soviet system, which implies that standard benchmarking is appropriate.

Table 12.7 Contributions to labor productivity growth: western Europe, USA, East Germany, and USSR (% per year)

	Capital deepening	Human capital deepening	TFP	Labor productivity growth
1960–70				
Austria	2.39	0.18	2.90	5.47
Belgium	1.36	0.42	2.33	4.11
Denmark	2.15	0.13	1.25	3.53
Finland	1.66	0.37	2.64	4.67
France	2.02	0.29	2.62	4.93
West Germany	2.10	0.23	2.03	4.36
Greece	3.63	0.26	4.45	8.34
Ireland	1.78	0.22	2.21	4.21
Italy	2.39	0.36	3.50	6.25
Netherlands	1.43	0.74	0.89	3.06
Norway	1.18	0.48	1.80	3.46
Portugal	2.05	0.35	3.99	6.39
Spain	2.45	0.38	3.73	6.56
Sweden	1.34	0.19	2.40	3.93
Switzerland	1.40	0.40	1.37	3.17
UK	1.45	0.17	1.24	2.86
USA	0.03	0.43	1.54	2.00
East Germany	1.10	n/a	1.71	2.81
USSR	1.84	n/a	0.90	2.74
1970–90				
Austria	1.32	0.22	1.00	2.54
Belgium	0.96	0.18	1.38	2.52
Denmark	0.82	0.24	0.02	1.08
Finland	0.98	0.62	0.90	2.50
France	1.28	0.36	0.84	2.48
West Germany	0.79	0.40	0.69	1.88
Greece	1.24	0.50	0.06	1.80
Ireland	1.47	0.38	1.18	3.03
Italy	0.98	0.32	1.22	2.52
Netherlands	0.72	0.25	0.65	1.62
Norway	0.90	0.70	0.84	2.44
Portugal	0.90	0.44	1.01	2.35
Spain	1.54	0.37	1.13	3.04
Sweden	0.67	0.36	0.27	1.30
Switzerland	0.72	0.30	−0.38	0.64
UK	0.83	0.32	0.74	1.89
USA	0.24	0.41	0.43	1.08
East Germany	1.05	n/a	0.75	1.80
USSR	1.14	n/a	−0.06	1.08
1990–2003				
Austria	0.86	0.27	0.37	1.50
Belgium	0.76	0.25	0.26	1.27
Denmark	0.72	0.19	0.95	1.86
Finland	0.49	0.31	1.49	2.29

Table 12.7 (cont.)

	Capital deepening	Human capital deepening	TFP	Labor productivity growth
France	0.58	0.27	0.13	0.98
Germany	0.76	0.17	0.60	1.53
Greece	0.61	0.35	1.25	2.21
Ireland	0.49	0.26	2.24	2.99
Italy	0.60	0.38	0.14	1.12
Netherlands	0.26	0.28	0.07	0.61
Norway	0.31	0.21	1.81	2.33
Portugal	1.13	0.47	−0.31	1.29
Spain	0.63	0.37	−0.37	0.63
Sweden	0.73	0.44	1.16	2.33
Switzerland	0.60	0.08	−0.23	0.45
UK	0.91	0.41	0.74	2.06
USA	0.90	0.10	0.82	1.82

Note: All estimates based on $\Delta(Y/L)/(Y/L) = \alpha\Delta(K/L)/(K/L) + \beta\Delta(HK/L)/(HK/L) + $ TFP growth assuming $\alpha = 0.35$; for USSR human capital deepening is subsumed in TFP.
Sources: estimates from Bosworth and Collins 2003, updated from website, except for USSR which is derived from data underlying Allen 2003, Figure 10.2, and, for employment, Harrison 1998c, both kindly supplied by the authors; East Germany is derived from Ritschl 1996, adjusted for revisions to labor productivity growth as reported in GGDC 2007. Irish estimates are adjusted to GNP basis.

good deal more to TFP growth and less to capital deepening than was the case in the East Asian Tigers from the 1960s through the 1980s.

Table 12.7 reveals that the slowdown in labor productivity growth in western Europe after the golden age reflected declines in both capital deepening and TFP growth in every country, the latter being generally more important. The unweighted average decrease between 1960–70 and 1970–90 was 1.00 percentage points per year for the capital deepening contribution, but 1.75 percentage points per year for TFP growth, which was largely the result of the evaporation of transitory components mentioned above. In the Soviet Union, TFP growth turned slightly negative, but the decline in labor productivity growth owed almost as much to a reduction in the contribution from capital deepening.

In the most recent period, 1990–2003, Table 12.7 shows a considerable diversity in performance among western European countries. Nine of these sixteen countries were no longer catching up with the United States in terms of labor productivity, and in eleven of them TFP growth was below that of the United States. While both capital deepening and TFP growth recovered from the lows seen in 1970–90 in the United States, they fell further in the majority of western European countries, though with some notable exceptions with regard

Table 12.8 Contributions to labor productivity growth: East Asian Tigers (% per year)

	Capital deepening	Human capital deepening	TFP	Labor productivity growth
1960–90				
Singapore	3.34	0.31	1.32	4.97
South Korea	2.84	0.80	1.42	5.06
Taiwan	3.17	0.60	2.30	6.07
1990–2003				
Singapore	1.76	0.82	0.93	3.51
South Korea	2.40	0.46	0.95	3.81
Taiwan	2.67	0.34	1.75	4.76

Source: derived as in Table 12.7 from Bosworth and Collins 2003, updated on website.

Table 12.9 Contributions to labor productivity growth: eastern Europe (% per year)

	Capital deepening	Human capital deepening	TFP	Labor productivity growth
1996–2006				
Czech Republic	2.1	n/a	1.1	3.2
Estonia	3.1	n/a	4.3	7.4
Hungary	1.8	n/a	1.7	3.5
Latvia	2.7	n/a	3.9	6.6
Lithuania	2.1	n/a	4.1	6.2
Poland	1.9	n/a	2.5	4.4
Slovakia	2.3	n/a	1.5	3.8
Slovenia	2.0	n/a	1.8	3.8
CIS	2.0	n/a	3.7	5.7
Russia	1.3	n/a	2.7	4.0

Source: derived from data in Iradian 2007, imposing same benchmarking assumptions as in Table 12.7 with human capital subsumed in TFP.

to TFP growth, including the Scandinavian countries, Greece, Ireland, and the UK. More detailed growth accounting confirms that these outcomes are quite closely related to differential success in exploiting the opportunities of the ICT era (Timmer and van Ark 2005), a theme which will be explored below (pp. 323–7).

Finally, Table 12.9 reports growth accounting estimates for the transition economies of eastern Europe starting from the mid-1990s. Labor productivity growth in the countries which have now joined the EU is still quite modest relative to the rates achieved by western European countries in the golden age, except in the Baltic countries. These outcomes seem to result more from TFP growth than from capital deepening contributions, although it should be noted that the data used to construct these estimates are more than usually imperfect. TFP growth in CIS countries has been relatively strong. In this region, strong TFP growth probably reflects a bounce back from an earlier output collapse, similar to post-war reconstruction but on a much larger scale, with in some cases (including Russia), a strong impetus from a high price of oil (Iradian 2007).

The golden age

From the late 1940s to the mid-1970s, growth in Europe was exceptional but performance was not uniformly good. This raises two questions which this section addresses, namely:

(1)   What explains the golden age?
(2)   What accounts for relative success and failure during the golden age?

In fact, examining the latter question gives further insight into the former, as the variance in growth outcomes is quite informative.

Western Europe had endured two world wars and the interwar depression, and so in 1950 many countries were well below the income level that a continuation of pre-1914 trend growth would have predicted. Recovery, and the correction of policy errors such as the disastrous protectionism of the interwar period, had the potential to deliver a phase of rapid growth. International economic relations would be different under the auspices of the Bretton Woods Agreement and the Marshall Plan from what they had been under the League of Nations and the Treaty of Versailles.

It is widely recognized that the Bretton Woods era of international monetary system, which coincided with the golden age, was a period when macroeconomic fluctuations were relatively gentle, and it has been argued that this provided a highly favorable context for rapid post-war growth (Boltho 1982). Theory is ambiguous about this claim, however, and economists have struggled to identify robust effects of output volatility on growth (Norrbin and Yigit 2005).

Rapid catch-up growth was, however based on more than this. The golden age can be seen as a period when western European growth was augmented by enhanced "social capability" and "technological congruence" (Abramovitz and David 1996). In terms of Figure 12.1, better institutions and policies promoted favorable shifts in both the Solow and Schumpeter lines.

The relative importance of these factors varied over time, as is revealed by the cross-country growth regressions in Temin 2002. In the 1950s, countries with relatively large scope for post-war reconstruction (e.g., West Germany) grew relatively quickly; in both the 1950s and early 1960s, countries with large agricultural sectors (e.g., Italy) performed relatively well, but after 1965 orthodox reduction of capital to labor and technology gaps took center stage.

The results from long-run time-series analysis of the "Janossy Hypothesis" obtained by Mills and Crafts (2000) confirm and extend these conclusions. Janossy (1969) maintained that the phase of super growth after the Second World War was based simply on a reversion to the pre-1914 trend growth path. This was shown to be incorrect, in that in all western European countries real GDP per capita was above the pre-1914 trend line by the end of the golden age. However, in the most war-affected economies – Austria, France, Netherlands, and West Germany – there is clear evidence of a slowdown in growth from the late 1950s.

The role of the Marshall Plan, whereby the United States provided $13 billion of grant aid to western Europe in the period 1948–51, has been the subject of significant research. It is now generally agreed that the direct effects were of little importance in the launching of the golden age. The investment rate was raised by perhaps 1 percent of GDP, but basic growth economics suggests that would have only a modest impact on growth and that there is no reason to think that the alleviation of supply bottlenecks mattered much either (Eichengreen and Uzan 1992).[3]

If the Marshall Plan had any substantial effects, they came through indirect channels. DeLong and Eichengreen (1993) suggest that it was a highly successful structural adjustment program – much more so than those designed by the World Bank in the 1980s and 1990s. These indirect effects worked through conditionality that changed the environment in which economic policy was made, both by strengthening commitments to the market economy and trade liberalization and by facilitating social contracts that underpinned high investment.

Trade liberalization can be expected to raise income levels by more than just the traditional welfare triangle effect. In addition, there may be positive impacts from greater investment, more technology transfer, intensified competition, and the realization of both internal and external economies of scale. Whether or not these have permanent effects on the growth rate, there is strong evidence that they have raised the level of income. Badinger (2005) finds that the process of European integration from the 1950s meant that European incomes were 26 percent higher in 2000. His index of integration shows that the strongest impact was felt between the late 1950s and the early 1970s, when about 55 percent of the initial trade barriers were eliminated through the

---

[3] Using standard neo-classical assumptions, with an initial capital to output ratio of around 2 and an output elasticity of 0.35, the growth effect of an increase in the investment rate of 1 percent of GDP would have been less than 0.2 percentage points per year.

establishment of the European Community, EFTA, and the Kennedy Round of GATT. The implication was an increase of the European growth rate of around 1 percent per year during this period.

External trade liberalization and the increased integration of the European market were factors that speeded up technology transfer and helped Europe to reduce the technology gap with the United States (Madsen 2007). There was more to it than this, however. Nelson and Wright (1992) also stressed the greater cost effectiveness of American technology in Europe, the increasing codification of technological knowledge, and increases in European technological competence based on increased investments in human capital and R&D. Even the most technologically advanced European countries were still obtaining over 40 percent of their technological progress from American research in the 1980s (Eaton and Kortum 1999).

In turn, it would be incorrect to see rapid TFP growth in golden age Europe as simply a reflection of technology transfer. Improvements in resource allocation played an important part, most notably in the context of a contraction of agricultural employment. Orthodox shift-share analysis does not capture this adequately, because it assumes that productivity growth rates in each sector would be unaffected by the absence of structural change, whereas rapid productivity advance in agriculture was predicated on the transfer of surplus labor out of small-scale family farms. Table 12.10 quantifies the contribution of

Table 12.10 Contribution of structural change to labor productivity growth, 1950–73 (% per year)

	Orthodox measure	Broadberry measure
Denmark	0.24	1.10
UK	−0.12	0.31
Sweden	0.00	0.60
Netherlands	−0.31	0.29
France	0.00	0.52
West Germany	0.18	0.77
Italy	0.83	1.77
Spain	0.80	1.77

Note: The orthodox approach assumes that the contribution of structural change equals $\Delta A_O/A_O - \sum \Delta A_i/A_i * A_i/A_O * S_i$ where A is labor productivity, S is share of employment, and subscripts o and i stand for the whole economy and sector i, respectively (Nordhaus 1972). Broadberry (1998) modified this so that labor productivity growth in declining sectors was measured using the overall rate of labor force growth, not the sectoral rate.
Source: derived from data in van Ark 1996 using a three-sector (agriculture, industry, services) decomposition where agriculture is assumed to be the declining sector.

structural change to labor productivity growth using the method proposed by Broadberry (1998), which implies that this had a major impact in Italy and Spain and a quite sizeable impact in France and West Germany.

Jerzmanowski (2007) provides a decomposition of TFP gaps between European countries and the United States which shows that while these gaps were still quite large in 1960, they were primarily due to shortfalls in efficiency rather than technology gaps. By 1985, big reductions in these efficiency gaps accounted for a good part of European catch-up. This tends to confirm both the importance of improvements in resource allocation and the fact that American technology was appropriate for early post-war western Europe.

The most striking hypothesis to explain enhanced social capability in post-war western Europe is that of Eichengreen (1999a), who argued that high investment rates (which allowed successful exploitation of catch-up opportunities) were facilitated by successful social contracts that sustained wage moderation by workers in return for high investment by firms. These "corporatist" arrangements provided institutions to monitor capitalists' compliance and centralized wage bargaining, which protected high-investment firms and prevented free-riding by sub-sets of workers. In addition, the state provided "bonds," in the form of an expanded welfare state, that would be jeopardized if labor defected on the agreements. The central foundation of a high investment/wage moderation equilibrium is that both sides are willing to wait for jam tomorrow.

It is certainly true that corporatist industrial relations were quite widespread in the golden age. Crouch (1993) puts Austria, Belgium, the Netherlands, Switzerland, West Germany, and the Scandinavian economies in this category. France and Italy, while not adopting the corporatist model as such, nevertheless enjoyed some of its advantages due to direct government intervention in the wage-bargaining process in the technologically advanced sectors where state-owned companies prevailed, thus providing guidelines to the overall wage-setting process (Toniolo 1998). The latter was, as in the corporatist countries, to a large extent centralized. Two of the most obvious "failures" of the golden age, Ireland and the UK, did not succeed in establishing these institutions, having strong but decentralized collective bargaining. But centralized wage bargaining does not appear to have been correlated with faster growth, *ceteris paribus* (Crafts 1992b). This is, however, at best, a crude test of the Eichengreen hypothesis on which the jury is still out.

A glance at Table 12.2 shows a strong inverse correlation between the level of real GDP per capita in a country in 1950 and its growth rate during the golden age, as would be expected given the evidence of unconditional convergence in this period. However, Table 12.2 also points to countries which appear to have done rather better or worse than their initial income might predict, and these do indeed include West Germany in the former and Ireland and the UK in the latter category. The residuals from the regression of Table 12.5 are +0.68 for West Germany and –1.70 and –0.68 for Ireland and the UK, respectively. Thus the diagnosis is that the UK could not have grown as fast as Italy or Spain, which had greater scope for catch-up, but should have been able to match Denmark or Sweden, while Ireland's growth might have been similar to that of Italy rather than Switzerland.

Going beyond the Eichengreen hypothesis, does the literature on these countries suggest further reasons for their apparent success or failure? In particular, is it possible to understand this in terms of the microfoundations of growth? Ireland is a particularly interesting case because the poor growth performance of the golden age was followed from the late 1980s by the famous Celtic Tiger phase of very rapid catch-up growth. Analysis of the reasons for this acceleration is also, either explicitly or implicitly, analysis of the reasons for Ireland's golden age failure.

It seems clear that the issues relate primarily to Irish economic policy rather than to peripherality, which Table 12.6 suggests was not an adverse factor. The most obvious initial error, which was corrected in the 1960s and 1970s, was to delay trade liberalization and instead pursue policies of import substitution (Ó Gráda and O'Rourke 1996). More than this, from the late 1960s, Ireland adopted a series of policies that facilitated technology transfer by attracting foreign direct investment (FDI) which could use Ireland as a platform from which to export, and thus to create a favorable shift in the Schumpeter line of Figure 12.1. These included a very generous corporate tax regime and a big (belated) upgrade in the educational standards of the Irish labor force. When macroeconomic stablization was achieved in the late 1980s in the context of a social contract, the ingredients for the Celtic Tiger were in place (Barry 2002).

With regard to West Germany and the UK, there were important differences in institutions and policies during the golden age. First, it is clear that West Germany was much more successful at human and physical capital accumulation. In 1973, capital per hour worked in West Germany was 35 percent above the UK level and in 1978/9 only 34.5 percent of West German workers were low skilled compared with 72.8 percent in the UK (O'Mahony 1999). This strong record of accumulation was based on corporatist institutions that incentivized vocational training, and an "insider" financial system that fostered relationship-specific long-term investments (Carlin 1996). Secondly, there was a major difference between the two countries in terms of industrial relations. Whereas West Germany established a system of industrial unions, multiple unionism was quite prevalent in the UK. Multiple unionism makes the "hold-up problem" for investments in fixed capital much more serious and encourages free-riding by unions; Bean and Crafts (1996) show that multiple unionism imposed a significant penalty in terms of productivity growth on the UK. Third, competition was relatively weak in the UK compared with West Germany, partly because the UK was slow to liberalize external trade and partly because competition policy was a low priority and badly designed. Price–cost margins were much higher and supernormal profits more persistent in the UK than in West Germany (Crafts and Mills 2005; Geroski and Jacquemin 1988). This mattered because UK firms suffered more from the agency problems that arise from separation of ownership and control, and to which competition is the antidote.[4] The UK evidence is that weak competition in the absence of a dominant external shareholder was associated with markedly inferior productivity performance (Nickell, Nicolitsas, and Dryden 1997).[5] In terms of the growth economics of Figure 12.1, West Germany was better placed than the UK.

The picture of golden age growth in western Europe that has emerged is as follows. First, the era was one of strong β-convergence. Second, fast growth was partly based on opportunities to recover from earlier adverse shocks and policy errors, but it is clear that European growth involved more than just that; both capital-to-labor and TFP gaps with the United States were considerably reduced over a prolonged period. Third, as modern growth economics stresses and as comparisons across European countries confirm, incentive structures mattered for growth performance.

The performance of eastern European economies during their silver age was less impressive, even though growth was rapid by historical standards. The diagnostics developed earlier reflect this. The regression of Table 12.5 suggested that there was a growth shortfall of about 1.3 percentage points, and the growth accounting of Table 12.7 points to weak TFP growth as a key reason.

Closer examination of growth in the USSR helps explain this outcome and also highlights important themes in the western European experience. Following the Second World War, the Soviet economy grew much as the Janossy hypothesis would predict, albeit with a modest trend growth in labor productivity. Worrying signs of a serious retardation in productivity growth on top of a Janossy-type slowdown did not appear until the 1970s (Harrison 1998c). The Soviet economy succeeded in producing "extensive growth," in that the investment/GDP ratio roughly doubled between 1950 and the early 1970s to just under 30 percent and the capital stock grew at about 8.5 percent per year in this period (Ofer 1987). Diminishing returns to capital accumulation (a rapidly rising marginal capital to output ratio), exacerbated by slow

---

[4] West Germany relied much less on public joint stock companies where these issues are likely to matter most. German companies almost always had shareholders owning 25 percent of the company, whereas in the UK only a small percentage did (Carlin 1996, p. 488). It should be noted that it is ownership concentration, not bank shareholdings *per se*, that delivers good performance (Edwards and Nibler 2000).

[5] In the one instance where UK competition policy was made considerably tougher – the 1956 Restrictive Practices Act which addressed the widespread cartelization that prevailed at the time – there was a marked improvement in productivity in the sectors which were collusive prior to the legislation (Symeonidis 2008).

TFP growth, implied that the rate of capital stock growth delivered by a given investment rate was falling over time.

Relatively low TFP growth was not the result of inadequate volumes of R&D, which by the 1970s was very high by world standards at around 3 percent of GDP. Rather the problem lay in the incentive structures that informed innovation at the firm level. This was a classic case of a failure in terms of "social capability." The planning system rewarded managers who achieved production targets in the short term rather than those who found ways to reduce costs or improve the quality of output over the long term. The balance of risk and reward was inimical to organizational and technological change, and the "kicking foot" of competition was absent (Berliner 1976). The Schumpeter line of Figure 12.1 was subject to a major adverse shift compared with western economies.

The post-golden age slowdown

After the early 1970s growth slowed down quite markedly right across Europe. The end of the golden age had a number of unavoidable aspects, including the exhaustion of transitory components of fast growth such as post-war reconstruction, diminishing returns to investment as the post-war boom went on, and reduction in the scope for catch-up as the gap with the leader narrowed and, in addition, growth of real GDP per capita in the United States weakened. In the east, the problems of slowdown became so acute as to trigger a regime-changing collapse.

On closer inspection, however, the story is clearly more complex and the context in which growth took place was changing. By 1973, deindustrialization had begun in much of western Europe and in the ensuing decades it became general (cf. Table 12.11); increasingly, the key to successful growth performance was going to reside in services rather than the manufacturing sector. This tendency was intensified by the rapidly increasing integration of world markets (globalization) and the switch of world industrial production and exports from Europe to Asia. And, since there was less scope for catch-up, slowdown was exacerbated by a sharp fall in the rate of catch-up, as reflected in the smaller coefficients on the initial income term in the regressions reported in Tables 12.5 and 12.6. Although the lower-income countries of western Europe continued to grow more quickly, in western Europe as a whole, since the early 1970s, catch-up has stalled with real GDP per capita at only about two thirds of the American level (Table 12.1). It is also noticeable that the pattern of relative success and failure changed after the golden age: for example, growth performance in Ireland has improved dramatically whereas that of France, Germany, and Italy has deteriorated.

Table 12.11 Sectoral employment shares

	Agriculture	Industry	Services
1950			
Austria	32.3	37.1	30.6
Belgium	12.2	48.9	38.9
Denmark	25.1	33.3	41.6
Finland	46.0	27.7	26.3
France	31.5	31.8	36.7
Germany	23.2	42.9	33.9
Greece	48.2	19.3	32.5
Ireland	39.6	24.4	36.0
Italy	42.2	32.1	25.7
Netherlands	17.8	38.4	43.8
Norway	25.9	36.9	37.4
Portugal	48.4	25.1	26.5
Spain	48.8	25.1	26.1
Sweden	20.3	40.9	38.8
Switzerland	16.5	46.6	36.9
UK	5.3	48.8	45.9
1974			
Austria	13.0	44.8	42.2
Belgium	3.8	41.0	55.2
Denmark	9.6	32.3	58.1
Finland	16.3	36.1	47.6
France	10.6	39.4	50.0
Germany	7.0	46.7	46.3
Greece	36.0	27.8	36.2
Ireland	22.8	32.6	44.6
Italy	17.5	39.3	43.2
Netherlands	5.7	35.9	58.4
Norway	10.6	34.3	55.1
Portugal	34.9	33.8	31.3
Spain	23.2	37.2	39.6
Sweden	6.7	37.0	56.3
Switzerland	7.5	44.3	48.2
UK	2.8	42.0	55.2
2004			
Austria	5.0	27.8	67.2
Belgium	2.0	24.9	73.1
Denmark	3.1	23.7	73.2
Finland	4.9	25.7	69.4
France	3.5	23.0	73.5
Germany	2.4	31.0	66.6
Greece	12.6	22.5	64.9
Ireland	6.4	27.7	65.9
Italy	4.5	31.0	64.5
Netherlands	3.0	20.3	76.7
Norway	3.5	20.9	75.6

Table 12.11 (cont.)

	Agriculture	Industry	Services
Portugal	12.1	31.4	56.5
Spain	5.5	30.5	64.0
Sweden	2.1	22.6	75.3
Switzerland	3.7	23.7	72.6
UK	1.3	22.3	76.4

Note: mining included in "industry."
Sources: Bairoch 1968; OECD 2001, 2005

With regard to labor productivity, although here too there was a marked drop in the size of the catch-up term in growth regressions (Crafts 2007), western European countries continued to narrow the gap with the United States until the mid-1990s, as Table 12.12 shows. However, the growth accounting estimates of Table 12.7 show that this was despite very big reductions in the contribution of capital deepening (the median fell to 1.0 from 2.0 percent per year in 1970–90 compared with 1960–70) and, especially, in TFP growth (the median fell from 2.5 to 0.9 percent per year).

This description prompts the following questions:

(1) What accounts for the differing trends in GDP per capita and labor productivity vis-à-vis the United States?
(2) Why did the European growth slowdown go beyond what was unavoidable?
(3) Why was the slowdown so much more serious for eastern Europe?

The short answer to the first of these questions is that, since the golden age, on average, Europeans work less than Americans (cf. Table 12.13), in particular, because they have more unemployment, longer holidays, and in some areas (e.g., Italy) lower female participation in the labor force. The implications for economic welfare depend on the extent to which shorter work years for the employed are attributed to distortions from tax (Prescott 2004) or from collective bargaining (Alesina, Glaeser, and Sacerdote 2005) rather than different preferences (Blanchard 2004). The experience across Europe is quite complicated; the literature has not yet reached a consensus on this issue and a satisfactory explanation has not yet been achieved. The elasticity of labor supply to tax changes seems too small to account for more than a modest part of the experience, and the cultural argument seems less than fully convincing given that the differential is recent, while strong collective bargaining produced work-sharing responses in some countries but not others (Faggio and Nickell 2007).

In considering labor productivity growth, it is helpful to divide the post-golden age period in the mid-1990s at the point where ICT had a major impact. Table 12.12 shows that from 1973 to 1995, western European countries

Table 12.12 Levels and rates of growth of real GDP/hour worked

(a) Levels (1990 GK $)

1973	(1)	(2)	1995	(1)	(2)	2005	(1)	(2)
Switzerland	18.88		Norway	31.67	28.78	Norway	39.78	36.68
Netherlands	18.01	17.69	W.Germany	30.08		France	35.24	31.44
Sweden	17.15	16.94	Belgium	29.21		Belgium	33.54	
Belgium	16.95		France	29.13	26.10	Netherlands	31.87	28.17
Italy	16.16	14.76	Italy	27.61	23.44	Austria	31.05	
W. Germany	16.05		Netherlands	27.47	23.28	Denmark	30.13	
Denmark	15.88		Denmark	27.01		Sweden	30.01	28.39
France	15.73	15.99	Austria	24.76		UK	29.62	28.56
Norway	15.70	14.96	Germany	24.50	21.31	Ireland	29.29	27.32
UK	14.05	14.05	UK	24.06	22.78	Italy	28.94	24.89
Austria	13.39		Sweden	23.47	21.89	Germany	28.86	24.88
Finland	11.61	12.40	Switzerland	23.33		Finland	28.13	26.79
Greece	10.15		Spain	22.24	18.44	Switzerland	26.82	
Spain	9.47	9.96	Finland	22.20	20.23	Spain	21.78	19.74
Ireland	9.45	10.41	Ireland	19.60	17.38	Greece	18.94	
Portugal	9.21		Greece	14.70		Portugal	17.20	
			Portugal	14.31				
USA	21.28		USA	27.77		USA	35.20	

(b) Rates of growth (% per year)

1973–95	(1)	(2)	1995–2005	(1)	(2)
Switzerland	0.97		Norway	2.31	2.46
Netherlands	1.94	1.26	Belgium	1.40	
Sweden	1.44	1.17	France	1.93	1.89
Belgium	2.51		Italy	0.48	0.62
Italy	2.47	2.13	Netherlands	1.50	1.93
W. Germany	2.90		Denmark	1.10	
Denmark	2.44		Austria	2.29	
France	2.84	2.25	Germany	1.66	1.57
Norway	3.24	3.02	UK	2.10	2.29
UK	2.48	2.22	Sweden	2.49	2.63
Austria	2.83		Switzerland	1.41	
Finland	2.95	2.25	Spain	−0.21	0.70
Greece	1.91		Finland	2.40	2.85
Spain	3.94	2.84	Ireland	4.10	4.62
Ireland	3.37	2.36	Greece	2.57	
Portugal	2.02		Portugal	1.87	
USA	1.22		USA	2.40	

Note: figures for Ireland are for GNP/HW. (1) refers to observed values and (2) refers to "structural values."
Sources: derived from Bourles and Cette 2006, and GGDC 2007.

Table 12.13 Annual hours worked/worker and total hours worked/population: western European countries and United States

	1950	1973	1995	2005
Annual hours/worker				
Austria	2100	1889	1561	1519
Belgium	2404	1851	1642	1611
Denmark	2145	1747	1499	1575
Finland	2035	1914	1776	1714
France	2233	2019	1650	1529
(West) Germany	2372	1870	1494	1437
Greece	2322	2111	1922	1912
Ireland	2437	2103	1835	1636
Italy	1928	1788	1635	1592
Netherlands	2299	1823	1456	1413
Norway	2039	1703	1414	1360
Portugal	2344	2024	1822	1709
Spain	2052	2124	1814	1774
Sweden	2016	1642	1626	1588
Switzerland	2092	1810	1598	1534
UK	2112	1919	1667	1624
United States	2016	1898	1853	1791
Total hours/population				
Austria	1037.9	839.2	729.0	709.7
Belgium	936.9	718.0	625.4	654.5
Denmark	1033.4	878.1	753.3	800.5
Finland	1055.1	955.2	714.2	786.4
France	1053.9	833.4	644.1	631.0
(West) Germany	982.5	819.5	643.9	685.6
Greece	787.9	754.4	702.1	785.2
Ireland	1000.8	728.4	648.9	785.8
Italy	686.2	658.1	623.5	665.3
Netherlands	885.1	726.3	673.8	706.9
Norway	892.1	721.1	685.3	684.3
Portugal	970.7	766.7	811.6	811.5
Spain	868.5	809.3	578.3	834.2
Sweden	988.8	786.8	751.6	763.5
Switzerland	1044.0	964.4	883.5	856.7
UK	943.6	856.2	731.1	756.7
United States	804.6	784.2	885.8	882.7

Note: 1995 figures are for West Germany; the data for Germany are 1534 and 704.0, respectively.
Source: GGDC 2007.

generally continued to catch up with the United States in terms of labor productivity and all except Switzerland had faster growth. Indeed, the raw data show that by 1995 six countries had apparently overtaken the United States and had a higher level of labor productivity. In fact, underlying performance was probably not quite that good, as European responses to the difficult macroeconomic environment of the 1970s and 1980s entailed reductions of labor inputs promoted both by collective bargaining and by government policies which disproportionately affected the employment of low-productivity (especially young and elderly) workers. The estimates in column (2) of Table 12.12 report the results of an econometric procedure to normalize for the productivity impact of different labor market structures. On the basis of these normalized estimates it seems probable that only Norway (which had become a major oil producer) actually overtook the United States, and that underlying European labor productivity growth was a fair bit lower than the raw data suggest. Even so, virtually all countries continued to catch up with the United States through the mid-1990s, albeit more slowly than before.

What may have accounted for this undue weakening of productivity growth? One very obvious point is that the fragility of the Eichengreen wage moderation/high investment equilibrium was revealed and it did not generally survive the turbulence of the 1970s, a time when union militancy and union power rose dramatically, as did labor's share of value added, and the rewards for patience fell in conditions of greater capital mobility, floating exchange rates, and greater employment protection. At the same time, the corporatist model of economic growth was becoming less appropriate in economies which now needed to become more innovative and less imitative in achieving productivity growth, as Eichengreen (2007) himself has recently emphasized.

Especially given the difficulties of the 1970s, in many countries the postwar settlements entailed a substantial rise in social welfare payments, financed to a considerable extent by "distortionary" taxation (Table 12.14).[6] The estimates in Kneller, Bleaney, and Gemmell (1999) indicate that an increase of one percentage point in the ratio of distortionary taxation to GDP reduces the growth rate by 0.1 percentage points, so the tax increases between 1965 and 1995 would on average entail a fall in the growth rate of about one percentage point.

Equally, the typical western European country also acquired a legacy of strong regulation (cf. Tables 12.15 and 12.17) which inhibited growth performance, but was politically difficult to reform. The evidence is that strict product market regulation raised mark-ups and lowered entry rates, thus reducing competitive pressure on managers with adverse impacts on both investment and innovation (Griffith and Harrison 2004; Griffith, Harrison, and Simpson 2006), and reduced TFP growth relative to the United States in this period by around 0.75 percentage points on average, based on the estimates in Nicoletti

---

[6] "Distortionary" is the term used by Kneller, Bleaney, and Gemmell (1999). This is basically direct taxation, which in many new growth models has adverse effects on growth whereas indirect taxes do not.

Table 12.14 Distortionary tax revenues and social transfers (% GDP)

(a) Distortionary tax revenues

	1965	1980	1995	2004
Austria	21.2	26.7	29.6	30.6
Belgium	19.5	30.0	32.4	33.7
Denmark	17.8	27.0	33.1	32.8
Finland	17.3	23.2	31.8	30.2
France	21.3	30.0	31.2	32.3
Germany	21.2	27.3	26.8	24.6
Greece	10.0	13.9	18.6	22.0
Ireland[a]	11.8	18.0	19.6	22.2
Italy	15.4	21.8	29.2	30.3
Netherlands	22.4	31.3	31.3	25.5
Norway	17.4	27.5	25.2	30.9
Portugal	8.8	12.6	19.2	21.2
Spain	8.7	17.9	22.9	25.0
Sweden	24.1	35.7	34.8	37.4
Switzerland	11.5	19.5	21.7	22.3
UK	20.3	24.9	22.7	24.5
USA	19.1	21.7	22.9	20.8

(b) Social transfers

	1960	1980	1995	2003
Austria	15.9	22.6	26.6	26.1
Belgium	13.1	23.5	26.4	26.5
Denmark	12.3	25.2	28.9	27.6
Finland	8.8	18.4	27.4	22.5
France	13.4	20.8	28.3	28.7
Germany	18.1	23.0	26.6	27.3
Greece	10.4	11.5	19.3	21.3
Ireland[a]	8.7	17.4	18.4	18.8
Italy	13.1	18.0	19.8	24.2
Netherlands	11.7	24.1	22.8	20.7
Norway	7.8	16.9	23.5	25.1
Portugal		10.8	18.1	23.5
Spain		15.5	21.5	20.3
Sweden	10.8	28.6	32.5	31.3
Switzerland	4.9	13.9	17.5	20.5
UK	10.2	16.6	20.4	20.6
USA	7.3	13.3	15.4	16.2

[a] For Ireland the figure represents % of GNP.
Sources: Lindert 2004; OECD 2006, 2007a.

Table 12.15 Product market regulation (0–10) and price–cost margins

	PCM manufactures	PCM services	PMR 1980	PMR 1998	PMR 2003
Austria	1.15	1.28	8.50	3.00	2.33
Belgium	1.10	1.20	9.17	3.50	2.33
Denmark	1.11	1.25	9.17	2.50	1.83
Finland	1.18	1.27	9.00	3.50	2.17
France	1.12	1.26	10.00	4.17	2.83
Germany	1.13	1.25	8.67	3.17	2.33
Greece			9.50	4.67	3.00
Ireland			9.50	2.50	1.83
Italy	1.15	1.38	9.67	4.67	3.17
Netherlands	1.13	1.24	9.33	3.00	2.33
Norway	1.13	1.26	9.17	3.00	2.50
Portugal			9.83	3.50	2.67
Spain	1.14		8.33	3.83	2.67
Sweden	1.11	1.17	7.50	3.00	2.00
Switzerland			7.00	3.67	2.83
UK	1.11	1.16	8.00	1.83	1.50
USA	1.12	1.19	4.50	2.17	1.67

Sources: PMR indicator for 1980 from Conway and Nicoletti 2006, and for 1998 and 2003 from Conway, Jarod, and Nicoletti 2005; the 1980 numbers are not strictly comparable with those for the later years. Price–cost margins from Hoj *et al.* 2007.

and Scarpetta 2005.[7] Similarly, high levels of employment regulation (if enforced) slow down the process of creative destruction and the labor force adjustment that it entails. The results in Caballero *et al.* (2004) could account for a difference of 0.5 percentage points per year between France and the United States in labor productivity growth in the 1980s and 1990s.

Two countries which were "growth failures" in the golden age and which were in crisis in the 1970s and early 1980s, namely Ireland and the UK, stand out as having made important reforms which improved their relative performance. The former represents an interesting permutation on the Eichengreen hypothesis because it developed a new kind of social contract, in which wage restraint was exchanged for tax cuts which were conducive to employment growth and to massive inflows of FDI already encouraged by Ireland's low corporate tax rates and strong connections with the United States (Barry 2002).

The UK was a country which had failed to establish a favorable Eichengreen equilibrium. Yet it held back on policy reform in areas such as fiscal policy,

---

[7] The concept of product market regulation employed by these authors and which the OECD PMR indicators seek to capture is the extent to which the regulatory environment is conducive to competition.

privatization, and collective bargaining in vain attempts to do so. The Thatcher years after 1979, when a radical prime minister, aided by the absence of restraints in the British political system on the exercise of executive power, finally gave up on corporatism and ended the implicit trade union veto were a period of deregulation and much increased competitive pressure on management, and of reform in industrial relations, thus addressing some of the weaknesses that had undermined the UK in the golden age (Crafts 2002b).

The Soviet economy suffered from problems which in a sense were similar but were much more severe. By the 1970s, the arithmetic of Soviet growth was becoming considerably less friendly as diminishing returns reduced the capital deepening associated with the constant investment rate of a little under 30 percent of GDP. The data constructed for the analysis in Allen 2003 show that the capital stock growth rate fell from 7.4 percent per year in the 1960s to 3.4 percent per year in the 1980s, and the scope for raising the investment rate was constrained by defense expenditure (16 percent of GDP). The situation was exacerbated by a decline in TFP growth, which turned negative at this point (cf. Table 12.7). This was driven by "waste of capital on a grand scale" (Allen 2003, p. 191) as old factories were re-equipped and expansion of natural resource industries in Siberia was pursued.

The incentive structures used by the Soviet leadership to motivate managers and workers were a complex mixture of rewards, punishments, and monitoring. Each of these became increasingly expensive over time, with the consequence that the viability of the system was threatened. Product innovation drove up monitoring costs, which also inhibited moves from mass to flexible production. A more educated population meant both that incarceration was more costly in terms of loss of human capital and that rewards needed to be higher. A TFP growth failure undermined the returns to extra effort. The interesting feature of this system is that it could be tipped from a high-coercion, high-effort equilibrium to a low-coercion, shirk-and-steal equilibrium if rewards and punishments were no longer credible – and this was perceived by the workers. Harrison (2002) argues that this accounts for the sudden collapse at the end of the 1980s.

The era of the "New Economy" and transition

It is well known that the United States has enjoyed a labor productivity growth revival since the mid-1990s and that for the first time in the post-war period this has outpaced average western European performance. At about the same time, it became clear that the Solow Productivity Paradox (you could see the computer everywhere except in the productivity statistics) no longer applied.

A standard American perspective on recent European growth is that it has been handicapped by too much taxation, too much regulation, and too little competition (Baily and Kirkegaard 2004).

This summary needs some qualification. Table 12.12 reports considerable diversity in western European productivity growth in the period 1995–2005, when seven countries exhibited stronger productivity growth than in 1973–95 and five (Finland, Greece, Ireland, Norway, and Sweden) had faster productivity growth than the United States. On the other hand, Italy and Spain experienced major declines in productivity growth.

Two questions deserve attention:

(1) Is the "American diagnosis" of weak European productivity growth correct ?
(2) How far does ICT explain productivity growth differentials?

Tables 12.14 through 12.16 show that the United States has relatively low "distortionary" taxation, product market and employment protection regulation, and price–cost margins in services, while the evidence reviewed in the previous section confirms that this would be conducive to stronger productivity growth. However, if these aspects of the European social market model were damaging, they had largely been already put in place by the 1980s. Moreover, they did not preclude catch-up prior to 1995.

Table 12.16 Employment protection (0–10)

	1960–4	1973–9	1988–95	2003
Austria	3.25	4.20	6.50	4.85
Belgium	3.60	7.75	6.75	5.00
Denmark	4.50	5.50	4.50	3.50
Finland	6.00	6.00	5.65	5.00
France	1.85	6.05	7.05	7.00
Germany	2.25	8.25	7.60	5.60
Greece			8.00	7.00
Ireland	0.10	2.25	2.60	2.80
Italy	9.60	10.00	9.45	4.85
Netherlands	6.95	6.95	6.40	5.50
Norway	7.75	7.75	7.30	6.50
Portugal	0.00	7.95	9.65	8.00
Spain	10.00	9.95	8.70	7.50
Sweden	0.00	7.30	7.65	5.50
Switzerland	2.75	2.75	2.75	2.75
UK	0.80	1.65	1.75	1.75
USA	0.50	0.50	0.50	0.50

Source: Nickell 2005.

Recent research has found that the adverse effects of regulation on productivity performance are strongest in the face of new technological opportunities and have impacted strongly on the diffusion of ICT. Cross-country regression evidence shows that employment protection deters investment in ICT equipment (Gust and Marquez 2004) because reorganizing working practices and upgrading the labor force, which are central to realizing the productivity potential of ICT, are made more expensive. Restrictive product market regulation has deterred investment in ICT capital directly (Conway *et al.* 2006), and the indirect effect of regulation by raising costs has been relatively pronounced in sectors that use ICT intensively. There has been a strong correlation between product market regulation and the contribution of ICT-using services (notably in distribution) to overall productivity growth (Nicoletti and Scarpetta 2005). Thus, the story is not that regulation has become more stringent but rather that existing regulation has become more costly in the context of a new technological era based on ICT.

The contribution that ICT made to labor productivity growth can be estimated using growth accounting techniques. In principle, this approach would identify contributions from ICT capital deepening, TFP growth in ICT production and (unremunerated) TFP spillovers from the use of ICT capital. In practice, this last aspect has proved somewhat elusive. Growth accounting estimates are reported in Table 12.17. They confirm that ICT contributed more

Table 12.17 Contributions to labor productivity growth in the market economy (% per year)

	1980–95	1995–2000	2000–5
EU			
Labor productivity	2.6	1.8	1.2
ICT capital deepening	0.4	0.7	0.4
TFP in ICT production	0.2	0.4	0.2
Other capital deepening	0.8	0.4	0.3
Other TFP	0.9	0.1	0.0
Human capital deepening	0.3	0.2	0.3
USA			
Labor productivity	1.9	3.0	2.9
ICT capital deepening	0.7	1.4	0.6
TFP in ICT production	0.3	0.6	0.6
Other capital deepening	0.3	0.3	0.2
Other TFP	0.4	0.5	1.0
Human capital deepening	0.2	0.3	0.4

Note: EU is based on ten countries (Austria, Belgium, Denmark, Finland, France, Germany, Italy, Netherlands, Spain, UK).
Source: derived from EUKLEMS data kindly provided by Bart van Ark.

to productivity growth in the United States than in the EU both before and after 1995, and that it played a significant role in the acceleration of American productivity growth after the mid-1990s.[8]

Another take on the role of ICT in recent growth can be obtained by considering the part that particular sectors have played. Here the big story is the contribution made by market services that are intensive in the use of ICT, in general, and the distributive trades, which account for close to 20 percent of employment in a typical OECD country, in particular. This may reflect the impact of TFP spillovers, and it certainly involves so-called "soft savings" achieved through the extra information that ICT provides, permitting better organization of inventories, logistics, etc. ICT-using market services contributed 1.3 percentage points per year to US labor productivity growth from 1996 to 2001 compared with −0.1 in France, 0.1 in Italy, and 0.2 in Germany (Nicoletti and Scarpetta 2005).

The UK has experienced a relatively strong contribution to productivity growth from the regulation-sensitive ICT-using services sector, and ICT capital deepening has been above the EU average. As a lightly regulated economy, the UK has been better positioned than the other big European economies to prosper in the ICT era. This has been reflected in TFP growth and relatively strong contributions to productivity growth from both ICT-using services and ICT capital deepening. In a sense, this can be seen as an unexpected bonus from the failure to establish a successful corporatist model in an earlier generation.[9]

Irish growth during the "Celtic Tiger" phase was sustained by both strong employment growth and strong productivity growth.[10] Fast growth represented a belated catch-up as policy errors from the golden age, such as protectionism and neglect of human capital formation, were corrected and macroeconomic stabilization was achieved; but it was augmented by a very elastic supply of labor in a regional economy starting with high unemployment where labor market reform dramatically reduced the non-accelerating inflation rate of unemployment (NAIRU) (Crafts 2005).

The key aspect of recent Irish productivity performance is the huge contribution of ICT production (almost entirely for export).[11] If this is taken out of labor productivity growth, it appears that the other components have not been exceptional. Clearly, the large ICT production sector in Ireland is a result of supply-side policies that have attracted FDI and have developed a successful

---

[8] However, in Finland, Sweden and, especially, Ireland, countries where ICT production comprised a relatively large share of GDP, ICT made a larger contribution than in the USA and labor productivity growth surpassed that of the USA.

[9] Though it should also be noted that recent legislation has substantially strengthened competition policy.

[10] Labor inputs grew at 2.1 percent per year from the start of the Celtic Tiger phase in 1987 up to 2004, during which period real GDP per capita grew 1.4 percent per year faster than real GDP per hour worked (GGDC 2007).

[11] TFP growth in ICT production contributed 3.62 percentage points per year to labor productivity growth between 1995 and 2001 (Timmer and van Ark 2005).

cluster. These include interventions that have improved the infrastructure and labor supply available to the multinationals. However, the success of the low-tax, light-regulation approach would have been much less spectacular if the composition of manufacturing output had happened to be less favorable. This suggests that Ireland is something of a special case, rather than an experience that can now easily be replicated across the European economies as a whole. Specialization in ICT exports is not possible for everyone, and low corporate taxes are most effective in attracting a large share of FDI if other countries do not follow suit.

ICT has mattered but is not the whole story, as is apparent from Table 12.17. The weakening of other capital deepening in the EU since 1995, and post-2000 the very strong performance of other TFP in the USA, stand out. Both may be transitory rather than permanent changes. The EU experience at the country level seems to be quite closely (inversely) correlated to hours per capita (cf. Table 12.13). Increases in employment reflecting attempts to reform the labor market, and social factors influencing female labor force participation, have not been matched by growth in the capital stock and have tended to reduce labor productivity growth, as in Spain, for example (Gordon and Dew-Becker 2008). In the United States, strong TFP growth seems to reflect huge pressure to reduce costs in the face of a profits squeeze (Oliner, Sichel, and Stiroh 2007).

The end of the communist regime ushered in a process of transition for central and eastern European economies, which now had an opportunity to go down the path of rapid catch-up growth but needed to be transformed into effective market economies. In some ways, the situation might be thought to have similarities to the beginning of the golden age in western Europe, but obviously there were also big differences in terms of social capability, access to foreign capital, and initial economic structure. The immediate experience of transition was traumatic as GDP fell dramatically in most countries. Since the mid-1990s, there has been rapid economic growth in many countries, but also considerable variance – for example, from 1992 to 2004 real GDP per capita rose by 64 percent in Poland but shrank by 26 percent in neighboring Ukraine (Beck and Laeven 2006).

This prompts two questions:

(1)   How does catch-up growth in eastern Europe since 1995 compare with the experience of golden age western Europe?
(2)   What accounts for early growth success and failure in the transition economies?

Four big differences between the east in the 1990s and the west in the 1950s deserve to be highlighted. First, the legacy of communism was an allocation of resources which reflected the extensive model of Soviet growth and was highly

Table 12.18 Economic structure of the transition economies in 1990

	% Agricultural employment	% Industrial employment	% Services employment	Industry % GDP	Overindustrialized % GDP
Bulgaria	18.5	49.3	32.2	59	23
Czech Rep.	12.9	44.0	43.1	58	21
Estonia	21.0	36.8	42.2	44	10
Hungary	15.6	36.4	48.0	36	−1
Latvia	16.4	40.6	43.0	45	10
Lithuania	18.9	41.2	39.9	45	10
Poland	23.4	36.4	40.2	52	13
Romania	31.1	41.5	27.4	59	22
Russia	13.2	42.3	44.5	48	7
Slovakia	10.0	44.5	45.5	59	23
Slovenia	9.7	49.2	41.1	44	6

Sources: Raiser, Schaffes, and Schuchhardt. 2004; De Melo *et al.* 2001.

distorted in many ways. One important corollary of this was the absence of a large reserve of low-productivity agricultural labor: none of the countries listed in Table 12.18 had a share of the labor force in agriculture in 1990 as high as France (or Italy or Spain etc.) in 1950. Another implication was that the starting point was one of "over-industrialization" and a very weak development of the service sector.

Second, while post-Second World War reconstruction in western Europe took about five years, during which there were extremely high growth rates, the post-Cold War transition from socialist to market economy in the former USSR was long and painful. In 1998, Russia's GDP per capita was only 56 percent of the 1990 level. The post-socialist slump in eastern Europe was less severe, but also entailed negative growth for several years in the early 1990s.

Thirdly, this new episode of catch-up growth is taking place in the context of a much more globalized world economy. This implies that the domestic savings constraint is no longer binding and that foreign capital and technology can be drawn upon more readily. Lucas (2000) argued that it was realistic to think that new countries joining the catch-up growth club could expect to achieve much faster growth than their predecessors; his calibrated model suggests a bonus of 2.5 percentage points per year nowadays compared with fifty years ago.

Fourthly, the institutions necessary for a successful market economy had to be developed *ab initio*. This was not a matter of fine-tuning the rules of the game for the capital market or wage bargaining but something much more fundamental: for example, establishing secure property rights and the rule of law to underpin investment and innovation, in some cases in economies which had been under communist control for over seventy years. As Table 12.19 shows, progress was quite rapid in central Europe and the Baltic states, but not

Table 12.19 The rule of law (−2.5 to 2.5)

	1996	2006
Bulgaria	−0.11	−0.17
Czech Republic	0.84	0.73
Estonia	0.50	0.91
Hungary	0.85	0.73
Latvia	0.13	0.52
Lithuania	0.29	0.45
Poland	0.66	0.25
Romania	−0.16	−0.16
Russia	−0.74	−0.91
Slovakia	0.21	0.43
Slovenia	0.86	0.79
Austria	1.86	1.87
Belgium	1.55	1.45
Denmark	1.91	2.03
Finland	1.92	1.95
France	1.45	1.31
Germany	1.80	1.77
Greece	0.90	0.64
Ireland	1.72	1.62
Italy	0.97	0.37
Netherlands	1.81	1.75
Norway	2.00	2.02
Portugal	1.13	0.97
Spain	1.33	1.10
Sweden	1.84	1.86
Switzerland	2.07	1.96
UK	1.83	1.73

Note: the rule of law indicator measures the extent to which agents have confidence in and abide by the rules of society. It is based on an aggregation of components which include the effectiveness and predictability of the judiciary and the enforceability of contracts.
Source: Kaufmann, Kraay, and Mastruzzi 2007.

in Russia. However, even in 2006 the rule of law indicator still shows a big gap between the best of western Europe and the best transition economy.

Beck and Laeven (2006) showed that weakness in institutional reform has been highly correlated with the number of years under communism and the importance of rents from natural resource exports. Indeed, some countries in this region appear to be vulnerable to the "natural resource curse."[12] In addition, the prospect of joining the EU acted as an effective form of

---

[12] The "natural resource curse" refers to the poor growth performance of countries rich in minerals. Sala-i-Martin and Subramanian (2003) report estimates suggesting that the channel through which this works is bad institutions.

Table 12.20 Labor productivity: growth and initial level

	Labor productivity growth, 1995–2005 % per year	GDP/worker, 1995 $ 1990 GK (% USA)	Predicted labor productivity growth % per year
Bulgaria	2.89	13294 (25.8)	5.49
Czech Republic	2.75	16974 (33.0)	5.02
East Germany	4.87	20525 (39.9)	4.57
Estonia	7.72	19478 (37.9)	4.70
Hungary	3.35	16422 (31.9)	5.09
Latvia	6.18	14676 (28.5)	5.32
Lithuania	6.36	12707 (24.7)	5.56
Poland	4.71	14539 (28.3)	5.33
Romania	3.47	7587 (14.7)	6.21
Russia	3.76	10761 (20.9)	5.81
Slovakia	4.24	17754 (34.5)	4.93
Slovenia	3.86	23028 (44.8)	4.26

	Labor productivity growth, 1950–73 (% per year)	GDP/worker, 1950 $ 1990 GK (% USA)
Austria	5.42	7498 (31.3)
Belgium	3.56	14018 (58.5)
Denmark	2.89	14410 (60.1)
Finland	4.42	8203 (34.2)
France	4.64	11166 (46.6)
(West) Germany	4.73	19338 (43.2)
Greece	5.99	5644 (23.6)
Ireland	3.79	8407 (35.1)
Italy	4.78	9840 (41.1)
Netherlands	3.31	15508 (64.7)
Norway	3.39	12407 (51.8)
Portugal	5.83	5037 (21.0)
Spain	6.08	5171 (21.6)
Sweden	3.17	13744 (57.4)
Switzerland	2.79	18161 (75.8)
UK	2.43	15529 (64.8)

Note: predicted labor productivity growth is based on the following estimated equation for golden age western Europe: LabProdGr = 7.168 − 0.065 Y/L%US, R^2 = 0.833
(19.815) (−8.718)
Source: GGDC 2007 and own calculations.

conditionality for the 2004 accession countries that needed to make reforms to qualify.[13]

Table 12.20 juxtaposes labor productivity growth rates in the west in the golden age and in the east in the early years of catch-up, and places them in the

[13] Clearly this has not worked very well for Bulgaria and Romania.

context of the initial labor productivity gap. The fast-growing Baltic countries have growth rates which, if sustained, will compare favorably with anything seen in the golden age, and which are based (as Tables 12.7 and 12.9 reveal) on very strong TFP growth. Generally, however, labor productivity growth has been appreciably below what would have been predicted on the basis of western Europe's experience. Certainly these growth rates are also lower than would be expected on the basis of early growth regressions that ignore the importance of institutional quality.[14] In fact, relative growth performance is well explained by the extent of liberalization and of (the exogenous component of) institutional reform, both of which have been shown to have strong positive effects on growth (Beck and Laeven 2006; Fidrmuc, 2003).

Conclusion

The aim of this chapter has been to describe and explain sixty-odd years of the European experience of economic growth as well as drawing some policy lessons from it. The framework that we have used to do this is based on the key concepts of growth based on endogenous innovation and catch-up. This concluding section seeks to pull together some important overview points from the details that have emerged in the course of our exposition.

First, it is clear that rapid, sustained catch-up growth in Europe was based on substantial contributions from both capital deepening and TFP growth. The latter obviously did benefit from technology transfer, but rapid TFP growth, as measured by conventional growth accounting, also reflected improvements in the allocation of resources and economies of scale. The Achilles heel of the Soviet economy was its inability to achieve strong TFP growth.

Secondly, evaluations of growth performance must take account of differential scope for catch-up. This matters for comparisons among both countries and periods. A notable case in point is comparison of golden age growth rates in eastern and western Europe. The raw data say that there was little difference – 3.81 percent per year compared with 4.06 percent per year – but normalizing for initial real GDP per capita, average eastern European growth was inferior by 1.3 percentage points.

Thirdly, and most important, incentive structures matter for growth, so institutions and policy make a real difference. This is confirmed throughout the chapter, notably in terms of understanding why growth was so strong in

---

[14] Initial optimism about growth in these transition economies was based on projections which emphasized high levels of education and big initial productivity gaps (cf. Fischer, Sahay, and Vegh 1998); these would suggest average productivity growth rates of around 5.5 percent per year.

the golden age and then slowed down so much thereafter; in explaining why Ireland's golden age failure was transformed into the emergence of the Celtic Tiger; and in making sense of the emerging pattern of success and failure among the transition economies. The demise of the Soviet Union exemplifies the importance of incentive structures rather than an unfavorable elasticity of substitution between capital and labor.

Fourthly, elaborating on this fundamental point about the role of incentive structures, several further insights deserve to be highlighted. These include the following:

(a) Contrary to conventional wisdom, European experience suggests that conditionality can sometimes be successfully deployed to improve long-term growth prospects through the promotion of institutional and policy reform. This is a plausible interpretation both of the main impact of the Marshall Plan and also of the EU accession process fifty years later.

(b) The evidence suggests that strengthening competition was conducive to faster productivity growth, notably in the context of adjusting rapidly to new technological opportunities and in mitigating agency problems within firms. The old (Schumpeterian) claim that market power is good for technological progress does not represent a good basis for anti-trust policy, as the UK experience, in particular, underlines.

(c) The relative failure of European countries generally to exploit the opportunities of ICT is, at least partly, a result of having more regulation than the United States. The point to note, however, is that this did not reflect more stringent regulation: rather the costs of existing regulation rose in the context of the new technology.

Finally, history matters. Western European countries developed institutions and policies that, generally speaking, served them well during the golden age. The downside of these arrangements was that they commanded political support that made them difficult to reform when this became necessary in the subsequent period.

Sectoral developments, 1945–2000

Stefan Houpt, Pedro Lains, and Lennart Schön

Contents

Introduction

Structural change has been comprehensive in Europe since 1945, with a shift from agriculture to industry and increasingly to services. It has also been an uneven process over time and space. In this chapter, trends and regional variations in output and productivity in each of the major sectors (agriculture, industry, and services) are presented and discussed in relation to the impact from primarily technological change and economic policy.

Agriculture

Growth and structural change

In the aftermath of the Second World War, agriculture still employed a large share of the workforce in most of Europe. Only the early developers – Great Britain, Belgium, and to a lesser extent the Netherlands and Germany – had by then already relatively low shares of labor employed in agriculture. During the half century that followed, employment in agriculture lost its importance across most of the Continent, due to the increase in factor productivity, which was crucial for catching-up and productivity convergence (Mellor 1995; Broadberry 2008). In 2000, agricultural employment was significant only in the most backward countries to the east, including Albania, Bulgaria, Romania, the Ukraine, and Turkey. The fall in the share of agricultural employment was in many places accompanied by a fall in the share of agriculture in total output. Yet these two changes were not closely correlated, because of differences in labor productivity across Europe. The sharp decline in the importance of European agricultural activity was a consequence of events within the agricultural sector, as well as changes in the industrial and service sectors.

The changes were motivated by market forces, but they were slowed down by government policies to protect the sector. Agriculture received special attention from governments for several reasons, including the need to provide food security, particularly in the aftermath of the Second World War, and also to limit welfare losses for the population in the rural areas. Government intervention occurred in the democratic west, where officials had higher incentives to respond to pressure groups, but also in the many dictatorial countries that existed in Europe before 1975 or 1990.

The changes in European agriculture are depicted in Table 13.1, which shows the evolution of the shares of agriculture in total employment and GDP in 1950, 1975, and 2000. Countries in the table are arranged according to levels of economic development in about 1950. The first group comprises the early

Table 13.1 Shares of agriculture in employment and GDP and labor productivity gaps, 1950–2000 (%)

	1950			1975			2000		
	Emp.	GDP	Prod. gap	Emp.	GDP	Prod. gap	Emp.	GDP	Prod. gap
Forerunners									
Belgium	9	8	88.9	4	3.3	82.5	1.8	1.4	77.8
France	23	13	56.5	10	5.9	59.0		2.8	
Germany	14	10	71.4	7	3	42.9	2.7	1.3	48.1
Luxembourg				2.6			1.5	0.7	46.7
Netherlands	10	13	130.0	6	4.6	76.7	3.1	2.6	83.9
Norway	22	13	59.1	9	4.8	53.3	4.1	2.2	53.7
Sweden	16	13	81.3	6	5.5	91.7	2.4	1.9	79.2
Switzerland	15			8			4.7	1.7	36.2
United Kingdom	5	5	100.0	3	2.8	93.3	1.5	1.0	66.7
Second comers									
Austria	23	17	73.9	13	6.6	50.8	5.8	2.1	36.2
Denmark	18	21	116.7	10	5.3	53.0	3.3	2.6	78.8
Czechoslovakia[a]		22		14	**8**	57.1	5.1	3.9	76.5
Slovak Republic							6.7	4.0	59.7
Finland	35	26	74.3	15	9.8	65.3	6.0	3.8	63.3
Italy	33	22	66.7	17	7.5	44.1	5.3	2.8	52.8
Spain	42	22	52.4	22	9.7	44.1	6.6	4.4	66.7
First Periphery									
Cyprus				15.7			5.3		
Greece	57	31	54.4	35	14.5	41.4	17.4	7.3	42.0
Hungary	**53**	26	49.1	**25**	15	60.0	6.5	5.4	83.1
Ireland	37	30	81.1	22	17	77.3	7.8	3.4	43.6
Poland	**57**	**35**	61.4	**30**	**16**	53.3	18.8	5.0	26.6
Portugal	44	31	70.5	34	26.5	77.9	12.6	3.8	30.2
Second Periphery									
Albania							71.8	29.1	40.5
Bulgaria	**64**	30	46.9	**24**			26.2	14.2	54.2
Romania	**70**	31	44.3				42.8	12.5	29.2
Turkey	76			58	35.8	61.7	36.0	15.4	42.8
USSR[b]		22		17			14.5	6.4	44.1
Estonia							7.2	4.9	68.1
Latvia							14.5	4.6	31.7
Lithuania							18.7	7.8	41.7
Georgia							52.1	21.9	42.0
Ukraine							20.5	17.1	83.4
Yugoslavia[c]		28		13				19.4	
Croatia							14.5	9.1	62.8
Slovenia							9.5	3.2	33.7

Figures in bold: 1950–54, 1955–59, 1960–64, 1965–69, 1970–74, 1975–79
(a) Czech republic from 1990. (b) Russian Federation from 1990. (c) Serbia in 2000.
Sources: World Bank Indicators Online & Mitchell 2003, pp. 929–34 & http://ddp-ext,worldbank,org/ext/
DDPQQ/showReport,do?method=showReport

developers in north-west Europe, where agriculture already had a small role in 1950, particularly in terms of its share in total output. There are important differences within this first group of countries, however. In fact, whereas the share of labor employed in agriculture in the UK, Belgium, and the Netherlands was 10 percent or below, France and Norway had agricultural employment shares above the 20 percent threshold. The most important unifying factor in this group of countries is the fact that structural transformation was very rapid, and that by 1975, in all of these countries, the shares of labor and GDP had converged to ratios within a small range. Table 13.1 also reports the labor productivity gap between agricultural and non-agricultural sectors, and again there are many differences in this indicator. The Netherlands, the UK, and Belgium had relatively low productivity gaps in 1950, but in the Netherlands that gap increased considerably in the years to 1975. Labor productivity gaps increased in most countries from 1975 to 2000.

The transformation of the structures of the economies of the second group of countries in Table 13.1 was less rapid than that of the forerunners, and continued to an important extent down to the end of the period. In 2000 the employment and output agricultural shares in this group of countries were much closer to those of the forerunners. The third and fourth groups of countries in Table 13.1 represent two very different patterns of development. The third group includes countries that had very large agricultural populations in 1950, but went through a period of strong structural transformation in both the 1950–75 and 1975–2000 periods. The fourth group consists of the countries in eastern and south-east Europe which lagged behind. It is however important to note that the labor productivity gap was very high in both groups of countries.

The data in Table 13.1 show that there is no significant correlation between the agricultural labor productivity gaps and the speed of structural transformation. In fact, the countries at the very bottom end of the table had large labor productivity gaps and yet their structures did not change more rapidly. This implies that either the productivity gaps were not matched by equivalent gaps in relative agricultural wages or, alternatively, labor did not move out of agriculture because of institutional factors, namely, sticky labor markets and government policies. This implies that an understanding of changes in European agriculture in the period from 1950 to 2000 needs also to take into account the role of economic policy.

European agricultural output expanded markedly, although there was a sharp decline in the labor force which was replaced by capital. Table 13.2 shows the very sharp decline in the absolute size of the agricultural workforce, which fell from 66.2 million in 1950 to 17.6 million in 2000. Despite this fall, the acreage was reduced by just 12 percent to 133 million hectares, but total fixed

Table 13.2 Agriculture in Europe, America, and the world

		1940s	1950	1960	1970	1980	1990	2000
1. Agricultural workforce (millions)	Europe		66.2	54.3	40.8	31.3	24.2	17.6
	N&C America		21.0	18.6	17.4	20.1	20.6	20.7
	World		809.5	843.0	928.7	1,067.1	1,221.2	1,318.6
	Eu/World		8.2%	6.4%	4.4%	2.9%	2.0%	1.3%
2. Acreage arable and tree crops (million hectares)	Europe	149		151[a]	146	141	139	133
	N&C America	240		260[a]	269	274	275	268
	World	1,217		1,346[a]	1,391	1,432	1,502	1,502
	Eu/World	12.2%		11.2%	10.5%	9.8%	9.2%	8.9%
3. Total fixed agricultural capital (billion 1990 US$)	Europe				348	333	691	621[c]
	N&C America				383	399	615	412[c]
	World				1,263	1,267	2,303	2,293[c]
	Eu/World				27.5%	26.3%	30.0%	27.1%
4. Irrigated acreage (million hectares)	Europe			8.3[b]	10.4	14.0	16.7	16.9
	N&C America			17.9[b]	20.9	27.6	28.9	31.4
	World			139.0[b]	167.8	209.7	244.3	274.2
	Eu/World			6.0%	6.2%	6.7%	6.8%	6.2%
5. Number of tractors (thousands)	Europe	270[d]	990	3,698[a]	6,077	8,454	10,356	9,650
	N&C America	1,576[d]	4,220	5,326[a]	6,038	5,606	5,841	5,808
	World	n/a	5,552	11,318[a]	16,102	21,932	26,526	26,424
	Eu/World		17.8%	32.7%	37.7%	38.5%	39.0%	36.5%
6. Tractors/ 1000 hectares	Europe		7.0		42.0			72.0
	N&C America		18.0		22.0			19.0
	World		5.0		12.0			18.0
7. Tractors/ 1000 workers	Europe		15.0		149.0			549.0
	N&C America		201.0		347.0			281.0
	World		2.0		17.0			20.0
8. Use of fertilizers (1000 tons)	Europe		6,990[e]	13,955[b]	24,883	31,196	26,414	19,472
	N&C America		4,798[e]	8,469[b]	17,614	25,636	23,605	22,868
	World		13,792[ef]	31,182[b]	69,308	116,720	137,819	136,435
	Eu/World		50.7%	44.8%	35.9%	26.7%	19.2%	14.3%

Table 13.2 (cont.)

	1940s	1950	1960	1970	1980	1990	2000
9. Fertilizer consumption (kg of nutrients)							
Europe		46.9		170.8			146.2
N&C America		20.0		65.5			89.0
World		11.3		49.8			90.9
10. Output (1989–91 = 100)							
W Europe		43.6[g]	62.0[a]	75.1	92.7	99.8	98.2
E. Europe			62.3[a]	74.4	93.4	101.2	79.3
N. America			57.9[a]	69.0	88.8	101.3	124.2
Asia inc. China		51.5[g]	38.3[a]	50.6	66.6	100.7	143.7
L. America		31.6[g]	44.1[a]	56.8	76.7	99.5	138.0
Africa		34.7[g]	50.1[a]	65.9	75.8	98.0	126.5
USSR		36.2[g]	63.4[a]	81.0	85.3	104.5	61.6
11. Labor productivity (1950 = 100)							
Europe		100.0	178.7	266.0	342.1	392.4	277.3
N&C America		100.0	131.7	166.2	187.1	199.1	240.3
World		100.0	134.1	149.5	175.6	200.2	202.0
12. Land productivity (1950 = 100)[i]							
Europe		100.0	144.1	175.8	223.3	246.7	254.2
N&C America		100.0	107.6	122.8	156.9	169.7	211.3
World		100.0	126.2	150.1	196.7	220.6	266.7

Source: Federico 2005, 1: p. 59, 2: p. 37, 3: p. 42, 4: p. 45, 5: p. 48, 6 and 7: p. 101, 8: p. 55, 9: p. 99, 10: pp. 236–7.
[a] 1961, [b] 1967, [c] 1992, [d] 1939, [e] 1950/51, [f] USSR excluded, [g] 1948–52, [h] =row 10/row 1, [i] =row 10/row 2

capital in the sector increased by 178 percent. This pace of change was peculiar to the European continent and contrasted with what occurred in the other more developed region for which Federico (2005) provides information, namely North and Central America, as shown in the same table.[1] The increase in capital invested in agriculture is associated with the expansion of irrigated acreage and the number of tractors used. Yet the use of fertilizers in Europe declined significantly after a peak in 1980.

Table 13.2 also provides data on the evolution of output, and labor and land productivity. The data on output is further disaggregated and depicts different trends for western and eastern Europe. Significantly, output growth in the west peaked in the 1980s, whereas in the east it continued to increase down to the 1990s and declined sharply thereafter. The differences in the two parts of the continent need to be related to changes in economic policies, respectively changes in the Common Agricultural Policy (CAP) and the changes that occurred in the communist regimes. Self-sufficiency within the CAP area was achieved in the 1980s, before the southern enlargement, and thus the CAP was a success in this respect. In the following decades the EEC's share in the OECD's agricultural exports increased to 56 percent, from 45 percent in the late 1960s (Neal 2007, p. 65). In the rest of the world, with the exception of the USSR/Russia, agricultural output growth proceeded down to the year 2000. The changes in the growth rate of output were reflected in the growth of labor and land productivity, as shown in the same table.

Agricultural policy

As a consequence of the effects of the war, by 1950 most European governments were concerned to secure self-sufficiency in terms of the supply of foodstuffs and raw materials. Governments in Europe, Japan, and the United States followed policies of promoting import substitution agriculture which were made possible by access to new technologies of production (Aparicio, Pinilla, and Serrano 2008, p. 66). European agriculture had been protected in the past, but some trade and international specialization was nevertheless allowed. This was not a problem of the agricultural sector alone, as industrial trade and international specialization were also affected by protection and state inter-vention. Yet European governments, particularly in the west, were much quicker to dismantle protection of the industrial sector, whereas liberalization of agriculture was only marginal. After the end of the Second World War, several important instruments were developed to promote trade liberalization,

---

[1] See Olmstead and Rhode 2008.

including the Bretton Woods institutions, namely the International Bank for Reconstruction and Development (IBRD) and the International Monetary Fund (IMF), the Organization of European Economic Cooperation (OEEC), which channeled the Marshall aid, and the General Agreement on Tariffs and Trade (GATT). These institutions helped the recovery of international trade, either by providing the funds to finance trade and multilateral balances, or by stimulating the reduction of trade barriers; but agricultural trade was largely unaffected by them.[2]

The liberalization of international trade in agriculture was only addressed directly within the limited group of six western industrialized countries that created the European Economic Community (EEC) in 1957, and the Common Agricultural Policy, which was agreed in 1962 and implemented between 1964 and 1968. The CAP had three main objectives: to stabilize agricultural markets; to assure the availability of food and agricultural raw material supplies; and to control prices (Ingersent and Rayner 1999, p. 151). The CAP worked by supporting agricultural product prices, and this implied major coordination planning problems, akin to those of the central planners in the east, though only at a sectoral level (Eichengreen 2007, p. 183). The option of price supports instead of income supplements to farmers may have been a lost opportunity to promote the integration of European agriculture into the international economy. Subsidies were ultimately replaced by aid to producers in 1995, following the GATT negotiations in the Uruguay Round (Neal 2007, p. 67). In 1999–2001 subsidies accounted for 36 percent of the total value of EU agricultural output, down from 42 percent in 1986–8, but ahead of the equivalent shares in the USA, which decreased from 25 percent to 22 percent in the same period. The CAP subsidies are complemented by national subsidies to a large extent. In 1999, the governments of France, Sweden, and the Netherlands transferred further to their farmers, respectively 31.8 percent, 46.8 percent and 77.6 percent of total EU subsidies (Neal 2007, p. 87). This makes total subsidies in the EU countries akin to those conceded by two non-EU countries, namely Norway and Switzerland, as well as Japan, where the equivalent rates were above 60 percent in the same years (Neal 2007, p. 80).[3] The objectives of the CAP were in tune with those of national interest groups and governments. The alternative would not have been the absence of support policies, but the proliferation of agricultural policies at the national level, which would have limited intra-European trade in agriculture. In fact, by coordinating agricultural policies, the governments of the Six allowed borders to open up to trade, as national agricultural sectors came under equivalent levels of external tariff or price protection or

---

[2] See Ingersent and Rayner 1999, pp. 121–6.   [3] See also Federico 2005, p. 201.

received similar amounts of subsidies (Milward 1992). The implementation of the CAP was accomplished the year before the completion of the Common Market, in 1968. The CAP ultimately also favored monetary integration, as it was the first area of intervention that was affected by exchange rate instability that followed the demise of the Bretton Woods System in 1971, and provided the background for the development of exchange rate mechanisms that led to the European Monetary System, created in 1979 (Ingersent and Rayner 1999, p. 151; Eichengreen 2007, p. 183).

Whatever its form, subsidies to agriculture within the EEC may have facilitated capital deepening and improvements in the sector, and thus the release of labor to the rest of the economy followed by large increases in both labor and land productivity. In any case, protection of agriculture did not prevent structural change, and between 1950 and 1975 the share of agriculture in total GDP declined substantially in the EEC Six, and also in the other six wealthy western countries that belonged to EFTA, namely Austria, Denmark, Norway, Sweden, Switzerland, and the United Kingdom.[4] In all of these countries agriculture's share of GDP was below 7 percent. A similar fall occurred in Czechoslovakia and Spain, where agriculture's GDP share declined from 22 percent in 1950 to 8 or 9 percent in 1975. Protective policies in the agricultural sector in those countries were much weaker than those that were imposed in the wealthier countries and thus the move towards the non-agricultural sector was possibly facilitated. In any case, the most important driving force behind the demise of agriculture in the two countries was the fact that industrialization was very rapid in the period 1950–73.

The United Kingdom, which joined the EEC only later and did not benefit from the CAP, also inherited interventionist policies from the interwar and the two world war periods, but protection was abandoned at an earlier phase. The demise of protection was important for the growth of agricultural exports from neighboring countries, particularly Denmark, Norway, and Ireland. In the countries that are grouped as second comers in Table 13.1, agricultural policies were designed at the national level and without international coordination, as these countries did not belong to any international organization that promoted policy coordination. Yet that was not an obstacle to rapid changes in these economies, as agriculture's share in total employment and output also declined rapidly. In fact, in Austria, Denmark, Finland, and Spain, as well as in communist Czechoslovakia, the importance of the agricultural sector fell to about 15 percent of GDP in 1975, and by 2000 its importance had reached the low levels of the EEC countries.

---

[4] Portugal was the seventh EFTA member. Because it joined as a developing economy, it managed to secure some trade liberalization for transformed agricultural products, such as canned tomatoes and fish, and cork.

In the countries grouped as the first periphery, the demise of agriculture was slower; this was due to the fact that liberalization came much later, and also that agriculture was heavily protected. The accession to the European Communities of the three southern European countries was followed by a more rapid transformation of the structure of their economies. The countries in the second periphery still have to endure that process and their agricultural sectors are still heavily protected.

As in many other areas, there are large differences between the speed of liberalization in the western democracies and the southern and central European dictatorships, but that political divide was not always important. In fact, Czechoslovakia had a rapid structural transformation during 1950–75 when it was a dictatorship, whereas the process was much slower in democratic Ireland.

The costs of protection

One major feature of European agriculture is that it was a heavily protected sector in the decades between 1950 and 2000. Despite protection, the share of agriculture in total employment and output fell sharply all over Europe, and only in the poorest parts of south-east Europe did agriculture still account for a considerable share of economic activity at the end of our period. Agricultural policies switched from protecting domestic producers from imports towards the protection of farmers' incomes, which was less harmful to growth. But even this more benign form of protection had large costs in terms of government budgets and, more importantly, in terms of European trade specialization in the wider world. It is hard to assess with precision whether agricultural policies in Europe impacted negatively on the pace of economic growth of the European nations and on the speed of economic convergence within the continent. By looking at how European agriculture was transformed in the half century here analyzed, we may posit that the impact was probably not too large. According to one estimate, the costs of the CAP in terms of overall economic efficiency were about 1.5 percent of GDP (Neal 2007, p. 83). CAP expenditures are the single most important item in the EU budget, and are of a regressive nature as they correlate positively with income levels (Sapir *et al.* 2004, p. 72).

But if the costs of protection were relatively low, it was certainly not because of the careful design of agricultural policies, but rather because the market forces that led to the growth of the manufacturing and service sectors were sufficiently strong to offset any wrongdoing by governments with regard to European agriculture. What happened outside agriculture was many times more important for overall macroeconomic performance.

Industry

The golden age (the 1950s and 1960s)

The golden age of European economic growth can perhaps most aptly be described as a virtuous cycle of growth. Demand and supply expanded hand in hand, attaining very high and sustained rates of change. Initially they expanded in a process of rapid reconstruction and recovery to the pre-war levels of income and production. But further on, the sustained high levels of growth were obtained through a fortunate combination of enhancing phenomena and lack of disequilibria. Among the growth-enhancing factors, population growth provided expanding markets and a growing labor force. Possible disequilibria in labor markets were avoided by in- or out-migration, female labor force allocation, and mechanization. Capital requirements and balance of payments tensions were overcome by export-led growth, which rapidly re-established exchange convertibility and permitted capital movements. Once expansion was under way, the profitability of investments drew capital into Europe at a low cost. In parallel, Keynesian policies stimulated demand and smoothed economic cycles.

The high growth rates of labor productivity during this period can be traced back to both the movements in employment between sectors and the relative growth of output with respect to the growth of sectoral employment. Both of these sources tended to diminish over time: First, because the shift of low-productivity labor from agriculture to high-productivity industry had nearly been exhausted – the shift from industry to services has no similar productivity differential – and secondly, because intra-sector improvements are limited by the reduced scope of productivity gains in services, which had become the most important sector in terms of output and employment.

But during this phase of European economic growth, new practices aimed at increasing efficiency, such as mass production, consumption, and distribution technologies, provided important productivity and utility gains. At the same time, these new modes of production and consumption combined well with trade liberalization and intra-European product market integration, because they allowed for specialization and economies of scale. New product lines, especially household appliances and motor vehicles, but also processed food and new leisure products, drove and responded to important changes in household decisions: more and more women joined the labor force; the accumulation of human capital received a higher priority in family household functions; appliances substituted for household labor; articles and services related to personal attire and appearance, leisure articles and activities, and health increased in household budgets and provided new markets mainly to the industrial and service sectors.

But overall, improvements in production tended to save all factors – labor, capital, and materials – thus leading to a general fall in costs within industry and so to a fall in the relative price of its products. This had a cumulative impact on costs and productivity in the industries using industrial intermediate goods. New and cheaper goods led to increases in demand. Thereby output and employment expanded, leading to economies of scale and further reductions in costs and prices.

Intra-European trade, mainly among nations with similar levels of income per capita and economic development, drove overall trade to grow faster than output, especially in manufactures. Large-scale industrial expansion evolved in a context of expanding home and foreign markets, elastic factor supply, and new technology with a high potential for increasing productivity and embracing economic policy. Furthermore, among others, Chandler (1977) and Freeman (1997) insist that large productivity gains were attainable in technological innovation via scale and flow economies in science-based industries by increasing R&D, education, and fixed capital investment.

In this context, an important part of the golden age productivity growth spurt was due to the imitation of technology, and in many cases, this high productivity growth potential was combined with new social and economic institutions: wage moderation and deployment of profits, large companies coexisting with a strong system of medium and small-sized firms, and good technical education and vocational training.

Three of the four regions examined in this chapter followed this pattern. Western Europe pushed into the age of mass consumption and developed welfare states; northern and southern regions experienced even higher rates of change, which allowed for catching up in terms of productivity, income, and sector composition.

And finally, although eastern Europe showed similar high growth and transformation, its political and institutional regime marked important differences. As satellite countries to the USSR, the political regimes maintained command economies with highly centralized planning and enforcement. A high overall priority was given to industrialization, especially to the heavy sectors as providers of durable investment goods for production. Resources and effort were channeled into iron and steel, chemicals, metals, electric power, and machinery. All eastern European countries experienced important shifts from agriculture to industry, in both output and employment. The potential for increasing output by shifting labor from low-productivity agriculture to industry was highest in the more backward countries. Bulgaria, Czechoslovakia, Hungary, Romania, and Yugoslavia strongly reduced their shares of agricultural labor by increasing their industrial labor force. Nonetheless income levels remained low in comparison to the rest of Europe. Consumer products showed moderate growth, combined with a limited choice in the range of products. Low-paid workers benefited from low prices for essential products, cheap housing, public health, and education, but skilled labor lost relative purchasing power and suffered strong economic disincentives.

Population and labor force in the east expanded at a higher rate than in the rest of Europe, but even so, forced investment drove an increase in fixed capital per person employed in all sectors. Extensive growth and lack of market dynamics to allocate and use resources efficiently led to lower capital, labor, and multi-factor productivity, resource underutilization and waste, slack labor discipline, misallocation of investment, and adverse incentives for technological change. From the 1960s, creeping economic reform introduced some degree of decentralization into decision making, market mechanisms for allocating resources, and private enterprise activity.

Slowdown (the 1970s and 1980s)

Stagflation and severe recession followed the economic boom of 1972–3. What was initially perceived as a trough in the cyclical movement of the post-war European economy languished on into an absolute decline in economic activity and two-digit rates of unemployment and inflation. Instability, the coming to an end of the Keynesian economic policy paradigm, and energy price hikes deepened the fall and dispersion of growth performance. Some scholars have interpreted these decades as a readjustment from previous abnormally high growth rates back to a sustainable growth path (Crafts and Toniolo 1996, pp. 16–20).

Much has been written on the favorable circumstances of previous decades and how changing adverse circumstances contributed to economic slowdown. We mentioned the virtues of adaptive labor supply, scale technologies, and efficient resource allocation in the previous section. A dimension which was to worsen the strains and imbalances of the early 1970s was energy costs. Terms of trade in general had been highly beneficial for Europe over the previous period. Commodity prices rose steadily, but food, energy, and raw material prices had lagged behind. Cheap energy had allowed the development of energy-intensive sectors. When the OPEC price hike hit production and consumption patterns, it required time and restructuring to adapt to the new relative prices.

Scope for further gains from catch-up in technology and allocating resources efficiently was limited by the 1970s. In industry, big was no longer beautiful: the "visible hand," as Chandler had termed the progressive replacement of

Table 13.3 Sectoral shares of value added at constant and current prices, and labor force (%)

	1950	1960	1970	1980	1990	2000
Western Europe (constant prices)						
Agriculture			3.0	2.7	2.5	2.2
Industry and construction			39.7	36.1	33.2	29.9
Services			57.8	61.5	64.3	67.9
Western Eurpoe (current prices)						
Agriculture			4.8	3.2	2.5	1.7
Industry and construction			34.2	31.2	27.0	22.0
Services			60.9	65.6	70.4	76.2
Western Europe (employment)						
Agriculture		12.8	8.4	5.4	5.0	4.6
Industry and construction		44.8	44.6	38.7	34.2	24.5
Services		42.4	46.9	55.8	60.8	70.9
Northern Europe (constant prices)						
Agriculture			5.4	4.5	4.1	3.5
Industry and construction			33.0	31.3	30.7	33.5
Services			62.1	64.2	65.2	64.5
Northern Europe (current prices)						
Agriculture			7.0	5.5	4.1	2.4
Industry and construction			27.1	27.0	24.3	27.1
Services			65.9	67.5	71.6	70.5
Northern Europe (employment)						
Agriculture		25.6	13.0	8.4	5.5	3.1
Industry and construction		35.1	37.4	32.4	28.5	24.5
Services		39.3	49.7	59.2	65.9	72.4
Southern Europe (constant prices)						
Agriculture			6.5	5.3	4.6	4.8
Industry and construction			33.4	33.7	31.8	30.1
Services			60.6	61.5	63.6	65.3
Southern Europe (current prices)						
Agriculture			17.8	13.1	9.2	7.5
Industry and construction			25.7	25.8	24.8	22.1
Services			56.5	61.2	66.0	70.5
Southern Europe (employment)						
Agriculture		46.8	35.0	29.8	22.7	20.1
Industry and construction		26.3	32.3	31.5	28.9	28.8
Services		26.9	32.7	38.8	48.3	51.1
Eastern Europe (constant prices)						
Agriculture	28.1	19.0	12.3	10.5	13.3	9.1
Industry and construction	31.0	46.7	48.8	50.7	42.4	45.3
Services	40.9	34.3	38.9	38.7	44.3	45.6
Eastern Europe (current prices)						
Agriculture			14.7	12.8	14.4	8.9
Industry and construction			41.2	41.4	36.3	25.6
Services			44.1	45.7	46.4	62.8
Eastern Europe (employment)						
Agriculture	50.2	38.0		12.5	12.3	18.5
Industry and construction	23.0	35.5		48.4	45.5	32.0
Services	18.2	26.6		39.1	42.2	49.5

market allocation mechanisms by large firm management, suffered a serious setback. Outsourcing, just-in-time or sub-contracting services previously done by company departments reduced the size and scope of firms. It helped make them more flexible and adaptive to rapid changes in a climate of instability. But at the same time, it shifted more and more resources out of industry and into services.

If we look back in European economic history for empirical regularities in economic development which might constitute what has been referred to as patterns of development, we can find two such patterns related to the allocation of labor: an initial phase, during which labor moved out of agriculture into industry, and a second phase when services grew at the expense of both industry and agriculture. We find that the 1970s were a period during which most European countries suffered a decline in the share of the labor force engaged in industry. Looking at the different areas of Europe, we find that the higher was the initial share of industry, the deeper was the subsequent fall. Deindustrialization was most pronounced in those countries where the proportion of the labor force in industry was already at or above 40 percent in 1960 (Feinstein 1999, pp. 37–8). Table 13.3 shows how the share of labor in western European industry dropped from around 45 percent in the 1970s to below 35 percent at the end of the 1980s. Less dramatic drops can be observed for northern and southern Europe, with falls from 35 percent to around 30 percent and 32 percent to 28 percent, respectively.

The fall in the share of industry has been steeper in the five big economies – France, Germany, Italy, the Netherlands, and the United Kingdom – which show a decline of more than ten points from 29 percent of value added in 1979 to less than 19 percent in 2003. Structural changes in the ten smaller EU-15 economies were far less pronounced. Industry fell from 22 percent to 19 percent and services rose from 75 percent to 79 percent. Thus, big and small economies became more similar in sector composition. Furthermore, most of the deindustrialization took place before the "New Economy" growth phase in the 1990s. Only after 2000 was there a renewed dip in industry shares for all the EU-15.

Table 13.3 *note:* division of Europe in geographical areas: northern Europe: Denmark, Finland, Norway, Sweden. Western Europe: Austria, Belgium, France, Germany, Ireland, Liechtenstein, Luxembourg, Netherlands, Switzerland, United Kingdom. Eastern Europe: Balkans (Bosnia-Herzegovina, Croatia, Moldavia, Montenegro, Serbia, Slovenia), former Czechoslovakia (Czech Republic, Slovakia), Bulgaria, Hungary, Poland, Romania, former USSR (Estonia, Latvia, Lithuania). Southern Europe: Andorra, Cyprus, Italy, Greece, Malta, Monaco, Portugal, Spain.
Sources: Constant VA: UN Data GDP at constant 1990 US Dollars. Current VA: UN Data GDP at current national currency. National shares weighted by population. Data for eastern Europe 1950 and 1960 from Aldcroft (2001), Table 6.2, weighted with population data from Maddison 2003.

Recovery and sluggish growth (the 1990s to the present)

The 1990s introduced important changes in European economies. The creation of European economic and monetary union provided fiscal and monetary discipline by limiting debt, deficit, and interest rate variation. Inflation was brought back under control and gradually increasing economic stability helped business, employment, and consumption to recover. But fixed exchange rates were also adopted to reduce risk and facilitate the efficient allocation of capital. Growing EU membership from the 1990s to the present has spread this stability and further increased scale. On the one hand, centripetal forces are concentrating high-tech industry in Europe's transport center in a clear example of Marshallian externalities – driven by skilled labor pools, the ease of technology spillovers, and most appropriate infrastructures. On the other hand, centrifugal forces are moving specialized activities and low-skill activities into the outer circles.

China's spectacular industrial growth performance – the awakening of the sleeping dragon – is moving assembly industries and labor-intensive activity in general towards East Asia. Europe has deindustrialized at a steady pace. The exception is northern Europe, which has been reindustrializing in terms of output. In this adverse economic context, the high growth of productivity in northern European industry compared to overall productivity growth has implied a lower share of labor inputs absorbed by that sector relative to its share in total output. The relatively good productivity performance also led to a relatively lower increase in prices, with a corresponding reduction in this region's share of output valued at current prices.

The revolution in information and communication technology (ICT) shows signs of constituting a "productivity paradox" similar to the replacement of steam power by electricity at the beginning of the twentieth century. Paper and digital formats continue to coexist and although ICT is providing higher speed and diversity and reduced storage space, the high pace of innovation – Schumpeterian creative destructive – may be contributing, as Solow (1987) observed, to a situation where we can "see the computer everywhere except in the productivity statistics."

Van Ark, O'Mahony, and Timmer (2008, pp. 25–6) hold the slower emergence of the knowledge economy in Europe responsible for the slowdown of labor productivity growth in Europe since 1995. They find lower growth contributions from investment in ICT and a small share of technology-producing industries in Europe. As Gordon (1997, 2004a, 2004b, 2006) has argued, part of the growing gap between Europe and the United States in productivity performance must be found in the rigidities of Europe's labor market. In Europe, labor force participation and working hours per person are low and there are higher preferences for leisure and high income taxes in support of a social welfare state system with generous unemployment benefits. In addition to these structural variables, increasingly poor primary and secondary education and high unionization are reinforcing a process of capital deepening.

The shift away from manufactures to services, which accompanies higher income per capita and the marketization of household production activities, reduces the potential for future productivity growth. Industry has often been considered the locus of innovation and technological change – the sector which has most intensively applied economies of scale, capital intensification and incremental innovation. However, from the 1990s, productivity growth related to the production of ICT equipment has been spectacular even in European industry. Thus, productivity increase in the European Union in the production of office machinery and electronic valves and tubes is calculated to have been in the range of 40 to 50 percent annually from 1990 to 2003![5] These branches are, of course, only a small fraction of total industry. In 2003 they represented one percent of the total industrial labor force. In the production of telecommunications equipment, comprising roughly another one percent of the total labor force, productivity growth has also been impressive, at around 10 percent annually over the same period. In industry at large, however, there was no similar quickening of productivity growth up to the beginning of the 2000s: productivity growth has hovered around 2 to 3 percent per annum in most branches since 1980.

Space and concentration in European industry

Progressive European economic integration over the last half century, from six to twenty-seven countries, has created growing interest in the spatial distribution of industry in Europe and the impact of European Union expansion into the periphery. Examining employment data for nine industrial activities from 1977 to 1999 for 197 NUTS2 regions, Ezcurra, Pascual, and Rapún (2006) have found an increase in geographic concentration in most industrial activities. The concentration of employment has increased in six of the nine sectors considered: non-metallic minerals; chemical products; metal products, machinery and electrical goods; transport equipment; textiles, clothing, and footwear; and other manufacturing. The greatest increase in concentration took place in the textiles, clothing, and footwear industry as a result of the shift of production to the southern periphery of the EU. The ores and mineral sector

---

[5] http://www.ggdc.net/dseries/totecon.html. The data refer to the EU15.

suffered dispersion, mainly due to the dismantling of the industry in formerly highly concentrated countries, and there was virtually no change in concentration in food, beverages, and tobacco or in paper and printing products, which are characterized by low-technology intensity and limited possibilities for exploiting economies of scale. The process of concentration has been increasing and the ergodic distributions the above-mentioned authors estimate seem to indicate a future trend to even higher concentration.

Rojec and Damijan (2008) analyze the relocation of economic activity from the EU-15 to the new member states. Although they find that inward foreign direct investment (FDI) to new member states is mainly efficiency-seeking FDI in manufacturing, the stock of such investments is very small in terms of overall EU-15 outward FDI. The low degree of relocation confirms Esteban's (2000) conclusions that differences in aggregate labor productivity in Europe are not to be attributed to the regional differences in the sector mix, where each sector has a different labor productivity, but rather to the fact that all sectors of a region have similarly high or low productivity. Sector mix is irrelevant. Infrastructures, social capabilities, and human capital are what matters. Ireland may stand as an example of this.

Services

For the last fifty years, services have been a dynamic part of the European economy, increasing their share of both output and employment. This structural change has been propeled by some major forces, from both the demand and the supply sides.

The demand for services has risen over these decades, for two main reasons. First, the level of knowledge intensity and specialization in European production has increased overall, which has meant a growing need for a number of services such as education, R&D, information, financial mediation, and transportation. Thus, inputs from the service sector have become more important in all production and a major factor behind productivity growth. Secondly, rising income has shifted demand to a number of services. From a consumer perspective, there is a high-income elasticity of demand for services such as education, healthcare, transportation, and tourism.

On the supply side, two major technological and organizational changes have exerted a strong influence on the service sector. First, during the period after the Second World War, possibilities of a catch-up with the more developed US service sector opened up in Europe, as part of the growth process of the golden age and the rapid transformation of large parts of Europe. Secondly, the ICT revolution that started in the 1970s and gained momentum in the 1980s and 1990s had a strong impact on service sector technology and organization. It also affected, of course, the demand for services, with a concomitant increase in knowledge intensity.

The interaction between the aggregate growth performance in Europe and the technological changes since 1945 gives a clear periodization of service sector performance. During the golden age of growth up to the mid-1970s, services were modernized in a way that was complementary to the expansion of the manufacturing sector. In the post-industrial society from the 1970s, however, services became a key sector in European growth. This periodization also fits with another major watershed in service sector production: the shift from public sector service growth to private sector service growth. Such a shift occurred in the late 1970s or early 1980s in large parts of Europe, when a political reorientation coincided with the technological changes that altered some of the conditions for public sector service provision. It is also evident that the increased emphasis on the role of services in economic growth has placed new items on the agenda for European integration.

There were, moreover, clear regional differences within Europe in all the developments outlined above. Income levels, sectoral composition, and institutional arrangements differed. As a general pattern, southern and eastern Europe were lagging in growth and modernization, while there were differences within northern and western Europe as well. Thus, catch-up within the service sector was not only a process between Europe and the USA but also an intra-European process that has widened in scope in the last decades.

The golden age (the 1950s and 1960s)

The acceleration of economic growth in Europe that occurred after recovery from war in the 1950s was a modernization and catch-up process that involved services to a very large extent. The productivity gap with the US economy that had widened over the interwar and war period was even more pronounced in services than in industry.[6] Mass education, particularly higher education, had a decisive lead in the USA over Europe, serving both industry and a growing service sector. From the end of the nineteenth century a new technology and a new organization of service production had developed and been diffused in the United States. It involved new office machinery with telephones, typewriters, calculators, cash registers etc. It also involved a new and more hierarchical organization suitable for standardized services in a high-volume production

---

[6] In combination with differences in the sector composition; cf. the emphasis on the shift out of agriculture in the golden age growth in Temin 2002.

adapted to the large and integrated American market (Broadberry 2006). Europe was slow to adopt the new technology before 1950. Services in Europe were generally more customized, adapted to the individual customer on narrow national markets and hence produced in low volumes with high margins. Furthermore, services were mainly an urban activity with low demand from traditional agriculture. The slowdown in the release of labor from agriculture to industry and services since the late nineteenth century had further limited the market for services in Europe (Broadberry, 2004, 2006).

Differences within Europe were large, however, in a number of respects. By 1950, Britain had a clear lead within Europe in service sector organization as a result of its radical urbanization, which provided a larger and more dynamic market for services, and also as a result of its international orientation in high-value-added services such as finance, insurance, and transportation. The rapid catch-up of the German economy in the 1950s and 1960s was to a large extent based on the flow of labor from agriculture to urban services, propeling a productivity-enhancing modernization of service production. Another region taking a lead was Scandinavia, characterized by small open economies. These adapted to the modernization and high-volume production of a number of services through a standardization process within the public sector, which was also integrated into a new welfare policy. Sweden, for instance, was also comparatively open to American ideas of standardization not only in industry but also in retailing, with early successes such as IKEA and HM (Schön 2000).

Comprehensive data for the service sector are still very scarce for the early post-war decades. It is clear, though, that in this golden age of growth there was a strong complementarity between the service sector and the rapid growth in the material production of manufacturing industry and construction, fueling urbanization in large parts of Europe.

The modernization of Europe, on different regional levels, provided new demands on the supply of human capital. Thus, one primary task of the service sector was to mobilize human resources. Education expanded explosively in the 1950s and 1960s due both to the high rates of population increase in the 1940s and 1950s and to the rise in the school-leaving age. Europe entered the era of mass education. Furthermore, the healthcare sector grew substantially in these decades, with both modernization of hospitals and medical treatments and extension of the supply of healthcare as part of post-war political programs.

During the 1960s and 1970s another labor-mobilizing service gained in importance: the provision of public childcare to release female labor from unpaid domestic work within the household. This link between the release of female labor and the growth of the public sector was particularly apparent in countries with comprehensive social programs for labor force mobilization and – progressively more outspoken – programs for gender equalization.

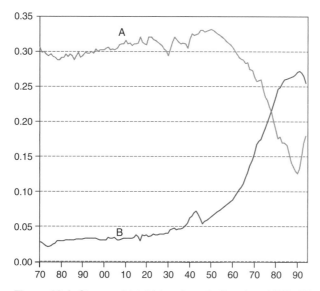

Figure 13.1 Shares of total labor force in Sweden, 1870–95.
A: women in unpaid domestic work; B: Public sector. *Source:* Schön 2000.

Thus, the link is clear in the northern European countries developing the Scandinavian model of public services as it appears from the Swedish historical national accounts used in Figure 13.1.

Education, healthcare, and childcare were to a large extent supplied by the public sector, by states or by local communities, and all over Europe employment in the public sector increased. This trend was further intensified by social democratic or Keynesian-inspired policies that gave a prominent role to the public sector in providing services to stabilize societies in the process of rapid modernization and reintegration into the world economy. Apart from more ambitious programs of income transfers, greater emphasis was put on social planning and this made the output of administrative services grow.

Consequently, the employment share of services grew particularly in northern Europe, i.e., in Scandinavia. Over the 1960s the service share grew by ten percentage points, and by 1970 roughly half the labor force was employed in services and close to one third in the public sector. During the 1960s Scandinavia overtook the mainly large economies of western Europe in service shares of employment, but all of these regions had high shares. Southern and eastern Europe were on a distinctly lower level with service shares increasing from a quarter to a third, marking the much more agricultural character of these regions.

Besides public sector provision of services (mainly public provision in the field of human capital mobilization), distribution was another main area of employment. In this branch employment stagnated, however, and decreased in relative importance within the service sector. The 1960s was a period of rather intensive rationalization in retailing, particularly in northern and western Europe. With the massive modernization of society, the diffusion of automobiles, and nationwide electrification, large-scale retailing was introduced more widely in Europe. Employment in transport and communications diminished relatively – an indication of technological change in this service area – but it was also an effect of the diffusion of private automobiles.

The financial sector was on a comparatively low level quantitatively, indicating the rather limited role that financial intermediation had to play in the Keynesian era, with nationally regulated markets. It was, however, relatively more important, in terms of employment, in the advanced economies of western Europe and particularly in the UK.

The service sector in the post-industrial society (the 1970s to the 1990s)

From the mid-1970s, Europe entered into a new era of accelerated growth of the service sector, particularly in terms of employment, at the expense of both the agricultural and the manufacturing sectors. There were certainly several factors behind this growth of the service sector. First, there was technological change. The advent of the microchip in the 1970s sparked off a new direction in the IT revolution with the massive diffusion of computer processing power, flexible communications, and low-cost information transfer. The intensity of information and knowledge rose steeply in most activities, creating scope and need for more and new services. Secondly, the prolonged income increases of the post-war period shifted demand in the direction of services such as personal care and domestic aid, tourism, media and cultural experiences, and financial intermediation. Thirdly, intensified global market integration and the diffusion of industrialization shifted European advantages in the direction of services – both internally by sustaining real income growth and externally by increasing demand for financial services or other business services.

Technological change and global market integration also changed the structure of services. The public sector growth ended in the 1980s and even went into reverse in the 1990s. There were two main reasons for this. First, there was a widespread political reaction against increasing levels of taxation, leading to new political ideas of deregulation and privatization from the 1970s and the 1980s (in eastern Europe this reaction to public sector redistribution took a very particular form in the 1980s and 1990s). Secondly, technological change created distinctly new possibilities of information flows and organization, reducing transaction costs as well as reducing information asymmetries. The pendulum shifted from the public to the private sector. It also shifted from national regulation to international integration. The financial sector was a forerunner, breaking down Keynesian-inspired regulations during the 1970s and 1980s. The media sector followed suit, and in the 1990s the Internet revolutionized most sectors of information and transactions.

When the bulk of growth forces shifted to the new service sector, taking both demand-side and supply-side factors into account, Europe was presented with both acute new possibilities and problems – particularly in relation to the American productivity lead and the American mode of production. On the one hand, technological change rendered a new flexibility in production and a new profitability to low-volume customized production that is more in line with European tradition and organization (Broadberry and Ghosal 2005). Such a reversal in technological trends may prove important for comparative European growth in the longer run, once the European catch-up in ICT investments has been carried through. On the other hand, services represent areas that to a large extent are difficult to integrate within Europe. Many services demand culture-specific competencies that have reduced the mobility of labor and of services (or increased the demand for a common language). The obstacles to integrating the European market were even more severe taking into account national regulations that had developed in the preceding period. Some of the most expansive and most knowledge-intensive sectors, such as the healthcare sector and the education sector, were deeply integrated into the public sector and had different national regulations. The Bologna process is one step in the direction of integrating higher education. Administrative integration and the integration of social insurance systems, in particular, are probably one of the keys to a more effective labor market and service sector in Europe. For any strategy to make Europe a world-leading area in terms of productivity, the integration of the service sector is vital, as expressed for instance in the Lisbon strategy of the year 2000.

Van Ark, O'Mahony, and Timmer (2008, pp. 39–42) relate the better performance in US market services to the large differences in financial and business services and multifactor productivity working through ICT. Common language and less diversity in consumption culture have also allowed the US to develop large-scale lean retailing with a high ICT input. Retailing was the leading sector in the productivity growth of US services in the 1990s, very much dependent upon spacious American towns and the massive use of automobiles. Europe was then handicapped by the restrictions of dense cities and more dependent upon collective transport systems. New trends in energy prices and climate change may however provide another reversal in favor of European organization.

The service sector growth can be seen clearly in employment shares all over Europe. In northern and western Europe, the service sector increased its share

Table 13.4 Relative service productivity levels, 1970–2000 (share of GDP/employment share)

	1970	1980	1990	2000
Western Europe	1.23	1.10	1.06	0.96
Northern Europe	1.24	1.08	0.99	0.88
Southern Europe	1.84	1.58	1.32	1.28
Eastern Europe	–	0.99	1.05	0.92

Source: Derived from Table 13.3 sectoral shares.

of employment from roughly half to close to three quarters from 1970 to the turn of the millennium in 2000. In southern and eastern Europe the increase was from one third to half of the total employment. Thus, by 2000 the southern and eastern periphery had reached the service shares of northern and western Europe in 1970, although with proportionately larger agricultural sectors and smaller manufacturing sectors.

The relative productivity of the service sector – in relation to the GDP productivity level – decreased considerably over the period. In part this was due to slower productivity growth in services than in manufacturing and agriculture.[7] It was also due to the fact that the agricultural sector, which has constantly had a lower productivity level, was rapidly shrinking, reducing the relative productivity advantage of services in a GDP perspective. In northern and western Europe this development was very similar, in both level and direction, although the decrease was more pronounced in northern Europe, where the female participation rate in the service sector has been the highest. From productivity levels distinctly above the average, the service sector fell below average by the year 2000. In southern Europe the relative level of service sector productivity was considerably higher than in central and northern Europe, which mainly reflects the large agricultural sector, debasing general productivity levels. It may also reflect differences in price structures and gender composition among regions. That may be the case in eastern Europe as well, with comparatively low relative service sector productivity despite a large agricultural sector. This may also be due to the composition of the services provided: a comparatively low share of highly productive financial services or other business services and a larger share of (female) care.

Employment in the various sub-sectors of services has mainly followed trends from the 1960s, with the public sector as the exception. Thus, the area

---

[7] The productivity growth rate of the service sector is low, at least it we take no account of the problem of measuring output in the service sector or the role of services as inputs contributing to productivity increases in other sectors. Cf. Gadrey and Gallouj 2002.

Table 13.5 Employment shares in different service sectors in Europe, 1960–2000 (%)

	1960	1970	1980	1990	2000
Trade and tourism	34.5	31.5	31.9	31.5	31.1
Transport and communication	15.9	13.6	11.8	10.4	9.9
Financial services, real estate, R&D	8.1	9.1	10.7	13.1	16.8
Public administration, community social work	41.5	45.8	45.6	45.0	42.2
Total	100	100	100	100	100

Source: OECD database.

of distribution (including not only wholesaling and retailing but also tourism activities such as hotels and restaurants) has followed an overall mild relative decline. While modernization of distribution has intensified, tourism activities have expanded. Employment in transport and communications bears witness to the impact of technological change. Despite the increase in transport and communication flows, employment has decreased. The financial sector and related business services and R&D, i.e., the highest value-added group of services with the most competence intensive processes, is the only category that increased its share of services. The employment share has doubled and the rate of increase risen over the decades.

From 1979 the Groningen 60 sector database gives a more detailed account of the service sector in terms of production, employment, and labor productivity per hour, mainly from the EU countries. The overall impression from the OECD data is corroborated. Employment in transport and communications has decreased while productivity has increased much more strongly than in any other service sector. Employment has been most expansive in business-related services, to a certain extent signifying the outsourcing of services earlier provided within manufacturing companies, but also signifying an increasing demand for more specialized competence in relation to new products and production processes. Real estate services have also been quite expansive in terms of employment, while employment in financial services more strictly defined has grown only slowly, despite considerable expansion of the financial markets. This is due primarily to the fact that the banking sector was the first service sector – besides communications itself – to apply modern IT technology, rationalizing heavily in front-office positions.

It is furthermore noticeable that employment in private household services has expanded rapidly, although productivity performance has been poor. Not only does this part of the service sector have the lowest level of productivity, but productivity is also on a downward slope. Admittedly, productivity in this and other service areas is hard to measure, and reflects mainly supply and demand conditions of the relevant labor.

Table 13.6 The service sector in the EU15, 1979–2003, annual growth rates

	Employment	Production	Productivity
Distribution and tourism	0.67	2.11	1.44
Transport and communication	−0.11	3.56	3.67
Financial	0.79	2.48	1.69
Real estate	2.62	2.68	0.06
R&D	1.27	2.43	1.16
Other business activities	4.06	4.33	0.27
Public administration, health, education	1.17	1.82	0.65
Private households	3.37	2.49	−0.88
Total services (excl. real estate)	1.26	3.10	1.84

Source: Groningen Growth and Development Center database, www.ggdc.net.

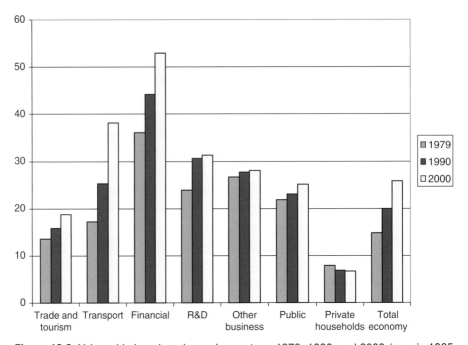

Figure 13.2 Value added per hour in service sectors, 1979, 1990, and 2000 (euro in 1995 prices). *Source:* see Table 13.6.

Labor productivity levels at three benchmark years are given in Figure 13.2. Labor productivity of real estate is not included – it is vastly inflated by the capital stock in the sector in which value added is mostly made up of interest rate charges. Evidently, labor productivity is the highest in the financial sector, engaging not only high competence but also much capital per employee. The same is true of the transport and communications sector, which has improved its position much and surpassed R&D, business activities, and the public sector – expressed in 1995 prices. Trade, tourism, and, in particular, private household work linger in the low-productivity realms. The decreasing value per hour in the latter case may also be the result of labor market deregulation, opening up new low-wage areas in the EU over recent decades.

Thus, development within the European service sector over the past decades involves both new opportunities for catch-up with the still leading American technologies, and an intensified intra-European catch-up from the eastern regions, and a divergence between the high-income and low-income sectors of service production.

Business cycles and economic policy, 1945–2007

Stefano Battilossi, James Foreman-Peck, and Gerhard Kling

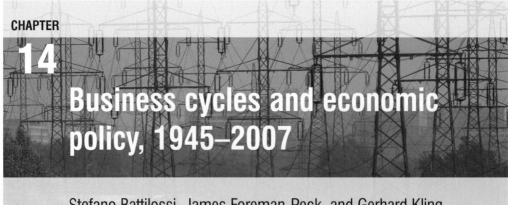

Contents

Introduction

In the first age of rapid economic growth after 1945, fluctuations in western European output and employment were so mild that the very notion of a "cycle" was transformed or even seemed obsolete. A second period of much slower average economic growth was marked by large and frequent oscillations, associated with the "oil shocks" and the Great Inflation of the 1970s and early 1980s. A third phase, characterized by smooth and modest swings in output and inflation which lasted until 2007, has been dubbed the "Great Moderation," reflecting the gradual reduction of inflationary trends.

Different reasons have been proposed for these changing patterns, but a common factor is that the conduct of economic policy was critical. In this chapter we explain how governments contributed and responded to fluctuations in economic activity in Europe during the second half of the twentieth century. In the second section we sketch the basic ideas essential to understanding the relationship between economic policy and business cycles. They include the notion that monetary and fiscal policies influence fluctuations in output, employment, and inflation according to the financial openness of the economy (free capital flows versus capital controls), as well as the currency regime chosen by policy makers (pegged versus flexible exchange rates). We also document the timing of financial liberalization in Europe and the persistent preference of most European governments for pegged exchange rate regimes over the entire period. We then examine the evolution of basic features of cycles in Europe, such as volatility and synchronization. We note the falling volatility of cycles in the 1960s and from the mid-1980s until 2007, explaining why changes in economic policy making were a fundamental driver. In the next section we support this analysis with narratives of the responses of national governments and central bankers to cyclical fluctuations before and after the global recession of 1974–5. Finally we look briefly at the historical and recent experience of eastern Europe, assessing the area's reintegration from 1989 after the long economic decoupling from the rest of the continent in 1945.

A conceptual framework

Policy objectives

Governments' preferences determine whether stable purchasing power of the currency or a high and stable level of production and employment will be their main policy focus. They assign different weights to fluctuations in the level of prices and economic activity when taking policy decisions.

Historically, policy preferences reflected a broader societal consensus about the desirability of alternative objectives. The great slump that began in 1929 was the catalyst for acceptance of Keynesian economic doctrine, and more generally a belief in the obligation of governments to prevent such a crisis from recurring. In most of the post-war industrialized world, government activism was legitimated, and heightened expectations of welfare turned the pursuit of social reforms and full employment into the major objective of economic policy. This approach has been blamed for creating a persistent inflationary bias, which judged large fluctuations in the price level as only a minor evil (Burns 1979; Ciocca and Nardozzi 1996). A notable exception was West Germany, where the public reaction to earlier twentieth-century economic history was an abhorrence of inflation and an independent central bank committed to price stability. Only after 1980 did a growing consensus about the undesirability of high and volatile inflation eventually change the macroeconomic regime, so that "taking on inflation" became the main priority of economic policy making (Volcker and Gyohten 1992). In the course of this regime shift, West German monetary arrangements became the model for European transnational money in the European System Central Banks set up by the 1991 Maastricht Treaty.

Policy instruments and optimization

Monetary and fiscal policies are the two principal means of stabilizing prices, output, and employment. During the 1950s and 1960s, the classic instruments of monetary policy – discount rate (Bank Rate), open market operations, and reserve requirements – were used in different combinations across western European countries; their mix also changed over time in the same country.

For example, Bank Rate was systematically employed by monetary authorities in the UK, West Germany, Belgium, the Netherlands, and Sweden. The French authorities also resorted frequently to this instrument in the 1950s, but much less frequently in the following decade. Conversely, the Italian authorities left discount rates almost unchanged for very long periods (Michaely 1971, pp. 33–7). Both French and Italian authorities gave increasing priority to the maintenance of low and stable nominal interest rates, in order to guarantee cheap funding for the government and the large state-owned industrial sector.

In many countries traditional instruments were complemented by a wide array of administrative controls, such as cash and liquidity ratios, quantitative limits on rediscounting and credit, regulation of banks' external position, and so on. This diversity of instruments was maintained in the transition to targeting the growth rates of the money stock for anti-inflationary purposes, initiated

by West Germany around 1974 (von Hagen 1999, pp. 421–36) and adopted by
the other major European governments by the end of the decade (Houben
2000, pp. 142–74).

After the Second World War the enhanced size of the typical central
government budget gave the state greater direct influence over the level of
spending in the economy. Total spending or aggregate demand determined the
short-term demand for workers and the pressure on prices. Countercyclical
use of taxation and government spending therefore seemed to some a way of
eliminating periodic slumps in employment. In practice the delays inherent in
approving and planning new public expenditure, coupled with political pressures not to cut spending, meant that fiscal policy was insufficiently responsive
to be used for "fine tuning" economic policy. Indeed there is evidence that in
many cases fiscal stances were the principal destabilizing force in the economy;
government spending and taxing policies were the sources of fluctuations in
employment and output (Darvasz, Rose, and Szapary 2005).

According to the theory of macroeconomic policy, governments should
choose policy instruments so as to optimize policy targets, and there is some
evidence that this is what they tried to do. Macroeconomic policy coordination,
in its earliest theoretical formulation, suggested that different policy instruments should be assigned to the various targets. In this way demand management would be more effective, particularly when the value of one target, such as
unemployment, required expansion and another, such as the balance of payments, warranted contraction. Modern reformulations in game-theoretic fashion also contend that fiscal and monetary authorities can achieve higher growth
and price stability if they choose cooperative strategies (Nordhaus 1994).

By the 1990s, there was something of a reversion to nineteenth-century
idealized gold standard policy that gave less scope to policy discretion. The
success of West German macroeconomic management encouraged the adoption of policy rules that constrained European governments' options in monetary and fiscal policy. The Maastricht criteria and the Stability and Growth
Pact were the most obvious examples. Governments were not competent, or
could not be trusted, to exercise macroeconomic policy discretion, or it simply
did not work.

How the economy worked

The relationship between policy instruments and targets depends on the
structure of the economy, which in our period was not fixed. Opinions as to
the relationship changed substantially in some countries over the sixty years
from 1945. Partly in consequence, direct controls and quantitative restrictions

were more widely employed in the early period, while a greater willingness to use prices and work with markets is apparent in later years.

Among structural factors, financial openness and currency regimes determined whether and to what extent economic policy instruments could achieve their targets. There is a close relationship between the possibilities of an independent monetary policy geared towards domestic goals, pegged exchange rates, and international capital mobility for small open economies. A government with a pegged exchange rate aims to counteract a recession by an expansionary monetary policy that initially lowers domestic interest rates. The interest rate differential opened up with foreign capital markets causes a capital flight. Investors convert domestic currency into foreign currency at the pegged exchange rate, and the country's international reserves fall as the central bank is obliged to intervene in foreign exchange markets (i.e., buys domestic currency and sells foreign) in order to stabilize the nominal exchange rate around the official peg. This foreign exchange operation contracts the monetary stock and offsets the initial expansion: the domestic monetary stock is endogenous to the economy and cannot be controlled by the monetary authorities, so that output and employment ultimately remain unaffected.

Attempts to "sterilize" this monetary offset with a new expansion of domestic monetary base will only accelerate the drain on reserves. Exchange and capital controls may block or slow the outflow, but otherwise foreign exchange reserves will eventually be exhausted. Before that happens investors will anticipate the abandonment of the pegged exchange rate and there will be a "speculative attack." Fundamentals are inconsistent with the target exchange rate: policy-makers face a "trilemma" (Obstfeld, Shambaugh, and Taylor 2005) that obliges them, in the absence of capital controls, either to abandon monetary expansion and keep the pegged rate, or to adopt a floating rate if they continue their inflationary policy. Policy makers wanting to use tight monetary policy to preserve price stability in an international inflationary environment will be equally frustrated by the expansionary effect of capital inflows and the accumulation of foreign reserves. In both cases, a weak form of monetary policy independence could be achieved through periodical realignments (i.e., devaluations or revaluations) of the nominal exchange rate, validating the accumulated inflation differential.

This conceptual framework helps explain post-war economic policy in western Europe. As shown in Table 14.1, over the second half of the century European governments exhibited remarkably consistent preferences for pegged exchange rates and a clear dislike of floating. Their choice reflected the harm that they believed exchange rate fluctuations would have caused to intra-European trade and the Common Agricultural Policy (Eichengreen 1996b, p. 137).

Table 14.1 Currency regime of sixteen western European countries, 1950–2007

	Time on pegged exchange rate (%)	Peg to US$	Peg to UK£	Peg to DM	Currency union (euro)	Peg to euro
Austria	96.5	1953–9		1959–98	1999–	
Belgium	94.7	1954–5		1955–71	1999–	
Denmark	100.0	1950		1951–71, 1978–98		1999–
Finland	71.9	1950–1, 1967–73		1973–92, 1993–8	1999–	
France	89.5	1956–71		1971–3, 1974–98	1999–	
Germany	47.4	1954–71, 1972			1999–	
Greece	96.5	1950–81		1984–98	1999–	
Ireland	100.0		1946–79	1979–98	1999–	
Italy	86.0	1951–73		1983–92, 1993–8	1999–	
Netherlands	100.0	1950–71		1971–98	1999–	
Norway	0.0					
Portugal	87.7	1950–1973		1981–98	1999–	
Spain	100.0	1951–80		1981–98	1999–	
Sweden	71.9	1951–73		1973–92		
Switzerland	70.2	1950–73		1981–88		
UK	43.9	1950–72		1991–2		

Notes: Definition based on *de facto* classification by Reinhardt and Rogoff (2004) and related background material. Pegs include: pre-announced peg or currency board, pre-announced band narrower than or equal to +/–2%, de facto peg, pre-announced and de facto crawling peg, and crawling band narrower than or equal to +/–2 percent.

Pegging to the US Dollar under the Bretton Woods System was definitely abandoned by most European governments in 1972–3, but quickly replaced by de facto pegging to the Deutschmark. Two periods of anchoring to the German currency as an external constraint on domestic economic policy were the "Snake" (1972–8) and the European Monetary System (1979–93). Both initially proved sustainable only for a group of northern European small economies with moderate inflation. But the peg was successfully adopted by large inflationary countries in the early 1980s as a disciplinary device to achieve disinflation (Gros and Thygesen 1992).

Capital mobility and arbitrage also increased over the period, both because of official financial liberalization and by circumvention of national capital controls (Marston 1995). As shown in Table 14.2, based on an index of external financial deregulation (Quinn 2003), European governments gradually relaxed

Table 14.2 Quinn index of capital liberalization, 1950–2000

	1950–60	1960–70	1970–80	1980–90	1990–2000	Year of full liberalization	Temporary controls after liberalization
Austria	12.5	62.5	62.5	75	87.5		
Belgium	75	75	75	75	100	1990	1996–8
Denmark	37.5	75	75	75	100	1988	
Finland	12.5	12.5	50	50	100	1994	
France	62.5	75	75	75	87.5	1998	
Germany	75	100	100	100	100	1957	1973, 1978–80
Greece	25	50	50	50	75	1997	
Ireland	50	50	75	75	100	1992	
Italy	37.5	75	75	75	100	1988	1990–2
Netherlands	75	75	75	100	100	1983	
Norway	37.5	37.5	37.5	62.5	100	1990	
Portugal	25	25	37.5	37.5	87.5		
Spain	12.5	50	50	75	75	1999	
Sweden	12.5	62.5	62.5	75	87.5		
Switzerland	100	100	100	100	100	1950	1964–65, 1974–8
UK	50	50	50	100	100	1979	

Note: Index of liberalization of capital account transactions. Scoring ranges from 0 (full restriction) to 100 (full liberalization). See details in Quinn 2003. Reported values are median score by decades.

capital controls from the late 1970s and eventually dismantled them during the 1980s, enhancing the prominence of the "trilemma."

From the mid-1950s to 1971, and again from the early 1980s to the adoption of the single currency in 1998, pegged currency regimes limited the policy discretion of governments. Pegged rates restricted how much inflation was possible without capital flight and a change in the exchange rate. They thereby contributed to holding down both expected and actual inflation.

In the last quarter of the twentieth century financial integration further tied the hands of governments. Only during the fifteen years between the demise of Bretton Woods and the last realignment within the EMS (1987) did floating or pegged-but-frequently-adjusted rates relax this external constraint and give policy makers significant leeway. As we show in the following section, this was also the period in which fiscal and monetary policies became less disciplined and business cycles in Europe more volatile. Government policy was more active and public uncertainty increased as to future inflation.

This uncertainty is demonstrated by the history of the Phillips curve, an empirical relation between inflation and unemployment. Originally estimated for the UK from 1861 to 1957, the data spanned a period of stable price expectations. Once figures from more inflationary subsequent years were introduced, the simplicity of the inverse relationship disappeared. It could only be recovered by introducing changing expected inflation (as well as determinants of shifts in the underlying equilibrium unemployment rate). Any idea that policy makers could trade off more inflation against less unemployment disappeared along with the basic Philips curve. For if policy makers chose any unemployment rate above the equilibrium rate, rising inflation quickly shifted the apparent trade-off by raising price expectations.

The Phillips curve has subsequently been interpreted as an aggregate supply curve. The apparent trade-off reflects aggregate demand fluctuations along a short-run supply curve. In the long run, with price expectations consistent with actual inflation, the supply curve is vertical at the equilibrium unemployment. Demand management cannot influence this level of unemployment. Markets have rational expectations and cannot be fooled by governments or central banks. This explains why expansionary demand management in the 1970s boosted inflation but not employment.

A European cycle?

Recessions

Whether or not policy stabilized or destabilized in practice, European economies were repeatedly struck by shocks, usually adverse, and oscillated accordingly. There are various ways of identifying these cycles. The widely adopted definition of the National Bureau of Economic Research (NBER) states that recessions are characterized by "a significant decline in activity, spread across the economy, lasting more than a few months, visible in industrial production, employment, real income, and trade." Peaks and troughs of output and employment mark the turning points of cycles; expansions – that is, the movement from trough to peak – represent the normal state of the economy, while recessions are "brief and relatively rare." In the post-war European experience they were so indeed.

Figure 14.1 shows two alternative indicators of fluctuations. Recent approaches define cycles in terms of deviations of output from underlying secular growth trends (Hodrick and Prescott 1997; Backus and Kehoe 1992). Extracting the cycle requires therefore detrending the (log) GDP series. This can be carried out either by assuming a linear trend and first-differencing the series, thus obtaining annual growth rates, or by applying a filter that removes a non-linear trend from the series. The trend is meant to capture potential output, and deviations from trend are interpreted as output gaps.

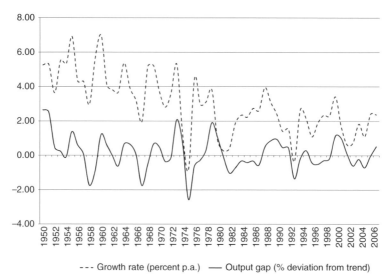

--- Growth rate (percent p.a.)   —— Output gap (% deviation from trend)

Figure 14.1 The European cycle, 1950–2007.
Weighted real GDP of sixteen European countries (weights are each country's share); includes Austria, Belgium, Denmark, Finland, France, West Germany (unified Germany after 1990), Greece, Ireland, Italy, Netherlands, Norway, Portugal, Spain, Sweden, Switzerland, UK. GDP is expressed in 1990 international $. Growth rate is year-to-year change in log (GDP). Cycles (output gap) are deviations from trend obtained by Hodrick-Prescott filtering with smoothing parameter 6.5. *Sources:* Data from the Conference Board and Groningen Growth and Development Center, Total Economy Database.

Level of output data and growth rates suggest that western Europe went through just three major episodes that can be classified as generalized recessions. The first two episodes were not exclusively European, but rather common shocks to industrialized economies: the extraordinary jump in the price of oil and food in 1974–5, and the second oil shock and the "austerity policies" implemented to keep their inflationary consequences under control in 1980–2. The third episode (1992–3) was more European in nature, for shocks were mainly related to German reunification, the ensuing unusually tight monetary policies and the crisis of the European Monetary System, although the crisis partially overlapped with the US recession of 1990–1.

However dampened the cycle was for western Europe as a whole before 1973–4, episodes of stagnation or even recession were far from absent at national level, as shown in Table 14.3. Country-specific recessions were rare between 1958 and 1974–5, but reappeared from the late 1970s until the early 1990s, reflecting the increased frequency of idiosyncratic shocks. These

Table 14.3 European recessions, 1950–2007: a synopsis

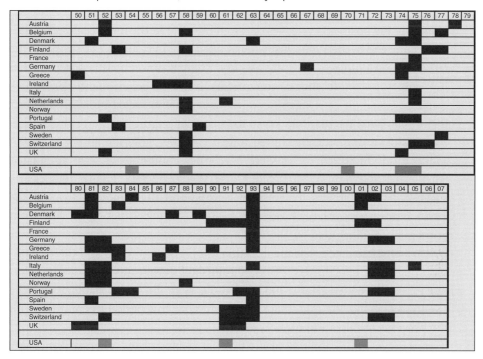

Notes: Recessions are indicated by years with annual real GDP growth either negative or in the range between 0 and 0.5.
Source: Total Economy Database.

shocks were often related to financial liberalization and the constraint imposed by rigidly pegged currency regimes. The most dramatic example was the deep crisis that hit the Nordic economies (Sweden and Finland in particular) in 1990–3, the severest for those countries since the Great Depression (Jonung, Schicknecht, and Tujula 2005).

The Nordic crisis was a particularly painful variation of a new type of economic fluctuation that emerged in Europe in the 1980s. According to this interpretation, successful disinflation, falling interest rates, and the liberalization of traditionally highly regulated banking and financial systems favored the excessive accumulation of debt, generating long boom cycles of credit and asset prices (Borio 2003). At the peak of the cycle, mounting inflationary pressures became incompatible with pegged exchange rates, and triggered contractionary intervention of monetary authorities, turning the boom into bust. Jaeger and Schuknecht (2004) identified sixteen episodes of asset prices boom and thirteen of bust in western Europe after 1984.

Volatility

Ironically the business cycle was declared obsolete in the industrialized econo-mies at the end of the 1960s, just when it was about to resume. The shocks of the 1970s caused a jump in cyclical volatility. There is now a broad consensus that not only supply-side shocks (oil prices), but also governments' pro-active response based on Keynesian demand management, fueled inflation and fur-ther destabilized fluctuations. From the mid-1980s until 2007, most industrial-ized countries dramatically shifted to low volatility, entering an era of "Great Moderation" in which cycles were barely perceptible, or at least attenuated (Blanchard and Simon 2001; Stock and Watson 2004). Figure 14.2 clearly suggests parallel stories for western Europe and the United States. By the 1990s output gap volatility reached historically low values in all European economies, as illustrated in Table 14.4.

It is well established that the duration of cycles lengthened and their ampli-tude (height of troughs and peaks) diminished during this period, which has now of course ended (Borio 2003, pp. 6–7). Why did cycles stabilize over the twenty years after the mid-1980s? And what has this period in common with the previous stabilization of the 1960s?

In the 1960s, the absence of the cyclical swings of the interwar years was often attributed to the greater role of government in the economy through ownership of swathes of industry, supplemented by budgets of historically unprecedented size. Heavier taxation and greater transfers, as well as bigger state bureaucracies, meant that a large component of aggregate demand was

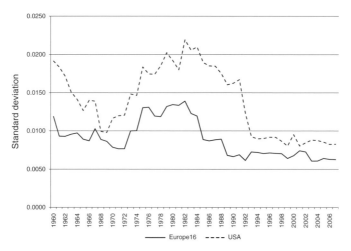

Figure 14.2 Transatlantic Great Moderation. Time-varying volatility of output gap. Values for each year are calculated as a ten-year rolling window ending in that year.

Table 14.4 The Great Moderation in western Europe

	1950–73	1974–93	1994–2007
	Output gap volatility		
Austria	2.8	1.09	0.73
Belgium	1.22	1.22	0.65
Denmark	1.51	1.38	0.74
Finland	1.82	2.37	1.01
France	1.16	0.99	0.64
Germany	2.5	1.21	0.74
Greece	2.11	1.62	0.35
Ireland	1.48	1.59	1.22
Italy	1.33	1.29	0.68
Netherlands	1.77	1.04	0.93
Norway	0.92	1.25	0.67
Portugal	1.65	2.2	1.15
Spain	2.39	1.11	0.65
Sweden	1.03	1.28	0.84
Switzerland	1.81	1.85	0.83
UK	1.27	1.5	0.31
Mean	*1.67*	*1.44*	*0.76*
Variance	*0.30*	*0.16*	*0.06*

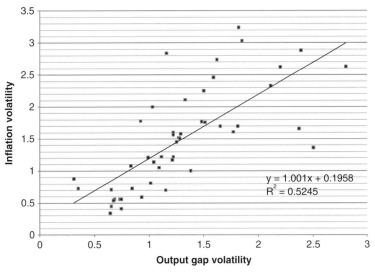

Figure 14.3 Inflation and output gap volatility, 1950–2007. Inflation volatility: standard deviation of consumer price index annual inflation in sixteen western European countries in the periods 1950–73; 1974–93; 1994–2007. Output gap volatility: standard deviation of output gap in the same periods. *Source:* CPI indices from IMF, International Financial Statistics. Real GDP from Total Economy Database.

less exposed to the vagaries of the market than in classic laissez-faire capitalism. Anglocentric interpretations of history were inclined to attribute this greater stability and high levels of employment to the Keynesian demand management of benign and omniscient governments (Boltho 1982). But even in what should have been the most Keynesian of economies, in Britain where the doctrine originated, the cause of the higher levels of employment in these decades was primarily higher investment, and secondarily higher exports, rather than public sector deficits (Matthews 1968). Policy was not Keynesian in the sense that fiscal policy targeted employment creation (Tomlinson 1984). Close observers noted that, while the larger government sector may have contributed to strong private sector demand by enhancing confidence, it was also government that triggered recessions with demand management (Maddison 1960).

Contrary to the Keynesian interpretation, even the most conservative of national economic policies met with apparently similar or greater success in minimizing the business cycle. Ludwig Erhard's economic miracle in West Germany, based on currency reform and price decontrol, and António de Oliveira Salazar's balanced budgets in Portugal, are cases in point. Growth was strong and prices stable also in Italy during the 1950s, where the Governor of the Bank of Italy, Donato Menichella, targeted the exchange rate and contended that unemployment was a structural problem, not one to be addressed by demand management (Fratianni and Spinelli 1997).

Governments' ability to keep inflation low and stable, by reducing uncertainty about future inflation, may have reduced output variability again after the 1980s. In turn this created a more favorable macroeconomic environment. Also thanks to lower inflationary expectations, monetary policy was able to respond more effectively to shocks. Consistent with this view, both in the USA and western Europe the steep drop in cycle volatility coincided with a clear anti-inflationary twist in the conduct of monetary policy. In Europe there is a robust positive empirical relationship between inflation and output gap variability, as shown in Figure 14.3.

The wide geographical spread of the Great Moderation points to common causal factors: anti-inflationary policies and successful macroeconomic coordination through the EMS, together with the increased independence of central banks, kept inflationary expectations low and stable. Constrained discretion and better coordination between monetary and fiscal policy may help explain the outstanding moderation of the British cycle since the 1990s, in spite of sustained economic growth (HM Treasury 2002).

Or possibly it was just good luck; that is, particularly benign economic conditions with only mild and infrequent adverse events (such as supply shocks). Stock and Watson (2004), for instance, find that the fall in G-7 countries' output variance in the 1980s and 1990s relative to the 1960s and 1970s is almost completely explained by the decline in the magnitude of shocks. But, if oil price hikes were the main driver of GDP volatility, the shift to the moderation era should have been synchronized. The significant lags with which different countries stabilized suggest that the role of the vanishing oil shocks in the Great Moderation is ambiguous at least (Summers 2005, pp. 15–20).

Links between the low inflation and low volatility of Figure 14.3 may be more subtle. Since the 1980s the amplitude and persistence of asset price cycles have increased in western Europe. The boom-and-bust fluctuations mentioned above have also been associated with large and persistent deviations of output growth from trend. This regularity is consistent with the financial system and the real economy becoming more closely associated, through household and corporate indebtedness, gross fixed investments, and asset prices. Some argue that this new environment is a return to that of the gold standard (Goodhart 2003).

Synchronization

Along with a secular fall in volatility, European cycles after 1950 also became more synchronized. By the end of the twentieth century a true "European" cycle seems to have emerged (see Figure 14.4). Why?

Increased synchronization of cycles across countries can be caused either by common shocks – such as the oil price hikes – or by the strengthening of

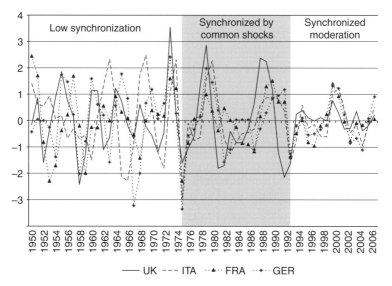

Figure 14.4 Increasing synchronization of main European cycles. Output gap based on (log) real GDP. *Source:* as for Figure 14.1.

mechanisms that transmit unanticipated events. One possible mechanism is international integration and interdependence created by increasing trade in goods and financial assets (Bayoumi and Eichengreen 1993). But trade might also increase the probability of sector-specific, asymmetric shocks, which could reduce cycle correlation (Krugman 1993).

Greater integration is not strictly necessary to explain closer cycle correlation, however. For any level of integration, cycles may be synchronized if common shocks become stronger or more frequent: the two oil shocks synchronized the recessions of 1974–5 and 1981–2 and explain the greater correlation of the 1970s and 1980s. But in the absence of large common shocks since the early 1990s, the causes of subsequent synchronization must be different.

Pegging exchange rates to the DM within the EMS may have enhanced cycle correlation through increased coordination of macroeconomic policies (Artis and Zhang 1997; Inklaar and de Haan 2001). Subsequently the EMU and the Growth and Stability Pact, by requiring countries to follow fiscal rules or disciplines, might create an optimum currency area, as Darvasz, Rose, and Szapary (2005) contend. Or simply introducing such rules might trigger common shocks and therefore a policy-induced cycle correlation.

In any case, the increased synchronization of national fluctuations with the German cycle is unquestionable. Table 14.5 shows that a limited number of European economies fluctuated with Germany before 1973. By the end of the century the German connection had become a salient feature of most European cycles, with the important exception of the UK's, which was decoupled from continental cycles and more synchronized with North America's (Artis, Marcellino, and Proietti 2004; Duecker and Wesche 2004).

Analytic narratives

Coordination failures

Under the Bretton Woods System, a target for both governments and central banks was to maintain the value of pegged exchange rates, but what this required was not always well understood. Uncertainty about the time that the economy took to respond to policy measures compounded the challenge.

As noted above, under the pegged exchange rate government policy was constrained by the external balance. Therefore economic policy should have responded to fluctuations in the exchange rate, international reserves, and the current account. Yet statistical evidence suggests demand management was

Table 14.5 Increasing German dominance?

	Synchronization of cycles with Germany		
	1950–73	1974–93	1994–2007
Switzerland	0.06	0.56	0.90
Italy	0.16	0.81	0.87
Netherlands	0.13	0.87	0.87
Austria	0.79	0.66	0.82
France	0.57	0.67	0.79
Belgium	0.49	0.63	0.78
Spain	−0.20	0.32	0.75
Denmark	0.44	0.58	0.70
Sweden	0.36	0.28	0.69
Finland	0.39	0.13	.65
Portugal	0.00	0.55	0.62
UK	0.21	0.35	0.60
Ireland	0.15	0.37	0.55
Norway	−0.04	0.35	0.17
Greece	−0.16	0.64	0.06
mean	*0.22*	*0.52*	*0.65*
variance	*0.08*	*0.04*	*0.06*

Note: Based on correlation (Pearson) of output gaps.

unresponsive to external imbalances in the vast majority of European countries. According to the most detailed study available for nine western economies between 1950 and 1966 (Michaely 1971), no consistent pattern of response by budgetary policies, as an instrument of aggregate demand policy, to the balance of payments can be found.

Even more strikingly, such unresponsiveness apparently cannot be explained by the use of the budget for competing policy targets. Rather, fiscal policy seemed unavailable for the correction of domestic, as well as balance-of-payments, disequilibria. Governments apparently did not combine fiscal and monetary policy in a manner consistent with the "policy mix" rule. Tighter monetary policy was appropriate to correcting a balance of payments deficit, for higher interest rates would draw in mobile capital. Expansionary fiscal policy, according to the Keynesian economic doctrine of the day in Britain and the USA, would address rising unemployment. With hindsight, governments probably did not use the policy mix rule simply because it would not have worked in most circumstances. More likely, the long run level of unemployment was determined by the structure of the labor market and the extent of competition between firms. Attempts to reduce unemployment below this level using demand policy would have been met with rising inflation. Then, as policy switched to bringing down inflation, unemployment would have begun rising.

Coordination between domestic monetary and fiscal policy could be a challenge, particularly with a formally independent central bank, for the central bank might object to financing government budget deficits by monetary expansion. It might prefer to rein in demand in order to stop price rises if the government budget was too inflationary. The German Bundesbank (until 1957 Bank Deutscher Länder) often resisted the expansionary fiscal policies of the West German Federal Government. A 1948 law imposed on the German central bank the primary task of "safeguarding the currency." From 1951 the Bank was also required to support the government's economic policy when there was no conflict with the currency objective. Economic performance was unlikely simply to have been a consequence of the accident of central bank independence; among other influences the intellectual climate created by the Freiburg School of Walter Eucken, which emphasized proactive policies to support and enhance competition – a supply orientated neo-liberalism – must have played a role (Denton, Forsyth, and Maclennan 1968).

History was perhaps even more important, as the following episode shows. In mid-1955 the West German central bank raised interest rates, after a long period of monetary ease, and publicly criticized the expansionary stance of Federal fiscal policy (Berger and de Haan 1999). The government was planning increased spending to improve its standing in the 1957 election, and therefore used its temporary veto over the next interest rate rise in March 1956. However, influential members of the government, Economics Minister Erhard and Finance Minister Schaffer, supported the bank policy against Adenauer, the Chancellor, in order to maintain price stability. These ministers also sat on the central bank's board and voted for yet another interest rate increase in May 1956. Together with the bank, they were publicly denounced by the Chancellor. But public opinion was against Adenauer and he was obliged to back down. More expansionary fiscal policy would not be accommodated by monetary policy, and therefore it was less likely to reduce unemployment sufficiently to boost re-election chances.

A similar conflict emerged ten years later. From 1964 strong expansion, driven by domestic demand, was compounded by sustained wage growth that was faster than the rise in productivity. Inflationary pressures were greater than at any time since the Korean War boom. The Federal government's budget deficit increased and the current account deteriorated. Again a strong correction was imposed by the Bundesbank through discount rate hikes between 1965 and 1966, against the protests of Cabinet members. The 1967 "mini-recession" – the first episode of negative growth experienced by West Germany since 1945 – was the result (Holtfrerich 1999, pp. 378–80).

Recent interpretations regard the Bundesbank's switching from tolerance of inflation in 1961–4 to a restrictive stance in 1965–6, in conflict with the Federal government, as a new episode of institutional rivalry. Marsh (1992, pp. 186–8) and Leaman (2001, pp. 138–42) underline the opportunistic behavior of the German central bank. According to this view, pre-eminence given to inflation-fighting should be evaluated against a broader political context, and could be interpreted as an attempt to absolve the central bank from government's responsibility for rising inflation, as well as a decisive step in the Bundesbank's ascent to political and economic dominance.

Formal or legal central bank independence may have mattered less for policy than the brief or target assigned to the institution or their ignorance of policy impacts. This is suggested by the conflict between the Governor of the Bank of England and British Chancellor of the Exchequer (Finance Minister), Peter Thorneycroft in 1957. The Bank Rate was raised to 7 percent in September, as inflation triggered short-term capital movements that threatened the exchange rate (Cairncross 1996). Thorneycroft wanted to increase his range of monetary instruments so that interest rates need not rise so high, adversely affecting industry and employment. He tried to persuade commercial banks to reduce their loans by 5 percent, but they refused, and the Governor would not issue the directive.

Despite the nationalization of the Bank of England in 1946, Thorneycroft lacked the authority to coerce the banks or dismiss the Governor, as he would have liked. Unemployment duly increased from autumn 1957 to a peak in November 1958. Reflationary measures, beginning in May 1958, were slow to take effect, but by the second half of 1959 were creating excessive expansion. No doubt this helped the re-election of the Macmillan government in October 1959. Removal of banking restrictions in the middle of 1958 almost doubled loans in the following three years. In addition there were tax concessions and greater public spending in the 1959 budget. Bank Rate was reduced from 6 percent in March 1959 to 4 percent in November. These measures interacted with each other to produce an unexpectedly strong expansion in spending. The balance of payments began to cause concern as imports soared, and the first experiments with incomes policy were discussed, to limit wage increases. The contrast with the German episode is more in the lack of coordination between the deregulation of banking and other policies than in lack of central bank independence.

Monetary brakes and the external constraint

During the 1960s, in a significant group of European countries, instruments of monetary policy – mainly the discount rate and the growth rate of money supply – moved in a direction (though not necessarily with a magnitude) consistent with the external position. That is, interest rates increased and growth of the money supply fell during periods of balance of payments deficit. This evidence is broadly compatible with monetary policy being flexible and effective, whereas fiscal policy was inflexible and inappropriate.

The IMF view was that countries affected by "temporary and reversible disequilibrium in the balance of payments … should not be expected to incur fluctuations in internal demand and activity." Rather, they should pursue "policies aimed at attracting appropriate equilibrating movements of private capital through international coordination of interest rates." But coordinating such policies between sovereign governments was a considerable challenge (Chalmers 1972). Pursuing domestic policies that maintained the confidence of internationally mobile capital turned out to be a surer bet.

Domestic monetary policy might offset contractions triggered by the balance of payments. When international reserves, a central bank asset partly balancing the liability of domestic money, fell without a change of policy, the domestic money stock would normally decline. However, policy could, and in the 1960s did, counteract this effect by increasing central bank holdings of domestic assets (government bonds and bills in particular) made easier by copious government borrowing. But the exchange rate, and the foreign reserves to support it, were not protected by this "sterilization" operation. Sterilization therefore meant more balance of payments crises, which could force exchange rate re-alignments.

The external constraint was binding on all governments, irrespective of their ideology. In Franco's Spain, still operating under a semi-autarkic regime in the late 1950s, inflation was fueled by populist wage measures taken to stem political unrest and uncontrolled creation of liquidity by the Bank of Spain. This led in 1959 to a mounting current account deficit and the virtual exhaustion of reserves. Assisted by the IMF and the OECD, the regime agreed to devalue the peseta and implement an orthodox package of fiscal adjustment and monetary restriction (Carreras and Tafunell 2004b, pp. 325–35). In Italy three years later, inflationary pressures at a peak of the expansionary cycle, a current account deficit approaching 4 percent of GDP, and massive capital flights (also caused by untimely nationalization of electric utilities) decided the Bank of Italy to implement a credit squeeze. Devaluation of the lira was avoided at the cost of a sudden contraction of economic activity (De Cecco 1969; Fratianni and Spinelli 1997, pp. 509–16). For those governments too timid to put on the brake when inflationary pressure accumulated, the only alternative in the end was reluctantly to accept exchange rate changes, as in the cases of the 1967–9 devaluations of the pound and the French franc (Eichengreen 1996b, pp. 125–8, 2007, pp. 233–41; Patat and Lutfalla 1990, pp. 207–10).

But "stop" policies could fail too. In West Germany in 1970–1 the Bundesbank's attempt to curb domestic liquidity and control rising inflation by using restrictive monetary and credit policies was swamped by massive inflows of foreign capital attracted by high interest rates. To allow the Bundesbank to regain control of the money supply, floating was judged a more feasible solution than an escalation of administrative capital controls (Emminger 1977, p. 28; von Hagen 1999, pp. 404–19).

Stop–go: responding to unemployment

The recession of the mid-1970s brought to an end the post-war epoch of stability: "stagflation" – rising unemployment and inflation – marked the next decade or more. In fact inflationary pressures, powered by high wage demands from trade unions and sustained expansion of governments' expenditures, had become evident in most European economies from 1970. But no longer was policy constrained by the pegged exchange rates of Bretton Woods, and attempts to control inflation with tight monetary policies in 1972–3 were soon abandoned. In the short run, both in the USA and in western Europe fiscal and monetary policies accommodated the oil shock, interpreted as transitory negative shocks to aggregate supply. Increasing budget deficits and government debt, fast money growth, and low or even negative real interest rates dominated until the early 1980s.

Proactive responsiveness to adverse shocks contributed to the creation of unusually large inflation differentials between European countries. One group, anchored to West Germany, switched earlier to price stability and learned coordination between fiscal and monetary policy – not without conflicts between the two arms of government. The other, including Britain, France, and Italy, was reluctant to abandon full employment as its main policy objective, and preferred the expansion followed by contraction of "stop–go" policies, rather than acknowledge the constraint that international capital mobility and confidence placed on their choices.

A policy innovation intended to contain rising wages and prices was to persuade unions and firms to limit these increases to less than a specified annual percentage. These "corporatist" patterns of economic policy making, based on "the co-ordinated, co-operative, and systematic management of the national economy by the state, centralized unions, and employers" (Siaroff 1999), succeeded in containing inflation where it had developed into a basic feature of the "post-war settlement," as in Austria, Germany, or Scandinavia. Here governments' commitment to raising living standards with economic growth policies and planning was reciprocated by wage restraint in the knowledge that such moderation would allow higher investment and therefore high future living standards (Eichengreen 1996a). But in countries with different political traditions and institutional setup, the "post-war settlement" failed in the face of mounting inflationary expectations. Prices and incomes policies in the UK, France, and Italy (in the two latter as part of indicative planning) were ineffective in controlling inflation for more than very short periods on those occasions when policies could be agreed (Ulman and Flanagan 1971).

The classic example of a Keynesian policy response is the British fiscal expansion of 1972–3. Following four disappointing years of low growth, rising unemployment, and mounting cost inflation and now in the cycle trough, the British government increased spending and cut taxes significantly. The abandonment of external equilibrium as a policy objective was announced by the Chancellor of the Exchequer, who declared that "it is neither necessary nor desirable to distort domestic economies to an unacceptable extent in order to retain unrealistic exchange rates" (James 1996, p. 239). Recovery of growth and employment in 1972–3 was therefore accompanied by a new bout of inflationary pressures, the worst deterioration of the current account in the post-war period, and a new external crisis forcing sterling out of the "Snake."

In spite of the removal of the balance of payment constraint by floating the exchange rate, growth remained slow and both unemployment and inflation kept rising. The end of demand-led growth policies came with the 1976 IMF crisis, when in order to obtain a loan to support the balance of payments, the Chancellor of the Exchequer was obliged to write a Letter of Intent to pursue "sounder" economic policies. By then, Labor Prime Minister Callaghan recognized that the option to "spend your way out of a recession" was no longer feasible (Budd 1998, pp. 275–6).

On the Continent, however, this notion had yet to spread. French policy makers proved the most reluctant to abandon demand expansion policies. The anti-inflationary "Plan Fourcade" of 1974–5, launched after the first withdrawal from the Snake, soon gave way to an expansionary "Relance Chirac" leading to mounting budget and current account deficits, a new exit from the Snake, and the resignation of its proponent. The "austerity plan" of the new prime minister, Raymond Barre, temporarily succeeded in achieving external balance and controlling the budget and inflation. But unemployment rose, and even the gains that had been made were wiped out by the second oil shock and the 1980 socialist victory in the presidential election.

The newly elected government, facing a global downturn, embarked on a program of nationalization to promote investment and heavily increased government spending. Under the "Plan Mauroy," the budget deficit reached 3 percent of GDP, the continuous devaluation of the exchange rate failed to reduce the mounting current account deficit, and inflation remained around

10 percent. Within eighteen months capital flight forced a reversal of policy. A stable exchange rate could not be maintained with such fiscal expansion. Between 1983 and 1986 a new "austerity plan," under the management of Jacques Delors, eventually achieved disinflation, although unemployment had reached 2.4 million at the end of 1984, four times greater than ten years earlier (Estrin and Holmes 1983; Patat and Lutfalla 1990, p. 232).

These overambitious aggregate demand policies were driven not only by mistaken economics but also by political party competition for the votes of electorates. Hence it is reasonable to wonder to what extent the political orientation of western European governments influenced their economic policies.

Parties want to be re-elected, but they may also have ideological commitments that appeal to only a section of the electorate. Debtors might be inclined to vote for left-wing parties and creditors for right-wing representatives, on the grounds that left-wing parties are expansionary and inflationary while right-wing parties pursue contractionary policies in the interests of price stability. Supposing this to be so, and bearing in mind that the outcomes of elections are often uncertain, when a left-wing government wins an election average expectations of inflation over the next year or two are likely to be lower than felt desirable by the new government, in so far as there was some chance that a low-inflation right-wing government could have been elected. Inflation expectations before an election are based on averaging the policies of the possible governments and weighting by the likelihood of their election. So long as inflation expectations are lower than actual inflation, real wages will be reduced and labor demand will expand. Eventually expectations will catch up with reality and the cycle upswing will stop. The converse is the case for the election of a right-wing government in this "rational partisan theory" (RPT) of business cycles.

The case of the French socialists is consistent with RPT. In a period of world recession (1981–3), the Mitterrand government at first pursued expansionary policies, keeping French economic growth positive while many other major industrial economies were in recession (Alesina 1989). The Swedish conservatives (1976) also offer a particularly good fit to the theory. In Sweden, output growth fell strongly from 1975–6 to 1978, consistent with inflation expectations being above the government's target.

Taking on inflation

The 1980s saw increasing acceptance of conservative macroeconomics by policy makers in the US and UK, especially the belief that there was no trade-off between inflation and unemployment. Most of western Europe shared in the recession of 1980–2, but the urgent task of eradicating inflation left governments with little countercyclical leeway. Especially in most inflationary countries, increasingly independent central banks carried out their task of "taking on inflation" with unprecedented tight money. Monetary authorities pushed nominal and real interest rates up to record highs until 1983, often in the face of offsetting fiscal policies (Ciocca and Nardozzi 1996).

Pegging weak European currencies to the DM within the EMS proved a successful mechanism for disinflation. By 1985 inflation in countries with past records of loose money and irresponsible budgets had substantially converged to the German rate. By anchoring to the Bundesbank, European monetary authorities could "buy" part of Germany's anti-inflationary reputation (Giavazzi and Pagano 1988). Perhaps helped by falling oil prices from 1986 as well, inflation was gradually squeezed out of the cycle through the 1980s. The Single Market initiative was probably also a benign supply-side shock.

New domestic equilibria emerged, based on the gradual relaxation of wage and pension indexation and novel relationships with trade unions that helped control wage dynamics. Unemployment fell when unions were either forced to cooperate by legislative changes, as in the United Kingdom, or chose to cooperate, as in the Dutch Wassenaar Agreement of 1982. In this Agreement, the unions moderated wage demands and in return management committed to expand part-time employment (Nickell and van Ours 2000). Government tax concessions were made for part-time employment and public sector employment, and wages were cut. Wage tax rates were reduced so that a lower nominal wage increase was required to maintain household incomes. Employment grew and real wage growth in the Netherlands was similar to that in the United States.

Less successful was West German government policy at the end of the decade, certainly turning what could have been a positive supply stimulus for Europe into a massive and sustained negative shock. With the breaking down of the Berlin Wall in 1989, the Cold War ended. The Soviet client states of eastern Europe were allowed to abandon their experiment with central planning, and shift to markets. Had Chancellor Kohl managed economic aspects of German reunification with the perspicacity shown half a century earlier by Ludwig Erhard, European economic history would have been transformed.

In July 1990 the Germanies were united monetarily at a rate of one Ostmark to one Deutschmark for two months' wages and two Ostmarks to one Deutschmark above that amount. Unfortunately the low productivity of the East German economy meant that this exchange rate massively overvalued East German labor and assets. Prices were controlled in former East Germany, creating a large new market but with impossibly low productivity. The currency conversion rate bankrupted eastern financial institutions. The burden of supporting a large population rendered unproductive by the terms of the monetary union pushed up unemployment.

This negative shock was superimposed upon what seemed to be a successful system of pegged European exchange rates, the EMS. Then the 1992 crisis forced the UK and Italy off what was effectively the DM peg, but other economies managed to stay on it. UK exports and economic activity generally began to expand while those of France stagnated. Momentum for a single currency was nevertheless maintained, and the euro was introduced for eleven countries on January 1, 1999.

Business cycles in eastern Europe and Russia, 1945–2006

Cycles under central planning

The USSR and the command economies of eastern Europe boasted that their economic systems were free of the periodic bursts of higher unemployment, swings in output, and price instability characteristic of the traditional western cycle. According to Loshkin (1964), central planning of production and distribution, together with state ownership of all productive resources, succeeded in replacing "the cyclical character of development which is organically inherent in capitalism" with "unswerving, continuous growth."

With Soviet national accounting systems and state control of information, this claim is not easy to evaluate. Levels of economic activity in Soviet systems were harder to measure than economic growth rates, and official data were censored. Nevertheless, large fluctuations of output growth rates (but not of employment) seemed to be characteristic of planned economies too, as suggested by Figure 14.5.

This cyclical output pattern almost certainly arose because of shocks, such as harvest failure, and because of the information and coordination challenges intrinsic to resource allocation in any large complex system. Absence of scarcity prices meant that there was a very limited role for monetary or fiscal policy. Policy was implemented instead by direct commands and controls. The changing phases of efforts to fulfill Plan targets were a significant source of fluctuations. At the end of a Plan period pressure to attain planned output could accelerate production and reduce quality, or bottlenecks in the system might require the planners to apply the brakes (Kornai 1992, pp. 186–93).

Besides this timing element, the system of capital grants provided without interest by the state, and the legal framework (absence of bankruptcy),

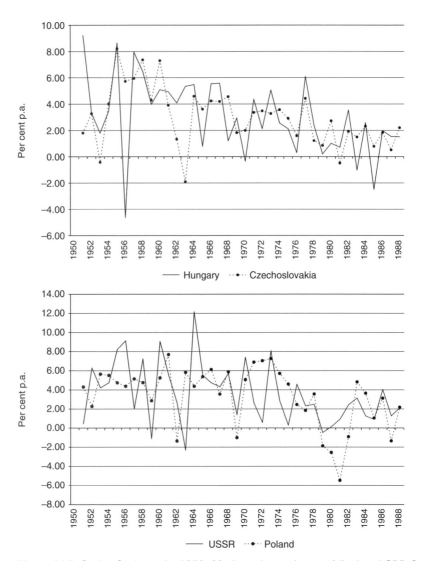

Figure 14.5 Cycles Soviet-style, 1950–88. Annual growth rate of (log) real GDP. *Source:* Data from Total Economy Database.

favored expansion of business over contraction. The allocation mechanism was biased towards dividing capital grants into smaller grants for various projects, for central planning tended to provide a similar amount to every project, failing to focus on especially attractive ones and ignore those with poorer prospects.

Consumption and investment targets were announced long before they were achieved, which may have increased the speed of adjustments and contributed to shorter cycles compared with market economies, in addition to the five-year plan planning horizon (Hutchings 1969). Kontorovich (1990) identified, as the driver of cyclicality of growth rates, mistakes in the allocation of investment. These triggered imbalances and declining capital utilization rates, which in turn caused the fluctuations. Examples of these mistakes were overfulfilment of plan targets in the Khruschev era of 1957–64 for heavy industry, and persistent underachievement in the consumer sector. In the following period down to 1985, that of Brezhnev and his successors, plans for industry tended to be less ambitious and more scientifically based. But information deficiencies ensured that plans continued to be inconsistent and therefore subject to continual revisions during implementation. This was a potential source of output fluctuation, but more importantly also of slow productivity growth, which widened the lag behind the western economies (Davis 1999).

Cycles in the post-1989 transition

In March 1985, the Communist Party elite chose Mikhail Gorbachev as General Secretary to implement reforms that would correct the many problems of the previous "stagnation era," while maintaining the communist system. Gorbachev's economic reforms were unsuccessful, with the consequence that industrial performance and living standards deteriorated. Economic collapse ignited deep-seated ethnic and regional grievances. The ensuing political reaction exploded in a coup attempt in August 1991 and the subsequent dissolution of the USSR along with its international system. Russia's and eastern Europe's transitions to market economies brought them distinctive shocks that continued to ensure that their economic experiences diverged from western Europe's.

As shown in Figure 14.6, after a period of collapsing output, the transition economies among the central and east European countries (CEECs) began to catch up with the west, achieving high rates of economic growth. However the former Soviet Union (FSU) generally followed a different path, with divergent patterns of prices and unemployment (Boeri and Terrel 2002). Underlying these paths, the shocks and their transmission processes differed for a number of reasons; proximity to western Europe both geographically and culturally, plus the opportunity to join the EU, appear to have been critical.

Whereas the "Washington consensus" of the World Bank, the IMF and influential US academics and policy makers, favored a "big bang" approach of sudden transition to markets and private enterprise, the Copenhagen criteria that had to be satisfied for eligibility for EU membership were more concerned with institution building, convergence, and stability. "Washington" and "Copenhagen"

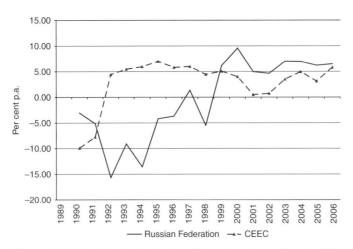

Figure 14.6 Growth rates in the transition. Annual growth rate of (log) real GDP. CEEC is weighted GDP of fifteen CEEC (weights are each country's share in total GDP); includes Albania, Bosnia-Herzegovina, Bulgaria, Croatia, Czech Republic, Estonia, Hungary, Latvia, Lithuania, Macedonia, Poland, Romania, Serbia, Montenegro, Slovakia, Slovenia. GDP is expressed in 1990 international $. *Source:* data from Total Economy Database.

combined seemed tolerably effective for most of the CEEC. "Washington" alone, as applied to the FSU in the 1990s, looked considerably less so.

In spite of moderate economic growth in the CEEC, unemployment increased quickly and stayed high. Regulation and (particularly) labor market policies were responsible for high unemployment rates, especially minimum wages and unemployment benefits. Those with low skills could not find jobs because the wage floor was above what they could contribute to an employer. In addition, benefits discouraged employment because they were a "negative subsidy"; the state took away benefits if people started working. Accordingly, excessive benefits were often blamed for creating a "poverty trap" and for fostering the black economy, especially in eastern Germany. Rising employment from the mid-1990s in the Baltic states, which took regulatory reform most seriously, is consistent with this interpretation.

Financial stability was a major concern of the transition. After a big financial shock, inflation rates fell quickly in the CEECs; high convergence with German rates was achieved by the turn of the century. For some of these economies, the synchronization of their fluctuations with the Eurozone countries also increased (Artis, Marcellino, and Proietti 2004). EU accession (eight CEECs joined in May 2004, and Bulgaria and Romania in 2007), fostering trade and foreign direct investment, contributed and also helped to enhance the quality of institutions (Andreff 2004). Improved institutional quality was much needed. Becoming a

Table 14.6 The Russian economy during transition, 1992–9

Indicator	Units	1992	1993	1994	1995	1996	1997	1998	1999
GDP growth	%	−14.5	−8.7	−12.7	−4.1	−3.4	0.8	−4.06	2.0
Industrial production	1991=100	82	71	55	54	52	53	50	54
Investment/GDP	%	23.9	20.4	21.8	21.3	21.2	19.4	17.6	15.3
Unemployment	%LF	4.8	5.3	7.1	8.3	9.2	10.9	12.4	12.6
Consumer price inflation	%	1526	875	311	198	48	15	28	87

Source: Davis and Foreman-Peck 2003.

EU member state was not an end of the transition to a fully fledged market economy.

In contrast in Russia, which dominated the FSU, the Gaidar government implemented a transition policy of privatization, liberalization, and free markets. They were impressed by the 1990 Polish "shock therapy" program, but the impact in Russia was very different. The policy shocks cut Russian gross industrial output by 40 percent in six years, as shown in Table 14.6. Most of this production decline was genuine rather than attributable to measurement error. Such a collapse of industrial output during peacetime in a major economy was unprecedented over the twentieth century. While the measurement of output must be subject to some controversy, there is no question that the most vital element of welfare, the health of the population, collapsed along with recorded production.

At the same time, inflation dropped from well over 1,000 percent in 1992 through to 1997, but unemployment rose in every year as well. Although aspects of economic performance had improved, they could not prevent the crash of August 1998. This was precipitated by falling oil prices and by the Asian economic crisis, but policy errors and internal weaknesses in the economic system – perhaps 70 percent of economic activity was conducted through barter – dragged down the Russian economy. The equity market bubble burst first, the stock market index dropping from a peak of 450 to 50 in August 1998. Unwise investments and speculative activities of most major Russian banks increased their vulnerability to shocks. So when in August the Kiriyenko government permitted the ruble exchange rate to crash and failed to service the government's debt (the GKOs), the banking system was paralyzed. Russian banks refused to honor forward exchange contracts with western banks and inflation jumped to over 80 percent (Davis and Foreman-Peck 2003).

The slump of 1998–9 showed that a rapid transition in Russia on the basis of the Washington consensus had failed. At the root of the problem was a weak and corrupt state, which had allowed mass privatization and expropriation of lucrative state assets with an ineffective legal system. Persistence of bureaucratic control, on the other hand, ensured the continuation of rationing. Soft budget constraints for government fueled inflation, the flight from money, and a barter economy. All this remained to be reformed if recovery was to be achieved.

A major contributor to the different paths in CEECs and the FSU was political stability. In 1991 the "Russian coup," the arrest of President Mikhail Gorbachev, and the breakdown of the "Emergency Committee" were not a good start to the transition process. The increasing power of "oligarchs," who benefited from privatization under Boris Yeltsin, created substantial political instability. Many companies paid no taxes at all and a tax collector's life was very dangerous. Insecurity was a breeding ground for high crime rates and widespread corruption, exacerbated by irregular payment of pensions, wages, and benefits, which weakened demand.

A lower exchange rate, and a rising oil price, respectively restored the competitiveness of Russian industry and replenished the state coffers from 1999. At the same time the authority of the central state was reasserted under Vladimir Putin. Yet in appointing Gref, a liberal reformer, Putin ensured that Russia remained committed to a market economy, and was duly rewarded by a long upswing of production and productivity during the eight years of his presidency.

Conclusion

The new millennium opened with much more of an international consensus about the potential and proper application of macroeconomic policy than was apparent at the end of the Second World War. Economists and policy makers had learned from history. Ambitions for state action were generally reduced, particularly for demand management with fiscal and monetary policy – or even with exchange rate regimes. "Stability" remained the watchword.

On the one hand, the supremacy of markets over state plans for delivering goods and services was established. On the other, periodic unemployment associated with business cycles, as well as structural unemployment, had not gone away in western Europe and had returned in the east. Shocks had not disappeared; the "sub-prime" financial crisis beginning in July 2007, linked to oil and other commodity price hikes, indicated that the recession of 2008–9 was likely to be especially severe and widespread. Financial innovation without appropriate regulation had created some very vulnerable structures, raising risk perceptions and interest rates.

The market fundamentalism of the Washington consensus had proved to be inadequate in Russia without the appropriate supporting institutions.

Fiscal policy had proved too rigid an instrument for general demand management. Monetary policy was more flexible and therefore more appropriate in normal times for smoothing the business cycle. In this respect the new policy orthodoxy resembled that under the late nineteenth-century gold standard, without the link between money and gold. In addition, confidence abounded that another Great Depression could be avoided by prompt action on the part of the monetary authorities to prevent collapses of large financial institutions.

Keynesian economic management was not responsible for the rapid growth of "the golden age." Nor were monetarism, independent central banks, and replacement of policy discretion by rules entirely to be credited with the stability of the Great Moderation of the 1990s. But much of the volatility of the 1970s and 1980s could be attributed to policy extravagances.

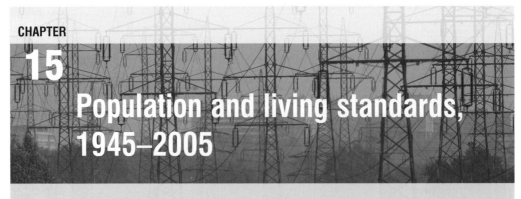

15 Population and living standards, 1945–2005

Dudley Baines, Neil Cummins, and Max-Stephan Schulze

Contents

Introduction

The sixty or more years since the end of the Second World War have seen an unprecedented increase in the average European's material standard of living. Europeans are now enjoying incomes that are, on average and in real terms, about three to five times as high as in 1950; those born now can expect to live about ten years longer than the generation born in the early 1950s, and access to secondary and tertiary education is far wider than it was sixty years ago.

The now widely-used Human Development Index (HDI) seeks to capture changes in the quality of life as a weighted composite measure of per capita income (GDP), longevity, and years of formal education cum literacy. A bounded, relative index of development, the HDI is useful as a convenient means to document *some* of the comparative quantitative dimensions of welfare change in Europe. Below we report HDI scores for nineteen European countries. Leaving aside, for the moment, changes in country rankings, regional variations and the behavior of the underlying series, the big message is clear: in HDI terms just as much as in terms of per capita GDP, Europeans are now much better off than they were in 1950, and variance in HDI across European countries is now only half the level it was then.

However, the HDI is certainly a less than perfect measure of broadly conceived living standards. It ignores the extent to which human rights, civil liberty, and political freedom are protected. It makes no allowance for how income and wealth are distributed among members of society or for the extent of unemployment. It incorporates longevity, but not the health status of the population. Most tellingly, perhaps, it does not inform us about what could be reasoned to be a fair expression of human well being – happiness. Richard Layard's recent work (2003) has shown that the happiness of the population in the western world has not increased, despite rapid growth in material living standards.

The changes in living standards across Europe since the end of the Second World War have been shaped by changes in incomes, demographics, and the institutional settings of "welfare delivery." The chapter starts by sketching out the Europe-wide rise of the public sector. The second section offers a comparative quantitative examination of changes in key welfare measures and the relationships between them. The final section explores the causes and economic consequences of demographic change.

The role of the state

Welfare expenditure

The origins of public involvement in the provision of welfare services reach back into the late eighteenth century. Initially this meant no more than "poor relief" and, to a very limited extent, also some provision for education. The introduction of basic social insurance schemes to cover industrial accidents, sickness, unemployment, and old age pensions for manual workers started in the late nineteenth century. By the interwar period most European countries had adopted some or all of such measures in some form. However, after 1945 public welfare provision changed in both its quantitative and qualitative dimensions (Johnson 1999, pp. 122–3; Lindert 2004, pp. 11–15). In most European societies, coverage across economic sectors, the labor force, and the population at large became almost universal. The objectives of public welfare provision were expanded beyond limited alleviation of hardship towards comprehensive social protection, encompassing unemployment and invalidity benefits, income support for those on low incomes or no income at all, the provision of pensions via public agencies, and free access to healthcare. The outcome was a long-term increase in the absolute level of social expenditure and its share in national product in practically every (western) European country (see Figures 15.1 and 15.2). This holds irrespective of the significant differences in the accounting conventions used by national and international agencies and the respective changes over time which so complicate the production of reasonably consistent comparative data.

A detailed treatment of the deeper causes of rapid advance of the modern "welfare state" after 1945 as reflected in the growth of "social" expenditure is beyond the scope of this chapter. It ought to be emphasized, however, that it was the rise in tax-based social spending that accounted for most of the growth in post-war total government spending and taxation, not, for example, national defense, public transport or public enterprises (Lindert 2004, p. 20). This shift in the composition of public expenditure reflects the shift in the role of the modern state beyond its traditional role of guarantor of the physical security of the citizens and their property rights towards that of provider of far more broadly conceived economic and social protection. In the literature this process has been linked to three "other great social transformations: the transition to fuller democracy, the demographic transition toward fewer births and longer life, and the onset of sustained economic growth" (Lindert 2004, p. 20). The effects of demographic change and economic growth will be dealt with in the following sections. Here it is important to note the fundamental change in the societal and political context within which welfare delivery occurred after

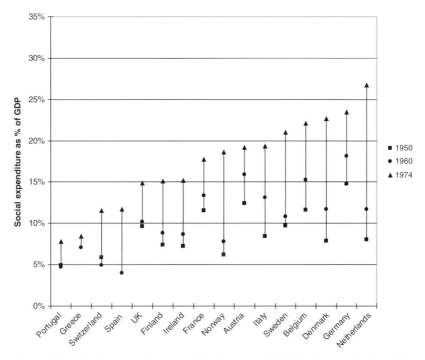

Figure 15.1 Social expenditure growth in Europe, 1950–74. *Source:* Castles 2001.

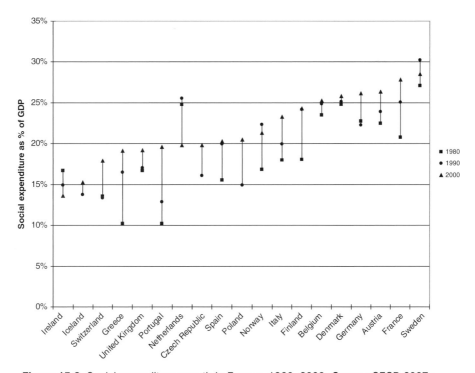

Figure 15.2 Social expenditure growth in Europe, 1980–2000. *Source:* OECD 2007a.

the Second World War as compared to earlier periods. Following Johnson (1999, p. 123), two broad explanations can be identified among the many on offer that speak directly to the hypothesis of political change and "democratization" as necessitating and engendering the expansion of public welfare spending in western Europe. Milward (1992) views both the rise in social spending and the inclusion of previously excluded social groups as a key component in post-war policies to re-establish the nation state and re-legitimize it in the eyes of the citizenry. Baldwin (1990) maintains that the creation of extensive post-war welfare systems was to a large extent an outcome of governments' attempts to fashion supportive electoral alliances among groups faced with similar exposure to social risks and similar needs of public support.

However, whilst there are strong common threads running through welfare policies across Europe, one should not lose sight of the fact that the specifics of welfare delivery within countries, its mechanisms, means, aims, objectives, and outcomes, were shaped by historical contingency as much as by deliberate political choices. The European Commission (1995, pp. 33–4) suggested that EU member countries in the early 1990s were clustered into four distinct groups. The first group includes the Scandinavian countries. Here social protection is a citizen's right and coverage is universal. The system is centrally administered and general taxation provides the main source of finance for social protection, augmented by additional occupational schemes for the gainfully employed. The second group comprises the United Kingdom and Ireland, where coverage of social protection is either universal or nearly so. Whilst administration is also centralized, benefits are more modest than in Scandinavia and means-testing of eligibility is more widespread. Healthcare is funded through general taxation, but social insurance contributions from both workers and employers play a major role in financing much of the remainder of social expenditure. The third group of countries is made up of Austria, the Benelux countries, Germany, and France. Here the emphasis is on a "Bismarckian"-type coverage whereby employment and family status, rather than citizenship, offer entitlements. The insurance principle underlies the determination of earnings-related benefits and often different regulations apply to different occupational groups. The system rests heavily on contributions from employers and employees, augmented by (tax-financed) social assistance schemes for those falling through the gaps in work-related social protection. The fourth group comprises the southern countries of Greece, Italy, Portugal, and Spain. Here we find a mixture of fragmented "Bismarckian" income maintenance schemes and separate social assistance for the uninsured. Benefit levels tend to be markedly lower than in the third group of countries and gaps in coverage are greater than elsewhere in the EU.

In central and eastern Europe and up until the fall of communism in 1989–90, social protection evolved under fundamentally different political, economic, and social conditions (Berend 1998; Eichengreen 2007). For most of the period under review, this makes east–west comparisons of social provision based on broad expenditure data practically impossible. Such comparisons are already problematic when looking only at the west European experience, since definitions of "social expenditure" change over time and vary between countries and the different international bodies charged with collecting comparative statistical material on the issue. Figures 15.1 and 15.2 should, therefore, be read with some caution: the definitions of social expenditure used in the Castles (2001) data set for 1950–74 are slightly different from those that apply to the OECD (2007a) data for 1980–2000. However, both data-sets broadly correspond with Lindert's (2004, pp. 6–7) delineation of social transfers as consisting of tax-based government spending, including basic material assistance to the poor, unemployment compensation, public (non-contributory) pensions, public health expenditure, and housing subsidies. What is of interest here is, first, the significant rise in social expenditure across virtually all western European societies up to the early 1980s, notwithstanding differences between countries in the relative levels of resources devoted to social protection (Figure 15.1). Starting from a range between about 7 to 15 percent of GDP, social expenditure rose to between 20 and 42 percent in 1980. To some extent, this is the outcome of post-war economic growth. As real per capita incomes grew rapidly (see Figure 15.4) and basic necessities became readily accessible to consumers, demand for goods with an income elasticity over one increased. Social protection, e.g., better health care or provision for old age, falls into this category: during the golden age all west European countries had social expenditure elasticities greater than unity, which means that for every one percent rise in GDP, social expenditure increased by more than one percent.

In the 1980s social expenditure growth slowed down, but so did GDP growth. With some variation between countries, social expenditure elasticities remained slightly above or at least near unity up until the end of the century. But there were no more such pronounced increases in social expenditure as a share of GDP as in earlier decades (Figure 15.2). The reasons for this are manifold, and the motives behind governments' attempts to limit the growth in social expenditure ranged from growing general concerns about the state of public finances to perceived adverse effects of welfare provision on incentives to find paid work.

For individual European economies there is strong evidence for a positive association between income levels and social expenditure. This impression is broadly confirmed in a cross-section of these economies at any one point in time (Johnson 1999, pp. 133–4). However, one ought not to read this as unequivocal support for the notion of social expenditure growth being a mere concomitant of economic growth. There is enough variation in the European sample to suggest that factors other than growth played a role as well: similar levels in GDP per capita were not necessarily associated with similar social expenditure shares. This is a clear pointer to historical contingency. As set out above, post-war national welfare regimes developed against a background of different historical conditions and different ideological traditions (cf. Esping-Anderson 1990). Further, the timing and extent of political and social pressures for substantial changes in welfare expenditure were only partially aligned across different European countries.

Outcomes

What were the outcomes of growth in European social expenditure over the longer term? Did the "welfare state" make for improvements in the standard of living of the European population? Two widely used criteria to assess public welfare performance are the extent of poverty prevalent in a society and the degree of income inequality. The proportion of people living in poverty is a basic, but reasonably useful indicator of the effectiveness of a welfare system, for it captures the success or otherwise of attempts to protect people from the potentially detrimental consequences of being unable to work, of being made redundant, or of having large families. As alternative indicators, measures of income inequality can point to broader welfare issues. "Poor" households in rich European countries may not be poor in an absolute sense: they may well be able to afford the basic necessities of life such as food, clothing, and housing and they may not be poor compared with households in developing economies. But they may have an income so much below the average or median in their society that they cannot fully participate in social life. Hence a very unequal distribution of income within a country may lead to the social exclusion of a significant number of its members. Wilkinson (1992) has argued that beyond certain threshold levels of income it is *relative* income, rather than absolute poverty, that matters for health outcomes. Further, while there appears to be no strong evidence suggesting an association between differences in per capita incomes and differences in life expectancy *across* developed economies, *within* these economies life expectancies and health are related to income distribution and social stratification (Wilkinson 2005; Wilkinson and Picket 2006).

However, consistent measurement over time in this area is as much of a problem as finding coherent and compatible indicators of social expenditure across countries. Modern, developed welfare states have a general tendency to equalize post-tax and post-transfer incomes and one may very well argue that this is an (if not *the* most) important part of the exercise in the first place. Yet transfers can go from poor to rich taxpayers just as much as the other way round:

the classic example being university education which, in most European countries, is still enjoyed disproportionately by students from families with above-
average income, but which is substantially financed out of general tax revenue.

Taking the European Community definition of people living in poverty if they
have an income of less than half the average income in their country, the
proportion of EC citizens living in poverty increased from 12.6 percent in 1975
to 14.7 percent in 1993 (Johnson 1999, p. 128). This rise coincided with the
slowdown in social expenditure growth documented in Figure 15.2 and a general
increase in income inequality in the 1980s. However, the comparative country
evidence suggests that there is a relationship between high levels of social expenditure and low levels of poverty. That social expenditure mattered in terms of
alleviating poverty is further borne out by different data which compare the
percentage of families in poverty (defined as living on half the median net income)
before and after social transfers. According to this evidence for the mid-1980s,
between 32 and 38 percent of families in seven western European countries had
incomes below half the median prior to transfers. Receipt of transfer payments
reduced that proportion to between 5 and 10 percent (Bradshaw 1993, p. 57).

Internationally comparative data on income inequality that reach back
in time are hard to come by. Here, the figures from World Development
Indicators (2007) have been used. They provide good geographical coverage
for the late 1990s and the early twenty-first century and have been augmented
by additional data for *c.* 1985 from Mitchell and Bradshaw 1992. Both studies
rest on the Luxembourg Income Study database, allowing for at least some
degree of broad compatibility over time and between countries. Five main
messages emerge from Table 15.1. First, prior to the collapse of communism,
the countries of central and eastern Europe displayed persistently lower levels
of income concentration than their western capitalist neighbors. Secondly, the
period since the fall of the Berlin Wall saw a sharp increase in income inequality
throughout the transition economies of the former eastern bloc countries.
Thirdly, in the west, too, income inequality increased significantly over the
last decade or two of the twentieth century: the evidence seems to suggest that
the post-golden age flattening out in the growth of social expenditure as a
proportion of national income (Figure 15.2) was associated with a marked rise
in income inequality as measured by Gini indices. In other words, the volume
and direction of transfer payments, taken together, now add up to comparatively less redistribution towards the relatively poor than in the 1980s. Fourthly,
the Scandinavian countries score highly in terms of their capacity to maintain a
relatively equal distribution of income through their tax regimes and/or social
security measures. In the cases of Denmark, Finland, and Norway this was
achieved against a background of relatively modest social expenditure to GDP
ratios of around 22 to 26 percent in 2000, pointing to either fairly flat pre-tax

Table 15.1 Income inequality: Gini indices (post-tax and post-transfer current incomes)

	c. 1985	c. 2000
Albania	..	29.1
Austria	..	29.1
Belgium	..	32.9
Bosnia and Herzegovina	..	26.2
Bulgaria	23.4	34.3
Croatia	22.8	29.0
Czech Republic	**19.4**	25.4
Denmark	..	**24.7**
Estonia	23.0	35.8
Finland	..	26.9
France	30.0	32.7
Germany	25.0	28.3
Greece	..	34.3
Hungary	20.9	26.8
Ireland	..	34.3
Italy	**31.0**	36.0
Latvia	22.5	37.7
Lithuania	22.5	31.8
Macedonia, FYR	..	39.0
Netherlands	26.0	30.9
Norway	..	25.8
Poland	25.2	34.5
Portugal	..	38.4
Romania	..	30.2
Russian Federation	23.8	**45.6**
Slovak Republic	19.5	25.8
Slovenia	23.6	28.4
Spain	..	34.7
Sweden	21.0	25.0
Switzerland	..	33.7
United Kingdom	28.0	36.0

Notes: Data refer to observations for or nearest to 1985 and 2000, respectively. Minima and maxima printed in bold. A low Gini index indicates a more equal income distribution, while a high Gini index reflects a more unequal distribution. An index value of 0 corresponds to perfect equality (everyone having exactly the same income) and 100 corresponds to perfect inequality (where one person has all the income and everyone else has zero income).
Sources: World Development Indicators (April 2007); Mitchell and Bradshaw 1992.

income distributions to start with or a strongly redistributive component in the tax system. In the case of Sweden, we find both a strong tax impact and a strong benefit impact on the distribution of net incomes (Bradshaw 1993, pp. 57–9). Finally, within the group of western European economies the gap between those with relatively modest degrees of income inequality (e.g., Scandinavia) and those with relatively high income concentration (e.g., Portugal, United Kingdom) widened over the last twenty or so years. Again, this is a pointer towards the significance of national welfare policies which, clearly, made for far less "convergence" in *within*-country distributional patterns than *between*-country income distribution.

Decomposing changes in the standard of living

Human Development Indices as a means to evaluate changes in living standards

The Human Development Index (HDI) is a useful tool for summarizing changes in historical living standards. It attempts to capture the *quality* of life by summarizing the core components of material wealth, longevity, and knowledge in a single index and measuring each of these components in terms of the distance traveled between an assumed minimum and maximum.[1] However, the HDI has its drawbacks as a welfare measure. For example, it fails to capture important issues such as economic inequality or respect for human rights. Every year (since 1990), the UN has published HDI estimates for almost all countries in the world.

The HDI represents a *relative* index of development. A country with a GDP per capita of $ 40,000 international dollars (at 2000 purchasing power parity), an average life expectancy at birth of eighty-five, enrollment rates for all levels of education of 100 percent and a 100 percent adult literacy rate, would score 1. Table 15.2 reports HDI scores for nineteen European countries, organized by rank for each year.

The average HDI score for Europe rose by almost 30 percent between 1950 and 2003 (0.699 → 0.905). There has also being a marked decline in the level of dispersion of HDI scores across the continent, as measured by the coefficient of variation (0.119→0.053) as well as some significant change in the country rank order. What does this mean? The HDI is primarily concerned with providing a comparative measure of development. For instance, we could think of the UK in 1950 (0.774) as having a level of development close to that of China in 2004 (0.768), or of Portugal in 1950 (0.530) being

---

[1] We use the following formula (as in Crafts 2002a, 395–396):

$$HDI = (E + I + L)/3$$

Where

$$E = 0.67LIT + .33Enrol$$
$$I = (\log y - \log 100)/(\log 40,000 - \log 100)$$
$$L = (e_0 - 25)/(85 - 25)$$

E = education, I = income, L = longevity, *Lit* = the adult literacy rate, *Enrol* = percentage of relative age group enrolled in primary education, y = GDP per capita, and e_0 = life expectancy at age 0.

Table 15.2 Historical HDI scores for Europe

1950		1975		2003	
Denmark	0.786	Switzerland	0.873	Sweden	0.957
Netherlands	0.784	Sweden	0.864	Norway	0.950
Switzerland	0.782	Netherlands	0.862	Switzerland	0.935
Sweden	0.780	Denmark	0.862	Finland	0.934
Norway	0.776	Norway	0.859	Ireland	0.929
UK	0.774	France	0.845	Italy	0.929
Germany	0.744	UK	0.841	Austria	0.928
France	0.729	Belgium	0.840	Netherlands	0.927
Belgium	0.727	Finland	0.839	France	0.926
Austria	0.720	Germany	0.837	Belgium	0.926
Finland	0.707	Austria	0.836	UK	0.924
Ireland	0.698	Italy	0.826	Denmark	0.924
Hungary	0.682	Spain	0.810	Spain	0.921
Italy	0.668	Ireland	0.807	Germany	0.919
Poland	0.657	Poland	0.790	Portugal	0.867
Spain	0.627	Hungary	0.788	Poland	0.856
Bulgaria	0.607	Bulgaria	0.774	Hungary	0.854
Portugal	0.530	Romania	0.763	Bulgaria	0.803
Romania	0.510	Portugal	0.727	Romania	0.784
Average	**0.699**		**0.823**		**0.905**
Coefficient of Variation	0.119		0.048		0.053

Sources: Own calculations and Crafts 2002a.

comparable to Bangladesh in 2004 (also 0.530). Of course, this also highlights the limitations of the HDI, as there are many reasons why most people would be reluctant to draw an equivalence between these countries at these points in time (Human Development Report 2006). Europe in 1950 can be categorized as a region of "medium human development," if we take an HDI of 0.8 as the threshold (in line with Human Development Report 2006). No countries (at least in this nineteen-country sample) could be categorized as countries of "low human development" (HDI below 0.5). By 1975, the vast majority of European countries could be described as having "high human development" (above 0.8). Only the countries of eastern Europe and Portugal were below 0.8. By 2003, most of Europe had achieved an HDI of greater than 0.9, except again for the countries of eastern Europe and Portugal. Today, in evaluating changes in living standards the HDI loses a lot of its power. This is because of the heavy discounting of growth in material living standards (as measured by GDP per capita), non-linear relationships between longevity and incomes, and also "bounds" on the values for the knowledge component (for instance, most of Europe is now achieving close to full enrollment and 100 percent adult literacy rates). Hence there is a need to investigate alternative and more comprehensive measures of living standards.

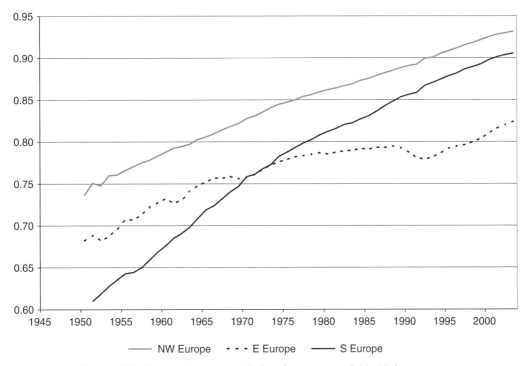

Figure 15.3 Human Development Index. *Sources:* see Table 15.2.

Within Europe, there has also been notable variation in rank of HDI score over the past fifty years: for instance, the relative improvement of Ireland (twelfth in 1950, fifth in 2003), and the relative decline of Denmark (first in 1950, twelfth in 2003). However, rank is not nearly as important in 2003 as it was in 1950, because the coefficient of variation is much lower in 2003, and differences between, say, the first and twelfth positions are much smaller in the later time period. The decline in variation in HDI in Europe is a rough indication of convergence in living standards over the period.

Regional variations in HDI

By aggregating annual HDI scores for individual European countries into regions, it is possible to identify three distinct trajectories in the growth of living standards in post-war Europe.[2] In 1950, north-west Europe was clearly more developed than both the southern and eastern regions of the Continent (Figure 15.3). However, the southern European experience since is very much

[2] Regional aggregation is as follows: north-west Europe: Austria, Belgium, Denmark, Finland, France, Germany, Ireland, Netherlands, Norway, Sweden, Switzerland, United Kingdom; eastern Europe: Bulgaria, Hungary, Poland, Romania; southern Europe: Italy, Portugal, Spain.

characterized by convergence. The HDI there grew far more rapidly than in north-west Europe, and the differential between the two regions declined from about 0.16 to 0.03 points.

The trend in eastern Europe's HDI is very different from the rest of Europe. From 1950 to about 1965, the HDI increased at a rapid rate, slightly above that of north-west Europe. After 1965, however, HDI growth in eastern Europe diminished strikingly, and in the late 1980s a period of decline followed, before the HDI picked up again in the 1990s (1991–2003). What drove these patterns? How can we explain southern Europe's convergence, and eastern Europe's relative failure in improving living standards to levels experienced elsewhere on the continent? The first step in answering these questions is to break up the HDI scores, and examine the trend in the three components of income, longevity, and knowledge.

Regional analysis of HDI components

Income

In terms of material standards of living, southern Europe's convergence with north-west Europe is magnified by the construction of the *income* component

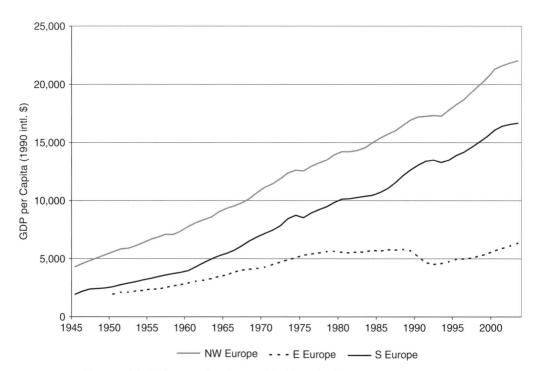

Figure 15.4 GDP per capita. *Source:* Maddison 2007.

in the HDI series, where growth is discounted at higher income levels. Analyzing the raw data (Maddison 2007), the overall picture is of persistent income growth and also a consistent movement towards similar levels in GDP per capita. Southern Europe's GDP per capita amounted to about 46 percent of north-west Europe's in 1950. By 2003, the differential had fallen to a level where southern Europe's GDP per capita was equivalent to 75 percent of north-west Europe's.

Eastern Europe, however, experienced a divergent trend in GDP per capita over the post-war period. Growth for the period as a whole was 2.6 percent per annum for north-west Europe, 3.6 percent for southern Europe, and 2.3 percent for eastern Europe. However, as with the HDI series, we can distinguish three different phases in the evolution of eastern European income. From 1950 to 1979, GDP per capita grew at 3.8 percent on annual average, but after 1979 income growth stagnated and GDP per capita even declined in the early 1990s. Average growth for 1979–93 was –1.2 percent per annum, recovering to 3.2 percent in 1994–2000. However, 1979 levels of GDP per capita were not achieved again until 2000.

The differential timing and pace of economic growth across the nineteen European countries generated three distinct phases of income convergence and divergence (Figure 15.5). First, the period between 1950 and 1978 is

Figure 15.5 Coefficient of variation, GDP per capita. *Sources:* see Figure 15.4.

characterized by a sharply diminishing coefficient of variation in GDP per capita. From 1978 to 1993, intercountry inequality increased, returning to 1965 levels by 1993. After 1993 variation declined again, albeit at a slower rate than before. This pattern was driven by eastern Europe's far more dramatic growth slowdown relative to the rest of Europe after the golden age.

The causes of western Europe's rapid economic advance during the golden age, and eastern Europe's initial success in keeping up with or even exceeding western rates of growth in national product and subsequent failure to do so in the post-golden age period, are discussed elsewhere in this volume (see Chapters 12 and 13). Here it suffices to say that the era of communism and central planning produced poor results at least from the early 1970s, and that the stagnation and relative decline in eastern living standards and incomes contributed to the collapse of these regimes (Dobrinsky, Hesse, and Traeger 2006, p. 1). Initially, strong growth during the golden age was primarily a result of the reallocation of labor, from the primary sector (agriculture etc.) to secondary industries (manufacturing). However, resource allocation was based on the motivations and political priorities of the central planners, not necessarily on any economic rationale. Eventually, such sub-optimal economic policy, together with insulation from international markets, would translate into slower growth (Dobrinsky, Hesse, and Traeger 2006, p. 11). It was only after the collapse of central planning and the subsequent "transitional recession" that income growth resumed during the early to mid-1990s.

The absolute and relative advance in material well being of the average western European is brought into even sharper relief when the decline in hours worked is accounted for. The average person in 1992 worked significantly fewer hours per year than the average person in 1950 (Figure 15.6), aided by strong growth in productivity. The resultant impact on welfare, ignored by measures such as GDP per capita and the HDI, is, of course, hugely important as people gained leisure time to pursue non-work-related but welfare-enhancing activities and had the material means to do so.

Life expectancy

Growth in life expectancy at birth for both sexes (e_0) was a great achievement of the post-war era and primarily a result of the spread of antibiotics and immunization (Mesle 2004, p. 46). North-west Europe added over a decade to average life expectancy between 1950 and 2002. Even more remarkable is the catch-up of southern Europe, adding a population average

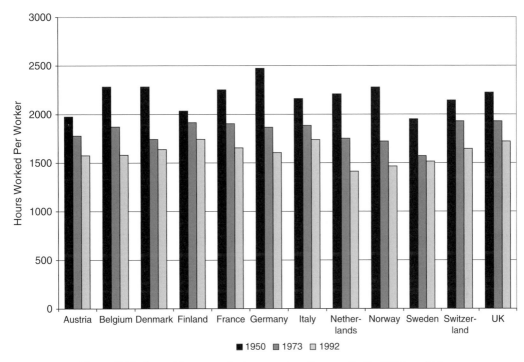

Figure 15.6 Annual hours worked per worker. *Source:* Crafts 1997, p. 316.

of sixteen years per person to life expectancy. Recently the trend in life expectancy has converged between north-west and southern Europe. However, the data on eastern European life expectancy are shocking, especially when viewed relative to the trends elsewhere in Europe. Southern and eastern Europe had a similar level of life expectancy in 1950, and both experienced a strong rate of growth until their paths diverged in the late 1960s. From 1973 to 1991, the growth rate of eastern European life expectancy was effectively zero. Only after 1997 did it display consistent growth again. In 2003, life expectancy was over seventy-eight years for both north-west and southern Europe, and just over seventy-two years for eastern Europe (Figure 15.7).

However, a more disaggregate country- and age group-specific perspective reveals some interesting features. Take the example of Hungary, where life expectancy, for both sexes, was sixty-two years in 1950. By 2003, this had increased to seventy-two years. However, male *age-specific* life expectancies actually *fell* for every year of age over ten, for the years 1950–1996. (In contrast, female age-specific life expectancy rose between 1950 and 1996.) For every age point after age ten, male life expectancy at that age was lower in 1996 than it was in 1950 and 1975. This contrasts with the experience in

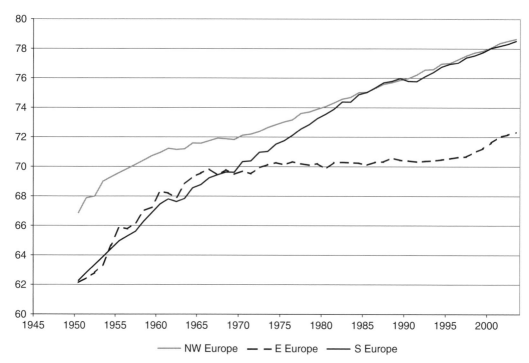

Figure 15.7 Life expectancy at birth. *Sources:* own calculations based on Rothenbacher 2005 and World Development Indicators (2003).

north-west and south-west Europe, where there is no evidence of decreases in age-specific life expectancy. We return to this point below.

Education

The knowledge component of the HDI comprises the combined general enrollment rate (⅓ weight), and the adult literacy rate (⅔ weight). Interestingly, eastern Europe scores relatively well in this regard, with only a slight divergence from the trend in north-west Europe (Figure 15.8). Southern Europe experienced strong catch-up and convergence, in the main driven by Portugal's very low initial levels in education and subsequent high growth. However, enrollment and literacy are only the very basic measures of human capital. The implied convergence as indicated by the HDI components series may be misleading. For example, if we examine a measure of knowledge at the higher end of the scale, such as scientific journal articles per capita, north-west Europe has currently about seven times eastern Europe's level.

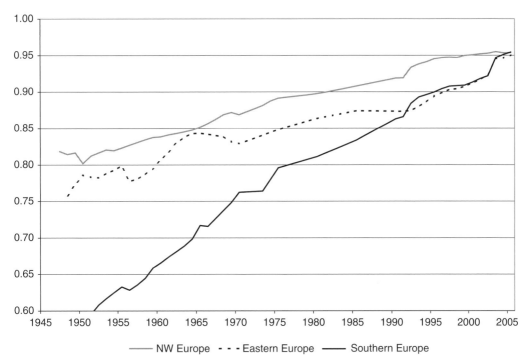

Figure 15.8 Education index. *Sources:* own calculations based on Flora 1986; Mitchell 2003; World Development Indicators (2007).

Causes and consequences of demographic change

Causes of the decline in mortality

In general, mortality decline in Europe has been substantial since the Second World War. Continuing pre-war trends, life expectancy in north-west and southern Europe at birth increased by some nine to eighteen years, for both males and females (Table 15.3). Southern European countries experienced strong convergence with the north-west, while improvements in eastern Europe were more modest. Life expectancy in Spain and Portugal, for example, was relatively low in 1950, but rose relatively fast. The fall was caused by the use of antibiotics, which were unknown before the war, better diet – a product of economic growth – and a large fall in the incidence of cardiovascular disease.

The components of the mortality fall are as follows. The widespread intro-duction of antibiotics further reduced adult mortality. It was already relatively low, because of the fall in deaths from infectious disease – along with war, the major cause of adult death. The fall in infant mortality was much more significant. Table 15.4 shows that in 1950 the variance in infant mortality

Table 15.3 Expectation of life at birth in selected European countries (years)

	1950	2005
W. EUROPE		
Belgium	64.68	79.48
France	66.57	80.21
Germany	66.51	78.93
Sweden	71.97	80.55
Switzerland	68.69	81.24
UK	68.80	78.95
S. EUROPE		
Greece	65.08	78.99
Italy	65.55	80.33
Portugal	59.12	78.07
Spain	62.15	80.57
E. EUROPE		
Bulgaria	n/a	72.56
Czech Republic	64.63	75.91
Hungary	62.13	72.85
Poland	61.57	75.00

Note: 1950 values are varying year averages centered around 1950.
Source: own calculations based on Rothenbacher 2005 and World Development Indicators (2007).

Table 15.4 Infant deaths in the first year, selected European countries (deaths per 1,000 live births)

	1950	2005
W. EUROPE		
Belgium	53.4	4
France	43.5	3
Germany*	55.7	4
Sweden	21.0	3
Switzerland	31.2	4
UK	31.2	5
S. EUROPE		
Greece	35.4	4
Italy	63.8	4
Portugal	94.1	4
Spain	64.2	4
E. EUROPE		
Bulgaria	45.0 (1960)	12
Czechoslovakia**	64.1	3
Hungary	85.7	7
Poland	108.0	6

*excludes GDR in 1950.
**excludes Slovakia in 2005.
Source: World Development Indicators (2007).

Table 15.5 Contribution of changes in age-specific mortality to the gains and losses in life expectancy between 1965 and 1995 (years)

Age group	Mediterranean Europe	N. Europe	E. Europe	Former USSR	All Europe
Males					
0–1	1.93	1.23	2.13	0.54	1.30
30–59	1.23	1.29	−1.41	−4.52	−1.25
All ages	6.69	5.59	1.31	−6.26	0.74
Females					
0–1	1.68	1.02	1.95	0.48	1.21
30–59	1.23	0.98	0.33	−1.21	0.21
All ages	7.73	5.56	4.07	−1.98	3.37

Source: Mesle and Vallin 2002, p. 171.

was extremely large. It was 21 per 1,000 live births in Sweden and 108 in Poland. By 2005, it had fallen to 3/000 and 6/000, respectively. This affected both eastern and western Europe. There were two main reasons. The effect of the fall in fertility meant that, on average, the mother's age at birth was lower and the baby was lower in the birth order, both of which are associated with lower infant mortality. Secondly, the fall in infant (and child) mortality was related to policy intervention, for example, government-owned clinics in both eastern and western Europe. This largely nullified the effect of differences in the level of urbanization (which was related to GDP growth) – so that infant mortality was not related to GDP growth. Finally, in recent years, there has been a rise in the life expectancy of older people. This has implications for age structure. (See below.)

However, governments in eastern Europe failed to implement the appropriate health policies to tackle cardiovascular disease mortality. This is the key source of the divergence in life expectancy between east and west (Mesle 2004, p. 66). In general, mortality in most eastern European countries failed to fall between the mid-1960s and the mid-1990s at a time when mortality was falling continuously in western and southern Europe. Table 15.5 shows this. For example, between 1965 and 1995, male life expectancy (30–59) gained nearly 1.2 to 1.3 years in western and southern Europe, but *fell* by 1.41 years in eastern Europe. In the former USSR it *fell* by 4.52 years.

The Russian life expectancy figure is a special case, with deaths from excessive drinking falling substantially when Gorbachev increased the price of vodka in 1985–6. During this brief period, life expectancy grew by three years for males and one year for females. It also briefly rose (by 5.7 and 3 years) during the economic crisis of 1991–4 (Mesle and Vallin 2002, p. 175). In other words, the further reduction in cardiovascular disease depended partly on individuals changing their behavior. Such behavioral changes occurred in other parts of Europe, but not in eastern Europe – as we may see in the former USSR, for example. The lack of government interest is important here. (Until recently, the population continued to smoke heavily, for example, and accidents and homicide also remained high.)

The unfavorable development in life expectancy in eastern Europe was also related to other factors. Apart from the former Czechoslovakia, the former USSR, and East Germany (the GDR), most of the east European economies were, after the Second World War, still characterized by large agricultural sectors in both absolute and relative terms. The eastern European economic model prioritized accelerated industrialization, i.e., the enforced shift of labor and material resources into industry and mining (cf. Eichengreen 2007, ch. 5). Thus at a time when the more developed western European economies began to "deindustrialize" (as reflected in changing employment shares) – i.e., from the mid-1950s to the mid-1970s – industrialization continued in the former USSR, Czechoslovakia, and the GDR, and began in earnest in the other countries. As a consequence, the share of industry in total employment rose from 37 percent in Czechoslovakia and 23 percent in both Hungary and Poland to 48, 45 and 34 percent, respectively, in 1971. These employment shares are comparable to those in early twentieth century Britain. A large proportion of the labor force became engaged in physically demanding work in an industrial environment that was far less severely governed by safety, health, and environmental protection laws and their enforcement than in western Europe. In reverse, the later upturn in east European life expectancy coincided with the process of deindustrialization that started with the post-1989 transition process.

Changes in fertility

Fertility was falling in most European countries before the Second World War. In general, fertility fell during the war, but there were important exceptions: it rose in Britain, France, and Scandinavia. Following the war, there was a brief post-war rise in fertility. This was essentially the births that had been postponed during the war. There was virtually no European equivalent of the "baby boom," and hence of the "baby boomer" generation, which was a phenomenon confined to the USA, Canada, Australia, and New Zealand. (The "baby boom" was a change in behavior, in effect an increase in the desired family size by one whole child.) European fertility then continued slowly to rise until the mid-1960s. But from then onward there was a major change. Fertility began to decline in every country and, eventually, to very low levels. The overall effect is

Table 15.6 Total fertility rate, selected European countries (children born per woman)

	1950	2005
W. EUROPE		
Belgium	2.35	1.72
France	2.93	1.92
Germany	2.10*	1.36
Sweden	2.28	1.77
Switzerland	2.40	1.42
UK	2.69 (1960)	1.80
S. EUROPE		
Greece	2.46 (1951)	1.28
Italy	2.49	1.32
Portugal	3.08	1.40
Spain	2.48	1.33
E. EUROPE		
Bulgaria	2.34 (1960)	1.31
Czechoslovakia	2.08	1.28**
Hungary	2.02 (1960)	1.32
Poland	2.98	1.24

*excludes GDR in 1950.
**excludes Slovakia in 2005.
The number of births is completed family size (cohort measure) except for later years, when future births to women who have not completed childbearing is estimated – i.e., a period measure. The latter is not expected to be significantly different from the former.
Source: World Development Indicators (2007).

shown in Table 15.6. There has been some recent recovery but, at the time of writing, no European country has replacement level fertility. (Clearly, a mean total fertility rate of just over two is necessary for the population to grow naturally in the long run.) In the 1990s, for example, only 15 percent of European population growth was natural; 85 percent was immigration.

Measurement

The expectation of life at birth shows the period a newly born person will live assuming s/he is subject to the relevant mortality at each age. This is a so-called period measure. Period measures are partly an abstraction. They do not account for changes in future mortality, which are known only for people who have already died. Similarly the total fertility rate (Table 15.6) shows the number of children that on average a woman will have assuming current fertility (normalized by age) continues. We do not know, for example, if younger women whose fertility is currently low will achieve a *completed family size* which is higher than that predicted, although most demographers do not expect this to happen. In the 1930s, for example, current fertility rates predicted large falls in population in most European countries. Fertility did not actually fall until the 1960s, which of course was a different female cohort.

Reasons for the fertility fall

Here, we are concerned with the trend fall in the total fertility rate (TFR). Fertility is subject to short-term fluctuations, but these are usually caused by economic uncertainty – i.e., the trade cycle – and the long-run effect on the economy is limited. Table 15.6 shows that the fertility decline was a Europe-wide phenomenon. Hence, we may discount those causes which are relevant to only one country. For example, it is tempting to relate falling fertility to the cost of children's education, religion, or the extent of child employment. But the variance in these factors across Europe was much greater than the variance in fertility. Similarly, the introduction of particular birth control methods, particularly the contraceptive pill, is a tempting hypothesis. But fertility fell in countries where the pill was rarely used. (Abortion was common, and legal, in most of eastern Europe from the 1950s to the 1980s.) This implies that the method used to prevent pregnancy was less important than changes in the desire to have children. (The low fertility of the 1930s was achieved in some countries using what today would be considered very inefficient methods.) In other words, there is an important distinction between sex and fertility. More efficient contraception affected coital frequency to a greater extent than fertility.

Consider the general and long-run changes in post-war European fertility. We might start with the rather nebulous concept of "modernization." But what we do know is that an increasing proportion of the population lived in cities; mass communication made people more aware of conditions in other parts of their own country or further afield; female education improved and the position of women in the labor market also improved. So far, so good. But we are left with a paradox. If, for example, children were substitutes for consumer durables, why did the increase in household income lead to rising fertility to the mid-1960s and then to falling fertility?

The most likely general explanation concerns the relation between income, female employment, and status. Assume that in an ideal world most women desire both to have children and a fulfilling occupation. In the 1950s, when most women were married, household income was rising, making it possible for a family to live (at then-current expectations) on a single income. On the other hand, employment opportunities for women were limited and poorly paid. Hence, for a woman, the opportunity cost of children in terms of both

Table 15.7 Participation rate, 15–64-year-old females, selected European countries, 2006 (full and part time; percent)

	Full time	Part time
W. EUROPE		
Belgium	38.5	20.4
France	49.3	14.6
Germany	41.7	26.8
Sweden	69.3	14.7
Switzerland	40.0	34.1
UK	43.0	27.3
S. EUROPE		
Greece	47.9	7.1
Italy	35.9	14.9
Portugal	59.4	9.0
Spain	48.1	13.0
E. EUROPE		
Czech Republic	58.9	3.4
Hungary	53.6	2.3
Poland	47.6	9.2

Source: OECD (2007b).

income and status was low. But by the later twentieth century, the labor market was different. Female occupations, particularly in services, were often well paid and had high status. But it was difficult for a woman to acquire sufficient human capital to establish a career if she had two or three children. This partly depends on the cost of childcare. Estimates of the impact of raising two children born before the mother reaches age thirty on a woman's lifetime income are very varied – ranging, for example, from –25 percent (France) to –50 percent (Britain). We show female participation rates in some European countries in Table 15.7.

One criticism of this approach is that it applies less to southern than to northern Europe. Fertility fell to exceptionally low levels in Spain and Italy, for example, but female labor force participation was somewhat lower (Table 15.7). It might be more instructive to stress the *rise* in the participation rate in southern Europe, which was exceptional. In other words, it is possible that we are observing lagged behavioral changes rather than cultural differences. To reiterate, we are not arguing that women forwent childbearing completely in order to enter the labor force. Most wanted both children and a job that was more fulfilling than domesticity.

Overall, female participation rates were high (60–80 percent of the 15–64-year-olds in western Europe). It follows that most of the women in the labor force must have had (one or two) children. The proportion of women who were working part time was much more varied – reflecting the cost and quality of childcare in the different countries.

There was also a major change in the timing of births in the years after the Second World War. The childbearing period became more compressed. Women completed childbearing at an early age or, alternatively, postponed having children until they had established a career. (The former was the more common.) Currently, about 20 percent of married women in Europe are childless (although that is not always from choice) and 80 percent have only one or two children. Hence, it is the decline of the three- and four-child family that has driven the fall in fertility. There have also been major changes in the composition of the household since the 1950s. In the 1950s, the nuclear house-hold (husband, wife, and children) was almost universal throughout Europe and most children were born within marriage. This was because marriage was the insurance against unwanted pregnancy. More recent years have seen the growth of single-person households, composed of both older and younger women. Children have been able to leave home at a younger age which is related to the growth of "cohabitation" (technically, heterosexual non-married partnerships). The fertility of unmarried couples is lower than that of married couples, however. Moreover, illegitimate births as a consequence of promiscu-ity are rare in most European countries other than Britain.

The consequences of demographic changes; changes in age structure

In recent years there have been two main reasons why populations are ageing: first, the effect of falling birth cohorts; secondly, the change in relative mortality rates, in particular falling mortality of older persons. The fastest ageing has been in southern Europe. This is because fertility in the past was relatively high, so that there are many older survivors of large earlier birth cohorts. Life expect-ancy at sixty five in the EU25 was 15.9 for males and 19.5 for females in 2004 (Carone and Costello 2005). In theory this has increased the number of "dependants" relative to "producers." In Europe, in 2000, there were about four people aged 15–64 to those aged over sixty-five. By 2025, this will fall to about three. (Children are an addition, of course.) But we may not be defining "dependency" correctly. For example, the demand for manual employment, which could not be undertaken by older people, is falling relative to the demand for service employment, some of which could. In other words, as the population ages, participation increases. In the UK, for example, changes in the male participation rate, which had been falling since 1931, had twice the effect of changes in age distribution (Johnson 1997, p. 1898). Moreover, many older workers have high levels of human capital. The latter point is critical. In the main, the increase in the participation rate of older workers did not cause the youth unemployment problem, which has become commonplace in virtually every European country, since that is caused by the low human capital embodied in many young people. Moreover, population ageing did not lead to a reduction in expenditure on education, as it might have, because educational expectations rose. There was a large increase in expenditure on tertiary education, for example.

Finally, dire predictions that the ageing of European populations would lead to a slowdown of economic growth have not occurred. This, it was argued (e.g., by Keynes), would lead to a fall in the savings ratio, and hence in investment. But, as we know, the most important component of economic growth since the Second World War has been total factor productivity. In other words, the investment rate has been largely determined by the growth rate, not *vice versa*.

Pensions do, however, provide a challenge

Under so-called "pay-as-you-go" pension schemes, which have been commonplace in post-war Europe, individuals, while working, pay for the pensions of retired people in return for an expectation that someone else will pay for their pension in the future. There is no fund, as in a private pension scheme. Such schemes became more generous in the 1950s and 1960s. It is easy to see why. Politicians were able to benefit from promises to improve pensions which, at the time, were easy to finance because there were relatively few existing pensioners and they had not built up large contributions. In most European countries pension scheme receipts increased faster than expenditure in the 1950s and 1960s, allowing pensions to increase without increases in taxation. In France and Italy, for example, many (but by no means all) workers could expect a retirement income at sixty of two thirds their average salary index-linked.

Table 15.8 Ratio of persons aged 15–64 to those aged sixty-five or more

	1960	1980	2000	2025
France	5.32	4.57	4.24	3.12
Germany	6.25	4.27	4.24	3.01
Italy	7.04	4.98	4.02	2.9
Spain	7.81	5.88	4.39	3.38
Sweden	5.52	3.94	3.72	2.6
UK	5.56	4.26	4.24	3.12

Source: OECD 2007b.

The equation

$$W(\%t.y) = P(\%p.w)$$

models a pay-as-you-go pension scheme, where W is the size of the labor force; P, the number of pensioners; %t, the contribution rate; %p, the replacement rate (the ratio of pensions to average income); y, average income and w the average wage. This shows that if the size of the labor force (W) falls (for example, because of population ageing), the level of pensions (P) can only be maintained if contributions (% t.y) rise or the value of pensions (% p.w) falls. Note that a rise in GDP will not solve the problem, since it would lead to a rise in average income (w) and hence a rise in pensions. The equation shows why changing the age of retirement has been the preferred policy response to the funding problem. Germany and the Scandinavian countries have already changed the retirement age – coupled with a small increase in contributions. As yet, no European government has abandoned a pay-as-you-go pension scheme, making pensions dependent on individual contributions. Such a policy would mean that existing taxpayers would have paid taxes (their "contributions") but would not receive adequate pensions. Moreover, in a privatized scheme, the government would have no option but to pay pensions to people with no savings – i.e., the very poor. Hence, changing the terms of the existing pay-as-you-go schemes has been politically more attractive. The UK is exceptional, however. The state pension was inadequate when it was introduced in 1948, and was subsequently eroded by inflation. Hence, personal (usually occupational) pensions were the norm. This meant that the UK government's exposure to pension problems was comparatively limited.

Migration

In the immediate post-war period, European migration was dominated by refugees and displaced persons. West Germany was the largest recipient because of expulsions from eastern Europe. But by the early 1950s, the immigrants were predominantly workers. Immigration increased until the early 1970s, when it peaked at 3 million (1.5 million net). By 1973, 12 percent of the German labor force were foreigners (and 10 percent of the French).

It is easy to see why immigration was so high. "Golden age" growth rates led to labor shortages. Transport costs were low. The domestic labor force could not increase fast enough – i.e., via increased participation and structural change (e.g., labor moving from low productivity sectors, such as agriculture) to compensate for the low fertility of the 1930s and the losses during the Second World War. About 10 percent of the increased labor demand in the golden age was met by immigration. Within the original EEC six, migration was uncontrolled but only Italy, where incomes were relatively low, had significant *intra*-EEC migration. Immigration from outside the EEC was strictly controlled. Immigrants entered on fixed-term labor contracts. Starting in the 1950s, workers were recruited from Turkey, former Yugoslavia, Portugal, Greece, North Africa, West Africa, Spain and – before its EEC entry in 1958 – Italy. The West German *Gastarbeiter* – literally "guest worker" – experiment of the 1960s is the best-known scheme, although it post-dated similar schemes in France and other countries. (Before 1961, when the Berlin Wall was built, West Germany could rely on immigration from the GDR.) The assumption of all the schemes was that the immigrants would return home when demand for their labor fell. Recruitment stopped in the early 1970s as growth slowed, but many temporary workers declined to leave. Since deportation would have been politically impossible, the European governments, and particularly the West German, had no choice but to transform them into permanent immigrants. In turn, this meant that more dependants entered than workers in the 1970s and 1980s. Britain was an exception. There were no *Gastarbeiter*, or their equivalent, in Britain, but immigration from the Irish Republic was uncontrolled, and high in the 1950s and 1960s.

The immigrant populations were clustered. Most immigrants from Turkey and former Yugoslavia were to be found in Germany, for example. There are three reasons. First, recruiters targeted certain nationalities. Secondly, the phenomenon of "chain migration." Migration is characterized by uncertainty and previous immigrants (sometimes relatives) are a key source of information about, for example, the labor market. And finally, because of colonial links. The most important of the colonial immigrants were people from North Africa in France, from the Indian sub-continent and the Caribbean in Britain, and the Caribbean in the Netherlands. However, the immigration of ethnic minority people from erstwhile colonies has been politically problematic. Following political pressures, most countries changed the status of colonial or ex-colonial citizens. For example, before the 1960s, any person born within the British Empire – e.g., anyone born in India or Pakistan before independence (1947), or in Hong Kong, was a British citizen and had the right to live and work in the UK. Following racial tensions in the 1960s, it became necessary for a British passport holder to have a British-born parent to exercise this right.

There were major changes in immigration patterns towards the end of the twentieth century (Table 15.9). Immigration rates increased. There was a large increase in south to north immigration – i.e., from Africa. The migration pattern in the southern European countries, Italy, Spain, and Portugal changed from net emigration to net immigration. The influx of immigrants from eastern Europe was less than expected. The number of immigrants

Table 15.9 Net migration, 1991 and 2006 (per 1,000 population)

	1995	2006
W. Europe		
Belgium	1.3	4.8
France	0.6	1.5
Germany	7.5*	0.3
Sweden	2.9	5.6
Switzerland	–	3.4
UK	1.3	2.6
S. Europe		
Greece	11.7*	3.6
Italy	0.1	6.4
Portugal	7.2	2.5
Spain	1.6	14.6
E. Europe		
Czech Republic	−5.5	3.4
Hungary	1.7	0.4
Poland	−0.4	−0.9

Note: net inflows except where marked as net outflows.
*exceptional (political) factors.
Source: Eurostat, *Demographic Yearbook* 2004, 2007.

claiming asylum increased and (net) emigration out of Europe fell. These trends are relatively easy to explain. Labor demand continued to increase in most European economies, but there were structural problems in some European labor markets. Natural increase in every European country was negative. At the same time, restrictions on non-European immigration continued. In effect, the only legal way to enter an EU country was to be an EU citizen, to obtain a work permit (increasingly, only given to skilled workers), or to claim asylum.

In economic theory, assuming no barriers to migration, trade, or capital movements, migration is explained by the difference in the return to labor in the origin and destination countries. In turn, this is determined by the relative abundance of capital. *Ceteris paribus*, labor moves to where capital is relatively cheaper and capital moves to where labor is cheaper, until a low net migration equilibrium is reached – so called "factor price equalisation." (Theoretically, the relative abundance of resources is important, but this is not relevant to recent European migration.) By the late twentieth century, there was free trade in manufactures and free movement of capital in the EU, resulting in real income convergence. Hence, we would expect net migration rates across EU borders to have been low and this was the case, although gross movement was high. The exception was migration from accession countries. Countries entering the EU were usually relatively poor. Moreover, as in many other parts of the world, on average the productivity of both labor and capital was lower in these countries than in the richer countries, predicting large migration flows. But existing EU members did not have to offer free labor mobility for up to six years. At the time of writing, immigrants from the Baltic States and Poland, for example, without a work permit may only (legally) enter the UK, Ireland, and Sweden. Bulgarian and Romanian nationals may not. The majority of permits were normally granted to skilled workers (and their dependants). Hence, in the later twentieth century, the mean level of skills of non-EU immigrants was rising and that of intra-EU immigrants was falling.

Obviously, the composition of the immigration flows was largely determined by the labor market in the main immigrant countries. Two of the three traditional immigrant sectors, manufacturing and agriculture, had declined. (Only construction continued to attract large numbers of immigrants.) The demand for skilled labor in high-end services was met by recruitment, some of which was within multinational corporations. But the main demand was for workers in low-end services, particularly in the larger and wealthier cities. Since these services could not be traded, the demand was met by unskilled immigration from within the EU and by undocumented immigrants. These relatively low-productivity jobs were not filled by natives, usually because their reservation wage was too high and internal migration too low. But there were also structural reasons from within the domestic labor market. There were still many (usually older) workers whose skills had become redundant because of industrial decline. They found it very difficult to retrain into the new service occupations. In some countries (e.g., the UK) they were sustained by social security payments on the grounds that they could not undertake heavy manual labor. Moreover, in several European countries, many young men (and, though not to the same extent, young women) had few marketable skills. For example, some of the declining industrial towns and rural areas of eastern Europe have surplus male populations because a large proportion of the young women have left to take up jobs in the larger cities – an option which is not open to young, low-skilled men.

The rate of immigration is affected by an additional structural factor: the extent of the secondary labor market. Undocumented immigrants work in the informal sector because they cannot obtain a social security card. They are to be found in every European country. But the largest number is to be found in those countries with the largest informal labor market, e.g., Portugal, Spain, Italy, and Greece. Social security contributions, mainly paid by employers in these countries, can increase the wage bill by 50–100 percent. This encourages employers to hire undocumented workers. (Attempts to regularize their position have often been unsuccessful because the workers would lose their jobs if the employers had to pay social security contributions.) There is no question that the demand for illegal immigrant labor is more than zero, for example because many of them provide low-cost domestic services. But in some countries they have a presence in several sectors. The source of undocumented immigrants was extremely wide, including Albania, north and west Africa, Latin America, and Russia. (Note that the undocumented immigrants did not cause the growth of the informal labor market. It was *vice versa*.) Finally, the number of immigrants claiming asylum increased in the late twentieth century. All the richer countries were affected, but Germany was the most important recipient, with large numbers of refugees from former Yugoslavia. Most of these returned, however. Asylum seekers were universally disliked by the electorate. Hence, policy in virtually all European countries has been seriously to discourage them. It is easy to see why. At its peak in the late 1990s, there were about 500,000 applications per year in Europe. Of these, some 50,000 were accepted. Of the 450,000 who were refused, only 150,000 were deported. This left some 300,000 living in Europe illegally.

Conclusion

The six decades since the end of the Second World War have seen a major increase in broadly conceived living standards in most parts of Europe. Welfare improvements in western Europe were easier to achieve, however, during the rapid economic expansion of the golden age, when incomes rose faster than in subsequent decades, when social expenditure as a proportion of rising output increased, and when demographics were more favorable than in the late twentieth century. The evidence for eastern Europe is far more ambiguous. While initially eastern Europe performed as well as southern Europe, if not better, in terms of the HDI, there was a distinct falling off in welfare levels relative to the west from the early 1970s onwards. This was, on the one hand, an outcome of slower economic growth and, on the other, the result of a flattening out in the growth of life expectancy. The stagnation in life expectancy, we hypothesize, may have been an outcome of the failure to match the continued fall in cardiovascular diseases in western Europe, and also the price paid for rapid post-war industrialization, with its emphasis on the expansion of heavy and pollutant-intensive industries. Alternatively, much of eastern Europe was experiencing after the Second World War what the economically most advanced parts of western Europe experienced during the industrial revolutions of the nineteenth century.

Bibliography

Abelshauser, W. 2000. Germany: Guns, Butter, and Economic Miracles. In Harrison 2000, pp. 122–76.

Abramovitz, M. 1961. The Nature and Significance of Kuznets Cycles. *Economic Development and Cultural Change* 9: 225–48.

1986. Catching Up, Forging Ahead, and Falling Behind. *Journal of Economic History* 46: 385–406.

Abramovitz, M. and P. A. David. 1996. Convergence and Delayed Catch-Up: Productivity Leadership and the Waning of American Exceptionalism. In *The Mosaic of Economic Growth*, ed. R. Landau, T. Taylor, and G. Wright. Stanford University Press, pp. 21–62.

Accominotti, O., M. Flandreau, R. Rezzik, and F. Zumer. 2008. Black Man's Burden: Measured Philanthropy in the British Empire, 1880–1913. CEPR Discussion Paper 6811.

Acemoglu, D., S. Johnson, and J. A. Robinson. 2002. Reversal of Fortunes: Geography and Institutions in the Making of the Modern World Income Distribution. *Quarterly Journal of Economics* 117: 1231–94.

A'Hearn, B. and U. Woitek. 2001. More International Evidence on the Historical Properties of Business Cycles. *Journal of Monetary Economics* 47: 321–46.

Aldcroft, D. H. 2001. *The European Economy 1914–2000*, fourth edition. London: Routledge.

Aldcroft, D. 2006. *Europe's Third World: The European Periphery in the Interwar Years*. Aldershot: Ashgate.

Alesina, A. 1989. Politics and Business Cycles in Industrial Democracies. *Economic Policy* 4: 57–98.

Alesina, A., E. Glaeser, and B. Sacerdote. 2005. Work and Leisure in the US and Europe: Why So Different? CEPR Discussion Paper 5140.

Allen, C., M. Gasiorek, and A. Smith. 1998. The Competition Effects of the Single Market in Europe. *Economic Policy* 27: 439–86.

Allen, R. C. 2003. *Farm to Factory: A Reinterpretation of the Soviet Industrial Revolution*. Princeton University Press.

Ambrosius, G. and W. Hubbard. 1989. *A Social and Economic History of Twentieth-Century Europe*. Cambridge, MA: Harvard University Press.

Andreff, W. 2004. Would a Second Transition Stage Prolong the Initial Period of Post-Socialist Transformation into Market Capitalism? *The European Journal of Comparative Economics* 1: 7–31.

Anfimov, A. M. and A. P. Korelin, eds. 1995. *Rossiia. 1913 god. Statistiko-dokumental'nyi spravochnik* (Russia, 1913: Statistical Documentary Handbook). St Petersburg: Blits.

Angell, N. 1972. *The Great Illusion. A Study of the Relation of Military Power in Nations to Their Economic and Social Advantage*. New York: Garland.

Antsiferov, A. 1930. *Russian Agriculture during the War*. New Haven: Yale University Press.

Aparicio, D., V. Pinilla, and R. Serrano. 2008. Europe and the International Trade in Agricultural and Food Products, 1870–2000. In *Agriculture and Economic Development in Europe since 1870*, ed. P. Lains and V. Pinilla. London: Routledge, 52–75.

Armstrong, P., A. Glyn, and J. Harrison. 1991. *Capitalism since World War II: The Making and Breakup of the Great Boom*. London: Fontana.

Artis, M., H.-M. Krolzig, and J. Toro. 2004. The European Business Cycle. *Oxford Economic Papers* 56: 1–44.

Artis, M., M. Marcellino, and T. Proietti. 2004. Characterizing the Business Cycle for Accession Countries. IGIER Working Paper no. 261.

Artis, M. J. and M. P. Taylor. 1994. The Stabilizing Effect of the ERM on Exchange Rates and Interest Rates. *IMF Staff Papers* 41: 123–48.

Artis, M. J. and W. Zhang. 1997. International Business Cycles and the ERM: Is There A European Business Cycle? *International Journal of Finance and Economics* 38: 1471–87.

Avramov, R. and S. Pamuk, eds. 2006. *Monetary and Fiscal Policies in South-East Europe. Historical and Comparative Perspective*. Sofia: Bulgarian National Bank.

Bachinger, K. 1973. Das Verkehrswesen. In *Die Habsburgermonarchie 1848–1918, Vol. 1, Die Wirtschaftliche Entwicklung*, ed. A. Brusatti. Vienna: Verlag der Österreichischen Akademie der Wissenschaften, pp. 278–322.

Backus, D. and P. Kehoe. 1992. International Evidence on the Historical Properties of Business Cycles. *American Economic Review* 82: 864–88.

Badinger, H. 2005. Growth Effects of Economic Integration: Evidence from the EU Member States. *Review of World Economics* 141: 50–78.

Bagge, G., E. Lundberg, and I. Svennilson. 1935. *Wages in Sweden, 1860–1930*. London: P.S. King & Son.

Baily, M. and J. F. Kirkegaard. 2004. *Transforming the European Economy*. Washington: Institute for International Economics.

Bain, G. S. and R. Price. 1980. *Profiles of Union Growth: A Comparative Statistical Portrait of Eight Industrial Countries*. Oxford: Blackwell.

Baines, D. 1999a. European Immigration since 1945. In Schulze 1999, pp. 177–90.

  1999b. European Demographic Change since 1945. In Schulze 1999, pp. 161–76.

  2007. Immigration and the Labour Market. In *Work and Pay in Twentieth-Century Britain*, ed. N. Crafts, I. Gazeley, and A. Newell. Oxford University Press, pp. 330–52.

Bairoch, P. 1968. *The Working Population and Its Structure*. Brussels: Institut de Sociologie.

  1974. General Structure and Trade Balance of European Foreign Trade. *Journal of European Economic History* 3: 557–608.

  1976. *Commerce extérieur et développement économique de l'Europe au XIXe siècle*. Paris: Mouton.

1982. International Industrialization Levels from 1750 to 1980. *Journal of European Economic History* 11: 269–333.

1989. European Trade Policy, 1815–1914. In *The Cambridge Economic History of Europe*, Volume VIII, *The Industrial Economies: The Development of Economic and Social Policies*, ed. P. Mathias and S. Pollard. Cambridge University Press.

1993. *Economics and World History: Myths and Paradoxes*. Hemel Hempstead: Harvester-Wheatsheaf.

Balderston, T. (1993). *The Origins and Course of the German Economic Crisis 1923–32*. Berlin: Hainde and Spener.

Baldwin, P. 1990. *The Politics of Social Solidarity*. Cambridge University Press.

Baldwin, R. 1989. The Growth Effects of 1992. *Economic Policy* 9: 247–81.

2006a. The Euro's Trade Effects. ECB Working Paper 594.

2006b. *In or Out: Does it Matter? An Evaluation-Based Analysis of the Euro's Trade Effects*. London: CEPR.

Barber, J. and R. Davies. 1994. Employment and Industrial Labour. In *The Economic Transformation of the Soviet Union*, ed. R. W. Davies, M. Harrison, and S. G. Wheatcroft. Cambridge University Press, pp. 81–105.

Barber, J. and M. Harrison. 1991. *The Soviet Home Front, 1941–1945: A Social and Economic History of the USSR in World War II*. London: Longman.

2005. Patriotic War, 1941 to 1945. In *The Cambridge History of Russia*, Vol. 3, (ed. R. G. Suny). Cambridge University Press, pp. 217–42.

Bardet, J.-P. 1999. La France: la fin d'une singularité? In Bardet and Dupâquier. 1999, pp. 437–88.

Bardet, J.-P. and J. Dupâquier, eds. 1999. *Histoire des populations de l'Europe*, Vol. 3, *Les temps incertains*, 1914–1998.

Barjot, D. *et al*. 1996. *Histoire de la France industrielle*. Paris: Larousse.

1997. *Industrialisation et sociétés en Europe occidentale du début des années 1880 à la fin des années 1960*. Paris: CNED-SEDES.

Barrell, R., S. Gottschalk, D. Holland, E. Khoman, I. Liadze, and O. Pomerantz. 2008. The Impact of EMU on Growth and Employment. European Commission Economic Papers 318.

Barro, R. 1996. Democracy and Growth. *Journal of Economic Growth* 1: 1–27.

Barro, R., G. Mankiw, and X. Sala-i-Martin. 1995. Capital Mobility in Neoclassical Models of Growth. *American Economic Review* 85: 103–15.

Barro, R. J. and X. Sala-i-Martin. 2003. *Economic Growth*, second edition. New York: McGraw-Hill.

Barry, F. 2002. The Celtic Tiger Era: Delayed Convergence or Regional Boom? *ESRI Quarterly Economic Commentary*, 84–91.

Barsky, R., and J. B. De Long. 1991. Forecasting Pre-World War I Inflation: The Fisher Effect and the Gold Standard. *Quarterly Journal of Economics* 106: 815–36.

Basu, S. and A. Taylor. 1999. Business Cycles in International Historical Perspective. *Journal of Economic Perspectives* 13: 45–68.

Baten, J. 2006. Global Height Trends in Industrial and Developing Countries, 1810–1984: An Overview. Working Paper, University of Tübingen.

Baten, J. and A. Wagner. 2003. Autarky, Market Disintegration, and Health: The Mortality and Nutritional Crisis in Nazi Germany 1933–37. *Economics and Human Biology* 1–1: 1–28.

Baumol, W. J. 1986. Productivity Growth, Convergence, and Welfare: What the Long-Run Data Show. *American Economic Review* 76: 1072–85.

Bayoumi, T. 1990. Saving–Investment Correlations: Immobile Capital, Government Policy, or Endogenous Behavior? *IMF Staff Papers* 37: 360–87.

Bayoumi, T. and B. Eichengreen. 1993. Shocking Aspects of European Monetary Unification. In *Adjustment and Growth in the European Monetary Union,* ed. F. Giavazzi and F. Torres. Cambridge University Press, 193–229.

1994. Economic Performance under Alternative Exchange Rate Regimes: Some Historical Evidence. In *The International Monetary System,* ed. P. Kenen, F. Papadia, and F. Saccomanni. Cambridge University Press, pp. 257–97.

1997. Is Regionalism Simply a Diversion? Evidence from the Evolution of the EC and EFTA. In *Regional versus Multilateral Trade Arrangements,* ed. T. Ito and A. Krueger. Chicago University of Chicago Press, pp. 141–68.

Bean, C. and N. Crafts. 1996. British Economic Growth since 1945: Relative Economic Decline … and Renaissance? In *Economic Growth in Europe Since 1945,* ed. N. Crafts and G. Toniolo. Cambridge University Press, pp. 131–72.

Beaudry, P. and F. Portier. 2002. The French Depression in the 1930s. *Review of Economic Dynamics* 5: 73–99.

Beck, T. and L. Laeven. 2006. Institution Building and Growth in Transition Economies. *Journal of Economic Growth* 11: 157–86.

Bell, F. and R. Millward. 1998. Public Health Expenditures and Mortality in England and Wales 1870–1914. *Continuity and Change* 13: 221–49.

Benavot, A. and P. Riddle. 1989. The Expansion of Primary Education, 1870–1940: Trends and Issues. *Sociology of Education* 61: 191–210.

Bengtsson, T. and Dribe, M. 2005. New Evidence on the Standard of Living in Sweden during the Eighteenth and Nineteenth Centuries: Long-Term Development of the Demographic Response to Short-Term Economic Stress. In *Living Standards in the Past. New Perspectives on Well-Being in Asia and Europe,* ed. R. C. Allen, T. Bengtsson, and M. Dribe. Oxford University Press, pp. 341–72.

Benjamin, D. and L. Kochin. 1979. Searching for an Explanation of Unemployment in Inter-War Britain. *Journal of Political Economy* 87: 441–78.

Berend, I. T. 1998. *Central and Eastern Europe, 1944–1993: Detour from the Periphery to the Periphery.* Reprint, Cambridge University Press.

2006. *An Economic History of Twentieth-Century Europe. Economic Regimes from Laissez-Faire to Globalization.* Cambridge University Press.

Berger, H. and J. de Haan. 1999. A State Within the State? An Event Study on the Bundesbank. *Scottish Journal of Political Economy* 46: 17–39.

Berger, H. and A. Ritschl. 1995. Germany and the Political Economy of the Marshall Plan, 1947–52: A Re-Revisionist Review. In *Europe's Postwar Recovery,* ed. B. Eichengreen. Cambridge University Press, pp. 199–245.

Berghahn, V. R. 1973. *Germany and the Approach of War in 1914*. New York: St. Martin's Press.

Bergman, M., M. Bordo, and L. Jonung. 1998. Historical Evidence on Business Cycles: The International Experience. In *Beyond Shocks: What Causes Business Cycles*, ed. J. Fuhrer and S. Schuh. Federal Reserve Bank of Boston, 65–113.

Bergman, M., S. Gerlach, and L. Jonung. 1992. External Influences in Nordic Business Cycles, 1870–1988. *Open Economy Review* 3: 1–22.

Berliner, J. S. 1976. *The Innovation Decision in Soviet Industry*. Cambridge, MA: MIT Press.

Bernanke, B. 1995. The Macroeconomics of the Great Depression: A Comparative Approach. *Journal of Money, Credit and Banking* 27: 1–28.

2000. *Essays on the Great Depression*. Princeton University Press.

Bernanke, B. and H. James. 1991. The Gold Standard, Deflation, and Financial Crisis in the Great Depression: An International Comparison. In *Financial Markets and Financial Crisis*, ed. G. Hubbard. Chicago: University of Chicago Press, 33–68.

Biraben, J. N. 1991. Pasteur, Pasteurization, and Medicine. In Schofield, Reher, and Bideau 1991, pp. 220–32.

Blanchard, O. J. 1984. The Lucas Critique and the Volcker Deflation. *American Economic Review* 74: 211–15.

2004. The Economic Future of Europe. *Journal of Economic Perspectives* 18(4): 3–26.

Blanchard, O. J. and P. A. Muet. 1993. Competitiveness through Disinflation: An Assessment of the French Macroeconomic Strategy. *Economic Policy* 16: 11–56.

Blanchard, O. J. and J. Simon. 2001. The Long and Large Decline in US Output Volatility. *Brookings Papers on Economic Activity* 1: 135–64.

Bloomfield, A. I. 1959. *Monetary Policy under the International Gold Standard, 1880–1914*. New York: Federal Reserve Bank of New York.

1968. *Patterns of Fluctuations in International Investment before 1914*. Princeton Studies in International Finance 21. Department of Economics, Princeton University.

Boeri, T. and K. Terrel. 2002. Institutional Determinants of Labour Reallocation in Transition. *Journal of Economic Perspectives* 16: 51–76.

Boesche, R. 1996. *Theories of Tyranny, from Plato to Arendt*. University Park, PA.: Pennsylvania State University Press.

Boltho, A. 1982a. Introduction to Boltho. 1982b, pp. 1–5.

1982b. *The European Economy: Growth and Crisis*. Oxford University Press.

Bonin, H. 1987. *Histoire économique de la IVe république*. Paris: Economica.

Borchardt, K. 1984. Could and Should Germany Have Followed Britain in Leaving the Gold Standard? *Journal of European Economic History* 13: 471–98.

1991 [1982]. *Perspectives on Modern German Economic History and Policy*. Cambridge University Press.

Bordo, M. D. 2006. Sudden Stops, Financial Crises and Original Sin in Emerging Countries: Déjà Vu? NBER Working Paper 12393.

Bordo, M. D., B. Eichengreen, D. Klingebiel, and M. S. Martinez-Peria (2001). Is the Crisis Problem Growing More Severe? *Economic Policy* 16: 51–82.

Bordo, M. D. and M. Flandreau. 2003. Core, Periphery, Exchange Rate Regimes and Globalization. In *Globalization in Historical Perspective*, ed. M. Bordo, A. Taylor, and J. Williamson. Chicago: University of Chicago Press, 417–68.

Bordo, M. D. and T. Helbling. 2003. Have National Business Cycles Become More Synchronized? In *Macroeconomic Policies in the World Economy*, ed. H. Siebert. Berlin and Heidelberg: Springer Verlag, 3–39.

Bordo, M. D. and L. Jonung. 1987. *The Long-Run Behavior of the Velocity of Circulation: The International Evidence*. Cambridge University Press.

Bordo, M. D., C. Meissner, and A. Redish. 2005. How 'Original Sin' Was Overcome: The Evolution of External Debt Denominated in Domestic Currencies in the United States and the British Dominions 1800–2000. In *Other People's Money: Debt Denomination and Financial Instability in Emerging Market Economies*, ed. B. Eichengreen and R. Hausmann. Chicago: University of Chicago Press, 122–53.

Bordo, M. D. and A. P. Murshid. 2000. Are Financial Crises Becoming Increasingly More Contagious? What is the Historical Evidence on Contagion? NBER Working Paper W7900.

Bordo, M. D. and H. Rockoff. 1996. The Gold Standard as a 'Good Housekeeping Seal of Approval'. *Journal of Economic History* 56: 389–428.

Bordo, M. D., A. M. Taylor, and J. G. Williamson, eds. 2003. *Globalization in Historical Perspective*, Chicago: University of Chicago Press.

Borio, C. 2003. A Tale of Two Perspectives: Old or New Challenges for Monetary Policy? BIS Working Papers no. 127.

Borodkin, L., B. Granville, and C. Leonard. 2008. The Rural–Urban Wage Gap in the Industrialization of Russia, 1885–1910. *European Review of Economic History* 12: 67–95.

Bosworth, B. P. and S. M. Collins. 2003. The Empirics of Growth: An Update. *Brookings Papers on Economic Activity* 2: 113–206.

Bourguignon, F. and C. Morrisson. 2002. Inequality among World Citizens: 1820–1992. *American Economic Review* 92: 727–44.

Bourles, R. and G. Cette. 2006. Les évolutions de la productivité 'structurelle' du travail dans les principaux pays industriells. *Bulletin de la Banque de France* 150: 23–30.

Boyden, R. 1928. Relation between Reparations and the Interallied Debts. *Proceedings of the Academy of Political Science in the City of New York* 12: 21–8.

Bradley, J. 1985. *Muzhik and Muscovite: Urbanization in Late Imperial Russia*. Berkeley: University of California Press.

Bradshaw, J. 1993. Developments in Social Security Policy. In *New Perspectives on the Welfare State in Europe*, ed. C. Jones. London: Routledge.

Brauer, J. and H. v. Tuyll. 2008. *Castles, Battles and Bombs. How Economics Explains Military History*. Chicago: University of Chicago Press.

Braun, H. 1990. *The German Economy in the Twentieth Century. The German Reich and the Federal Republic*. London: Routledge.

Bringas Gutiérrez, M. A. 2000. *La productividad de los factores en la agricultura española*. Estudios de historia económica no. 39. Madrid: Banco de España.

Broadberry, S. N. 1986. Aggregate Supply in Interwar Britain. *Economic Journal* 96: 467–81.

1986. *The British Economy between the Wars. A Macroeconomic Survey*. Oxford: Blackwell.

1992. *Britain in the International Economy, 1870–1939*. Cambridge University Press.

1997. *The Productivity Race: British Manufacturing in International Perspective, 1850–1990*. Cambridge University Press.

1998. How did the United States and Germany Overtake Britain? A Sectoral Analysis of Comparative Productivity Levels, 1870–1990. *Journal of Economic History* 58: 375–407.

2004. Explaining Anglo-German Productivity Differences in Services Since 1870. *European Review of Economic History* 8: 229–62.

2005. Italian GDP During World War I. In Broadberry and Harrison, 2005a, 305–9.

2006. *Market Services and the Productivity Race, 1850–2000: British Performance in International Perspective*. Cambridge University Press.

2008. Agriculture and Structural Change: Lessons from the UK Experience in an International Context. In *Agriculture and Economic Development in Europe since 1870*, ed. P. Lains and V. Pinilla. London: Routledge, 76–94.

Broadberry, S. N. and C. Burhop. 2007. Comparative Productivity in British and German Manufacturing Before World War II: Reconciling Direct Benchmark Estimates and Time Series Projections. *Journal of Economic History* 67: 315–49.

Broadberry, S. N. and N. F. R. Crafts. 1992a. British Macroeconomic History 1870–1939: Overview and Key Issues. In Broadberry and Crafts 1992b, pp. 1–27.

Broadberry, S. N. and N. F. R. Crafts, eds. 1992b. *Britain in the International Economy 1870–1934*. Cambridge University Press.

Broadberry, S. N. and S. Ghosal. 2002. From the Counting House to the Modern Office: Explaining Anglo-American Productivity Differences in Services, 1870–1990. *Journal of Economic History* 62: 967–98.

Broadberry, S. and S. Ghosal. 2005. Technology, Organisation and Productivity Performance in Services: Lessons from Britain and the United States since 1870. *Structural Change and Economic Dynamics* 16: 437–66.

Broadberry, S. and M. Harrison (eds.) 2005a. *The Economics of World War I*. Cambridge University Press.

2005b. The Economics of World War I: An Overview. In Broadberry and Harrison, 2005a, pp. 3–40.

Broadberry, S. and P. Howlett. 2005. The United Kingdom During World War I: Business as Usual? In Broadberry and Harrison 2005a, pp. 206–34.

Broadberry, S. and A. Klein. 2008. Aggregate and Per Capita GDP in Europe, 1870–2000: Continental, Regional and National Data with Changing Boundaries. Unpublished manuscript, University of Warwick.

Broadberry, S. N. and A. J. Marrison. 2002. External Economies of Scale in the Lancashire Cotton Industry, 1900–1950. *Economic History Review* 55: 51–77.

Broadberry, S. and A. Ritschl. 1995. Real Wages, Productivity, and Unemployment in Britain and Germany during the 1920s. *Explorations in Economic History* 32: 327–49.

Brown, J. 2000. Economics and Infant Mortality Decline in German towns, 1889–1912: Household Behaviour and Public Intervention. In *Body and City: Histories of Urban Public Health*, ed. S. Sheard and H. Power. Aldershot: Ashgate, pp. 166–93.

Bruno, M. and J. D. Sachs. 1985. *The Economics of Worldwide Stagflation*. Cambridge, MA: Harvard University Press.

Budd, A. 1998. Three Views of Macroeconomics. *Bank of England Quarterly Bulletin* 38: 274–80.

Buiter, W. H. and M. Miller. 1981. The Thatcher Experiment: The First Two Years. *Brookings Papers on Economic Activity* 2: 315–79.

Burnett, J. 1991. Housing and the Decline of Mortality. In *The Decline of Mortality in Europe*, ed. R. Schofield, D. Reher, and A. Bideau. Oxford: Clarendon.

Burns, A. F. and W. Mitchell. 1946. *Measuring Business Cycles*. New York: NBER.

Burns, A. F. 1979. The Anguish of Central Banking. *The 1979 Per Jacobsson Lecture*. Belgrade: Per Jacobsson Foundation.

Buyst, E. 2004. Economic Growth in an Era of Severe Macroeconomic Imbalances: Belgium, 1910–1934. In *Exploring Economic Growth. Essays in Measurement and Analysis*, ed. S. Heikkinen and J. L. Van Zanden. Amsterdam: Aksant, 167–81.

Caballero, R., K. Cowan, E. Engel, and A. Micco. 2004. Effective Labor Regulation and Microeconomic Flexibility. NBER Working Paper 10744.

Cain, P. J. and A. G. Hopkins. 2002. *British Imperialism 1688–2000*, second edition. Harlow: Longman.

Cairncross, A. 1996. *Managing the British Economy in the 1960s: A Treasury Perspective*. London: Macmillan.

Calot, G. and C. Blayo. 1982. The Recent Course of Fertility in Western Europe. *Population Studies* 36: 349–72.

Calvo, G. 1998. Capital Flows and Capital-Market Crises: The Simple Economics of Sudden Stops. *Journal of Applied Economics* 1: 35–54.

  1999. Contagion in the Emerging Markets: When Wall Street is a Carrier. Mimeo.

Calvo, G., A. Izquierdo, and L.-F. Mejía. 2004. On the Empirics of Sudden Stops: The Relevance of Balance-Sheet Effects. NBER Working Paper 10520.

Cameron, R. 1985. A New View of European Industrialization. *Economic History Review* 38: 1–23.

Canning, K. 1996. Social Policy, Body Politics: Recasting the Social Question in Germany, 1825–1900. In *Gender and Class in Modern Europe*, ed. L. L. Frader and S. O. Rose. Ithaca and London: Cornell University Press, pp. 211–37.

Carlin, W. 1996. West German Growth and Institutions, 1945–90. In Crafts and Toniolo 1996b, pp. 455–97.

Carlin, W. and D. Soskice. 2006. *Macroeconomics: Imperfections, Institutions and Policies*. Oxford University Press.

Caron, F. 1979. *An Economic History of Modern France*. London: Methuen.

Caron, F. *et al.* 1995. *Innovations in the European Economy between the Wars*. Berlin: de Gruyter.

Carone, G. and D. Costello. 2005. Can Europe Afford to Grow Old? *Finance and Development* (IMF) 43–3.

Carreras, A. 2005. Spanish Industrialization in the Swedish Mirror. In *Different Paths to Modernity: A Nordic and Spanish Perspective*, ed. M. Jerneck, M. Mörner, G. Tortella, and S. Akerman Lund: Nordic Academic Press, 151–65.

Carreras, A. 2006. The Twentieth Century. In *An Economic History of Europe: from Expansion to Development*, ed. A. Di Vittorio. London: Routledge.

Carreras, A. and X. Tafunell. 2004a. The European Union Economic Growth Experience, 1830–2000. In *Explorations in Economic Growth*, ed. S. Heikkinen and J. L. Van Zanden Amsterdam: Aksant, 63–87.

2004b. *Historia económica de la España contemporánea*. Barcelona: Crítica.

2008. *Western European Long Term Growth, 1830–2000: Facts and Issues*. Barcelona: CREI (Opuscles del CREI, no. 20).

Carter, S. *et al.*, eds. 2006. *Historical Statistics of the United States. Millennial Edition*, Vol. 1. Cambridge University Press.

Caselli, F. 2005. Accounting for Cross-Country Income Differences. In *Handbook of Economic Growth*, Volume 1, ed. P. Aghion and S. Durlauf. Amsterdam: Elsevier.

Caselli, G. 1991. Health Transition and Cause-Specific Mortality. In *The Decline of Mortality in Europe*, ed. R. Schofield, D. Reher, and A. Bideau. Oxford: Clarendon, 142–57.

Caselli, G., F. Meslé, and J. Vallin. 1999. Le triomphe de la médecine. In Bardet and Dupâquier 1999, pp. 125–81.

Cassidy, M. 2004. Productivity in Ireland: Issues and Trends. *Central Bank of Ireland Quarterly Bulletin*, Spring: 83–105.

Castles, F. G. 2001. The Dog that Didn't Bark: Economic Development and the Postwar Welfare State. In *Welfare States Futures*, ed. Stephan Leibfried and Gialiano Bonoli. Cambridge University Press, 37–56.

Catão, L. 2006. Sudden Stops and Currency Drops: A Historical Look. IMF Working Paper 06/133.

Catão, L. and S. Solomou. 2005. Effective Exchange Rates and the Classical Gold Standard Adjustment. *American Economic Review* 95: 1259–75.

Chalmers, E. 1972. *International Interest Rate War*. London: Macmillan.

Chandler, A. D. Jr. 1977. *The Visible Hand*. Cambridge, MA: Belknap.

1990. *Scale and Scope: The Dynamics of Industrial Capitalism*. Cambridge, MA: Harvard University Press.

Charle, C. 1994. *La République des universitaires*. Paris: Seuil.

Chesnais, J.-C. 1999. La fécondité au XXe siècle: une baisse irrégulière, mais profunde et irrésistible. In Bardet and Dupâquier 1999, pp. 183–222.

Child, F. 1958. *The Theory and Practice of Exchange Control in Germany*. The Hague: Mouton.

Chiswick, B. R. and T. J. Hatton. 2003. International Migration and the Integration of Labor Markets. In Bordo, Taylor, and Williamson 2003, pp. 65–120.

Choudri, E. and L. Kochin. 1980. The Exchange Rate and the International Transmission of Business Cycle Disturbances: Some Evidence from the Great Depression. *Journal of Money, Credit, and Banking* 12: 565–74.

Churchill, W. S. 1948. *The Gathering Storm*. Volume I of *The Second World War*. Boston: Houghton Mifflin.

Ciocca, P. L. and G. Nardozzi. 1996. *The High Price of Money: An Interpretation of World Interest Rates*. Oxford: Clarendon.

Claessens, S., R. Dornbush, and Y. C. Park. 2000. Contagion: Understanding How It Spreads. *World Bank Research Observer* 15: 177–97.

Clarida, R., M. Gertler, and J. Gali. 1999. The Science of Monetary Policy: A New Keynesian Perspective. *Journal of Economic Literature*, 37: 1661–707.

Clark, C. 1951. *The Conditions of Economic Progress*, second edition. London: Macmillan.

Clark, G. 1987. Why Isn't the Whole World Developed? Lessons from the Cotton Mills. *Journal of Economic History* 47: 141–73.

Clark, G. and R. C. Feenstra. 2003. Technology in the Great Divergence. In Bordo, Taylor, and Williamson 2003, pp. 277–322.

Clarke, S. 1976. *Central Bank Cooperation 1924–31*. New York: Federal Reserve Bank of New York.

Clemens, M. A. and J. G. Williamson. 2004. Wealth Bias in the First Global Capital Market Boom, 1870–1913. *Economic Journal* 114: 304–37.

Coale, A. J. 1986. The Decline of Fertility in Europe since the 18th Century as a Chapter in Demographic History. In *The Decline of Fertility in Europe*, ed. A. J. Coale and S. C. Watkins. Princeton University Press, 1–30.

Coale, A. J., B. A. Anderson, and E. Härm. 1979. *Human Fertility in Russia since the Nineteenth Century*. Princeton University Press.

Cohen, J. and G. Federico. 2000. *The Growth of the Italian Economy, 1820–1960*. Cambridge University Press.

Cole, H. and L. Ohanian. 2002. The Great U.K. Depression: A Puzzle and Possible Resolution. *Review of Economic Dynamics* 5: 19–44.

Connelly, S. and M. Gregory. 2007. Women and Work since 1970. In *Work and Pay in Twentieth-Century Britain*, ed. N. Crafts, I. Gazeley, and A. Newell. Oxford University Press, pp. 142–77.

Conway, P., D. de Rosa, G. Nicoletti, and F. Steiner. 2006. Regulation, Competition and Productivity Convergence. OECD Economics Department Working Paper 509.

Conway, P., V. Janod, and G. Nicoletti. 2005. Product Market Regulation in OECD Countries: 1998 to 2003. OECD Economics Department Working Paper 419.

Conway, P. and G. Nicoletti. 2006. Product Market Regulation in the Non-Manufacturing Sectors of OECD Countries: Measurement and Highlights. OECD Economics Department Working Paper 530.

Cooper, R. N. 1990. Comments on A. Giovannini: *European Monetary Reform: Progress and Prospects*. *Brookings Papers on Economic Activity* 2: 217–91.

Coppola, M. and G. Vecchi. 2006. Nutrition and Growth in Italy, 1861–1911: What Macroeconomic Data Hide. *Explorations in Economic History* 43: 438–64.

Corbino, E. 1964. La soluzione migliore è quella di fare l'Europa. In *Cronache economiche e politiche*, ed. E. Corbino. Naples: Istituto editoriale del Mezzogiorno.

Corsini, C. A. and P. P. Viazzo. 1997. Introduction: Recent Advances and Some Open Questions in the Long-term Study of Infant and Child Mortality. In *The Decline of*

Infant and Child Mortality. The European Experience: 1750–1990, ed. S. Ogilvie and R. Overy. Florence: Nijhoff.

Cottrell, P. H., ed. 1997. *Rebuilding the Financial System in Central and Eastern Europe, 1918–1994*. Aldershot: Scolar Press.

Crafts, N. 1992a. Productivity Growth Reconsidered. *Economic Policy* 15: 387–426.

1992b. Institutions and Economic Growth: Recent British Experience in an International Context. *West European Politics* 15: 16–38.

1997. The Human Development Index and Changes in the Standards of Living: Some Historical Comparisons. *European Review of Economic History* 1: 299–322.

2002a. The Human Development Index, 1870–1999: Some Revised Estimates. *European Review of Economic History*, 6: 395–405.

2002b. *Britain's Relative Economic Performance, 1870–1999*. London: Institute of Economic Affairs.

2005. Interpreting Ireland's Economic Growth. Background paper for UNIDO *Industrial Development Report*.

2007. Recent European Economic Growth: Why Can't It Be Like the Golden Age? *National Institute Economic Review* 199: 69–81.

Crafts, N., S. J. Leybourne, and T. C. Mills. 1990. Measurement of Trend Growth in European Industrial Output before 1914: Methodological Issues and New Estimates. *Explorations in Economic History* 27: 442–67.

Crafts, N. and T. C. Mills. 1996. Europe's Golden Age: An Econometric Investigation. In Van Ark and Crafts 1996, pp. 415–31.

Crafts, N. and T. C. Mills. 2005. TFP Growth in British and German Manufacturing, 1950–1996. *Economic Journal* 115: 649–70.

Crafts, N. and G. Toniolo. 1996a. Postwar Growth: An Overview. In Crafts, N. F. R. and G. Toniolo, 1996b, pp. 1–37.

Crafts, N. F. R. and G. Toniolo, eds. 1996b. *Economic Growth in Europe since 1945*. Cambridge University Press.

Craig, L. and D. Fisher. 1992. The Integration of the European Business Cycle 1871–1910. *Explorations in Economic History* 29: 144–68.

1997. *The Integration of the European Economy, 1850–1913*. Basingstoke: Macmillan.

2000. *The European Macroeconomy: Growth, Integration and Cycles 1500–1913*. Cheltenham: Edward Elgar.

Crouch, C. 1993. *Industrial Relations and European State Traditions*. Oxford: Clarendon.

Crouzet, F. 1970. Un indice de la production industrielle française au XIXe siècle. *Annales* 25: 92–7.

Darvasz, Z., A. K. Rose, and G. Szapary. 2005. Fiscal Divergence and Business Cycle Synchronization: Irresponsibility is Idiosyncratic. NBER Working Paper no. 11580.

Davenport, M. 1982. The Economic Impact of the EEC. In Boltho 1982b, pp. 225–58.

Davies, R. W. and S. Wheatcroft. 2004. *Years of Hunger. Soviet Agriculture, 1931–1933*, London: Palgrave Macmillan.

Davis, C. M. 1999. Russian Industrial Policy and Performance, 1890–2000: A Comparative Economic Systems Interpretation. In *European Industrial Policy:*

The Twentieth Century Experience., ed. J. Foreman-Peck and G. Federico. Oxford: Oxford University Press.

Davis, C. M. and J. Foreman-Peck. 2003. The Russian Transition through the Historical Looking Glass: Gradual Versus Abrupt De-Control of Economic Systems. In *Economic Challenges of the 21ˢᵗ Century in Historical Perspective*, ed. P. David and M. Thomas. Oxford: Oxford University Press and the British Academy.

Davis, L. E. and Engerman, S. L. 2006. *Naval Blockades in Peace and War: An Economic History since 1750*. Cambridge University Press.

Davis, L. E. and R. A. Huttenback. 1986. *Mammon and the Pursuit of Empire: The Political Economy of British Imperialism, 1860–1912*. Cambridge University Press.

Deacon, B. 1993. Developments in East European Social Policy. In *New Perspectives on the Welfare State in Europe*, ed. C. Jones. London: Routledge.

Deane, P. and W. A. Cole. 1962. *British Economic Growth 1688–1959: Trends and Structure*. Cambridge University Press.

De Cecco, M., 1969. The Italian Payment Crisis of 1963–64. In *Problems of the International Economy*, ed. A. Swoboda and R. Mundell. Chicago: University of Chicago Press.

DeLong, J. B 1988. Productivity Growth, Convergence, and Welfare: Comment. *American Economic Review* 78: 1138–54.

2000. *Cornucopia: The Pace of Economic Growth in the Twentieth Century*. NBER Working Paper No. W7602. Cambridge, MA.: National Bureau of Economic Research.

DeLong, J. B. and B. Eichengreen. 1993. The Marshall Plan: History's Most Successful Structural Adjustment Programme. In *Postwar Economic Reconstruction and Lessons for the East Today*, ed. R. Dornbusch, W. Nölling, and R. Layard, Cambridge, MA: MIT Press, pp. 89–230.

De Melo, M., C. Denizer, A. Gelb, and S. Tenev. 2001. Circumstance and Choice: The Role of Initial Conditions and Policies in Transition Economies. *World Bank Economic Review* 15: 1–31.

De Santis, G. and M. Livi Bacci. 2005. La population italienne au xxᵉ siècle. In Bardet and Dupâquier 2005, pp. 517–38.

Denton, G., M. Forsyth, and M. Maclennan. 1968. *Economic Planning and Policies in Britain France and Germany*. London: Allen & Unwin.

Dobrinsky, R., D. Hesse, and R. Traeger. 2006. Understanding the Long-term Growth Performance of the East European and CIS economies. UNECE Discussion Paper Series, no. 9.

Dormois, J.-P. 2004. Episodes in Catching-Up: Anglo-French Industrial Productivity Differentials in 1930. *European Review of Economic History* 8: 337–73.

2004. *The French Economy in the Twentieth Century*. Cambridge University Press.

Dornbusch, R. 1987. Lessons from the German Inflation Experience of the 1920s. In *Macroeconomics and Finance: Essays in Honor of Franco Modigliani.*, ed. R. Dornbusch *et al*. Cambridge University Press, 337–66.

Dowrick, S. and B. DeLong. 2003. Globalization and Convergence. In Bordo, Taylor, and Williamson 2003, pp. 191–226.

Duecker, M. and K. Wesche. 2003. European Business Cycles: New Indices and Their Synchronicity. *Economic Inquiry* 41: 116–31.

Dugec, Z. 2005. New Public Health for a New State: Inter-War Public Health in the Kingdom of the Serbs, Croats and Slovenes (Kingdom of Yugoslavia) and the Rockefeller Foundation. In *Facing Illness in Troubled Times: Health in Europe in the Inter-War Years*, ed. I. Borowy and W. D. Gruner. Frankfurt am Main: Lang.

Dungey, M. and D. Tambakis. 2005. *Identifying International Financial Contagion: Progress and Challenges*. Oxford University Press.

Duranton, G. and D. Puga. 2004. Micro-Foundations of Urban Agglomeration Economies. In *Handbook of Regional and Urban Economics*, Volume 4, ed. V. Henderson and J.-F. Thisse. Amsterdam: North-Holland.

Easterlin, R. 1968. *Population, Labor Force, and Long Swings in Economic Growth: The American Experience*. New York: National Bureau of Economic Research.

Easterly, W., and R. Levine. 2003. Tropics, Germs, and Crops: How Endowments Influence Economic Development. *Journal of Monetary Economics* 50: 3–39.

Eaton, J. and S. Kortum. 1999. International Technology Diffusion: Theory and Measurement. *International Economic Review* 40: 535–70.

Edelstein, M. 1982. *Overseas Investment in the Age of High Imperialism*. New York: Columbia University Press.

2004. Foreign Investment, Accumulation and Empire, 1860–1914. In *The Cambridge Economic History of Modern Britain*, ed. R. Floud and P. Johnson. Cambridge University Press.

Edwards, J. and M. Nibler. 2000. Corporate Governance in Germany: The Role of Banks and Ownership Concentration. *Economic Policy* 31: 239–67.

Egebo, T. and A. S. Englander. 1992. Institutional Commitments and Policy Credibility: A Critical Survey and Empirical Evidence from the ERM. *OECD Economic Studies* 18: 45–84.

Eichengreen, B. 1992a. Conducting the International Orchestra: Bank of England Leadership Under the Classical Gold Standard, 1880–1913. *Journal of International Money and Finance* 6: 5–29.

1992b. *Golden Fetters: The Gold Standard and the Great Depression 1919–1939*. Oxford University Press.

1992c. The Origins and Nature of the Great Slump Revisited. *Economic History Review* 45: 213–39.

1992d. The Gold Standard since Alec Ford. In Broadberry and Crafts 1992b, 49–79.

1996a. Institutions and Economic Growth. In Crafts and Toniolo 1996b, pp. 38–94.

1996b. *Globalizing Capital: A History of the International Monetary System*. Princeton University Press.

2007. *The European Economy since 1945: Coordinated Capitalism and Beyond*. Princeton University Press.

Eichengreen, B. and M. Flandreau. 1997. *The Gold Standard in Theory and History*. London: Routledge.

Eichengreen, B. and T. Hatton, eds. 1988. *Inter-War Unemployment in International Perspective*. Dordrecht: Kluwer.

Eichengreen, B. and J. Sachs. 1985. Exchange Rates and Economic Recovery in the 1930s. *Journal of Economic History* 45: 925–46.

Eichengreen, B. and P. Temin. 2000. The Gold Standard and the Great Depression. *Contemporary European History* 9: 183–207.

Eichengreen, B. and M. Uzan. 1992. The Marshall Plan: Economic Effects and Implications for Eastern Europe and the Former USSR. *Economic Policy* 14: 13–76.

Einzig, P. 1934. *Germany's Default: The Economics of Hitlerism*. London: Macmillan.
    1937. *The Theory of Forward Exchange*. London: Macmillan.

Ellis, H. 1941. *Exchange Control in Central Europe*. Cambridge University Press.

Eloranta, J. 2002a. European States in the International Arms Trade, 1920–1937: The Impact of External Threats, Market Forces, and Domestic Constraints. *Scandinavian Economic History Review* 50: 44–67.

    2002b. External Security by Domestic Choices: Military Spending as an Impure Public Good Among Eleven European States, 1920–1938. Ph.D dissertation. Department of History and Civilisation. Florence: European University Institute.

    2003. National Defense. In *The Oxford Encyclopedia of Economic History*, ed. J. Mokyr, Oxford University Press, 30–3.

    2007. From the Great Illusion to the Great War: Military Spending Behaviour of the Great Powers, 1870–1913. *European Review of Economic History* 11: 255–83.

Emerson, M. *et al.* 1988. *The Economics of 1992*. Oxford University Press.

Emminger, O. 1977. *The D-Mark in the Conflict between Internal and External Equilibrium*. Essays in International Finance, Princeton University, no. 122.

Emmons, T. and W. S. Vucinich (eds.). 1982. *The Zemstvo in Russia: An Experiment in Local Self-Government*. Cambridge University Press.

Engerman, S. L., and K. L. Sokoloff. 1997. Factor Endowments, Institutions, and Differential Paths of Growth Among New World Economies: A View from Economic Historians of the United States. In *How Latin America Fell Behind*, ed. S. Haber. Stanford University Press, pp. 260–304.

Escurra, R., P. Pascual, and M. Rapún 2006. The Dynamics of Industrial Concentration in the Regions of the European Union. *Growth and Change* 37: 200–29.

Esping-Andersen, G. 1990. *The Three Worlds of Welfare Capitalism*. Reprint, Cambridge: Polity.

Esteban, J. 2000. Regional Convergence in Europe and the Industry Mix: A Shift–Share Analysis. *Regional Science and Urban Economics* 30: 353–64.

Estevadeordal, A., B. Frantz, and A. M. Taylor. 2003. The Rise and Fall of World Trade, 1870–1939. *Quarterly Journal of Economics* 118: 359–407.

Esteves, R. 2007. Between Imperialism and Capitalism. European Capital Exports before 1914. Mimeo, Oxford University.

Esteves, R. and D. Khoudour-Castéras. 2009. A Fantastic Rain of Gold: European Migrants' Remittances and Balance of Payments Adjustment during the Gold Standard Period. *Journal of Economic History* 69: 951–85.

Estrin, S. and P. Holmes. 1983. *French Planning in Theory and Practice*. London: Allen & Unwin.

Etémad, B. 2000. *La possession du monde. Poids et mesures de la colonisation*. Bruxelles: Editions Complexe.

2006. Colonial and European Domestic Trade: A Statistical Perspective Over Time. In *A Deus Ex Machina Revisited: Atlantic Trade and European Economic Development*, ed P. C. Emmer, O. Pétré-Grenouilleau, and J. V. Roitman. Leiden and Boston: Brill.

European Commission. 1995, 1997. *Social Protection in Europe*. Luxembourg: Directorate for Employment, Industrial Relations and Social Affairs.

2002. The Macroeconomic Effects of the Single Market Programme after 10 Years. ec.europa.eu/internal_market/10years/background_en.htm.

Eurostat. *Demographic Yearbook* (2004, 2007). Luxembourg: Eurostat.

Faggio, G. and S. Nickell. 2007. Patterns of Work Across the OECD. *Economic Journal* 117: F416–F440.

Falkus, M. E. 1972. *The Industrialisation of Russia, 1700–1914*. London: Macmillan.

Faron, O and P. George. 1999. Les migrations européennes, de la Grande Guerre à nos jours. In Bardet and Dupâquier. 1999, pp. 323–58.

Fassmann, H. and R. Munz. 1994 *European Migration in the Late Twentieth Century. Historical Patterns, Actual Trends and Social Implications*. Aldershot: Edward Elgar.

Federico, G. 1986. Mercantilizzazione e sviluppo economico in Italia (1860–1940). *Rivista di Storia Economica* 3: 149–86. English translation in *The Economic Development of Italy since 1870*, ed. G. Federico, 1994. Aldershot: Edward Elgar.

2003a. Heights, Calories and Welfare: A New Perspective on Italian Industrialization, 1854–1913. *Economics and Human Biology* 1: 289–308.

2003b. A Capital-Intensive Innovation in a Capital-Scarce World: Steam-Threshing in 19th Century Italy. *Advances in Agricultural Economic History* 2: 75–114.

2004. The Growth of World Agricultural Production, 1800–1938. *Research in Economic History* 22: 125–81.

2005. *Feeding the World: An Economic History of World Agriculture, 1800–2000*. Princeton University Press.

Federico, G. and K. G. Persson. 2007. Market Integration and Convergence in the World Wheat Market, 1800–2000. In *The New Comparative Economic History: Essays in Honor of Jeffrey G. Williamson*, ed. T. J. Hatton, K. H. O'Rourke, and A. M. Taylor. Cambridge, MA: MIT Press, pp. 87–113.

Federico, P. J. 1964. Historical Patent Statistics, 1791–1961. *Journal of the Patent Office Society*, 46: 89–171.

Federn, W. 1910. Das Problem gesetzlicher Aufnahme der Barzahlungen in Österreich-Ungarn. *Schmollers Jahrbuch* 34: 151–72.

Feinstein, C. H. 1972. *National Income, Expenditure and Output of the United Kingdom, 1855–1965*. Cambridge University Press.

1999. Structural Change in the Developed Countries during the Twentieth Century. *Oxford Review of Economic Policy* 15 (4): 35–55.

Feinstein, C. H., ed. 1995. *Banking, Currency, and Finance in Europe between the Wars*. Oxford University Press.

Feinstein, C. H., P. Temin, and G. Toniolo, 1997. *The European Economy between the Wars*. Oxford: Oxford University Press.

Feis, H. 1930. *Europe the World's Banker 1870–1914: An Account of European Foreign Investment and the Connection of World Finance with Diplomacy Before the War*. New Haven: Yale University Press.

Feldman, G. 1993. *The Great Disorder. Politics, Economics, and Society in the German Inflation, 1914–1924*. Oxford University Press.

Feldstein, M., and C. Horioka. 1980. Domestic Saving and International Capital Flows. *Economic Journal* 90: 314–29.

Fenoaltea, S. 1988. International Resource Flows and Construction Movements in the Atlantic Economy: The Kuznets Cycle in Italy, 1861–1913. *Journal of Economic History* 48: 605–37.

2003. Notes on the Rate of Industrial Growth in Italy, 1861–1913. *Journal of Economic History* 63: 695–735.

1999. *The Pity of War. Explaining World War I*. New York: Basic Books.

2001. *The Cash Nexus: Money and Power in the Modern World, 1700–2000*. New York: Basic Books.

2006. *The War of the World: Twentieth-Century Conflict and the Descent of the West*. New York: Penguin.

Ferguson, N., and M. Schularick. 2006. The Empire Effect: The Determinants of Country Risk in the First Age of Globalization, 1880–1913. *Journal of Economic History* 66: 283–312.

Fidrmuc, J. 2003. Economic Reform, Democracy and Growth during Post-Communist Transition. *European Journal of Political Economy* 19: 583–604.

Field, A. J. 2003. The Most Technologically Progressive Decade of the Century. *American Economic Review* 93: 1399–414.

2006. Technical Change and U.S. Economic Growth: The Interwar Period and the 1990s. In *The Global Economy in the 1990s: A Long Run Perspective* (ed. P. Rhode, and G. Toniolo). Cambridge University Press, 89–117.

Findlay, R., and K. H. O'Rourke. 2003. Commodity Market Integration, 1500–2000. In Bordo, Taylor, and Williamson 2003, pp. 13–64.

Findlay, R. and K. H. O'Rourke. 2007. *Power and Plenty: Trade, War, and the World Economy in the Second Millennium*. Princeton University Press.

Fischer, F. 1967. *Germany's Aims in the First World War*. London: Chatto & Windus.

Fischer, S., R. Sahay, and C. A. Vegh. 1998. How Far is Eastern Europe from Brussels? IMF Working Paper **98**/53.

Fisher, J. and A. Hornstein. 2002. The Role of Real Wages, Productivity, and Fiscal Policy in Germany's Great Depression 1928–1937. *Review of Economic Dynamics* 5: 100–27.

Fisher, K. 2000. Uncertain Aims and Tacit Negotiations: Birth Control Practices in Britain, 1925–50. *Population and Development Review* 26: 295–317.

Fishlow, A. 1985. Lessons from the Past: Capital Markets during the 19th Century and the Interwar Period. *International Organization* 39: 383–439.

Flandreau, M. 2003a. *Money Doctors. The Experience of International Financial Advising 1850–2000*. London: Routledge.

2003b. Caveat Emptor: Coping with Sovereign Risk under the International Gold Standard. In *International Financial History in the Twentieth Century: System and Anarchy*, ed. M. Flandreau, C.-L. Holtfrerich, and H. James, Cambridge University Press.

2004. *The Glitter of Gold: France, Bimetallism and the Emergence of the International Gold Standard*. Oxford University Press.

2006. 'Home Biases', 19th Century Style. *Journal of the European Economic Association* 4: 634–43.

Flandreau, M. and C. Jobst. 2005. The Ties that Divide. A Network Analysis of the International Monetary System, 1890–1910. *Journal of Economic History* 65: 977–1007.

Flandreau, M. and J. Flores. 2009. Bonds and Brands: Foundations of Sovereign Debt Markets, 1820–1830. *Journal of Economic History* 69: 646–84.

Flandreau, M. and J. Komlos. 2006. Target Zones in History and Theory: Efficiency, Credibility and Policy Autonomy. *Journal of Monetary Economics* 53: 1979–95.

Flandreau, M., J. Le Cacheux, and F. Zumer. 1998. Stability Without a Pact? Lessons from the European Gold Standard 1880–1913. *Economic Policy*: 117–62.

Flandreau, M. and M. Maurel. 2005. Monetary Union, Trade Integration, and Business Cycles in 19th Century Europe: Just Do It. *Open Economies Review* 16: 135–52.

Flandreau, M. and C. Rivière. 1999. La grande 'retransformation'? Contrôles de capitaux et intégration financière internationale, 1880–1996. *Economie Internationale* 78: 11–58.

Flandreau, M. and N. Sussman. 2005. Old Sins, Exchange Rate Clauses and European Foreign Lending in the 19th Century. In *Other People's Money: Debt Denomination and Financial Instability in Emerging Market Economies*, ed. B. Eichengreen and R. Hausmann. Chicago: University of Chicago Press, 154–89.

Flandreau, M. and F. Zumer. 2004. *The Making of Global Finance, 1880–1913*. Paris: OECD.

Flora, P. 1987. *State, Economy and Society in Western Europe, 1815–1975. A Data Handbook in Two Volumes*, Vol. 2. Frankfurt: Campus; London: Macmillan, New York: St James Press.

Flora, P., ed., 1986. *Growth to Limits: The Western European Welfare States since World War II*, Vol. 4. Berlin: de Gruyter.

Flores, J. 2007. Information Asymmetries and Financial Intermediation during the Baring Crisis: 1880–1890. Working Papers in Economic History, Universidad Carlos III, 07–16.

Fogel, R. 1964. *Railroads and American Economic Growth: Essays in Econometric History*. Baltimore: Johns Hopkins University Press.

1986. Nutrition and the Decline in Mortality since 1700: Some Preliminary Findings. In *Long-Term Factors in American Economic Growth*, ed. S. L. Engerman and R. E. Gallman. Chicago: Chicago University Press, 439–555.

Fohlin, C. 1998. Fiduciari and Firm Liquidity Constraints: The Italian Experience with German-Style Universal Banking. *Explorations in Economic History* 35: 83–107.

Forbes, K. and R. Rigobon. 2002. No Contagion, Only Interdependence: Measuring Stock Market Comovements. *Journal of Finance* 57: 2223–61.

Ford, A. G. 1960. Notes on the Working of the Gold Standard Before 1914. *Oxford Economic Papers* 12: 52–76.

1962. *The Gold Standard 1880–1914: Britain and Argentina*. Oxford: Clarendon.

1981. The Trade Cycle in Britain 1860–1914. In *The Economic History of Britain since 1700*, Vol. 2: 1860 to the 1970s, ed. R. Floud and D. McCloskey. Cambridge University Press, pp. 27–49.

1989. International Financial Policy and the Gold Standard 1870–1914. In *The Cambridge Economic History of Europe*. Cambridge University Press, pp. 197–249.

Foreman-Peck, J. 1983. *History of the World Economy*. Brighton: Harvester Press.

1991. International Technology Transfer in Telephony, 1876–1914. In *International Technology Transfer: Europe, Japan and the USA, 1700–1914*, ed. D. J. Jeremy. Aldershot: Eldward Elgar.

Foreman-Peck, J. and R. Millward. 1994. *Public and Private Ownership of British Industry, 1820–1990*. Oxford: Clarendon.

Førland, T. E. 1993. The History of Economic Warfare: International Law, Effectiveness, Strategies. *Journal of Peace Research* 30: 151–62.

Fourquet, F. 1980. *Les comptes de la puissance. Histoire de la comptabilité nationale et du plan*. Paris: Recherche.

Frader, L. L. 1996. Engendering Work and Wages: The French Labor Movement and the Family Wage. In Frader and Rose 1996, pp. 142–64.

Frader, L. L. and S. O. Rose, eds. 1996. *Gender and Class in Modern Europe*. Ithaca and London: Cornell University Press.

Frankel, J. A. and D. Romer. 1999. Does Trade Cause Growth? *American Economic Review* 89: 379–99.

Fratianni, M. and M. Spinelli. 1997. *A Monetary History of Italy*. Cambridge University Press.

Freeman, C. and L. Soete. 1997. *The Economics of Industrial Innovation*. Third edition. Cambridge, MA: MIT Press.

Freixas, X., P. Hartmann, and C. Mayer. 2004. European Financial Integration. *Oxford Review of Economic Policy* 20: 475–89.

Frieden, J. 2006. *Global Capitalism: Its Fall and Rise in the Twentieth Century*. New York: Norton.

Friedman, M. and A. Schwartz. 1963. *A Monetary History of the United States 1867–1960*. Princeton University Press.

Gadisseur, J. 1973. Contribution à l'étude de la production agricole en Belgique de 1846 à 1913. *Revue Belge d'Histoire Contemporaine* 4: 1–48.

Gadrey, J. and Gallouj, F., eds. 2002. *Productivity, Innovation and Knowledge in Services: New Economic and Socio-Economic Approaches*. Aldershot: Edward Elgar.

Galassi, F. 1986. Stasi e sviluppo nell'agricoltura toscana 1870–1914: primi risultati di uno studio aziendale. *Rivista di Storia Economica* 3: 304–37.

Galassi, F. and J. Cohen. 1994. The Economics of Tenancy in Early Twentieth Century Italy. *Economic History Review* 47: 585–600.

Galley, C. 2006, 'George Newman – A Life in Public Health'. In *Infant Mortality: A Continuing Social Problem*, ed. E. Garrett, C. Galley, N. Shelton, and R. Woods. Aldershot: Ashgate.

García Iglesias, C. 2002. Interest Rate Risk Premium and Monetary Union in the European Periphery: New Lessons from the Gold Standard. *Scandinavian Economic History Review* 50: 31–54.

Gatrell, P. 1986. *The Tsarist Economy, 1850–1917*. London: Batsford.

  2005. Poor Russia, Poor Show: Mobilising a Backward Economy. In Broadberry and Harrison 2005a, pp. 235–75.

Geroski, P. and A. Jacquemin. 1988. The Persistence of Profits: A European Comparison. *Economic Journal* 98: 375–89.

Gerschenkron, A. 1962. *Economic Backwardness in Historical Perspective*. Cambridge, MA: Harvard University Press.

  1966. Agrarian Policies and Industrialisation in Russia, 1861–1917. In *The Cambridge Economic History of Europe*, Volume 6, Part 2, ed. M. M. Postan and H. J. Habakkuk. Cambridge University Press, pp. 706–16, 763–7.

Giavazzi, F. and M. Pagano. 1988. The Advantage of Tying One's Hands: EMS Discipline and Central Bank Credibility. *European Economic Review* 32: 1055–75.

Giersch, H., ed., 1994. *Economic Aspects of International Migration*. Berlin: Springer.

Gillingham, J. 1995. The European Coal and Steel Community: An Object Lesson? In *Europe's Postwar Recovery*, ed. B. Eichengreen. Cambridge University Press, pp. 151–68.

  2003. *European Integration 1950–2003: Superstate or New Market Economy?* Cambridge University Press.

Goetzmann, W. and A. Ukhov. 2006. British Overseas Investment 1870–1913: A Modern Portfolio Theory Approach. *Review of Finance* 10: 261–300.

Goldin, C. and Katz, L. F. 1998. The Origins of Technology–Skills Complementarity. *Quarterly Journal of Economics* 113: 693–732.

Goldsmith, R. W. 1961. The Economic Growth of Tsarist Russia, 1860–1913. *Economic Development and Cultural Change* 9: 441–75.

  1985. *Comparative National Balance Sheets: A Study of Twenty Countries, 1688–1978*. Chicago: University of Chicago Press.

Good, D. F. 1978. The Great Depression and Austrian Growth after 1873. *Economic History Review* 31: 290–4.

  1984. *The Economic Rise of the Habsburg Empire, 1750–1914*. Berkeley: University of California Press.

Goodhart, C. 2003. The Historical Pattern of Economic Cycles and Their Interaction with Asset Prices and Financial Regulation. In W. Hunter *et al.* (eds.), *Asset Price Bubbles*. Cambridge, MA.: MIT Press, pp. 467–80.

Gordon, R. J. 1997. Is There a Tradeoff between Unemployment and Productivity Growth? In *Unemployment Policy: Government Options for the Labour Market*, ed. D. Snower and G. de la Dehesa. Cambridge University Press, pp. 433–63.

  2004a. Two Centuries of Economic Growth: Europe Chasing the American Frontier. CEPR Discussion Paper 4415.

2004b. Why was Europe Left at the Station when America's Productivity Locomotive Departed? CEPR Discussion Paper 4416.

2006. The Slowdown in European Productivity Growth: A Tale of Tigers, Tortoises and Textbook Labor Economics. Paper presented at NBER Summer Institute, Macroeconomics and Productivity Workshop, Cambridge, MA, July 20.

Gordon, R. J. and I. Dew-Becker. 2008. The Role of Labour Market Changes in the Slowdown of European Productivity Growth. CEPR Discussion Paper 6722.

Goubert, J.-P. (1988). The Development of Water and Sewerage Systems in France, 1850–1950. In *Technology and the Rise of the Networked City in Europe and America* (Philadelphia: Temple University Press), pp. 116–36.

Gould, J. 1979. European Inter-Continental Emigration, 1815–1914: Patterns and Causes. *Journal of European Economic History* 8: 593–679.

Grantham, G. 1989. Agricultural Supply During the Industrial Revolution: French Evidence and European Implications. *Journal of Economic History* 49: 43–72.

Greasley, D. 1990. Fifty Years of Coalmining Productivity: The Record of the British Coal Industry before 1939. *Journal of Economic History* 50: 877–902.

Gregory, P. R. 1982. *Russia's National Income, 1885–1913.* Cambridge University Press.

1994. *Before Command: An Economic History of Russia from Emancipation to the First Five-Year Plan.* Princeton University Press.

Griffith, R. and R. Harrison. 2004. The Link between Product Market Regulation and Macroeconomic Performance. European Commission Economic Papers 209.

Griffith, R., R. Harrison, and H. Simpson. 2006. Product Market Reform and Innovation in the EU. IFS Working Paper 06/17.

Groningen Growth and Development Centre (GGDC). 2007. *Total Economy Database.*

Gros, D. and N. Thygesen. 1992. *European Monetary Integration. From the EMS to the EMU.* London: Longman.

Guinnane, T. W. 2002. Delegated Monitors, Large and Small: Germany's Banking System, 1800–1914. *Journal of Economic Literature* 40: 73–124.

2003. Population and the Economy in Germany, 1800–1990. In *Germany. A New Social and Economic History, Vol 3: Since 1800*, ed. S. Ogilvie and R. Overy. London: Arnold, pp. 35–70.

Gust, C. and J. Marquez. 2004. International Comparisons of Productivity Growth: The Role of Information Technology and Regulatory Practices. *Labour Economics* 11: 33–58.

Guttormson, L. 2002. Parent–Child Relations. In *The History of the European Family*, Vol. 2, Family Life in the Long Nineteenth Century, 1789–1913, ed. D. Kertzer and M. Barbagli. London: Yale University Press, pp. 251–81.

Gwartney, J. D. and R. A. Lawson. 2006. *Economic Freedom of the World: 2006 Annual Report.* Vancouver: Fraser Institute.

Haas, E. B. 1958. *The Uniting of Europe: Political, Social and Economic Forces, 1950–1957.* Stanford University Press.

Habakkuk, H. J. 1962. *American and British Technology in the Nineteenth Century.* Cambridge University Press.

Hajnal, J. 1965. European Marriage Patterns in Perspective. In *Population in History: Essays in Historical Demography*, ed. D. Glass and D. Everett. London: Arnold, pp. 101–43.

Hall, R. E., and C. I. Jones. 1999. Why Do Some Countries Produce So Much More Output Per Worker than Others? *Quarterly Journal of Economics* 114: 83–116.

Hannah, L. 1983. *The Rise of the Corporate Economy*. Second edition. London: Methuen.

Hansen, S. A. 1974. *Økonomisk Vaekst i Danmark*, Vol. II: 1914–1970. Copenhagen: University of Copenhagen.

Harris, B. 1998. The Height of Schoolchildren in Britain, 1900–1950. In *Stature, Living Standards, and Economic Development: Essays in Anthropometric History*, ed. J. Komlos. Chicago: University of Chicago Press, 25–38.

Harrison, M. 1996. *Accounting for War: Soviet Production, Employment, and the Defence Burden, 1940–1945*. Cambridge University Press.

Harrison, M. (ed.) 1998a. *The Economics of World War II. Six Great Powers in International Comparisons*. Cambridge University Press.

Harrison, M. 1998b. The Economics of World War II: An Overview. In Harrison 1998a, pp. 1–42.

1998c. Trends in Soviet Labour Productivity, 1928–85: War, Postwar Recovery, and Slowdown. *European Review of Economic History* 2: 171–200.

2002. Coercion, Compliance, and the Collapse of the Soviet Command Economy. *Economic History Review* 55: 397–433.

2003. Counting Soviet Deaths in the Great Patriotic War: Comment. *Europe–Asia Studies* 55, 939–44.

Hatton, T. 1988. Institutional Change and Wage Rigidity in the UK, 1880–1985. *Oxford Review of Economic Policy* 4: 74–86.

Hatton, T. J. and J. G. Williamson. 1998. *The Age of Mass Migration: An Economic Analysis*. Oxford University Press.

2005. *Global Migration and the World Economy: Two Centuries of Policy and Performance*. Cambridge, MA: MIT Press.

Hautcoeur, P.-C., and P. Sicsic. 1999. Threat of a Capital Levy, Expected Devaluation, and Interest Rates in France During the Interwar Period. *European Review of Economic History* 3: 25–56.

Hayami, Y. and V. W. Ruttan. 1971. *Agricultural Development. An International Perspective*. Baltimore: The Johns Hopkins Press.

Heikkinen, S. 1997. *Labour and the Market. Workers, Wages and Living Standards in Finland, 1850–1913*. Helsinki: Finnish Society of Sciences and Letters.

Henrekson, M., J. Torstensson, and R. Torstensson. 1997. Growth Effects of European Integration. *European Economic Review* 41: 1537–57.

Heritage Foundation. 2009. Index of Economic Freedom. www.heritage.org/index/.

Herranz-Loncán, A. 2006. Railroad Impact in Backward Economies: Spain, 1850–1913. *Journal of Economic History* 66: 853–81.

Hjerppe, R. 1996. *Finland's Historical National Accounts 1860–1994. Calculation Methods and Statistical Tables*. Jyväskylä: Kivirauma.

Hjerppe, R. and J. Jalava. 2006. Economic Growth and Structural Change – A Century and a Half of Catching-up. In *The Road to Prosperity. An Economic History of Finland*, ed. J. Ojala, J. Eloranta, and J. Jalava. Helsinki: SKS, pp. 33–64.

HM Treasury. 2001. *Reforming Britain's Economic and Financial Policy: Towards Greater Economic Stability*, ed. E. Balls and G. O'Donnell. London: Palgrave Macmillan.

2003. *EMU and Trade*. www.hm-treasury.gov.uk/media/721/27/adsuf03_456.pdf.

Hobsbawm, E. J. 1996. *The Age of Extremes: A History of the World, 1914–1991*. New York: Vintage Books.

Hobson, J. M. 1993. The Military-Extraction Gap and the Wary Titan: The Fiscal Sociology of British Defence Policy 1870–1914. *Journal of European Economic History* 22: 466–507.

Hoch, S. L. 1994. On Good Numbers and Bad: Malthus, Population Trends and Peasant Standard of Living in Late Imperial Russia. *Slavic Review* 53: 41–75.

Hodrick, R. J. and E. C. Prescott. 1997. Postwar US Business Cycles: An Empirical Investigation. *Journal of Money Credit and Banking* 29: 1–16.

Hoffmann, W. G. 1965. *Das Wachstum der deutschen Wirtschaft seit der Mitte des 19. Jahrhunderts*. Berlin: Springer-Verlag.

Hoj, J., M. Jimenez, M. Maher, G. Nicoletti, and M. Wise. 2007. Product Market Competition in OECD Countries: Taking Stock and Moving Forward. OECD Economics Department Working Paper 575.

Holtfrerich, C.-L. 1986. *The German Inflation*. New York: de Gruyter.

Holtfrerich, K. L. 1999. Monetary Policy under Fixed Exchange Rates (1948–1970). In *Fifty Years of the Deutsche Mark: Central Bank and the Currency in Germany since 1948*, ed. Deutsche Bundesbank. Oxford University Press, 307–401.

Honeyman, K. and J. Goodman. 1991. Women's Work, Gender Conflict, and Labour Markets in Europe, 1500–1900. *Economic History Review* 44: 608–28.

Houben, A. C. F. 2000. *The Evolution of Monetary Policy Strategies in Europe*. Dordrecht: Kluwer.

Hu, M. Y., C. X. Jiang, and C. Tsoukalas. 2004. The Volatility Impact of the European Monetary System on Member and Non-member Currencies. *Applied Financial Economics* 14: 313–25.

Huberman, M. 2004. Working Hours of the World Unite? New International Evidence of Worktime, 1870–1913. *Journal of Economic History* 64: 964–1001.

2008. A Ticket to Trade: Belgian Workers and Globalization before 1914. *Economic History Review* 61: 326–59.

Huberman, M. and W. Lewchuk. 2003. European Economic Integration and the Labour Compact, 1850–1913. *European Review of Economic History* 7: 3–41.

Huberman, M. and C. Minns. 2007. The Times They Are Not Changin': Days and Hours of Work in Old and New Worlds, 1870–2000. *Explorations in Economic History* 44: 538–67.

Huffman, W. and J. Lothian. 1984. The Gold Standard and the Transmission of Business Cycles, 1833–1932. In *A Retrospective on the Classical Gold Standard, 1821–1931*, ed. M. D. Bordo and A. Schwartz. Chicago: University of Chicago Press, 455–511.

Huntington, S. P. 1996. *The Clash of Civilizations and the Remaking of World Order.* New York: Simon & Schuster.

Hutchings, R. 1969. *Periodic Fluctuation in Soviet Industrial Growth Rates. Soviet Studies* 20: 331–52.

Imlah, A. H. 1952. British Balance of Payments and Export of Capital, 1816–1913. *Economic History Review* 5: 208–39.

Ingersent, K. A., and A. J. Rayner. 1999. *Agricultural Policy in Western Europe and the United States.* Cheltenham: Edward Elgar.

Inklaar, R. and J. de Haan. 2001. Is There Really a European Business Cycle? *Oxford Economic Papers* 53: 215–20.

Iradian, G. 2007. Rapid Growth in Transition Economies: Growth Accounting Approach. IMF Working Paper 07/164.

Jacks, D. S. 2005. Intra- and International Commodity Market Integration in the Atlantic Economy, 1800–1913. *Explorations in Economic History* 42: 381–413.

2006. What Drove 19th Century Commodity Market Integration? *Explorations in Economic History* 43: 383–412.

Jaeger, A. and L. Schuknecht. 2004. Boom–Bust Phases in Asset Prices and Fiscal Policy Behavior. IMF Working Paper WP/04/54.

James, H. 1985. *The Reichsbank and Public Finance in Germany, 1924–1933: A Study of the Politics of Economics during the Great Depression.* Frankfurt am Main: Knapp.

1986. *The German Slump: Politics and Economics, 1924–1936.* Oxford: Clarendon.

1996. *International Monetary Cooperation since Bretton Woods.* Washington: IMF.

2000. *The End of Globalization: Lessons from the Great Depression.* Cambridge, MA: Harvard University Press.

Janossy, F. 1969. *The End of the Economic Miracle.* White Plains, NY: IASP.

Janssens, A. 1997. The Rise and Decline of the Male Breadwinner Family. A Review of the Debate. *International Review of Social History* 42, Supplement: 1–23.

2003. Economic Transformation, Women's Work and Family Life. In *Family Life in the Twentieth Century. The History of the European Family,* ed. D. Kertzer and M. Barbagli, Vol. 3. London: Yale University Press, pp. 55–110.

Jeremy, D. J., ed. 1991. *International Technology Transfer: Europe, Japan and the USA, 1700–1914.* Aldershot: Edward Elgar.

Jerome, H. 1926. *Migration and Business Cycles.* New York: NBER.

Jerzmanowski, M. 2007. Total Factor Productivity Differences: Appropriate Technology vs. Efficiency. *European Economic Review* 51: 2080–110.

Jobst, C. 2009. Market Leader: The Austro-Hungarian Bank and the Making of Foreign Exchange Intervention, 1896–1913. *European Review of Economic History* 13: 287–318.

Johnson, P. 1997. Fiscal Implications of Population Ageing. *Philosophical Transactions: Biological Sciences* 352: 1895–903.

1999. Welfare States. In Schulze 1999, pp. 122–39.

Jolly, R., L. Emmerij, and T. G. Weiss. 2005. *The Power of UN Ideas. Lessons from the First 60 Years.* New York: United Nations Intellectual History Project.

Jones, M. T. and M. Obstfeld. 2001. Saving, Investment, and Gold: A Reassessment of Historical Current Account Data. In *Money, Capital Mobility, and Trade: Essays in Honor of Robert A. Mundell*, ed. G. A. Calvo, M. Obstfeld, and R. Dornbusch. Cambridge, MA: MIT Press.

Jonung L., L. Schicknecht, and M. Tujula. 2005. The Boom–Bust Cycle in Finland and Sweden 1984–1995 in an International Perspective. European Economy Economic Papers no. 237.

Joslin, D. 1963. *A Century of Banking in Latin America*. Oxford University Press.

Juglar, C. 1862. *Des crises commerciales et de leur retour périodique en France, en Angleterre et aux Etats-Unis*. Paris: Guillaumin.

Juuti, P. S. and T. S. Katko. 2005. Water, Time and European Cities. History Matters for the Futures. http://www.watertime.net/Docs/WP3/WTEC.pdf.

Kaminsky, G. and C. Reinhart. 2000. On Crises, Contagion, and Confusion. *Journal of International Economics* 51: 145–68.

Kaminsky, G., C. Reinhart, and C. Végh. 2003. The Unholy Trinity of Financial Contagion. *Journal of Economic Perspectives* 17: 51–74.

Kaufmann, D., A. Kraay and M. Mastruzzi. 2007. Governance Matters VI: Aggregate and Individual Governance Indicators 1996–2006. World Bank Policy Research Working Paper 4280.

Kay, A. J. 2006. *Exploitation, Resettlement, Mass Murder: Political and Economic Planning for German Occupation Policy in the Soviet Union, 1940–1941*. New York: Berghahn Books.

Keegan, J. 1999. *The First World War*. London: Hutchinson.

Kennedy, P. 1989. *The Rise and Fall of the Great Powers. Economic Change and Military Conflict from 1500 to 2000*. London: Fontana.

Kenwood, A. and A Lougheed. 1992. *The Growth of the International Economy, 1820–1990*. London: Routledge.

Khan, Z. 2005. *The Democratization of Invention: Patents and Copyrights in American Economic Development, 1790–1920*. Cambridge University Press.

Khoudour-Castéras, D. 2002. Taux de changes fixes et migrations internationales: l'étalon-or à l'aune de la théorie des zones monétaires optimales. *Revue de l'OFCE* 82: 82–116.

    2005. International Adjustment during the Classical Gold Standard: The Migration Nexus. Working Paper, Chaire Finances Internationales, Sciences Po.

Kindleberger, C. P. 1964. *Economic Growth in France and Britain, 1851–1950*. Cambridge, MA: Harvard University Press.

    1973. *The World in Depression, 1929–1939*. London: Allen Lane.

    1985. *Keynesianism vs. Monetarism and Other Essays in Financial History*. London: George Allen & Unwin.

    1987. *International Capital Movements*. Based on the Marshall lectures given at the University of Cambridge. Cambridge University Press.

    1989. Commercial Policy Between the Wars. In *The Cambridge Economic History of Europe*, Vol. 8, ed. P. Mathias and S. Pollard. Cambridge University Press, pp. 161–96.

Kintner, H. J. 1985. Trends and Regional Differences in Breastfeeding in Germany from 1871 to 1937. *Journal of Family History* 10: 163–82.

Kirk, D. 1946. *Europe's Population in the Interwar Years*. New York, London, and Paris: Gordon and Breach Science Publishers.

Kirkaldy, A. W. [1914] 1973. *British Shipping: Its History, Organisation and Importance*. New York: Augustus Kelly Reprints.

Klug, A. 1993. *The German Buybacks 1932–1939: A Cure for Overhang?* Princeton University Press.

Kneller, R., M. Bleaney, and N. Gemmell. 1999. Fiscal Policy and Growth: Evidence from OECD Countries. *Journal of Public Economics* 74: 171–90.

Komlos, J. 1978. Is the Depression in Austria after 1873 a 'Myth'? *Economic History Review* 31: 287–9.

     1983. *The Habsburg Monarchy as a Customs Union: Economic Development in Austria–Hungary in the Nineteenth Century*. Princeton University Press.

     1985. Stature and Nutrition in the Habsburg Monarchy: The Standard of Living and Economic Development in the Eighteenth Century. *American Historical Review* 90: 1149–61.

Komlos J. and Baten J., eds. 2004. *Social Science History – Special Journal Issue on Anthropometric History*. Vol. 28–2. Durham, N.C.: Duke University Press.

Kondratiev, N. 1926. Die langen Wellen der Konjunktur. *Archiv für Sozialwissenschaft und Sozialpolitik* 56: 573–609.

Kontorovich, V. 1990. Utilization of Fixed Capital and Soviet Industrial Growth. *Economics of Planning* 23: 37–50.

Kornai, J. 1992. *The Socialist System: The Political Economy of Communism*. Oxford: Clarendon.

Krantz, O. 1987. Schweden, Norwegen, Danemark, Finnland, 1914–1970. In *Handbuch der Europäischen Wirtschafts- und Sozialgeschichte*, ed. W. Fischer, J. A. van Houtte, H. Kellenbenz, I. Miek, and F. Vittinghoff, Vol. 6. Stuttgart: Klett-Cotta, pp. 222–93.

     1988. New Estimates of Swedish Historical GDP since the Beginning of the Nineteenth Century. *Review of Income and Wealth* 34: 165–82.

Krantz, O. and L. Schön. 2007. Swedish Historical National Accounts, 1800–2000. Lund University Macroeconomic and Demographic Database, www.ehl.lu.se/database/LU-MADD/National%20Accounts/default.htm.

Krause, K. 1992. *Arms and the State: Patterns of Military Production and Trade*. Cambridge University Press.

Krause, K. and M. K. MacDonald. 1993. Regulating Arms Sales Through World War II. In *Encyclopedia of Arms Control and Disarmament*, Vol. 2, ed. R. D. Burns. New York: Charles Scribner's Sons.

Krugman, P. 1991a. Target Zones and Exchange Rate Dynamics. *Quarterly Journal of Economics* 106: 669–82.

     1991b. *Geography and Trade*. Cambridge, MA: MIT Press.

     1993. Lessons of Massachusetts for EMU. In *The Transition to Economic and Monetary Union*, ed. F. Giavazzi and F. Torres. Cambridge University Press, 241–69.

Krugman, P. R. and A. J. Venables. 1995. Globalization and the Inequality of Nations. *Quarterly Journal of Economics* 110: 857–80.

Kulischer, E. M. 1948. *Europe on the Move: War and Population Changes 1917–47.* New York: Columbia University Press.

Kuznets, S. 1961. *Capital in the American Economy.* Princeton University Press.

1958. Long Swings in the Growth of Population and in Related Economic Variables. *Proceedings of the American Philosophical Society* 102: 25–52.

Kydland, F. and E. Prescott. 1982. Time to Build and Aggregate Fluctuations. *Econometrica* 50: 1345–70.

Kynaston, D. 1995. *The City of London,* Vol. 2: *Golden Years, 1890–1914.* London: Pimlico.

Lains, P. 1995. *A economia portuguesa no século XIX. Crescimento económico e comércio externo, 1851–1913.* Lisbon: Imprensa Nacional (French edn. L'Harmattan, 1999).

2003. *Os progressos do atraso. Uma nova história económica de Portugal.* Lisbon: Imprensa de Ciências Sociais.

2006. Growth in a Protected Environment: Portugal, 1850–1950. Unpublished paper, University of Lisbon.

Lains, P. and V. Pinilla, eds. 2008. *Agriculture and Economic Development in Europe Since 1870.* London: Routledge.

Landes, D. S. 1969. *The Unbound Prometheus: Technological Change and Industrial Development in Western Europe from 1750 to the Present.* Cambridge University Press.

La Vecchia, C., F. Levi, F. Lucchini, and E. Negri. 1998. Trends in Mortality from Major Diseases in Europe, 1980–1993. *European Journal of Epidemiology* 14: 1–8.

Layard, R. 2003. Happiness: Has Social Science a Clue? Lionel Robbins Memorial Lectures 2002/3, London School of Economics.

League of Nations. 1931. *Statistical Yearbook of the League of Nations 1931/32.* Geneva: League of Nations.

1940. *Statistical Yearbook of the League of Nations 1939/40.* Geneva: League of Nations.

Leaman, J. 2001. *The Bundesbank Myth: Towards a Critique of Central Bank Independence.* New York: Palgrave.

Lee, S. J. 1987. *The European Dictatorships, 1918–1945.* London: Methuen.

Leibenstein, H. 1966. Allocative Efficiency Versus X-Efficiency. *American Economic Review* 56: 392–415.

Lenin, V. I. 1963 (original edition 1916). Imperialism, the Highest Stage of Capitalism. In *Selected Works,* Vol. 1. Moscow: Progress, pp. 667–766.

Leonard, C. S. 2009. *Agrarian Reform in Russia: The Road from Serfdom.* Cambridge University Press.

Lévy-Leboyer, M. 1979. L'héritage de Simiand: prix, profit et termes d'échange au XIXe siècle. *Revue Historique* 243: 77–120.

Lévy-Leboyer, M. and F. Bourgignon. 1990. *The French Economy in the Nineteenth Century: An Essay in Econometric Analysis.* Cambridge University Press.

Liberman, P. 1996. *Does Conquest Pay? The Exploitation of Occupied Industrial Societies.* Princeton University Press.

Lindert, P. H. 1969. Key Currencies and Gold, 1900–1913. Princeton Studies in International Finance 24. International Section, Department of Economics, Princeton University.

　　2004. *Growing Public: Social Spending and Economic Growth Since the Eighteenth Century*. Cambridge University Press.

Link, W. 1970. *Die amerikanische Stabilisierungspolitik in Deutschland 1921–32*. Düsseldorf: Droste.

Linz, J. J. 2000. *Totalitarian and Authoritarian Regimes*. Boulder, CO: Lynne Rienner Publishers.

Little, I. M. D., T. Scitovsky, and M. Scott 1970. *Industry and Trade in Some Developing Countries*. Oxford University Press.

Ljungberg, J. 1997. The Impact of the Great Emigration on the Swedish Economy. *Scandinavian Economic History Review* 45: 159–89.

Lokshin, E. Y. 1964. *Promyshlennost SSSR: Ocherk istorii 1964–1963*. Moscow: Mysl', 1964.

López-Córdova, J. E. and C. M. Meissner. 2003. Exchange-Rate Regimes and International Trade: Evidence from the Classical Gold Standard Era. *American Economic Review* 93: 344–353.

Lucas, R. E. 1990. Why Doesn't Capital Flow from Rich to Poor Countries? *American Economic Review* 80: 92–6.

　　2000. Some Macroeconomics for the 21st Century. *Journal of Economic Perspectives* 14(1): 159–78.

McCloskey, D. N. 1971. International Differences in Productivity? Coal and Steel in America and Britain Before World War I. In *Essays on a Mature Economy: Britain After 1840*, ed. D. N. McCloskey. London: Methuen, 285–304.

McCloskey, D. and J. R. Zecher. 1976. How the Gold Standard Worked, 1880–1913. In *The Monetary Approach to the Balance of Payments* J. A. Frenkel and H. G. Johnson, ed. London: Allen and Unwin, pp. 357–85.

　　1984. The Success of Purchasing Power Parity: Historical Evidence and Its Implications for Macroeconomics. In *A Retrospective on the Classical Gold Standard 1821–1931*, ed. M. Bordo and A. J. Schwartz. Chicago: NBER, University of Chicago Press, pp. 121–50.

McKeown, T. 1976. *The Modern Rise of Population*. London: Arnold.

McNeill, W. H. 1982. *The Pursuit of Power. Technology, Armed Force, and Society since A.D. 1000*. Chicago: University of Chicago Press.

Maddison, A. 1960. The Postwar Business Cycle in Western Europe and the Role of Government Policy. *Banca Nazionale del Lavoro Quarterly Review*, June, 100–48.

　　1982. *Phases of Capitalist Development*. Oxford University Press.

　　1987. Growth and Slowdown in Advanced Capitalist Economies: Techniques of Quantitative Assessment. *Journal of Economic Literature* 25: 649–98.

　　1989. *The World Economy in the 20th Century*. Paris: OECD.

　　1991. *Dynamic Forces in Capitalist Development. A Long-Run Comparative View*. Oxford University Press.

　　1995. *Monitoring the World Economy 1820–1992*. Paris: OECD.

　　2001. *The World Economy: A Millennial Perspective*. Paris: OECD.

2003. *The World Economy. Historical Statistics.* Paris: OECD.

2007. *Historical Statistics for the World Economy: 1–2003 AD.* www.ggdc.net/maddison/.

Madsen, J. B. 2007. Technology Spillover through Trade and TFP Convergence: 135 Years of Evidence for the OECD Countries. *Journal of International Economics* 72: 464–80.

Maizels, A. 1965. *Industrial Growth and World Trade.* Cambridge University Press.

Malanima, P. 2003. Measuring the Italian Economy, 1300–1861. *Rivista di Storia Economica* 19: 265–95.

2006a. Alle origini della crescita in Italia, 1820–1913. *Rivista di Storia Economica* 22: 307–30.

2006b. An Age of Decline. Product and Income in Eighteenth–Nineteenth Century Italy. *Rivista di Storia Economica* 22: 91–133.

Mankiw, N., D. Romer, and D. N. Weil. 1992. A Contribution to the Empirics of Economic Growth. *Quarterly Journal of Economics* 107: 407–37.

Marsh, D. 1992. *The Bundesbank. The Bank that Rules Europe.* London: Heinemann.

Marshall, A. [1920] 1977. *Principles of Economics.* Eighth edition. London: Macmillan Reprint.

Marston, R. C. 1995. *International Financial Integration.* Cambridge University Press.

Martínez-Galarraga, J. 2007. New Estimates of Regional GDP in Spain, 1860–1930. Paper presented to Workshop on Historical Economic Geography of Europe, 1900–2000, Madrid.

Mášová, H. and P. Svobodný. 2005. Health and Health Care in Czechoslovakia 1918–38: From Infectious to Civilization Diseases. In *Facing Illness in Troubled Times: Health in Europe in the Inter-War Years*, ed. I. Borowy and W. O. Grunes. Frankfurt am Main: Lang, 165–206.

Matthews, R. C. O. 1968. Why has Britain Had Full Employment Since the War? *Economic Journal* 78: 555–69.

Matthews, R. C. O., C. H. Feinstein, and J. Odling-Smee. 1982. *British Economic Growth, 1856–1973.* Oxford University Press.

Mauro, P. 1995. Corruption and Growth. *Quarterly Journal of Economics* 110: 681–712.

Mauro, P., N. Sussman, and Y. Yafeh. 2002. Emerging Market Spreads: Then Versus Now. *Quarterly Journal of Economics* 117: 695–733.

2006. *Emerging Markets and Financial Globalization: Sovereign Bond Spreads in 1870–1913 and Today.* Oxford University Press.

Mellor, J. W. 1995. Introduction to *Agriculture on the Road to Industrialization*, ed. J. W. Mellor. Baltimore: Johns Hopkins University Press, pp.1–22.

Mesle, F. 2004. Mortality in Central and Eastern Europe: Long-term Trends and Recent Upturns. *Demographic Research*, Special Collection 2–Article 3. www.demographic-research.org/special/2/3/.

Mesle, F. and J. Vallin. 2002. Mortality in Europe: The Divergence Between East and West. *Population* 57: 157–97.

Metzer, J. 1974. Railroad Development and Market Integration: The Case of Tsarist Russia. *Journal of Economic History* 34: 529–550.

Michaely, M. 1971. *The Responsiveness of Demand Policies to Balance of Payments: Postwar Patterns*. New York: Columbia University Press.

Millett, A. R., W. Murray, and K. H. Watman. 1988. The Effectiveness of Military Organizations. In *Military Effectiveness*, Volume 1: *The First World War*, ed. A. R. Millett and W. Murray. Boston: Unwin Hyman.

Mills, T. C. and N. Crafts. 2000. After the Golden Age: A Long-Run Perspective on Growth Rates that Speeded Up, Slowed Down and Still Differ. *The Manchester School* 68: 68–91.

Millward, R. 1999. Industrial Performance, the Infrastructure and Government Policy. In *The British Industrial Decline*, ed. J Dormois, and M. Dintenfass. London: Routledge, 47–64.

   2005. *Private and Public Enterprise in Europe: Energy, Telecommunications and Transport, 1830–1990*. Cambridge University Press.

Millward, R. and F. Bell. 2001. Infant Mortality in Victorian Britain: The Mother as Medium. *Economic History Review* 54: 699–733.

Milward, A. S. 1965. *The German Economy at War*. London: Athlone Press.

   1992. *The European Rescue of the Nation State*. Berkeley: University of California Press.

Milward, A. S. and S. B. Saul. 1977. *The Development of the Economies of Continental Europe, 1850–1914*. London: Allen & Unwin.

Mironov, B. N. 1999a. *A Social History of Imperial Russia, 1700–1917*. Boulder: Westview Press.

   1999b. New Approaches to Old Problems: The Well-Being of the Population of Russia from 1821 to 1910 as Measured by Physical Stature. *Slavic Review* 58: 1–26.

Mitchell, B. R. 1976. Statistical Appendix. In *The Fontana Economic History of Europe: Contemporary Economies: Part Two*, ed. C. M. Cipolla. Glasgow: Collins/Fontana, 648–55.

   1988. *British Historical Statistics*. Cambridge University Press.

   2003. *International Historical Statistics: Europe, 1750–2000*. London: Macmillan.

Mitchell, D. and J. Bradshaw. 1992. *Lone Parents and Their Incomes: A Comparative Study of Ten Countries*. York.

Mitchener, K. J. and M. Weidenmier. 2007. *Trade and Empire*. Mimeo, Santa Clara University and Claremont McKenna College.

Modelski, G. and W. R. Thompson. 1996. *Leading Sectors and World Powers. The Coevolution of Global Politics and Economics*. Columbia, SC: University of South Carolina Press.

Moggridge, D. 1969. *The Return to Gold 1925: The Formulation of Economic Policy and its Critics*. Cambridge University Press.

Mokyr, J. 2000, Why "More Work for Mother?" Knowledge and Household Behavior, 1870–1945. *Journal of Economic History*, 60: 1–41.

   2002. *The Gifts of Athena. The Historical Origins of the Knowledge Economy*. Princeton University Press.

Molle, W. 1980. *Regional Disparity and Economic Development in the European Community*. Farnborough: Saxon House.

Moravcsik, A. 1998. *The Choice for Europe*. Ithaca and London: Cornell University Press.

Morel, M-F 1991. The Care of Children: The Influence of Medical Innovation and Medical Institutions on Infant Mortality, 1750–1914. In Schofield, Reher, and Bideau. 1991, pp. 196–219.

Morgenstern, O. 1959. *International Financial Transactions and Business Cycles*. Princeton University Press.

Morys, M. 2006. The Classical Gold Standard in the European Periphery: A Case Study of Austria–Hungary and Italy, 1870–1913. PhD thesis, London School of Economics and Political Science.

Moser, P. 2005. How Do Patent Laws Influence Innovation? Evidence from Nineteenth-Century World Fairs. *The American Economic Review*, 95: 1214–36.

Moser, T. 2003. What Is International Financial Contagion? *International Finance* 6: 157–78.

Mouré, K. 1991. *Managing the Franc Poincaré: Economic Understanding and Political Constraints in French Monetary Policy*. Cambridge University Press.

2002. *The Gold Standard Illusion: France, the Bank of France, and the International Gold Standard 1914–1939*. Oxford University Press.

Mundell, R. 1961. A Theory of Optimum Currency Areas. *American Economic Review* 51: 657–65.

Munting, R. and B. Holderness. 1991. *Crisis, Recovery, and War: An Economic History of Continental Europe, 1918–1945*. London: Philip Allan.

Myrdal, G. 1970. *The Challenge of World Poverty*. New York: Kingsport Press.

Neal, L. 2007. *The Economics of Europe and the European Union*. Cambridge University Press.

Nelson, R. R. and G. Wright. 1992. The Rise and Fall of American Technological Leadership: The Postwar Era in Historical Perspective. *Journal of Economic Literature* 30: 1931–64.

Newman, G. 1906. *Infant Mortality. A Social Problem*. London: Methuen.

Nickell, S. 2005. What Has Happened to Unemployment in the OECD since the 1980s? Unpublished presentation to Work and Pensions Economics Group, HM Treasury.

Nickell, S., D. Nicolitsas, and N. Dryden. 1997. What Makes Firms Perform Well? *European Economic Review* 41: 783–96.

Nickell, S. and J. van Ours. 2000. The Netherlands and the UK: a European Unemployment Miracle? *Economic Policy* 30: 135–75.

Nicolau, R. 2005. Población, salud y actividad. In *Estadística histórica de España, siglos XIX–XX*, ed. A. Carreras and X. Tafunell, Bilbao: Fundación BBVA, 77–154.

Nicoletti, G. and S. Scarpetta. 2005. Regulation and Economic Performance: Product Market Reforms and Productivity in the OECD. OECD Economics Department Working Paper 460.

Nordhaus, W. D. 1972. The Recent Productivity Slowdown. *Brookings Papers on Economic Activity* 3: 493–531.

Nolte, E. 1965. *Three Faces of Fascism; Action Française, Italian Fascism, National Socialism*. London: Weidenfeld and Nicolson.

Nordhaus, W. D. 1994. Policy Games: Coordination and Independence in Monetary and Fiscal Policies. *Brookings Papers on Economic Activity* 25: 139–216.

Norrbin, S. and P. Yigit. 2005. The Robustness of the Link between Volatility and Growth of Output. *Review of World Economics* 144: 343–56.

North, D. C. 1990. *Institutions, Institutional Change and Economic Performance.* Cambridge University Press.

Nurkse, R. 1944. *International Currency Experience: Lessons of the Inter-War Period.* Princeton: League of Nations.

    1954. International Investment To-Day in the Light of Nineteenth-Century Experience. *Economic Journal* 64: 744–58.

O'Brien, P. K. 1983. Transport and Economic Development in Europe, 1789–1914. In *Railways and the Economic Development of Western Europe, 1830–1914,* ed. P. K. O'Brien. Basingstoke: Macmillan, pp. 1–27.

O'Brien, P. K. and C. Keyder. 1978. *Economic Growth in Britain and France 1780–1914: Two Paths to the Twentieth Century.* London: Allen & Unwin.

O'Brien, P. K. and L. Prados de la Escosura, eds. 1998. *The Costs and Benefits of European Imperialism from the Conquest of Ceuta, 1415, to the Treaty of Lusaka, 1974. Revista de Historia Económica* Special Issue XVI, 1, winter.

Obstfeld, M. and A. M. Taylor. 2003. Globalization and Capital Markets. In Bordo, Taylor, and Williamson 2003, pp. 121–87.

    2004. *Global Capital Markets: Integration, Crisis, and Growth.* Cambridge University Press.

Obstfeld, M., J. Shambaugh, and A. M. Taylor. 2005. The Trilemma in History: Tradeoffs among Exchange Rates, Monetary Policies, and Capital Mobility. *Review of Economics and Statistics* 87: 439–52.

OECD. 2001. *Historical Statistics.* Paris.

    2005. *OECD in Figures.* Paris.

    2006. *Revenue Statistics, 1965–2005.* Paris.

    2007a. *Social Expenditure Database.* Paris. www.oecd.org/els/social/expenditure

    2007b. *Employment Outlook.* Paris.

    2007c. *International Migration Statistics.* Paris: OECD.

Ofer, G. 1987. Soviet Economic Growth: 1928–1985. *Journal of Economic Literature* 25: 1767–833.

Offer, A. 1989. *The First World War: An Agrarian Interpretation.* Oxford: Clarendon.

    1993. The British Empire, 1870–1914: A Waste of Money? *Economic History Review* 46: 215–38.

Ó Gráda, C. and K. H. O'Rourke. 1996. Irish Economic Growth, 1945–88. In Crafts and Toniolo 1996b, pp. 388–426.

Oliner, S. D., D. E. Sichel, and K. J. Stiroh. 2007. Explaining a Productive Decade. *Brookings Papers on Economic Activity* 1: 81–152.

Olmstead, A. L. and P. W. Rhode. 2008. Conceptual Issues for the Comparative Study of Agricultural development. In *Agriculture and Economic Development in Europe since 1870,* ed. P. Lains and V. Pinilla. London: Routledge, 27–51.

Olson, M. 1963. *The Economics of the Wartime Shortage: A History of British Food Supplies in the Napoleonic War and in World Wars I and II*. Durham, NC: Duke University Press.

Olsson, U. 1973. *Upprustning och verkstadsindustri i Sverige under det andra världskriget*. Göteborg: Göteborgs Universitet, Ekonomisk-historiska Institutionen.

O'Mahony, M. 1999. *Britain's Productivity Performance, 1950–1996*. London: NIESR.

O'Rourke, K. H. 1997. The European Grain Invasion. *Journal of Economic History* 57: 775–801.

O'Rourke, K. H. and J. G. Williamson. 1994. Late 19th Century Anglo-American Factor Price Convergence: Were Heckscher and Ohlin Right? *Journal of Economic History* 54: 892–916.

  1995. Open Economy Forces and Late Nineteenth Century Swedish Catch Up. A Quantitative Accounting. *Scandinavian Economic History Review* 43: 171–203.

  1997. Around the European Periphery, 1870–1913: Globalization, Schooling and Growth. *European Review of Economic History* 1: 153–90.

  1999. *Globalization and History: The Evolution of a Nineteenth Century Atlantic Economy*. Cambridge, MA: MIT Press.

Owen, N. 1983. *Economies of Scale, Competitiveness, and Trade Patterns within the European Community*. Oxford: Clarendon.

Palairet, M. 1995. Real Wages and Earnings in Long-Run Decline: Serbia and Yugoslavia since 1862. In *Labour's Reward. Real Wages and Economic Change in 19th- and 20th-Century Europe*, ed. P. Scholliers and V. Zamagni. Aldershot: Edward Elgar, pp. 76–86.

Pallot, J. 1991. Women's Domestic Industries in Moscow Province, 1880–1900. In *Russia's Women: Accommodation, Resistance, and Transformation*, ed. B. Clements, B. Engel, and C. Worobec. Berkeley: University of California Press.

Pamuk, S. 2005. The Ottoman Economy in World War I. In Broadberry and Harrison 2005a, 112–36.

  2006. Estimating Economic Growth in the Middle East since 1820. *Journal of Economic History* 66: 809–28.

Panic, M. 1992. *European Monetary Union: Lessons from the Classical Gold Standard*. New York: St. Martin's Press.

Patat, J.-P. and M. Lutfalla. 1990. *A Monetary History of France in the Twentieth Century*. London: Macmillan.

Peck, M. J. 1989. Industrial Organization and the Gains from Europe 1992. *Brookings Papers on Economic Activity* 2: 277–99.

Peeters, S., M. Goossens, and E. Buyst. 2005. *Belgian National Income during the Interwar Period. Reconstruction of the Database*. Leuven University Press.

Pericoli, M. and M. Sbracia. 2001. A Primer on Financial Contagion. Temi di discussione (Economic Working Papers) 407. Bank of Italy, Economic Research Department.

Petith, H. C. 1977. European Integration and the Terms of Trade. *Economic Journal* 87: 262–72.

Phelps Brown, E. and M. Browne. 1968. *A Century of Pay: The Course of Pay and Production in France, Germany, Sweden, the United Kingdom, and the United States of America, 1860–1960*. London: Macmillan.

Pinilla, V. and M.-I. Ayuda, 2002. The Political Economy of the Wine Trade: Spanish Exports and the International Market, 1890–1935. *European Review of Economic History* 6: 51–86.

Polanyi, K. 1944. *The Great Transformation*. New York: Rinehart.

POLITY IV: www.systemicpeace.org/polity/polity4.htm.

Pollard, S. 1981. *Peaceful Conquest: The Industrialization of Europe 1760–1970*. Oxford University Press.

Pounds, N. J. G. 1957. *Coal and Steel in Western Europe: The Influence of Resources and Technique on Production*. Bloomington: Indiana University Press.

Prados de la Escosura, L. 2000. International Comparisons of Real Product, 1820–1990: An Alternative Dataset. *Explorations in Economic History* 37: 1–41.

2003. *El progreso económico de España, 1850–2000*. Madrid: Fundación BBVA.

2005. *El progreso económico de España, 1850–2000*. Bilbao: Fundación BBVA.

2007. European Patterns of Development in Historical Perspective. *Scandinavian Economic History Review* 55: 187–221.

Prati, A. 1991. Poincaré's Stabilization: Stopping a Run on Government Debt. *Journal of Monetary Economics* 27: 231–9.

Prescott, E. C. 2004. Why Do Americans Work So Much More than Europeans? *Federal Reserve Bank of Minneapolis Quarterly Review* 28(1): 2–13.

Quinn, D. 2003. Capital Account Liberalization and Financial Globalization, 1890–1999: A Synoptic View. *International Journal of Finance and Economics* 8: 189–204.

Raiser, M., M. Schaffer, and J. Schuchhardt. 2004. Benchmarking Structural Change in Transition. *Structural Change and Economic Dynamics* 15: 47–81.

Rajan, R. and L. Zingales. 2003. Banks and Markets: The Changing Character of European Finance. In *The Transformation of the European Financial System*, ed. V. Gaspar, P. Hartmann, and O. Sleijpen. Frankfurt: ECB, pp. 123–68.

Ravn, M. and H. Uhlig. 2002. On Adjusting the HP-Filter for the Frequency of Observations. *Review of Economics and Statistics* 84: 371–6.

Regalsky, A. 2002. *Mercados, inversiones y elites: las inversiones francesas en la Argentina 1880–1914*. Caseros (B.A.): UTREF.

Reinhardt, C. M. and K. S. Rogoff. 2004. The Modern History of Exchange Rate Arrangements: A Reinterpretation. *The Quarterly Journal of Economics* 119: 1–48.

Reis, J. 1993. *O atraso económico Português, 1850–1930*. Lisbon: Imprensa Nacional Casa da Moeda.

2007. An 'Art', Not a 'Science'? Central Bank Management in Portugal under the Gold Standard, 1863–87. *Economic History Review* 60: 712–41.

Riley, J. C. 2001. *Rising Life Expectancy. A Global History*. Cambridge University Press.

Ritschl, A. 1996. An Exercise in Futility: East German Economic Growth and Decline, 1945–1989. In Crafts and Toniolo 1996b, pp. 498–550.

1998. Reparation Transfers, the Borchardt Hypothesis, and the Great Depression in Germany, 1929–1932: A Guided Tour for Hard-Headed Keynesians. *European Review of Economic History* 2: 49–72.

2001. Nazi Economic Imperialism and the Exploitation of the Small: Evidence from Germany's Secret Foreign Exchange Balances, 1938–40. *Economic History Review* 54: 324–45.

2002a. *Deutschlands Krise und Konjunktur, 1924–1934. Binnenkonjunktur, Auslandsverschuldung und Reparationsproblem zwischen Dawes-Plan und Transfersperre.* Berlin: Akademie-Verlag.

2002b. International Capital Movements and the Onset of the Great Depression: Some International Evidence. In *The Interwar Depression in an International Context*, ed. H. James. Munich: Oldenbourg, pp. 1–14.

2003. Dancing on a Volcano: The Economic Recovery and Collapse of the Weimar Republic. In *World Economy and National Economies in the Interwar Slump*, ed. T. Balderston. London: Macmillan, pp. 105–42.

2004. The Marshall Plan, 1948–1951. In *EH.Net Encyclopedia*, ed. R. Whaples. February 10, 2008. www.eh.net/encyclopedia/article/Ritschl.Marshall.Plan.

2005. The Pity of Peace: Germany's War Economy, 1914–1918 and Beyond. In Broadberry and Harrison 2005a, pp. 41–76.

Ritschl, A., and M. Spoerer 1997. Das Bruttosozialprodukt in Deutschland nach den amtlichen Volkseinkommens- und Sozialproduktstatistiken 1901–1995. *Jahrbuch für Wirtschaftsgeschichte* 1997: 11–37.

Rockoff, H. 1998. The United States: From Ploughshares to Swords. In *The Economics of World War II: Six Great Powers in International Comparison*, ed. M. Harrison. Cambridge University Press.

Rojec, M. and J. Damijan 2008. Relocation via Foreign Direct Investment from Old to New EU Member States. Scale and Structural Dimension of the Process. *Structural Change and Economic Dynamics* 19: 53–65.

Romer, C. D. 1989. The Prewar Business Cycle Reconsidered: New Estimates of Gross National Product, 1869–1908. *Journal of Political Economy* 97: 1–37.

Romer, P. M, 1990. Endogenous Technological Change. *Journal of Political Economy* 98: S71–102.

Rose, A. K. 2000. One Money, One Market: The Effect of Common Currencies on Trade. *Economic Policy* 30: 7–45.

Rose, A. K. and E. van Wincoop. 2001. National Money as a Barrier to International Trade: The Real Case for Currency Unions. *American Economic Review* 91: 386–90.

Rose, S. O. 1996. Protective Labor Legislation in Nineteenth Century Britain: Gender, Class and the Liberal State. In *Gender and Class in Modern Europe*, ed. L. L. Frader and S. O. Rose. Ithaca and London: Cornell University Press, pp. 193–210.

Rostow, W. W. 1961. *The Stages of Economic Growth*. Cambridge University Press.

Rothenbacher, F. 2005. *The European Population since 1945*. Basingstoke: Palgrave Macmillan.

Rothschild, J. 1974. *East Central Europe between the Two World Wars*. Seattle and London: University of Washington Press.

Rowe, D. 2005. The Tragedy of Liberalism: How Globalization Caused the First World War. *Security Studies* 14: 407–47.

Rudolph, R. L. 1976. *Banking and Industrialization in Austria-Hungary: The Role of Banks in the Industrialization of the Czech Crownlands, 1873–1914*. Cambridge University Press.

Sáiz, J. P. 2005. Investigación y desarrollo: patentes. In *Estadística histórica de España, siglos XIX–XX*, ed. A. Carreras and X. Tafunell. Bilbao: Fundación BBVA, 835–72.

Sala-i-Martin, X., G. Doppelhofer, and R. I. Miller. 2004. Determinants of Long-Term Growth: A Bayesian Averaging of Classical Estimates (BACE) Approach. *American Economic Review* 94: 813–35.

Sala-i-Martin, X. and A. Subramanian. 2003. Assessing the Natural Resource Curse: An Illustration from Nigeria. NBER Working Paper 9804.

Salin, E. 1928. Standortverschiebungen der deutschen Wirtschaft. In *Strukturwandlungen der deutschen Volkswirtschaft*, ed. B. Harms. Berlin: Reimar Hobbing, 75–106.

Sandberg, L. G. 1974. *Lancashire in Decline: A Study in Entrepreneurship, Technology and International Trade*. Columbus: Ohio State University Press.

Sapir, A. 1992. Regional Integration in Europe. *Economic Journal* 102: 1491–506.

Sapir, A. *et. al.* 2004. *An Agenda for a Growing Europe. The Sapir Report.* Oxford University Press.

Sargent, T. 1982. The End of Four Big Inflations. In *Rational Expectations and Inflation*, ed. T. Sargent New York: Harper & Row, pp. 40–109.

Sargent, T. and C. Sims. 1977. Business Cycle Modelling Without Pretending to Have Too Much A Priori Economic Theory. In *New Methods in Business Cycle Research*, ed. Christopher Sims. Minneapolis: Federal Reserve Bank of Minneapolis, pp. 45–109.

Saul, S. B. 1969. *The Myth of the Great Depression, 1873–1896*. Basingstoke: Macmillan.

Saz, I. 1999. Foreign Policy under the Dictatorship of Primo de Rivera. In *Spain and the Great Powers in the Twentieth Century*, ed. S. Balfour. and P. Preston. New York: Routledge, pp. 53–72.

Schnabel, I. 2004. The German Twin Crisis of 1931. *Journal of Economic History* 64: 822–71.

Schofield, R. and D. Reher 1991. The Decline of Mortality in Europe. In Schofield, Reher, and Bideau, 1991, pp. 1–17.

Schofield, R., D. Reher, and A. Bideau. 1991. *The Decline of Mortality in Europe.* Oxford: Clarendon.

Schön, L. 2000. *En modern svensk ekonomisk historia. Tillväxt och omvandling under två sekel* (A modern Swedish economic history. Growth and transformation in two centuries). Stockholm: SNS Förlag.

Schubert, A. 1991. *The Credit-Anstalt Crisis of 1931*. Cambridge University Press.

Schuker, S. 1976a. *The End of French Predominance in Europe*. Chapel Hill: University of North Carolina Press.

  1976b. Finance and Foreign Policy in the Era of the German Inflation. In *Historische Prozesse der deutschen Inflation 1914–1924*, ed. O. Büsch and G. Feldman. Berlin: de Gruyter, 343–61.

1988. *American Reparations to Germany, 1924–1933*. Princeton University Press.

Schulze, M.-S. 2000. Patterns of Growth and Stagnation in the Late Nineteenth Century Habsburg Economy. *European Review of Economic History* 4: 311–40.

2005. Austria–Hungary's Economy in World War I. In Broadberry and Harrison 2005a, pp. 77–111.

Schulze, M.-S., ed. 1999. *Western Europe: Economic and Social Charge since 1945*. London: Longman.

Schulze, M.-S. and N. Wolf. 2009. On the Origins of Border Effects: Insights from the Habsburg Empire. *Journal of Economic Geography* 9: 117–36.

Schumpeter, J. 1939. *Business Cycles: A Theoretical, Historical and Statistical Analysis of the Capitalist Process*. New York: McGraw-Hill.

Scranton, P. 1997. *Endless Novelty: Specialty Production and American Industrialization, 1865–1925*. Princeton University Press.

Sereni, E. 1968. *Il capitalismo nelle campagne*. Turin: Einaudi.

Shearer, J. R. 1997. The Reichskuratorium für Wirtschaftlichkeit. Fordism and Organised Capitalism in Germany, 1918–1945. *The Business History Review* 71 (4): 569–602.

Shorter, F. C. 1985. The Population of Turkey after the War of Independence. *International Journal of Middle East Studies* 17: 417–41.

Siaroff, A. 1999. Corporatism in 24 Industrial Democracies: Meaning and Measurement. *European Journal of Political Research* 36: 175–205.

Sicsic, P. 1993. Was the Franc Poincaré Undervalued? *Explorations in Economic History* 29: 69–92.

Siegenthaler, H. 1987. Die Schweiz 1914–1970. In *Handbuch der Europäischen Wirtschafts- und Sozialgeschichte*, Vol. 6, ed. W. Fisher, J. A. van Houtte, H. Kellenbenz, I. Miek, and F. Vittinghoff. Stuttgart: Klett-Cotta, pp. 482–512.

Simonov, N. S. 1996. Strengthen the Defence of the Land of the Soviets: The 1927 War Alarm and Its Consequences. *Europe–Asia Studies* 48: 1355–64.

Simpson, J. 1995. Real Wages and Labour Mobility in Spain, 1860–1936. In *Labour's Reward. Real Wages and Economic Change in 19th- and 20th-Century Europe*, ed. P. Scholliers and V. Zamagni. Aldershot: Edward Elgar, pp. 182–200.

1939. *The Refugee Problem*. Oxford University Press.

Smith, M. S. 2006. *The Emergence of Modern Business Enterprise in France, 1800–1930*. Cambridge, MA: Harvard University Press.

Smits, J.-P., E. Horlings, and J. L. van Zanden. 2000. Dutch GNP and its Components, 1870–1913. N.W. Posthumus Institute, University of Groningen, www.nationalaccounts.niwi.knaw.nl/start.htm.

Solomou, S. 1998. *Economic Cycles: Long Cycles and Business Cycles since 1870*. Manchester University Press.

Solomou, S. and W. Wu. 1999. Weather Effects on European Agricultural Output, 1850–1913. *European Review of Economic History* 3: 351–72.

Solow, R. M. 1956. A Contribution to the Theory of Economic Growth. *Quarterly Journal of Economics* 70: 65–94.

1957. Technical Change and the Aggregate Production Function. *Review of Economics and Statistics* 39: 312–20.

1987. We'd Better Watch Out. *New York Times Book Review* (12 July).

Spree, R. 1988 [1981]. *Health and Social Class in Imperial Germany*. Hamburg: Berg.

Stachura, P. D. 2003. Social Policy and Social Welfare in Germany from the Mid-Nineteenth Century to the Present. In *Germany: A New Social and Economic History*, ed. S. Ogilvie and R. Overy. London: Arnold, 227–50.

Statistisches Bundesamt Deutschland. 2007. *Aktuelle Kreisergebnisse fur Deutschland*.

Steckel, R. H. 1995. Stature and Standard of Living. *Journal of Economic Literature* 33: 1903–40.

Steckel, R. H. and R. Floud. 1997. *Health and Welfare during Industrialization*. Chicago: University of Chicago Press.

1998. Height and the Standard of Living. Health and Welfare during Industrialization. *Journal of Economic History* 58: 866–70.

Stern, R. 1960. A Century of Food Exports. *Kyklos* 13: 44–57.

Stiglitz, J. E. 2002. *Globalization and Its Discontents*. New York: Norton.

Stock, J. H. and M. W. Watson. 2004. Understanding Changes in International Business Cycle Dynamics. NBER Working Paper no. 9859.

Stone, I. 1999. *The Global Export of Capital from Great Britain, 1865–1914: A Statistical Survey*. London: Macmillan.

Stone, J. F. 1996. Republican Ideology, Gender and Class: France 1860s–1914. In Frader and Rose, 1996, pp. 238–59.

Studenski, P. 1958. *The Income of Nations: Theory*. New York University Press.

Summers, P. M. 2005. What Caused the Great Moderation? Some Cross-Country Evidence. *Federal Reserve Bank of Kansas City Economic Review*, Third Quarter, 5–30.

Svensson, L. 1995. *Closing the Gender Gap. Determinants of Change in the Female-to-Male Blue Collar Wage Ratio in Swedish Manufacturing, 1913–1990*. Lund, University.

2004. Technology Shifts, Industrial Dynamics and Labour Market Institutions in Sweden, 1920–95. In *Technology and Human Capital in Historical Perspective*, ed. J. Ljungberg and J.-P. Smits. Basingstoke: Palgrave Macmillan, pp. 79–101.

Svennilson, I. 1954. *Growth and Stagnation in the European Economy*. Geneva: United Nations.

Swan, T. W. 1956. Economic Growth and Capital Accumulation. *Economic Record* 32: 334–61.

Sylos-Labini, P. 1970. *Problemi dello sviluppo economico*. Bari: Laterza.

Symeonidis, G. 2008. The Effect of Competition on Wages and Productivity: Evidence from the United Kingdom. *Review of Economics and Statistics*. 90: 134–46.

Taylor, A. M. and J. G. Williamson. 1997. Convergence in the Age of Mass Migration. *European Review of Economic History* 1: 27–63.

Teichova, A. 1988. *The Czechoslovak Economy, 1918–1980*. London: Routledge.

Temin, P. 1987. Capital Exports, 1870–1914: An Alternative Model. *Economic History Review* 40: 453–8.

1989. *Lessons from the Great Depression*. Cambridge, MA: MIT Press.

2002. The Golden Age of European Growth Reconsidered. *European Review of Economic History* 6: 3–22.

Thomas, B. 1954. *Migration and Economic Growth: A Study of Great Britain and the Atlantic Economy.* Cambridge University Press.

Thomas, M. 2004. The Service Sector. In *The Cambridge Economic History of Modern Britain*, ed. R. Floud and P. Johnson. Cambridge University Press, 99–132.

Timmer, A. and J. G. Williamson. 1998. Immigration Policy Prior to the Thirties: Labor Markets, Policy Interactions and Globalization Backlash. *Population and Development Review* 24: 739–71.

Timmer, M. and B. van Ark. 2005. Does Information and Communication Technology Drive EU–US Productivity Growth Differentials? *Oxford Economic Papers* 57: 693–716.

Tinbergen, J. 1942. Zur Theorie der langsfristigen Wirtschaftsentwicklung. *Weltwirtschaftliches Archiv* 55: 511–49.

Tolliday, S. 1991. Competition and Maturity in the British Steel Industry, 1870–1914. In *Changing Patterns of International Rivalry: Some Lessons from the Steel Industry*, ed. E. Abé and Y. Suzuki. Tokyo University Press, pp. 20–72.

Tomlinson, J. D. 1984. A 'Keynesian Revolution' in Economic Policy-Making? *Economic History Review* 37: 258–62.

Toniolo G. 1995. Italian Banking, 1919–1936. In *Banking, Currency, and Finance in Europe between the Wars*, ed. C. H. Feinstein. Oxford: Clarendon, pp. 296–314.

1998. Europe's Golden Age, 1950–73: Speculations from a Long-Run Perspective. *Economic History Review* 51: 252–67.

2005. *Central Bank Cooperation at the Bank for International Settlements, 1930–1973.* Cambridge University Press.

Tooze, J. A. 2001. *Statistics and the German State, 1900–1945: The Making of Modern Economic Knowledge.* Cambridge University Press.

2007. *The Wages of Destruction: The Making and Breaking of the Nazi Economy.* London: Penguin.

Toutain, J. C. 1997. Le produit intérieur brut de la France, 1789–1990. *Economies et Sociétés, Histoire économique quantitative*, Série HEQ 1(11): 5–136.

Travis, A. S. *et al.* 1998. *Determinants in the Evolution of the European Chemical Industry 1900–1939: New Technologies, Political Framework Markets and Companies.* Dordrecht: Kluwer.

Trebilcock, C. 1981. *The Industrialization of the Continental Powers, 1780–1914.* London: Longman.

Triner, G. and K. Wandschneider. 2005. The Baring Crisis and the Brazilian Encilhamento, 1889–1891: An Early Example of Contagion among Emerging Capital Markets. *Financial History Review* 12: 199–225.

Tugan-Baranovskiy, M. I. 1970. *The Russian Factory in the 19th Century*, trans. A. Levin and C. Levin. Homewood, IL.: Published for the American Economic Association by R. D. Irwin. [Original 1922, *Russkaia fabrika v proshlom i nastoiashchem: istoricheskoe razvitie russkoi fabriki v XIX v.* Moscow: Moskovskii rabochii.]

Turnock, D. 2006. *The Economy of East Central Europe, 1815–1989. Stages of Transformation in a Peripheral Region.* London: Routledge.

Twarog, S. 1997. Heights and Living Standards in Germany, 1850–1939: The Case of Württemberg. In *Health and Welfare during Industrialization*, ed. R. H. Steckel and R. Floud. Chicago: University of Chicago Press, pp. 285–330.

Ulman, L. and R. J. Flanagan. 1971. *Wage Restraint: A Study of Income Policy in Western Europe*. Berkeley: University of California Press.

UNDP. 2006, 2007. *Human Development Report*. New York. www.hdr.undp.org/hdr2007/.

Union des Associations Internationales. 1957. *Les 1978 Organisations Internationales fondées depuis le Congrès de Vienne*. Brussels.

 1960. *Les Congrès Internationaux de 1681 à 1899 / International Congresses 1681 to 1899*. Brussels.

Urlanis, B. 1971. *Wars and Population*. Moscow: Progress.

US Department of Commerce. 1975. *Historical Statistics of the United States: Colonial Times to 1970*. Washington, DC: GPO.

Vallin, J. 1991. Mortality in Europe from 1720 to 1914: Long-Term Trends and Changes in Patterns by Age and Sex. In Schofield, Reher, and Bideau 1988, 38–67.

Van Ark, B. 1996. Sectoral Growth Accounting and Structural Change in Postwar Europe. In Van Ark and Crafts 1996, pp. 84–164.

Van Ark, B. and N. Crafts 1996. *Quantative Aspects of Post-War European Economic Growth*. Cambridge University Press.

Van Ark, B., M. O'Mahony, and M. Timmer 2008. The Productivity Gap between Europe and the United States: Trends and Causes. *Journal of Economic Perspectives* 22: 25–44.

Van Zanden, J. L. 1991. The First Green Revolution: The Growth of Production and Productivity in European Agriculture, 1870–1914. *Economic History Review* 44: 215–39.

 1994. *The Transformation of European Agriculture in the 19th Century: The Case of the Netherlands*. Amsterdam: Vu Uitgeverij.

Van Zanden, J. L. and A. van Riel. 2004. *The Strictures of Inheritance: The Dutch Economy in the Nineteenth Century*. Princeton University Press.

Vernon, R. 1966. International Investment and International Trade in the Product Cycle. *Quarterly Journal of Economics* 80: 190–207.

Villa, P. 1993. *Une analyse macroéconomique de la France au XXe siècle*. Paris: CNRS.

Ville, S. 1991. Shipping Industry Technologies. In *International Technology Transfer: Europe, Japan and the USA, 1700–1914*, ed. D. J. Jeremy. Aldershot: Eldward Elgar, pp. 74–94.

Vögele, J. 1998. *Urban Mortality Change in England and Germany, 1870–1913*. Liverpool University Press.

Volcker, P. and T. Gyohten. 1992. *Changing Fortunes: The World's Money And The Threat to American Leadership*. New York: Times Books.

Von Hagen, J. 1999. A New Approach to Monetary Policy (1971–8). In *Fifty Years of the Deutsche Mark: Central Bank and the Currency in Germany since 1948*, ed. Deutsche Bundesbank. Oxford University Press, 403–38.

Voth, H.-J. 2006. La discontinuidad olvidada: provisión de trabajo, cambio tecnológico y nuevos bienes durante la Revolución Industrial. *Revista de Historia Industrial* 15: 13–31.

Watkins, S. C. 1986. Regional Patterns of Nuptiality in Western Europe, 1870–1960. In *The Decline of Fertility in Europe*, ed. A. J. Coale and S. C. Watkins. Princeton: Princeton University Press, pp. 314–36.

Webb, S. N. 1989. *Hyperinflation and Stabilization in Weimar Germany*. Oxford University Press.

Weitzman, M. L. 1970. Soviet Postwar Economic Growth and Capital-Labor Substitution. *American Economic Review* 60: 676–92.

Wheatcroft, S. G. 1999. The Great Leap Forward: Anthropometric Data and Indicators of Crises and Secular Change in Soviet Welfare Levels, 1880–1960. *Slavic Review* 58: 27–60.

White, E. 2001. Making the French Pay: The Cost and Consequences of Napoleonic Reparations. *European Review of Economic History* 5: 337–65.

Wilkins, M. 1970. *The Emergence of Multinational Enterprise: American Business Abroad from the Colonial Era to 1914*. Cambridge, MA: Harvard University Press.

Wilkinson, R. 1992. Income Distribution and Life Expectancy. *British Medical Journal* 304: 165–8.

2005. *The Impact of Inequality*. London: Routledge.

Wilkinson, R. and K. Picket. 2006. Income Inequality and Population Health: A Review and Explanation of the Evidence. *Social Science and Medicine* 62: 1768–84.

Williamson, J. G. 1995. The Evolution of Global Labor Markets since 1830: Background Evidence and Hypotheses. *Explorations in Economic History* 32: 141–96.

1997. Globalization and Inequality, Past and Present. *World Bank Research Observer* 12: 117–35.

2002a. Land, Labor and Globalization in the Third World, 1870–1940. *Journal of Economic History* 62: 55–85.

2002b. Winners and Losers Over Two Centuries of Globalization. NBER Working Paper No. 9161.

Wirth, M. 1893. The Crisis of 1890. *Journal of Political Economy* 1: 214–35.

Wolf, N. 2008. Scylla and Charybdis. Explaining Europe's Exit from Gold, 1928–1936. *Explorations in Economic History*. Forthcoming.

Woods, R. 2006. Newman's *Infant Mortality* as an Agenda for Research. In *Infant Mortality: A Continuing Social Problem*, ed. E. Garrett, C. Galley, N. Shelton, and R. Woods. Aldershot: Ashgate, pp. 33–49.

World Bank. 2003, 2007. *World Development Indicators*. Washington DC.

Wrigley, C. 2000. *The First World War and the International Economy*. Cheltenham: Edward Elgar.

Yeager, L. B. 1976. *International Monetary Relations: Theory, History, and Policy*. New York: Harper & Row.

Zilbert, E. R. 1981. *Albert Speer and the Nazi Ministry of Arms*. Rutherford, NJ: Fairleigh Dickinson University Press.

Zimmermann, K. F. 2005. European Labour Mobility: Challenges and Potentials. *De Economist* 153: 425–50.

Zurcher, E. J. 2000. *Turkey: A Modern History*. London: Tauris.

Zylberman, P. 2005. Mosquitos and the Komitadjis: Malaria and Borders in Macedonia. In *Facing Illness in Troubled Times: Health in Europe in the Inter-War Years*, ed. I. Borowy and W. D. Gruner. Frankfurt am Main: Lang, pp. 305–43.

Index